AN

INTRODUCTION

TO

EDUCATION

IN

AMERICAN

SOCIETY

The Country School by Winslow Homer

A N INTRODUCTION TO EDUCATION I N AMERICAN SOCIETY

A Text with Readings

BY

RAYMOND E. CALLAHAN

WASHINGTON UNIVERSITY

FOREWORD BY *George S. Counts*

SECOND EDITION

Alfred · A · Knopf   NEW YORK   1960

L. C. catalog card number 60–6471

© RAYMOND E. CALLAHAN, 1956, 1960

THIS IS A BORZOI BOOK,
PUBLISHED BY ALFRED A. KNOPF, INC.

PUBLISHED 1956, REPRINTED FIVE TIMES

SECOND EDITION, REVISED, 1960

FOREWORD

BY GEORGE S. COUNTS

I

SOMETHING OVER A CENTURY AGO THE AMERICAN PEOPLE LAUNCHED the great struggle to establish their system of public schools— a struggle which they eventually carried through successfully throughout the nation. While we maintain private schools in great diversity in accordance with our traditions of freedom, the unique American contribution to the history of educational institutions is the "educational ladder" composed of elementary, secondary, and higher schools, all supported by public taxation. Within the limits of family circumstance and the assistance of various benefactions, the individual may climb as high on this ladder as his abilities permit and his inclinations dictate. The content of programs and the level of standards are adjusted to a wide range of talents, aptitudes, and interests.

The growth of this system from its simple beginnings, and particularly since the opening of the present century, has shattered the conceptions and surpassed the expectations of its founders. Today, despite the fact that other nations have been engaged for some time in the radical extension of the opportunities of organized education to more and more children and youth, our secondary and higher schools enroll a far larger proportion of young people of appropriate age than do those of any other country. Here without doubt is one of the most distinctive features and one of the most authentic expressions of our democracy. It is as truly American as our constitutional system.

The total achievement of this system of schools, as it has ministered to the needs of each succeeding generation, cannot be measured by any calculus known to man. Yet we do know that with all of its deficiencies and imperfections it has contributed mightily to the building of America. Without it the course of our history would have been profoundly different. Without it our democratic institutions could scarcely have endured. Without it a regime of liberty could not have been established over such a vast territory. Without it the fabulously productive industrial economy, with its insatiable demands for skills, knowledges, resourcefulness, and creative talent, would have been impossible. Without it the formation of a single people out of the many nations, races, and religious sects coming to our shores from the Old World would have faltered. Also the public school, even the one-room district school on the frontier and in the rural neighborhood, was almost invariably a civilizing influence. It at least symbolized, however modestly and unwittingly, the finest and most enduring achievements of Western Man.

From time to time this system of public schools has been subjected to more or less severe criticism and reappraisal. Today we are passing through such a period. It is charged that the public school is neglecting the "fundamentals" of reading, writing, and arithmetic, that it has abandoned the time-tested methods of drill and recitation, that it has exchanged the rigorous discipline of the past for the "soft pedagogy" of the Progressives, that it has lowered intellectual standards and placed a premium on mediocrity, that it has failed to inculcate habits of work and prepare the young to live in a competitive world, and that it has slighted the teaching of facts and introduced children to the study of controversial issues beyond their understanding. It is charged also that the school has become insensitive to the cultivation of moral and spiritual values, and has thus weakened the moral fiber of our people and contributed to the spread of juvenile delinquency. It is even charged in some quarters that many teachers have sought to convert the school into an agency for the subversion of our American way of life.

Many of these charges are not new. As a matter of fact, they have been with us in varying degree of emphasis and intensity since the founding of the public school. Although criticism is sometimes malicious and uninformed, the process of criticism itself is the very essence of the democratic way and the finest flower of political freedom. Moreover, the institution has always had its staunch defenders. And friends of public education in every age should welcome the most searching criticism of current practice. Here lies the road to better schools. Because of the vast expansion of education, the invention of new methods, the advance of relevant knowledge, and the profound changes in the social order during recent decades, the present period *should* be a period of reappraisal.

II

IT IS proverbial that the teacher is the key factor in any educational enterprise. For the teacher there is no substitute, whether in the course of study, the pattern of administration, the form of organization, or the mechanics of instruction. Peschel, speaking of the Seven Weeks' War between Prussia and Austria, observed that "the victory of the Prussians over the Austrians was a victory of the Prussian over the Austrian schoolmaster." It would seem quite possible that the world-wide struggle in our time between freedom and tyranny may be won or lost by the teacher in free society and particularly in America. The reappraisal of the training of the teacher should therefore be at the center of any reappraisal of the public school.

The tradition of teacher-training in America is inadequate for these times. This situation is due largely to the conception of teaching which prevailed at the time of the launching of our system of public schools. A century and a quarter ago the demands made upon the schools by society were relatively few. As a matter of fact, the rearing of the young was largely a by-product of growing up in the family and the rural neighborhood. The school year was short, attendance was irregular, the years of instruction were brief, the high school was in its embryonic stage, and overwhelming emphasis was placed on the acquisition of an elementary command of the so-called "tools of learning." The development of the social and behavioral sciences of biology, psychology, sociology, anthropology, economics, and others which undergird the process of education was still in the future. Under these circumstances teaching was scarcely regarded as a fit life career for either man or woman. Persons in the later years of youth, or even younger, were commonly recruited to discharge the responsibilities of tuition. The training provided for these teachers was only a little less meager than the curriculum of the school itself. It was designed to prepare for what was often appropriately called "school keeping." One of the major tasks of the teacher was to maintain order and prevent the "big boys" from disrupting the process of learning.

In the intervening years the total situation has been transformed. Because of profound changes in the nature of our society, because of the movement from the simple rural society of our ancestors to the marvelously complex, dynamic, and far-reaching industrial society of today, the burdens placed on the school have increased rapidly and steadily from generation to generation. The school has consequently evolved, not only into a major educational institution, but also into a major *social* institution. At the same time the sciences basic to education and knowledge about the entire process of education have developed. In a word, our intellectual resources for the conduct of the educational undertaking have been immeasurably increased. Clearly the time has come for the fullest utilization of these resources.

Our program of teacher training has of course been greatly improved since the launching of our earliest normal school. Yet the program today reveals all too clearly its humble and simple beginnings. Even in the best of our teacher training institutions the emphasis is placed altogether too largely on the mastery of the mechanics of the teaching process and on the school apart from the society and civilization which it serves.

In the present epoch, when our society is rushing ever more swiftly toward an unknown destination, when the cause of human liberty hangs in the balance throughout the earth, and when the very structure of the world is being transformed, there is obvious need for the formulation of a more generous conception of the work of the teacher. Potentially teaching is indeed a profession, but it is much more. At any rate it is a unique profession. Beyond any other, unless it be the ministry, it is concerned with the future of our society, with the future of both its forms and its values. Ineluctably, teaching is deeply involved in the shaping of the minds and hearts, as well as the bodies, of the members of the coming generation. This would appear to mean that the teacher should be at least as carefully selected, as broadly and deeply prepared for his work, as the practitioner of any other calling, not excluding the physician or the jurist.

III

An Introduction to Education in American Society represents an attempt to meet this challenge to teacher-training institutions. Though designed merely to introduce the student to the program of professional preparation, it is not elementary in its basic concepts. It draws upon all the sciences and philosophies relevant to the tasks of education and it does this in the framework of our American civilization in its historical and world relationships. It thus repudiates completely the conception of education as an autonomous or quasi-autonomous process conducted according to its own laws. The student who works his way through the materials of this book, including the suggested supplementary readings, should be on his way to becoming the kind of teacher which our American democracy requires in this "time of troubles" and this "time of promise." I am glad to commend this book to our institutions of teacher training. Professor Callahan has performed successfully an arduous and important service to the cause of education. *An Introduction to Education in American Society* is an inspiring achievement in the realm of educational statesmanship.

PREFACE

THE PURPOSE OF THIS BOOK IS TO PRESENT TO THE READER THE FACTS and concepts essential for an understanding of American education in general and the school system in particular. The book was designed primarily for college students entering the teaching profession, but it was also intended to serve as a general work for laymen interested in American education. The selection of material was determined in part by the pattern and sequence of courses that have been established in the institutions of higher learning that prepare teachers. That pattern is to begin the prospective teacher's professional program of study with a course generally entitled "An Introduction to American Education" or "An Orientation to Teaching." For the most part, students are required to take this course in their freshman or sophomore years. This is generally followed in the sequence by a course in educational psychology. After these two basic courses the common core of the sequence is ended and the student goes into the specialized sequence of courses for either elementary or secondary education. Therefore, this book does not attempt to provide subject matter that rightfully belongs in these other courses. It does attempt to provide subject matter that will serve as a solid foundation for the later courses. In pursuit of this goal, material has been included from other disciplines where it has seemed advisable in order to contribute to a better understanding.

The book is organized as a text with readings for two reasons. The first is that these selections do an excellent job of presenting the desired facts and concepts. The second is the author's belief that students who are prospective teachers should be exposed to the best minds in education and should have an opportunity to read them in the original. It is a serious indictment of our undergraduate programs in education that so few of our graduates have read any of the works of outstanding educators such as Dewey, Counts, Hook, Conant, and Hutchins. My experience in having students read these materials over the last several years has been encouraging. None of the students has complained that the materials were too easy, but most of them have found them stimulating and informative. This is especially true when the readings are followed by a probing analysis and discussion in the classroom. My experience has been that this procedure for the use of a textbook can result in genuine understanding, involving as it does careful, thoughtful reading followed by active participation in a directed class discussion.

Each of the six major divisions of the text is designed to develop more limited objectives which in turn contribute to the over-all objective of developing an understanding of American education. The purpose of Part I is to provide an understanding of the nature and urgency of the challenge facing American education; to indicate the tremendous potential as well as the great power of education for good or evil; and to present some of the factors that provide a basis for our efforts to create the kind of educational institutions and programs required in the continuing crisis of the mid-twentieth century. The purpose of Part II is to help the student gain some insight into the nature of culture and personality as a basis for understanding the nature of education and the major educational institution—the school. In Part III the intent is to lead the student to an understanding of the relationship between education and the rise of American civilization, as well as the relationship between the school and the society in which it functions. This problem is handled by a study of the history of American education with particular emphasis upon the origin and development of the public school system, in addition to an analysis of the major characteristics of contemporary American society and their reflections in American education. Part IV presents a descriptive account of the organization, support, and control of American education on all levels, including the international. This section also considers the aims of American education and the nature and organization of the curriculum. Part V is designed to acquaint the student with three major philosophies of education with the hope that he may take some steps toward developing his own philosophy as he progresses in his professional work. Finally, in Part VI, an attempt is made to show the growth, development, and present status of the teaching profession. Although the entire text is concerned in an indirect way with helping the student answer the question "Do I want to become a teacher?" this section deals with the question directly. In this section the problems of academic freedom and tenure, salaries, retirement, and job opportunities are treated along with an analysis of the qualities of a good teacher.

I am indebted to many persons for their invaluable assistance on this text. Professor George S. Counts gave me the benefit of his vast knowledge and experience in many hours of discussion, in addition to reading and criticizing parts of the manuscript. Professor Dietrich Gerhard helped in the formulation and organization of Chapters 7 and 8, "Ideological Characteristics of American Society and Education" and "Social and Economic Characteristics of American Society and Education," and gave other sections a critical reading. Professor R. Freeman Butts made important recommendations in the organization of the work and in the selection of readings, as well as reading the chapter on the history of American education. I am most grateful to my colleagues at Washington University for their counsel and inspiration—especially Charles Lee, Earl Herminghaus, Ralph Patrick, Lewis Hahn, Ryland Crary, and Robert Schaefer.

I wish to express my appreciation to the following persons for their help in the preparation of the manuscript: Lyn Kreps Hendry who read the manuscript critically and offered many helpful suggestions; Dorris Wilson who not only typed and edited the manuscript but also was a steady source of encouragement; and finally my wife, Helen Davidson Callahan, who assisted in editing and revising the manuscript and who gave constant encouragement and support.

I would especially like to acknowledge my debt to my great teachers Dietrich Gerhard, George S. Counts, and John L. Childs, without whom this book could not have been written. They are of course in no way responsible for its shortcomings.

RAYMOND E. CALLAHAN

St. Louis, Missouri
April, 1956

NOTE

IN THIS REVISION I MAINTAIN THE BASIC PHILOSOPHY OF THE FIRST EDI-
tion and approach American education as an integral part of American civilization. Of course, the statistical information has been
brought up to date and material incorporated on some of the important
recent developments such as James B. Conant's report on the American
high school. I have also included data which has been gathered in the
past four years by myself and my students in the history of American
education. The most important addition in this connection is a more
elaborate treatment of the important work of the Commission on the
Reorganization of Secondary Education which functioned from 1913
to 1922 and which produced the design for the modern comprehensive
high school. The most extensive revisions, however, have been made in
the last part of the book which contains the material on the teaching
profession and on teaching as a career. Specifically I have introduced
some of Myron Lieberman's interesting and controversial proposals on
the profession and a section on the art and science of teaching.

RAYMOND E. CALLAHAN

St. Louis, Missouri
April, 1960

CONTENTS

PART II. Culture, Education, and the School

PART III. American Society and American Education

Education
and the Future of
Civilization

*Human history becomes more and more a race be-
tween education and catastrophe.*

H. G. WELLS

CHAPTER 1

THE CHALLENGE TO EDUCATION

A BOOK WHOSE SUBJECT IS AMERICAN EDUCATION, AND ESPECIALLY ONE designed for prospective teachers, may properly—even, perhaps, necessarily—begin with a discussion of the nature and extent of the challenge facing American educators in the middle of the twentieth century. For the plain truth is that man in his long history has never faced problems of such complexity and such consequence as he faces to-day. On the other hand he has never before had at his disposal the means that exist today for elevating himself and his civilization. Therefore, the challenge facing mankind has its negative and positive aspects. The nega-tive side involves the task of preventing World War III, which would almost surely bring incomparable human suffering and misery, if not the destruction of civilization itself, while at the same time preventing totalitarianism in any form from engulfing the earth. The positive side involves the possibility of harnessing man's intelligence and creative genius for his own welfare. Arthur Compton, one of America's leading nuclear physicists and one of the pioneers in the development of the atomic bomb, stated the case very well when he said:

> Science and technology have put great new powers into the hands of men. If rightly used, they can give strength, a fuller freedom and a better human life for individuals and society.
> Because these powers released by science affect peoples' lives so deeply, it becomes increasingly important that the choices in the hands of men shall be made wisely and maturely with a sense of human responsibility and with the commitment of the higher goals of mankind.[1]

Unfortunately, men are not born with wisdom, maturity, and human responsibility; as we shall see, these patterns of behavior must be learned.

[1] *Student Life* (Washington University, St. Louis, Mo., Student Newspaper) September 28, 1954, p. 1.

Thus the task is essentially an educational one and therein lies the great challenge to education.

A brief review of the human record during the first half of the twentieth century will illustrate the complexity and gravity of the problems now facing mankind. In a sense this record has been one of great paradoxes. For example, in the twentieth century more schools have been built, more teachers have been trained, and more human beings have had more education than in any other period in history. On the basis of these facts it would be reasonable to expect that the twentieth century would be the most peaceful and the most prosperous in history. Exactly the reverse has been true, as any schoolboy knows. As George Counts has stated it:

> The horrors of Buchenwald, Dachau and Auschwitz, though thoroughly documented, remain incredible. A British parliamentary commission after visiting these camps reported with restraint and discrimination that they constituted the lowest point in moral degradation yet reached by the human race.[2]

Another of the great paradoxes of the twentieth century is the fact that we have seen hunger and poverty in the midst of plenty. Since the beginning of time men have labored to raise enough food and produce enough goods to keep themselves alive. But in our time we have witnessed the "absurdity of overproduction" in which farmers plowed crops under while human beings went hungry. Factories were closed when men needed goods.

The question is: What has happened? Why after all our education and all our technical progress are we in serious danger of destroying ourselves? One of the reasons is that man's technical skills have been developed far in advance of his sense of moral responsibility and of his social organization. But to understand what has happened and to comprehend the nature of the challenge to education, it is necessary to study and analyze some of the forces and events that have been responsible for bringing the modern world to its present dangerous state.

Advances in Science and Technology

PERHAPS the most basic factor in the emergence of modern civilization, with its resultant problems, has been the development of science and technology. In the twentieth century, through application of the scientific method, man has accumulated a vast amount of knowledge which has helped him to understand both himself and the world in which he

[2] George S. Counts, *Education and American Civilization* (New York: Bureau of Publications, Teachers College, Columbia University, 1952), pp. 5–6.

lives. Consider, for example, the achievements in the fields of biology, chemistry, physics, psychology, and sociology-anthropology. But man has done more than accumulate knowledge; he has also applied it, and the results have been startling. As a result of recent achievements in biology and chemistry man has a high degree of control over disease and, therefore, a healthier, longer life. Knowledge of physics and chemistry has enabled man to harness energy and to use it to produce the millions of mechanical devices which characterize our society. Knowledge in the fields of psychology, social psychology, and sociology-anthropology has enabled man to understand better himself, his motives, and his behavior, as well as the society in which he lives.

In the future it is likely that the changes resulting from science on the one hand and its practical application, technology, on the other will be occurring at a faster rate because advances in one tend to make possible advances in the other. The relationship between science and technology can be seen in the development of the atomic bomb. Knowledge about nuclear fission was accumulated by physicists but the production of the nuclear bomb involved engineering. Also, technical improvements such as the electronic microscope, made possible by scientific knowledge in the first place, enabled the scientist to open new frontiers of knowledge heretofore closed. The introduction of these new factors into human societies has been like a double-edged sword. Man has been able to conquer hunger and disease and to live a better life, but he has also produced engines of destruction that threaten to destroy him. Even before the H-bomb heightened the tension, scientific and technological knowledge had been used destructively by Hitler, Tojo, and Stalin. The destructive power at man's disposal is a prime factor in the precarious world situation, and men seeking a solution to the problem must understand this power, take it into account, and eventually control it.

The Impact of Industrialization

THE application of scientific and technical knowledge to the production of goods in the last century has produced our modern industrialized societies. Based upon mechanical power and the machine, and utilizing specialization of labor and mass-production techniques, industrialism has provided modern man with comforts and conveniences that would have been unbelievable a century ago. Industrialism has also created such problems as depressions and unemployment which, with the insecurity and fear they breed, have been among the major causes of the rise of the modern totalitarian state. Today all over the world one of the most critical issues is whether free men can handle their economic, industrial problems. In France, Germany, Japan, India, and many other countries a severe depression with its unemployment and acute economic suffering would in all probability pave the way for communism. Modern industrialization, based as it is upon extreme specialization, has made men more and more dependent upon one another. This interdependence requires a degree of co-operation and social planning difficult to attain among peoples with a strong belief in the individualism which characterized the preindustrial period. It has also caused major changes in family relations because the father and, in many instances, the mother work away from home. The result is that the school has assumed more and more of the responsibility for the education of the child. Finally, industrialization has produced the weapons of modern war which of course have been used in both World Wars to slaughter human beings.

It seems clear that men with knowledge, wisdom, and maturity will be needed to handle a complex, delicately balanced, industrialized economy. We in the United States have taken important strides forward in this direction since 1929, but our present level of employment is still based upon our defense effort. Moreover, in the years ahead we will have to be prepared to handle the social and economic problems that are bound to result from automation.

The Growth of Nationalism

WHILE science, technology, and industrialization have been pulling mankind together, nationalism has tended to keep groups of men apart. In the mid-twentieth century the human race is divided into some seventy-odd nation-states, many of which are separated by imaginary boundary lines. For individuals who are born and reared within a given nation-state, their country is the center of the universe. From childhood the individual is conditioned to accept the institutions, values, and military and political leaders of his own nation as naturally superior to those of other nations. This conditioning is informal in the home and in the nation at large, but it is systematic in the schools, particularly in the teaching of history and citizenship. In its extreme form, it is expressed in an inflated sense of national egoism which holds that the nation can do no wrong, that all the wars it has fought have been defensive, and that its actions are always just. In foreign policy, decisions are always based upon national interests and only incidentally upon the interests of the human race, and this pattern is accepted without question by diplomats and citizens alike.

Most historians are agreed that nationalism was one of the major causes of World War I and many observers believe it is still the major obstacle in the path of the creation of a world community. Hitler in Germany, and Mussolini in Italy, developed nationalism to such an emotional state that it resembled religious fanaticism and was the basis for the aggressive actions of the German and Italian people. But even in nations where it is not a basis for military aggression, nationalism often results in an inflated sense of national pride that causes resentment and suspicion between nations and makes genuine co-operation between them very difficult. The problem of developing an intelligent sense of national loyalty that recognizes man as part of a human family is one of the foremost educational tasks of the twentieth century.

The Consequences of Imperialism

IMPERIALISM has been closely related to nationalism as a source of trouble in the world. It may be defined as the attempt by a nation—in theory and practice—to extend its control, dominion, or empire. Imperialism has taken many forms since it was successfully carried out by Alexander the Great in ancient Greece. In most instances the conquest was through force of arms, and control was maintained in the same way.

In modern history the building of empires began in the sixteenth century with Britain, France, the Netherlands, and Spain competing for colonies. The purpose of the early imperialists was to build up the mother country by bringing back from the colonies gold or silver or, as in Britain's case, materials needed for the British fleet. Even in those days the competition for colonies tended to involve nations in wars. In the early nineteenth century the competition for empires slowed as most European countries had to cope with domestic problems and Napoleon. However, after 1870 the competition began anew with the field of conquest shifting from the Americas to Asia and Africa. In the new imperialism Britain again led the world, followed by France and Belgium and later by Germany, Italy, and the United States.

There were probably two basic reasons for this upsurge of imperialism in the late nineteenth century. First and foremost was the impact of industrialism. All the colonial powers were becoming industrialized and needed both raw materials for their factories and markets for their manufactured products. Secondly, the force of nationalism was reaching its peak and national pride demanded colonies, since the extent of empire was a yardstick for measuring national prestige.

Basically, imperialism has meant the exploitation of the backward nations for the benefit of the great powers, the welfare of the people themselves being secondary, if it was considered at all. The net result of this exploitation of the colored races has been a deep distrust of and a resentment against the West. For this reason the Japanese propaganda slogan "Asia for the Asiatics" used before and during World War II was very effective, and the theme is being replayed today by the communists in Asia. Of course in time the Asiatics found that the Japanese substituted an even more aggressive form of imperialism that could be more accurately described as "Asia for the Japanese." This indicates that imperialism need not involve feelings of racial superiority but, in most cases, since the imperial powers were white and the people of the colonies black or brown, a feeling of racial superiority was developed. There is no doubt that much of the present difficulty between East and West is due to the lingering odor of imperialism. The Russians continually attempt to make capital of this fact, keeping the issue before the Asians and the Africans by referring to the Western powers, especially the United States, as "imperialists."

After World War I it seemed that imperialism was on its way out. Colonial nations everywhere were either gaining their independence or had promise of it in the near future. Cases in point are India and the Philippines. Unfortunately the period between the wars saw the rise of three dictatorships whose policies were to be more viciously imperialistic than anything known to history—that is, until the world became familiar with postwar Soviet imperialism. These imperialists, backed by force and ruthlessness, were not and have not been tempered by any feelings of humanitarianism.

The judgment of imperialism can be clearly drawn. It has been a major cause of competition, conflict, and, ultimately, war between nations. It has alienated large portions of the earth's population from the Western democracies, and it has been the cause of untold suffering in Ethiopia, Manchuria, China, and many other nations. Finally, in its latest form in Korea, Indochina, and Hungary, it has been responsible for hundreds of thousands of human casualties, as well as the increased possibility of a third world war.

The Effects of Militarism

ANOTHER factor that has contributed to the problems of the twentieth century has been the emphasis upon militarism. In a world composed of nation-states, often competing with and suspicious of each other, there have been and will be conflicts from time to time. Because no international court with the power to enforce its decisions has existed, it has been up to the diplomats of the states involved to work out problems. In many critical situations the states involved have been unable to compromise for fear of suffering a loss of face or prestige—in other words, a slight on the national honor—and the only resource was the threat or use of force. Thus, in bargaining between nation-states, the strength and size of their armed forces and, later, their industrial capacity could be used as aids to the diplomats in their bargaining. Sometimes if the states were of unequal strength the mere threat of force would suffice to settle the dispute in favor of the more powerful state and war could be avoided. Thus the world has come to recognize the unpleasant reality of "power politics," whose basis in modern times is military force backed by industrial potential.

In this situation of law-of-the-jungle politics it was necessary for each nation-state to maintain its armed strength on a par with its rivals if possible. This competition to maintain a superior military establishment and the inevitable armament race that followed produced a national state of mind that was in itself a cause of war. For example, it became necessary for the military, if they were to defend the nation, to keep ahead of the potential enemy in industrial strength, weapons, and tactics. Therefore it was necessary to be informed about the potential enemy's strength in these areas. For this purpose spies—"intelligence agents" is the term used when they are representing one's own nation —were required, and spying, in turn, increased the suspicion and enmity between nations. Also, in order to assure the nation's full support for the armed forces and to induce young men to serve in the armed forces willingly and enthusiastically, it was necessary to build up and glorify the martial spirit. Once built up, this martial spirit has been difficult to control. It not only prepared the way for war psychologically but, once war started, contributed to its intensity and, of course, made a peaceful settlement more difficult.

Militarism has contributed toward war in another way, and it is here that the fineness of the line between offense and defense may be seen. Most military leaders have stated, at least for public consumption, that their actions are purely defensive. The Russian leaders, for example, have justified their huge military establishment, which prevents the Russian people from having a higher standard of living, on the grounds that the Soviet Union is surrounded by enemies. However, even military men who really desire peace instead of war have, by merely carrying out the responsibilities of their jobs, created a psychological atmosphere that has been a cause of war.

Europe before World War I is an example of the way in which the martial spirit contributes to the outbreak of war. Probably most of the generals and admirals in the nations of Europe were not eager to plunge their countries into war. Yet they were responsible for the fitness of the armed forces and for strategic planning. For example, France, England, and Russia, who were allied, planned the steps to be taken in the event Germany attacked. The German military leaders, for their part, had worked out detailed plans for the invasion of France through Belgium if war came. Also, joint planning was done by Germany and Austria as to what that nation's role would be. Each general staff kept pressure on the political leaders. They warned that a good offense was the best defense, and if war became inevitable they must strike the enemy first; otherwise victory could not be guaranteed. The result was that Europe, nervously watching and waiting, in 1914 literally held a bomb. When the Austrian Archduke was assassinated in Serbia, and Austria mobilized, the fuse was ignited. A chain reaction quickly spread over a jumpy and jittery Europe, and World War I, with all its misery and suffering, had begun. Today, despite the fact that President Eisenhower has stated repeatedly that victory is impossible for either side in an atomic war, we are spending vast sums on arms and are continuing to stockpile atomic bombs. The other great nations are doing likewise.

This is not to say that armies and navies can be done away with, for unilateral disarmament probably is not the way to peace. It is simply a historical fact that militarism has led to war. Most of the nations in the United Nations have realized this fact in their continuing efforts to reduce armaments. Our own policy after the war was also based on this premise, and earnest efforts were made to reduce and control armaments to avoid both the expense and the "psychology of war" which go with militarism. Unfortunately, faced with a nation such as the Soviet Union, with its aggressive intentions, our only hope is for the free world to be well armed. However, this fact should not blind us to the dangers inherent in militarism nor should it prevent us from continuing to search for a more adequate basis for handling international problems.

The Use of Propaganda

THE effects of propaganda should not be overlooked in any analysis of the factors responsible for the anarchy of the twentieth century. The use of propaganda has come about slowly since the development of the media of mass communication (chiefly the newspapers), in the late nineteenth and early twentieth centuries, and the development of universal education. The propaganda used in this period was of a nationalistic, patriotic nature and was not considered propaganda by those who used it. Certainly when we compare it with the later efficient use made of deliberate lying by men such as Goebbels and Stalin, it was mild indeed. Nevertheless a beginning was made before 1914. In France, for example, sensationalist newspapers urged Frenchmen to revenge their defeat by Germany in the Franco-Prussian War of 1870. In the French schools textbooks full of anti-German sentiment were used.

This was in fact only a beginning. The full exploitation of propaganda was developed during World War I as both sides attempted to marshal the emotions of their nations in order to attain a maximum of effort and participation. Propaganda ministries (usually called "offices of information") were set up in every nation and they began to pour out their "information." Below is a description by a French editor of the work done by one French propaganda organization during World War I.

> Its principal work consisted in making photographs and cuts of wooden figures with cut-off hands, torn-out tongues, gouged-out eyes, crushed skulls and brains laid bare. The pictures thus made were sent as unassailable evidence of German atrocities to all parts of the globe, where they did not fail to produce the desired effect. In the same rooms fictitious photographs were made of bombarded French and Belgian churches, violated graves and monuments, and scenes of ruins and desolation. The staging and painting of those scenes were done by the best scene-painters of the Paris Grand Opera.[3]

Since World War I, propaganda has been developed to a high degree by unscrupulous individuals who have deliberately distorted the truth in order to achieve their ends. Thus, Hitler, Mussolini, and Stalin stopped all freedom of the press in their respective countries. They then substituted their own organs of information which expressed the "official version" of the truth. In Germany, Goebbels was the master-mind who decided what information the German nation was to receive and every important means of communication—including press, radio, cinema, and the schools—was brought into line to support the Nazi program. In the Soviet Union Stalin, learning from Hitler, developed his techniques of propaganda to some sort of zenith. All outside sources of information were cut off from the Russian people. Then the Russians were given the party line not only in *Pravda* and through the radio channels but also by a careful writing of school textbooks and even by a rewriting of the dictionary to make the meaning of words conform to the "truth." Under the circumstances it is not surprising that hatred, suspicion, and misunderstanding have existed among the nations of the world.

The Tragedy of the "Great War"

ALTHOUGH it is true that the advancement of science and industrialism and the emergence of nationalism, imperialism, and militarism have been basic causes of troubles of the modern world, the real curse is war. The two great global wars that have occurred in the modern era have left in their wake a scarred and troubled world. No segment of human society involved has escaped the impact—in fact, many have been profoundly changed. In retrospect, World War I appears the most tragic event of the twentieth century. The long years of that struggle started

---

[3] Frederick E. Lumley, *The Propaganda Menace* (New York: Appleton-Century-Crofts, 1933), p. 230.

Europe on the downward path physically, economically, politically, and morally. It took the cream of European youth and weakened her economically to such an extent that democratic governments were overthrown outright in Germany and Italy and were seriously weakened in the other states. The moral conditions created undoubtedly played a part in paving the way for fascism and communism and, once they were established, contributed to their spread. The French and British turned away from Hitler's crimes, took the easy way out, and, in a crucial moment, let the League of Nations down. The dominant feeling in these democracies in the thirties was one of pessimism and despair, expressed vividly in the slogan "peace at any price." Nor was the situation much better in America. We rejected the League, spurned our responsibilities, and buried our heads in the sand while the world was rising in turmoil about us. Late in the 1930's thousands of American college students took the Oxford Pledge, solemnly swearing they would never go to war, and many classroom instructors were told by students that they did not care to hear about Hitler's atrocities against the Jews.

One of the factors responsible for this condition was of course the dreadful suffering involved in World War I. All the legendary glamor of great military campaigns was gone because in modern war men lived and died in mud and filth, often killing and being killed by men they could not even see. Nor did it take an Einstein to see that the next war would make the first one seem like child's play. But perhaps even more important was the realization of the utter senselessness of the war. It had started for no good reason and had solved none of the world's problems. Finally, publication of the details of the propaganda techniques used to fire men's emotions was disillusioning, to say the least.

The Failure of the League of Nations

WORLD WAR I destroyed the myth that had surrounded the concept of the balance of power as a means of keeping the peace. It is true that the idea was not and has not been abandoned; nevertheless, most responsible statesmen realized its inadequacies. The result was that, under the leadership of Woodrow Wilson, the League of Nations organization was set up in 1919. The changeover to an attempt at collective security through the League did not involve a change in human nature. The simple truth was that men had been driven to this step by the violent logic of war. Until 1914, war had been troublesome, and even cruel to the unfortunate individuals involved, but it had not become a threat to civilization and could therefore be tolerated. The introduction of total war plus the changed modes of warfare brought the entire nation to the front line. It was clear that something had to be done. The means employed in the nineteenth century to settle disputes between nations were no longer adequate.

The need for international co-operation had been felt in many areas long before 1913 and many international organizations had been set up. Among these were the Universal Postal Union and the International Health Control, formed, in each instance, to meet an intolerable situation. Gradually their areas of operation were broadened and these beginning movements constituted the first steps toward international government. Added to the control of public health and the postal service were regulations for telegraph and wireless and other matters in which conflicting national interests had been forced to give way before the interests of the whole. The final step remained in the field of politics, and it took a world war to shake a sufficient number of people out of their lethargy and to spur them to create a world political organization.

The failure of the League is a matter of history but the reasons for its failure have been a topic of controversy for twenty years. Certainly the failure of the United States to join was a severe blow. More important, perhaps, was the lack of any power to enforce decisions. This fact was continually emphasized by the men who wrote the United Nations Charter in 1945 as *the* weakness and a concerted effort was made to correct this lack in the new charter. Undoubtedly another factor was the rule of unanimity, which meant that every country had to agree before any action could be taken, and this certainly made decisions difficult. However, other critics claim that these facts were but symptoms of a weakness that had its roots in the structure of the League itself.

The League of Nations was an organization of sovereign states. Each nation maintained its own military establishment and accepted the jurisdiction of the League only when such jurisdiction happened to coincide with narrow national interest. The international situation after World War I required a political institution to provide a minimum of government on an international scale. The League had none of the attributes of government and was therefore unable to enact or to enforce the world law necessary to prevent disputes between states from breaking into war. The basic weakness of the League was exemplified by the statement of Sir John Simon, the British Foreign Minister in 1931 during the Manchurian crisis. Defending his position of noninterference he said: "The object of my policy is to keep my own country out of trouble." The nations were unwilling, and therefore the League was unable, to stop the Japanese aggression in China in 1931 or the Italian invasion of Ethiopia in 1935.

It is not meant to imply here that the League of Nations was not a valuable organization. Much of its work was worthwhile and, in fact, many disputes between smaller powers were settled. Most important, however, was the *idea* of the League as a symbol of world unity and co-operation. The fact that it failed to preserve peace permanently was tragic but the fact that it existed at all was a great step forward. It is obvious that war had not become intolerable, for at least three nations used war in the 1930's as an instrument of national policy.

The Rise of Dictatorships and the Totalitarian States

As a result of the social, economic, political, and moral disorganization caused by World War I, there appeared a new phenomenon in Western civilization—the modern dictator. Using the forms and slogans of democracy and the devices of technology, these men gained an unprecedented degree of control over the lives of the individuals within their respective states. And so the world was faced with the spectacle of these ruthless and efficient dictators—Mussolini, Hitler, and Stalin—in complete control of three powerful nation-states organized under the now-familiar totalitarian pattern.

The history of Germany between the two wars furnishes an example of the way in which several of the forces that have been discussed have contributed to the crisis of the twentieth century. In 1932, Germany, a powerful, interdependent, industrial nation, was economically prostrate with her factories closed and millions unemployed, hungry, and insecure. Hitler promised to put people to work. He did that and more. He blamed the Jews for Germany's economic distress and thus provided a scapegoat. He played upon the fear of communism held by the industrialists and the middle classes. He charged that the party in power (the Social Democratic) was inept and was responsible for Germany's plight. He associated the Social Democrats with responsibility for the humiliation of the Versaille Treaty and aroused the latent national resentment of the Germans against them. He inflated national and individual egos by preaching the doctrine of Aryan racial superiority. The record of history shows that the German people—hungry, unemployed, insecure, humiliated, and frustrated—were fair game for Hitler's propaganda. Once in power he consolidated his position into that of absolute dictator and led Germany on the aggressive path that was directly responsible for World War II.

World War II and the United Nations

Unlike the first great war World War II involved clear-cut issues. Either the democracies would fight or dictatorship would overwhelm them. So they fought, and the victory won is a magnificent record of courage, sacrifice, and co-operation. The war, which was the most devastating in history, resulted in the prostration of Germany, Japan, and Italy, the exhaustion of Britain and France, and the emergence of two military and industrial giants—the United States and the U.S.S.R. Also of great importance was the harnessing of atomic energy and development of the atomic bomb, which was used on Japan.

The violence, brutality, and destructiveness of the war, plus the terrifying possibilities of the atomic bomb, led to the almost universal demand that future wars be prevented. To this end the United Nations was created and set into motion, with the high hopes and prayers of mankind. But the urge for peace was not strong enough to overcome the temptation to exploit the situation for national interest. Consequently, the institution that was created was not substantially stronger than the League, and moreover it concentrated power in the hands of the Big Five. Some of the smaller nations fought in vain to democratize the charter. Attempts were made to alter the amending process, to give the Assembly more power, to place more emphasis upon economic and social problems, and last but not least, to temper the veto power. The situation was described by Herbert Evatt, the Australian delegate, as follows:

> We were told over and over again that preservation of the principle of unanimity among the Great Powers was vital, and when amendments to the formula were moved or discussed, we were accused of wanting to be "perfectionists" or of wanting to "tear up the charter." In the end we were told flatly that no change in the text would be accepted and that we would have to take the charter with this text or have no world organization at all.[4]

From the beginning the Soviet Union thwarted the new organization with its vetoes, its stalling, and its general disruptive tactics. Apparently the Russian leaders had no intention of letting the new organization function. The United States plan for the control of atomic energy, known as the Baruch Plan, which was one of the most intelligent and generous proposals ever made by a nation-state, was delayed and eventually killed by the Soviet leaders, although recently they have apparently reconsidered their position and have participated in discussions of variations of the original plan. The efforts of the UN did not of course prevent the "cold war," or the hot wars in Korea and Indochina. But the organization took a firm stand against the communist aggression in Korea and established the principle of collective security. The fact is that the United Nations has achieved a great deal despite the obstructionist tactics of the Soviet leaders and there is every indication that it could do more if it received more support from the nations and peoples

[4] Herbert Evatt, *The United Nations* (Cambridge, Mass.: Harvard University Press, 1948), p. 24.

of the world, especially the United States and Great Britain. We have been guilty too often of using the UN as an instrument of our foreign policy. The fact that the United Nations is even in existence is an encouraging sign, but the organization must be strengthened and supported if it is to keep the peace. Probably the greatest obstacle to a strengthened and successful United Nations is the power of nationalism. Nation-states seem unwilling to give up any degree of sovereignty, even if some semblance of world order could be created thereby.

The Threat of Russian Communism

THE present world crisis is largely a result of the activity of the Russian communists. It is true, of course, that if by some magic the Russian communists were to disappear from the face of the earth, we would still have the legacy of problems created by the forces and events already mentioned and, therefore, no guarantee of peace and security. But it is Russian communism that presently threatens the very existence of the free world.

The communist threat has at least three dimensions: military, economic, and ideological. The military is certainly the most immediate and probably the most dangerous. If the Russians did not have an army of two hundred divisions, a powerful air force, and nuclear weapons the world situation would not be as ominous as it is. But too often, the other aspects of the communist challenge are overlooked and in the long run this oversight could be fatal. The economic challenge lies in the fact that communism promises people, such as the Chinese, the benefits of industrialization without the evils of the exploitation of labor and without the dangers of depression. It has been said of the Russian communists that they consigned depressions to the wastebasket of history. It was this aspect of their program that attracted many intelligent, sensitive persons to their ranks during the years of the Great Depression, and it is this part of their program that is attracting many in the underdeveloped areas of the world. As Chester Bowles sees it, this problem of economic reorganization is the basic issue in Asia. The question is whether nations, such as India and China, can have both rapid industrialization and higher standards of living under a democratic system. China, according to Bowles, has accepted the communist program of industrialization under a ruthlessly totalitarian system. India, on the other hand, is attempting to secure the benefits of industrialization and still maintain its progress toward the democratic pattern of individual freedom, dignity, and self-government. It is clear that this question must be answered in all nations, including the United States. As the economic pattern began to unfold in the Soviet Union during the thirties, it became clear that economic security was being achieved at the price of individual freedom, and so that pattern has been rejected by thoughtful men who believe that both values—security and freedom —can be achieved. Still, where democratic patterns are weak and not meeting the needs, the communist economic solutions are being accepted.

The third dimension of the communist challenge is related to the second but goes beyond it. In effect, it promises the end of unemployment and of economic suffering. It promises the end of the exploitation of man by man and the equality of all races, and as a result of the record of imperialism, this promise is most effective in Asia, as it could be in Africa. On the negative side it blames "capitalistic imperialism" for the wars, depressions, and exploitation of the twentieth century. Of course, well-informed persons the world over are aware of the real nature of Russian communism, based on evidence from within the U.S.S.R. and from the satellite countries. But to millions of hungry, exploited men who are without hope the communist ideology offers a chance for something better than they have. As in all effective propaganda, the communist platform contains enough truth, e.g., on racial discrimination and imperialism, to make it effective.

The Challenge to Education

THE powerful forces and events discussed in the preceding pages have produced the problems that must be faced by educators in the second half of the twentieth century. Somehow, science, technology, and industrialization must be used for man's welfare and not for his destruction. Somehow, the divisive force of nationalism must be understood, tempered, and counteracted by an emphasis upon human unity. The evils of imperialism, militarism, and propaganda must be understood and gradually eliminated from our social fabric. Last, but not least, we must meet the challenge not only of Russian communism, but also of totalitarianism in any form if the human race is to move forward toward ever-higher levels of civilization. Of course, teachers alone through the schools cannot solve this complex legacy of problems. But these problems were created by human beings and they can be solved by intelligent, mature, sensitive, well-informed human beings. It is in the development of such individuals that education can make its contribution. Obviously our efforts may be in vain for there is no way of telling what course the Russian communists may take in the years ahead. But if they realize the futility of modern atomic war and if they are convinced that the democracies will not collapse, perhaps a modus vivendi can be worked out between the United States and Russia. If so, the issue will settle down to a long-range struggle and in this kind of struggle, over the long pull, education can be decisive.

In our educational as well as our political planning we have to assume that the human race will not be destroyed in an atomic war, but we dare not forget that both the United States and Russia have enough bombs in their respective stockpiles to bring on such destruction. An intelligent approach is neither one of hopeless despair because of the possibility of atomic war nor one of naïve optimism each time world tension eases a little. Rather, we must realize that to achieve and maintain world peace and freedom a persistent, concerted effort must be made with educators at the forefront. This places the individual teacher and the teaching profession as a whole in a new perspective. We cannot afford to continue believing and acting on the belief that teaching is essentially a job of "keeping order" or that "he who can, does; he who cannot, teaches!" To meet the challenge education will need the most intelligent, the most sensitive, and the most dedicated of our young people to go into teaching. It must then provide them with the finest education possible, regardless of the cost.

Individuals just beginning to prepare themselves for the teaching profession will have an especially heavy responsibility. Our teachers will have more influence than any other group on the intellectual, moral, social, and aesthetic development of the next generation of Americans. Therefore, in the long run, the fate of our country and of civilization itself will depend in large part upon their quality. Thus the prospective teacher, more than any other college student, must approach his work with the seriousness of purpose necessary to professional excellence. In addition, the colleges and universities must focus their attention upon improving the quality of their teacher education programs so that we will have eventually an excellent teacher in every classroom in America. By settling for less we are gambling with the future.

Suggested Readings

Anderson, Howard R., ed.: *Approaches to an Understanding of World Affairs.* Twenty-fifth Yearbook of the National Council for Social Studies. Washington, D.C.: National Council for the Social Studies, 1954.

Arndt, Christian O., and Everett, Samuel, eds.: *Education for a World Society.* New York: Harper & Brothers, 1951.

Bowles, Chester: *Africa's Challenge to America.* Berkeley and Los Angeles: University of California Press, 1956.

Bowles, Chester: *The New Dimensions of Peace*. New York: Harper & Brothers, 1955.

Childs, John L.: *Education and Morals*. New York: Appleton-Century-Crofts, 1950.

Conant, James B.: *Education in a Divided World*. Cambridge, Mass.: Harvard University Press, 1948.

Counts, George S.: *Education and American Civilization*. New York: Bureau of Publications, Teachers College, Columbia University, 1952.

Cousins, Norman: *Who Speaks for Man*. New York: The Macmillan Company, 1953.

Crossman, Richard, ed.: *The God That Failed*. New York: Harper & Brothers, 1949.

Kennan, George F.: *American Diplomacy 1900–1950*. Chicago: University of Chicago Press, 1951.

Kohn, Hans: *The Twentieth Century*. New York: The Macmillan Company, 1949.

Lippmann, Walter: *The Public Philosophy*. New York: A Mentor Book, The New American Library of World Literature, Inc., 1956.

Meyer, Cord: *Peace or Anarchy*. Boston: Little, Brown & Company, 1948.

Stevenson, Adlai E.: *Friends and Enemies*. New York: Harper & Brothers, 1959.

———: *The New America*. New York: Harper & Brothers, 1959.

Wecter, Dixon: *The Age of the Great Depression*. New York: The Macmillan Company, 1948.

CHAPTER 2

THE POTENTIAL OF EDUCATION

GRANTED THAT THE HUMAN RACE FACES AN UNPARALLELED CHALLENGE in a world situation that gives every indication of being continuously critical, the question is: Is man capable of meeting this challenge? Does man have the potential to control his destiny and to rise to higher levels of civilization, or has he reached his limit and is he now unable to cope with the complex problems he himself has created? If man is capable, how can he use education in attempting to solve his problems? Does education have the *potential* to contribute to the solution of these problems? Obviously the tremendous expansion of formal education in the twentieth century has not *prevented* world war and totalitarianism. In fact, as we have seen, the reverse appears to be true. Are we really justified in expecting so much from education? In short, what potential does man have and how is education involved? To help answer these questions we will consider evidence, first, from the field of biological science and then from the field of social science.

Man's Biological Potential

THE evidence of man's biological potential will be presented by one of the world's leading biological scientists, Julian Huxley. The selection printed constitutes the greater part of a chapter entitled "The Path of Biological Progress" from his recent book, *Evolution in Action*. The student of education should be particularly concerned with the role that education plays in the "new process of evolution" described by Mr. Huxley.

JULIAN HUXLEY

FROM

Evolution in Action [1]

Thirty years ago, Professor Bury wrote a very interesting book on *The Idea of Progress*. When I read it, I was surprised at the modernity of the notion. Its history dates back to little more than three hundred years ago, and it is eminently a nineteenth-century concept. Other periods thought in terms of deterioration from a Golden Age, or of cyclical recurrence, or of the mere persistence of human sin and misery, tempered by hopes of salvation in another life. The idea of progress could not have become part of general thought until men could see that, in one respect or another, they were improving their lot. In the eighteenth century, the chief emphasis seems to have been on the superiority of the civilized and cultured life of the period. In the nineteenth it was switched to the rapid improvement in man's technological control of nature; but there were many variants of the idea, ranging from the perfectibility of man through universal education to the Hegelian doctrines about the National State. Darwin's work added scientific respectability to the general concept; but in practice it was used to justify any philosophy of progress in vogue, including the Prussian conception of progress through struggle and war.

One of my earliest essays was on this subject of progress. As a young zoologist, I had become impressed with the overall trends to be discerned in evolution, and the need for studying and thinking about them as well as about the minor details of the process, or its underlying mechanisms. In particular, I realized the need of reaching a scientific definition of the term "progress" itself. On re-reading this youthful production, I find that my ideas on the subject are still much the same. The only difference is that I then thought that biological progress could be wholly defined by its results; I now realize that any definition must also take into account the path that it has followed.

It is easy to confuse the two ideas of progress and improvement; so, at the risk of repeating myself tediously, I want to remind you of a few salient points. There are all kinds of biological improvement. There are adaptations which benefit certain individuals at the expense of the species; minor adjustments of the species; specializations of a type for a particular way of life; and advances in the general efficiency of biological machinery. But improvements are not something ready-made, they are trends in time. And most of them turn out to be finite; sooner or

[1] Julian Huxley, *Evolution in Action* (New York: Harper & Brothers) Copyright, 1953, by Julian S. Huxley. Pp. 124–6, 129–41, 147–50.

later, they come to a stop. Occasionally, one line of advance continues after related lines have come to a stop; and then you get what I called successional replacement, where a later deployment replaces an earlier one as a dominant type. The fact of replacement is itself a demonstration that there has been general improvement or advance. Putting the matter in another way, there is continuity of improvement between one group and its successor, as for instance between reptiles and mammals. We need a term for the sum of these continuities through the whole of evolutionary time, and I prefer to take over a familiar word like progress instead of coining a special piece of esoteric jargon.

In the light of these considerations, the human species, as the latest successional deployment, represents the furthest step yet taken in evolutionary progress. This is not just anthropomorphic wish-fulfillment, but a direct and necessary deduction from biological fact. Man may not be the measure of all things, but the difference between man and the simplest organisms is certainly the measure of biological progress. However, though biological progress has culminated in man, progress had been going on during the hundreds of millions of years before man came into existence. It was there, merely waiting to be detected. . . .

I once tried to list the series of all the major steps in biological progress, but gave it up when I got to the fortieth. Here all I can do is to pick out a few illuminating instances. Before beginning on this I must make one point. The story of life's advance is not made up out of the imagination; even though the evidence is often indirect or circumstantial, it is none the less evidence. The biologist knows that evolution has happened. He looks at the results of it, as many of them as possible, and then reconstructs the picture of its course which will best fit the facts. When the facts are available in the shape of actual fossils, his picture will be more detailed and more accurate. But the facts of comparative anatomy and embryology and biochemistry and genetics are equally relevant, and any picture which fits them will not be a false picture; it will give a reasonable approximation to the truth.

One of the earliest necessary steps in progress was the reduction of the rate at which mutation occurs. I remember the surprise with which I first realized this fact. We know that mutation rate can be controlled genetically: genes have been discovered which alter the rates of mutation of other genes, though we do not yet know just how this is effected. We also know that any molecule so immensely large and complicated as a gene would be expected to undergo changes in its chemical structure— in other words to mutate—at a rate too high for reasonable genetic stability, and certainly much higher than all normal mutation rates actually found. Selection must have mutations to build with; but if the mutation rate is too high, the building will keep falling apart. The necessary reduction of mutation rate to a manageable level seems to have been one of the very first steps in progress. With the possible exception of some of the viruses (perhaps not fully fledged organisms at all), this step was taken by all forms of life.

The first forms of life can have been little more than naked genes; an early step in progress was from this simplicity to the cellular level of organization. A cell, for our purpose, is a microscopic but highly complicated unit of living substance, enclosing a nucleus with an accurately self-producing genetic outfit in it—in other words, chromosomes with an array of different genes along their length, and a mechanism for distributing them accurately each time the cell divides. This seems to have been combined, probably from the outset, with another vital step, the development of sex—in other words, a mechanism for recombining mutant genes from different lines. It used to be supposed, until very recently, that the whole enormous group of bacteria were so primitive that they possess neither chromosomes nor sex. One of the most spectacular discoveries of the past few years is the fact that, in their chromosomes and their mechanisms of sexual recombination, they possess essentially the same genetic equipment as you or I or any other organism.

Next, I want to say a word about the step to the many-celled condition in animals. This was indispensable for the attainment of more than microscopic size and more than an elementary degree of division of labor among the tissues and the organs of the body. But it was not universally taken. The protozoa are organized on the basis of a single cell unit; but they are among the most successful of animals, swarming in the sea, in the soil, in fresh water, in the interiors of other animals. This fact well illustrates the differences between success and advance. There is room in the world for microscopic animals as well as large ones. The protozoa fill a large part of the microscopic niche very successfully, and in a way that would be impossible for animals of larger bulk. Theoretically, the step to the many-celled condition could have been taken in two rather different ways—either by way of a colony of separate cells, or by the cutting up of a single highly differentiated cell with several nuclei in it, into a number of cellular units. It looks as if the first was the method adopted by the sponges. In any case, the sponges have remained throughout their evolution as rather loosely knit aggregates of cells; and they have never evolved such elementary prerequisites of further progress as a mouth or a nervous system. They represent a branch that came inevitably to a dead end. . . .

The next indispensable step involves three apparently different but actually interconnected developments. These are bilateral symmetry; the exploration of the environment for food by forward movement; and finally the formation of a head—the gradual concentration in the front part of the body, of the mouth, the primitive brain, and the main sense organs. We are apt to take these improvements for granted; but, though they were indispensable for progress, they were not present in the great majority of earlier forms of life, and one or other of them has often been abandoned during the further evolution of animals. This happened with all the creatures that took to a fixed existence, or went over from active searching for food to filter feeding or tentacle feeding, to random crawling or floating—sea anemones and jellyfish, sea lilies and clams, sea urchins and barnacles. And it is quite clear that any animals that lost any one of this set of improvements were thereby put out of the path of further progress. Headless animals are often successful; but they are in a blind alley. . . .

Now I must make a big jump. In the next stage of animal progress, over hundreds of millions of years, there must have been parallel advances in many different lines—advances in efficiency and in integrated complexity. Thus, the three main groups which have evolved out of the early many-celled Metazoa—the molluscs, the arthropods and the vertebrates—all developed highly organized digestive and circulatory systems, highly efficient tissues like muscles and nerves, and highly elaborate sense organs, like pattern-forming eyes, while they were still aquatic. It comes as something of a shock to realize that this could not have been achieved without death, in the sense of the obligatory death of all the body except its germ cells. The distinction between non-reproducing individual body or *soma* and immortal reproductive tissue or *germ plasm*, first made by Weismann, is an important one, even though it is not always quite so clear-cut as he supposed. In protozoa, death in this sense does not exist: the individual simply divides into two. In Metazoa the separation begins; and it grows sharper during their evolution. It grows sharper in two rather different ways. The continuing sexual germ plasm becomes more rigidly separated at an early stage in development, and the somatic tissues lose their capacity for non-sexual reproduction. Many polyps and worms, for instance, can still reproduce by fission or make new individuals by budding. But even this seems to be impossible after a certain level of organization has been reached. At any rate it never occurs in animals with a highly organized body consisting of specialized tissues. For the Metazoa, death was thus a prerequisite for further progress; it is the price life had to pay for individuality and the efficiency of its biological machinery; and we continue to pay that price.

Among the molluscs and the arthropods are to be found some very successful groups, like the snails or the crabs or the insects: the insects indeed are in one way the most successful of all types, in that they have given rise to more different species than any other. But of all these none was capable of indefinite progress. This was reserved for the vertebrates. The earliest vertebrates had many prerequisites for further progress. They were active searchers for food; their method of swimming with the aid of a tail gave them greater speed and power than any of their

competitors; and they were capable of growing to larger size. Perhaps I
should say that the scale of their construction is larger than that of any
other kind of animal. The smallest vertebrate is hundreds or thousands
of times larger than the smallest mollusc or arthropod, and no mollusc
attains even one-tenth, or arthropod even one-hundredth, of the bulk of
the biggest fish, still less of the biggest mammals.

Further, a point which is often forgotten, their organization is more
flexible. Their skeleton is made of living and adjustable material, like
bone and cartilage, instead of dead secretions; and their tendons can
adapt themselves to the tensions to which they are subjected during
growth. Thus their whole structural framework can grow and adjust itself continuously, instead of molting from one predetermined piece of
body armor into another, as in arthopods. In addition, they are capable
of attaining a much greater flexibility of behavior. They have evolved an
internal environment which is both more flexible and more independent
of outer changes than that of any other group. The blood stream of
higher vertebrates regulates its chemical composition with extraordinary
accuracy, and in this way, as well as by its self-regulatory mechanism of
temperature control, lays the foundation for a high degree of continuity
and accuracy of mental activities. Meanwhile the development of the
system of endocrine glands, secreting hormones into the blood, makes
possible a new and more flexible integration.

Before the appearance of the early vertebrates we have reached the
stage at which evolution is documented by well-preserved fossils—the
stage comparable to that of recorded history in the affairs of man. Accordingly, we can now often detect the actual twists and turns of progress. Take the successful occupation of the land by animals—a step
which only occurred well on in the last quarter of evolutionary time. On
land, the animal is confronted with a greater range and rapidity of
change in environmental conditions than in water. This means a need
for greater acuteness and range of sense organs, and puts a premium on
learning rapidly by experience. On land, again, not only was there an
obvious advantage in attaining a high constant body temperature, but it
was easier, for various physiological reasons, to attain it. The stimuli of
land life thus provided various opportunities for progress; and only the
vertebrates were capable of taking full advantage of those opportunities.
Even the insects could not climb these further steps—they are too small
to have a constant temperature or to be very intelligent, and too rigidly
made for flexibility of structure or behavior. In passing, their inflexibility
and their small size are the reasons for the enormous number of their
species—each species tends to have a smaller coverage, so to speak, of
the environment.

However, for the vertebrates to achieve land life they had to pass
through a narrow and devious channel, some three hundred million

years ago, during the Devonian period. There were various prerequisites for this step in progress. In the first place, there had to be a change of climate—a desiccation which led to a drying out of the fresh waters of the world. Then, the invaders of the land, the future ancestors of ourselves, had to be fresh-water fish; marine fish were out of the running. They had still to retain lobe-shaped fins, widely spaced out along the body, on which they rested while on the bottom of the water; so all fish which had specialized for streamlined speed in open waters were out of the running also. Finally, they had to have a swim bladder which was open to the gullet, and was therefore capable of acting as an accessory organ of respiration by gulping in air.

In the Devonian period there was a whole group of fish of this type, adapted to bottom living in stagnant fresh waters—the lungfish, in the broad sense of the word. When they were caught in increasingly stagnant water by the change of climate, they could survive by getting from one pool to another in case of need. In those which adopted this method, the air bladder became a little more of a lung; their fins became better able to support their weight when out of water. So the first step in the conquest of the land was, strictly speaking, not an adaptation to land life at all, but merely an adaptation for continuing aquatic life by getting from one pool of water to another as quickly as possible. However, once this step had been taken, a new evolutionary opportunity was open. By means of minor further improvements their fins could become walking legs, and their air bladders could become nothing but lungs. With these improvements the animals were able to spend the whole of their adult life out of water, so long as they spent it in moist conditions.

Another striking twist in the path of progress occurred during the origin of the mammals. They had, it seems, to pass through a phase of their existence as small and insignificant nocturnal creatures, in the course of which they lost the capacity for color vision. Their very insignificance enabled them to survive during the long period when the land was dominated by powerful and specialized types of reptile. Their opportunity came when a great mountain-building revolution occurred, at the close of the Mesozoic epoch. The accompanying changes in climate, and in the distribution of land and sea, eventually resulted in the extinction of many of their reptilian competitors and put the rest at a disadvantage. The mammals were then able to profit by their new combination of capacities—temperature regulation, and caring for their young; and so were able to emerge into the light of day, and to spread and multiply exceedingly, though they seem not to have reacquired color vision until the emergence of monkeys and apes.

Meanwhile, the birds had replaced the pterodactyls as conquerors of the air, and during the subsequent period they arrived at a delicacy of temperature regulation equal to that of the mammals. They also became capable of speeds greater than that of any other organism—speeds which were only excelled by airplanes a bare twenty years ago. They were very successful, and they achieved a number of important advances, but they cut themselves off from progress by their specialization. Their fore limbs are so thoroughly specialized as flying organs that they have become unusable for any other function; they are incapable of use as hands, and hands were a prerequisite for further progress.

Long before the end of the Cenozoic epoch, most of the possibilities available to living substance had been exhausted, in one animal group or another. Speed I have just mentioned. Size had reached a point where it became self-defeating; the chemical composition of the blood had become fully constant; the efficiency of nervous conduction, of sense organs, of digestive systems, and of mechanical construction had all reached limits of one sort or another. Only one feature remained capable of improvement—brain organization and behavior. Only a greater flexibility of behavior, and a higher organization of awareness, enabled living substance to become capable of conceptual thought and symbolic language; and these, as we saw, are the two distinguishing marks of man, and the basis of the latest deployment of life.

Here again the new step could not be reached except through a tortuous channel. The precursor of man had to pass through the stage of being a monkey. It had to give up the usual practice of mammals, of producing many young at a birth. As J. B. S. Haldane has pointed out, the presence of many young in the uterus gives rise to an acute struggle for existence between them before birth; and in this competition, general rapidity of growth and development is at a premium. Only in creatures which normally produce one young at a birth was it possible for the general rate of development to be slowed down, so as to provide a longer learning period. Monkeys live in trees, and they use their hands as well as feet for climbing. They also use their hands for manipulating their food, and have developed binocular vision for its better detection. This combination of handling and seeing was necessary for the better organization of experience. Tree life thus laid the foundation both for our clearer definition of objects by conceptual thought, and for our fuller control of them by tools and machines tens of millions of years later. However, two further turnings had to be taken before this could come about. First, monkeys had to become apes. Apes get around mainly by swinging with their arms, not by climbing with all four limbs. This made it possible for their hind limbs to become differentiated as supporting feet. Finally, it was necessary for the apes to descend from the trees. This paved the way for the fully erect posture of our own species; and made possible the freeing of the hands for the sole job of manipulation. And this, in turn, was the prerequisite for the last step in biological progress—the attainment of true speech and conceptual thinking.

Looking back into the past we see clearly enough that conceptual thought could only have arisen in an animal as against a plant; in a multicellular animal; in an actively feeding animal, with bilateral symmetry and a head; in one with a highly differentiated bodily organization, which was therefore doomed to die; in a vertebrate as against a mollusc or an arthropod; in a land vertebrate as against a fish; and among land vertebrates, only in a placental mammal with a constant temperature. And finally, it could have arisen only in a mammal which had become gregarious, which had a long period of learning and experience, which produced only one young at a birth, and which had recently become terrestrial after a long spell of life in the trees. Clearly, the path of progress is both devious and unique! . . .

Purely biological progress, in fact, has come to an end, but human progress is just beginning. There is a radical difference between them, which is correlated with the equally radical difference between any kind of animal life and any kind of human life. We begin by minimizing the difference between animals and ourselves by unconsciously projecting our own qualities into them: This is the way of children and of primitive peoples. Though early scientific thinkers, like Descartes, tried to make the difference absolute, later applications of the method of scientific analysis to man have, until quite recently, tended to reduce it again. This is partly because we have often been guilty of the fallacy of mistaking origins for explanations—that we may call the "nothing but" fallacy: if sexual impulse is at the base of love, then love is to be regarded as nothing but sex; if it can be shown that man originated from an animal, then in all essentials he is nothing but an animal. This, I repeat, is a dangerous fallacy.

We have tended to misunderstand the nature of the difference between ourselves and animals. We have a way of thinking that if there is continuity in time there must be continuity in quality. A little reflection would show that this is not the case. When we boil water there is a continuity of substance between water as a liquid and water as steam; but there is a critical point at which the substance H_2O changes its properties. This emergence of new properties is even more obvious when the process involves change in organization as in all cases when chemical elements combine to produce a chemical compound.

The critical point in the evolution of man—the change of state when wholly new properties emerged in evolving life—was when he acquired the use of verbal concepts and could organize his experience in a common pool. It was this which made human life different from that of all other organisms; and we can now begin to grasp the nature and profundity of the difference. The development of animals is always closed; their evolution is always sooner or later restricted. Man's individual development, on the other hand, is potentially open. It continues throughout his life, and it can take place in all sorts of directions; while in animals there is only one normal pattern to be realized. The same sort of thing holds for man as a type—his pooled experience can be indefinitely added to, and it can be organized in an indefinite number of different ways. Animal types have limited possibilities, and sooner or later exhaust them: man has an unlimited field of possibilities, and he can never realize all of them. He has developed a new method of evolution: the transmission of organized experience by way of tradition, which supplements and largely overrides the automatic process of natural selection as the agency of change in the human phase.

This puts mind, in all its aspects, into the business of evolution. Thus, under this new dispensation, beliefs are inevitably brought into being; and once they have been brought into being, they become tools of living. And the same is true of ideals or purposes or scientific theories or religious systems—they are among the emergent properties of the new, human type of organization. They cannot help coming into existence, and then they cannot help becoming operative factors for further change. Thus, once life had become organized in human form it was impelled forward, not merely by the blind forces of natural selection but by mental and spiritual forces as well.

In the light of evolutionary biology man can now see himself as the sole agent of further evolutionary advance on this planet, and one of the few possible instruments of progress in the universe at large. He finds himself in the unexpected position of business manager for the cosmic process of evolution. He no longer ought to feel separated from the rest of nature, for he is part of it—that part which has become conscious, capable of love and understanding and aspiration. He need no longer regard himself as insignificant in relation to the cosmos. He is intensely significant. In his person, he has acquired meaning, for he is constantly creating new meanings. Human society generates new mental and spiritual agencies, and sets them to work in the cosmic process: it controls matter by means of mind. . . .

Thus we see that from Huxley's point of view man has the potential for almost unlimited development. But as Huxley has pointed out, this is no longer a matter of biological progress but rather, because of man's mental powers and his verbal ability, a matter of the accumulation and transmission of knowledge, as well as the creation of new social patterns. It is through the use of these abilities that his future rests.

Since biological change in man has now been slowed because of interference with the process of natural selection, we need to study the nature of this organism who is the end-product of biological evolution.

If, for example, it could be proved that man is by nature aggressive and warlike, any attempt to educate for peace would seem to be an obvious waste of time and effort. Under these circumstances it would seem more reasonable to attempt to channel man's aggressive tendencies in such a way that they would not destroy him and his civilization, as modern total war threatens to do. It might be desirable to educate men to find outlets for this aggressive drive by fighting wars with boxing gloves, a system that has obvious advantages over using hydrogen bombs.

The question is, therefore, what is the nature of the organism we call man? Is he basically good but corrupted by his environment, as Rousseau believed? Or is he a depraved creature, by nature evil, as Calvin and later the Puritans in colonial America believed? Is man by nature competitive, as certain business groups have maintained? Or is he by nature co-operative, as some sociologists and anthropologists have claimed? Certainly the answers to these questions are of tremendous importance for teachers and must be taken into account in any educational program.

Human Nature and Its Potential

It should be realized at the outset that these questions concerning the nature of man are not of recent origin but have vexed and fascinated men in all walks of life for centuries. And for centuries, as during our own day, men have yielded to the temptation to make sweeping generalizations about man's nature. All of us, I suppose, have at one time or another made or heard the statement "that is just human nature." This statement may be made, and usually is, to describe cussedness, selfishness, or some other pattern of behavior that is not approved by society and the implication is that nothing can be done about it. This type of judgment is usually based upon the so-called "common sense" approach to the study of human nature.

The historical conceptions of the nature of man that have been held can be of value in helping us to understand man and his institutions, including the schools. Therefore, let us look briefly at some of these conceptions. During the Greek period, thinkers such as Plato and Aristotle held that men were by nature inherently unequal. They felt that it was right that some men should be slaves, because they were intellectually inferior to others and incapable of a high type of rational activity. In one respect, these thinkers had a point. Modern psychologists tell us that individuals differ greatly in ability, and certainly in this sense men are unequal. However, whether this inequality should carry over into the political and social realm is another matter. As a matter of fact, there is no evidence that the political condition of the inhabitants of Athens was determined in any way by intellectual capacity. It is quite possible that the slave group in Athens could have produced some of the most intelligent men in Greece.

During the Roman period, partially because of the impact of Christianity with its emphasis on the equality of men before God, many men, and particularly the Stoics, held that men were by nature equal and that this equality was to be found somewhere in a natural law, a natural arrangement of things in the universe. During the period of the Reformation another conception about the nature of man appeared in the teaching and writing of John Calvin. Calvin believed that men were by nature bad and that their natural tendencies had to be restrained. This conception has had a tremendous impact on Western civilization, and was particularly strong in colonial Massachusetts. As a result of their conception of the nature of man, these Calvinists—we call them Puritans—lived a very austere, sober existence. They believed that any form of play or recreation was undesirable since it would tempt man and lead him off the beaten path. Their distrust of human nature is evident in their laws and their institutions, including their schools.

During the period of the Enlightenment, from approximately 1750 to 1825, writers and thinkers began to question Calvin's theories regarding the nature of man. The new age of reason had begun and men were beginning to think and probe into all areas of human knowledge and belief. Rousseau developed the idea that man was by nature good and that it was through contact with human society and human institutions that he was corrupted. This basic belief in the inherent goodness of man is expressed in the Declaration of Independence. It is the basis of the belief held by our founding fathers in the possibility of the almost infinite perfectability of man and his institutions. Unlike Calvin, the approach of such men as Rousseau, Jefferson, and Paine was one of hope for the future, and a belief and faith not only in man's innate goodness but in his potential for development. But, of course, this was the period of the great revolutions, in France and America. The old feudal system had broken down and men seemed to be going forward in establishing democracy everywhere. The famous words of the French Revolution— liberty, equality, and fraternity—typify the spirit of the period. It is not surprising that in this era of hope men should believe in the inherent goodness of man.

During the nineteenth century still another conception of the nature of man was developed. This was the period of the Industrial Revolution and the change from an agricultural to an industrial society. This was the period of the rise of the middle class, with its emphasis on manufacturing, trade, and, above all, profit; in short, the nineteenth century was the period of the flowering of capitalism. This economic system, which was based on competition, sought support and justification for its existence by developing a theory of human nature as being essentially competitive. Capitalism's advocates received support at a very opportune moment from the field of science in the person of Charles Darwin in 1859. In that year Darwin published his *Origin of Species*, in which he developed the ideas of natural selection and the survival of the fittest as laws of nature. Thus the free-enterprise economic system of capitalism based upon competition was buttressed by the fact that it seemed to be in harmony with natural law. Conveniently overlooked was the fact that Darwin also pointed out, in a book published a few years later, that in a state of nature there was as much co-operation as competition.

Down through history men have studied themselves and their institutions and have formulated theories concerning the nature of man. In most instances, these theories have been formulated without benefit of scientific data and have therefore been both inaccurate and incomplete, and they have always been conditioned by the social environment. In some instances these theories have been developed to bolster the *status quo* or to justify certain economic, political, or social philosophies. The theory of the competitive nature of man and the capitalistic system, developed during the nineteenth century, and the master-race concept of the Nazis in our own time are examples of the practice. In both cases certain findings of science were used to strengthen the theory developed.

In the twentieth century, research in the fields of psychology and anthropology has enabled us to place these controversies on a more scientific, objective basis. It seems reasonable to assume, if we are interested in human nature, that we should study man wherever we find him. This is exactly what the anthropologists have done. They have studied man all over the earth. They have studied him in complex industrial societies like the United States and Russia; they have studied him in underdeveloped areas like India and China; and they have studied him in primitive tribes in the southwestern United States and in Australia. As a result of their efforts, it has been established that human beings, wherever they are found, have certain things in common. For example, whether an individual is living in a primitive tribe or in a society like our own, he has certain basic needs. He needs food to eat and air to breathe, he needs sleep, and he needs to reproduce in order to maintain his group. In addition, human beings, wherever we find them, have the ability to learn and to adapt; they have the power of conceptual thought and the ability to make tools. Thus they have been able to exert a certain amount of control over their environment and in this respect they differ from other members of the animal kingdom. In addition, they live in groups and are, therefore, social beings. Everywhere we find that man has developed a spoken language and, more often than not, a written language, so that he is able to communicate orally and graphically with his fellows. Finally, we find that man has developed institutions and customs. Every human group has some form of government, some kind of law, some form of religion, some system for obtaining food, and socially acceptable and unacceptable patterns of behavior.

So far as any specific patterns of human behavior are concerned, certain valuable data have been collected through the study of man in many societies. We may assume that if man were by nature competitive, then he would be competitive in whatever society we found him. But research indicates that there are some human groups in which competition is virtually unknown and the whole emphasis is on co-operation. On the other hand, there are human groups in which co-operation is not stressed and in which competition is the dominant value. The fact seems to be that man at birth has certain potentialities. He is by nature neither good nor bad, neither competitive nor co-operative. An individual has the potential for becoming, morally, a Hitler or a Lincoln. He can develop in either direction. How he develops depends largely upon what happens to him after he is born, that is, the sum of his experiences. One anthropologist has stated it this way:

> Children are not born selfish little egotists whose drives are mainly aggressive and competitive, "original sinners," evil, destructive creatures, brats who have to be "disciplined" into human beings by being sedulously and efficiently frustrated for the good of their actual or metaphoric souls. Aggressors are made, not born. On the other hand, the baby is born with drives which properly satisfied lead to co-operation. It is we, in our ignorance, who, failing to satisfy those needs, produce anxiety and hostility and then blame the child for being hostile! And so at every stage of the process.[2]

There seem to be differences in inherited tendencies—for example, some individuals at an early age are more aggressive while others are rather timid—but the way in which these tendencies develop is determined by the environment in which the individual lives and learns. These facts about human nature—namely, that man at birth is a bundle of potentiality and is extremely flexible—provide great hope for the future. If we can suppress the social conditions which engender bitter, hostile, selfish human beings and encourage those which produce co-operative, generous individuals, we can reduce the possibility of conflict and war. Certainly there is nothing in human nature which requires that man periodically engage in the slaughter of his fellows.

This neutrality and flexibility also gives us great hope in education. It makes the work of the teacher and the parent (and all adults for that matter, since all adults are teachers) more important. We know that man is not predisposed by nature to be brutal, but that he can be brutal the inmates of Dachau and Buchenwald learned. On the other hand,

[2] M. F. Ashley Montagu, "New Frontiers in Education," *School and Society*, November 17, 1951, p. 311.

neither is he necessarily predisposed to be gentle; he has to be taught. Thus the human potential is there; the question is whether we can develop it in the right way. Dewey has said: "Although schools abound, education as a controlled process of modification of disposition is hardly even in its infancy." [3] That Dewey was right is evidenced by the fact that we have had the bloodiest wars in human history in the recent past. There is also evidence that we are not aware of the potential in education for developing better individuals. We in the United States spend twenty billion dollars a year on the prevention of crime and approximately fourteen billion on public elementary and secondary schools.

The Power of Education to Modify Human Nature

THE tremendous potential of education and therefore the great importance of schools and teachers are emphasized by the scientific facts which prove, first, that man is at birth a neutral, plastic organism capable of becoming a Hitler or a Lincoln; and, second, that he can profit from past experience and has, as Huxley points out, the possibility of almost unlimited cultural evolution. But there is an important concept that every educator needs to understand: education, like science, is, in and of itself, neutral. Everything depends on the way in which it is used by man. One of the harsh realities of the modern world is the way in which the great potential of education has been harnessed by the totalitarian states. In a way, these efforts by the Nazis and the Russian communists have opened the eyes of political leaders and educators in the West to the great power of education for freedom and peace or slavery and war. We in America have held the rather naïve view that education was something cherished by free men and feared by tyrants, and that the more of it we have, the better. Now we know that education can be used to free men or to enslave them. The reading given below illustrates how the communist leaders in Russia have utilized education as a means of controlling the thoughts of an entire nation. The selection was written by Professor George S. Counts and consists of edited sections of the chapter, "Education as a Weapon," from his book, *The Country of the Blind.* Dr. Counts, who is Emeritus Professor of Education at Teachers College, Columbia University, is one of the few American authorities on Russian education. His research has been strengthened by his three extended visits to the U.S.S.R. in 1927, 1929 and 1936 and his knowledge of the Russian language, which enables him to read the original Russian sources. This book, published in 1949, has the appropriate subtitle, *The Soviet System of Mind Control,* and records one of the most amazing developments in

[3] John Dewey, "Human Nature," *Encyclopedia of the Social Sciences,* VII (New York: The Macmillan Company, 1932), 536.

human history. The Russians, learning from the Nazis and utilizing the coercive power of the state and the modern media of communication, have mobilized what Counts calls the entire cultural apparatus to achieve their ends. In this endeavor they are following the dictum laid down by Stalin in his famous statement to H. G. Wells that "Education is a weapon whose effect depends upon who holds it in his hands and at whom it is aimed."

GEORGE S. COUNTS and NUCIA LODGE

FROM

The Country of the Blind [4]

. . . The fact is difficult to conceive in the West that in the Soviet Union the term "education" is made to embrace all the processes and agencies involved in the moulding of the mind of both young and old. This means that the ways of life and all institutions have a recognized educational function and are under perpetual scrutiny from the standpoint of current Party policy. But it means more especially that certain branches of the culture which in other countries are supposed to enjoy a measure of independence are judged in the Soviet Union first of all in terms of their bearing on political education and propaganda. The resolutions of the Central Committee stress this point over and over again.

This vast educational enterprise includes the school system as one of its important branches. But it also includes as major divisions the press in all of its aspects, other media of mass communication such as the radio and television, all agencies of entertainment such as the theatre and the moving picture, literature and art in all of their forms, libraries, museums, and "parks of culture and rest," and all basic institutions of family and community. The trade union, the co-operative, the Red Army, and all organizations of the people are expected to perform educational functions. The Party, of course, with its societies for children and youth, falls under this category. Indeed, the Society of Young Pioneers and the League of Young Communists, the one enrolling about twelve million boys and girls from ten to sixteen years of age and the other with approximately seven million youth from fourteen to twenty-three, are powerful and faithful arms of the Party. The Soviet educational system constitutes the most gigantic and comprehensive marshalling of forces to shape the human mind in the whole history of mankind. It is under the close supervision of the central organs of the Party and is directed toward the

[4] George S. Counts and Nucia Lodge, *The Country of the Blind* (Boston: Houghton Mifflin Company, 1949), pp. 244–5, 247–50, 256–61.

achievement of Party purposes. It is, indeed, as the Soviet leaders never tire of repeating, a "weapon of Communism.". . .

In the ideological struggle the daily press could not long be overlooked, for Stalin once said that "it is the sharpest and most powerful weapon of our Party." So in the spring of 1948 the entire Soviet press was haled before the bar of Party criticism and asked to render an account of its stewardship. Very fittingly this movement was launched on May 5, the day of the year long celebrated in the Soviet Union as "Bolshevik Press Day," commemorating the first issue of *Pravda* on May 5, 1912. An All-Moscow Conference of Workers of the Press was held in the famous Hall of Columns.[5] From Moscow the conference spread during the following month to other great centers of the country.

The Moscow conference was called by the Department of Propaganda and Agitation of the Central Committee of the All-Union Communist Party and was addressed, according to Party custom, by the Acting Director of the Department, L. F. Ilichev. The following brief account of the conference appeared in *Pravda*, May 6:

"In his address Comrade Ilichev pointed to the great role which the Bolshevik press, created by V. I. Lenin and I. V. Stalin, has played in the revolutionary struggle of the peoples of our Motherland. 'The press,' so teaches Stalin, 'is the most powerful weapon with which the party speaks daily and hourly to the working class in its own language. No other comparable instrument, no other comparable apparatus, exists in nature for strengthening the spiritual ties between Party and class.'

"The entire road of our press is illuminated with the light of scientific socialism. It is precisely for this reason that it fulfills successfully its role of collective propagandist, agitator, and organizer. The fundamental characteristics of our press are inherent in its very nature: its mass character, its truthfulness, its closeness to the people.

"The Soviet press confronts the great tasks of educating the working people in Communism and of struggling with the vestiges of capitalism in the consciousness of the people.

"Comrade Ilichev emphasized that the Bolshevik Party attaches tremendous significance to the improvement of ideological work among the wide masses of the working people. Soviet journalists must remember that propagation of the great ideas of Communism is the noblest task of our press. . . .

" 'The Party has entrusted to the workers of the Bolshevik Press,' said L. F. Ilichev in conclusion, 'one of the most responsible and militant tasks in the universal struggle for the building of Com-

[5] *Pravda*, May 6, 1948.

munism. Let us therefore give all our strength, knowledge, and experience to the cause of serving the great Party of Lenin and Stalin, to our heroic Soviet people!'

"With tremendous enthusiasm those participating in the conference agreed to send a letter of greetings to Comrade Stalin."

On May 19 and 20 another conference was held in Moscow under the auspices of the Division of Propaganda of the Central Committee of the Party. The meeting was directed primarily to the book press and was attended by directors of publishing houses, editors of central newspapers and journals, representatives of ministries and administrative organs, and various Party workers. This conference, which was followed by similar meetings in the capitals of the Union Republics, devoted itself primarily to questions of ideology and Party loyalty in the work of the publishing houses.[6]

At the conference in Moscow the discussion was led again by L. F. Ilichev, Acting Director of the Division of Propaganda and Agitation. He declared that the resolutions of the Central Committee on literature, the drama, the cinema, and music "raise the level of all the means of socialist culture and mark a new stage in the ideological work of our Party." He also called upon "all workers on the ideological front to be guided in all their activities by the principles of the Bolshevik Party loyalty." The May 21 issue of *Kultura i Zhizn* reports the conference in a leading article entitled "For Bolshevik Party Loyalty and High Ideology in the Work of Publishing Houses." The following excerpts give the substance of the article:

"An examination of the activity of certain central publishing houses and the discussion of the question of publishing at the conference revealed serious shortcomings and mistakes in . . . this important field of ideological work. . . . In 1947 the Publishing House of the State Planning Commission published a number of injurious books in which the contemporary problems of bourgeois economics are treated objectively. Most publications suffer from a non-political approach in analyzing the economics of imperialistic countries. The books fail to expose the organic relation between economics and the policy of imperialism and to analyze the basic differences between socialist and bourgeois economics. Such mistakes are the result of the dulling of Bolshevik vigilance among some workers in publishing houses. . . .

"A care-free and complacent spirit is intolerable everywhere and is especially intolerable on the ideological front. Workers in pub-

[6] *Kultura i Zhizn*, May 21, 1948.

lishing houses must raise their revolutionary vigilance and strengthen their warfare against bourgeois ideology. . . . Publishers must realize fully their responsibility before the Party and the Soviet people and take all necessary steps to improve the ideological and scientific level of books published.

"A Soviet publishing house (said Comrade Ilichev), regardless of its literary specialty, cannot be merely a mailbox which accepts everything sent to it. It must be an ideological fortress against which each and all attempts to drag in an ideology alien to our Party and our people are shattered to bits.

"Soviet publishing houses must abandon once and for all their care-free and complacent mood and raise their Bolshevik viligance. Party members commissioned to supervise publishing work must assume a more active role in the struggle against the depraved and infamous ideology of capitalism and against bourgeois objectivity. They must battle for purity of Communist ideology. . . .

"Some publishers (said Comrade Ilichev) regard scientific and technical literature as unrelated to ideology. They think that such literature is ideologically and politically unconditioned and presumably stands outside of politics and ideology. They assume it is to be judged only by scientific and technical standards. That such a view is evil is entirely obvious.

"In speaking of translations of foreign literature, the speaker emphasized particularly that books written by bourgeois authors require qualifying introductions which explain to the readers the basic content of the book and subject its shortcomings to Marxian criticism. . . .

"Party organizations and directors of publishing houses are not insisting sufficiently that editors master Marxian theory and acquaint themselves fully with questions of the domestic and foreign policy of the USSR. Workers in publishing houses must constantly improve their Marxist-Leninist education in order to carry the principle of Party loyalty into literature and wage successful warfare against all signs of bourgeois ideology.

"Publishers and particularly their directing personnel, said the speaker, are assigned by the Party of Lenin and Stalin to one of the most important positions on the ideological front, to its advanced line. The abundance of the spiritual culture of our Soviet people, creator and builder of Communist society, depends in large measure on the work of publishers. And it is our task to launch with Bolshevik passion and enthusiasm an immediate campaign for the correction of errors. We must fulfill those lofty and honorable demands which Comrade Stalin makes on workers on the ideological front. . . ."

Few Americans realize that in addition to the regular system of schools open to the people generally there is in the Soviet Union a second system at the youth and adult level designed to provide that special kind of preparation necessary for Party members and particularly for Party functionaries and leaders. Since its central function is the training of the Communist priesthood, it may be likened to the theological schools which have been maintained by religious sects and theocratic states from time immemorial. Moreover, wherever the Party may be found in strength in other countries, it endeavors to establish schools after the Russian model. There are several such schools in the United States which are to be distinguished primarily from their prototypes in the Soviet Union, not by their doctrinal emphasis, but by their names. After some years of experience American Communists sought the protective coloration of such glorious democratic names as Benjamin Franklin, Thomas Jefferson, and Abraham Lincoln.

The Soviet system in its postwar structure, according to Malenkov, is organized on three levels. At the first level, as of September, 1947, there were 177 "two-year Party Schools and nine-month courses" enrolling "about 30,000 Party, Soviet, Komsomol, and newspaper workers." These institutions prepare for the lower posts in Party and state. At the second level is a three-year Higher Party School which prepares a smaller number for positions in the upper ranges of the Party and state apparatus. In 1947 approximately one thousand students were enrolled. At the third and highest level is the Academy of Social Sciences. This institution is "called upon to prepare theoretical workers for central Party institutions, Central Committees of the Communist Parties of the Union Republics, regional and provisional committees of the Party, and also qualified teachers for higher technical schools and universities and theoretical workers for scientific-research institutions and scientific journals." That the Academy, though only recently organized, is destined to play a central role in the entire cultural life of the country in the years to come is indicated by the nature and breadth of its program. It is supposed to prepare "workers in the following special fields: political economy, the economics and politics of foreign states, political and legal theory, international law, history of the USSR, general history, international relations, history of the All-Union Communist Party, dialectical and historical materialism, history of Russian and West European philosophy, logic and psychology, science of literature, and science of art." [7] This system of Party schools rests upon a comprehensive network of "polit-schools" or "political schools" which are supposed to carry Party doctrine to the rank-and-file membership in factories, in shops and mines, and on collective farms.

[7] G. Malenkov, *Informational Report on the Activity of the Central Committee of the All-Union Communist Party* (Moscow, 1947), pp. 25–6. (In Russian.)

The attention given to this system of Party schools and the founding of the Academy of Social Science demonstrate the utter seriousness of the postwar domestic and foreign policy on which this action of the Party rests. The power of the ideological drive is also suggested by the unprecedented scale of the publication and distribution of the sacred scriptures of Communism. Thus, according to Malenkov, during the first two postwar years "the various classical works of Marxism-Leninism were published to the number of more than ninety million copies." There were printed in the same period also ten million copies of the *Short History of the All-Union Communist Party*. And a *Short Biography of Stalin* which presents the "Great Leader" in a purified and glorified version, is being published and sold in millions of copies.[8] The Party is throwing the entire weight of its propaganda behind a campaign to arouse the people to read and study all the books of the Soviet Bible. The emphasis throughout is on the authenticity of the Communist apocalypse and the authority of the Communist prophets. By way of contrast one should know that approximately twenty-five million copies of the Christian Bible, published in over one thousand languages and dialects, are distributed throughout the world annually.

. . . The Soviet system of public schools embraces a vast network of institutions from the nursery school and kindergarten through the primary and secondary schools and the various vocational, technical, and professional schools of different grades to the universities and scientific institutes and academies. By 1939, according to Stalin's report to the Eighteenth Congress of the Party, the total number of pupils and students of all ages attending these schools and classes part time or full time reached the tremendous figure of 47,422,100. After generous allowance is made for the "use of statistics as a political weapon," the material growth of the Soviet school system is extremely impressive.

The school of course is also a weapon. The Central Committee therefore has shaped and guided its development with great care. It has devoted time and energy not only to broad matters of philosophy, ideology, and program, but also to details of textbook preparation, teaching methods, and classroom organization. Nothing is too small or insignificant to engage its attention. On one occasion it issued a resolution fixing the number and length of the recess periods for the primary school.

The ideological resolutions of the Central Committee of August and September, 1946, calling for an assault on Western "bourgeois" culture and for the glorification of Soviet life and institutions, had an immediate impact on the schools and on all references to the educational practices of other countries and particularly of the United States. The first issue thereafter of *Sovietskaia Pedagogika*, official organ of the Academy of

[8] *Ibid.*, p. 27.

Pedagogical Science of the RSFSR, devoted its leading editorial to the resolutions under the title, "For Bolshevik Ideology in Soviet Pedagogical Science." [9] The editorial proclaimed that "the serious shortcomings exposed recently by the Central Committee on the ideological front are unquestionably present in our pedagogical sciences," that "the ideologocial training of our youth is above all political," that "we must not forget for a moment that every science is Party science," that "teaching cannot be divorced from the politics of Party and state," that "workers in pedagogical science must first of all study stubbornly, persistently, and consistently the science of sciences—the Marxist-Leninist theory," and that they "must become bold and militant propagandists of the great Communist ideas of educating the new man." The editorial reported also that the resolutions "stirred profoundly the whole of Soviet society." It is entirely appropriate to note here that in the Middle Ages under the dominion of the Church theology was called the "queen of the sciences." The parallel would appear to be quite close.

During the next twelve months meetings and conferences of teachers and educators were held throughout the country to consider the work of the schools in the light of the resolutions of the Central Committee. At a meeting of the members of the Academy of Pedagogical Science on October 11, 1946, the President of the Academy, I. A. Kairov, delivered an address in which he drew the obvious conclusions. "The Central Committee of the Party," he said, "demands that all workers on the ideological front, and consequently workers in pedagogical science, understand that they are placed in the advanced line of fire." [10] On April 17 and 18, 1947, the Ministry of Education of the RSFSR held a conference with teachers and educational workers from Moscow and Leningrad. The addresses and reports given at the meeting revealed that the resolutions of the Central Committee had "shaken the Moscow and Leningrad teaching body and aroused a great creative upsurge in their work," and had stimulated the majority to study "independently the history of the All-Union Communist Party and the writings of Comrade Stalin." [11] An All-Russian conference of heads of departments of pedagogy, psychology, and methods of teaching in pedagogical institutes and teacher training schools met in conference from July 1 to 8, 1947, in Moscow. The leading speaker warned that conditions in the institutions represented were far from satisfactory, that "many faculties have not as yet understood their tasks," and that their work had not improved "in the light of the resolutions of the Central Committee." He declared further that "some faculties and their leaders" had "failed to draw the necessary inferences" and had "not grasped as yet the fact that the

[9] *Sovietskaia Pedagogika*, No. 10–11 (October–November, 1946), pp. 3–8.
[10] *Ibid.*, No. 12, December, 1946, p. 3.
[11] *Ibid.*, No. 6, June, 1947, p. 120.

resolutions on literature and art have significance in principle for all ideological work." [12]

The attention of teachers was quickly directed to the application of the resolutions to the various subjects of study in the public schools. The teachers of natural science are told that their "chief aim" is "to arm the students with knowledge" so that they may "achieve a conscious mastery of the natural-scientific foundations of the Communist world outlook." [13] A reviewer of a volume on the history of the Middle Ages says that "the very greatest fault of the textbook is its insufficiently high Bolshevik ideology." [14] Geography of course has its obvious uses. Thus, "in comparing the USSR with capitalist countries" the teacher should "show the superiority of socialist over capitalist economy" and point out "that the USSR is certain to develop much more rapidly than any capitalist country, including the United States of America." [15] Literature should reveal to the young that "love for the socialist Motherland in Soviet people is joined with burning hatred toward her enemies." The writer then quotes from Stalin: "You cannot defeat an enemy without learning to hate him with all your soul." [16]

The program of teacher training was sharply criticized at many points. Instruction in psychology was subjected to careful review. A writer on this question opens with the observation that "psychology is first of all a world-view subject." He then asserts that the "correct formation of the Communist world-view demands a knowledge of scientific psychology" and that "this thesis acquires peculiar significance because of the necessity for a decisive and irreconcilable struggle against foreign idealistic and decadent teachings." [17] In the teaching of the history of education it is necessary to present a "much clearer picture of the *latest contemporary bourgeois pedagogy*." The instructor should point out "that the majority of the representatives of *contemporary* West-European and American educational theory actually serve reactionary political purposes under a mask of 'objectivity,' 'scientific approach,' and 'love for the child.' " The writer notes that the "role of Dewey is very significant in this connection." [18] Soviet educational journals overflow with materials of this general character.

Since this material was written, Stalin has died, Khrushchev has taken over the leadership of the Party, and the world has had convincing evidence of the excellence of some aspects of Russian education. But the basic pattern of using the entire cultural apparatus, and especially the schools, to mold the minds of the Russian people according to the wishes of the leaders of the Party has not changed, as George Counts has

[12] *Ibid.*, No. 9, September, 1947, p. 116.
[13] *Ibid.*, No. 1, January, 1947, p. 27.
[14] *Ibid.*, No. 8, August, 1947, p. 23.
[15] *Ibid.*, No. 9, September, 1947, p. 30.
[16] *Ibid.*, No. 2, February, 1948, p. 10.
[17] *Ibid.*, No. 7, July, 1947, p. 73.
[18] *Ibid.*, No. 10, October, 1947, p. 84.

shown in his recent book *The Challenge of Soviet Education*. And we have evidence that the molding process has been effective in producing loyalty to the Party, enthusiasm for communism, and a distorted picture of the world outside of the U.S.S.R. Perhaps the most reliable data was gathered by a small group of American students from the Russian Institute at Columbia University who traveled extensively throughout the Soviet Union and who, because they spoke Russian, had an opportunity to actually talk to the people. They found not only enthusiasm for communism among young Russians but a genuine sympathy for "poor Americans who were missing out on the joys of communism." They also found that the Russians believed that South Korea had invaded North Korea, that the U.N. was a puppet of Wall Street, that workers were starving in Times Square, and that the United States was intent on starting a war.[19]

On the positive side of the ledger, we know that education can be a powerful force for liberating human beings. It is difficult to see how Jefferson, Lincoln, Emerson, Dewey, and Einstein could have made the contributions they did to American civilization without the education each received. Lincoln, of course, had little formal schooling, but he had the freedom to read and learn. The others were well educated formally, and fine teachers helped Jefferson and Dewey develop their potentials. The evidence from psychology is clear: if the right kind of learning environment is provided, the child can not only become highly skilled, but also a stable, mature, sensitive, responsible human being. So education is a two-edged sword. It can be used to promote human welfare and to liberate, or it can be used to enslave.

To illustrate what education (formal and informal) can do to develop fine human beings, a short selection by Dr. Anne Roe is reprinted here. Dr. Roe, a clinical psychologist, spent four years studying sixty-four of America's top scientists and recorded the results in her book, *The Making of a Scientist*. The following discussion of the influences responsible for their development contains material of value to anyone concerned with education of the young in a democratic society.

Anne Roe

from

The Making of a Scientist [20]

There are distinct patterns in these life histories. These scientists come from rather selected families, since half of them had fathers who

[19] "They Let Us Talk to the Russians," *Ladies' Home Journal*, June, 1955.
[20] Reprinted by permission of Dodd, Mead & Company from *The Making of a Scientist* by Anne Roe. Copyright 1952, 1953 by Anne Roe. Pp. 230–1, 234–5, 238–41.

were professional men, and none of them had fathers who were unskilled laborers. . . .

Not all the sons of professional fathers become scientists, but this background more than others, seems to have a predisposing effect. Why? By and large the intelligence of people in professional occupations is relatively high, and so their children would be expected to be relatively bright, hence there may be some hereditary factor. But the inheritance of intelligence is a very complicated matter, and not too well understood, and I think here of relatively less importance than other things. What seems to be important in the home background is the knowledge of learning, and the value placed on it *for its own sake,* in terms of the enrichment of life, and not just for economic and social rewards. This high evaluation placed on learning and on intellectual satisfactions was also operative in many of the homes in which the father was not a professional man. The few scientists whose homes lacked this had always had close contact with some one else, usually a teacher, who held this attitude. . . .

One of the first things one notes about scientists is the fact that a large part of their time is spent in thinking about things, in a question-answering way. They want to find out something, and all of their activities are designed to bring them answers to questions. (Of course a good part of the trick to being a first-rate scientist is in asking the right questions, or asking them in ways that make it possible to find answers.) One way of putting this is to say that they are curious, even though each may be chiefly curious about very specialized things and not very curious about all the other things in the world. All children are curious, I think, but not all adults are. For one reason or another, many adults are unable to be curious to any great degree, or are able to be curious about few things. It is true, of scientists, too, that some of them seem to be curious only about some things, but most of them have a more general sort of curiosity. This limitation of a healthy and intelligent person's normal reaction of interest in the world around him may result from repressive training, from discouragement of questioning by weary parents or teachers, from an adult attitude of know-it-all, and insistence on a child's conformity. . . .

There are other implications for educational practice in these stories. The discovery that it is possible to find things out for oneself is not a natural part of growing up for every child in our culture. It can be seen clearly in these life histories that for many of these men it was just chance,—the chance, usually, of getting in a class in school where this type of activity was encouraged. Whether it was encouraged because the teacher was genuinely interested in encouraging the children to think for themselves, or whether it was encouraged because the teacher did not want to be bothered with the students and so left them pretty much on their own does not seem to matter too much. The important thing is that they learned that they could satisfy their curiosity by their own efforts. Once they did learn this, good teaching encouraged them, but bad teaching did not stultify them.

It is no easy matter to so design teaching in general that individual thinking is encouraged. For one thing in our public schools our classes are large, and, especially in the grades, there are so many things that must be learned by rote (multiplication tables, reading, spelling) that the atmosphere becomes overwhelmingly one of accepting what is in the book and giving it back unchanged. This carries over strongly to subjects of other sorts, where rote learning actually is not essential, and where it would often be a good idea if the children have an attitude of "it ain't necessarily so" just because the teacher or the book said so. It is chiefly, I think, the carry-over of this authoritarian attitude that is most stultifying. After all the multiplication table, the forms of spelling, are all conventions, designed for greater convenience in manipulating and conveying ideas, and they should be taught as such, not as basic truths, but I wonder if they ever are. The teachers, themselves, have been brought up by the book and naturally most of them teach as they have been taught. And I must say that the psychologists' invention of the time-saving and effort-saving and hence very popular true and false tests, and similar devices, has not helped matters any in this respect but has probably actually exacerbated the situation.

I mentioned the public schools particularly, but I do not mean to imply that private schools are better in this respect. In fact, with the exception of the anthropologists, very few of this group went to private schools, and I am strongly of the impression that private schools do not produce scientists in any numbers,—they go in much more strongly for the "humanities." Certainly church schools do not produce scientists, even at the college level. Some of the progressive schools have done a good deal, however, to encourage children to follow out their own pursuits. Unfortunately a good many of them have carried this so far that they have neglected to insist upon the children also learning the conventions which are really necessary.

Let me make it clear that I do not think the major function of any school is to produce scientists. The major function of our schools is to aid in the production of good citizens. It is true, I think, that scientists are usually very good citizens,—they mind their own business, they pay at least as much attention to civic duties as the average man does, they do not enrich themselves at others' expense, they and their families rarely become public charges, and the more violent crimes are practically unknown among them. You will remember that even on test material they show up as an unaggressive group, on the whole. (The scientists involved in espionage have been very few, indeed, and misguided as they may have been, they have acted on principle and not for personal gain.) But obviously scientists are not the only good citizens. The point that is important here, and much more important than the production of scientists, is that the things that make good scientists are also the things that make good citizens, in a democracy. This is true only for democratic forms of government. A democracy can only exist effectively if the citizens are able to participate freely and intelligently. If they are not free to think and to feel, they are not free. We give a good deal of lip service to the concept of an enlightened electorate, but we are often still not quite sure that people can be trusted. There is a good deal of evidence in the clinical literature that people, freed of neurotic needs and in a position to make a really conscious choice, will not choose asocially. We are more hampered by our own fear of ourselves, and of our nature than we are by anything else.

The Potential of American Education

So far we have seen on the basis of available scientific evidence that man has the potential for meeting the challenge discussed in Chapter 1, and that education properly developed can be a valuable resource. It is entirely possible, however, even with man's potential and the potential in education that the requisites in terms of money, schools, teachers, etc., make this impossible in America. Before we leave the subject, then, we must inquire into the resources that exist or are available in American society and American education for creating an educational program equal to the task. Is present knowledge in America sufficient for the goal we have set for education? Have we the professional, institutional, and economic resources necessary? And, finally, has American education the moral potential to cope with the problems of the twentieth century? Each of these questions will be considered briefly.

Perhaps our greatest resource in our efforts to improve the human race through education is the vast reservoir of knowledge that man has at his disposal. To attempt to indicate even in outline form the extent of this vast accumulation would take volumes; therefore a few general statements will have to suffice to illustrate the point. Of primary importance in this reservoir is scientific method, the means through which the great bulk of man's knowledge has been obtained. In the twentieth century through use of this method, man has learned much about the earth and the universe in which he lives. He has learned, if not the origin, at least much of the evolution and nature of life. He has learned much about the behavior of man, the causes of aggression, and the essentials of physical and mental health. He has learned much about the origin and nature of culture and institutions. In the field of education he has learned much about the growth and development of children and the learning process, knowledge which can be used to do a better job in educating. In short, man already possesses enough knowledge to enable him, through education, to produce fine human beings with the knowledge, attitudes, and skills needed to solve their problems. This is not to say that man knows everything or even that he knows enough. It is to say that the knowledge available from the various sciences, if used, could provide the minimum essentials for a sound, healthy civilization. If we can judge by what has been accomplished in the relatively short time that the scientific method has been used by man, it would seem that what is already known is only a slight beginning compared to what will be known, perhaps fifty years from now.

Increasingly in the last few decades there have been efforts by the teaching profession to apply knowledge gained through science in our educational institutions. As we shall see in the closing chapters of this volume, progress in the teaching profession has been too slow. This is partially a result of sheer overload on the teaching profession, owing to the unprecedented growth of our school population. It is also partially a result of the lack of an inquiring approach on the part of teachers. Nevertheless, much has been achieved in the direction of establishing a strong professional group with high professional standards. Much remains to be done but certainly the tremendous strides that have been made in the last generation provide at least a professional foundation for creating an excellent school system and making a fine education available to all American youth. We have more than a million teachers in America, and we are moving rapidly toward the day when the vast majority of them will have completed four years of college work, and a large percentage, five years.

Furthermore, although we have a serious teacher shortage, with a little imagination and additional financial support we could go a long way toward solving the problem. For example, there are thousands of well-educated, able men and women who could be induced to become teachers. In many colleges today special professional programs are being set up to prepare men and women who are college graduates. Other schools are inducing intelligent married women, with their children in school, to come to college and prepare for teaching. These intelligent, mature women are excellent material, and if properly educated, make excellent teachers. The point is, there is no lack of talent in America. By spending one-tenth of the effort and only a small fraction of the money involved in World War II, we would be well on the way toward solving our problem.

In our consideration of the potential of American education we must consider the educational institutions which exist. The school is the primary educational institution in America, and there are some 175,000 schools in the country. Even though we have a critical shortage of classrooms, more children receive more years of formal education in America than in any other country. We have more than 1800 colleges and universities, many of which are equal to the best schools in any part of the world. All of our states have fine state universities, and there are numerous private schools offering advanced graduate work. Moreover, the American people believe in education and send their children to school willingly. Despite the work that needs to be done, we have an elaborate and extensive school system already in existence. In addition to the schools, we have other important agencies of education, such as radio and television and the press, that have hardly been utilized by educators. Unfortunately, these great agencies of education may actually be doing more harm than good. We allow our children to watch movies and television programs indiscriminately. We provide flashy (and often indecent) and sadistic comics at virtually every newsstand while many children seldom see the inside of a library.

The question that is frequently raised when the problem of providing educational facilities is discussed is: Can we afford it? The present estimate of our gross national product, that is, the wealth America produces measured in dollars, is about 436 billion dollars and is rising steadily. In 1958–59 the United States Office of Education estimates that we spent a total of 20 billion dollars on all our schools, public and private, from kindergarten through the universities. This figure includes money used for current expenditures, capital outlay, and interest. We are spending between 14 and 15 billion per year, or approximately 3 per cent of our national product, on our public elementary and secondary schools. The fact is that we spend as much on advertising as we do on our public elementary and secondary schools, and a good deal more on liquor and tobacco. The average American spends much more on owning and operating his car each year than he does on the education of his children. Therefore, insofar as our economic potential is concerned, our capacity for supporting education is almost unlimited. If we ever become serious about the education of our children, it can be provided easily.

Perhaps our greatest resource for creating an education equal to the challenge of the twentieth century is the great moral potential latent in American civilization. From the end of the eighteenth century through the nineteenth century America was the haven and hope of the oppressed peoples of the world. Of course, part of the attraction of America was in the economic opportunity that it offered to the underprivileged. But equally important were the great moral principles upon which the country was founded. The nation that had been "conceived in liberty and dedicated to the principle that all men are created equal" had set a standard for the world. Carl Becker, the noted American historian, in his essay, "Some Generalities That Still Glitter," has summarized the values which America at its best has represented.

> To have faith in the dignity and worth of the individual man as an end in himself, to believe that it is better to be governed by persuasion than by coercion, to believe that fraternal good will is more worthy than a selfish and contentious spirit, to believe that in the long run all values are inseparable from the love of the truth and the disinterested search for it, to believe that knowledge and the power it confers should be used to promote the welfare and the happiness of all men rather than to serve the interests of those individuals and classes whom fortune and intelligence endow with temporary advantage—these are the values which are affirmed by the traditional democratic ideology.[21]

And these great principles of human dignity, freedom, and equality were not merely verbal enunciations in our Declaration of Independence and Constitution, for they are put into practice in our government, our courts, and our schools. Again and again in our history this moral potential has been drawn upon to sustain and lift our nation when difficult problems were faced. Men like Horace Mann and Henry Barnard drew upon this moral potential to establish the public school system. Lincoln drew upon it to urge a nation that had suffered four years of a bitter civil war to meet its problems "with justice for all and malice toward none." Woodrow Wilson drew upon it to support a League of Nations which was to abolish war. President Truman drew upon it in formulating and supporting the Point Four program to aid the underdeveloped regions of the world.

In the critical years ahead we shall need to draw upon this great moral potential even more, for we seem to be in a period of cynicism in which we have forgotten or have become ashamed of the great principles upon which our nation was founded. We have drifted into the habit of thinking in military terms in seeking to solve world problems, and we are becoming dangerously materialistic at home. For this reason Norman Cousins urged us to use what he calls "moral imagination" in solving our world problems. He asked what might happen if instead of sending ten thousand soldiers overseas we sent ten thousand farmers, workers, teachers, or technicians. It was partly to the use of this great moral potential that James Conant referred when he suggested a "strong and vigorous rival to the Soviet Views." And Chester Bowles, our former am-

[21] Carl L. Becker, *New Liberties for Old* (New Haven, Conn.: Yale University Press, 1941), p. 149.

bassador to India, speaking of this potential, pointed out that: "If we can recover some of Lincoln's democratic faith and apply it to the world, we will find that our own American Revolution in all its dynamic implications has come to life again, and we will see the people of Europe, Asia, Africa, and South America reach out their hands to us in new confidence and in friendship." [22]

Like Cousins and Conant, Bowles did not have in mind simply preaching democracy at the rest of the world but actually living and applying it at home and abroad. Our use of this great moral potential in our education can serve as a kind of self-generating chain reaction. We can draw upon it as an inspiration to provide a fine education for all our children, and this kind of education will in turn nourish, strengthen, and extend these values which are the heart of our democratic heritage.

Suggested Readings

Bowles, Chester: *The New Dimensions of Peace.* New York: Harper & Brothers, 1955.

Childs, John L.: *Education and Morals.* New York: Appleton-Century-Crofts, 1950.

Counts, George S.: *The Challenge of Soviet Education.* New York: McGraw-Hill Book Company, Inc., 1957.

———: *Education and American Civilization.* New York: Bureau of Publications, Teachers College, Columbia University, 1952.

———, and Lodge, Nucia: *The Country of the Blind.* Boston: Houghton Mifflin Company, 1949.

Dewey, John: *Human Nature and Conduct.* New York: Henry Holt and Company, 1922.

Frank, Lawrence: *Nature and Human Nature.* New Brunswick, N.J.: Rutgers University Press, 1951.

Huxley, Julian: *Evolution in Action.* New York: Harper & Brothers, 1953.

Kelley, E. C., and Rasey, M. I.: *Education and the Nature of Man.* New York: Harper & Brothers, 1952.

Roe, Anne: *The Making of a Scientist.* New York: Dodd, Mead & Company, 1953.

[22] Chester Bowles, *The New Dimensions of Peace* (New York: Harper & Brothers, 1955), p. 386.

PART
II

Culture, Education,
and the School

The attributes and the abilities that we prize as distinctively human are due in no small part to the fact that man lives in this culturally transformed, and educationally more potent, environment. As the child matures in this cultural environment his responses are directed by "weighted" stimuli—by stimuli that are charged with the meanings which his human group has acquired, from that which it has appropriated from other human groups, together with those meanings it has discovered through its deliberately controlled efforts to get knowledge of the behaviors and the connections of things. Without his superior organic endowment, man would never have got started on the enterprise of the development of culture—but once he began to remake "nature" into culture his own powers of understanding, of prediction, and of control began to expand. Nature was in a real sense rationalized as it became progressively instrumentalized through the activities of man.

JOHN L. CHILDS

CHAPTER 3

THE NATURE OF CULTURE

WE SHALL BEGIN OUR ANALYSIS OF AMERICAN EDUCATION BY A CONsideration of what might be described as the social foundations of education. A moment's reflection will bring the realization that man is a social animal. The human infant, at birth and for the first years of his life, is the most helpless of creatures and would perish were it not for the care and protection he receives from his parents and from the social group in which he lives. We have already seen that this long period of learning plus his ability to learn—to use symbols, to communicate, and therefore to pass on his social heritage—is also his great strength. As he lives in a human group man, using his unique talents, learns those skills, attitudes, understandings, and beliefs which are characteristic of his group. Thus man *learns* his human nature within a specific social context. Our first step is to understand the nature of this social context, or social framework, within which man lives.

One other point should be made before we proceed: man lives in two environments. One is the natural environment composed of land, sea, air, and the plant and animal life which preceded man and was not created by him. The other is the man-made or "cultural" environment consisting of tools, buildings, institutions, customs, and ideas. The word "natural" rather than the word "physical" is used in order to distinguish this aspect of man's environment from the physical man-made environment such as buildings, etc. This is not to say that the man-made environment is unnatural, for man himself is a part of nature and so in a sense everything he produces is natural. But the distinction is made for the purpose of pointing up the difference between the two environments. It is important to remember also that the natural environment— soil, climate, topography, etc.—in a given locale provides the raw material with which man works. This fact accounts to some extent for the great diversity of cultures to be found on the earth.

With this important distinction in mind our next step is to consider the nature of the man-made environment or "culture." For this purpose a statement by Bronislaw Malinowski, one of Britain's foremost anthropologists, is included. This statement is taken from his article, "Culture," which was written for the *Encyclopedia of the Social Sciences*. As is true with most anthropologists, Malinowski's research work was done primarily with primitive groups (in his case, in New Guinea).

BRONISLAW MALINOWSKI

FROM

"Culture" [1]

Culture. Man varies in two respects: in physical form and in social heritage, or culture. The science of physical anthropology, employing a complex apparatus of definitions, descriptions and terminologies and somewhat more precise methods than common sense and untutored observations, has succeeded in cataloguing the various branches of mankind according to their bodily structure and physiological characteristics. But man varies also in an entirely different aspect. A pure blooded Negro infant, transported to France and brought up there would differ profoundly from what he would have been if reared in the jungle of his native land. He would have been given a different social heritage: a different language, different habits, ideas and beliefs; he would have been incorporated into a different social organization and cultural setting. This social heritage is the key concept of cultural anthropology, the other branch of the comparative study of man. It is usually called culture in modern anthropology and social science. The word culture is at times used synonymously with civilization, but it is better to use the two terms distinctively, reserving civilization for a special aspect of more advanced cultures. Culture comprises inherited artifacts, goods, technical processes, ideas, habits and values. Social organization cannot be really understood except as a part of culture; . . .

Man in order to live continually alters his surroundings. On all points of contact with the outer world he creates an artificial, secondary environment. He makes houses, or constructs shelters; he prepares his food more or less elaborately, procuring it by means of weapons and implements; he makes roads and uses means of transport. Were man to rely on his anatomical equipment exclusively, he would soon be destroyed or perish from hunger and exposure. Defense, feeding, movement in space, all physiological and spiritual needs, are satisfied indirectly by means of

[1] "Culture" by Bronislaw Malinowski in E. R. A. Seligman, *The Encyclopedia of the Social Sciences*. Copyright 1930 by The Macmillan Co. and used with their permission. Vol. IV, pp. 621–3, 626–9, 633–4, 645.

artifacts even in the most primitive modes of human life. The man of nature, the *Naturmensch*, does not exist.

This *material* outfit of man—his artifacts, his buildings, his sailing craft, his implements and weapons, the liturgical paraphernalia of his magic and religion—are one and all the most obvious and tangible aspects of culture. They define its level and they constitute its effectiveness. The material equipment of culture is not, however, a force in itself. Knowledge is necessary in the production, management and use of artifacts, implements, weapons and other constructions and is essentially connected with mental and moral discipline, of which religion, laws and ethical rules are the ultimate source. The handling and possession of goods imply also the appreciation of their value. The manipulation of implements and the consumption of goods also require cooperation. Common work and common enjoyment of its results are always based on a definite type of social organization. Thus material culture requires a complement less simple, less easily catalogued or analyzed, consisting of the body of intellectual knowledge, of the system of moral, spiritual and economic values, of social organization and of language. On the other hand, material culture is an indispensable apparatus for the molding or conditioning of each generation of human beings. The secondary environment, the outfit of material culture, is a laboratory in which the reflexes, the impulses, the emotional tendencies of the organism are formed. The hands, arms, legs and eyes are adjusted by the use of implements to the proper technical skill necessary in a culture. The nervous processes are modified so as to yield the whole range of intellectual concepts, emotional types and sentiments which form the body of science, religion and morals prevalent in a community. As an important counterpart to these mental processes there are the modifications in the larynx and tongue which fix some of the crucial concepts and values by associating them with definite sounds. Artifact and custom are equally indispensable and they mutually produce and determine one another.

Language is often regarded as something distinct from both man's material possessions and his system of customs. This view is frequently coupled with a theory by which meaning is regarded as a mystical content of the word, which can be transmitted in utterance from one mind to another. But the meaning of a word is the sound uttered within a context of situation. The utterance of sound is a significant act indispensable in all forms of human concerted action. It is a type of behavior strictly comparable to the handling of a tool, the wielding of a weapon, the performance of a ritual or the concluding of a contract. The use of words is in all these forms of human activity an indispensable correlate of manual and bodily behavior. The meaning of words consists in what they achieve by concerted action, the indirect handling of the environment through the direct action upon other organisms. Speech therefore is a bodily habit and is comparable to any other type of custom. The learning of language consists in the development of a system of conditioned reflexes which at the same time become conditioned stimuli. Speech is the production of articulate sounds, developed in childhood out of the inarticulate infantile utterances which constitute the child's main endowment in dealing with his environment. As the individual grows his increase of linguistic knowledge runs parallel with his general development. A growing knowledge of technical processes is bound up with the learning of technical terms; the development of his tribal citizenship and social responsibility is accompanied by the acquisition of a sociological vocabulary and of polite speech, commands and legal phraseology; the growing experience of religious and moral values is associated with the development of ritual and ethical formulae. The full knowledge of language is the inevitable correlate of the full attainment of a tribal and cultural status. Language thus is an integral part of culture; it is not, however, a system of tools but rather a body of vocal customs.

Social organization is often regarded by sociologists as remaining outside culture, but the organization of social groups is a complex combination of material equipment and bodily customs which cannot be divorced from either its material or psychological substratum. Social organization is the standardized manner in which groups behave. But a social group consists always of individuals. The child, attached to its parents through the satisfaction of all its needs, grows up within the shelter of the parental house, hut or tent. The domestic hearth is the center around which the various necessities of warmth, comfort, food and companionship are satisfied. Later in every human society communal life is associated with the local settlement, the town, village or compound; it is localized within definite boundaries and associated with private and public activities of an economic, political and religious nature. In every organized activity therefore human beings are bound together by their connection with a definite portion of environment, by their association with a common shelter and by the fact that they carry out certain tasks in common. The concerted character of their behavior is the result of social rules, that is, customs, either sanctioned by explicit measures or working in an apparently automatic way. The sanctioned rules—laws, customs and manners—belong to the category of acquired bodily habits. The essence of moral values by which man is driven to definite behavior by inner compulsion has in religious and metaphysical thought been ascribed to conscience, the will of God or an inborn categorical imperative; while some sociologists have explained it as due to a supreme moral being—society, or the collective soul. Moral motivation when viewed empirically consists in a disposition of the nervous system and of the whole organism to follow within given circumstances a line of behavior dictated by inner constraint which is due neither to innate impulses nor yet to obvious gains or utilities. The inner constraint is the result of the gradual training of the organism within a definite set of cultural conditions. The impulses, desires and ideas are within each society welded into specific systems, in psychology called sentiments. Such sentiments define the attitudes of a man toward the members of his group, above all his nearest kindred; toward the material objects of his surroundings; toward the country which he inhabits; toward the community with which he works; toward the realities of his magical or metaphysical *Weltanschauung*. Fixed values or sentiments often condition human behavior so that man prefers death to surrender or compromise, pain to pleasure, abstention to satisfaction of desire. The formation of sentiments and thus of values is always based on the cultural apparatus in a society. Sentiments are formed over a long space of time and through a very gradual training or conditioning of the organism. They are based on forms of organization, very often world wide, such as the Christian church, the community of Islam, the empire, the flag—all symbols or catchwords, behind which, however, there exist vast and living cultural realities. . . .

The real component units of cultures which have a considerable degree of permanence, universality and independence are the organized systems of human activities called institutions. Every institution centers around a fundamental need, permanently unites a group of people in a cooperative task and has its particular body of doctrine and its technique of craft. Institutions are not correlated simply and directly to their functions: one need does not receive one satisfaction in one institution. But institutions show a pronounced amalgamation of functions and have a synthetic character. . . .

The form of cultural objects is determined by direct bodily needs on the one hand and by instrumental uses on the other, but this division of needs and uses is neither complete nor satisfactory. The ceremonial staff used as a mark of rank or office is neither a tool nor a commodity, and customs, words and beliefs cannot be referred either to physiology or to the workshop.

Man like any animal must receive nourishment, and he has to propagate if he is to continue individually and racially. He must also have permanent safeguards against dangers coming from the physical environment, from animals or from other human beings. A whole range of necessary bodily comforts must be provided—shelter, warmth, a dry lair and means of cleanliness. The effective satisfaction of these primary bodily needs imposes or dictates to every culture a number of fundamental aspects; institutions for nutrition, or the commissariat; institutions for mating and propagation; and organizations for defense and comfort. The organic needs of man form the basic imperatives leading to the development of culture in that they compel every community to carry on a number of organized activities. Religion or magic, the maintenance of law or systems of knowledge and mythology occur with such persistent regularity in every culture that it must be assumed that they also are the result of some deep needs or imperatives.

The cultural mode of satisfaction of the biological needs of the human organism creates new conditions and thus imposes new cultural imperatives. With insignificant exceptions, desire for food does not bring man directly in touch with nature and force him to consume the fruits as they grow in the forest. In all cultures, however simple, staple food is prepared and cooked and eaten according to strict rules within a definite group and with the observance of manners, rights and tabus. It is usually obtained by more or less complicated, collectively carried out processes, such as agriculture, exchange or some system of social cooperation and communal distribution. In all this man is dependent on the artificially produced apparatus of weapons, agricultural implements, fishing craft and tackle. He is equally dependent upon organized cooperation and upon economic and moral values.

Thus out of the satisfaction of physiological needs there grow derived imperatives. Since they are essentially means to an end they may be called the instrumental imperatives of culture. These are as indispensable to man's commissariat, to the satisfaction of his nutritive needs, as the raw material of food and the processes of its ingestion. For man is so molded that if he were deprived of his economic organization and of his implements he would as effectively starve as if the substance of his foodstuffs were withdrawn from him.

From the biological point of view the continuity of race might be satisfied in a very simple manner: it would be enough for people to mate, to produce two or occasionally more children per couple, enough to insure that two individuals survive for every two who die. If biology alone controlled human procreation, people would mate by rules of physiology which are the same for the whole species; they would produce offspring in the natural course of pregnancy and childbirth; and the animal species man would have its typical family life, physiologically defined. The human family, the biological unit, would then present exactly the same constitution throughout humanity. It would also remain outside the scope of cultural science—as has been in fact postulated by many sociologists, notably by Durkheim. But instead, mating, that is, the system of courtship, love making and selection of consorts, is in every human society traditionally defined by the body of cultural customs prevalent in that community. There are rules which debar some people from marriage and make it desirable if not compulsory for others to marry; there are rules of chastity and rules of license; there are strictly cultural elements which blend with the natural impulse and produce an ideal of attractiveness which varies from one society and one culture to another. In place of biologically determined uniformity a bewildering variety of sexual customs and courtship arrangements regulating mating exist. Marriage within each human culture is by no means a simple sexual union or even cohabitation of two people. It is invariably a legal contract defining the mode in which man and wife should live together and the economic conditions of their union, such as cooperation in property, mutual contributions and contributions of the respective relatives of their consort. It is invariably a public ceremony, a matter for social concern, involving large groups of people as well as the two main actors. Its dissolution as well as its conclusion is subject to fixed traditional rules.

Nor is parenthood a mere biological relationship. Conception is the subject of a rich traditional folklore in every human community and has its legal side in the rules which discriminate between children conceived in wedlock and out of it. Pregnancy is surrounded by an atmosphere of moral values and rules. Usually the expectant mother is compelled to lead a special mode of life hedged in by tabus, all of which she has to observe on account of the welfare of the child. There is thus a culturally established, anticipatory maternity which foreshadows the biological fact. Childbirth is also an event deeply modified by ritual, legal, magical and religious concomitants, in which the emotions of the mother, her relations to the child and the relations of both to the social group are molded so as to conform to a specific traditional pattern. The father also is never passive or indifferent at childbirth. Tradition closely defines the parental duties during early pregnancy and the manner in which they are divided between husband and wife and partly shifted to more distant relatives.

Kinship, the tie between the child and its parents and their relatives, is never a haphazard affair. Its development is determined by the legal system of the community, which organizes on a definite pattern all emotional responses as well as all duties, moral attitudes and customary obligations. The important distinction between matrilineal and patrilineal relatives, the development of the wider or classificatory kinship relations as well as the formation of clans, or sibs, in which large groups of relatives are to a certain extent regarded and treated as real kindred, are cultural modifications of natural kinship. Procreation thus becomes in human societies a vast cultural scheme. The racial need of continuity is not satisfied by the mere action of physiological impulses and physiological processes but by the working of traditional rules associated with an apparatus of material culture. The procreative scheme, moreover, is seen to be composed of several component institutions: standardized courtship, marriage, parenthood, kinship and clanship. In the same way the nutritive scheme may be divided into the consuming institutions, that is, household or clubhouse with its men's refectory; the productive institutions, of tribal gardening, hunting and fishing; and the distributive institutions, such as markets and trading arrangements. Impulses act in the form of social or cultural commands, which are the reinterpretations of physiological drives in terms of social, traditionally sanctioned rules. The human being starts to court or to dig the soil, to make love or to go hunting, or fishing, not because he is directly moved by an instinct but because the routine of his tribe makes him do these things. At the same time tribal routine insures that physiological needs are satisfied and that the cultural means of satisfaction conform to the same pattern with only minor variations in detail. The direct motive for human actions is couched in cultural terms and conforms to a cultural pattern. But cultural commands always bid man to satisfy his needs in a more or less direct manner, and on the whole the system of cultural commands in a given society leaves but few of the physiological needs unsatisfied.

An amalgamation of functions occurs in most human institutions. The household is not merely a reproductive institution: it is one of the main nutritive institutions and an economic, legal and often a religious unit. The family is the place where cultural continuity through education is served. This amalgamation of functions within the same institution is not fortuitous. Most of man's fundamental needs are so concatenated that their satisfaction can be best provided for within the same human group and by a combined apparatus of material culture. Even human physiology causes birth to be followed by lactation, and this is inevitably associated with the tender cares of the mother for the child, which gradually shades into the earliest educational services. The mother requires a male helpmate, and the parental group must become a cooperative as well as an educational association. The fact that marriage is an economic as well as an educational and procreative relation influences courtship deeply, and this becomes a selection for lifelong companionship, common work and common responsibilities, so that sex must be blended with other personal and cultural requirements.

Education means training in the use of implements and goods, in the knowledge of tradition, in the wielding of social power and responsibility. The parents who develop in their offspring economic attitudes, technical dexterities, moral and social duties, have also to hand over their possessions, their status or their office. The domestic relationship therefore implies a system of laws of inheritance, descent and succession. . . .

The primary biological needs of a community, that is, the conditions under which a culture can thrive, develop and continue, are satisfied in an indirect manner which imposes secondary or derived conditions. These may be designated as the instrumental imperatives of culture. The whole body of material culture must be produced, maintained, distributed and used. In every culture therefore a system of traditional rules or

commands is found which defines the activities, usages and values by
which food is produced, stored and apportioned, goods manufactured,
owned and used, tools prepared and embodied in production. An economic organization is indispensable to every community, and culture
must always keep in touch with its material substratum.

Regulated cooperation exists even in such simple activities as the
search for food among the lowest primitives. They at times have to ap-
provision big tribal gatherings, and this requires a complicated system of
commissariat. Within the family there is a division of labor, and the
cooperation of families within the local community is never a simple
economic matter. The maintenance of the utilitarian principle in production is closely related to artistic, magical, religious and ceremonial
activities. . . .

Cooperation means sacrifice, effort, subordination of private interests
and inclinations to the joint ends of the community, the existence of
social constraint. Life in common offers various temptations, especially
to the impulses of sex, and as a result a system of prohibitions and re-
straints as well as of mandatory rules is unavoidable. Economic production provides man with things desirable and valuable, not unrestrictedly
accessible for use and enjoyment to everybody alike, and rules of property, of possession and use are developed and enforced. Special organization entails differences in rank, leadership, status and influence. Hierarchy develops social ambitions and requires safeguards, which are
effectively sanctioned. This whole set of problems has been signally
neglected because law and its sanctions are in primitive communities
very rarely embodied in special institutions. Legislation, legal sanctions
and effective administration of tribal rules are very often carried out as
by-products of other activities. The maintenance of law is usually one
of the secondary or derived functions of such institutions as the family,
the household, the local community and the tribal organization. But although not laid down in a specific body of codified rules nor yet carried
out by specially organized groups of people the sanctions of primitive law
function none the less in a special manner and develop special features
in the institutions to which they belong. For it is essentially incorrect to
maintain, as has often been done, that primitive law works automatically
and that the savage is naturally a law abiding citizen. Rules of conduct
must be drilled into each new generation through education: that is,
provision must be made for the continuity of culture through the instrumentality of tradition. The first requisite is the existence of symbolic
signs in which condensed experience can be handed over from one generation to another. Language is the most important type of such symbolic signs. Language does not contain experience; it is rather a system
of sound habits which accompanies the development of cultural experience in every human community and becomes an integral part of this

cultural experience. In primitive cultures tradition remains oral. The speech of a primitive tribe is full of set sayings, maxims, rules and reflections, which in a stereotyped manner carry on the wisdom of one generation into another. Folk tales and mythology form another department of verbal tradition. In higher cultures writing is added to carry on spoken tradition. The failure to realize that language is an integral part of culture has led to the vague, metaphorical and misleading parallels between animal societies and human culture which have done much harm to sociology. If it were clearly realized that culture without language does not exist, the treatment of animal communities would cease to be a part of sociology and animal adaptations to nature would be clearly distinguished from culture. Education in primitive society seldom commands specific institutions. The family, the group of extended kindred, the local community, age grades, secret societies, initiation camps, the professional groups or guilds of technical, magical or religious craft—these are the institutions which correspond in some of their derived functions to schools in more advanced cultures.

The three instrumental imperatives, economic organization, law and education, do not exhaust all that culture entails in its indirect satisfaction of human needs. Magic and religion, knowledge and art, are part of the universal scheme which underlies all concrete cultures and may be said to arise in response to an integrative or synthetic imperative of human culture.

In spite of the various theories about a specific non-empirical and prelogical character of primitive mentality there can be no doubt that as soon as man developed the mastery of environment by the use of implements, and as soon as language came into being, there must also have existed primitive knowledge of an essentially scientific character. No culture could survive if its arts and crafts, its weapons and economic pursuits were based on mystical, non-empirical conceptions and doctrines. When human culture is approached from the pragmatic, technological side, it is found that primitive man is capable of exact observation, of sound generalizations and of logical reasoning in all those matters which affect his normal activities and are at the basis of his production. Knowledge is then an absolute derived necessity of culture. It is more, however, than a means to an end, and it was not classed therefore with the instrumental imperatives. Its place in culture, its function, is slightly different from that of production, of law or of education. Systems of knowledge serve to connect various types of behavior; they carry over the results of past experiences into future enterprise and they bring together elements of human experience and allow man to coordinate mental attitude, a diathesis of the nervous system, which allows man to carry on the work which culture makes him do. Its function is to organize and integrate the indispensable activities of culture.

The material embodiment of knowledge consists in the body of arts and crafts, of technical processes and rules of craftsmanship. More specifically, in most primitive cultures and certainly in higher ones there are special implements of knowledge—diagrams, topographical models, measures, aids to orientation or to counting. . . .

By the very forethought and foresight which it gives, the integrative function of knowledge creates new needs, that is, imposes new imperatives. Knowledge gives man the possibility of planning ahead, of embracing vast spaces of time and distance; it allows a wide range to his hopes and desires. But however much knowledge and science help man in allowing him to obtain what he wants they are unable completely to control chance, to eliminate accidents, to foresee the unexpected turn of natural events or to make human handiwork reliable and adequate to all practical requirements. In this field, much more practical, definite and circumscribed than that of religion, there develops a special type of ritual activities which anthropology labels collectively as magic.

The most hazardous of all human enterprises known to primitive man is sailing. In the preparation of his sailing craft and the laying out of his plans the savage turns to his science. The painstaking work as well as the intelligently organized labor in construction and in navigation bears witness to the savage's trust in science and submission to it. But adverse wind or no wind at all, rough weather, currents and reefs are always liable to upset his best plans and most careful preparations. He must admit that neither his knowledge nor his most painstaking efforts are a guaranty of success. Something unaccountable usually enters and baffles his anticipations. But although unaccountable it yet appears to have a deep meaning, to act or behave with a purpose. The sequence, the significant concatenation of events, seems to contain some inner logical consistency. Man feels that he can do something to wrestle with that mysterious element or force, to help and abet his luck. There are therefore always systems of superstition, of more or less developed ritual, associated with sailing, and in primitive communities the magic of sailing craft is highly developed. . . .

Culture is then essentially an instrumental reality which has come into existence to satisfy the needs of man in a manner far surpassing any direct adaptation to the environment. Culture endows man with an additional extension of his anatomical apparatus, with a protective armor of defenses and safeguards, with mobility and speed through media where his direct bodily equipment would have entirely failed him. Culture, the cumulative creation of man, extends the range of individual efficiency and of power of action; and it gives a depth of thought and breadth of vision undreamed of in any animal species. The source of all this consists in the cumulative character of individual achievements and in the power to share in common work. Culture thus transforms individuals into organized groups and gives these an almost indefinite continuity. Man is certainly not a gregarious animal in the sense that his concerted actions are due to physiological and innate endowment and carried on in patterns common to the whole species. Organization and all concerted behavior, the results of traditional continuity, assume a different form for every culture. Culture deeply modifies human innate endowment, and in doing this it not only bestows blessings but also imposes obligations and demands the surrender of a great many personal liberties to the common welfare. The individual has to submit to order and law; he has to learn and to obey tradition; he has to twist his tongue and to adjust his larynx to a variety of sounds and to adapt his nervous system to a variety of habits. He works and produces objects which others will consume, while in turn he is always dependent upon alien toil. Finally his capacity of accumulating experience and letting it foretell the future opens new vistas and creates gaps which are satisfied in the system of knowledge, of art and of magical and religious beliefs. Although culture is primarily born out of the satisfaction of biological needs, its very nature makes man into something essentially different from a mere animal organism. Man satisfies none of his needs as mere animal. Man has his wants as an implement making and implement using creature, as a communing and discoursing member of a group, as the guardian of a traditional continuity, as a toiling unit within a cooperative body of men, as one who is haunted by the past or in love with it, as one whom the events to come fill with hopes and with anxieties and finally as one to whom the division of labor and the provisions for the future have given leisure and opportunities to enjoy color, form and music.

From the above reading it is clear that the anthropologist's conception of culture is quite different from the common usage of the term. The anthropologist would say that every human being is "cultured" whether he is a connoisseur of fine art or not. And a simple digging stick tells him as much about a people as does an electric generator.

Custom

INSTITUTIONS, as Malinowski pointed out, were created (and, of course, are still being created) by man out of need to help him discharge his functions more effectively and more efficiently. The origin and development of customs, since many of them seem irrational, is not quite so obvious. The theory advanced by William Graham Sumner in his classic work, *Folkways*, published in 1907, is that customs or folkways develop in much the same way as institutions. Sumner's theory is that men in meeting their individual day-to-day needs worked out certain behavior patterns on a trial-and-error basis. Gradually those actions which were most successful or least painful were retained. From recurrent need these actions were developed into customs which were then passed on to the next generation. According to Sumner the whole process was not planned or thought out but was done almost unconsciously. As time passed a whole series of customs were developed which provided ready-made patterns for the child born into the group. When these *folkways*, or customs, reached the point where they were regarded as necessary for the group welfare they became *mores* that defined the standards of right and wrong conduct for the individuals in the group. In modern societies these mores are generally in the form of laws, but many of them are not. There is no law which prevents an individual from going to church in a bathing suit, but it simply is not done.

The customs and mores of a group can even affect physiological functions as is evidenced by this story related by Clyde Kluckhohn.

> I once knew a trader's wife in Arizona who took a somewhat devilish interest in producing a cultural reaction. Guests who came her way were often served delicious sandwiches filled with a meat that seemed to be neither chicken nor tuna fish yet was reminiscent of both. To queries she gave no reply until each had eaten his fill. She then explained that what they had eaten was not chicken, not tuna fish, but the rich, white flesh of freshly killed rattlesnakes. The response was instantaneous—vomiting, often violent vomiting. A biological process is caught in a cultural web.[2]

It is important to remember that cultures vary in their level of complexity and this complexity has a direct influence upon the individuals concerned. In our society, human beings have been conditioned to a high standard of living and our needs and expectations are greater. We could live as the Mexicans do on corn and beans, but we would be most unhappy if we had to do so. In the same way if we had to live without electricity and the home appliances which depend upon it (refrigerators, radios, electric lights, etc.) we would have to readjust our whole way of life. These luxury items are not necessary to meet our biological needs but most Americans would say they were essentials. The story is told of the individual who committed suicide because as a result of the stock market crash in 1929 he was reduced to an annual income of $25,000. His needs were obviously far beyond food, shelter, and clothing.

[2] By permission from *Mirror for Man* by Clyde Kluckhohn. Copyright 1949. McGraw-Hill Book Company, Inc. P. 19.

Cultural Continuity and Social Change

It is clear from what has been said that all cultures have continuity and that all cultures are changing. Even when violent revolutions have occurred, as in Russia in 1917, the characteristically Russian patterns of culture appeared in the new regime that emerged. The fact is that the adults in any culture are creatures of that culture, and the habits and customs and experiences of a lifetime cannot be changed overnight. This is not to say that cultures cannot be changed; they can. For men are creators as well as creatures of culture, but the very factors that provide the continuity in cultures also work against rapid change.

So far as social change is concerned, it is clear that not all cultures change at the same rate. In some primitive groups the rate of change is almost imperceptible whereas in modern, technical, industrial societies, the rate of change is rapid. Furthermore, not all of the segments within a culture develop at the same rate and this results in what sociologists call "culture lag." In our culture, developments in science and technology have far outdistanced our social and political patterns, often with resultant serious problems of readjustment. For example, part of our problem in the years of the Great Depression was that our social, political, and economic ideas were fashioned in an agrarian, individualistic society. By 1929 America had become a highly industrialized, interdependent society but we still adhered to our nineteenth-century belief: the government that governs least, governs best. Since then we have made real progress in adapting our ideas and institutions to our new society and both political parties are agreed that government must play a strong active role in keeping our economy on an even keel. Because of the interrelatedness, or organic nature, of culture, changes in one segment, e.g., science, are bound to have repercussions in other segments.

The Diversity of Culture

We have seen that all human beings have certain basic needs in common but the way in which these needs are satisfied varies greatly from culture to culture. Both the Eskimo and the Mexican must eat to live, but one lives on fish and whale blubber and the other lives on corn and beans. Partly this cultural diversity is a result of soil, climate, and topography, but even when these factors are comparable, the food that is eaten, and the way it is prepared, vary greatly. The fact is that no two cultures are alike although all have certain common elements. The geographic and climatic factors are of course vitally important. It is no accident that the level of culture in the tropical areas is comparatively low. Any American who has lived in the tropics or in some areas of the United States in July and August knows that one's total energy is used for mere existence with nothing left for raising the level of culture. It is no accident either that most of the advanced civilizations have developed in the temperate zones. In ancient Egypt and the Mesopotamian Valley, with climatic conditions neither strictly temperate nor tropical, rich fertile areas made it possible for men to have leisure time—time that could be and was devoted to developing language, institutions, and knowledge. In other areas where the resources for sustaining human life are scarce, man still lives in a primitive way. Thus the Siriono Indians of Bolivia devote their entire time and energy to gathering food and barely manage to keep themselves alive. However, favorable soil and climate alone do not guarantee that a group will reach a high level of civilization. Once a group reaches an advanced level of culture, it can to some extent use its technical knowledge to overcome the physical environment, for example, to convert a desert into life-sustaining farmland. In the American culture, for example, we have the knowledge and the technical means to reclaim much of the land that is now barren.

The explanation for the origin and development of cultures and their great diversity has intrigued social scientists for years. The diversity is explained by the geographic isolation of human groups owing to lack of transportation and the resulting adaptation of these groups to their natural environments. As groups lived in isolation they developed ways and means of meeting their basic physiological needs and created a secondary or cultural environment. The various aspects of culture—tools, language, institutions, and customs were blended together to form what Ruth Benedict called a "pattern" of culture in which all of the parts were interrelated. This pattern operating upon the members of the group produces a group character or what Sumner called "ethos," which sets them off from all other groups. Thus it is quite simple to pick out a group of Americans in Calcutta or even in Paris by their dress, speech, and mannerisms. It is important to realize that very often there are subcultures within cultures, especially in large groups scattered over a wide geographic area. For example, consider the Negro group within the United States or some of the groups such as the Tatars of the Crimea or the Kalmucks of the Lower Volga within the Soviet Union.

This diversity has unquestionably enriched human life as each group has made its own unique contributions. But it has also made it difficult for human groups to live in peace. In the twentieth century this difficulty has been aggravated as the human family is pulled closer and closer together owing to progress in transportation and communication. Every culture must have agreement on basic values or it cannot endure, and the lessons of our own Civil War are clear on this point. The problem is, as the world becomes more and more a community, to achieve the essential unity which will enable men to live and work together while maintaining the richness of diversity which prevents deadening uniformity. A tremendous stride toward achieving this basic unity was taken when the Declaration of Human Rights was signed by most of the nations of the world. To be sure these rights will be violated repeatedly by the signatory nations themselves, but the important thing is agreement as to what the basic values of the human family *should be*. Within the framework almost unlimited diversity is possible and yet the danger of complete cultural relativism is avoided. Thus there is plenty of room for religious diversity but no room for the aggressive anti-Semitic doctrine of Nazism. This problem of unity and diversity was faced and solved in the colonization and development of America into a nation as the peoples from many nations were Americanized, partly through the public school system. It should be remembered, however, that the English groups dominated the country and established the basic pattern before the strong influx of Germans and southern Europeans started. Also, the vast majority of the immigrants had the benefit of a common European cultural background.

All of the facts and ideas presented in this chapter have an important bearing upon education and the schools. There is no pretense, of course, that this brief treatment could be anything but a beginning of the study of the nature and function of culture. Nevertheless, even from the limited treatment, it should be clear that an understanding of culture in general and of American culture in particular is essential for understanding American education. For American education functions within the framework of and is an integral part of American culture. It is from our culture that the aims, the content, and the organization of the schools are derived. This understanding can help us avoid the pitfall of considering the school and its operation as an entity complete in itself and functioning independently. Furthermore, an understanding of culture can assist us in meeting the challenge presented in Chapter 1, for, as Lawrence Frank has said:

> In the years to come it is probable that this discovery of the human origin and development of culture, will be recognized as the greatest of all discoveries, since heretofore man has been helpless before these cultural and social formulations which generation after generation have perpetuated the same frustration and defeat of human values and aspirations. So long as he believed this was necessary and inevitable, he could not but accept this lot with resignation. Now man is beginning to realize that his culture and social organization are not unchanging cosmic processes, but are human creations which may be altered. For those who cherish the democratic faith this discovery means that they can, and must, under-

take a continuing assay of our culture and our society in terms of its consequences for human life and human values. This is the historic origin and purpose of human culture, to create a human way of life. To our age falls the responsibility of utilizing the amazing new resources of science to meet these cultural tasks, to continue the great human tradition of man taking charge of his own destiny.[3]

Suggested Readings

Benedict, Ruth: *Patterns of Culture*. Boston: Houghton Mifflin Company, 1934.

Herskovits, Melville J.: *Cultural Anthropology*. New York: Alfred A. Knopf, 1955.

Kluckhohn, Clyde: *Mirror for Man*. New York: McGraw-Hill Book Company, 1949.

Linton, Ralph: *The Study of Man*. New York: Appleton-Century-Crofts, 1936.

————: *The Tree of Culture*. New York: Alfred A. Knopf, 1955.

Malinowski, Bronislaw: *Freedom and Civilization*. New York: Roy Publishers, 1944.

Mannheim, Karl: *Ideology and Utopia*. New York: Harcourt, Brace and Company, 1936.

Mead, Margaret: *Growing Up in New Guinea*. New York: William Morrow & Company, 1930.

————: *Sex and Temperament in Three Primitive Societies*. New York: William Morrow & Company, 1935.

Ogburn, William F.: *Social Change*. New York: The Viking Press, 1922.

Sumner, W. C.: *Folkways*. Boston: Ginn & Company, 1906.

Wissler, Clark: *Man and Culture*. New York: Thomas Y. Crowell Company, 1923.

[3] Lawrence K. Frank, "Science and Culture," *The Scientific Monthly*, L (June 1940), 497.

CHAPTER 4

THE INDIVIDUAL IN CULTURE— PERSONALITY

K NOWLEDGE OF THE NATURE OF CULTURE IS ESSENTIAL, BUT IS NOT adequate for even an elementary understanding of the social foundations of education. For although education is a distinctly social undertaking, it always centers about individuals. It is true that individuals are creatures of culture in the sense that their language, customs, beliefs, etc., are determined by the culture into which they happen to be born. It is also true that individual human beings from the same culture tend to resemble one another, that is, they have certain characteristics in common; but they only resemble, they are not identical. One of the commonplace but nevertheless astounding facts of human life is that no two individual human beings are exactly the same. Each person has, as we say, a unique personality. Even identical twins who are formed from the same germ cell and receive the same genetic equipment are distinctly different.

Understanding the Determinants of Personality

THE question is: How can this uniqueness of individual personality be explained, and in what way is it important for an understanding of American education? The first part of this question might be answered in part by the influence of subculture. However, even individuals within subcultures differ; therefore other factors must be operating that produce the differences in personality. The answer to the second part of the question might be that we need to understand human beings and the development of personality so that we can do a better job of teaching. This is certainly true, but there are other important reasons why a knowledge of personality is essential to an understanding of American education.

However, before dealing with this question, let us first consider what the factors are that determine personality. Once these factors are before us our question can be considered more intelligently. To discuss the determinants of personality a statement by Clyde Kluckhohn and Henry A. Murray from the book *Personality in Nature, Society, and Culture* has been chosen. Both authors are outstanding in their fields, Kluckhohn in anthropology and Murray in psychology, and their collaboration enables us to have the benefit of knowledge from the two disciplines most concerned with personality. The reader is urged to study the entire volume, which is a collection of research findings by scholars who have pioneered in the study of personality.

CLYDE KLUCKHOHN and HENRY A. MURRAY

FROM

Personality in Nature, Society, and Culture [1]

Every man is in certain respects

a. like all other men,
b. like some other men,
c. like no other man.

He is like all other men because some of the determinants of his personality are universal to the species. That is to say, there are common features in the biological endowments of all men, in the physical environments they inhabit, and in the societies and cultures in which they develop. It is the very obviousness of this fact which makes restatements of it expedient, since, like other people, we students of personality are naturally disposed to be attracted by what is unusual, by the qualities which distinguish individuals, environments, and societies, and so to overlook the common heritage and lot of man. It is possible that the most important of the undiscovered determinants of personality and culture are only to be revealed by close attention to the commonplace. Every man experiences birth and must learn to move about and explore his environment, to protect himself against extremes of temperature and to avoid serious injuries; every man experiences sexual tensions and other importunate needs and must learn to find ways of appeasing them; every man grows in stature, matures, and dies; and he does all this and much more, from first to last, as a member of a society. These characteristics he shares with the majority of herd animals, but others are unique to

[1] Clyde Kluckhohn and Henry A. Murray with the collaboration of David M. Schneider, *Personality in Nature, Society, and Culture*, rev. ed. (New York: Alfred A. Knopf, copyright 1948, 1953), pp. 53–67.

him. Only with those of his own kind does he enjoy an erect posture, hands that grasp, three-dimensional and color vision, and a nervous system that permits elaborate speech and learning processes of the highest order.

Any one personality is like all others, also, because, as social animals, men must adjust to a condition of interdependence with other members of their society and of groups within it, and, as cultural animals, they must adjust to traditionally defined expectations. All men are born helpless into an inanimate and impersonal world which presents countless threats to survival; the human species would die out if social life were abandoned. Human adaptation to the external environment depends upon that mutual support which is social life; and, in addition, it depends upon culture. Many types of insects live socially yet have no culture. Their capacity to survive resides in action patterns which are inherited via the germ plasm. Higher organisms have less rigid habits and can learn more from experience. Human beings, however, learn not only from experience but also from each other. All human societies rely greatly for their survival upon accumulated learning (culture). Culture is a great storehouse of ready-made solutions to problems which human animals are wont to encounter. This storehouse is man's substitute for instinct. It is filled not merely with the pooled learning of the living members of the society, but also with the learning of men long dead and of men belonging to other societies.

Human personalities are similar, furthermore, insofar as they all experience both gratifications and deprivations. They are frustrated by the impersonal environment (weather, physical obstacles, etc.) and by physiological conditions within their own bodies (physical incapacities, illnesses, etc.). Likewise, social life means some sacrifice of autonomy, subordination, and the responsibilities of superordination. The pleasure and pain men experience depend also upon what culture has taught them to expect from one another. Anticipations of pain and pleasure are internalized through punishment and reward.

These universalities of human life produce comparable effects upon the developing personalities of men of all times, places, and races. But they are seldom explicitly observed or commented upon. They tend to remain background phenomena—taken for granted like the air we breathe.

Frequently remarked, however, are the similarities in personality traits among members of groups or in specific individuals from different groups. In certain features of personality, most men are "like some other men." The statistical prediction can safely be made that a hundred Americans, for example, will display certain defined characteristics more frequently than will a hundred Englishmen comparably distributed as to age, sex, social class, and vocation.

But being "like some men" is by no means limited to members of social units like nations, tribes, and classes. Seafaring people, regardless of the communities from which they come, tend to manifest similar qualities. The same may be said for desert folk. Intellectuals and athletes the world over have something in common; so have those who were born to wealth or poverty. Persons who have exercised authority over large groups for many years develop parallel reaction systems, in spite of culturally tailored differences in the details of their behaviors. Probably tyrannical fathers leave a detectably similar imprint upon their children, though the uniformity may be superficially obscured by local manners. Certainly the hyperpituitary type is equally recognizable among Europeans, African Negroes, and American Indians. Also, even where organic causes are unknown or doubtful, certain neurotic and psychotic syndromes in persons of one society remind us of other individuals belonging to very different societies.

Finally, there is the inescapable fact that a man is in many respects like no other man. Each individual's modes of perceiving, feeling, needing, and behaving have characteristic patterns which are not precisely duplicated by those of any other individual. This is traceable, in part, to the unique combination of biological materials which the person has received from his parents. More exactly, the ultimate uniqueness of each personality is the product of countless and successive interactions between the maturing constitution and different environing situations from birth onward. An identical sequence of such determining influences is never reproduced. In this connection it is necessary to emphasize the importance of "accidents," that is, of events that are not predictable for any given individual on the basis of generalized knowledge of his physical, social and cultural environments. A child gets lost in the woods and suffers from exposure and hunger. Another child is nearly drowned by a sudden flood in a canyon. Another loses his mother and is reared by an aged grandmother, or his father remarries and his education is entrusted to a stepmother with a psychopathic personality. Although the personalities of children who have experienced a trauma of the same type will often resemble each other in certain respects, the differences between them may be even more apparent, partly because the traumatic situation in each case had certain unique features, and partly because at the time of the trauma the personality of each child, being already unique, responded in a unique manner. Thus there is uniqueness in each inheritance and uniqueness in each environment, but, more particularly, uniqueness in the number, kinds, and temporal order of critically determining situations encountered in the course of life.

In personal relations, in psychotherapy, and in the arts, this uniqueness of personality usually is, and should be, accented. But for general scientific purpose the observation of uniformities, uniformities of elements and uniformities of patterns, is of first importance. This is so because without the discovery of uniformities there can be no concepts, no classifications, no formulations, no principles, no laws; and without these no science can exist.

The writers suggest that clear and orderly thinking about personality formation will be facilitated if four classes of determinants (and their interactions) are distinguished: *constitutional, group-membership, role, and situational.* These will help us to understand in what ways every man is "like all other men," "like some other men," "like no other man."

1. CONSTITUTIONAL DETERMINANTS

The old problem of "heredity *or* environment" is essentially meaningless. The two sets of determinants can rarely be completely disentangled once the environment has begun to operate. All geneticists are agreed today that traits are not inherited in any simple sense. The observed characters of organisms are, at any given point in time, the product of a long series of complex interactions between biologically-inherited potentialities and environmental forces. The outcome of each interaction is a modification of the personality. The only pertinent questions therefore are: (1) which of the various genetic potentialities will be actualized as a consequence of a particular series of life-events in a given physical, social, and cultural environment? and (2) what limits to the development of this personality are set by genetic constitution?

Because there are only a few extreme cases in which an individual is definitely committed by his germ plasm to particular personality traits, we use the term "constitutional" rather than "hereditary." "Constitution" refers to the total physiological make-up of an individual at a given time. This is a product of influences emanating from the germ plasm and influences derived from the environment (diet, drugs, etc.).

Since most human beings (including scientists) crave simple solutions and tend to feel that because simple questions can be asked there must be simple answers, there are numberless examples both of overestimation and of underestimation of constitutional factors in theories of personality formation. Under the spell of the spectacular success of Darwinian biology and the medicine of the last hundred years, it has often been assumed that personality was no less definitely "given" at birth than was physique. At most, it was granted that a personality "unfolded" as the result of a strictly biological process of maturation.

On the other hand, certain psychiatrists, sociologists, and anthropologists have recently tended to neglect constitutional factors almost completely. Their assumptions are understandable in terms of common human motivations. Excited by discovering the effectiveness of certain determinants, people are inclined to make these explain everything instead of something. Moreover, it is much more cheerful and reassuring to believe that environmental factors (which can be manipulated) are all important, and that hereditary factors (which can't be changed) are comparatively inconsequential. Finally, the psychiatrists, one suspects, are consciously or unconsciously defending their livelihood when they minimize the constitutional side of personality.

The writers recognize the enormous importance of biological events and event patterns in molding the different forms which personalities assume. In fact, in the last chapter personality was defined as "the entire sequence of organized governmental processes in the brain from birth to death." They also insist that biological inheritance provides the stuff from which personality is fashioned and, as manifested in the physique at a given time-point, determines trends and sets limits within which variation is constrained. There are substantial reasons for believing that different genetic structures carry with them varying potentialities for learning, for reaction time, for energy level, for frustration tolerance. Different people appear to have different biological rhythms: of growth, of menstrual cycle, of activity, of depression and exaltation. The various biologically inherited malfunctions certainly have implications among those who share the same physical handicap (deafness, for example).

Sex and age must be regarded as among the more striking constitutional determinants of personality. Personality is also shaped through such traits of physique as stature, pigmentation, strength, conformity of features to the culturally fashionable type, etc. Such characteristics influence a man's needs and expectations. The kind of world he finds about him is to a considerable extent determined by the way other people react to his appearance and physical capacities. Occasionally a physically weak youth, such as Theodore Roosevelt was, may be driven to achieve feats of physical prowess as a form of over-compensation, but usually a man will learn to accept the fact that his physical make-up excludes him from certain types of vocational and social activities, although some concealed resentment may remain as an appreciable ingredient of his total personality. Conversely, special physical fitnesses make certain other types of adjustment particularly congenial.

2. GROUP-MEMBERSHIP DETERMINANTS

The members of any organized enduring group tend to manifest certain personality traits more frequently than do members of other groups. How large or how small are the groupings one compares depends on the problem at hand. By and large, the motivational structures and action patterns of Western Europeans seem similar when contrasted to those of Mohammedans of the Near East or to Eastern Asiatics. Most white citizens of the United States, in spite of regional, ethnic, and class differences, have features of personality which distinguish them from Englishmen, Australians, or New Zealanders. In distinguishing group-membership determinants, one must usually take account of a concentric order of social groups to which the individual belongs, ranging from large national or international groups down to small local units. One must also know the hierarchical class, political or social, to which he belongs within each of these groups. How inclusive a unit one considers in speaking of group-membership determinants is purely a function of the level of abstraction at which one is operating at a given time.

Some of the personality traits which tend to distinguish the members of a given group from humanity as a whole derive from a distinctive biological heritage. Persons who live together are more likely to have the same genes than are persons who live far apart. If the physical vitality is typically low for one group as contrasted with other groups, or if certain types of endocrine imbalance are unusually frequent, the personalities of the members of that group will probably have distinctive qualities.

In the greater number of cases, however, the similarities of character within a group are traceable less to constitutional factors than to formative influences of the environment to which all members of the group have been subjected. Of these group-membership determinants, culture is with little doubt the most significant. To say that "culture determines" is, of course, a highly abstract way of speaking. What one actually observes is the interaction of people. One never sees "culture" any more than one sees "gravity." But "culture" is a very convenient construct which helps in understanding certain regularities in human events, just as "gravity" represents one type of regularity in physical events. Those who have been trained in childhood along traditional lines, and even those who have as adults adopted some new design for living, will be apt to behave predictably in many contexts because of a prevailing tendency to conform to group standards. As Edward Sapir has said:

> "All cultural behavior is patterned. This is merely a way of saying that many things that an individual does and thinks and feels may be looked upon not merely from the standpoint of the forms of behavior that are proper to himself as a biological organism but from the standpoint of a generalized mode of conduct that is imputed to society rather than to the individual, though the personal genesis of conduct is of precisely the same nature, whether we choose to call the conduct 'individual' or 'social.' It is impossible to say what an individual is doing unless we have tacitly accepted the essentially arbitrary modes of interpretation that social tradition is constantly suggesting to us from the very moment of our birth."

Not only the action patterns but also the motivational systems of individuals are influenced by culture. Certain needs are biologically given, but many others are not. All human beings get hungry, but no gene in any chromosome predisposes a person to work for a radio or a new car or a shell necklace or "success." Sometimes biologically-given drives, such as sex, are for longer or shorter periods subordinated to culturally acquired drives, such as the pursuit of money or religious asceticism. And the means by which needs are satisfied are ordinarily defined by cultural habits and fashions. Most Americans would go hungry rather than eat a snake, but this is not true of tribes that consider snake meat a delicacy.

Those aspects of the personality that are not inherited but learned all have—at least in their more superficial and peripheral aspects—a cultural tinge. The skills that are acquired, the factual knowledge, the basic assumptions, the values, and the tastes, are largely determined by culture. Culture likewise structures the conditions under which each kind of learning takes place: whether transmitted by parents or parental substitutes, or by brothers and sisters or by the learner's own age mates; whether gradually or quickly; whether renunciations are harshly imposed or reassuringly rewarded.

Of course we are speaking here of general tendencies rather than invariable facts. If there were no variations in the conceptions and applications of cultural standards, personalities formed in a given society would be more nearly alike than they actually are. Culture determines only what an individual learns as a member of a group—not so much what he learns as a private individual and as a member of a particular family. Because of these special experiences and particular constitutional endowments, each person's selection from and reaction to cultural teachings have an individual quality. What is learned is almost never symmetrical and coherent, and only occasionally is it fully integrated. Deviation from cultural norms is inevitable and endless, for variability appears to be a property of all biological organisms. But variation is also perpetuated because those who have learned later become teachers. Even the most conventional teachers will give culture a certain personal flavor in accord with their constitution and peculiar life-experiences. The culture may prescribe that the training of the child shall be gradual and gentle, but there will always be some abrupt and severe personalities who are temperamentally disposed to act otherwise. Nor is it in the concrete just a matter of individuality in the strict sense. There are family patterns resultant upon the habitual ways in which a number of individuals have come to adjust to each other.

Some types of variation, however, are more predictable. For example, certain differences in the personalities of Americans are referable to the fact that they have grown up in various sub-cultures. Jones is not only an

American; he is also a member of the middle class, an Easterner, and has lived all his life in a small Vermont community. This kind of variation falls within the framework of the group determinants.

The values imbedded in a culture have special weight among the group membership determinants. A value is a conception, explicit or implicit, distinctive of an individual or characteristic of a group, of the desirable which influences the selection from available modes, means, and ends of action. It is thus not just a preference, a desire, but a formulation of the desirable, the "ought" and "should" standards which influence action.

The component elements of a culture must, up to a point, be either logically consistent or meaningfully congruous. Otherwise the culture carriers feel uncomfortably adrift in a capricious, chaotic world. In a personality system, behavior must be reasonably regular or predictable, or the individual will not get expectable and needed responses from others because they will feel that they cannot "depend" on him. In other words, a social life and living in a social world both require standards "within" the individual and standards roughly agreed upon by individuals who live and work together in a group. There can be no personal security and no stability of social organization unless random carelessness, irresponsibility, and purely impulsive behavior are restrained in terms of private and group codes. If one asks the question, "Why are there values?" the reply must be: "Because social life would be impossible without them; the functioning of the social system could not continue to achieve group goals; individuals could not get what they want and need from other individuals in personal and emotional terms, nor could they feel within themselves a requisite measure of order and unified purpose." Above all, values add an element of predictability to social life.[2]

Culture is not the only influence that bears with approximate constancy upon all the members of a relatively stable, organized group. But we know almost nothing of the effects upon personality of the continued press of the impersonal environment. Does living in a constantly rainy climate tend to make people glum and passive, living in a sunny, arid country tend to make them cheerful and lively? What are the differential effects of dwelling in a walled-in mountain valley, on a flat plain, or upon a high plateau studded with wide-sculptured red buttes? Thus far we can only speculate, for we lack adequate data. The effects of climate and even of scenery and topography may be greater than is generally supposed.

Membership in a group also carries with it exposure to a social en-

[2] Fuller treatment of the concept of values will be found in C. Kluckhohn, "Values and Value-Orientations in the Theory of Action: An Exploration in Definition and Classification," in T. Parsons and E. Schills (eds.), *Toward a General Theory of Action* (Cambridge, Mass.: Harvard University Press, 1951).

vironment. Although the social and cultural are inextricably intermingled in an individual's observable behavior, there is a social dimension to group membership that is not culturally defined. The individual must adjust to the presence or absence of other human beings in specified numbers and of specified age and sex. The density of population affects the actual or potential number of face-to-face relationships available to the individual. Patterns for human adjustment which would be suitable to a group of five hundred would not work equally well in a group of five thousand and vice versa. The size of a society, the density of its population, its age and sex ratio are not entirely culturally prescribed, although often conditioned by the interaction between the technological level of the culture and the exigencies of the physical environment. The quality and type of social interaction that is determined by this social dimension of group membership, has, likewise, its consequences for personality formation.

Before leaving the group-membership determinants, we must remind the reader once more that this conception is merely a useful abstraction. In the concrete, the individual personality is never directly affected by the group as a physical totality. Rather, his personality is molded by the particular members of the group with whom he has personal contact and by his conceptions of the group as a whole. Some traits of group members are predictable—in a statistical sense—from knowledge of the biological, social, and cultural properties of the group. But no single person is ever completely representative of all the characteristics imputed to the group as a whole. Concretely, not the group but group agents with their own peculiar traits determine personality formation. Of these group agents, the most important are the parents and other members of the individual's family. They, we repeat, act as individuals, as members of a group, and as members of a sub-group with special characteristics (the family itself).

3. ROLE DETERMINANTS

The culture defines how the different functions, or roles, necessary to group life are to be performed—such roles, for example, as those assigned on the basis of sex and age, or on the basis of membership in a caste, class, or occupational group. In a sense, the role determinants of personality are a special class of group-membership determinants; they apply to strata that cross-cut most kinds of group membership. The long-continued playing of a distinctive role, however, appears to be so potent in differentiating personalities within a group that it is useful to treat these determinants separately.

Moreover, if one is aware of the role determinants, one will less often be misled in interpreting various manifestations of personality. In this connection it is worth recalling that, in early Latin, *persona* means "a mask"—*dramatis personae* are the masks which actors wear in a play, that is, the characters that are represented. Etymologically and historically, then, the personality is the character that is manifested in public. In modern psychology and sociology this corresponds rather closely to the role behavior of a differentiated person. From one point of view, this constitutes a disguise. Just as the outer body shields the viscera from view, and clothing the genitals, so the public personality shields the private personality from the curious and censorious world. It also operates to conceal underlying motivations from the individual's own consciousness. The person who has painfully achieved some sort of integration, and who knows what is expected of him in a particular social situation, will usually produce the appropriate responses with only a little personal coloring. This explains, in part, why the attitudes and action patterns produced by the group-membership and role determinants constitute a screen which, in the case of normal individuals, can be penetrated only by the intensive, lengthy, and oblique procedures of depth psychology.

The disposition to accept a person's behavior in a given situation as representative of his total personality is almost universal. Very often he is merely conforming, very acceptably, to the cultural definition of his role. One visits a doctor in his office, and his behavior fits the stereotype of the physician so perfectly that one says, often mistakenly, "There indeed is a well-adjusted person." But a scientist must train himself to get behind a man's cultivated surface, because he will not be able to understand much if he limits his data to the action patterns perfected through the repeated performance of the roles as physician, as middle-aged man, as physician dealing with an older male patient, etc.

4. SITUATIONAL DETERMINANTS

Besides the constitutional determinants and the forces which will more or less inevitably confront individuals who live in the same physical environment, who are members of a society of a certain size and of a certain culture, and who play the same roles, there are things which "just happen" to people. Even casual contacts of brief duration ("accidental"—i.e., not foreordained by the cultural patterns for social interrelations) are often crucial, it seems, in determining whether a person's life will proceed along one or another of various possible paths. A student, say, who is undecided as to his career, or who is about equally drawn to several different vocations, happens to sit down in a railroad car next to a journalist who is an engaging and persuasive advocate of his profession. This event does not, of course, immediately and directly change the young man's personality, but it may set in motion a chain of events which put him into situations that are decisive in molding his personality.

The situational determinants include things that happen a thousand times as well as those that happen only once—provided they are not standard for a whole group. For example, it is generally agreed that the family constellation in which a person grows up is a primary source of personality styling. These domestic influences are conditioned by the cultural prescriptions for the roles of parents and children. But a divorce, a father who is much older than the mother, a father whose occupation keeps him away from home most of the time, the fact of being an only child or the eldest or youngest in a series—these are situational determinants.

Contact with a group involves determinants which are classified as group-membership or situational, depending on the individual's sense of belongingness or commitment to the group. The congeries of persons among whom a man accidentally finds himself one or more times may affect his personality development but not in the same manner as those social units with which the individual feels himself allied as a result of shared experiences or of imaginative identification.

5. INTERDEPENDENCE OF THE DETERMINANTS

"Culture and personality" is one of the fashionable slogans of contemporary social science and, by present usage, denotes a range of problems on the borderline between anthropology and sociology, on the one hand, and psychology and psychiatry, on the other. However, the phrase has unfortunate implications. A dualism is implied, whereas "culture *in* personality" and "personality *in* culture" would suggest conceptual models more in accord with the facts. Moreover, the slogan favors a dangerous simplification of the problems of personality formation. Recognition of culture as one of the determinants of personality is a great gain, but there are some indications that this theoretical advance has tended to obscure the significance of other types of determinants. "Culture and personality" is as lopsided as "biology and personality." To avoid perpetuation of an over-emphasis upon culture, the writers have treated cultural forces as but one variety of the press to which personalities are subjected as a consequence of their membership in an organized group.

A balanced consideration of "personality in nature, society, and culture" must be carried on within the framework of a complex conceptual scheme which explicitly recognizes, instead of tacitly excluding, a number of types of determinants. But it must also not be forgotten that any classification of personality determinants is, at best, a convenient abstraction.

A few illustrations of the intricate linkage of the determinants will clarify this point. For example, we may instance a network of cultural, role, and constitutional determinants. In every society the child is differently socialized according to sex. Also, in every society different behavior is expected of individuals in different age groups, although each culture makes its own prescriptions as to where these lines are drawn and what behavioral variations are to be anticipated. Thus, the personalities of men and women, of the old and the young, are differentiated, in part, by the experience of playing these various roles in conformity with cultural standards. But, since age and sex are biological facts, they also operate throughout life as constitutional determinants of personality. A woman's motivations and action patterns are modified by the fact of her physique as a woman.

Some factors that one is likely to pigeonhole all too complacently as biological often turn out, on careful examination, to be the product of complicated interactions. Illness may result from group as well as from individual constitutional factors. And illness, in turn, may be considered a situational determinant. The illness—with all its effects upon personality formation—is an "accident" in that one could predict only that the betting odds were relatively high that this individual would fall victim to this illness. However, when the person does become a patient, one can see that both a constitutional predisposition and membership in a caste or class group where sanitation and medical care were substandard are causative factors in this "accidental" event. Similarly, a constitutional tendency towards corpulence certainly has implications for personality when it is characteristic of a group as well as when it distinguishes an individual within a group. But the resources of the physical environment as exploited by the culturally-transmitted technology are major determinants in the production and utilization of nutritional substances of various sorts and these have patent consequences for corpulence, stature, and energy potential. Tuberculosis or pellagra may be endemic. If hookworm is endemic in a population, one will hardly expect vigor to be a striking feature of the majority of people. Yet hookworm is not an unavoidable "given," either constitutionally or environmentally; the prevalence and effects of hookworms are dependent upon culturally enjoined types of sanitary control.

Complicated interrelations of the same sort may be noted between the environmental and cultural forces which constitute the group membership determinants. On the one hand, the physical environment imposes certain limitations upon the cultural forms which man creates, or it constrains toward change and readjustment in the culture he brings into an ecological area. There is always a large portion of the impersonal environment to which men can adjust but not control; there is another portion which is man-made and cultural. Most cultures provide technologies which permit some alterations in the physical world (for example, methods of cutting irrigation ditches or of terracing hillsides). There are also those artifacts (houses, furniture, tools, vehicles) which serve as instruments for the gratification of needs, and, not infrequently, for their incitement and frustration. Most important of all, perhaps, culture directs and often distorts man's perceptions of the external world. What effects social suggestion may have in setting frames of reference for perception has been shown experimentally. Culture acts as a set of gliders, or series of lenses, through which men view their environments.

Among group-membership determinants, the social and cultural factors are interdependent, yet analytically distinct. Man, of course, is only one of many social animals, but the ways in which social, as opposed to solitary, life modifies his behavior are especially numerous and varied. The fact that human beings are mammals and reproduce bi-sexually creates a basic predisposition toward at least the rudiments of social living. And the prolonged helplessness of human infants conduces to the formation of a family group. Also, certain universal social processes (such as conflict, competition, and accommodation) are given distinct forms through cultural transmission. Thus, while the physically strong tend to dominate the weak, this tendency may be checked and even to some extent reversed by a tradition which rewards chivalry, compassion, and humility. Attitudes towards women, towards infants, towards the old, towards the weak will be affected by the age and sex ratios and the birth and death rates prevalent at a particular time.

The social and cultural press likewise interlock with the situational determinants. There are many forces involved in social interactions which influence personality formation and yet are in no sense culturally prescribed. All children (unless multiple births) are born at different points in their parents' careers, which means that they have, psychologically speaking, somewhat different parents. Likewise, whether a child is wanted or unwanted and whether it is of the desired sex will make a difference in the ways in which it will be treated, even though the culture says that all children are wanted and defines the two sexes as of equal value.

A final example will link the constitutional with both the group-membership and situational determinants. Even though identical twins may differ remarkably little from a biological standpoint, and participate in group activities which are apparently similar, a situational factor may intrude as a result of which their experiences in social interaction will be quite different. If, for instance, one twin is injured in an automobile accident and the other is not, and if the injured twin has to spend a year in bed, as the special object of his mother's solicitations, noticeable personality differences will probably develop. The extent to which these differences endure will depend surely upon many other factors, but it is unlikely that they will be entirely counteracted. The variations in treatment which a bed-ridden child receives is partly determined by culture (the extent to which the ideal patterns permit a sick child to be petted, etc.), and partly by extra-cultural factors (the mother's need for nurturance, the father's idiomatic performance of his culturally patterned role in these circumstances, etc.).

6. SIMILARITIES AND DIFFERENCES IN PERSONALITY

In conclusion, let us return for a moment to the observed fact that every man is "like all other men, like some other men, like no other man." In the beginning there is (1) the organism and (2) the environment. Using this division as the starting point in thinking about personality formation, one might say that the *differences* observed in the personalities of human beings are due to variations in their biological equipment and in the total environment to which they must adjust, while the similarities are ascribable to biological and environmental regularities. Although the organism and the environment have a kind of wholeness in the concrete behavioral world which the student loses sight of at his peril, this generalization is substantially correct. However, the formulation can be put more neatly in terms of field. There is (1) the organism moving through a field which is (2) structured both by culture and by the physical and social world in a relatively uniform manner, but which is (3) subject to endless variation within the general patterning due to the organism's constitutionally-determined peculiarities of reaction and to the occurrence of special situations.

In certain circumstances, one reacts to men and women, not as unique organizations of experience, but as representatives of a group. In other circumstances, one reacts to men and women primarily as fulfilling certain roles. If one is unfamiliar with the Chinese, one is likely to react to them first as Chinese rather than as individuals. When one meets new people at a social gathering, one is often able to predict correctly: "That man is a doctor." "That man certainly isn't a businessman, he acts like a professor." "That fellow over there looks like a government official, surely not an artist, a writer, or an actor." Similarities in personality created by the role and group-membership determinants are genuine enough. A man is likely to resemble other men from his home town, other members of his vocation, other members of his class, as well as the majority of his countrymen as contrasted to foreigners.

But the variations are equally common. Smith is stubborn in his office as well as at home and on the golf course. Probably he would have been stubborn in all social contexts if he had been taken to England from America at an early age and his socialization had been completed there. The playing of roles is always tinged by the uniqueness of the personality. Such differences may be distinguished by saying, "Yes, Brown and Jones are both forty-five-year-old Americans, both small-businessmen with about the same responsibilities, family ties, and prestige—but somehow they are different." Such dissimilarities may be traced to the interactions of the constitutional and situational determinants, which have been different for each man, with the common group-membership and role determinants to which both have been subjected.

Another type of resemblance between personalities cuts across the boundaries of groups and roles but is equally understandable within this framework of thinking about personality formation. In general, one observes quite different personality manifestations in Hopi Indians and in white Americans—save for those common to all humanity. But occasionally one meets a Hopi whose behavior, as a whole or in part, reminds one very strongly of a certain type of white man. Such parallels can arise from similar constitutional or situational determinants or a combination of these. A Hopi and a white man might both have had several long childhood illnesses which brought them an exceptional amount of maternal care. While an over-abundance of motherly devotion would have had somewhat different effects upon the two personalities, a striking segmental resemblance might have been produced which persisted throughout life.

In most cases the observed similarities, as well as the differences, between groups of people are largely attributable to fairly uniform social and cultural processes. When one says, "Smith reminds me of Brown," a biologically inherited determinant may be completely responsible for the observed resemblance. But when one notes that American businessmen, for example, have certain typical characteristics which identify them as a group and distinguish them from American farmers and teachers it can hardly be a question of genetic constitution. Likewise, the similarities of personality between Americans in general as contrasted with Germans in general must be traced primarily to common press which produces resemblances in spite of wide variations in individual constitutions.

To summarize the content of this chapter in other terms: The personality of an individual is the product of inherited dispositions and environmental experiences. These experiences occur within the field of his physical, biological, and social environment, all of which are modified by the culture of his group. Similarities of life experiences and heredity will tend to produce similar personality characteristics in different individuals, whether in the same society or in different societies.

Importance of Personality in Education

With this knowledge of the factors that influence personality, many human actions can be understood. Consider for example, a 5–4 decision by the Supreme Court. All of the judges on the Court have the same information, the same briefs on the case being decided. All of them have had similar training in law, and the wording of the laws themselves is constant. Why then in some cases do five judges vote one way and four another? Obviously a difference in interpretation is involved but what factors influence the interpretations? The answer is of course all of the factors that have operated to determine the personality of the individual judge. Each judge has his own point of view, his own frame of reference, his own values and beliefs, which combine to produce his bias. Complete objectivity is impossible because decisions must be made by human personalities who are at any given moment the product of all the experience of a lifetime blended into a unique biological heritage.

What is true for Supreme Court justices is true for people everywhere, including teachers and students. This fact explains the difference of opinion, of outlook, of value between individuals and these differences are reflected in their actions. This knowledge is essential to an understanding of American education because it is human personalities who establish schools and decide on their aims, content, and organization, with their beliefs and values inevitably reflected in them. Later in this volume we will consider conflicting philosophies of education. It will be obvious that Robert Hutchins and John Dewey disagreed on many points and these differences can be understood in part by knowing something of the background of the life experiences of the two men. With this knowledge we can better understand the position of the southerners on the issue of segregation in the schools, or of the Catholic Church on the question of federal aid to parochial schools. A knowledge of the determinants of personality can help teachers to understand their students, their biases, their motivations, and their interests. And it can help them to understand themselves. How often have teachers made the statement: "I just don't understand Johnny"? The reason probably is that they attempt to understand Johnny in terms of their own background and experience. And how often have teachers of literature with a rich background and a real love for the subject been impatient with students who did not appreciate the works of Shakespeare or Dickens? Here it is a matter of the teacher expecting the student to accept his values, failing to realize that the student may not have the background necessary to enable him to appreciate fine literature.

Suggested Readings

Allport, Gordon W.: *Personality, a Psychological Interpretation*. New York: Henry Holt and Company, 1937.

Kluckhohn, Clyde: *Mirror for Man*. New York: McGraw-Hill Book Company, 1949.

————, and Murray, Henry A., eds.: *Personality in Nature, Society, and Culture*, rev. ed. New York: Alfred A. Knopf, 1953.

Linton, Ralph: *The Cultural Background of Personality*. New York: Appleton-Century-Crofts, 1945.

Mead, George H.: *Mind, Self and Society*. Chicago: University of Chicago Press, 1934.

Murphy, Gardner: *Personality*. New York: Harper & Brothers, 1947.

Murray, Henry A., *et al.*: *Explorations in Personality*. New York: Oxford University Press, 1938.

CHAPTER 5

EDUCATION AND THE SCHOOL

THE MATERIAL PRESENTED IN CHAPTERS 3 AND 4 MAKES IT CLEAR THAT the cultural accumulation passed on to each new generation enables men to rise above the level of the animal. We have seen also how this social heritage is interwoven with the genetic characteristics of the individual to produce personality. From the standpoint of the continuity of culture or the determination of personality, the role of education is central. For it is through the *process of education* that culture is transmitted and that personality is *learned*. Death is inevitable for each member of a human group, but if the culture of that group is to continue, what has been learned by one generation must somehow be passed on to the next. Therefore, without education culture could not exist; education is as much a necessity of life for the individual and the group as biological reproduction. As Dewey has said: "What nutrition and reproduction are to physiological life, education is to social life." [1]

The Nature of the Process of Education

THE nature of the process of education or learning is of primary concern to teachers who are directly involved in trying to educate the young. Obviously, the more teachers know of the process whereby knowledge, attitudes, and skills are transmitted, the more effective they can be. But aside from its practical value to method, understanding of this process is essential for a general understanding of education and the school system. This problem has been studied intensively by both educators and psychologists in the last fifty years and a great deal of knowledge has been accumulated. For the most part the emphasis has been upon the nature of *learning*, not the nature of *education*, but insofar as education

[1] John Dewey, *Democracy and Education* (New York: The Macmillan Company, 1916), p. 11.

is thought of as *process* the two words can be used and are used synonymously. Probably when we think of education we think of *teaching and learning* but we are likely to speak of a man such as Lincoln as being *self-educated*. It is also true that much learning can go on without teaching. In any case, in the following paragraphs we will use the two terms interchangeably.

It should be pointed out that the following brief analysis of the process of education is not intended as a substitute for the systematic study of learning given in educational psychology. Rather, the intent is to present here enough information about education so that its nature is understood, partly for its own sake but also because such understanding is necessary to an understanding of much of the material presented in subsequent chapters.

Education has been defined by Dewey as "that reconstruction or reorganization of experience which adds to the meaning of experience, and which increases ability to direct the course of subsequent experience." [2] From the moment the individual is born he begins to learn. He interacts with his environment and has a continuous series of life experiences. The baby learns that if he cries he gets attention. He learns that the white substance in the bottle tastes good and satisfies his hunger. Later he learns that this substance is called "milk." At this stage, learning is on an unconscious level. The infant does not reflect upon or consciously understand the relationship between milk and hunger. He is only aware that certain responses bring certain results or satisfaction. This type of learning is known as "conditioning" and accounts for most of the learning in the early years, including the learning of language. In the early years the child learns that certain actions bring pain and others bring pleasure. If he sticks his finger into a flame, he learns that his finger pains him and he is taught that his finger is "burned." He may learn from warnings from his mother that something bad will happen to him if he touches the flame, or falls down the stairs, or goes into the street. In these instances the child has learned *vicariously*, that is, without direct experience.

In the early years the child also learns through trial and error. Certain things work, others do not. If the learning is not on the conscious level, that is, if relationships are not intellectualized, trial and error blends easily into conditioning, especially if the action occurs over and over again, as in learning to ride a bicycle. As the child grows older, he is able to intellectualize his experience and to recognize relationships. The normal child of six or seven recognizes these relationships and establishes meanings daily as he learns to adjust to his environment. A good illustration of this type of learning is provided by Boyd Bode in his account of an individual walking along a path.

[2] *Ibid.*, pp. 89–90.

In approaching the problem of learning, our clue must come from the idea that mind is such a process of "progressively shaping up the environment." This process was illustrated earlier by the example of the pedestrian making his way along a difficult path. He picks and chooses, as we say; which means that a whole field, consisting of environmental relationships and bodily reactions, is in continuous reorganization. This process of reorganization is not, indeed, the same as learning, since no new elements may be involved. The case is different if our pedestrian discovers, as a result of his experience, that clay is slippery, whereas sod or gravel affords a firm footing. He learns about clay, for example, provided that he notes the connection between the appearance of clay and what the clay does to him when he tries to walk on it. To note the connection is to learn something, and the learning takes the form of changing the experience. The clay now *looks* slippery; it has acquired meaning. Such change in an experience whereby it becomes more serviceable for the guidance of behavior is what is meant by learning.[3]

From this example of a learning situation better insight can be gained into Dewey's definition of education. The pedestrian has reorganized his experience, has added to the meaning of his previous experience, and is able to direct the course of his future activity so that he avoids slipping and falling—an outcome obviously to be desired.

Education always goes on within an individual human being and always involves the reorganization of his experience. One experience is added to another continually throughout life. In facing a situation at any given point in his life the individual consciously and unconsciously interprets that situation in the light of his past experience. Thus the words written on this page will be interpreted by each reader in terms of his own experience and background. An individual never faces a situation as a blank tablet, so to speak. All that a pupil, in a fifth-grade class, for instance, can do is to try to understand what the teacher is saying on the basis of his own experience. He receives certain impulses from the environment, absorbs them into his own experience, and perhaps changes his behavior as a result. Therefore a learning situation to be effective should contain elements that the student recognizes. For example, if a child has had no experience with arithmetic, he will obviously be frustrated when he is asked to solve a problem in algebra. On the other hand, if the elements in the learning situation are "old stuff" to him, he will probably be bored. The ideal in a learning situation is to have enough old elements so that the student has a basis for understanding and enough new elements to challenge him. If the problem is too

[3] Boyd H. Bode, *How We Learn* (Boston: D. C. Heath and Company, 1940), pp. 233-4. Reprinted by special permission of D. C. Heath and Company.

easy, he is bored; if it is too difficult, he will be frustrated and give up. When this factor of experience as background for learning is understood, and when differences in native ability among children are taken into account, some notion can be gained of the difficulties encountered in teaching children. Even if children have substantially similar backgrounds or life experiences, the more intelligent child will gain more from each experience and thus be far advanced.

Another aspect of the process of education that must be understood is that although the process goes on within the individual it is essentially a social process. As we have seen, the individual in isolation is an abstraction; he does not exist. The individual lives in a social group from the time he is born. As he interacts and communicates with other individuals, he learns. He is never a passive agent, but he is molded by his environment. He learns by living the language, customs, and values of his group, but he is also selective. He learns those things which are rewarding or satisfying to him. This is not to imply that he learns only that which is pleasant, for we know that individuals will subject themselves to most unpleasant learning experiences (e.g., studying for examinations) if those experiences bring satisfying results. This is the well-known law of effect developed by Thorndike early in the twentieth century and it still applies. We know that individuals learn what is necessary to satisfy their needs and the strength of the need influences the degree of determination or motivation that the individual has to learn a given task. These needs may be primary or secondary. For example, it would be a relatively easy matter to induce an Indian youngster, whose food supply depended on his ability to shoot a bow and arrow, to learn to shoot that weapon. The need in this instance is primary; food is necessary for survival. The same strong motivation may be evident in a medical student, but in this case the need is of a secondary nature, that is, medical training is not a necessity for survival.

Formal and Informal Education

THE facts presented above about the process of education or learning are universal. Education must be and is present in all human groups. But there is great variation among the cultures of the world in the kind and content of education. In primitive cultures, education is just as essential as it is in a complex, industrial, democratic society. However, in most primitive cultures, formal education and specialized educational institutions do not exist. In these groups the child is taught by his parents and by other members of the group. Here education is a natural part of living. The child is taught the skills and techniques as well as the customs and values of his group. To these groups, as Dewey has pointed out, ". . . it would seem preposterous to seek out a place where nothing but learning was going on in order that one might learn." [4]

However, even in primitive societies the process of education is not automatic, but must be deliberate and careful. The immature individual being inducted into the group learns by sharing in the experiences of the adults, e.g., hunting, fishing, farming, etc., but the skills and techniques involved in these activities are taught to the young carefully, not haphazardly, for the very existence of the group depends upon them.

In some primitive groups some formal education is given, generally at the time of puberty. Dr. David Scanlon records the way in which this type of education was arranged in a tribe in West Africa:

> The Poro, a secret society for men, provided Baima's first formal education. As a young boy he had been taken into the "little bush," where a circumcision rite had been performed. He had remained in the "little bush" for two days. During this period, he had participated in an elaborate ritual which stressed the teachings of his mother, ancestor worship, and respect for the elders.
>
> At the age of nine, Baima had been sent to the "big bush" of the Poro. In this restricted area of the forest he had been given what might be considered advanced courses in law, religion, agricultural methods, and medicine. At the end of the training period, which in Baima's case lasted two years, he returned to the village, where he was considered no longer a boy but an adult. The Poro experiences bind together all men in the village. The rites and rituals are known only to members of the society. [5]

In more advanced cultures education is provided in specialized institutions called schools. At what stage of cultural development schools were established in societies is a moot question, but in all probability their origin was closely associated with a written language. For a written language to be developed, leisure was necessary, and leisure requires a cultural level above that of mere sustenance. In groups where all of the efforts of individuals are devoted to raising and gathering food, written languages have not been created. Once a written language was developed a special skill—writing—was added to the culture. Whereas the oral use of language was picked up naturally by the young, the teaching of writing required a more thorough, systematic effort, and specialists in the art of teaching were developed. From these crude beginnings, the development of formal schooling has paralleled the progress of civilization. The more advanced the culture the more highly organized the school system.

[4] Dewey, op. cit., p. 9.
[5] David Scanlon, "Education and Social Change in West Africa," *Teachers College Record*, December 1954, p. 130.

The development of specialized educational institutions has its advantages and disadvantages. If they are handled intelligently, schools can condense, select, and organize in a few years the important knowledge and skills accumulated by countless men over a period of hundreds of years. Consider the skill and knowledge of one of our doctors or engineers or teachers, for example. Because of the specialization that is possible, we have individuals who are able to devote their entire lives to teaching the young. Obviously this is a tremendous advance over education by parents, who have no special skill or training and who lack time. In the best modern schools the combined talents of specially educated men and women are devoted to creating a *special environment for learning*. But there are disadvantages in this system, too. Whereas the informal education of the savage (or of the farmer's son) is close to his primary needs and a part of everyday living, the school, because it deals largely with symbols that are far from the child's felt needs and experience, runs the risk of being remote and dead. Consider the difference between teaching an African boy to hunt and teaching an American youngster American history. A good case could be made to show that the study of history is just as important to the American boy who is to be a citizen in a complicated democracy as learning to hunt is to the African but the task of getting the American high school student to understand this fact is not easy.

The fact is that the higher the level of culture, the greater is the gap between child and adult. A child in a primitive group quickly grasps the skills and techniques his father uses in fishing. But consider the possibility of having an American child understand the work of his father who is a nuclear physicist. Because of this gap the teaching of the young is more difficult and the modern teacher gives a great deal of attention to motivating the child. Also when the social heritage is stored in symbols, there is real danger that the school will become removed from reality. The result is that as Dewey has pointed out:

> . . . we reach the ordinary notion of education: the notion which ignores its social necessity and its identity with all human association that affects conscious life, and which identifies it with imparting information about remote matters and the conveying of learning through verbal signs: the acquisition of literacy.[6]

Despite the fact that in advanced societies the primary educational institution is the school, it should not be inferred that informal education does not exist in these societies. On the contrary, there is a great deal of informal education. What the child learns in the first six years of his life before he comes to school is learned largely on an informal basis and many psychologists believe this early education to be the most im-

[6] Dewey, *op. cit.*, p. 10.

portant in the child's life. After he enters school the child continues to learn from his peers, from comic books, from television, and this informal learning continues throughout his life. The educative or miseducative effect of these informal influences, e.g., comic books, is difficult to measure but the research that has been done indicates that they have an influence. Professor Earl Herminghaus of Harris Teachers College in St. Louis, in a carefully controlled study, found that the social and personal adjustment of a group of teen-agers was improved by the reading of certain carefully selected books. It seems safe to assume that if attitudes and behavior can be changed in a *desirable* direction by good books they can be changed in an *undesirable* direction by brutal, sadistic comics. In the years ahead it is likely that scientific research in this area will be accelerated as educators and parents seek to determine the effect of these informal educative influences, such as having a child watch television programs indiscriminately.

The Moral Nature of Deliberate Education

ANOTHER dimension of the analysis of education and the school needs to be explored. This dimension John Childs calls "the moral nature of deliberate education." It has to do with problems of freedom and indoctrination, of the rights of the child and the nature of democracy, and it can be focused by such questions as these: In a democracy should the schools be neutral or should we indoctrinate the child with democratic patterns? If we chose the latter course, are we really any better than Hitler or Stalin and is not all this talk of freedom of teaching and learning a sham? If we are not to indoctrinate, are we to sit back and *hope* that our children grow up to be little democrats and not little communists or fascists? Or to put the question another way, should we teach the child *how* to think or *what* to think? And what has the maturity of the child to do with the matter? Would we be willing to censor the reading materials of a child but not of an adult? Or is censorship at any level undemocratic? To help answer these questions a short statement by Dr. John L. Childs, Emeritus Professor of Education at Teachers College, Columbia University, has been included here. These excerpts were taken from Chapters 1 and 7 of his book, *Education and Morals,* published in 1950.

JOHN L. CHILDS

FROM

Education and Morals [1]

As we have already indicated, men everywhere reveal by their actual deeds that they regard the immature human being as the kind of creature who should go to school. This universal tendency to organize and support schools is a concrete expression of the basic human conviction that patterns of conduct and personality are not wholly predetermined, but are created, at least in some significant sense, by experience—that is, by that which human beings learn and become as a result of what they do and undergo. Faith in this capacity of man to learn, and to benefit from that which he learns, is implicit in every attempt of adults to plan and maintain an organized program of education.

Schools are also public testimony to man's faith in the possibility of control over his own destiny. They are founded because man believes that he has some measure of power to shape the course of his own ways of living. A school system is organized whenever a human group begins to become conscious of its own experience, and desires to select from the totality of its beliefs and practices certain things which it is concerned to preserve and foster by reproducing them in the lives of its young. In other words, the organization of a system of schools signifies the deliberate attempt of a human group to control the pattern of its own evolution. Through the responsible guidance of the experiencing and learning of their young, adults hope to make of them and of their society something different and more satisfactory than would eventuate if affairs were left to take their own course. Organized education is thus the antithesis of a laissez-faire practice; it is an activity that deliberately involves itself in the destinies of human beings.

In fine, the enterprise of education is grounded in two basic and interrelated faiths—faith in the modifiability of the human form, and faith in the possibility of controlling the human enterprise in the interest of cherished ends, or values. Man demonstrates by this universal tendency to found and support schools that he is not a fatalist. Were he really convinced that his preferences and efforts were without power to ameliorate his own estate, he would not progressively expand his investments in deliberate education. This increasing tendency to trust in the art of education is associated with a growing respect for the powers and potentialities of man. Implicit in the practice of the school is the

[1] John L. Childs, *Education and Morals* (New York: Appleton-Century-Crofts, 1950), pp. 5–17, 136–8.

faith that human effort, guided by intelligence, can make a real difference in the course of those things that matter most. . . .

The moral nature of education stems from the fact that schools are organized and maintained by adults, not by the children who attend them. Adults engage in deliberate education because they are concerned to direct the processes by which their children mature and learn to become participating members of their society. A manifestation of preference for certain patterns of living as opposed to others is therefore inherent in every program of deliberate education. Schools always exhibit in their purposes and their programs of study that which the adults of a society have come to prize in their experience and most deeply desire to nurture in their own children. Hence the curriculum of a school is an index to the values of the particular human group that founds the school. It is because some conception of what is humanly significant and desirable is implicit in all nurture of the young that we may say without exaggeration that each program of deliberate education is, by nature, a moral undertaking.

Our thought about education will be confused at its very root if we do not perceive that a school can never be a morally indifferent institution. Each school operates within a definite historical-social situation. This situation is marked by genuine life alternatives. Amid these plural and competing patterns of living, the school seeks to emphasize and to foster certain types of growth, and to hinder and to avert other types of growth. Were one invariant line of development alone open to the young, there would be no need for adult guidance. Thus, both lay and professional educational leaders misconceive the essential meaning of a school whenever they pretend to be neutral or indifferent to what happens to the children under their jurisdiction. In the last analysis, the success or failure of a school is measured in moral terms, that is, by what it does with and for the human beings entrusted to its care. All of the other functions of a school are ancillary to this primary responsibility of directing the growth of the immature members of its society.

Obviously, there can be important differences in judgment about what kinds of human behavior are so fundamental and desirable that they should be cultivated in the school. In view of our present limited knowledge of the process of human maturation and learning, there can also be legitimate differences about the best means of nurturing cherished attitudes, techniques, interests, tastes, outlooks and patterns of conduct in the young. But the fact that we still have much to learn about both the ends and the means of education provides no sound ground for the notion that we can educate, and at the same time avoid responsibility for making judgments about the kind of person, or persons, we want the immature to become. This elemental moral responsibility is inherent in each program of deliberate education, for the cultural selections and rejections inescapably involved in the construction and direction of an educational program necessarily have consequences in the lives of those who are nurtured in it.

This tendency to pattern the intellectual and emotional dispositions of the young is present in every type of educational program—democratic as well as humanist, liberal as well as vocational, individualist as well as collectivist. In sum, the making of choices that have to do with the destinies of human beings cannot be eliminated from that directing of experience and learning which is the distinctive function of the school. It is choice among significant life alternatives that is the essence of the moral act, and choice among values necessarily pervades those human actions by which the program of a school is organized and communicated. . . .

Bernard Shaw has contended that "the vilest abortionist is he who attempts to mold the mind of a child." In this striking phrase he has summarized a view held by some of those who have been identified with the "child-centered" educational movement. Shaw, however, both mistakes and mis-states the issue. The primary fact is that the life and the mind of the child is necessarily molded, for it is through the nurture provided by other human beings that each child achieves its most distinctive human traits. Apart from this group nurture, were the child fortunate enough to survive, he would not achieve a type of existence much above that of other animals. It is through this association with others that the infant acquires the characteristics that we designate as mind. The actual choice therefore is not between a process of unfolding from within and a process of molding from without; it is a choice between alternative ways of having the human surroundings effect this molding of the child. The real question is whether the development of the child is to come as a by-product of the accidents and pressures of his own unplanned and unguided interactions with his surroundings, or whether his growth is to come as the result of an experience in a special environment planned for this educational purpose. Schools are organized and supported because adults have faith that better results will be attained if the young grow to maturity in an environment that has been deliberately organized for the purpose of introducing them to the life and thought of their society. If we really oppose any and all molding of the life of the child, we should in consistency repudiate the whole enterprise of deliberate education because this patterning of the development of the individual is its basic purpose and justification. The actual moral problem therefore is not one of molding versus not molding; it is rather the problem of discovering the means by which the nurture of the child can be made a process of enrichment and liberation, not one of exploitation and enslavement. . . .

Viewed from the standpoint of their founders and supporters all schools are activity schools. A school, it should be noted, is not primarily a building, it is an organized program of human activity. It is an enterprise of purpose. Like other purposeful activities, it involves the selection and the ordering of means to attain projected and desired outcomes. As we have emphasized in the foregoing, these educational outcomes have to do with the lives of human beings. A program of education is therefore intelligent only to the degree that those who have constructed it are aware of the results they desire to attain in the lives of the young and have adapted their means accordingly.

A harmful fallacy is thus imbedded in the notion that teachers can do more satisfactory work if they simply seek the growth of each child and are not encumbered with definite ideas about either the outcomes they hope to attain or the means by which they expect to achieve these outcomes. Ignorance, vagueness, and aimless "busy-work" have no greater value in education than in other spheres of human effort. Certainly those who have faith in intelligence will believe that our prospect of getting satisfactory results will be greater if we know what we are about when we undertake this very important task of directing the experiencing of the young. . . .

It is important for educators to recognize that education in and for democracy in no way lessens our responsibility for being aware of the values we are seeking to nurture in the young. Democracy is not a form of anarchy, it is a definite system of social and political life. The democratic way of life is indeed a distinctive mode of associated life and it makes its definite demands on its members. It therefore should have its own distinctive educational program. But a distinctive program of education is still a program, and the adults who are to introduce the young to the principles and the practices of democracy carry a definite and demanding intellectual and moral responsibility.

Democracy is not nature's own unique mode of life. It is the product of a long and costly human struggle, and its life of freedom, of shared responsibility as well as its basic principle of government of, by and for the people make demands on the individual that are ethically more, not less, exacting than the practices of authoritarian social and political systems. Nor is democracy inevitably fated to be the pattern of the future. The future of democracy depends upon the depth of our commitment to it, and upon what we are prepared to do to preserve it. Now all of this carries its implications for the way we should think of the function of education in a democratic society. Democratic attitudes, behaviors and values do not spontaneously unfold in the bosom of the child; he acquires them only as he learns them. The democratic way of life can renew itself only as the children of each successive generation reproduce in their own lives its principles, its techniques, its disciplines, its loyalties and its responsibilites. Our schools must be clear about their part in all of this. It is a confused and misleading interpretation which holds that since democracy is a life of freedom based on respect for each person, we offend against its morality when we take positive steps to cultivate its distinctive attitudes and behaviors in the personalities of our young. Tolerance is a great virtue, but tolerance does not imply moral indifference. Tolerance, moreover, is but one of many values comprehended in what we call our democratic way of life, and educators can be intelligent about the various human attitudes and practices which make this life of freedom and tolerance possible. It is a dubious allegiance to democracy that leads one to be indifferent to its foundations, particularly those foundations that are constituted by the attitudes, the loyalties, the habits, and the dispositions of its citizens. . . .

It is also important for educators to recognize that a scientifically grounded pedagogy is no substitute for clear ideas about the values and purposes of education. The scientific study of both the nature of the child and the process of human maturation and learning is making indispensable contributions to the work of education. No teacher worthy of the name can afford to ignore these tested findings. But knowledge of these scientific findings does not in and of itself define our educational objectives. For example, knowledge of the fact of individual differences, and of the uniqueness of each child, does not relieve us of responsibility for making judgments about the way in which that inherited uniqueness is to find its appropriate expression within the context of our changing modes of life and thought.

Studies of human learning show that learning is an active, dynamic affair, and the leaders of progressive education have rendered an important service by developing an activity curriculum to provide more adequately for these dynamic aspects of the learning process. But "pupil initiative" and "wholehearted purposeful projects" are in no sense a substitute for adult guidance; they should rather be viewed as improved means of making that guidance more effectual. The more knowledge that we can get about the process by which the powers of the child ripen, the better we shall be able to plan the program of the school, but knowledge of "the human maturation sequence" does not justify a "hands-off" policy in education. As a matter of fact, such findings as we have about child development show that "the human maturation sequence" is by no means exclusively an affair of the biological organism; it is deeply influenced by environmental factors, and after the first years, the role of a culturally conditioned experience becomes primary in determining the further lines of personal growth. Confronted with plural and conflicting cultural patterns, educators cannot escape responsibility for choosing main lines of human development.

Those educators who have combined the psychological principles of child growth with the moral principles of democracy and have developed the conception that the supreme aim of education should be the nurture of an individual who can take responsibility for his own continued growth have made an ethical contribution of lasting worth. But acceptance of the objective of developing a person who can eventually take over his own education does not at all imply that the school should arrange its affairs so that each child, unhindered by adult guidance, will be left "free to develop in his own way." To attempt to do this is to negate the very purpose of deliberate education. We establish schools because we recognize that the child does not know the principles and the means of his own development, and because we also realize that the kind of scientific and humane conduct we call "mature" and which is presupposed in the principle of responsible "self-education" is not an original endowment. It is a genuine ethical insight that distinguishes intellectual and emotional maturity from mere slavish conformity to custom, but we err whenever we assume that what is prized as "maturity" is the product of an unguided, spontaneous unfolding of an inborn pattern of human personality. . . .

In fine, education is a value-conditioned activity. The schools seeks to cultivate selected values in the young by means of both the subject-matters and the methods that it employs in its program. In education, as in other human arts, our practice becomes intelligent as it grows, both in its awareness of the ends that it is seeking to attain and in its mastery of the means which it must use to attain these ends. The fact that these ends or outcomes involve the lives of the immature deepens—it does not diminish—our responsibility to know what we are trying to accomplish when we undertake to educate. . . .

The democratic criterion has far-reaching educational implications. Not all of the educational programs that profess allegiance to the supreme worth of human personality measure up in their practices to this avowed democratic standard. A school may even be a "child-centered" school, yet fail to manifest this basic respect for the child. If a school construes the pedagogical doctrine of "interest" to imply approval of mere impulsive or random activity on the part of pupils, rather than the effort to secure their whole-hearted participation in activities that enrich meaning and increase their capacity for control of life-affairs, its program is not really in accord with the democratic conception. We show respect for the child in the school, not by indulging or coddling him, but by enlisting him in significant undertakings that result in the development of his resourcefulness as a human being.

Even programs of so-called "moral education" fail, at times, to exhibit this regard for the nurture of intelligence which is an essential part of any educational program that has genuine respect for the individual human being. Whenever concern for a "revealed" code prompts those who serve as its trustees to try to transmit the code by a process of indoc-

370.973

trination that involves the withholding of pertinent knowledge, the young are not treated as ends in themselves. To treat a child as an end, means so to conduct his education that he will progressively grow in his ability to make up his own mind about that which he shall believe, and about that which is to be considered worthy of his allegiance. Measured by this standard, alleged interest in the ultimate welfare or future salvation of the child does not give adults the right to deprive him of the opportunity to develop a mind of his own. One of the deplorable features in the present confused situation is that certain groups, purporting to have the spiritual interests of man at heart, are trying to impose special programs of "moral education" on the public school that actually involve an abridgement of the processes of historical and critical study. There is nothing "spiritual" about suppression, and it is difficult to see how the moral life of a democratic community will be strengthened by a program of "moral education" that strives to keep the young in ignorance about any aspect of human experience. A faith that fears knowledge cannot be counted on the side of the forces that are working to develop a democratic civilization based on respect for all men. Cal

Nor are those groups who desire to indoctrinate the young in outmoded historic outlooks and institutionalized practices, the only ones who offend in these matters. Revolutionary groups may also organize authoritarian programs for social change that fail to measure up to the searching democratic criterion of respect for human personality. Leaders of movements for revolutionary change may proclaim that their aim is the welfare of the masses, but whenever they try to win their adherents, not by persuasion based on enlightenment, but by a process of disguised manipulation, they do not manifest this basic regard for the worth of the individual human being. Any program of education ceases to treat individuals as ends in themselves once its concern about a particular social outcome or goal—revolutionary or reactionary—overrides its desire to provide people with the knowledge they must have if they are to be in a position to evaluate the cause to which they are invited to commit their lives. So far as democratic educational values are concerned, a program of animal training remains a program of animal training, irrespective of whether it is organized to breed militant warriors for a new social order, or to train docile defenders of the status quo.

In brief, democratic education believes in the nurture of human personality. It holds that the nurture of human personality involves as its very essence the nurture of mind, and that the nurture of mind is incompatible with any attempt to inculcate beliefs and attitudes by a process that involves the deliberate withholding of knowledge. Such a process of suppression and indoctrination can breed a "mind in the individual," but it cannot nurture "individual mind"—the kind of mind a person must have if he is to be equipped to carry on his own education.

We cultivate individual minds only as we nurture individuals who have the capacity for moral responsibility; that is, the capacity to co-operate in the development of life purposes as well as the capacity to evaluate the consequences that flow from their life activities. Any program of education that is committed to the development of individual minds is democratic in character—it necessarily has regard for the capacity of men to inquire, to evaluate, and to take responsibility for their own actions. Similarly, any program of education that seeks to restrict the development of mind is undemocratic in nature, no matter how much it may profess to believe in the worth and dignity of human personality. Such a program fails to satisfy the basic moral criterion of democracy, namely, that individual human beings be treated not as mere means, but as ends in themselves.

Democracy, Deliberate Education, and Freedom

FROM what Professor Childs has said, the relationship between deliberate education and freedom in a democracy should be clear. Democratic education and all deliberate education are necessarily moral in the sense that choices between possibilities, especially of values, must inevitably be made by teachers. But democratic education, committed as it is to respect for the individual, precludes indoctrination. Therefore, all aspects of human experience, including communism and fascism, must be available for study. But these problems of freedom and indoctrination in education can be understood and dealt with intelligently only when an important variable, namely, the *maturity* of the individual being taught, is known. This is also true with the problem of censorship or with the question of whether the student should be taught *how* to think or *what* to think in the schools in a democratic society.

In most instances Americans, and particularly American college students, believing as they do in the democratic way of life rebel at the notion either of censorship or of teaching the student *what* to think. But some reflection upon our experience will indicate that we do both of these things regularly in American education in the schools and in the home. On the question of censorship every parent worthy of the name attempts to select or help the child select what he will read. With very young children the parents make the selection arbitrarily, but as soon as possible the parents should be in the position of *helping* the child select or of *selecting with* the child. No normal, intelligent American parents would permit their ten-year-old child to read obscene or sadistic literature. The better the parents, the more careful they are in helping the child select the books he reads, as well as the television programs he watches and the movies he sees. And they give more attention to the problem of helping the child develop standards of his own so that he will make better selections. The same is true for teachers. Good teachers in the elementary schools do a careful job of screening the books used in the classroom, and they work very hard to help the child develop high standards so that he will select and read good books on his own. The same procedure is followed with reference to teaching the child what to think. Every parent from the time the child is born teaches his child what to think. From the beginning parents are continually teaching the child that some things are wrong and others are right; that he must obey his parents; that he must love, not hate, his brothers and sisters; etc. Likewise, in the school the child is taught to be honest, not dishonest; to be truthful, not a liar; to be industrious, not lazy; etc. The fact is that in the home and the school the child is taught *what* to think as well as *how* to think, and this process is inevitable in guiding the immature toward maturity. Again, the child does not accept these values simply by being told to accept them. Generally the child is taught through a process of reward and punishment which is made most effective by his dependence on the parent.

As the child grows older he should be led gradually toward the time when he will have complete freedom of thought and action. Then, of course, he must assume complete responsibility for his acts, for this responsibility is the essence of democracy and of "self" government. The role of the teacher is to decide upon the desirable values and beliefs to be taught (for example, belief in freedom, respect for individuals, honesty, decency, gentleness, co-operation), as well as behavior patterns. He then attempts to provide an environment in which they will be likely to be accepted and learned by the children.

Decisions must be made at each stage in the child's development as to how much freedom and responsibility he is able to assume. At some point, probably in the senior high school, all censorship except that imposed by law (e.g., on obscene materials) should be eliminated. Certainly there should be no censorship in any aspect of adult America. Censorship of adult life is as inconsistent with democracy as it is consistent with fascism, communism, or any other form of totalitarianism. If censorship in any form is to be permitted in colleges, libraries, or in the press, the question is: Who are to be the censors? But these adult problems are not analogous with the problems of educating the young. In the education of the young a selection of materials and ideas (censorship) is inevitable, but it must be lifted gradually as the child matures.

Much of the controversy over the question of indoctrination is related to the meaning attached to the word. If it is used to mean "to teach or to instruct," it is of course not incompatible with freedom. But if it is used to mean "to imbue with an opinion or with a partisan or sectarian point of view"—and this definition is applicable to the educational activity in the totalitarian states—then indoctrination is certainly not compatible with freedom. Again, however, the maturity of the individual being taught has to be taken into consideration. Our efforts in teaching values to very young children can be labeled accurately as indoctrination. The important thing is that as the child matures value choices are placed before him. As for factual knowledge, even young children should be given all the facts they are mature enough to understand. The deliberate withholding of evidence, which is the essence of indoctrination in totalitarian states, is never acceptable in a free society.

There is, of course, no guarantee that the free individual after he has examined all of the facts will not reject democracy, just as there is no guarantee that a free individual may not become a thief. But we must have faith in the democratic way of life and in human intelligence set free. We, as teachers engaged in educating our children, have the task of getting them to accept and to develop intelligent faith in the basic democratic patterns. Although our commitment to principles of democracy as well as to standards of scholarship requires that we encourage students to inquire freely and make their own decisions, we certainly are not indifferent about the kind of people they turn out to be.

Suggested Readings

Bode, Boyd: *How We Learn.* Boston: D. C. Heath and Company, 1940.

Childs, John L.: *Education and Morals.* New York: Appleton-Century-Crofts, 1950.

Counts, George S.: *The Social Foundations of Education.* New York: Charles Scribner's Sons, 1934.

Dewey, John: *Democracy and Education.* New York: The Macmillan Company, 1916.

———: *Experience and Education.* New York: The Macmillan Company, 1938.

Garrett, Henry E.: *Great Experiments in Psychology.* New York: Appleton-Century-Crofts, 1941.

Hopkins, Thomas L.: *The Emerging Self.* New York: Harper & Brothers, 1954.

———: *Interaction.* Boston: D. C. Heath and Company, 1941.

Kelley, Earl C.: *Education for What Is Real.* New York: Harper & Brothers, 1945.

Rugg, Harold: *Foundations for American Education.* New York: World Book Company, 1947.

American Society
and
American Education

Above all things, I hope the education of the common people will be attended to; convinced that on their good senses we may rely with the most security for the preservation of a due degree of liberty.

THOMAS JEFFERSON

CHAPTER 6

THE HISTORY OF AMERICAN EDUCATION

FROM WHAT HAS BEEN SAID IN PREVIOUS CHAPTERS IT FOLLOWS that education is always influenced by the time and place in which it occurs. Education never exists in a vacuum or in the abstract; it always goes on in a particular society at a particular time in history. It is true that some elements of the process of education are universal. As we have seen, wherever education occurs it generally involves a social group —that is, at least two human beings—and generally the more mature teach the immature. Also, the nature of learning is such that wherever education occurs it takes place within an individual human being and requires the reorganization of his experience. Even so, the *ends* and *means* of education as well as the *content* of education vary with time and place.

So far as time is concerned this variation can be seen by comparing the aims, methods, and content of education of the schools in colonial America with the aims, methods, and content of education in America today. If to the difference in time a difference in culture is added, even greater variation exists. Some similarities are apparent in a comparison of education in colonial and modern America since there is a strong thread of continuity between colonial and modern America, especially if one looks beneath the surface, for both were in the stream of Western civilization. But consider the sharper differences existing within the same time span when completely different societies are compared. Compare, for instance, the education of an Indian child living in the area of St. Louis in 1650 with the education of an American child living in that area in 1960. The young Indian was taught the skills, customs, and beliefs that would enable him to live in a group that was primarily a hunting and agricultural society. The young American must be taught the skills, customs, and beliefs to enable him to live in a modern, democratic, industrial society. Thus the factors of time and place are always interrelated and must be considered in the analysis of any educational system.

Even when the time factor is not present, variation in education in different societies can be considerable. Compare the educational systems of some contemporary primitive societies with our own. Or compare the aims, methods, and content of education in America with those of education in China, India, Japan, Germany, Liberia, or Peru. In each instance there are the similarities noted above which are common to all groups, plus others, such as the existence of special educational institutions called "schools" and the emphasis upon reading, writing, and figuring as a bare minimum. But even here the differences are sharp. In each country a different language is used and the reading material, even in the simplest stages, reflects the beliefs, values, and customs of the particular society.

As a result, in order to understand the educational system of any society, one must know something about that society. Therefore, in any analysis of the American school system it is necessary to analyze and understand American society. On the other hand, one of the best ways of studying a given society is to study its school system, for in the schools each society (or the governing group in that society) presents from its total experience those elements it considers essential to the maintenance of the group. But neither the schools nor the society in which they function can be understood by studying them as they are presently constituted without some knowledge of their origin and development. Therefore in this chapter we will be concerned with the historical relationship between American schools and American society. Then, after tracing the historical development we will turn our attention to the contemporary scene.

Our Educational Heritage

THE early settlers who came to America brought a rich cultural heritage to the New World. Among other things they had a fully developed language with a wealth of fine literature. They had a highly developed social organization which included elaborate economic, political, legal, and religious systems. And they had an educational system that extended from the elementary school through the university. When the colonists began the task of setting up schools they did not create new institutions. Rather, they did what men have always done when faced with problems, —they drew upon their past experience and established the kinds of schools with which they were familiar. Therefore, in order to understand better the origin and development of American education, we should examine briefly the nature of the society and the institutions with which the colonists were familiar.

Although our colonial heritage was European, the roots of our heritage and therefore of our educational system can be traced all the way back to the Greeks. Moreover, the literary heritage of Greece and Rome was revived during the Renaissance and, although it was given a religious emphasis after the Reformation, it remained the basis for secondary and higher education in Europe and America until well into the nineteenth century. However, despite the obvious thread of continuity from Greek times to the present, significant changes had occurred in European education by the time American colonization started. During the Middle Ages education was controlled by the church and was therefore strongly religious. This pattern was altered somewhat during the Renaissance and for a time a strong humanistic movement emerged.

Unfortunately the full impact of the Renaissance, with its study of Latin and Greek and its emphasis upon human beings and their life on this earth (patterned, of course, after the Greeks), was cut short by the religious revolution known as the Reformation. Starting in 1519 in Germany and gathering momentum rapidly, the religious struggle was to dominate European life for almost two centuries, and this dominance was reflected in the education of the time. The first important characteristic of European society, then, just prior to the settlement of America was this emphasis upon religion.

The Protestants, who by 1700 were the dominant group in most of Northern Europe, believed in having their children read the Bible in line with Luther's idea of the "priesthood of all believers." Therefore, they translated the Bible from the Latin into the vernacular and began to encourage the establishment of schools so that individuals would be able to read the word of God. The Catholics for their part renewed their interest in and attempted to strengthen their control over education chiefly through their new religious order, the Jesuits.

Thus it happened that in the Protestant areas of Europe and particularly in the Lutheran and Calvinist areas, education on the lower levels tended to be encouraged. Nevertheless this movement, aided as it was by the invention of printing almost a century earlier, did not result in all children being sent to school. We know from our experience what a difficult task it is to establish a system of schools even when the will and the means to do so exist. Despite the Reformation and the leadership of Luther and Calvin, the majority of Europeans lacked both the will and the means. As George Counts has said, "only in Puritan Massachusetts, was the logic of the Protestant position applied." [1]

[1] George S. Counts, "Education," *Encyclopedia of the Social Sciences*, V (New York: The Macmillan Company, 1931), p. 410.

Another important aspect of the Reformation was to have implications for education. That aspect was the change in relationship between church and state. Until the Reformation the Catholic church had been able (at times with difficulty) to maintain at least nominal control over the countries of Europe. Then Luther disturbed this relationship by teaching that the civil government should have authority over the church and that it was the duty of every Christian to obey the civil governors. This proposal was in part responsible for the success of Lutheranism in Germany as the many princes, eager to get away from church control, joined the movement and confiscated church properties. This course was also taken by Henry VIII in England.

Calvin differed slightly from Luther in his conception of the relationship between church and state. Calvin believed in a degree of cooperation that amounted to union. This union known as "theocracy" was developed in colonial Massachusetts where church and state were one. A clear idea of Calvin's system can be gained through a study of the kind of government he established in Geneva in the middle of the sixteenth century. Naturally, under these conditions the schools were strongly religious in nature.

In England the pattern was slightly different and the Anglican church, established as a result of the struggles of Henry VIII and Elizabeth with the papacy, was clearly subservient, although closely related to the state. Although he maintained the basic patterns of organization and much of the doctrine and ritual of the Catholic church, the King replaced the Pope at the top. This arrangement, of a state church supported by taxation in which the Crown made decisions regarding matters of conscience, drove many Englishmen to the New World. In general, the Anglican church placed less emphasis on education, especially on the lower levels, and in this respect differed fundamentally from most of the other Protestant sects. This fact was to be significant educationally in the colonies in explaining the differences between Virginia, which was largely Anglican, and Massachusetts, which was largely Calvinistic.

A second important feature of European society which had a great influence upon American education was its rigid class structure. There was no democratic conception of equality in either school or society in seventeenth-century Europe. What did exist was a corporate society in which each person had his life role assigned, generally at birth. There was no chance of going from "rags to riches" nor was there desire to do so. The emphasis was upon stability and upon maintaining the group, and although it is true that such a society provided little opportunity for "rugged individualism" there was also very little individual isolation, for each person had his place and therefore his rights and responsibilities in the group.

At the top of the social structure were the landed nobility—men who owned, operated, governed, and passed on to their sons the great estates or manors. The king was one of this group and generally vied with them for supremacy in running the country. A king who could keep the nobility under control or on his side ruled without too much difficulty. One who could not, certainly ruled with difficulty. On their estates the nobles ruled supreme. In collaboration with other members of their class they ruled Europe. The clergy on the highest levels was a part of this group and controlled religion and education and, given the close relationship that existed between church and state, exerted a strong influence on political life.

Next came the landed gentry, less wealthy and less powerful than the higher nobility, with a great deal of land and influence. Then came the many officials or civil servants and the professional groups such as lawyers. Next in line was the merchant group, becoming ever more powerful as Europeans spread over the earth. This group worked its way into recognition through its wealth, and eventually in the nineteenth and twentieth centuries became dominant. Members of this class were among the staunchest supporters of education—especially for their own children.

Beneath these groups were the small independent farmers or yeomen, then the craftsmen, and finally the servants and tenant farmers. This last group was quite large and, as in England after the enclosure, often largely destitute. It constituted a real problem for society. One attempt to alleviate this problem was the Poor Law of 1601 which provided for public taxation to take care of the poor and the compulsory apprenticeship of poor boys and girls. Since the apprenticeship generally involved religious and moral as well as vocational training, the law undoubtedly established a precedent that influenced educational practices in England and in the colonies.

European education in the seventeenth century reflected the European class structure. The lowest level consisted of elementary schools in which the teaching was done in the vernacular, generally either German, English, or French. For the most part these schools were located in the towns and evidence suggests that few of them existed. Students, generally from the lower classes, attended for a few years, or until they had learned to read and write, and this constituted their formal education. Occasionally it happened that pupils from the middle class would attend these schools for a few years prior to their entrance into a secondary school, but more often they received their early education from tutors as did the sons of the nobility. The requirements for teaching in these vernacular schools consisted first and foremost of religious orthodoxy, and then some knowledge of the fundamental subjects. In England and in the colonies these schools were often taught by widows in their own homes and have been appropriately labeled "dame schools." The curriculum usually consisted of the three "R's" plus religion, although frequently writing and arithmetic were not taught, the former because of the scarcity of writing materials. Music, history, and physical education were sometimes added to the curriculum.

The situation in general was that comparatively few of these schools existed and that their curricula were limited, although it seems that in some places fairly good primary schools were established. Usually in these instances some philanthropic individual, or some organization such as the church, either Catholic or Protestant, was responsible. Despite the teaching of Luther that the ability to read the Bible was a prerequisite to salvation, and the teaching of Comenius who urged that all children be educated, elementary schools were meager in number and in content. Most children, especially in the rural areas, received little if any formal education.

The secondary schools of the period were classical in nature and designed to prepare the upper-class youths who attended them for their future roles in church, government, business, or the professions. The Gymnasium in Germany, the *lycée* and the Jesuit Collège in France, and the Latin grammar schools in England were the dominant institutions. In each, the study of Latin and Greek formed the basis of the curriculum with the objective being (particularly in the Protestant countries) to enable students to read the Scriptures in the original. The program of instruction varied from seven to ten years in length. Students generally entered between the ages of seven or eight and were ready to enter the university when they finished. Although the students attending were largely from the upper classes, it was possible for poor youngsters to get scholarships. The conception of a secondary school for all youth, which we take for granted in America today, was nonexistent.

At the top of the educational systems of Europe in the seventeenth century were the universities, which reflected the dominant role that religion played in this period. The schools of Oxford and Cambridge, for example, supported different creeds but both were primarily concerned with training clergymen. Cambridge is of special interest since its colleges were the "centers of a militant puritanism which trained many of the Puritans who came to America." [2] Also of interest was its pattern of organization described by one historian as follows:

> The system of college instruction as opposed to University instruction was more firmly imbedded than ever by the Reformation emphasis upon discipline, mental, moral and religious. The college retained its communal aspects, marked by the hall and quadrangle, in which masters and students lived and studied together. The con-

[2] By permission from R. F. Butts, *A Cultural History of Western Education* (2nd ed.). McGraw-Hill Book Company, Inc. P. 234.

tinued enforcement of celibacy upon masters and tutors also helped to preserve the communal life of the English college long after the Reformation had seen its disappearance in German universities. The English conception of a college with its discipline and pre-scribed curriculum was most influential in the development of higher education in America. Harvard, the first American College, was virtually a copy of one of the colleges at Cambridge.[3]

This, in brief, was the educational heritage of the men who came to America in the early part of the seventeenth century. It was not demo-cratic, it was dominated by sectarian religion, and its program of study was obviously poorly suited to the conditions of life in colonial America. Yet the fact that the schools existed at all was important. More impor-tant was the faith the early settlers had in schools as a means for achieving desired ends. It was, perhaps, this legacy of faith that led men such as Horace Mann to turn to the school as the instrument to be used in forging a democratic society.

Education in Colonial America, 1620–1775

THE history of American education dates back to the earliest settlements in New England in the first half of the seventeenth century. A Latin grammar (secondary) school was established in Boston in 1635 and Harvard College was founded a year later in 1636. Within a few years many towns, including Dorchester, Dedham, Roxbury, and Salem, had set up schools. An agreement signed in Roxbury in 1645 by a number of the inhabitants will illustrate the general climate of opinion that pre-vailed in some communities:

> Whereas, the Inhabitantes of Roxburie, in consideration of their relligeous care of posteritie, have taken into consideration how nec-essarie the education of theire children in Literature will be to fitt them for public service, both in Churche and Commonwealth, in succeeding ages. They therefore unanimously have consented and agreed to erect a free schoole in the said town of Roxburie, and to allow twenty pounds per annum to the schoolemaster, to bee raised out of the messuages and part of the lands of the severall donors (Inhabitantes of said Towne) in severall proportions as hereafter followeth under their hands. And for the well ordering thereof they have chosen and elected some Feoffees who shall have power to putt in or remove the Schoolemaster, to see to the well ordering of the schoole and schollars, to receive and pay the said twenty pounds per annum to the Schoolemaster and to dispose of any other gifte

[3] *Ibid.*

or giftes which hereafter may or shall be given for the advancement
of learning and education of children . . .[4]

Massachusetts took the lead in providing for schools in colonial America. Laws passed in 1634 and 1638 required all persons to pay taxes for
community projects and thereby established the basis for the public support of schools. In 1642 the first compulsory education law was passed.
Apparently parents had not been educating their children—at least not
in a satisfactory manner—and so the church appealed to the colonial
legislature for legal backing. The law, which compelled parents to educate children, read as follows:

> This Court, taking into consideration the great neglect of many
> parents and masters in training up their children in learning, and
> labor, and other implyments which may be proffitable to the com-
> mon wealth, do hereupon order and decree, that in every towne ye
> chosen men appointed for managing prudentiall affaires of the same
> shall henceforth stand charged with the care of the redresse of this
> evil, so as they shalbee sufficiently punished by fines for the neglect
> thereof, upon presentment of the grand jury, or other information
> on complaint in any Court within this jurisdiction. And for this
> end they, or the greater number of them, shall have power to take
> account from time to time of all parents and masters, and of their
> children, concerning their calling and implyment of their children,
> *especially of their ability to read and understand the principles of
> religion and the capitall lawes of this country,*[5] and to impose fines
> upon such as shall refuse to render such account to them when they
> shall be required; and they shall have power, with consent of any
> Court or the magistrate, to put forth apprentices the children of
> such as they shall [find] not to be able and fitt to imploy and bring
> them up. They shall take . . . that boyes and girles be not suffered
> to converse together, so as may occasion any wanton, dishonest, or
> immodest behavior.[6]

Five years later a second law was passed which specifically required
towns to establish schools. The law, known as the "Old Deluder Act"
reads as follows:

> It being one chiefe project of that old deluder, Satan, to keepe
> men from the knowledge of the Scriptures, as in former times by
> keeping them in an unknown tongue, so in these latter times by
> persuading from the use of tongues, that so at least the true sence

---

[4] Quoted in E. P. Cubberley, *Readings in Public Education in the United States*
(Boston: Houghton Mifflin Company, 1934), p. 15.

[5] [Italics the author's.]

[6] Quoted in Cubberley, *op. cit.*, pp. 16–17.

and meaning of the originall might be clouded by false glosses of saint seeming deceivers, that learning may not be buried in the grave of our fathers in church and commonwealth, the Lord assisting our endeavors,—

It is therefore ordered that every township in this jurisdiction, after the Lord hath increased their number to 50 householders, shall then forthwith appoint one within their towne to teach all such children as shall resort to him to write and reade, whose wages shall be paid either by the parents or masters of such children, or by the inhabitants in general, . . . and it is further ordered that where any towne shall increase to the number of 100 families or house-holders they shall set up a grammar schoole, the Master thereof be-ing able to instruct youth so farr as they shall be fitted for the Uni-versity, provided that if any town neglect the performance hereof above one year, that every such town shall pay five pounds to the next school till they shall perform this order.[7]

Thus by 1647 in Massachusetts the legal basis for a system of public schools had been established. Historians differ in their interpretations of the significance of these laws. One maintained that they represented "the very foundation stones upon which our American public school sys-tems have later been constructed." [8] Others have disagreed, especially in regard to the pattern of state control of education which was regarded as having established the basis for our public school system two centuries later. It has been pointed out that the fact that education was ordered by "the state" was of no special significance, for state and church were one in Massachusetts at the time. Probably both views are partially cor-rect. Certainly the Puritan leaders in Massachusetts had no thought of establishing a free, democratic school system. They were concerned with raising little Puritans. Yet the fact that the schools were established and supported by public taxation for the welfare of the community, regard-less of how narrowly this was conceived, still set a precedent.

It is important to remember that Puritan Massachusetts was not, and made no claim to be, democratic. The Puritans established a society based on Calvin's idea of a Bible State with control in the hands of God's Elect, and in which freedom of conscience or of thought had no place—as Roger Williams discovered. The Puritans' basic religious tenets included the (1) omnipotence of God, (2) depravity of man, (3) au-thority of the Scriptures, and (4) idea of predestination. This set of be-liefs explains the close relationship between church and state in which the former dominated (for example, only church members could vote)

[7] *Ibid.*, pp. 18–19.

[8] E. P. Cubberley, *Public Education in the United States* (Boston: Houghton Mifflin Company, 1934), p. 18.

and, of course, it had important implications for education. The Puritan belief in the depravity of man was reflected in the strict moral codes and the basic distrust of human beings. These ideas were, in turn, sprinkled through the materials of instruction used in the schools. Edmund Burke, the British statesman, is reported to have said of this religion that it "didn't keep the Puritan from sinning, but kept him from enjoying it."

The school system of Massachusetts in the seventeenth century consisted of semipublic and dame schools on the elementary level, Latin grammar schools and, later (1750), academies on the secondary level, and colleges on the higher level.

The chief instructional material or "textbook" in the lower grades was called a "hornbook." This "book" consisted of a thin piece of wood with a handle, on which was tacked a sheet of paper with the alphabet and the Lord's Prayer printed on it. This sheet was covered by a thin sheet of transparent horn and served as a "handy and practically indestructible text." When the child finished with the hornbook he graduated into the catechism where his knowledge of fundamentals was applied to learn the religious tenets of his group. The *Westminster Catechism* was most widely used in the American colonies although a text prepared by the Reverend John Cotton entitled *Spiritual Milk for American Babes Drawn out of the Breasts of Both Testaments, for Their Souls' Nourishment* was also used a great deal. After the catechism, if he got that far, the child was ready for the Bible.

About 1690 the famous *New England Primer* was introduced and was adopted in all of the colonies except Anglican Virginia. The *Primer* replaced the hornbook as well as the catechism since it incorporated much of the *Westminster Catechism* within its covers. This little book, which reflects the society that produced it, became the basic (and often the only) text for more than 100 years and was still being used well into the nineteenth century. It is estimated that more than three million copies were sold and copies were to be found in every home and bookstore in the Colonial period. It is said of the *Primer* that "it taught millions to read, and not one to sin." Full of moral maxims, its content was gloomy to the point of morbidity, and one cannot help but wonder what kind of an impression it made on very young children.

Determination of the exact number of colonial children who attended elementary schools is impossible. It is likely that in the towns most of the children of the middle and upper classes received several years of schooling, whereas the children in the poorer groups were fortunate if they learned to read. In the rural areas it is unlikely that many of the children received any formal education. Because of the compactness of the settlements, children in New England had more of an opportunity than children in the South where the settlements were farther apart. However, in both areas life was rugged, transportation was limited, and books were few. Under the circumstances formal education was not as essential as it is today and the "school of hard knocks" was adequate. Certainly until well into the nineteenth century only a small percentage of American children went to school, and for those who did the instruction was poor and the program limited. No comparison is possible with the extensive program of the modern elementary school.

Virginia lagged behind Massachusetts in developing a school system, partly because it was Anglican and did not have the religious motivation of the Calvinist Puritans and partly because the economic basis of life was the plantation so that people were not clustered in towns as they were in New England. Because of the lack of transportation and the scattered nature of the settlements, schools would have been difficult to establish even if the religious factor had not been present. Wealthy parents either hired tutors for their children or sent them to private schools, sometimes in England. Poorer youngsters were neglected, unless they were unfortunate enough to be orphans or paupers in which case they were trained as apprentices or placed in pauper schools. In the South, in this period, education was not considered the business of the state and it was not until 1693 that the Anglican church indicated an awakening interest in education by setting up William and Mary College to train ministers.

The dominant and virtually the only type of secondary school in colonial America until 1750 was the Latin grammar school. This institution originated in England and served to prepare students for Oxford and Cambridge. Since instruction in the colleges was given in Latin the preparatory institution was of necessity primarily concerned with teaching Latin, hence the name for this type of school.

The pupil entered the Latin grammar school at the age of seven or eight and remained until age fifteen. During this time he was expected to prepare himself to meet the entrance requirements to Harvard. These requirements, stated in 1642, were as follows:

> When any scholar is able to read Tully, or such like classical Latine author *extempore*, and make and speak true Latin in Verse and Prose, and decline perfectly the paradigms of nounes and verbes in the Greek tongue, then may he be admitted into the college, nor shall any claim admission before such qualifications.[9]

The Latin grammar school remained the only type of secondary school until about 1700, when, in response to the demand created by the development of trade and commerce and the emergence of a merchant group in the colonies, a few new private schools were established. These schools taught such practical subjects as arithmetic, navigation, and

[9] Quoted in E. W. Knight and C. L. Hall, *Readings in American Educational History* (New York: Appleton-Century-Crofts, 1951), p. 4.

surveying, in both day and evening classes. The following advertisement which appeared in the American Weekly Mercury in Philadelphia in October–November of 1723 provides an indication of the nature of these schools.

There is a school in New York, in the Broad Street, near the Exchange where Mr. John Walton, late of Yale-Colledge, teacheth Reading, Writing, Arethmatick, whole Numbers and Fractions, Vulgar and Decimal, the Mariners Art, Plain and Mercators Way; also Geometry, Surveying, the Latin tongue, and Greek and Hebrew Grammers, Ethicks, Rhetorick, Logick, Natural Philosophy and Metaphysicks, all or any of them for a Reasonable Price. The School from the first of October till the first of March will be tended in the Evening. If any Gentleman in the Country are disposed to send their sons to the said School, if they apply themselves to the Master he will immediately procure suitable Entertainment for them, very cheap. Also if any Young Gentleman of the City will please to come in the Evening and make some Tryal of the Liberal Arts, they may have opportunity of Learning the same things which are commonly taught in Colledges.[10]

The most significant change in secondary education in the Colonial period occurred in 1750 when Benjamin Franklin opened his Academy. Franklin had attended a Latin school for a time but was withdrawn by his father because of the expense and apprenticed to a printer. He learned the printing trade, educated himself, and became wealthy as a printer in Philadelphia. Franklin believed that the emphasis in secondary schools should be placed upon modern languages and especially English, as well as on practical subjects such as surveying and navigation. Also included in his program were history, geography, logic, rhetoric, algebra, geometry, and astronomy. Although Latin and Greek were also included, Franklin suggested that the cultural value of these subjects could be obtained by reading translations and spending the time on other subjects. Franklin's Academy which grew into the University of Pennsylvania started a movement, and by the time of the Revolutionary War, several academies were in existence. Among the first of these were Phillips Academy at Andover, Massachusetts, established in 1778, and Phillips Exeter Academy at Exeter, New Hampshire, established in 1783.

For most of the seventeenth century the only college that existed in the colonies was Harvard, established at Cambridge in 1636. The college was named after John Harvard who made the original donation to establish the school. Shortly afterward the General Court of Massachusetts appropriated £400 and set up a governing board, composed of six

[10] Quoted in Cubberley, Readings, op. cit., p. 83.

magistrates from surrounding towns, to oversee the college. The purpose of the college can be seen from an excerpt from a pamphlet which was originally a letter written from Boston in 1642 and published in London in 1643:

> After God had carried us safe to New England, and wee had builded our houses, provided necessaries for our livelihood, rear'd convenient places for God's worship, and setled, the Civill Government; one of the next things we longed for, and looked after was to advance Learning, and perpetuate it to Posterity, dreading to leave an illiterate Ministery to the churches, when our present Ministers shall lie in the Dust.[11]

The first president of Harvard was a man named Dunster who was a graduate of Cambridge University. His salary was supposed to have been £60 a year, and he did all the teaching for the small group of students who attended. The curriculum was designed to train ministers, and was rigidly prescribed and uniform for all students. It consisted of the study of logic, physics, ethics, politics, arithmetic, geometry, astronomy, Latin, Greek, and Hebrew. In order to graduate students had to be able to read the "Originalls of the Old and New testament into the Latine tongue, and to resolve them logically." As one historian has said, "turning Hebrew and Greek into Latin is not child's play today, nor was it in that day." The original curriculum, which remained virtually unchanged in the Colonial period, as well as the graduation requirements were part of the Harvard statutes, written by Dunster in 1642. Dunster himself remained at Harvard until 1654 when he was forced to resign because he had doubted the doctrine of infant baptism.

The second college in the colonies was William and Mary, established in Virginia in 1693 with a grant of £2000 from the English monarchs. Like Harvard, the college was founded for the purpose of furnishing the church of Virginia with a "seminary of the ministers of the gospel" and to promote "true philosophy, and other good and liberal arts and sciences" to the end that "the Orthodox Christian faith may be propagated."[12] A few years later (1701) a group of ministers obtained a charter from the General Assembly of Connecticut and established a small college, again to train ministers. The school was moved from town to town and was in a difficult financial position when in 1720 Elihu Yale, a prosperous merchant, donated a rather large sum of money which enabled the college to build and settle at New Haven.

In the middle of the eighteenth century higher education in the colonies was given a tremendous impetus by the strong religious revival led

[11] *Ibid.*, p. 13.
[12] *Ibid.*, pp. 28–9.

by Jonathan Edwards and known in American history as the Great Awakening. As a result of the religious fervor a number of denominational colleges were established. Foremost among these was the College of New Jersey, now Princeton, created by the Presbyterians in 1746 to train ministers to preach the Gospel. Preach they did and establish other colleges too, including an academy in Virginia which developed into Washington and Lee, and one in North Carolina which developed into Davidson College. Later, in 1764, the Baptists set up a religious training school in Rhode Island which became Brown University, and in 1766 the Dutch Reformed Church established Rutgers College in New Jersey for the same purpose.

Perhaps the most significant development in higher education in the eighteenth century in America was the attempt in 1754 to establish Kings College (now Columbia) in New York on a nonsectarian basis. The attempt failed and the college was controlled by the Church of England. Nevertheless the school was established with "no intention to impose on the Scholars the peculiar tenets of any particular Sect of Christians." In its philosophy and its program Kings College reflected the growing influence of the Enlightenment and the changes that were taking place in America. This new spirit is clearly indicated in a statement issued by the President, Samuel Johnson, in announcing the opening of the school. Students attending the college would find that:

> A serious, virtuous and industrious Course of Life being first provided for, it is further the Design of this College, to instruct and perfect the Youth in the learned Languages, and in the Arts of Reasoning exactly, of Writing correctly, and Speaking eloquently: And in the Arts of Numbering and Measuring, of Surveying and Navigation, of Geography and History, of Husbandry, Commerce and Government; and in the Knowledge of all Nature in the Heavens above us, and in the Air, Water and Earth around us, and the various Kinds of Meteors, Stones, Mines and Minerals, Plants and Animals, and of every Thing useful for the Comfort, the Convenience, and Elegance of Life, in the chief Manufactures relating to any of these Things—And finally, to lead them from the Study of Nature, to the Knowledge of themselves, and of the God of Nature, and their Duty to him, themselves, and one another; and every Thing that can contribute to their Happiness both here and hereafter.[13]

Thus by the time of the Revolutionary War the American colonies could boast a rather extensive school system—a system that played no small part in producing the leadership that was so important in the critical period from 1775–1825.

[13] Quoted in Knight and Hall, *op. cit.*, pp. 82–3.

The Early National Period, 1775–1825

IN THE first fifty years of our history as an independent nation, education was shoved into the background, as it has always been in periods of crisis. During this period the neglect may have been justifiable for it was by no means certain that the United States would emerge or survive as a nation. First came the war with England which brought chaos and was uncomfortably close to being lost. Then after the war friction between the states was such that it seemed the European pattern of a system of rivaling states might be developing. The Constitutional Convention was in serious danger of producing no constitution at all and even after the Constitution was adopted, bitterness between the Republicans and the Federalists prevented domestic tranquility and political stability. Finally, the War of 1812 was a severe test for a young nation. With its capitol in ruins and internal dissension strong, the United States was indeed in a "time of trouble." It is not surprising therefore that schools and the means of education were neglected. However, it is not correct to assume that this period was of no importance in the development of American education.

Perhaps the most important development in this period was the blossoming of the great ideas that we generally associate with democracy. Growing out of the Enlightenment and gathering strength as the eighteenth century wore on, these ideas found in the young America a fertile soil for growth. Perhaps best expressed in the writings of Thomas Paine and Thomas Jefferson, the democratic concepts of freedom, equality, and individual rights were the topic of discussion in pamphlets and town meetings all over the colonies. In addition there was a new faith in reason that, coupled with belief in equality, developed into a faith in the common man and in his ultimate perfectability. The immediate consequence of the impact of these ideas was the new Constitution and the Bill of Rights. A later consequence was the development of a free public school system.

Even though the development of a system of schools consistent with the ideals of democracy was delayed until the middle of the nineteenth century, much concrete evidence exists that a real concern for education existed as early as 1776. Such evidence may be found in the state constitutions, which were written by many of the original states between 1776 and 1784 and by the newer states such as Ohio, Indiana, and Illinois as they came into the Union. Thus the new Pennsylvania constitution of 1776 contained the following statement:

> A school or schools shall be established in each county by the legislature, for the convenient instruction of youth, with such sala-

ries to masters, paid by the public, as may enable them to instruct the youth at low prices; and all useful learning shall be duly encouraged and promoted in one or more universities.

The Vermont constitution of 1777 and the North Carolina constitution of 1776 contained provisions similar to Pennsylvania's, whereas others like Georgia's of 1777 and Delaware's of 1792 simply provided that schools should be established and supported by the state. The constitutions of Massachusetts in 1780 and New Hampshire in 1784 contained sections supporting the diffusion of knowledge through many institutions, including the public schools.

Most of the western states as they came into the Union inserted similar statements in their constitutions, and it is interesting to note the amount of word-for-word repetition. For example, the Ohio constitution of 1803 contained a statement identical to one written into the Northwest Ordinance of 1787. It reads as follows: "Religion, morality, and knowledge, being necessary to good government and the happiness of mankind, schools and the means of education shall forever be encouraged." The Ohio Constitution inserted the word *essentially* before *necessary* and tacked on at the end *encouraged by legislative provision, not inconsistent with the right of conscience.* The Indiana constitution of 1816 contained a statement that duplicated the wording of the New Hampshire document but then went beyond it, stating that:

> It shall be the duty of the general assembly, as soon as circumstances will permit, to provide by law for a general system of education, ascending in a regular graduation from township schools to a state university wherein tuition shall be gratis, and equally open to all.

The reasons for the similarities are apparent. Ohio was settled under the provisions of the Northwest Ordinance and this document was well known to the men who wrote the Ohio constitution. In Indiana it is quite possible that some of the men who wrote the state constitution came from New Hampshire, or that the constitution of that state, as well as all the others, was available to them for study.

The Indiana constitution was the first to set the legal basis for a complete and comprehensive free school system from the elementary school through the university; however, it was decades before such a system was brought into existence in any state. In Indiana itself, despite the constitution, a free school system was delayed until after 1850, partly because of the opposition in the southern part of the state. This sectional difference over education was evident in other midwestern states. For example, in Illinois, where southerners were in control, no mention was made of education in the constitutions of 1818 and 1848, and not until 1870 was a provision on education inserted. However, in most states such provisions were included from the beginning.

In addition to these constitutional provisions which supported public schools, other actions taken by the states contributed to the development of American education. The first of these occurred in Massachusetts in 1789 and 1801 when laws were passed establishing the district system as the basic pattern of organization on the local level. Early in the seventeenth century the districts had included a town and the land immediately around it. As the population began to spread, it became more and more difficult to get families who lived some distance from the towns either to send their children to or give support to the schools. Instead they established schools in their own districts. The laws of 1789 and 1801 legalized this system and placed responsibility for running it in the hands of local committees. These committees, similar to our present boards of education, had authority to raise funds by taxation, hire teachers, and supervise the operation of the schools. Because of its simple and democratic nature this district system has become the dominant pattern of organization for public education on the local level in the United States.

The district system was adopted by other New England states and, finally, by New York in 1812. New York had taken steps toward the establishment of a free school system in 1795, when the legislature appropriated $100,000 a year to aid the schools. Within three years 1,350 schools, enrolling almost 60,000 pupils, were established. Unfortunately the aid was cut off in 1800 and the school system collapsed. When a new law was written it provided for education on a basis that was used in many states in this period. This was the rate bill system under which parents paid a certain amount for each child in school. Thus in New York, as in other states, the free-school idea had to wait, and it is apparent that the idea of free tax-supported schools for all children had not been accepted. In Pennsylvania the free-school movement was side-tracked and the famous "Pauper Schools" were established for the education of the poorer children.

Although the district system resulted in broadening the base of education and provided at least some education for most children, the problem of support was not solved. Many devices were used, from the fund established in Connecticut through the sale of its western lands, to the use of funds raised through taxes on liquors, lotteries, and marriage licenses, to the rate bill system. The result was that support was inadequate and erratic. In the middle and southern colonies, school support was even more erratic than in New England, since the prevailing belief was that education was either a matter for the church or a private matter. Evidence of this lack of support occurred in Virginia in 1779 when Jefferson submitted his plan for education in that state. He proposed that each county be divided into districts five miles square, and that each district establish a school which would be free to all children for three years. Then from each district the best student whose parents were too poor to continue his education would be selected and sent to a secondary school at state expense for a possible maximum of six years if he succeeded in facing another elimination contest held after the first or second year. After six years the upper half of the group would be sent to William and Mary, also at state expense. However, even a man of Jefferson's stature was unable to get the bill passed. When the bill was finally passed twenty years later it was not put into effect because of lack of funds.

Other educational developments that were important occurred in this period. One was the Sunday School, established originally in England in 1780 to provide some semblance of education in reading and religion for the children working in factories. The movement took hold and flourished in the colonies in the late eighteenth and early nineteenth centuries. Later it was taken over by church groups and the program reduced from a day of secular work to a short period of religious teaching. Another important development was the introduction of the Lancastrian, or monitorial, schools. Founded by an Englishman, Joseph Lancaster, in 1797, these schools were enthusiastically received both in England and in America. In these schools a single teacher could teach several hundred students by using monitors, or older children, who could teach the younger. Generally, the teacher taught the monitors a lesson from a printed card, then the monitors, "youthful corporals of the teacher's regiment," took their rows of children to "stations" about the wall and proceeded to teach the other boys what they had just learned. Apparently, the system was efficient, which explains its enthusiastic reception, but it was also formal and mechanical. The schools began to decline in 1820 and by 1830 few were to be found, although at least one monitorial school existed as far west as St. Louis as late as 1850.

On the national scene this period of our history is significant because of the grants of land given to the states by the federal government as they came into the Union. The provision for these grants was made in the Ordinance of 1785. The Ordinance divided the land in the Northwest Territory into townships six miles square. These townships were then divided into sections one mile square, and the sixteenth section (640 acres) of each township was given to the state to be used for education. This procedure was followed with all the western states except Texas, which owned its own land when it came into the Union. Most of the states west of the Mississippi received two sections of land from each township, and Utah, Arizona, and New Mexico received four sections. These grants amounted to approximately 145,000,000 acres (226,-

562 square miles) or an area of land almost as large as the original Northwest Territory.

Thus, despite the troubled condition of the country between 1775 and 1825, important contributions were made to American education. Perhaps as important as anything, in the long run, was the strong belief held by the Founding Fathers regarding the relationship between democracy and education. An indication of this belief can be seen in Washington's Farewell Address, given in 1796.

> Promote then, as an object of primary importance, institutions for the general diffusion of knowledge. In proportion as the structure of a government gives force to public opinion it is essential that public opinion should be enlightened.

Washington also favored the plan, proposed by Charles Pinckney during the Constitutional Convention, for the establishment of a national university free of religious control, and advised the creation of such an institution in his message to Congress in 1790. There had been some consideration of inclusion in the Constitution of a provision on this matter but it was deemed unnecessary because it was felt that such power was implied in other provisions. Thus the fact that education is not mentioned in the Constitution does not mean that it was considered unimportant.

In addition to Washington and Pinckney, many of the other leaders of the time, including Franklin, were vitally interested in education and schools. But perhaps the individual most concerned was Jefferson. His classic statement, "If a nation expects to be ignorant and free in a state of civilization it expects what never was and never will be," remains as true today as it was when he wrote it. Jefferson showed his interest and concern for education in his proposal in Virginia, mentioned above, and in an action that he considered one of his most important, the founding of the University of Virginia in 1825. So while it is true that men such as Washington and Jefferson were unable to establish a system of schools they did help lay the foundation for such a system partly through their efforts in helping to create a democratic society in America and partly through their proposals on education.

The Formative Period, 1825–60

By 1825 the United States had achieved a certain amount of stability and the nation began to develop rapidly. Rails were being laid and factories built. Immigrants were pouring into the country and the population was increasing with concentration in the urban areas. The barons of industry were beginning to make themselves felt, and labor associations

were being formed. America was started on the road toward industrialization.

In other areas, notably the political and the social, changes just as
significant were taking place. Universal manhood suffrage had been
achieved and the results were apparent as Andrew Jackson was elected
to the presidency in 1828. The frontier had become the great equalizer
and a great breeding ground for democracy, and as the West gained
strength and asserted itself its equalitarianism surged back into the East.
Alexis de Tocqueville, a French scholar and statesman who visited
America in the 1830's wrote:

> Amongst the novel objects that attracted my attention during
> my stay in the United States, nothing struck me more forcibly than
> the general equality of conditions among the people. I readily dis-
> covered the prodigious influence which this primary fact exercises
> on the whole course of a society; it gives a peculiar direction to pub-
> lic opinion, and a peculiar tenor to the laws; it imparts new maxims
> to the governing authorities, and peculiar habits to the governed
> . . . the more I advanced in the study of American society, the
> more I perceived that this equality of condition is the fundamental
> fact from which all others seem to be derived, and the central point
> at which all my observations constantly terminated.[14]

This concern for equality in the political and social areas was carried
over into the field of education and became an important factor in the
struggle for free public schools. For example, several of the groups that
were most active in their support of the public school movement were
labor associations, since they viewed the schools as a means for attaining
a degree of equality of opportunity for their children.

Also important at this time was the surge of humanitarianism that
produced the many social reformers. Some of these men fought for the
softening of the criminal code which imposed severe punishments for
minor crimes, and for reform of the prisons. Others, like Samuel Howe,
worked to establish schools for the blind and the deaf. This was also the
period of the well-known experiment by Robert Owen at New Harmony,
Indiana, and of the campaign against slavery led by William Lloyd Garrison. The struggle for the public schools was a part of this larger movement and its great spokesman, Horace Mann, was one of the ablest and
most dedicated of all these reformers. His crusading spirit was perhaps
best expressed in a speech he gave to the graduates of Antioch College
when he told them, "Be ashamed to die until you have won some victory
for humanity."

Related to the development of democracy in the young nation was the

[14] Alexis de Tocqueville, *Democracy in America* (New York: Alfred A. Knopf.
1946), I, 3.

growth of a strong national spirit. Men began to think of themselves first and foremost as Americans and then as New Yorkers or Virginians. By this time that love of country which is a basic characteristic of nationalism was becoming strong. Pride in country and the logic of democracy were combined in the minds of men to support the idea that education for citizenship was essential.

Although the battle for free "common" schools had been started in the eighteenth century, the struggle began in earnest in the late 1820's. Led by men like Horace Mann and James Carter in Massachusetts, Henry Barnard in Connecticut, Thaddeus Stevens in Pennsylvania, and Lyman Beecher and Calvin Stowe in Ohio, the fight was carried on by men from all walks of life—from workingmen to the governors of the states. In the course of the next twenty years hundreds of groups such as the Pennsylvania Society For the Promotion of Public Schools were organized to promote the public schools. Letters and pamphlets were written and circulated all over the country. Conventions were held, such as the one held by the Friends of Education in Trenton in 1838, in which action was urged upon the people. The legislatures were flooded with petitions, resolutions, and letters presenting arguments for and against free schools. The campaign for the public schools was as spirited and vigorous, and at times as emotional, as our current political campaigns.

What was the nature of this common school that was causing all of this controversy? Certainly many of the individuals working in the movement had no clear idea. They wanted free schools and that was that. However, the leaders in the movement had a clear conception of the kind of school they believed essential for the American democracy. The basic elements in this "ideal" common school were as follows: [15]

1. That the common school would be free and open to all. It was thought that no other system, least of all the dual system used in Europe, was acceptable for a democracy.
2. That the common school would be of such excellent quality that all parents would be willing to send their children.
3. That the common school would be common in the sense that all children would attend and that it would serve as a unifying force to weld communities together. This was of particular importance since large numbers of immigrants were pouring into the country and had to be assimilated. It was also thought that if children from all classes would attend the same school that they would understand each other and the class conflicts that were causing so much difficulty in the old country might be avoided.

[15] Lawrence A. Cremin, *The American Common School* (New York: Bureau of Publications, Teachers College, Columbia University, 1951), pp. 49–82.

4. That the common school would be publicly supported through taxation of the whole community.
5. That the common school would be publicly controlled through elected or appointed public officials responsible to the whole community and not to any particular political, economic or religious group.
6. That the common school should be non-sectarian in character. Mann's view was that morality could be taught without teaching the tenets of any particular sect.
7. That the common school provide the basic knowledge and skills essential to enable students of diverse backgrounds to assume the responsibilities of citizenship in the young Republic.

The men who argued for the public schools had marshaled their case in the following way. In the first place they pointed out that the suffrage had been extended to include all men, and if men were going to vote they had to be educated. They argued that the pauper schools and the private and religious schools were inadequate for several reasons: the former, because the social stigma connected with the schools kept many from attending; the latter, because the fees charged kept some children out and were used as an excuse for not sending their children to school by those parents who were looking for an excuse. In addition, the religious schools were not acceptable because of America's commitment to freedom of conscience, which ruled out the possibility of forcing religion on any child, or of forcing any person to pay taxes to support a religious school. In addition, they were not acceptable because of the extreme religious diversity that existed in America which logically would have required a school system for each sect. But the need for schools extended beyond the requirements of citizenship. They were necessary, it was argued, to prevent pauperism and crime, to reduce poverty and distress, and in general to preserve the well-being of the state. They were necessary to help assimilate the immigrants who were pouring into the country, and to prevent a class society from developing in America. In answering the charge of the merchant industrial group that by supporting public schools the industrious would be taxed to support the lazy, supporters of the public school movement argued that education would serve to increase productivity and to eliminate radical ideas about the distribution of wealth. Finally, they argued that education was the God-given, natural right of all children and it was up to the communities to provide it.

The opponents of the free public schools argued just as vigorously that the whole scheme was utopian and visionary and that the country couldn't afford it. Besides, it was wrong, they said, to take a man's property to educate his neighbor's child, and if a man had no children he

should pay no school tax. They challenged the right of the state to interfere in the education of the child. This, they said, was the responsibility
of the family or the church, and naturally the private and parochial
schoolmen supported this position. The aristocratic elements argued that
free schools would educate people out of their proper station in life and
break down desirable social barriers. They believed that education was
for those who had leisure time, and since the poor had no leisure time,
they had no need of education.

Perhaps the most serious problems that had to be solved were, first,
that of gaining public support through general taxation, and, second,
that of keeping the schools on a nonsectarian basis. In the first case, the
struggle was won through the kind of reasoning used by Thaddeus
Stevens in a speech in 1835 before the Pennsylvania Legislature in which
he opposed the repeal of the Common School Law of 1834.

> Many complain of the school tax, not so much on account of its
> amount, as because it is for the benefit of others and not themselves.
> This is a mistake. It is *for their own benefit*, inasmuch as it per-
> petuates the government and ensures the due administration of the
> laws under which they live, and by which their lives and property
> are protected. Why do they not urge the same objection against all
> other taxes? The industrious, thrifty, rich farmer pays a heavy
> county tax to support criminal courts, build jails, and pay sheriffs
> and jail keepers, and yet probably he never has had and never will
> have any direct personal use for either. He never gets the worth of
> his money by being tried for a crime before the court, allowed the
> privilege of the jail on conviction, or receiving an equivalent from
> the sheriff or his hangmen officers! He cheerfully pays the tax which
> is necessary to support and punish convicts, but loudly complains
> of that which goes to prevent his fellow being from becoming a
> criminal, and to obviate the necessity of those humiliating instruc-
> tions.[16]

On the second problem, that of establishing a public school system
that would be nonsectarian, Mann ran into a storm of controversy. His
dedication to the idea of freedom of conscience and his realization of
the diversity of religious beliefs in America led him to propose the
teaching of the common elements of Christianity through a study of
the Bible. For this he was attacked from two sides. The idea of using the
Bible as the moral foundation was attacked as sectarian by the Catholics.
On the other hand some Protestant clergymen believed that even using
the Bible had the effect of producing religious relativism. Although there
was evidence to disprove this claim it was clear that whatever religious
program was adopted, it would displease many groups. The result was

[16] Quoted in Cremin, *op. cit.*, p. 78.

that the trend during the nineteenth century was more and more toward the policy of teaching morals and ethics in the public schools and leaving the teaching of religious doctrine to the other great agencies of education—the home and the church.

By 1860 the free public elementary school was firmly established in America, and it generally resembled the ideal that its founders had in mind. It is impossible to say exactly how many children attended these schools and for how long. Certainly the urban areas were far ahead of the rural in this respect and it seems likely that most of the children living in towns and cities received at least a basic education. Gradually through the years the level of schooling was raised as compulsory attendance laws were passed, first in Massachusetts in 1852, and in most of the other states before 1890. As the elementary schools developed, so did the organization of the school system. Thus, by 1860 every state in the Union had a state superintendent of schools. At the same time the office of county superintendent was established to serve as a liaison office between the state and the local districts. On the local level the schools were in the hands of small lay committees who raised funds, hired teachers, and generally supervised the operation of the schools. This system worked fairly well in a district with one teacher and one school. However when the systems began to grow and many schools were established in one system, it became necessary to have a unified control under a person who knew something about education, and so the office of local superintendent of schools was created. Thus, in this period the basic pattern of organization was formed—a pattern that is still in use at the present time.

The period from 1830 to 1860 saw not only the establishment but also the expansion of the public school system. In the curriculum this expansion consisted of a more extensive training in the three "R's," but it included also such new subjects as geography, grammar, and history. In 1848 a graded system of instruction was introduced into the Boston schools, and then spread rapidly all over the country where the schools were of any size. The graded system required a large number of pupils and several teachers and this combination generally existed in the towns. In the rural areas grading was introduced much later. As the high schools increased in number the trend toward arranging a continuous program from the elementary schools through the high school began. Finally, the state universities were connected with and extended out from the high schools and the famous American "ladder system" was a reality. The ladder was extended downward when shortly before 1860 the kindergarten, which originated in Germany under Frederich Froebel, was introduced into this country. A few years later it was incorporated into a public school system in St. Louis through the efforts of Susan Blow.

In 1830 the dominant form of secondary education was the academy which was privately controlled but often supported in part by public funds. The first public high school was established in Boston in 1821 for the purpose of providing a noncollege preparatory secondary education. In the next decades public high schools were established in the other large cities and most of them adopted a pattern of including a college preparatory program in their curriculum. By 1860 the public high school was replacing the academy although in many instances the two schools differed only in the matter of support. In this period only a small percentage of children attended the high schools and most of those who did were preparing for college.

The middle decades of the nineteenth century were also formative years for higher education in America. In this period a great many publicly supported state universities were established and there were significant changes in the purposes and programs of the existing private schools. The basis for state colleges had been established under the Northwest Ordinance which provided land for this purpose, and all of the new states eventually set up such schools. Jefferson's University of Virginia opened in 1825, Indiana University in 1824, and Alabama University in 1831. Provisions for state universities were made in Michigan in 1835, in Wisconsin in 1836, in Missouri in 1839, in Mississippi in 1844, and in Iowa in 1847. Also many private schools, most of them supported by religious groups but many of them nondenominational insofar as philosophy and program were concerned, were established. Among these were Amherst in 1821, Haverford in 1830, Western Reserve in 1826, Oberlin in 1833, Rochester in 1851, and Washington University in St. Louis in 1853. In the matter of philosophy and program the colleges began to turn away from the religious and classical and to emphasize the scientific and professional although the greatest changes occurred after the Civil War.

Of considerable importance to the tremendous expansion of higher education was the Dartmouth College decision handed down by Chief Justice John Marshall in 1819. The case grew out of the attempt of the State of New Hampshire to take over Dartmouth College. The Supreme Court decided the attempt was illegal and Dartmouth remained a private college. This decision gave private schools a boost since it insured their freedom from government expropriation; however, it also boosted the development of state schools since the decision made clear that if the legislatures wanted colleges under their control they would have to build them.

Thus by the time of the Civil War the basic pattern of the American public school system had been formed. The task then became one of improving the quality of instruction and of extending the system upward.

Education in the Early Industrial Period, 1865–1914

THE period between the Civil War and World War I was a time of change in America. The development of industrialism, accelerated by the Civil War and aided by progress in science and technology, constituted the most important change. Based on power and the machine the new industrial system developed the factory and its modern concomitants, mass production and specialization, into the present-day pattern of production. With the factory system came the corporation with its board of directors, its stockholders, its engineering managers, and its emphasis upon efficiency. With it also came increasing urbanization and new problems in health and sanitation, political corruption, and juvenile delinquency. In short, this was modern industrial America in its embryonic stages. It held out tremendous potential for human comfort and well-being, but it also brought with it the problems of a highly interdependent society and the dangers of depression.

At the same time that more and better goods were being produced important developments were occurring in the field of medicine. Disease was being controlled through individual and public measures. The infant mortality rate began to drop and life expectancy began to rise. The result was a tremendous increase in the native population which, when added to the millions of immigrants who continued to stream into the country, formed the basis for a modern mass society.

The schools felt the impact of the new industrialism and the rapid growth of population. The free public elementary school idea, already accepted, now spread over the country and thousands of new schools were established. Reflecting the growth of the country the schools not only increased in number but also in size. Year by year, from 1865 on, more and more children attended public elementary schools for a greater number of years until by 1914, especially in the cities, the majority of children went through the eighth grade. In rural areas the development was not as rapid. Most of the schools were one-room ungraded institutions with a school year that had to be adapted to the crops being raised. In most cases the "children" (some were fully grown) attended school only long enough to learn to read, write, and figure.

Coinciding with these developments in the schools were those in the training of teachers. To meet the growing demand for teachers two-year normal schools were established which students could enter directly from the elementary schools. Gradually the standards were raised until a high school education was a prerequisite. Then in the early years of the twentieth century the two-year normal schools began to be converted into four-year institutions, and were called teachers colleges. During this period, women began to enter the profession in ever greater numbers and as early as 1870 they outnumbered the men.

In the cities the scope of education became so great that school "systems" were established. The pattern was similar to our present arrangement and generally included several elementary schools and one or more high schools. The system was administered by one superintendent for the entire district and by principals for each school in the system. A school board of lay members elected by the people was the body responsible for hiring the superintendent and for the over-all operation of the system.

Just as the period from 1825–60 was the formative period for the common school so was the period from 1865 to 1914 the formative period for the public high school in America. One important event that gave an impetus to this development was the decision handed down in the Kalamazoo Case by the Supreme Court of Michigan in 1872, in which the Court recognized the right of a community to tax itself for secondary schools. However little impetus was needed. The country was growing and becoming more complex and the demand for more and more schooling followed naturally. Between 1860 and 1880 alone, some 500 high schools were established, and by 1890 about 10 per cent of the youngsters between fourteen and seventeen were enrolled in secondary schools. Again the greatest developments occurred in the cities; still, a surprising number of small country communities established high schools, some of them while they were not much more than frontier towns.

As a result of this growth, important changes began to take place in the nature and character of the high school. Throughout the eighteenth and most of the nineteenth centuries, secondary education was essentially college preparatory in nature and the curriculum was strongly weighted with Latin, Greek, and mathematics. With the expansion of knowledge on the one hand and the demand of the public for a more practical education on the other, pressure to change the curriculum began to mount. The result was that new subjects such as modern languages, chemistry, physics, zoology, botany, English, history, geography, manual arts, and commercial subjects were introduced and taught, although not without spirited resistance from the colleges who fought to maintain the classical curriculum.

What was to be the nature of the high school in a democracy? Would it be an extension of the common school which all children would attend? If so, what kind of a program would be offered? If the classical curriculum was not acceptable for all students, was it the best preparation for college? If so, how could such a program be set up alongside the noncollege preparatory curriculum? In this situation the famous Committee of Ten was appointed by the National Education Association in 1892 to study the problem.

The Committee, which was made up primarily of college people and chaired by President Eliot of Harvard, in submitting its report recognized that:

> The Secondary schools of the United States, taken as a whole, do not exist for the purpose of preparing boys and girls for colleges. Only an insignificant percentage of the graduates of these schools go to colleges or scientific schools. . . . A secondary school program intended for national use must therefore be made for those children whose education is not to be pursued beyond the secondary school.[17]

While cognizant of this basic fact, the committee was also aware that it was quite possible that a student might not know, when he started high school, whether he would want to go to college when he finished, and they did not want to penalize such a student. Therefore they decided that a system should be devised that would enable any graduate of any "good secondary school" to be admitted to college regardless of the subjects he had taken. However the Committee felt that much of the high school work was "of a very feeble and scrappy nature." To remedy the "scrappy nature" they recommended that fewer subjects be studied by students, but that more time be spent on each one. Thus they suggested that a college might say:

> We will accept for admission any groups of studies taken from the secondary school programme, provided that the sum of the studies in each of the four years amounts to sixteen, or eighteen, or twenty periods a week . . . and provided, further, that in each year at least four of the subjects presented shall have been pursued at least three periods a week, and that at least three of the subjects shall have been pursued three or more years.[18]

As a result, the Committee created the concept of "equivalents," that is, that one subject was as acceptable as another if it were on the approved list and were studied for an equal length of time. Later the term "unit" was used to describe a certain quantity of work and high school and college programs measured in units or credits, each designating a specific number of hours in class, were established. These recommendations were accepted in school after school, until shortly after the turn of the century the unit and credit system was well entrenched and had become a basic part of the American educational system. Devised as a means of coping with the mass education that was emerging, the credit system has had a disastrous effect upon American education. It has be-

[17] *Report of the Committee of Ten on Secondary School Studies* (New York: American Book Company, 1894), p. 51.
[18] *Ibid.*, p. 52.

come so well established that neither teachers nor students think of questioning its merit. It has led teachers and students to think of education in mechanical, quantitative terms, and a college education for many students has degenerated into a race to accumulate credits, regardless of what is learned. In recent years the disease has spread to the graduate schools and thousands of masters degrees are granted yearly on the basis of the routine accumulation of so many credit hours.

This period in American education saw the emergence of regional accrediting agencies, such as the North Central Association of Colleges and Secondary Schools established in 1895. These associations grew out of the need for some means of standardizing the programs and evaluating the many schools that were opening. As a result, if a high school met certain standards set up by the Association it received a rating, which meant that it would be recognized and that the work its students took would be accepted at other schools and colleges. In other words the school was then "accredited." These agencies are still active and quite important today especially since so many students transfer from one school to another, and the evaluation of schools and credits is constantly going on.

In the period from 1865 to 1900, the American university as we know it today emerged. The first such school was Johns Hopkins University, established in 1876 at Baltimore and patterned after the German universities in which research was emphasized. In the next few years Johns Hopkins became the center for advanced study in America and it was there that John Dewey received his Ph.D. degree in 1884. Shortly afterward, other schools followed the pattern and by 1900 several other institutions, including Harvard and Yale, had become "universities"; that is, they consisted of a group of schools offering graduate and professional work in addition to the undergraduate liberal arts program.

Another important development in this period was the establishment of the United States Office of Education. The office was created in 1867 as the Department of Education. In 1870 it was changed into the Bureau of Education and then into its present status in 1929. Recently the U.S. Office has been transferred from the Federal Security Agency and is now a part of the newly created Department of Health, Education, and Welfare, which has cabinet rank in the federal government. The U.S. Office of Education is headed by the U.S. Commissioner of Education who is appointed by the President for an indefinite term. The first commissioner, Henry Barnard, was appointed in 1867 by President Johnson and served until 1870. Since then, some outstanding educators have served as commissioners, including William T. Harris, who held office from 1889 to 1906. In general, the U.S. Office has administered those areas of education which are outside the scope of the states or which could not be handled effectively by them. Thus the U.S. Office has administered the Indian and territorial schools. The office collects information, carries on research, and publishes reports that are of interest and importance to American schoolmen. It has also provided assistance to the states at their request and co-operates with them in promoting education.

In this period the federal government also passed a series of laws designed to promote industrial and agricultural education. The first of these was the Morrill Act passed by Congress and signed by President Lincoln in 1862. This law provided 30,000 acres of land to each state for each congressman representing that state in the Congress. The proceeds from the sale of the land were to be used to establish colleges of agriculture and mechanical arts. This has provided the basis for many of our "A. and M." colleges. In 1887 the Hatch Act was passed, appropriating $15,000 annually to each state having an agricultural college, in order to promote scientific research in agriculture. As a result of this law, agricultural experiment stations were established which have made important contributions to the development of scientific farming in the United States. Continuing in this pattern the Congress in 1914 passed the Smith-Lever Act which provided funds to the states on a matching basis, to be used for extension work in agriculture and home economics. This law served to bring the fruits of research into the homes and onto the farms of America; however, the matching principle, whereby the federal government matched the amount put up by the state, has been abandoned in its original form since it provided more funds to the wealthier states than to the poorer states that needed it the most. A few years later (1918) the Smith-Hughes Act was passed which provided funds, again on a matching basis, for vocational education in public schools below the college level. The funds were and are used to pay vocational and agricultural teachers and supervisors, to help train teachers in these fields, and to promote research in vocational education. This succession of bills reflects the increasing importance of agriculture and industry in this period, and also indicates the faith that Americans had in science and in education. It also illustrates the role that the federal government has played and can play in an educational system controlled by the states.

Thus by 1914 American education had taken on most of the characteristics it has today. The common school had been extended upward to include the high school, and in terms of the number of children being educated, it was fast becoming a mass system. Owing to the influence of industrialization the schools were becoming more technical; owing to the influence of industrialization and urbanization, and the resultant changes in the family, the school began to take on more and more of the educational functions formerly handled by the parents in the home.

Education in Industrial America

AFTER World War I America emerged as an industrial giant—the most powerful and wealthy nation in the world—and American education developed into a gigantic enterprise. By 1959 more than 31,000,000 children were attending elementary schools, and of these more than 27,000,-000 were enrolled in public schools. The secondary-school attendance had jumped to over 8,880,000, and of this total more than 7,000,000 were in public high schools. Approximately 3,623,000 Americans were enrolled in schools beyond the secondary level, making a staggering total of more than 44,000,000 students enrolled in American schools. In addition, and as an indication of the changes that had occurred, more than 30,000 foreign students from all over the world were attending American schools mostly colleges and universities. As might be expected, the nation has lagged behind in coping with this situation and there is a serious shortage of teachers, buildings and, of course, money.

The elementary schools have not only expanded numerically, but they have expanded their programs to include such subjects as social studies and science, and more and more emphasis was being placed on the creative arts. As a result of research, new knowledge about child growth and development is available and is being applied. Partly as a result of this research and partly through other experimentation, great strides have been made in improving teaching methods, especially in the primary grades. At their best—that is, with a capable teacher and a decent class size—the elementary schools are doing a tremendous job. The whole school atmosphere is more humane; the day of severe punishment of little children is past. Teachers in general are more concerned about children as individuals, and understand, as great teachers always have, that education involves more than the mental development of the child. Unfortunately, too many teachers are still not adequately prepared, and too many elementary classrooms contain thirty, forty, or fifty children. Under these circumstances, it is idle to speak of teaching each individual child, and the best teacher can do little more than keep order. In too many instances rich and wealthy America is neglecting its most precious resource—its children.

These great changes in the elementary schools are partly due to the writing and teaching of John Dewey. In his experimental laboratory school in Chicago in 1898 and in his famous *Democracy and Education* published in 1916, Dewey laid the basis for modern educational theory and practice. He pointed out that education was a matter of individual experience and that learning was an active not a passive process. He pointed out that much of the work of the traditional school was so far removed from the experience of the child that it was often meaningless, and frequently resulted in mere verbalization, which gave the appearance but not the substance of real learning. He also taught that the interests and purposes of the child should be respected and the curriculum of the school adapted to them. These ideas, which were the basis of progressive education, gained wide acceptance in American education after 1920. For the most part they have resulted in an improved educational opportunity for children. In some cases, however, Dewey's teaching was interpreted to mean allowing the child to do as he pleased, with a resultant lack of direction and, often, activity for its own sake. Dewey responded to this misunderstanding as follows:

> Because the older education imposed the knowledge, methods and the rules of conduct of the mature person upon the young, it does not follow, except on the basis of the extreme *Either-Or* philosophy, that the knowledge and skill of the mature person has no directive value for the experience of the immature. On the contrary, basing education upon personal experience may mean more multiplied and more intimate contacts between the mature and the immature than ever existed in the traditional school, and consequently more, rather than less guidance by others.[19]

Not only does this statement correct the misunderstanding that in a progressive school the teacher is a mere bystander, but it also raises interesting questions for some of our very large schools. Consider the possibility of "multiple" and "intimate" contacts between teacher and student in some of our high schools when the teacher has five classes a day with thirty to thirty-five students in a class, or in an elementary classroom with fifty pupils.

Similarly, Dewey's teaching about discipline, in which he expressed the view that self-discipline, springing from within the person, was the only real discipline, was interpreted to mean no discipline at all. In this connection Dewey wrote that:

> The ideal aim of education is self control. But the mere removal of external control is no guarantee for the production of self control. It is easy to jump out of the frying-pan into the fire. It is easy, in other words, to escape one form of external control only to find oneself in another and more dangerous form of external control. Impulses and desires that are not ordered by intelligence are under the control of accidental circumstances. It may be a loss rather than a gain to escape from the control of another person only to find one's conduct dictated by immediate whim and caprice; that is, at the

[19] John Dewey, *Experience and Education* (New York: The Macmillan Company, 1938), p. 8.

mercy of impulses into whose formation intelligent judgment has not entered. A person whose conduct is controlled in this way has at most only the illusion of freedom. Actually he is directed by forces over which he has no command.[20]

Dewey was a forthright critic of the education of his time and especially of the emphasis upon formalism and rote learning that he saw in the schools. He asked of these schools:

> How many students were rendered callous to ideas, and how many lost the impetus to learn because of the way in which learning was experienced by them? How many acquired special skills by means of automatic drill so that their power of judgment and capacity to act intelligently in new situations was limited? How many came to associate the learning process with ennui and boredom? How many found what they did so foreign to the situations of life outside the school as to give them no power of control over the latter? How many came to associate books with dull drudgery, so that they were "conditioned" to all but flashy reading matter? [21]

One might ask whether this same indictment might not be made of many contemporary schools, despite Dewey's efforts. However, in general there has been a wholesome departure from formalism and rote learning and much more attention has been given to the interests and needs of children. Often, as noted, this situation has been carried to extremes with the teacher believing it to be her job to let the child "grow naturally." Often, too, in reaction against the traditional school and in line with making schoolwork interesting, teachers neglected the intellectual training of their students and did not lead them to work and think deeply and rigorously. Whereas many teachers seemed to shy away from such words as "intellectual" or "discipline" Dewey, the father of progressive education, had this to say in 1938 about the importance of the intellectual aspect of experience:

> The experimental method of science [the basis for his whole philosophy] attaches more importance, not less, to ideas as ideas than do other methods. . . . The method of intelligence manifested in the experimental method demands keeping track of ideas, activities, and observed consequences. Keeping track is a matter of reflective review and summarizing, in which there is both discrimination and record of the significant features of a developing experience. To reflect is to look back over what has been done so as to extract the net meanings which are the capital stock for intelligent

[20] *Ibid.*, pp. 75–6.
[21] *Ibid.*, p. 15.

dealing with further experiences. It is the heart of intellectual organization and of the disciplined mind.[22]

The fact is that learning situations can be interesting and meaningful to the child and still require him to think and to develop the ability to do intensive intellectual work. When this combination exists, Dewey's teaching is bearing fruit.

Dewey's work has had a tremendous influence on American education, especially on the elementary school. But other factors were working in the same direction. The most important of these was the great progress made in the sciences, particularly the social sciences. In the field of psychology, for example, outstanding contributions of Thorndike in learning theory, G. Stanley Hall in child study, and Alfred Binet in intelligence testing enabled teachers to understand the child and the learning process. At the same time, progress in sociology and anthropology provided educators with new insights into the nature and function of societies. The pioneer work of Freud in psychology and psychiatry provided the basis for the mental hygiene movement, which has enabled teachers to understand the elements of emotional development. These achievements and many others were gradually brought into the professional preparation of teachers and, eventually, into the classrooms of America.

In the secondary schools, although the curriculum had been broadened somewhat from its classical base as a result of the recommendations of the Committee of Ten, the major emphasis was still upon academic work and preparation for college. After 1905, however, for a number of reasons the public high school became a center of controversy, and it was changed significantly by 1925. First, in the years 1905–14 there was tremendous pressure by business and industrial leaders on American educators to offer vocational training. The major factor in this drive was the strong competition for world markets being exerted by Germany. American industrialists believed that Germany's great productive efficiency was based on her system of industrial schools, and they maintained that the United States could compete successfully only if the German plan was copied. The need for vocational education was granted, but there was much debate as to whether separate vocational schools should be established (the German arrangement) or training provided in a comprehensive high school which offered both college preparatory and technical education. In the end, although some separate schools were established, the idea of the comprehensive school won out because American educators feared separate schools would limit equality of opportunity by forcing a career choice too soon, and because it was believed such schools would tend to contribute to a stratified class

[22] *Ibid.*, p. 109.

society. One leader in this movement, Clarence Kingsley, urged successfully that the high school period be conceived of as a testing time in
which the interests and abilities of students could be assessed prior to a
definite career choice. The decision against copying the German system
was reinforced, of course, after the outbreak of World War I, especially
when America entered the war and all things German were in disrepute.

There were other forces at work that were destined to change the
American high school. In the years after 1905 child labor laws were
passed, compulsory attendance laws were tightened and the upper age
limit extended to sixteen, and of course the population was increasing
rapidly (fourteen million immigrants entered the U.S. between 1900
and 1914). At the same time the public high schools were subjected to
severe criticism, especially from such journals as *The Saturday Evening
Post* and *The Ladies' Home Journal,* which had circulations of well over
a million. The high schools were accused of being "medieval," of placing too much emphasis upon "culture" and book learning, and were
urged to introduce more practical programs to meet the "needs" of
students, both boys and girls. Coupled with this bitter criticism was a
growing demand on the part of secondary-school administrators for escape from the control of the colleges, and especially college entrance requirements, and for the autonomy of the high school. Finally, when
research studies began to cast doubt on the claims which had been made
for the classics as mental disciplines, the bonds were broken, and the
secondary schools took their destiny in their own hands.

The dramatic change can be seen in the development of two major
committees appointed by the National Education Association. The
first, appointed in 1911, was on the Articulation of High School and
College. This group, composed of secondary school men, gradually came
to the conclusion that its basic problem was not "articulation" but reorganization of the high school. As a result, the committee recommended changing its title to Commission on the Reorganization of Secondary Education. This recommendation was accepted by the N.E.A.,
and under the leadership of Clarence Kingsley the Commission published a total of sixteen reports between 1913 and 1922. Most famous of
these was the *Report on the Cardinal Principles of Secondary Education,* issued in 1918, which broadened the aims of secondary education
and recommended the comprehensive high school. It constituted a blue-
print for the new, uniquely American secondary school designed to
serve all American youth in a democratic, industrial society.

In the twenties, as secondary school enrollment continued to increase,
school administrators were subjected to pressure to economize, and they
did this by building larger schools, increasing class size, eliminating small
classes, and increasing the teaching load. These steps did save money,
but they complicated the already difficult problems of providing high

quality education in a multipurpose school to students differing greatly in ability, interests, and motivation. In the large cities the larger schools and the increase in the teachers' load made the schools extremely impersonal and factory-like in their operation. And in all schools new courses were introduced and old ones dropped (especially Latin) as American educators responded to the continued demands to make the schools more functional.

By the early thirties frequent criticism was being directed at the high schools by college and university personnel who charged that the changes toward a functional curriculum were having an adverse effect upon those students who came to college. They urged a return to the traditional type of secondary program. In an attempt to solve some of these problems, the famous Eight-Year Study was launched in 1933. This study, carried on under the auspices of the Progressive Education Association, turned out to be one of the most significant developments in secondary education in the twentieth century. Experimenting with students from thirty high schools, the investigators found that students who had graduated from the newer, progressive schools with a diversified program did as well in college as those who had attended traditional schools. Some educators have interpreted the study to mean that there was no relationship between the subjects taken in high school and success in college, but the director of the Study drew no such conclusion. His conclusion was that it was not the type or number of subjects studied that mattered. What was important was the quality of work done and the kind of education the student received.[23] The result of the Study was a further freeing of the high schools from the control of the colleges, although most colleges still require units in language, social studies, science, and mathematics for entrance.

By mid-century the high school had grown to the point where almost all American youth attended and the vast majority remained to graduate. Dissatisfaction with the quality of work continued, however, especially on the part of the college instructors who claimed their students were inadequately prepared. Then in 1956 the Russians launched their first satellite, and in the ensuing months American secondary education came under renewed attack and was compared unfavorably with both Russian and European schools. In this context, James B. Conant, an outstanding scientist, a former president of Harvard University, and later our Ambassador to West Germany, undertook a study of the American high school. In his first report, issued in 1959 and based on an extensive study of a selected group of secondary schools in eighteen states, Conant reaffirmed his belief in the soundness of the comprehensive high school. He suggested, however, a series of steps which he believed

[23] W. Aiken, *The Story of the Eight-Year Study* (New York: Harper & Brothers, 1942), pp. 118–19.

would correct some of its inadequacies. These included the elimination of very small schools, the improvement of student counseling, subject-by-subject ability grouping, more effective instruction for slow learners, the improvement of vocational education so that it would not remain a "dumping ground," and more challenging programs, especially in science, mathematics, and foreign languages, for academically talented students. Because of the importance of the problem, and because of Conant's stature and his record of concern for public education, his words will receive careful attention and his reports will be among the most significant documents in the history of American education.

On the college level, too, important changes had taken place. Emphasis on scientific, technical, and professional studies, begun in the nineteenth century, was increased until the liberal arts college, especially in those aspects concerned with the humanities and to some extent the social sciences, seemed in danger of being pushed into obscurity. The elective system, also started in the nineteenth century, reached its peak and began to decline as more and more colleges came to believe that the "cafeteria" style of education left something to be desired. By mid-century the social sciences and humanities were being restressed as scientists and professionals realized the dangers made obvious by the atomic bomb. Also, the reaction against the elective system set in and the pattern adopted was a prescribed general education program with options in the first two years, followed by specialization in the last two.

Like elementary and secondary education, higher education at mid-century was on a mass-production basis, with New York University enrolling 39,000 students and many other schools, public and private, enrolling over 20,000. It had reached the point where a college enrolling less than 5,000 students was classified as small. At the same time the number of courses offered was increasing, and this, plus the mass enrollment and the frequent transferring of students, made the emphasis upon a quantitative measure more prominent. If it was true that high school students were more concerned with accumulating credits than with learning, it was just as true in the colleges. Moreover many college educators felt there was little unity or continuity in the college program. As in the high schools, students were advised *en masse*, and if any sense of direction or purpose resulted from the experience, it came from the student himself, not from advice received or the program of studies.

The departmentalization and specialization so much a part of modern America was painfully obvious in the universities. From a research standpoint this specialization made sense, but it made the development of an integrated, meaningful curriculum difficult. If the high schools were impersonal, the great universities were equally so, and again it was primarily a matter of costs. Small classes and light teaching loads—essentials of a genuine teaching-learning situation—were pipe dreams in all but the wealthiest schools, and it was the exceptional professor in the large school who knew more about the undergraduate than his name. For the most part this situation was at its worst in the lower division of colleges, somewhat better in the upper division, and generally much better on the graduate levels. Unfortunately, there were signs that graduate instruction too was becoming an impersonal, mass-production affair.

Another development after World War I was what has become known as "big-time football." Almost every college and university fielded a team, and for many it became big business, with as many as 100,000 spectators watching a single game. The best techniques of public relations work and salesmanship, as well as thousands of dollars, went into the persuasion and recruitment of star athletes from the high schools. Some of the schools limited themselves to their own states or regions, but other schools used the whole country as their hunting grounds and held out lowered entrance requirements and lucrative scholarships as bait. Some schools, such as Chicago, abandoned football altogether, whereas others, such as Washington University in St. Louis, experimented with an "amateur" program in which sports were an important part, but only a part, of the educational program. The emphasis upon football led to a situation in which a college was often better known for its football team than for its academic work.

But the veterans' educational program of World War II known as the GI bill gave the colleges a real shot in the arm, and for more than financial reasons. Older and more experienced than other students, the veterans were generally more serious about their work and had more of a sense of direction. In addition, many colleges were concerned with improving their programs and began searching for ways and means of providing a better quality of education despite their financial handicaps. It seemed clear that if the money could be obtained, salaries could be raised, teaching loads could be reduced, and more adequate facilities, particularly libraries, could be provided. If so, there was no reason why American colleges could not provide a caliber of education equal to any in the world, for if the ferment evident among the faculty on many a college campus was any indication, the will to provide such an education existed. Furthermore, America had an abundance of excellent scholars who, if given the means, could do the job. Unfortunately, colleges all over the country, public as well as private, were having budgets cut, not raised, as the tax burden for armaments became increasingly heavy. The private schools, with their tuition charges providing only a part of their costs, looked to big industry for support to build up endowments that had not seen much growth since the depression.

Looking back over the development of the American school system in the last century, one can only marvel at what has been done. Despite its deficiencies, the American public school, in its conception and in its operation, must be ranked with our institutions of law and of representative government among the foremost achievements of man. Without our public schools our democracy would surely wither and die.

However, the fact is that, perhaps without realizing it, we in American education have taken hold of one of the most formidable problems man has ever faced. The problem can be stated simply. We are committed to the democratic proposition that each child—genius or moron, black or white, rich or poor—should be educated to bring out the best that is in him. But there are some 40,000,000 children of school age in America! Moreover, we know that genuine education is a long, slow process. It cannot be handled on a mass-production basis. When we face up to these facts, we realize that to do the job well will take many more teachers and many more classrooms than we had dreamed would be necessary. We have been deluded into thinking that our aim to "educate all the children" can be translated into reality as easily as it can be stated.

Looking back over the development of the public school system in America, it seems clear we have reached a new stage. We have almost done the quantitative job; that is, we have crammed all of our youngsters into schools. The question is: Can we go beyond and provide a high-quality education for all our children, or will we falter and accept the easy solution of mass-production education? It may be, as one foreign educator remarked, that this mass state was a necessary step on the road to the establishment of a fine school system. There is no question of our ability to afford or create such a system, but it will take effort.

Suggested Readings

Butts, R. Freeman: *The American Tradition in Religion and Education.* Boston: The Beacon Press, 1950.
———: *A Cultural History of Western Education,* 2nd ed. New York: McGraw-Hill Book Company, 1955.
———, and Cremin, Lawrence A.: *A History of Education in American Culture.* New York: Henry Holt and Company, 1953.
Cremin, Lawrence A.: *The American Common School.* New York: Bureau of Publications, Teachers College, Columbia University, 1951.
Curti, Merle: *The Social Ideas of American Educators.* New York: Charles Scribner's Sons, 1935.
Noble, Stuart C.: *A History of American Education,* rev. ed. New York: Rinehart & Company, 1954.
Reisner, Edward H.: *The Evolution of the Common School.* New York: The Macmillan Company, 1930.
———: *Historical Foundations of American Education.* New York: The Macmillan Company, 1928.

CHAPTER 7

IDEOLOGICAL CHARACTERISTICS OF
AMERICAN SOCIETY AND EDUCATION

Wᴵᵀᴴ ᴏᴜʀ ꜱᴜʀᴠᴇʏ ᴏꜰ ᴛʜᴇ ʜɪꜱᴛᴏʀʏ ᴏꜰ ᴀᴍᴇʀɪᴄᴀɴ ᴇᴅᴜᴄᴀᴛɪᴏɴ ᴄᴏᴍ-
pleted, we can now turn to the American education system as
it is today. In our historical analysis an attempt was made to
show the relationship between school and society and to show how
changes in society caused changes in the schools. Our next step, before
we go into a detailed account of the school system itself, is to understand
the relationship between contemporary American society and contemporary American education. We have said repeatedly that schools
inevitably reflect their cultures. The problem now is to give this concept meaning by analyzing the basic characteristics of American society
and then showing how these characteristics are reflected in the schools.

At the outset it should be stated that any attempt to analyze a society
as complex as ours is bound to deal in generalizations which will at
every step do violence to reality. For example, the generalization that
America is a democratic society is true, but it is equally true that America
is not completely democratic. Many individual Americans are undemocratic and so are many of our institutions. In the same way the generalization that America is a nationalistic society, although certainly true,
must be qualified by the fact that many Americans are strongly inter-
nationalist or world-minded, whereas some place their allegiance to God
above the nation. Nevertheless, both of these generalizations are so
obviously true that they must be listed as two of the basic ideological
characteristics of American society. Furthermore, no claim is made that
the following analysis is exhaustive and complete, for America is a complicated society. Still the characteristics discussed in this chapter and
Chapter 8 do exist in our society, and they do have their parallels in
the schools. Our obligation to understand and improve both our schools

and our society requires us to make the effort to understand the relationship between the two.

One other fact must be established before we attempt our analysis. All of the aspects of our society are interrelated and, in reality, cannot be separated except for purposes of analysis. Growing knowledge of the nature of this interrelationship has led social scientists to develop the concept of the organic nature of society described by Professor Childs:

> A society is neither an organism nor is it a mere aggregation of discrete interests and practices. Its various activities—technological, economic, social, political, scientific, artistic, religious and educational have mutually conditioned one another in a common process of social development, and as a result they now function as an interrelated whole.[1]

Therefore it should be kept in mind that all of the aspects of our society and our schools are closely linked and constantly interact with and condition one another. When changes occur in one segment, for example in science or technology, the impact is bound to be felt in other areas.

Democracy and Education

ONE of the most basic ideological characteristics of American society is that it is democratic. Although volumes have been written on the meaning of democracy, in essence it is a system in which the individual human being is the center of value and in which all political, social, and economic institutions serve his well-being. Thus Jefferson in the Declaration of Independence declared that:

> Governments are instituted among Men, deriving their just powers from the consent of the governed,—That whenever any Form of Government becomes destructive of these ends, it is the Right of the People to alter or abolish it, and to institute new Government, laying its foundation on such principles, and organizing its power in such form, as to them shall seem most likely to effect their Safety and Happiness.

And Lincoln in his Gettysburg Address speaks of "government of the people, by the people, and for the people."

The ends of democracy, then, are individual human beings. The means of democracy are the principles, the values, and the institutions that serve these ends. It does not follow that individuals in a democratic

[1] John L. Childs, *Education and Morals* (New York: Appleton-Century-Crofts, 1950), p. 208.

society are passive beneficiaries of some mysterious force called the "democratic way of life," although many Americans seem to take this attitude. Rather these principles, values, and institutions have been, and will continue to be, created by individuals on the basis of their individual and group experience. In each generation decisions must be made as to whether institutions promote or hinder human dignity and welfare, and each generation must apply meaning and give substance to these principles and values. For example, slavery as an institution, as well as the body of beliefs that supported it, was considered to be in conflict with the democratic ideal and was therefore eliminated from our society. On the other hand, an institution such as the public school, consistent with our democratic ideal, has been accepted and maintained as a basic element in our society, although the schools have been undergoing change, for example, to give substance to our idea of equality of opportunity.

If we were to set forth the basic values and ideals of democracy they would include the following: First and foremost, as has been mentioned, are the worth of the individual human being and the concept that the enhancement of individual life is the end of all social and political institutions. Second is a series of values which may be thought of as means of achieving our first ideal. These include concepts such as the equality of all individuals regardless of race, creed, or national origin. Closely related to equality is the concept of equality of opportunity which is so fundamental in our society. Since it is fact that not all human beings are equal in ability or interests, the concept of *equality of opportunity* is most applicable in the realm of education and economics. On the other hand *absolute equality* should prevail in the field of social, political, and legal activities. In addition to equality are the great rights and freedoms expressed in our Bill of Rights. Freedom of conscience, of speech, of thought, and of press are foremost among the freedoms. Among the rights are those of assembly and association, trial by jury, and freedom from arbitrary arrest.

Also inherent in democracy are other values, such as faith in reason and in freedom of thought, which are products of the humanistic tradition started by the Greeks. During the Enlightenment faith in reason was applied to man and the universe, and the result was a faith in the common man and his potential for progress and perfectibility which is a basic ingredient in our democracy. This faith finds expression in our conception of *self*-government—that is, that man can and should govern himself.

These basic values and ideals have been translated into certain democratic practices which are also characteristic of democracy. Among these are: representative and constitutional government, including our system of law and courts; rule of the majority while recognizing the rights of the minority; periodic elections; a plural party system; the absence of privileged groups, whether they be based on birth or position or wealth; civilian control of the military; separation of church and state and development of the secular state; and finally, a system of public schools.

A good example of the application of the logic of democracy in American society can be seen in the degree of freedom and equality that women enjoy. American women have a high degree of legal equality with men and certainly are not socially inferior, or in any way subservient, to men. Since 1919 when they were granted suffrage women have been on an equal political footing with men and we have had women in both the House and the Senate and occasionally in the Cabinet of the federal government. Women are prominent in most professions including medicine, law, and teaching, and more and more of them are entering scientific fields. Women are to be found working in factories and driving buses, and they are enlisted in great numbers in the armed forces although they are not used in combat. It is true, of course, that women do not have absolute equality with men in many fields. Moreover, because of the biological fact of child bearing, the roles of men and women are bound to be different in some respects. Nevertheless, women have come a long way since they received the right to vote in 1919 and are, apparently, well on their way toward equality in all areas of our society.

The fact that America is a democratic country in which men are free to assemble and to associate, plus the fact that America is a complex industrial nation with many competing interests have led to the development of a group society. Despite the fact that America is extremely individualistic, it is probably correct to say that in our country's actual functioning these competing interests—sometimes called "pressure groups"—have superseded the individual as the unit of power. It is generally believed, and probably true, that if an individual wishes to achieve something he must work through a group or organization. Certainly in the political field it is the well-organized "pressure group" which makes itself felt and gets results.

There are literally thousands of organizations in America, and it is not unusual for an individual to belong to several at the same time. As one American historian put it, "Americans are a nation of joiners." There are political, business, labor, farm, religious, professional, military, patriotic, and fraternal organizations in almost every community in America. Each group has its own reason for being. Many represent vested interests of some kind, and the individual members feel that something is to be gained by joining. Often membership in such organizations as business and professional groups or fraternities and sororities is related to the individual's striving for success and may give him status in the community.

The influence of democracy upon the schools can be seen in many ways. Most important of all is the concern of the school with the fullest development of the individual. As one of our leading educators put it, our education "involves nothing less than the guiding of the individual to full maturity and freedom." [2] Considering that the individual is the center of value in our society this is a logical and natural development. Moreover, especially in the last generation, partly because of the influence of the mental hygiene movement, but partly through a better understanding of the nature of democracy, children are being treated with more respect and not beaten about as they were in many a school a generation ago. This concern for the individual can be seen in the elementary schools in the attempt to provide a suitable environment for the varying talents of all the children. The same is true in the secondary schools and in colleges, both of which provide a wide assortment of programs. The elective system now used in virtually all secondary schools and colleges was developed in part at least because it was more consistent with democracy. The whole guidance movement is based upon the desire to help children to help themselves academically, socially, and vocationally. The Liberal Arts college with its emphasis upon leading students to be independent, inquiring individuals is also one of the clear manifestations of democracy in education. It is no accident that institutions of higher learning that emphasize these points have been either severely limited or entirely absent in the totalitarian states.

The influence of democracy can be seen in many other ways in our schools. Our belief in freedom of conscience has led us to protect children from religious indoctrination in the public schools but has also enabled religious schools to flourish. The concept of self-government has its logical development in our practice of compulsory education, for if all individuals are to be citizens participating in government, they need to be educated. At first glance it would seem that forcing a child to go to school is not very democratic, but the important point is that this decision was made by the adult Americans (who presumably know better than the child what he needs) and can be changed by them at any time.

The influence of democracy can be seen in the development of the single or common-school system which all children attend as opposed to the dual system "one for the masses and one for the classes" that has been used in many societies. Horace Mann's idea in setting up the common school was that it would be a democratic institution in which all children would get to know each other and thereby avoid class conflicts. Of course the strength of the belief in equality of opportunity made a class system of schools impossible. It is this belief which is gradually but surely breaking down segregation in the schools since it is obvious that the Negro schools are not equal.

[2] George S. Counts, *Education and American Civilization* (New York: Bureau of Publications, Teachers College, Columbia University, 1952), p. 460.

The influence of democracy can also be seen in the education of women. All of our public schools are coeducational and although few girls take machine shop and few boys take home economics, this is a reflection of the probable difference in function after graduation. In other aspects of the school program the equality of women is evident. Women far outnumber men in teaching positions. More and more of them are going into administrative positions, particularly as principals. In both of these areas the majority of women are on an equal basis with men so far as salary is concerned. Finally, more and more women are serving on school boards.

The fact that America is a group society has had some important implications for the schools. The primary reason is that many of these groups have attempted at various times to interfere with the operation of the school. Most often this has taken the form of attempts to determine what should or should not be taught in the schools. Thus at times the teaching of the theory of evolution was forced out of the schools. In New York in 1950 the Christian Science Church succeeded in having a law passed by the state legislature which permitted its children to be excused from attending health and hygiene courses that conflicted with the principles of their religion.[3] At other times groups have constituted special committees to see that nothing un-American was being taught and they have had their own definitions of what constitutes un-American. In recent years pressure groups have been successful in some cities such as Los Angeles in having United Nations and UNESCO programs and materials removed from the schools because these materials were supposedly subversive.[4] These attacks upon the contents of instruction may be made directly upon the school, or indirectly either through the legislature (for example, in the form of loyalty oaths) or through influencing public opinion by means of newspaper or radio.

The other line of attack taken by special interest groups has been to bring pressure upon individuals—teachers, administrators, and board members—who are connected with the schools. Thus in recent years such outstanding American educators as Willard Goslin and George Stoddard have been removed from their jobs. In Houston, Texas, a few years ago Dr. George W. Ebey, an assistant superintendent of schools, was accused of being pro-communist in anonymous letters. An exhaustive investigation was carried out by a group of former FBI men who cleared him of the charges. Nevertheless, the board of education voted against rehiring him on the ground that the public had probably lost confidence in him.[5]

Not all groups in America have attempted to bring pressure to bear

[3] *New York Times*, March 15, 1950, p. 22.
[4] *Ibid.*, January 21, 1953, p. 33.
[5] *St. Louis Post-Dispatch*, July 16, 1953, p. 16.

upon the schools. On the contrary, many groups including business, labor, religious and professional groups, have actively supported and defended the schools. For example, Walter Reuther, president of the powerful Automotive Workers Union, has vigorously supported the schools and their right to the freedom of teaching and learning. However, the main defense of the schools against the attacks of pressure groups has come from the professional teachers' organizations. In 1952 in California a high school social studies teacher was accused by a radio commentator of being friendly to communism. Almost immediately she was shunned by students, and parents began calling the school. Both her job and her reputation were in jeopardy. At this point the California State Teachers Association investigated the charges, found them to be false and provided the teacher with legal counsel. The result was that both the commentator and the station were sued, found guilty, and forced to pay some $50,000 in damages.[6] Alone, this teacher would have been helpless. With a strong professional organization behind her, she and the schools were saved.

It is clear that the actions of these groups upon the schools are more pronounced in periods of stress and strain. It can be shown, for example, that in each period of crisis the demand for the administration of loyalty oaths to teachers is greater, as though this action would solve the problem. The results of tension of the last decade can be seen in the emphasis upon loyalty oaths and in the reluctance of many teachers, administrators, and textbook publishers to handle controversial issues.

In a free society such as ours the formation of groups is inevitable. Moreover it is evident that very many of them have contributed to human welfare. However, the public schools, because they are public, are inevitably affected by public opinion and by public pressure. The question, then, is not one of doing away with pressure groups since this would be possible only in a totalitarian state, but rather one of how they should function in a democracy. Specifically, what should be the relationship between these groups and the public schools which must serve *all* the people and not just one segment of them?

In the organization, operation, and administration of our schools the influence of democracy is apparent. The public schools are controlled by a board of lay citizens elected by the people. The people decide upon the amount of taxes that are to be levied to raise funds to support the schools. In recent years great efforts have been made to bring parents into the schools through the Parent Teacher Associations and to have them participate in the running of the schools. Parents and citizens are

[6] *NEA Journal*, October, 1953, p. 397.

free to visit the schools and talk to the teachers at any time. In the classroom the friendly relationship between teachers and students and the stress placed upon student discussion, activity, and participation is certainly democratic. Many schools and many classrooms have student councils, in an attempt to give students a voice and to have them represented. Unfortunately, the student government movement has often bogged down and is either dropped or becomes window dressing without any real function. This is likely to occur when teachers are unwilling to give the students any real responsibility and authority, and the students learn this quickly. It may also occur (although less frequently) that students are given responsibility they are unable to assume.

In the administration of the schools, of course, the election of the school board is a democratic pattern. But even within the schools the pressure to develop democratic administration is great, and while it has by no means been achieved, as an ideal it is unquestioned. The idea is that any person who is affected by a policy should have a voice in formulating that policy with, of course, due regard to maturity and competence. In any group of American school administrators the question of what is democratic administration and how can it be put into practice is a main topic of discussion.

In the school itself any list of objectives will reflect the democratic concept. Teachers are likely to try to develop behavior patterns such as co-operation, initiative, responsibility, concern for others, open mindedness, critical thinking, etc. Moreover, if an examination were made of any course of study or of any textbook in use in the American schools, the emphasis upon the aspects of democracy that have been mentioned would be immediately apparent. For example, the strong faith in law as an essential element of democracy is reflected in the schools from the first grade on through college. Particular emphasis is placed upon the Constitution as the basic law of the land and upon gaining the pupils' loyalty and respect for that document. Courses in civics and government are a part of every curriculum in every school in the country. In the literature the young American reads he is reminded again and again of the desirability of law and order. In the stories about the development of the frontier—the westerns—the central theme is the bringing of law and order to the West so that decent people could live in peace.

In these ways, therefore, democracy and education are interrelated in America. More important perhaps is their mutual dependence for it is not too much to say that democracy could not endure without education and especially public education. Nor could free public school systems, in which freedom of inquiry and of teaching and learning is central, exist apart from a democratic society. Thus the relationship, that of mutual dependence, is the closest of all possible relationships.

Nationalism and Education

AMERICA is a nation-state. The human beings who live within her boundaries are Americans and somehow this sets them apart from the human beings that inhabit the rest of the earth. A person who lives north of an imaginary line drawn across the continent of North American is different from us—he is a Canadian. This same pattern is in existence all over the world, and in the middle of the twentieth century the human race is divided into some seventy-odd nations. In each of these political entities the inhabitants or citizens are apt to regard their nation as the center of the universe. In each nation strong loyalties exist for the political entity and this loyalty is symbolized by flags, national anthems, national heroes, and national myths and legends. In each nation the individual is a "citizen" which involves certain rights and duties. One of the worst punishments that can be inflicted upon an individual is to lose his citizenship. Consider the plight of the "man without a country" in the famous story read by millions of American school children.

Historically, nationalism as we know it orginated in Europe in the eighteenth century and its nature and development can best be seen there. As originally developed it was simply an awakening of a people to an appreciation of a common historic, cultural, and linguistic heritage. Such things as folk songs and legends were revived and hailed as bonds of union among certain people who claimed some kind of geographical or linguistic unity. As thus expressed, nationalism was a beautiful and enriching series of life experiences for peoples. However, in the storm and stress of the nineteenth century, nations began, through the media of the newly established daily newspapers and through the educational system, to channel this force toward other ends.

It was almost inevitable, given the system of competitive national states that existed in Europe in the nineteenth century, that friction would develop among them. Given this friction, it was almost inevitable that enterprising men would rally the national forces, because bargaining power at the conference table was directly related to the strength of the nation. In building up the national power the mass educational facilities and the cheap newspaper (the result of new printing processes) were made to order. Men were taught love of country and, especially in time of war, hatred toward the enemy. Moreover, much of the indoctrination was carried on unconsciously, even on the highest levels, and therefore made each national group's superiority appear as natural as sunlight. Thus presented, the nationalistic tradition became part of the man and he could not easily escape its influence.

Judging from the way nationalism has spread and been received by human beings (most recently in Asia, Africa, and the Middle East), it must be conceded that it has a strong psychological basis. This basis is the strong attachment or sense of belonging men have or can develop through education for the land in which they live. One has only to realize the emotional effect that a picture of the flag, coupled with the playing of a military air and marching soldiers, sailors, or marines has on the citizen. Once developed, it has a powerful emotional hold on the individual and the unfortunate fact is that this emotional potential can be stirred to a white heat in time of war or near war. As one historian has stated it: "When anxious nations faced one another across fortified frontiers, the sentiment of nationalism inevitably intensified." [7]

It is no mere accident that all four dictators—Hitler, Mussolini, Stalin, and Tojo—have made their appeal on the basis of love of country, fatherland, or motherland. But the power of nationalism preceded the dictators and was a powerful factor in the European conflicts throughout the nineteenth century as well as in World War I. Indeed it has been so potent that one historian has described it as follows:

> For millions of deluded folk it became a stronger force than religion, surpassing Christianity in its appeal to the emotion and to the spirit of sacrifice in a holy cause. Men died for the honor of the flag as cheerfully as any martyrs had ever laid down their lives for the glory of the Cross.[8]

Thus it is not difficult to understand why millions of men were willing to fight and die in World War I against men whom they did not know and had no reason to dislike, and this for four long years.

The pride in country which is the essential element of nationalism is everywhere evident in America. And when this feeling is coupled with the great beauty and the fabulous natural wealth of the country, which has been developed into power and production through industrialization, this pride has easily developed into a feeling of superiority. Thus we hear that America is the "greatest land of all" and we accept this as self-evident. Our sporting events are preceded by a playing of the national anthem and a raising of the flag. Our public buildings, our schools, our business houses and even our churches are bedecked with flags and other nationalistic symbols. We have set aside days honoring national heroes and great national events. America has many patriotic organizations which constantly remind the public of how patriotic they are and urge other Americans to do as they do.

Other examples of the reality of nationalism abound in America. We justify actions taken in the operation of our foreign policy on the

[7] Ralph H. Gabriel, *The Course of American Democratic Thought.* Copyright 1940, The Ronald Press Company. P. 345.

[8] E. M. Burns, *Western Civilization* (New York: W. W. Norton & Company, 1941), p. 709.

grounds of "national self-interest." Our president, as well as other government officials, is committed to a program that will "further the interests of the United States" and we accept this as natural and right. We sometimes fail to realize that other nations act upon the same policy and when they do and their action conflicts with our own interests, we are likely to be unhappy. To some of us, America has always been just and honorable, and in any dispute with another nation we often view the other nation as causing the difficulty. It is sometimes a shock to Americans to learn that America has not always been saintly in her dealings with other nations, particularly those in Latin America and Asia. It is clear that America as a nation has on the whole acted fairly and justly with other nations. Only through the rosy glasses of national pride can it be seen that we have always done so.

In our thinking, if something can be shown to be American, and especially "typically American" or the "American way" we are for it; if it is foreign we are suspicious and generally we are against it. In our emphasis upon Americanism some of us become concerned (especially in a time of trouble) with un-American activity and we have an Un-American Activities Committee in Congress. Some of us, because of our concern for nationalism, are fearful of words like internationalism, worldmindedness, and world citizenship. This fear has led to the removal of materials on the United Nations and UNESCO from the schools in some cities. This fear of foreign "isms" has led to loyalty oaths and to laws requiring the study of the Constitution in schools. It has led to the demand that the time-honored story of Robin Hood be taken from the schools because it was, someone thought, un-American. It has led us to be disturbed when some religious group has refused to salute the flag.

We also tend to associate nationalism with the army and navy and thus our holidays are generally marked by parades by these organizations. This association of patriotism with the military is of course a characteristic of nationalism wherever it is found. To some extent the modern conception of a nation does not differ significantly from that presented by Admiral Mahan in 1890 when he said that a nation must be thought of as a fort with its boundaries being its exterior walls and its population its garrison.[9] One distinguished American historian has summed up the consequences of nationalism in America as follows:

> From the beginning nationalism has been an essential part of the pattern of the American democratic faith. Nationalism has been the core of the doctrine of the mission of America. The time has now come, however, when twentieth century nationalism, in the form evolving upon the continent of Europe, threatens every other doctrine of the American democratic pattern. Nationalism, creating the

[9] Gabriel, *op. cit.*, p. 346.

leviathan State, challenges the ideal of the free individual. The exact uniformity of the column marching under orders becomes the approved behavior for the individual. Nationalism threatens also that old belief in a fundamental law governing nations as well as men, the belief in a natural and moral law before which not only all men but all nation-states are equal and from which men and nations derive equal and unalienable rights. When nationalism evolves into State worship, the nation becomes a law unto itself. Its moral code is founded on pragmatic expediency. The logic of twentieth century nationalism, with its emphasis upon power and self-sufficiency, drives inexorably toward increasing the size and the resources of the national group. If the power of a particular nation-state can be augmented by devouring a smaller neighbor, the conquest is good. Under the influence of this logic international relations have undergone a devolution toward the code of the jungle. The result is a paradox. Extreme collectivism, totalitarianism within the nations has bred the opposite extreme, anarchy, among the nations. Nationalism, the security formula of the twentieth century, has filled the peoples of the world with apprehension.[10]

That America is a nationalistic society is a reality which, like many other things, has its good and bad sides. On the one hand, there is a tremendous amount of security and satisfaction and sheer happiness in being an American, especially when we recall the great words of the Declaration of Independence and the Gettysburg Address and the great achievements of our people, including our role in Korea. On the other hand, we should be aware of the fact that nationalism has had its unfortunate side. It has puffed nations up with false pride, led to feelings of superiority, and has been a major factor in the anarchy of the twentieth century.

The basic fact so far as nationalism and education are concerned is that nationalism is nurtured and developed through the process of education both in schools and out. From the time a child is born he is influenced by the fact that he is an American and not a Russian, a Frenchman, or a Mexican. Once he is old enough to speak, he will speak our language. As soon as he is able to understand, his parents will tell him perhaps the story of the cherry tree or of the battle of Bunker Hill or of the struggles with the Indians. Once he is able to read, he will encounter constantly the symbols of Americanism. After a while he will study history and citizenship. He will salute the flag and learn the pledge of allegiance and the national anthem. He will be surrounded by pictures of Washington, Lincoln, and Jefferson and will study the lives of these great men and what they have done for America. It is no exag-

[10] *Ibid.*, pp. 416–17.

geration to say that developing citizens loyal to our country is the first concern of the American schools, as it is the first concern of schools in every other nation-state.

A few years ago a great deal of national bias was to be found in textbooks, particularly in the history texts. It is interesting to compare the account of the battle of Bunker Hill in some of these books with the account in a British text of the same period. There were some who defended this lack of objectivity on the grounds that it was wrong to teach the young anything unfavorable about their country. It is obvious that such a practice would make international understanding more difficult, to say the least. In the last generation, however, the texts are much improved and a more objective account is given. Even so, *UNESCO* thought the problem important enough to commission a group of historians to write an objective history of mankind that would not represent the point of view of any nation, and would attempt to record what had actually happened insofar as this was humanly possible.

One of the problems created by the strength of nationalism is the emphasis placed upon the particular nation in the schools while practically excluding the rest of the world. Where this occurs, it breeds a very strong feeling of ethnocentrism which is anachronistic in our modern interdependent world. Since World War II, real efforts have been made to place more emphasis upon other countries and people, both in the schools and in the teacher training institutions. For example, some colleges are providing opportunities for young teachers to spend some time studying in other countries. In addition, teacher exchanges are being encouraged. Many American teachers are teaching abroad and many foreign teachers are teaching in America. The problem of developing an intelligent national loyalty that recognizes the rights as well as the contributions of other nations is one of the foremost tasks in American education.

Individualism and Education

A COMBINATION of circumstances has worked to make America a highly individualistic society, and this individualism has been channeled into the striving for achievement or "success." These circumstances are: the nature of democracy which makes the individual the center of value; the influence of the frontier where rugged individualism came close to being a reality and where a man was judged not on the basis of who his father was but upon his own action; the influence of the free enterprise, capitalistic, profit-motive system based on competition; and finally, the fact that America was a fabulously rich country and the opportunities for accumulating wealth were great. Combine all these factors and then remember that Americans were largely from the poorer classes of Europe who had come to this country seeking a better life, it is not difficult to understand the emphasis placed upon success.

To say that this emphasis upon individualism and success is pervasive is to understate the case. It is probably the dominant force in the life of the average American. It spurs men on to almost superhuman efforts in terms of work and sacrifice. In our society the ideal for a human being is to be "successful," and usually, although not always, success is based upon the accumulation of wealth. Generally the business executive or the banker is placed at the top of the social scale by Americans themselves. Similarly, when an American speaks of a successful lawyer or doctor, he generally means one who has succeeded financially. A successful farmer is one who has a big, fine farm, etc. On the other side, if a man loses out financially he is generally regarded as a failure, whatever else he may have achieved. There are of course other criteria for success in a complex society like America. For example, many parents would consider a son successful who went into the ministry. However, for the society as a whole, all-important success is generally measured in financial terms.

One well-known saying that reflects the emphasis upon success as well as the democratic nature of America, is the saying that "any boy can grow up to be president." While it would not be possible at this time for a Negro boy to be president, it is true that Abraham Lincoln, Harry Truman, and Dwight Eisenhower were certainly just plain, ordinary people. Here the relationship between the democratic concept of equality of opportunity and individual success becomes important. If all individuals are to strive for success in a democratic society, there must be no handicaps. As one author has stated:

> To Americans the world is an arena and life is a race. And they are less inclined to inquire after the nature of the stakes than they are to ask whether the conditions are fair and the best man wins.[11]

This combination, together with America's great natural wealth, is responsible for the label given America as the "land of opportunity." This whole characteristic of America was exemplified in a story entitled "What America Means to Me" by Kirk Douglas, one of Hollywood's leading actors.

> That's what America means most to me—opportunity. Can you imagine a fellow like me getting the breaks I've had in any country but America? I'm just a plain, ordinary guy from plain, simple folks. But I've had a good education and I have a good job. . . . My

---

[11] George S. Counts, *The American Road to Culture* (New York: The John Day Company, 1930), p. 60.

parents came from Russia. They were simple, peasant people. They arrived here with their hearts full of dreams. They heard that the streets were paved with gold and they believed it! It wasn't too long ago that my mother told me that she had found something better than gold bricks in the United States. She found freedom and a country where she and my father could raise a family of seven children and see all of them grow up in comfort. Each one was able to get an education and to choose a way of life.[12]

At its finest the emphasis upon individual success has been a source of inspiration and of hope for a better future, and who can say how many times the rags to riches story has been a reality in America. At its worst it has degenerated into a selfish seeking for wealth with a callous disregard for anything or anyone in the way. In many cases it has resulted in setting goals too high and has produced frustrated individuals who are never satisfied with what they have and spend their lives in a restless seeking for something better, while making themselves and their entire families miserable. This philosophy would seem to be at odds with the Christian doctrine of spurning material wealth and giving to the poor. However, somewhere, somehow, Americans have developed a saying that "God helps him who helps himself." And so God is used as an authority to bolster individualism. This saying could be interpreted to mean that the individual has to make some effort and that God can't or won't do it all. But it is used more often to mean that "It's every man for himself and the devil take the hindmost."

Individualism has also tended to promote the illusion of the "self-made man" as though the individual existed in isolation from society and as though his success or failure depended entirely upon his own behavior. This has led many Americans to overlook the fact that they must co-operate with their fellowmen to create a society in which individual initiative and creative ability can have a chance. During the thirties many a high school graduate was given a stirring send-off by a commencement speaker exhorting him to conquer the world, only to find after walking the streets for several months that something was wrong. He was given little inkling that the country was in bad shape (of course, he could sense it at home and in the community) or that he and others like him working together could do something about it.

The desire to have the material comforts of life, to be well fed, to be warm, well housed, and well clothed, and even the desire for the luxuries of life are certainly understandable, as is the need for recognition. And many of those in other countries who criticize our "crass materialism" would be only too happy to have our plumbing and sewage systems and many of our other luxuries that can make life so much more

<hr>

[12] *Parade*, February 14, 1954, p. 2.

pleasant. However, when the material things become the end of life we may be in danger. In a sense the American people are pioneers in a vast experiment. We are the first people in history to achieve such a high standard of living, a standard that the other peoples of the world will probably achieve in time. The question is whether we can use the material things to produce a richer, fuller life or whether the material side will be dominant. If the latter, American life will degenerate into a rat race to accumulate more and better gadgets. George Counts stated the problem very well when he wrote that:

> As life is more than the bare physical necessities of food, clothing, shelter, so civilization is more than economics. . . . Men may be free, equal, secure and well fed, they may fly around the earth in a few hours and to the moon in as many days, they may even be able to remove mountains and change the courses of great rivers, yet they may fail in some realms of the mind to reach the heights scaled by the ancient Athenians or the men of the Elizabethan age. The central purpose of economic and political institutions is to provide the material base and social conditions essential to the release and fulfillment of the creative powers of the species.[13]

In recent years the concept of "rugged individualism" has been tempered somewhat as Americans are apparently beginning to recognize the interdependent nature of our society. The factory worker, for example, is helpless when the factory shuts down. He can go to another factory but if the conditions of the depression years prevail, there will be many more applicants than there are jobs. If this man lives in a city, he probably couldn't grow more than a few potatoes in his small yard. The same is true for any of our professional people. All are specialists and while we have been able to progress because of this specialization, it is important to remember that we are dependent on each other. Even the farmer has become a specialist and is dependent on the market. If our government stopped price supports to farmers and they were left on their own, they, as well as the rest of the country, would soon be in extreme difficulty.

As a result such things as social security and unemployment insurance, as well as government planning to prevent economic depression are accepted by both major parties. We are apparently beginning to realize that the individual can achieve true individuality only by cooperating with his fellow men. There are signs, too, that more and more Americans are beginning to realize that success is more than the amassing of wealth. Finally, there are indications that Americans are setting more reasonable goals for themselves, goals that are consistent with their abilities. We know that not every child has the ability to be a doctor, a

[13] George S. Counts, *Education and American Civilization* (New York: Bureau of Publications, Teachers College, Columbia University, 1952), p. 383.

lawyer, an engineer, or a teacher and this is no disgrace. We know all too well the disastrous effects of telling a youngster that he can be what he wants to be if he will only work hard enough, if the child aims for a career for which he doesn't have the ability. On the other hand, we should not forget that willingness to work and work hard can compensate to some extent for lack of natural ability.

Since individual success is one of the dominant values in America, it is natural that this value should be nurtured through education. And since in modern America the school is the chief educational agency, it is natural that individual success should be emphasized there. Actually the concern over individual success and its corollary, equality of opportunity, were two of the main reasons for the founding of the free, public, common elementary school in the 1830's and for the extension of that free public system upward through the nineteenth and twentieth centuries. More than any other agency, the American public schools have equalized opportunity and thereby made a contribution to the struggle for individual success in America. This is done through the famous "ladder system" which one author described:

> The pride of the American school system and a major contribution to the advance of civilization is the educational ladder. This ladder, composed of the elementary school, the secondary school, and the state university, constitutes a continuous and unbroken program of instruction from early childhood to maturity and from the first beginnings of school education to the most advanced forms of professional training and graduate study. If the influence of family fortune and tradition is disregarded, the individual in his progress up this ladder encounters no barrier beyond the increasing difficulty of the ascent and the limitations set by his own capacities. The entire range of institutions involved is supported by the state and any individual able to meet the very modest scholastic requirements enforced is free to attend.[14]

Thus if the world is an arena and life is a race, education is a track and Americans intend to see to it that there are no handicaps imposed. This accounts for the efforts to provide federal aid to education. Some poorer states that make a real effort are still unable to provide an education equal in quality to that provided by the wealthier states. The same principle is applied in the granting of state school funds within the states as they attempt to see that the children in the poorer sections get an education equal to that of other children in the state.

The school cannot completely equalize opportunity. Despite the schools, most youngsters follow in the footsteps of their parents. The

[14] George S. Counts, *The American Road to Culture* (New York: The John Day Company, 1930), p. 65.

study of youth in Elmtown indicated that, in general, students from the lower socio-economic groups took the general and the commercial programs, while the majority of those from the upper groups went into the college preparatory programs.[15] Also, a recent study of the background and training of sixty-five of our leading scientists showed that most of them came from the upper-middle socio-economic groups.[16] Nevertheless, despite the fact that climbing to the top of the educational ladder and therefore lifting oneself in society is a difficult task, it can be done, and it is done in America.

The emphasis placed upon individual success in America is also partly responsible for our belief in the monetary value of schooling. Studies have been made which attempt to show that a positive relationship exists between the time spent in schools and income.[17] A reading of the advertisement section of an American newspaper will reveal ads which make this same point. Getting a high school diploma will mean a better job. Attending night classes will result in a promotion. A survey of public opinion made a few years ago by Elmo Roper indicated that the overwhelming majority of American parents wanted their sons to go to college and the reason given in most cases was that this would enable them to get better jobs and help them be successful. It seems clear that:

> The assumption that educational opportunities, provided at public expense, should be judged in terms of their money value to the person receiving them reveals the extent to which the new pecuniary order and the ideal of individual success have come to dominate their theory of education.[18]

In many instances this emphasis upon the cash value of education has led to an attitude on the part of the student that a college education has to be gone through and put up with in order to get into a desired position. With this attitude it is clear that the more quickly and easily the thing can be accomplished, the better.

In the schoolroom itself the stress upon individual success is obvious. It can be seen in the contents of the texts that tell of the rags-to-riches success stories, although that theme is not stressed as much as it used to be. Combined with the emphasis upon competition, it can be seen in the grading system and the awarding of stars in the elementary school, and awards and honors in the upper grades for achievement, both academic and otherwise. The basis for motivation largely stresses individual success and competition with other students. Unfortunately,

[15] A. B. Hollingshead, *Elmtown's Youth* (New York: John Wiley & Sons, 1949), p. 168.
[16] A. Roe, *The Making of a Scientist* (New York: Dodd, Mead & Company, 1953), pp. 66–8.
[17] Counts, *The American Road to Culture*, p. 68.
[18] *Ibid.*, pp. 68–9.

very often the tangible symbols of achievement, the grades, become the dominant factor and the knowledge that was learned or not learned is considered unimportant. In these cases grades, not knowledge and understanding, become the ends of education.

In most school systems in the country teachers who have a master's degree receive more money than those who do not regardless of their teaching ability. In many school systems teachers are required to earn a certain number of credits to get their salary increases. Regardless of what they know or learn, if they accumulate the "hours" they get the increase. Part of the problem is due to the difficulty of evaluating the ability of teachers. It is much easier to determine whether they have so many hours of credit. In this way we force the teacher into gathering credits instead of knowledge.

Individualism is also manifested in the schools in the sports programs. Although these activities are generally team sports and require a high degree of co-operation the recognition is in the form of individual rewards. Athletes who make the teams are awarded honors in the form of "letters" and gain wide acclaim from students, faculty, and community alike. In recent years achievement in athletics has often become more important than the academic work, and many high schools and colleges are better known for their athletic teams than they are for their teaching or research. Recently the entire sports program has been examined and aspects of it criticized by the Educational Policies Commission, probably the most influential group of educators in America. The crux of the criticism was that sports were being overemphasized and that steps should be taken to place them in their proper place within the total educational program.

Christianity, Secularism, and Education

CLOSELY related to democracy in its influence upon Americans have been the moral and ethical values and religious beliefs of Christianity. Actually democracy and Christianity have been so closely interrelated in the history of western civilization as to be in reality inseparable. The basic values in both reflect this interrelationship. In both the dignity and worth of the individual are foremost. In both, the concepts of the essential equality and brotherhood of man are central. In both, the value of peace is prevalent over the value of war. It is no accident that some of the great Christians like John Wycliffe and Roger Williams were also great democrats.

Of course, many Christians have been anything but democratic and the Christian faith has been used to justify such an undemocratic practice as slavery. Moreover, some of the most brutal wars ever fought have been fought ostensibly for Christianity, while some of the most brutal acts of torture have been committed in its name. It is also true that some of the great human beings, such as Mahatma Gandhi, were not Christians. Furthermore, many of these great values, such as equality and brotherhood, preceded Christianity, can be traced back to the Old Testament and beyond, and are to be found in the other great religions of the world. As was mentioned earlier, the values of the Judaic and Christian traditions are so similar and have been blended for so long that they are often considered together as part of the cultural heritage of Western civilization. Certainly, this mixture continues to exist and influence American society, since 6,000,000 Americans are Jews. Nevertheless, it is the Christian tradition that has had the most influence upon America.

The majority of Americans today belong to a Christian church, and many who do not still consider themselves Christians. They are apt to accept without question such practices as monotheism and monogamy as well as the other aspects of the Ten Commandments. The churches of America are prominent in both urban and rural areas. Sunday morning will find millions of Americans in churches and Sunday schools, and the overwhelming majority of them will be in one of the hundreds of different Christian churches that thrive here. Moreover, for millions of Americans in both city and country the church is the center of social as well as religious life. The most prominent holidays in America—Christmas and Easter—are of course the great and important days for all Christian groups.

It is true, of course, that not all Americans are Christian, even some who claim to be. In some instances those who attend church regularly violate in their daily lives the basic tenets of the faith. In many cases conflicts and contradictions exist side by side in the same individual. For example, an American's religious beliefs tell him to love his fellowmen, while his business philosophy may be "every man for himself and the devil take the hindmost." Or his religion may tell him to take what he has and give it to the poor, while social pressure urges him to accumulate wealth. His religion may tell him that all men are equal before God, but his church may not admit Negroes. His religion may tell him that the meek and humble shall inherit the earth, but he strives to get into a position of authority.

It seems that, to some extent at least, Americans are able to compartmentalize their lives. They often accept one set of values in the home and church and another in the business world. If they realize the inconsistency, they may justify it on the grounds that the teachings of Jesus "are all right in their place but a man would starve if he practiced them in his business." In the world of sports the "great competitors" are often quoted to the effect that "nice guys don't win pennants." Finally, there are those among us in America, such as Gerald L. K. Smith, who, while calling their groups "Christian" groups and while mentioning God's name in every other line of their propaganda, actually preach a doctrine of hate.

The majority of Americans accept and believe in the basic moral and ethical values of Christianity, however, and for the most part, act upon them. When we consider the dog-eat-dog competition that the individual encounters, especially in periods of economic difficulty, it is surprising that there is as much gentleness, kindness, and charity as there is, and there is a great deal.

Despite the fact that America is a strongly Christian society, it is also a secular society. Inasmuch as the term *secular* has been used to mean the very opposite of spiritual, this may seem to be a contradiction in terms. However, *secular* is not used in that respect here. Rather, it is used to describe the fact that no official, state-supported church exists in America. Of course America is also secular in the sense of being worldly and materialistic and this inconsistency with the spirit of Christianity was pointed out above. However, in this analysis *secular* is being used to describe the institutional relationship between church and state in America and in this sense a society could be deeply religious and yet secular. From the beginning of their history as a nation, Americans have believed in the concept of the separation of church and state as being essential to freedom of conscience. Jefferson and Madison thought it so important that they placed it first on the list of amendments to the Constitution. The amendment states that Congress shall make no law respecting an establishment of religion, or prohibiting the free exercise thereof. Jefferson was well aware of the lack of religious freedom and of even the persecution that had existed under the state church in many of the countries of Europe as well as in some of the American colonies. He knew that this fact had caused many a European to come to America. He believed also that both church and state suffered from the interference of each in the affairs of the other. These factors, plus his strong belief in freedom of conscience and his awareness of the extreme religious diversity in America, led him to take his stand in favor of a secular society.

The secular nature of American society has meant that religion is a private, individual matter. No religious group is favored by the state, but neither is any persecuted. All are permitted to function freely and are even aided by tax exemption. Thus a nation that encourages all religious groups to function by providing the legal framework in which this is possible can hardly be charged with being "godless." Moreover, there are many religious aspects to our official life as a nation. Jefferson in the Declaration of Independence spoke of "men being *created* equal" and of "*God* given rights." Our official oaths prerequisite to taking office (including those of the Presidency) are taken on the Bible and end with the phrase "so help me God." The same is true for the oath administered in every court in the country. Our coins are engraved with the words "In God We Trust." There are clergymen stationed in the Congress and each session of the legislature is opened with a prayer. In the armed forces clergymen of the various sects are permitted and encouraged to function.

Most Americans now believe that freedom of conscience is desirable and that individuals should be allowed to worship in their own way or not at all. Furthermore, they believe that no man should be compelled to pay taxes to support another man's religion. Although some religious prejudice still exists, it is perhaps less strong than at some times in the past. In general, every American is free to worship as he pleases. He is also free to disbelieve although this action is less acceptable socially. The prevalent feeling in many parts of America seems to be that a person is free to believe as long as he believes in something. An avowed atheist is often regarded with suspicion.

The institutional separation of church and state has been carried out effectively in the public schools. Almost from the beginning of the free, public common school the policy has been established that no sectarian religious teaching would be permitted in the school and this policy is still in effect today. Also, the policy of not providing public support for parochial schools is the general policy in effect all over the United States. Many states have provisions in their constitutions which make this quite explicit. The following is quoted from the Illinois Constitution.

—Neither the General Assembly nor any county, city, town, township, school district, or other public corporation, shall ever make any appropriation, or pay from any public fund whatever, anything in aid of any church or sectarian purpose, or to help support or sustain any school, academy, seminary, college, university, or other literary or scientific institution, controlled by any church or sectarian denomination whatever; nor shall any grant or donation of land, money or other personal property ever be made by the State or any such public corporation, to any church, or for any sectarian purpose.

In the United States all religious groups have the right to establish and operate their own school systems if they so desire, and at the present time approximately ten per cent of all school children are enrolled in private and parochial schools. In this connection, the decision in the famous Oregon case of 1925 is important. The Oregon legislature had passed a law requiring all children to attend public schools. The Supreme Court of the United States decided the law was unconstitutional on the grounds that the parent, not the state, had the primary responsibility for the education of the child and that the law deprived the private schools of their means of existence. Today the right of the parochial schools to operate is unchallenged and is evidence of the religious freedom that has been established in a secular society which does not support religious groups with public funds.

Despite the apparent definiteness of the two basic principles that no sectarian religious beliefs should be taught in the schools and that no parochial school should receive public funds, in practice the issue is not so clear cut. In some states Bible reading is permitted in the schools, and the Supreme Court of Pennsylvania said recently that this practice was legal and did not violate the First Amendment because the Bible was not a sectarian book. Publicity was given to a situation in Johnsburg, Illinois in which a Catholic school with nuns as teachers was receiving public support and in effect was the public school.[19] This was clearly a violation of the First Amendment, but nothing was done until a Lutheran couple moved into the town and discovered that their child would be attending a Catholic school and that they would have to support it. They complained to the State of Illinois, and apparently changes will be made, since the state has a responsibility to provide public education for all children and cannot violate the First Amendment in doing it. Undoubtedly there are many situations of this kind in America, but they are the exception not the rule, and if any person is willing to take the matter to court there is little doubt concerning the outcome.

In recent years there has been a strong movement to have religion taught in the schools. However, the matter is not as simple as it sounds. In the first place, the freedom of conscience of any child cannot be violated. In the second place, there is such religious diversity in America that it is next to impossible to agree on what will be taught, how it will be taught, and who will do the teaching. The National Education Association has recommended that moral and spiritual values be taught apart from any particular creed.[20] Many schools have tried to solve the problem by providing released time (usually the last period in the day) for religious instruction. Originally this was often offered in the school building until the Supreme Court in the McCollum Case in 1947 ruled by an eight-to-one vote that this practice violated the First Amendment. Recently in the Zorach case the court ruled, in a five-to-three decision, that the released time program was legal if the instruction was carried on outside the school. In most instances the youngsters go to the church of their choice.

Equally difficult is the matter of deciding what does and what does not constitute support to a parochial school. There seems to be no question but that direct aid to parochial schools is unconstitutional and cer-

[19] *The Christian Century*, May 13, 1953, pp. 564–5.
[20] Educational Policies Commission, *Moral and Spiritual Values in the Public Schools* (Washington, D.C.: National Education Association, 1951), p. 4.

tainly would not be tolerated by the American people. However, problems have arisen over such fringe benefits as aid for transportation, textbooks, and school lunches. In 1947 the Supreme Court in the Everson case, while upholding the idea of the separation of church and state, decided by a five-to-four vote that public funds could be used for transportation of children to parochial schools and that this was aid to the child and not the church. Many state courts have ruled in an opposite manner, and the situation at the present time is unclear, to say the least.

The dominant pattern in the public schools of America is one of no sectarian religious instruction and no public funds for parochial schools. This latter principle has held up the passage of federal aid to education bills for the last decade as some religious groups have attempted to get federal aid for their schools and, failing that, have blocked all legislation.

The secular nature of American society described in the section above obviously places limitations upon the schools in America so far as religion is concerned. Nevertheless, the fact that America is a strongly Christian society is reflected in the schools. The majority of teachers in America are Christians and to expect them to divest themselves of such a vital part of their personality when they enter the classroom is to expect the impossible. Certainly the moral and ethical values of Christianity are present in the classroom through the teacher. Moreover the fact that the teacher believes in God is bound to exert an influence, subtle though it may be, upon the development of the child.

In addition to being introduced through the teacher, Christian values are manifested in the schools in other ways. The content of the materials used in the curriculum is filled with references to the dignity and equality and brotherhood of man as well as such values as charity, kindness, and gentleness. The textbooks used in the schools contain frequent references to morals (and these are Christian morals), to churches (most of these are Christian churches), and to God. For example, in a civics textbook used in the Missouri schools, there is a chapter on moral training and a chapter on the influence of religions. In the chapter on moral training the golden rule is emphasized, and in the chapter on religions the reader is told that "Jesus explained his teaching in the Golden Rule." [21] In many schools, units on religion are taught and twelve states actually require that the Bible be read in the public schools although seven of these also have laws prohibiting sectarian instruction.[22] Studies also indicate that as many as 2,000,000 children may be taking part in released time programs,[23] and of course most of these children are receiving instruction in one of the Christian churches. The great

[21] C. L. Blough and D. S. Switzer, *Fundamentals of Citizenship* (Chicago: Laidlaw Brothers, 1951), p. 86.

[22] R. F. Butts, *The American Tradition in Religion and Education* (Boston: The Beacon Press, 1950), p. 191.

[23] *Ibid.*, p. 200.

Christian religious holidays of Christmas and Easter are celebrated in the schools, and to some extent at least the Christian story associated with these days is emphasized. The same is true for the Thanksgiving holiday period. Finally, many schools open the school day with the Lord's Prayer, while many others open their assembly programs with a religious statement.

To these manifestations of the influence of Christianity upon the schools must be added the fact that there are thousands of religious schools in America which are supported by the churches themselves. Most of these are full-time day schools, although some of them, particularly those of the Jewish church, are late afternoon and Saturday schools. The most important religious schools in America from a numerical standpoint are those supported, maintained, and operated by the Roman Catholic Church. They enroll approximately ninety per cent of the students who attend church schools and have a complete system that includes institutions on the elementary, secondary, and higher levels.

Suggested Readings

Becker, Carl: *Freedom and Responsibility in the American Way of Life.* New York: Alfred A. Knopf, 1945.

Commager, Henry S.: *The American Mind.* New Haven, Conn.: Yale University Press, 1950.

Counts, George S.: *The American Road to Culture.* New York: The John Day Company, 1930.

————: *Education and American Civilization.* New York: Bureau of Publications, Teachers College, Columbia University, 1952.

Curti, Merle: *The Growth of American Thought.* New York: Harper & Brothers, 1943.

Gabriel, Ralph H.: *The Course of American Democratic Thought.* New York: The Ronald Press Company, 1940.

Laski, Harold J.: *The American Democracy.* New York: The Viking Press, 1948.

Mead, Margaret: *And Keep Your Powder Dry.* New York: William Morrow & Company, 1942.

Parrington, Vernon L.: *Main Currents in American Thought.* New York: Harcourt, Brace and Company, 1927.

Perry, Ralph B.: *Characteristically American.* New York: Alfred A. Knopf, 1949.

Riesman, David: *The Lonely Crowd.* New Haven, Conn.: Yale University Press, 1950.

Williams, Robin: *American Society,* 2nd ed. New York: Alfred A. Knopf, 1960.

CHAPTER 8

SOCIAL AND ECONOMIC CHARACTERISTICS OF AMERICAN SOCIETY AND EDUCATION

Social Class and Education

As SOCIOLOGISTS HAVE DOCUMENTED IN THE LAST THIRTY YEARS, America is a class society. Well known among the studies in this field are those by Lloyd Warner in his Yankee City series and those by Allison Davis in his work in the deep south. These studies were conducted on the basis of asking Americans to classify themselves and their neighbors. The result was that while many sociologists disagreed with Warner on certain points, there seemed to be substantial agreement among them on the existence and operation of the over-all pattern of social class in America. The class system in America is usually divided by sociologists into six major divisions: the upper-upper, the lower-upper, the upper-middle, the lower-middle, the upper-lower and the lower-lower. The factors that determine social class were found to be vocation, income and source of income, family background, and type of house and residential area. It is clear that the social-class structure in America is essentially a status system.

The individuals who comprise the various classes are indicated by the research in the following manner. The upper-upper consists of the very wealthy and socially prominent families, and represent a very small percentage of the total population. The lower-upper consists of families who are wealthy and prominent but who have not enjoyed this high status as long as the upper-upper. The upper-middle class consists of professional people and businessmen not as wealthy or as well established socially and generally without the family background of the upper classes; this group is usually quite active in community affairs and tends to associate itself with the upper classes. The lower-middle class, which represents approximately a quarter of the population, is comprised of small businessmen and some professional and white-collar workers. The upper-lower class is comprised mostly of workers, skilled and unskilled, and this group constitutes over a third of the population. The lower-lower class consists of manual laborers, migrant workers and domestic servants, and in many communities is composed largely of Negroes. This group is generally regarded by the other groups as lazy, shiftless, and lacking in ability and ambition.

It should be remembered that all American communities do not fall into these neat classifications. In many cases it is impossible to draw distinctions and the above analysis does some violence to reality. Also the above classification tends to be more accurate in smaller, well-established communities. Although the difference in social class exists in larger cities, it is not so easy to catalogue. In new communities, class lines tend to be more fluid and not so sharply drawn by the communities themselves. This pattern was characteristic of our western communities a few years ago. Also it should be remembered that there is a distinction between class and caste. This distinction was made by a group of sociologists:

> Class is present in a community when people are placed by the values of the group itself at general levels of inferiority and superiority and when the highly and lowly valued symbols are unevenly distributed among the several levels. Social mobility in a class system permits an individual during his lifetime to move up or down through the several social strata. A man may be born lower-class but in time climb into the upper ranges of the society, although ordinarily a person stays in the class into which he was born. Class rules also permit an individual to marry outside his own level as well as within his social group. A man or woman can marry above, below, or in his or her level. A class structure, then, is flexible, and there is always movement in it.

> Caste, found in many parts of the world in addition to India, is a rank order which classifies all people and all the behavior of the society. Like a class order it unequally distributes the things which are prized and those not wanted. But here the resemblance between caste and class ends. Where class approves of outmarriage, caste prohibits it. A man must marry in his own caste, for the rules forbid and custom punishes marriage outside the caste. There is another major distinction between the two: whereas class positively sanctions and rewards efforts to climb from a lower social level to a higher one, caste disapproves and punishes such behavior. The rules of caste demand that an individual be born, live and die in one caste.[1]

Thus in America the class lines are not rigid and the possibility of vertical mobility up the status scale exists. But it is equally true that Ameri-

[1] W. L. Warner, R. J. Havighurst, and M. B. Loeb, *Who Shall Be Educated?* (New York: Harper & Brothers, 1944), p. 19.

cans tend to associate and to intermarry within their own class. Consider the improbability of a member of one of our socially prominent families marrying a person from the lower-lower class. It should also be pointed out that in some respects the Negro in America is more a member of a caste than a class. While there are class distinctions within the Negro group itself, especially in the large cities, it is illegal for Negroes and whites to intermarry in some states and it is socially unacceptable all over the United States.

While America is a class society, it is not a class society in the Marxian sense. There is little class consciousness and less class conflict in America. Probably in any free society class lines will develop for people tend to associate and to intermarry with those with whom they have common interests, even when the element of snobbishness and prestige is eliminated. However, in a democracy legal and political equality is essential as is equality of opportunity in the economic and educational areas. And although individuals certainly have every right to associate with whomever they choose it would seem to be desirable to have a society in which individuals are judged for what they are and not on the basis of family and, therefore, of social-class background.

Education is influenced by this social-class pattern in many ways. In general the amount of schooling an individual receives depends upon his social-class membership, and his class status is in turn influenced by his educational background. Almost all of the three upper classes will send their sons and their daughters through college whereas it is rare for a lower-lower family to send a son, much less a daughter, to college. Some families from the upper-lower will send their children to college, and more, but by no means all, from the lower-middle will do so. The result is that education is one of the factors used in determining a person's status and a college education can be the main vehicle through which the individual can raise himself from a lower-class to a middle-class standing. This is so partly because the college degree carries with it some prestige and partly because it enables the individual to get a job that is generally associated with a higher status. In the upper classes, a college education is almost taken for granted. More important at this level is which college the individual attends, with graduation from certain colleges such as Harvard, Princeton, Yale, Smith, Wellesley, and Radcliffe carrying great prestige values. Attendance at these schools is also an important factor in enabling the individual to rise from the middle-class to an upper-class standing.

The social-class pattern of American society is reflected in the schools in other ways. The majority of school board members are from the upper-middle and lower-upper classes with the lower classes being inadequately represented. In the high schools the curriculum is influenced by the social-class background of the students attending. For example, a school in a wealthy neighborhood emphasizes a college preparatory program whereas just the opposite is true in a poor neighborhood. In general there is a relationship between the social-class background of students and the type of program they select in high school, with the upper groups selecting the college preparatory and the lower groups the commercial or vocational.

Perhaps the most important fact concerning the relationship between social class and education is the influence that social-class background has on the education of the child outside of the school. Each social class has its own pattern of life and its own scheme of values. For example, a middle-class family may regard success in school as being most important while a lower-class family may be indifferent in the matter. A middle-class family may impress upon their child that honesty is the best policy while a lower-lower family may tell their child that whatever he can get away with is acceptable. From the moment he is born the individual is influenced in countless ways and his whole outlook toward life is fashioned by his environment, chiefly his home, family and neighborhood. His concepts of right and wrong, his attitudes toward school and his hopes for the future are all influenced by his family background. If he is from an upper-middle class home—say the son of a professional person—he will probably be surrounded by books; his parents probably discuss world affairs and take an active part in community life. If he is from a lower class home, books are probably absent and there is likely to be little intellectual stimulation. Thus the social-class background of the individual has extremely important implications for the school. Consider the difficulty of getting a youngster with a barren home background interested in Chaucer or Shakespeare in a high school classroom.

This leads us to another important aspect of social class and education. This aspect is that the other half of the teaching-learning equation, namely the teacher, is also a product of her social-class background. Most teachers in America are from middle-class families and generally have a philosophy of life or a frame of reference typical of that group. As long as the students being taught are also from the middle class, there is little reason for misunderstanding. However, when teachers have students from the lower groups, conflicts may arise which can convert the schoolroom into a semipenitentiary. In this situation the teacher may fail to understand the child and condemn him as inherently bad when the child is simply behaving in a manner which he has learned at home. Therefore, it is essential for teachers to understand the social-class structure of American society if they are to do an effective job of teaching.

Since their establishment the free public schools in America have been a powerful factor in promoting social mobility and in keeping class lines fluid. Still, as we have seen, the school is perhaps not the great equalizer that some Americans would like to believe it is, and the evidence shows that home and family background exerts a strong influence. Nevertheless, the public school is the institution that does the most to keep our ideal of equality of opportunity a reality and to keep class lines from hardening. To appreciate this fact, we need only consider what social conditions would prevail in America if the public schools did not exist.

Segregation and Education

DESPITE the fact that America is a democratic society committed to the idea of equality and equal opportunity, the country is segregated according to race. Although the degree of segregation differs in various parts of the country and the extent of segregation is decreasing year by year, the white and Negro races are still segregated. In most sections of the country Negroes live in one neighborhood and whites in another. In most communities Negro children attend one school and white children another. In most cases the Negro is severely limited in terms of the type of job that is open to him. Social mixture, including interracial marriage, dating, and general social mingling, is virtually nonexistent. To all intents and purposes, the Negroes in America live in one world and the whites in another. Even in churches and burial places segregation exists.

In many parts of our country, Negroes, who pay taxes like everyone else, are not allowed in certain public places and must sit in specified sections of common carriers. It is usual in public eating places to see the sign "We reserve the right to refuse service to anyone," which usually means that Negroes will not be served. Until recently segregation was commonly practiced in the District of Columbia, where the capital of our great democracy is located. Apparently Negroes are good enough to fight and die for their country but not good enough to deserve social equality, and in a very real sense the Negro in America is treated as a second-class citizen. This aspect of our society proves to be particularly troublesome to our government in its handling of foreign policy, especially when the Asian, African, and Latin American countries are involved. Of course, the Russians seldom miss an opportunity for reminding them or us of this obvious inconsistency. It is troublesome also when colored foreign students come to our country and are embarrassed. This often has the effect of undermining the purpose of the student exchange program, which is to build understanding, since these individuals often leave America quite bitter over their experiences.

Especially since World War II, segregation barriers have been breaking down in many areas of American society. Negroes are being admitted for the first time into many schools and colleges that were formerly closed to them. Through the co-operative efforts of industry, labor, and government, the latter through the establishment of fair employment practices legislation, many new opportunities are open in the economic field. Negroes have been admitted more and more in recent years into organized sports and into the entertainment field. Official segregation has been eliminated in the armed forces. Finally, segregation in the public schools was ruled unconstitutional by the Supreme Court of the United States, in a unanimous decision. Nevertheless, despite this progress, America in mid-twentieth century is still a segregated society.

The pattern of segregation which predominates in American society also predominates in the schools, although such segregation has now been ruled unconstitutional by the Supreme Court. In many states segregation had been enforced by law. In Missouri, for example, the Constitution stated that: "Separate schools shall be provided for white and colored children, except in cases otherwise provided for by law." And Section 163.130, Missouri Revised Statutes, 1949, provides that no colored child shall attend a white school and no white child shall attend a colored school. Moreover, education, both in and out of school (particularly the latter), is the means through which the discrimination and prejudice is learned. It is not inborn. Generally the discriminatory values are picked up incidentally in the home and neighborhood and are not deliberately taught. Also, in most instances the fact of segregation is a reality which the child grows into in the same way that he comes to accept the rest of his cultural heritage.

In most cases the fact of segregation is not discussed in the schools. This is so partly because it is such a controversial issue and partly because of the obvious contradiction between the fact of segregation and the concepts of equality and brotherhood which are basic in both democracy and Christianity, both of which have a central place in the schools. In a sense it seems that we have a guilty conscience over this situation and would rather not talk or think about it. Moreover, it is a difficult thing to tell the Negro youngster that many of the fine phrases of democracy do not apply to him. This teaching by omission is also evident in the content of the reading materials that are used in the schools. Not often is a Negro family used as a model in picturing family life in America.

Segregation turns into discrimination in many ways. Although the pattern is changing, Negroes are not admitted to some of our finest schools. Negro schools are generally overcrowded, and less money is spent per pupil on Negro than on white children. Except in the large cities, Negro teachers receive lower salaries and have heavier teaching loads.

In the last twenty years, and particularly since World War II, more and more schools have been abandoning their segregation policies. Even before the Supreme Court decisions in 1950, which forced the admittance of Negro students to the Universities of Texas and Oklahoma, many colleges and universities, including some in southern states, had been admitting Negroes. The same was true in the northern states for elementary and secondary schools, both public and private. Then in 1954 the legal basis for segregation was destroyed by the Supreme Court. In a unanimous decision the Court ruled that separate schools were "inherently unequal" and that Negroes were being deprived of the equal protection of the laws guaranteed by the Fourteenth Amendment. The ruling of the Court was obeyed, generally without incident, in the North and in many places in the South. But there was also strong opposition in the South, and in some states political leaders closed the public schools rather than submit to integration. Some southern legislators tried various legal devices to get around the Court's ruling. The most tragic episode in the desegregation story occurred in Little Rock, Arkansas, where the Governor, Orval Faubus, defied the Supreme Court and forced President Eisenhower to send federal troups to Little Rock to enforce compliance and to protect the Negro children. The tragedy was that the school board had worked out a gradual, sensible program for integrating the schools. The actions by Faubus, and by some fanatic segregationists from other parts of the country, not only ruined this program but encouraged the defiance of the law and the unleashing of human passion and hatred. In August of 1959 the police in Little Rock had to use force to disperse mobs who had gathered to prevent a handful of Negro children from attending a reopened public high school with over 1,000 white pupils.

So far as education is concerned, integration will be limited because of residential segregation. Even so, great progress has been made in the last decade. This is true also in other aspects of American life, and each year more states are passing laws preventing discrimination in employment, in housing, and in public accommodations. More important in the long run is the fact that many teachers have worked hard and with success to eliminate the senseless poison of racial prejudice from our society.

Science, Technology, and Education

ANOTHER obvious characteristic of American society is its scientific-technical nature. Perhaps more than any other single factor, science and the practical application of its findings—technology—are responsible for the development of modern America. It is not overstating the case to say that of all the areas of human endeavor the developments in the field of science have had the greatest impact on man's environment. We need only think back to the days of Washington and Jefferson, a comparatively short time when we consider the long course of human history. It has been pointed out that a wheel turned no faster in 1776 than it did in 44 B.C. It took nearly as much time and effort to raise wheat in 1800 as it did in Egypt in 5000 B.C. The speed with which clothing could be made remained almost unchanged from the days of the Greeks until Washington's day. Certainly Washington could send a message no faster than Caesar could eighteen hundred years before.

Then science changed man's life. Scientists began to spend long hours in their laboratories studying the laws of nature. Before long an army of men probed into the secrets of nature, and practical men were quick to adapt their findings. The steam engine was developed and man crossed the oceans and laid rails over the land. Bessemer developed a process for converting iron into steel, and a thousand uses were found for the new metal, from the building trades to the production of armaments and battleships. The dynamo, a machine for converting mechanical energy into electrical energy, was developed, and electricity replaced steam and gave man control over darkness. A short time later the internal combustion engine was developed, releasing the energy of petroleum to run millions of automobiles, airplanes, and tanks. Amazing developments have been made in transportation and communication, bridging space and pulling men together and making them dependent upon one another. It is possible today to talk to other men on any part of the earth by wireless or by telephone. And it is possible to travel to any place on the earth in a matter of hours. Finally, in 1945 the energy of the atom was released, and men had control of an endless source of energy to be used as they chose—for human welfare or for human destruction.

The essential element of modern science is the scientific method, which is based upon observation, experimentation, and analysis. This method has had a tremendous impact upon society and upon man's patterns of thinking. Some of the physical changes have been mentioned. But science and the scientific method have also changed man's patterns of thinking. Not so many years ago if a man were struck down by a disease, the cause was likely to be attributed to demons or evil spirits, and men often lived in dread of these unseen and unknown forces. Today if an unfamiliar phenomenon occurs, we seek a scientific explanation. We believe in cause and effect, and in most cases the causes are natural causes. If our children are struck down by a new disease, we are confident that we can find the cause if enough money is provided to enable the scientific research to go forward. There is hardly an American who does not take it for granted that a cure will eventually be found for cancer. As a people we have great confidence in science. Moreover, Americans are using the scientific experimental method in their own lives.

Americans have taken to the scientific experimental method like a duck to water. Part of the reason may be that the new method of science coincided to a great extent with the willingness to experiment that was characteristic of Americans as they toiled to build a civilization out of a wilderness. It is probably no accident that this emphasis upon experimentation was to have a central place in the thinking of one of America's foremost philosophers, John Dewey, who spent some years close to the frontier before the turn of the century. Americans today are often mechanically minded and inventive, and at home with tools. From Franklin and Jefferson on down, mechanical gadgets seem to have had a strange fascination for Americans. We are intrigued by a new automatic transmission, or a new atomic battery, and professional advertisers capitalize on this fact. It is the exceptional product that does not have a new ingredient or a secret formula, and the implication is that science and scientists are behind it all. Commercial after commercial will offer "scientific proof" that its product is superior.

The net result of the impact of science and technology has been change, first technical change and then the inevitable change in patterns of living and thinking. Moreover, not only is America a changing society, it is obviously a *rapidly* changing or dynamic society. This dynamism is evident everywhere in America. A short forty years ago there were few automobiles on the streets; today there are millions. New subdivisions may be built in a few months, and it is getting to the place where whole communities may emerge from bare fields in a few years' time. Americans themselves seem to have caught the fever in their daily lives.

> The people living in the American community are in almost ceaseless motion. In a sense the locality into which one is born or in which one dwells is merely the point of entrance into or of contact with this vast community—a sort of home base from which one may sally forth on all kinds of exploits. . . . According to a report of the Bureau of the Census made public in March, 1950, twenty-eight million persons, or about 1 out of every 5, in April, 1949, were living in a different house from the one they had lived in a year earlier.[2]

Finally, there is much evidence that man has been far more willing to apply the scientific method to the control of nature than to himself or his institutions. The result has been that man's practical inventiveness has run ahead of his moral and social development; the terrible destruc-

[2] George S. Counts, *Education and American Civilization* (New York: Bureau of Publications, Teachers College, Columbia University, 1952), p. 437.

tion of the last half century is grim evidence of that fact. Whether man will apply this scientific method, which is one of his most remarkable achievements, to the solution of his economic, political, and human problems remains to be seen.

That America is a scientific, technological society is apparent through even a superficial look at the schools. The modern elementary schools abound with the objects of scientific study, and the visitor will note immediately birds, fish, and animals, as well as flowers and plants. If he will open the storage cabinet in one of the intermediate grades, he is likely to find a magnet or a coil of wire or perhaps even a microscope. The school probably will have a moving-picture projector, a slide projector, and possibly a radio or television set. And, of course, in a modern school the physical environment—the lights, the design of the windows, etc.—are all concrete evidence of the application of science. If the visitor stays a while, he will learn that science is an important part of the school program. If he talks with the teacher, he will find that she has training in science and in science education. He will learn that even in the primary grades the scientific experimental methods are taught, although in a form that is within the experience of the child and therefore understandable to him. The school probably has a doctor, a dentist, and a nurse ready to use their scientific training, and a cafeteria whose physical characteristics and menu have been scientifically designed. In the principal's office the visitor will find the records of scientific tests especially designed to aid the school in providing better education.

In the secondary schools the impact of science is even more evident. Here our visitor will find laboratories in which students are actually carrying out experiments in chemistry, physics, and biology. If the school is a technical school, radio and electronic shops as well as drafting and designing rooms will be seen. In the American secondary schools all students are required to take some courses in science, and some students major in this area. As in the elementary school, the visitor will find that scientific measures, such as intelligence tests, are used to help fit the program to the individual students and that the health and nutritional aspects of the lower school are continued.

In the colleges the emphasis upon science found in the high schools is carried to higher levels with better equipment and more opportunity for the student. Special schools with highly trained instructors exist in which engineering and medicine are taught. Even in the social sciences and the humanities the scientific method has a central place, and the student will find special courses in methodology and logic. In the universities the emphasis upon science is even more pronounced, especially in the graduate schools, where the active search for new knowledge is a primary concern.

In the field of professional education the emphasis upon science and the scientific method is pervasive. In fact, so much emphasis has been placed upon it in the last three decades that it is common to refer to the "scientific movement in education." Research has been and is being carried out in every area of education. Through research in psychology, particularly in the areas of learning and of child growth and development, great strides have been taken in improving the schools. Likewise, knowledge in the field of sociology and anthropology has enabled us to have a better understanding of ourselves and our institutions (including the school) and therefore gives us the possibility of having greater control of our future. Even so, it is clear we have barely scratched the surface and much remains to be done. We need to know more, for example, about the factors involved in motivation for learning, about the education of the mentally retarded, about how to develop such skills as critical thinking and problem solving, and about measuring the effects of teaching. Our progress has been slow, partly because we have had inadequate support for research, partly because the sciences upon which education is based (psychology, social psychology, and sociology-anthropology) are young, and partly because too few researchers in the field of education have been adequately prepared.

Industrialism and Education

ANOTHER of the most basic characteristics of American society is that it is industrial. In towns, in cities, and on the farms the basis of industrialism—machine production and mechanical power—is evident. Fundamentally, industrialism is a means of production, and, while it is generally associated with manufacturing and the factory system, it is being used more and more in agriculture. Industrialization has changed life in America from a simple agrarian pattern into the complex, dynamic, mass production society we know today.

Although it is clear that industrialism and capitalism are closely interrelated, it is also clear that the whole industrial system had to be preceded by the developments in science and technology discussed above. It was the application of the findings of science to the production of goods that resulted in what has come to be known as the industrial revolution. Of course, science and industrialization are and have been closely related. In the field of medicine, for example, new scientific developments have cut down the infant mortality rate and extended the life span, thereby providing workers for the factories and buyers for the manufactured products. Moreover, the constant emphasis upon the utilization of scientific knowledge by technologists in industry has rapidly raised production levels and lowered costs. On the other hand the growth of industry has provided laboratories for thousands of research scientists who are constantly probing into nature's secrets.

The basic features of the industrial system are: first, the mechanization of industry or the use of machines that are power driven; and second, the factory system in which machines and workers are concentrated in one building in producing goods. Through the years, the factory system itself has undergone changes until today we have what is known as "mass production" in which huge quantities of standardized products are manufactured. Along with mass production has developed specialization of labor in which one man becomes a specialist in one phase of the manufacturing process.

There was a time when individual craftsmen produced whatever products were manufactured. The process was slow but there was a sense of pride in the work that was done and the worker was more or less his own boss. The industrial revolution changed this completely. The individual became a cog in a wheel. Instead of having one man handle all of the steps in the manufacturing process each man came to be a specialist in a certain operation, and after doing the same thing over and over again attained an amazing degree of speed and dexterity. Thus the main features of the factory system developed—mass production and specialization. The result so far as production was concerned was amazing—a fine product was produced at low cost and living standards were raised. However, the factory system created new problems. Men no longer had as much of a sense of pride in their work. No longer was there as much opportunity for contact between employee and employer, and the tendency was toward impersonal relationships. In order to keep costs down wages were kept as low as possible, and it was necessary for workers to organize into unions to bargain for higher wages. Moreover, when workers reached a certain age and began to slow down in their work they were not wanted and were unable to maintain themselves and their families. Finally, the factory system made the workers completely dependent upon the factory for their subsistance. When business was poor and the factory closed the worker faced the spectre of unemployment—a fear that replaced the fear men had of famine in the preindustrial period.

What has this industrial revolution meant to American society? How has it changed America? In the first place the industrial system has led to unprecedented increases in populations, for the simple reason that with an increase in the production of goods more men could be fed and clothed. Of course advances in medicine have also been a factor here, but without the increased production of food and other items, the saving of human life from disease would have meant instead death from starvation. Industrialization has not only provided the material foundation for an increase in population but because of the nature of the factory system has led to the concentration of populations into small areas of land. The factory could not operate without men, and the larger (and therefore, up to a point, more efficient) the factory, the more men were required. Since it was impractical and expensive for men to travel great distances to the factory, workers tended to concentrate around the factory. Societies were thus faced with the problems of masses of men living jammed together, often in squalid slums. These people, completely dependent upon the factory and usually unable to save any money, were destitute when, through a slack in business, the factory had to be closed down. It was the insecure masses of people in the cities who were the first victims of the emotional rantings of Hitler and Mussolini. This concentration or urbanization also brought with it complicated problems of housing, sanitation, and education and has been partly responsible for creating the mass society of our time.

Also characteristic of industrialism in America in the last fifty years has been the creation of larger and larger patterns of industrial organization. Today in America we have a handful of giant oil companies such as the Standard Oil Company and the Texas Company. We have a handful of giant grocery companies such as Kroger and the A. & P. We have a handful of giant automotive firms such as General Motors, Chrysler, and Ford. We have a handful of corporations that produce most of our steel, our copper, our aluminum, and our chemical products. Industrial America is characterized by huge corporations while the small manufacturer can exist only in some highly specialized field or through producing products for the larger firms. On the other hand, the last two decades have seen the emergence of giant labor unions such as the AF of L and the CIO, each with millions of members. America is then an industrial society characterized by huge corporations and huge unions and a degree of human interdependence unequalled in human history.

The coming of industrialization solved many problems but created many new ones. In the twentieth century for the first time in history industrialized countries could produce all of the food, clothing, and shelter that men could use. No longer was the age-old problem of raising enough food a critical problem. However, in his industrial society man has not been able to solve the problem of distribution and has periodically experienced business slow-downs that have come to be called depressions. In this state of affairs millions of workers are out of work, banks closed, and insecurity and fear become dreadful realities. In the twentieth century the depression that began with the stock market crash of 1929 had the most far-reaching effects. By 1932 in the United States alone over 14,000,000 men were unemployed and the situation was similar in western Europe. There were bread lines, soup kitchens, and relief handouts. The civilized world was shaken to its foundations. Partly as a result of this economic chaos of the twenties and thirties great industrial nations like Italy, Germany, and Japan came under the control of powerful and ruthless dictators who were to be directly responsible for World War II. This occurred because the masses of the people in these countries were in desperate circumstances and could see no hope of making a better future for themselves. They were persuaded to follow leaders who promised to bring a better way of life to the whole nation. The lesson to be learned seems clear. If we are to have peace and if democracy is to survive, we must somehow learn to cope with these economic problems that industrialism has produced. If we can do this, industrialization can be a real boon to mankind with the horizons unlimited, particularly with the development of new sources of energy and power.

The fact that America is an industrial society is clearly reflected in the schools. In the elementary school a glance at any textbook, whether it be in arithmetic, social studies or the language arts, will reveal the tractor, the automobile, and the million and one other products of the factory. In the secondary schools the content of the materials used will be even more heavily weighted with the evidence of industrialization. In these schools the student may choose a vocational curriculum in which he will receive preparation in the manual arts for either farm or factory. In the larger systems special vocational schools exist which are devoted entirely to the training of vocational skills necessary for an industrial society. In many high schools pupils are engaged in on-the-job training which takes them into the industrial plant for at least part of the day, usually in their senior year. The universities, too, gear their programs, especially in the upper division, to the professional training necessary for industry, particularly in the field of engineering. However even in the general education program in the lower division the impact of industrialization is studied, especially in the social sciences.

Perhaps the most important impact of industrialism upon education is to be found in the organization, administration, and operation of the schools. There is a striking similarity between the organization of a corporation with its stockholders, its board of directors, its production managers and its workers, and a large school system with its board of education, its superintendent, its various consultants, and its teachers. More important, however, is the extent to which the schools have adopted, since the late nineteenth century, the basic values of industrialism—namely, efficiency and production—as their basic criteria. The educational literature since then abounds with such terms as "efficiency of operation," "school plant and management," "educational workers," and "raising output." No less a figure than E. P. Cubberley, the well-known educational historian, provides a good example. Discussing the benefits derived from the introduction of specialized classes after 1890 he writes:

The effect of the introduction of the specialized classes has been to reduce waste, speed up the rate of production, and increase the value of the output of our schools. The condition of our schools before about 1900, and to a certain degree this condition still persists, was that of a manufacturing establishment running at a low grade of efficiency. The waste of material was great and the output small and costly—in part because the workmen in the establishment were not supplied with enough of the right kind of tools; in part because the supervision emphasized wrong points in manufacture; but largely because the establishment was not equipped with enough pieces of special-type plant, to enable it to work up the waste material and meet modern manufacturing conditions. Since about 1900, through the introduction of flexible promotions, parallel courses of study, differentiated courses, and special-type classes and schools, we have been engaged in improving the business by speeding it up, supplying it with new and specialized machinery; saving wastes, and increasing the rate and the value to society of the output. The public schools of the United States are, in a sense, a manufactory, doing a two-billion dollar business each year in trying to prepare future citizens for usefulness and efficiency in life. As such we have recently been engaged in revising our manufacturing specifications and in applying to the conduct of the business some of the same principles of specialized production and manufacturing efficiency which control in other parts of the manufacturing world.[3]

In the last thirty years as the number of children attending the school grew into the millions, more and more of the highly efficient and successful patterns of industrial plant organization and management have been adopted. Huge schools have been built in which thousands of pupils have been housed and taught. Because of the size a highly developed system of organization had to be established and this involved schedules that had to function with machinelike precision or the whole complicated apparatus was in chaos.

With the adoption of this industrial pattern in the organization and operation of the schools has come the tendency to regard the school administration job as essentially that of a business executive rather than that of an educator or a scholar. This trend is certainly understandable for in the last decades the administrator has had to handle, more and more, a multitude of legal and financial details. The fact is that these are a part of the administrator's job and he has these tasks thrust upon him. The result has been that in the professional education of the school

[3] E. P. Cubberley, *Public Education in the United States* (Boston: Houghton Mifflin Company, 1934), pp. 527–8.

administrator more and more emphasis has necessarily been placed on these aspects of the job.

However, regardless of the trends the fact remains that a school is not a factory or a business and the administrator's training should be shaped accordingly. What does the administrator need to know and how should he be trained? Certainly he needs to know and understand children. He needs to understand the learning process and the essentials of a good learning situation. He needs to understand the nature and function of the school and of the curriculum. Since he is the leader in the school, he needs to be a fine teacher and a scholar. Finally, he needs to have a real understanding of the world in which he lives, including the nature of communism and democracy. It would seem like false economy to have a highly educated individual devoting his time to checking on whether the doors are locked or the windows are closed instead of devoting time to the philosophy and program of the school. There are signs that this fact is being realized as more and more schools are hiring business managers to handle the financial details so that the administrator can be freed for education. The problem so far as industrialization and education is concerned was clearly grasped by Professor Kandel twenty years ago. He wrote:

With the enlargement and expansion of the scope of education and its supply, there has developed the position of the superintendent of schools who has applied to the vast enterprise principles of administrative efficiency borrowed from big business. If the administration of American education is open to criticism, it is not because these principles are unsound or inapplicable, but because an adequate distinction has not been made between those aspects of administration which can be mechanized and reduced to standards and routine and those which concern those human relations which are properly called education. There is a very real weakness in carrying the analogy between the administration of education and the administration of big business too far; in the one the whole machinery must be so organized that waste motion is eliminated and the result is a standardized, marketable product; in the other the mechanical organization is important only to the extent that it removes difficulties and leaves the well-trained teacher free but responsible in carrying out the task for which the school is created. To standardize costs, accounting, building, equipment, reports and records is one thing and necessary for efficiency; to attempt in the interests of efficiency to standardize curricula, courses of study, textbooks, and even methods of instruction by administrative procedures and to measure the results by standardized tests, which should serve as guides rather than ends, is another, and tends to defeat the purpose for which education exists—the liberation of the individual, the teacher as much as the pupil. Between bureaucratic control and methods of efficiency as applied to the educative and instructional process there is on the whole not much to choose. It is doubtful whether much is gained by applying industrial terminology to educational administration, if the school becomes a plant and the teacher the operator of the machine.[4]

When the close relationship between school and society is grasped, the resemblance between industry and education is understandable. Indeed it would be more surprising if it were not so. After all, America is the most highly industrialized country in the world, and the system has brought wealth and luxury to Americans. Moreover, the men and women who support and run the schools—the parents, board members, principals, and teachers—have been raised in an industrial society, and its patterns of culture inevitably affect the schools, as they do all other institutions in our society. However, understanding the relationship should not blind us to the dangers Professor Kandel has pointed out. When efficiency becomes the overriding criterion in the operation of the schools, the education of children is bound to suffer.

Mass Society and Mass Education

THE latest census reports show that the population of the United States is well over 175,000,000 people and growing rapidly. The factors responsible for this tremendous increase are, first, the advances in the field of medicine which lowered the infant mortality rate and extended the life span and, second, the increasing production of food and goods which have resulted from the application of the findings of science in these areas. The result is that America is already a "mass" society. Picturing Times Square on New Year's Eve, or the Rose Bowl Stadium at Pasadena on New Year's Day, or the shopping district of any large city on a Saturday afternoon will make this clear. Our national elections now involve almost 60,000,000 voters, and one senator may represent several million people. Whether we like it or not, whatever we do in America will be done in a big way. It is quite probable that in the next century the whole United States will be as thickly populated as the eastern part of the country.

The combination of a mass society and a highly developed industrial system continuously aided by technology has produced powerful pressures which work toward uniformity, standardization, and conformity in

[4] I. L. Kandel, *Comparative Education* (Boston: Houghton Mifflin Company, 1933), p. 347.

the realm of human behavior as they have done in the production of goods. In America today we are likely to wear the same clothes, to drive the same cars, to play the same games, and to laugh at the same jokes. In our giant chain stores we buy the same food products prepared in the same way and sold at the same price. So far as the material products are concerned, for example food, clothing or automobiles, this is because these items are produced on a mass production basis which means higher quality at lowered costs. In the nonmaterial realm, that is in the area of ideas, news, entertainment, etc., a similar situation exists. With the modern mass media of communication—newspapers, radio, and television—we hear the same news written and edited by a few gigantic news services. Through the same media we are bombarded with the same advertising and the same jokes.

Psychologically this tendency toward conformity is understandable. Individuals want to be accepted by their group and can hardly bear to be ostracized from it. Unfortunately our patterns of acceptance generally favor similarity. We tend to accept those who dress as we do, think as we do, etc., and to reject and even to ridicule those who are different. The parents who themselves value conformity can hardly be expected to encourage individuality in their children. Even if the parents are aware of the problem, they are generally helpless against the pressures of society and of the youngster's peer group, especially in adolescence. However, if the child gains the recognition of his group and gains confidence in himself, the home and the school can do much to help him become a personality who will think for himself, and not always follow the crowd.

To these tremendous pressures for uniformity must be added the pressure of nationalism. The whole development of the nation-state in the last two centuries has been in the direction of national unity in language, customs, and institutions. Thus as the national pattern developed in America in the nineteenth century, men ceased to think of themselves primarily as New Yorkers or Virginians and thought of themselves as Americans. This process has been characteristic of the unification of every nation, such as Russia, Germany, France, or Italy, that evolved from a number of independent groups. The process in its early stages can be seen in Asia and Africa at the present time.

Undoubtedly a certain amount of uniformity is necessary and desirable and obviously no community can exist without some common features such as language, law, etc. Moreover, basic agreement must exist in the field of values, for as Lincoln said, no nation can endure half slave and half free. If there were disagreement on basic values chaos would result and this has occurred on the international scene in recent years just as it did in 1860 in America. The problem, on an individual, a national, and a world basis is to achieve the basic unity necessary for communication and understanding and to enable men to live and work together, and yet to preserve the diversity and the richness of difference which will enable us to avoid the monotony of uniformity and, instead, to enjoy the unique contributions of individuals and nations. Such a minimum basis in the political field might be a strengthened United Nations. In the moral realm the Declaration of Human Rights, one of the great achievements of the human race, could provide the basic moral unity since all the members of the UN have given it their approval. Our contribution here in America has been considerable, and in a sense this problem was faced and solved here. We provided the basic political and moral unity through the Constitution and the Bill of Rights, which might be compared with the United Nations Charter and the Declaration of Human Rights. We are also the first nation to feel the full impact of the powerful forces mentioned above which are at work pressing us toward conformity. It may be that in the generation ahead another kind of battle will be fought to see whether this nation or any nation can resist these forces and maintain the richness of individual differences while still enjoying the products of the mass industrial system.

As a result of the emergence of America as a mass society in the twentieth century and its democratic commitment to educate all its children, American education in this period has developed into a mass education system. At the present time we have some 44,000,000 pupils in American schools and over 1,300,000 teachers. Literally millions of diplomas are granted each year, and hundreds of thousands of degrees. Even graduate schools are turning out graduates en masse, and thousands of advanced degrees are granted each year.

The sheer number of students, the premium placed upon efficiency, and the success of large-scale production in industry has led to the adoption of industrial patterns in education, especially in the large cities. Thus it is not unusual to find secondary schools with enrollments of 2,000 to 4,000 students and some enroll as many as 6,000. In many high schools teachers teach five classes a day with anywhere from twenty to forty students in each class and a total number of well over a hundred students a day. Under these circumstances, teachers are hardly able to know their students' names, much less teach them or find out what they have learned. In the elementary schools the situation is better because the teacher has one class all day. Even here, however, there are many classes with forty-five, fifty, and fifty-five pupils. In higher education the situation is almost as bad. Between classes, graduate students, and his own research, the instructor is generally overwhelmed by sheer numbers. Because of the numbers, a high degree of organization is essential even to keep track of the students.

The result is that the large schools resemble factories. They are precise and machinelike, and the whole operation of getting students from room to room depends upon having the bells ring on time. Whatever is in progress in a classroom must stop for the student must get to his next class every fifty minutes. Moreover, once the routine is established it is difficult to have any flexibility even if the learning of the students could be facilitated thereby. For like an assembly line or an army marching in formation, any unusual action may upset the whole complicated apparatus. Thus, while no rule restrains teachers from taking students into the community to visit a factory, the system makes it virtually impossible, and after a while teachers resign themselves to the classroom and to the clocklike routine.

The sheer masses of children to be educated has posed a formidable challenge. It has been a tremendous achievement to obtain enough teachers and enough classrooms even to house 38,000,000 students let alone teach them. Unfortunately too many Americans, both teachers and laymen, acquiesce in this mass education system, failing to realize that children cannot be educated as machines are manufactured. Emerson in his essay on Education pointed this out in 1867 when he wrote:

> . . . there is always the temptation in large schools to omit the endless task of meeting the wants of each single mind, and to govern by steam. But it is at frightful cost. Our modes of Education aim to expedite, to save labor; to do for masses what cannot be done for masses, what must be done reverently one by one.[5]

There is evidence that we have not really come to grips with this problem of educating all our children. If we do, we will realize that genuine teaching and genuine learning take time and require constant and continuous interaction between teacher and student. Real learning occurs with difficulty in a mass, impersonal environment. Although there are other problems in American education, that of providing a quality education suited to each child in a mass society is the most difficult. To do the job we so innocently accept will take more teachers and more classrooms than we have ever dreamed would be necessary.

In such a mass system the path of least resistance is uniformity and conformity whereas the nurturing of individual uniqueness is extremely difficult. Although teachers often make valiant efforts in this direction, too often if the child is a good boy, that is if he causes no trouble and fits into the group inconspicuously, teachers are satisfied. And with the load many of them carry, little else is possible. Also students themselves regard the child who does not conform as odd or queer; particularly for the adolescent, this pressure exerted by the peer group is almost irresistible. Therefore the school, as the other great educational agencies —the home, the church, and the mass media of communication—actually becomes an agent that produces uniformity.

[5] R. W. Emerson, *Education* (Boston: Houghton Mifflin Company, 1883), p. 29.

Capitalism and Education

THIS characteristic permeates the very fiber of American society and no individual American can escape its influence. This commercial-capitalistic-business system was brought over from Europe in the eighteenth and nineteenth centuries and it has flowered in wealthy, expanding America. The essence of the capitalistic system is profit and the accumulation of wealth, while also of major importance in the system are competition and individual initiative. Originally the system included a laissez faire concept of the function of government but today, although the term *free enterprise* is used a great deal, the real question is not whether government should or should not interfere with business, but rather how and how much it should interfere, regulate, or assist.

The most obvious manifestation of this characteristic is in the form of advertising. In the newspapers, on the radio and television, on the streetcar or on the highway (marring our lovely country), the individual is constantly reminded to buy certain products and the reminders are ceaseless and incessant. Our entertainment and recreation, even our cherished holidays such as Christmas, Easter, and Mother's Day are commercialized. Millions and millions of dollars and tremendous energy and ingenuity are expended each year to convince Americans that one product is superior to another. It was this that led Thomas Wolfe to blurt out:

> America—the magnificent, unrivaled, unequalled, unbeatable, unshrinkable, supercolossal, 99-and 44-one-hundredths-percent-pure, schoolgirl complexion, covers the earth, I'd-walk-a-mile-for-it, four-out-of-five-have-it, his-master's-voice, ask-the-man-who-owns-one, blueplate-special home of advertising, salesmanship and special pleading in all its many catchy and beguiling forms.[6]

In this endeavor full use is made of other basic values in American life. One of these is our faith in science and research which has been discussed. Advertisements are full of statements such as "scientific tests prove" or "laboratory tests show." Very often the individual presenting the ad is dressed in a doctor's attire or is standing in a laboratory. Even our well-staged political speeches on television have the speaker on a stage with library and books in the background. These men are not doctors or scientists or scholars, but the idea is to give the audience the impression that they are and that therefore their product is reliable and superior. At times when genuine research has indicated that certain products are far from meeting the claims of the ads or are actually harm-

[6] Thomas Wolfe, *You Can't Go Home Again* (Garden City, N.Y.: The Sun Dial Press, 1934), p. 396.

ful, the real scientists are denounced. A case in point is the work of one of the great medical scientists in America, Dr. Evarts Graham, when, after painstaking and carefully controlled research with mice proved that there was a link between smoking and lung cancer.[7] Dr. Graham's findings were reinforced a few months later when the American Cancer Society reported that on the basis of more than two years of study on 187,766 men between the ages of fifty and seventy lung cancer deaths were three to nine times as common among cigarette smokers as among nonsmokers, and five to sixteen times as high among heavy smokers as among those who never smoked regularly.[8] The philosophy seems to be to use science as long as it is profitable but reject it when it is not.

Another appeal of the ads is directed toward taking advantage of the admiration that Americans have for success. Thus we find leading actors, actresses, and sportsmen telling us how much they enjoy and use a certain product such as a cigarette, a razor blade, or a deodorant, and the implication of these ads is that if these great humans use them, these products must be superior. If a "name" person is not used, the same effect is achieved by having the model pose and dress and appear in an environment that makes it self-evident that he is a "successful" person. The effect of all this on Americans is difficult to measure, but it is hard to see how insincerity and deceit can produce a wholesome effect. Everyone knows that the "name" giving the testimonial is doing so for a price. Many of the advertisements border on fraud and the buyer must be most discerning to keep from being cheated.

Still another appeal of advertising is directed toward the admiration for youth and beauty that is prevalent in America. Countless products are available which improve the complexion, the figure, and in general keep Americans (and especially women) looking young. Of course life would be rather dull, especially for men, if women were not concerned with their appearance. However, in too many cases the worship of youth has caused many a person to feel that life was practically over at forty and to attempt to forestall the inevitable aging process through the use of beauty devices. In recent years Americans have begun to reconsider this attitude, realizing that the years of later maturity, although less active, can be just as enjoyable. Yet the pressures from Hollywood and the "school girl complexion" advertisements continue to glorify youth.

The emphasis upon selling, plus the tremendous pressure on the individual to succeed, has led to some unfortunate results. A pattern known as high-pressure salesmanship has been developed that operates in a manner similar to the Communist brainwashing. Not so revolting but perhaps more dangerous in the long run is the approach based upon the "how to win friends and influence people" principle. The idea is to

[7] New York Times, February 3, 1954, p. 20.
[8] Ibid., June 22, 1954, p. 1.

maintain a smiling, friendly, handshaking, back-slapping attitude with the prospective customer even if you dislike him intensely. If possible, get acquainted with the customer and his family—and make him think you are genuinely interested in them, using flattery if necessary. The essence of this approach in both advertising and salesmanship is insincerity and pretending to be something you are not, for a price. This is not to say that there are not many sincere individuals who are selling—individuals who would rather lose a sale than distort the truth. But there are too many others of whom "let the buyer beware." The alarming thing is that we have come to accept the insincerity and the deceit as normal and natural. We are even adopting this blandness, insincerity, and back-slapping in other areas of our society sometimes, under the guise of "human relations."

In the lives of Americans the emphasis upon business is evident. One of the great ambitions of many Americans is to be able to go into business for themselves. In part this reflects the desire for independence and the unwillingness to take orders from anyone, which is a part of our heritage, but it also reflects the fact that Americans are in the habit of buying and selling. When they buy a home, the possibility of reselling it is always a consideration. The same thing is true in the purchase of automobiles. Also, of course, a great many Americans earn their living as salesmen or in buying and selling on the stock exchange. Other millions of Americans own stock in corporations and draw dividends, and it is commonplace for Americans to think of their plans, whether they be educational or vocational, as "investments." Even farmers are businessmen. Crops will be planted or not planted, and taken or not taken to market, on the basis of the state of the market, and livestock will be bought and sold on the same basis.

The fact that America is a capitalistic society and the individual freedom of democracy have combined to produce the competition which is a basic characteristic of our society. Competition is generally regarded by Americans as the zest of life, and they compete in almost everything they do. The role of government regarding competition between individuals and corporations is to see that it is maintained on a fair basis. Monopoly is regarded as undesirable because it stifles competition. Americans believe in a free competitive economy as providing the best products at lowest costs. If a company is inefficient, it should go out of business; the same criterion is applied to individuals. So far as the individual is concerned, he is in constant competition with his fellowmen, especially in his job. Although some Americans believe that competition is harmful and that more emphasis should be placed on co-operation, the country has faith in it and believes that it is responsible for our high standard of living. Even its strongest supporters, however, oppose "cutthroat competition," at least in theory.

Another aspect of commercialism in American life is the widespread use of credit. Practically everything is bought on credit with a small down payment and the remainder on the installment plan. In modern America everything from a house to a cemetery lot may be purchased on "time." The large department stores have whole divisions that devote their entire time to this aspect of business. Large corporations hiring thousands of people do nothing but investigate people who apply for credit. The banks, of course, handle a great deal of this activity especially if any large sum is involved. Through the use of credit some remarkable transactions occur and it is possible to buy and sell property with only a small fraction of the total value in cash. It is literally true that American business runs on credit and if it were stopped suddenly, the whole business world would undoubtedly collapse.

It is clear that business and trade is one of the foundations and probably the lifeblood of our society. Without it our highly specialized industrial system could not function. But when this emphasis upon buying and selling is combined with intense competition and the drive for success, the temptation to use unethical practices is great.

As with the other dominant characteristics of American society the emphasis upon business is clearly reflected in the schools. Starting in the elementary school the content of the curriculum is permeated with the symbols of the business world. Thus the child in learning arithmetic will be faced with the problem of how many apples John has left in a dozen after he has sold six to Mary. Or how much one apple costs if apples are so much a dozen. In the intermediate grades it is even probable that the child will be asked the reason for buying two cans of beans for twenty-nine cents rather than one for fifteen cents. Certainly this approach is based on sound learning principles and has real meaning for the child, since this kind of behavior is all around him in the home and is therefore a part of his experience. Also in his reading the child is apt to read and see pictures of Father going to the office or Mother going to the grocery store.

In most of the high schools a special commercial curriculum is available (usually for girls) offering typing, shorthand, and general business practice. In many schools courses on consumer buying or retailing are given in addition to the traditional course in economics. In many schools special programs have been established in distributive education as part of which the student spends some time working in shops or department stores. In many other schools Junior Achievement programs have been established in which students form companies, invest capital, and in general run a business on a small scale.

In the colleges and universities the student will study aspects of the business world in most of his courses in the social sciences in addition to his courses in economics. For example, if he studies government, he will probably be introduced to the Full Employment Bill and to the Presidents Council of Economic Advisers. If he is planning to be a teacher he will doubtless encounter the problems of the support of education and of school finance. In addition there are special schools of business in which the student may concentrate in personnel management, salesmanship, retailing, or a number of areas.

In the over-all operation and administration of the school system great stress is laid upon doing things on a "businesslike basis," and as a result most school administrators have some training in business methods. This is true in the public schools as well as private. It is due in part to the pervasiveness of the business psychology in our culture but is also due to the fact that many of the members of the boards of education in America, especially in the larger communities, are businessmen. Even in the rural areas, this tends to be true since farmers consider themselves to be in business and some of the board members, if not the majority, are merchants in the small towns.

The private schools are, of course, business enterprises and even when they are heavily endowed must pay their own way. The tendency to consider higher education a big business is especially prevalent in America at the present time. Robert Hutchins, former Chancellor of the University of Chicago and now President of the Fund for the Republic, has said:

> I believe that the educators of America are largely responsible for the present confusion in and about education. They have felt obligated in my day to seek for money, first, last, and all the time. They have always supposed, I think erroneously, that money could be obtained only for activities that harmonized with the interests and opinions of those who had it. What they have done and what they have not done has been determined by financial considerations. When New York University dropped intercollegiate football the other day it did not say it was doing so because football is an outrageously immoral activity, not only a departure and diversion from the purpose of the university, but also directly contrary to it. No, New York University said that it was abandoning football because football lost money.
>
> I admit that this is a business civilization and that businessmen understand profit-and-loss statements and balance sheets. But one of the functions of educational leadership is to explain to businessmen that since a university has no profit-and-loss statement, and since its balance sheet is meaningless, there must be other standards by which its work is judged. These standards are supplied by its purpose.[9]

[9] *The Saturday Review*, October 17, 1953, p. 12.

Perhaps the two most important influences of our commercial-capitalistic-business culture upon our schools have been the emphasis placed upon competition and the adoption of the credit system. Competition permeates the whole school program from the elementary schools through the university and is intimately associated with individual success. Generally the competition in the schools is waged through the struggle for grades (although in the elementary school the prize may be a star) but it is also carried into sports and other activities as well. The emphasis upon competition has been heightened in the secondary schools and colleges by the normal probability curve. With this device the student must do better than his fellows if he is to receive a high grade.

In recent years, because of the knowledge of individual differences and of the harmful effects of an overemphasis upon competition, some changes have been introduced into the schools. Report cards, instead of indicating grades on an absolute scale, attempt to show whether the child is working up to his ability. In the classroom teachers are trying more and more to get students to work for achievement for what it will mean to them personally and not for the purpose of outdoing the other children.

The adoption of the credit system has also had an important effect upon the American schools. The use of the word *credit* in and of itself is an indication of the way that education is regarded as kind of a business asset or an investment. As one American educator put it:

> Once a credit was earned, it was as safe as anything in the world. It would be deposited and indelibly recorded in the registrar's saving-bank, while the substance of the course could be, if one wished, happily forgotten.[10]

Finally, the "how to win friends and influence people" technique has been adopted in many schools under the guise of human relations. The story is told of the teacher who was always positive and always smiling. One day a class that she had the previous year put on an outstanding performance for the entire school. After the performance the teacher came in to praise her former class. After she had gone the current teacher asked the class if they were not happy with the praise. Whereupon one youngster said, "It doesn't mean anything. Mrs. _____ would smile and tell us we were wonderful even if we stunk." The fact was that she had been so obviously insincere so many times in the past that even the children were aware of it. As a result they didn't believe her, even when she was being sincere. While there is something to be said for avoiding

[10] Norman Foerster, *The American State University* (Chapel Hill, N.C.: The University of North Carolina Press, 1937), p. 97.

rudeness even at the cost of telling a white lie, the continued insincerity so prevalent in our society can have unfortunate consequences.

These, then, are some of the dominant characteristics of American society, together with their reflections in the American schools. It is obvious that the American schools are characteristically American; they could not be otherwise. If a study were made of the Soviet Union or of any other country, the characteristics would be different, but in each case there would be the same close relationship between school and society.

Suggested Readings

Becker, Carl: *Freedom and Responsibility in the American Way of Life.* New York: Alfred A. Knopf, Inc., 1945.

Commager, Henry S.: *The American Mind.* New Haven, Conn.: Yale University Press, 1950.

Counts, George S.: *The American Road to Culture.* New York: The John Day Company, 1930.

———: *Education and American Civilization.* New York: Bureau of Publications, Teachers College, Columbia University, 1952.

Curti, Merle: *The Growth of American Thought.* New York: Harper & Brothers, 1943.

Gabriel, Ralph H.: *The Course of American Democratic Thought.* New York: The Ronald Press Company, 1940.

Hollingshead, August B.: *Elmtown's Youth.* New York: John Wiley & Sons, 1949.

Laski, Harold J.: *The American Democracy.* New York: The Viking Press, 1948.

Lynd, Robert S., and Lynd, Helen M.: *Middletown.* New York: Harcourt, Brace and Company, 1929.

Mead, Margaret: *And Keep Your Powder Dry.* New York: William Morrow & Company, 1942.

Myers, Gustavus: *History of the Great American Fortunes.* New York: Modern Library, 1936.

Myrdal, Gunnar: *An American Dilemma.* New York: Harper & Brothers, 1944.

Parrington, Vernon L.: *Main Currents in American Thought.* New York: Harcourt, Brace and Company, 1927.

Perry, Ralph B.: *Characteristically American.* New York: Alfred A. Knopf, Inc., 1949.

Riesman, David: *The Lonely Crowd.* New Haven, Conn.: Yale University Press, 1950.

Williams, Robin: *American Society*, 2nd ed. New York: Alfred A. Knopf, 1960.

The American School System

We have made great progress in the last twenty-five years in our attempt to provide adequate schools for all American Youth. For the future we must endeavor to combine the British concern for training the "natural aristocracy of talents" with the American insistence on general education for all future citizens. If we can do that, then our industrialized society will prosper and at the same time the necessary degree of instruction will be provided for all the people so that in their hands "our liberties will remain secure."

JAMES B. CONANT

CHAPTER 9

THE ORGANIZATION AND ADMINISTRATION
OF AMERICAN SCHOOLS

THE AMERICAN SCHOOL SYSTEM CONSISTS OF A VAST SERIES OF INSTI-
tutions that provide instruction from the nursery school, which
admits children between the ages of 2½ and 5, to the advanced
graduate schools in the universities. The system might best be described
as a ladder system, since, in general, graduation from a lower school is
prerequisite to entrance to the next higher school. In all, there are
approximately 175,000 schools in the United States, including 140,000
elementary schools, 30,000 secondary schools, and 1,850 colleges and
universities. In addition, there are special schools such as schools for the
blind, trade schools, schools of nursing, etc. The American school system
has an enrollment of approximately 44,000,000 students and employs
some 1,300,000 teachers. Because education is compulsory, every American child, except the severely handicapped, attends school and the vast
majority attend for a period of from 10 to 12 years. These figures are of
value because they indicate both the extent and scope of the American
school system and give evidence that from the standpoint of numbers
alone the school is one of the basic institutions of our culture.

The American school system consists of public and private schools.
This classification is based upon the way in which the schools are supported and controlled and not on the basis of whether they are open to
the public. With few exceptions the private schools of the United States
are open to the public, provided that academic or other requirements
for entrance can be met and, of course, that the tuition can be paid. The
significant difference is that the public schools are supported by public
taxation and controlled by officials elected by the people. The private
schools, on the other hand, while they are generally favored by being tax
exempt, must seek their support through private means, and they are not
under public control although they can be legally controlled by the

state, as we shall see. In terms of numbers, the public schools outnumber the private schools on the elementary and secondary level about eleven to one. Of the total of 32,000,000 children in the elementary school 27,-000,000 are in public schools, while slightly less than 8,000,000 of the total of 8,880,000 in secondary schools are in public schools. In the colleges and universities the situation is reversed. Out of the total of 1,850 schools, 1,210, with an enrollment of approximately 1,800,000, are private; 641, with approximately the same enrollment, are public. Thus there are twice as many private colleges and universities, but they have about half the total enrollment, indicating that in general public colleges and universities are much larger.

The Private Schools

THE private schools of the United States can be divided into two major categories: those operated by religious groups, that is, those known as denominational schools; and those that are not. On the elementary and secondary levels better than ninety per cent of the private schools are denominational, and ninety per cent of these are supported and controlled by the Roman Catholic Church.

Of the many religious groups existing in America only a few maintain schools from the nursery school through the university. Of these the Catholic church is by far the leader, as it maintains elementary, secondary, and higher schools, including such well-known universities as Notre Dame and Fordham. For the most part the Catholic church provides separate high schools for boys and girls, although some of the newer schools are coeducational. Generally the teaching is done by the nuns in the elementary school, by the teaching brothers in the high schools, and by the Jesuits in the colleges and universities. In these schools the main burden of support falls upon the church, although part of the cost is met through tuition charges to the individual student. The Lutheran church, which probably leads the Protestant group, maintains some schools on all three levels, but the total number of these schools is relatively small. The main efforts of the Protestant group have been in the establishment and support of the many denominational colleges that are to be found all over the country. The Jewish group maintains day schools in a few of the larger cities.

The other classification of private schools, the nondenominational schools, enroll only a small percentage of American youth, with this enrollment concentrated in the secondary schools and the colleges. There are very few nondenominational private elementary schools in the United States. On the secondary level this type of school is more numerous and tends to be rather specialized when compared with the multipurpose public high school. A large percentage of these schools are college preparatory and because of their tuition charges are attended, with very few exceptions, by students from the upper socio-economic groups. Among the better known of these schools are Exeter and Groton which in many respects are similar to the famous English prep schools such as Eton, Harrow, and Rugby. For the most part these schools are located in the East, especially in New England, but in recent years they have been established in most of the large cities of the Midwest and the Far West. Another type of private nondenominational school is the military academy which is generally, although not always, a boarding school and which also is basically a prep school for the well-to-do.

By far the largest group of private nondenominational schools are found on the college level. Many of these schools, such as Harvard, Princeton, and Columbia, originally had connections with a religious organization but today the support or control by the church is nominal. Other well-known schools in this category are Chicago, Northwestern, Stanford, and Washington University in St. Louis.

The Public Schools

As was pointed out in Chapter 6, the American people on the basis of their experience decided during the nineteenth century that private and parochial schools were inadequate as a basis for education in a democratic society. They were forced by the logic of the situation in which they found themselves in the 1830's and forties to move toward the establishment of the free, public, "common" school. The story of American education since then has been in the main an extension upward and an elaboration of that "common" school. There is no question that the ideals that Horace Mann had in mind have been essentially realized. Certainly the public school system has been a unifying force in our society and certainly a degree of equality of educational opportunity unparalleled in human history has been realized. One of the best and most convincing evidences of the soundness of the principle of public education in a democracy is the fact that as the other free nations have struggled to improve their democracies, they have followed (with their own variations) essentially the same pattern of free public education developed in the United States. The most conclusive evidence, of course, is the fact that better than ninety per cent of American children attend the public schools and it is obvious that the American people approve of the compulsory school laws.

Despite these impressive facts, it has also been true that in recent years more and more upper class Americans have been sending their children to private schools. Moreover, in recent years the public schools have been subjected to bitter and prolonged attacks, often by individuals who do not believe in public education.

One of the criticisms leveled against the public schools is that they do not teach religion and therefore, it is contended, they cannot teach moral and spiritual values. Another criticism is that the public secondary

AGE

Graduate
and
Professional
Schools

22

21 — 4 Year Colleges

20 — and Universities   Junior College

19

18 _____

17 — 4 Year | 4 Year Voca-tional and Tech-nical | 3 Year High School | 3 Year Voca-tional or Tech-nical | | 4 Year Advanced School | Compulsory Attendance in Calif., Utah, Idaho, Pa., Nev., Okla., Oregon

16 — High School

15 — School

14 ___

13 — Junior High School | 6 Year Second-ary School | 4 Year Second-ary School

12

11 — Compulsory Attendance

10 — 8 Year Elementary School

9 — 6 Year Elementary School | 6 Year Elementary School

8

7

6

5 — KINDERGARTEN

4

3 — NURSERY SCHOOL

2 _____

THE AMERICAN SCHOOL SYSTEM

schools are not providing adequate stimulus to the gifted student. So once again the issue of private versus public schools, which was apparently settled in the nineteenth century, has been raised. The result is that it has become necessary for educators to take stock of the public schools and to re-think the philosophy underlying them. Are the public schools essential for the existence of a democratic society? Or can private and parochial schools do the job? If the public schools are essential what is to be the role of the private schools? Do they have a vital function to perform? Can the public schools teach religion in a nation that has such religious diversity and is committed to freedom of conscience and of religion? Can moral and spiritual values be taught apart from religious dogma? These and many others are the questions that the American people need to answer. One of America's foremost scientists and educators, James B. Conant, the former president of Harvard University, has addressed himself to these questions in his book, *Education and Liberty*, published in 1953. A short selection from that book has been included here. Dr. Conant of course speaks for himself but many if not most educators, especially those who believe in public schools, would agree with his point of view. Certainly in this statement he presents a strong case for the public schools while recognizing the important role that private schools have to play. It should also be remembered that Dr. Conant was president of one of the world's leading private universities and that his views undoubtedly have had a great influence upon Americans both in and outside the teaching profession.

JAMES B. CONANT

FROM

Education and Liberty [1]

This American pattern of education is quite different from that which has evolved in the other English-speaking nations. We have already noted the high percentage of the youth attending school in this country on a full-time basis; in addition, our pattern is characterized by the small numbers attending private schools. The absence of tax-supported denominational schools is in contrast with England and Scotland. Is this American pattern now so widely accepted that one need not argue for its preservation? Twenty or thirty years ago I think the answer would have been in the affirmative. But not so today. Any frank discussion of the future of education in the United States must recognize the existence

[1] Reprinted by permission of the publishers from James Bryant Conant, *Education and Liberty*, Cambridge, Mass.: Harvard University Press, Copyright, 1953, by the President and Fellows of Harvard College. Pp. 77–87.

of many powerful church leaders who do not accept the present pattern as a permanent feature of American life. One must likewise realize that while only some 10 per cent of the youth of the country now in school attend private schools, in some cities the figure is as high as 40 per cent. Furthermore, the percentage of students attending private schools is increasing in certain sections of the country. Therefore I believe it of importance for all citizens to consider carefully the basic issue—the continuance of the American pattern.

I shall not detain the reader by reciting the attacks on the public schools that have taken place in the last few years (1949 to 1952). The formation in many localities of citizens' groups to defend the public schools is clear evidence of the devotion to them of a vast majority of the citizens of most towns and cities. Irresponsible attacks will certainly be warded off, and though some damage will be done, one need not fear the drastic alteration of the American pattern from violent, prejudiced criticism. But I am convinced that it is wise to discuss the fundamental criticisms of the American pattern of public education and to explore the alternative patterns which some critics favor. As a matter of convenience I shall call them the Australian and English patterns. In the one, a large proportion of the youth attending school at ages 15 to 17 is enrolled in church-connected private schools financed *without* tax support; in the other, the private school—church-connected or not—may receive tax money.

Public education, like all other education and all public institutions, needs critics. But critics who believe in the continuation of the American pattern and seek to improve the schools within this framework must be clearly distinguished from those who wish to bring about an educational revolution. Therefore I think it is only fair to insist that the critics of our public schools should make clear their stand on two important points. To each one who questions the performance of our public schools, I would ask the question: "Would you like to increase the number and scope of the private schools?" If the answer is in the affirmative, I would then ask a second question: "Do you look forward to the day when tax money will directly or indirectly assist these schools?" If the answer is again in the affirmative, the lines have been clearly drawn and a rational debate on a vital issue can proceed.

Needless to say, I would find myself on the opposite side from those who answer either or both of these questions in the affirmative. But what I am more concerned with in the year 1952 is that the critics of the public schools in the United States should show their colors. This is not an issue involving any single denomination. The proponents of the expansion of sectarian secondary schools are to be found in several Christian churches. One of the most vocal of the critics of public high schools is a Protestant clergyman who reveals himself when he writes: "The

Communist is not, as a matter of fact, much of a revolutionist. The Communist would only substitute the logical secularism of Karl Marx for the pragmatic secularism of John Dewey." If this clergyman would start off all his attacks on modern education by stating that for him secularism and communism are equal dangers, the reader would be in a better position to evaluate what he was about to read.

There are many sincere Protestants, Jews, and Catholics who believe that secondary education divorced from a denominational religious core of instruction is highly unsatisfactory education. They assume—erroneously, I believe—that the tax-supported schools because they must be free of any denominational bias cannot be concerned with moral and spiritual values. This is essentially the point of view of the headmasters of the Australian private schools referred to in Chapter 1. Such people, to my mind, are wrong in equating a religious outlook with a strictly denominational viewpoint, yet that they have a right to organize their own schools is beyond question. The United States Supreme Court settled the law on that point in the famous Oregon Case of 1925. But over and beyond the legal issue is the fundamental belief in tolerance of diversity so basic to our society. I know of no one today who wishes to suppress private schools. If there were anyone who had such a notion, the means of putting the idea into effect would involve such drastic state action as to be repugnant to our fundamental ideas of liberty.

But unwillingness even to consider advocating state or national action to suppress private schools is quite a different matter from being indifferent to their expansion. It is certainly a very different thing from acquiescing in the use of tax money directly or indirectly for the support of private schools.

Public funds are used to assist private schools including denominational schools in England and Scotland. No one can object to an open advocacy of the adoption of the English pattern here in the United States. Indeed, for those who believe that education divorced from denominational control is bad education, such an advocacy would seem highly logical. It is important for every American citizen to examine this issue as unemotionally as possible and see where he or she stands. For there is more than one way of changing a social pattern; we could easily drift by slow stages into a situation where in some states the adoption of the English pattern would be inevitable. If in a number of cities and towns the public high schools no longer received popular support, their successful rivals—the private schools—would be logical recipients of tax money. By one method or another the present constitutional barriers against the use of public funds for religious schools would be swept aside.

During the past seventy-five years all but a few per cent of the children in the United States have attended public schools. More than one foreign observer has remarked that without these schools we never could have assimilated so rapidly the different cultures which came to North America in the nineteenth century. Our schools have served all creeds and all economic groups within a given geographic area. I believe it to be of the utmost importance that this pattern be continued. To this end the comprehensive high school deserves the enthusiastic support of the American taxpayer. The greater the proportion of our youth who fail to attend our public schools and who receive their education elsewhere, the greater the threat to our democratic unity. To use taxpayers' money to assist private schools is to suggest that American society use its own hands to destroy itself. This is the answer I must give to those who would advocate the transformation of the American pattern into that of England.

What is the basic objection to the Australian or English pattern, you may ask. Or, to put it the other way around—what are the advantages of free schools for all? To ask these questions is almost to give the answers. If one accepts the ideal of a democratic, fluid society with a minimum of class distinction, the maximum of fluidity, the maximum of understanding between different vocational groups, then the ideal secondary school is a comprehensive public high school. Of this much there can be no doubt: If one wished generation after generation to perpetuate class distinction based on hereditary status in a given society, one would certainly demand a dual system of schools; this is the case in the Province of Quebec where a majority of the people wish to perpetuate two different cultural groups. A dual system serves and helps to maintain group cleavages, the absence of a dual system does the reverse. This is particularly true of the secondary schools. Indeed, I would plead with those who insist as a matter of conscience on sending their children to denominational schools that they might limit their insistence on this type of education to the elementary years.

In terms of numbers involved, the dual nature of our present pattern may seem slight—about 92 per cent of our secondary school pupils are in public schools. In terms of a stratification of society on economic and religious lines, however, the duality is marked. In socio-economic terms we are not as far from the English "Public School" system as we sometimes like to think. Chancellor McConnell of the University of Buffalo, reporting on English education, notes the predominance of "Public School" graduates over grammar school graduates in the entrants to Oxford in 1948. A half dozen of the best-known Eastern colleges in the United States would show a similar social phenomenon; they enroll something like half their students from private Protestant schools which encompass only a few per cent of an entire age group. But it is only fair to point out that these same colleges have been trying desperately hard in the last twenty-five years to attract a larger number of public high-school graduates. They aim to be national in terms of geography and representative of all income groups; that they have to some degree succeeded in moving nearer their goal is, to me, a hopeful sign.

I cannot help regretting that private schools have been established in the last twenty years in certain urban areas where a generation ago a public high school served all the youth of the town or city. In some of our Western cities in particular, the trend toward private education for the sons and daughters of the well-to-do has recently been pronounced, but there is no use for those of us who are committed to public high schools as schools for all to denounce or bemoan the growth of private secondary schools. The founding of a new independent school in a locality is a challenge to those connected with public education. Granted the "snob appeal" of some of these new independent schools, nevertheless I feel sure in many cases they would never have come into existence if the management of the local high school had been wiser. Education is a social process. This is a free country and people will not be pushed around by educators. What is required is for those concerned to improve the high schools; public school administrators must recognize the validity of some of the criticisms now directed against them in terms of the failure of the high school to provide adequate education for the gifted. The problem is especially acute in metropolitan areas. The success of the private school in Australian cities should be a reminder of where we may be headed.

Private schools exist and will continue to exist in the United States. Parents have the privilege of deciding whether to send their children to private or public schools. If they have doubts about the ability of secular schools to promote the growth of moral and spiritual values, then these doubts must be weighed against the advantages of a pupil's attending a free school for all denominations. Similarly, if a family questions the ability of the local high school to prepare a gifted boy or girl adequately for university work (and the question unfortunately must be raised in many communities today), the family will have to balance these misgivings against the advantage of mixing with all sorts of people while at school. It is hardly worth debating whether or not under ideal conditions in the United States all the public high schools would be so excellent that there would be no room for the private nonsectarian school. Many of those actively engaged in teaching in private schools hope that their efforts will so challenge the public schools that fewer and fewer parents will have to decide in favor of the private school for the gifted child.

Within limits, competition between private schools and public schools can be of advantage to the latter. I have used the phrase "competition within limits" advisedly, for it is difficult to run a private school without continuously recruiting students and it is difficult to recruit students without undermining public confidence in the tax-supported schools. Since the amount of money available for public education depends largely on the enthusiasm of the taxpayer, a chain reaction inimical to public education in a community may easily be started by zealous proponents of a private school. This is obvious in regard to a denominational school. If a religious group starts a school in a community, it is difficult for the promoters to avoid showing a derogatory attitude towards the rival public school. Thus even if the members of the denomination in question have no desire to receive tax money for their own private school, their criticism of the public schools may often tend to discourage the taxpayer. The same thing may happen as a result of schools that draw sons and daughters from well-to-do homes. That the growth of private schools, quite apart from the numbers enrolled, may endanger public education in a community is a fact often overlooked by those actively concerned with private education.

A comparable situation does not exist as between private colleges or universities on the one hand and state or municipal institutions on the other. There has been no such attack on state universities as the recent attacks on the public secondary schools. There is no movement, as far as I am aware, to have denominational colleges or universities supported by public funds. Universities and colleges serve only a small fraction of an age group; whether state or private, they cannot, by their nature, have the unifying influence of the comprehensive high school. Some proponents of an expansion of private secondary schools have attempted to win the allegiance of private colleges by equating the function and status of a school and a college. If a private college is worth supporting, why are not all private schools worthwhile, it is asked. This argument misses the point at issue: namely, the value to our society of a school enrolling essentially *all* the youth of a community.

A line of rational debate becomes possible if attention is centered on a community now served only by a comprehensive high school. The question is: "Would you favor the dispersion of a considerable proportion of the present student body into a group of parallel private schools, some free and church connected, some charging fees and nonsectarian?" If your answer is yes, then a subsidiary question is whether you advocate the present Australian pattern (no tax money for the private schools) or the English pattern. But the important question is the first, for it brings to a focus the issue of the American public school as an instrument for strengthening the spirit of national unity. If a given community does not now have a comprehensive high school, or has a very poor one, the question is: "Would you try to establish a first-rate public school or a group of private schools?" The basic issue is the same.

We Americans desire to provide through our schools unity in our national life. On the other hand, we seek the diversity that comes from freedom of action and expression for small groups of citizens. We look with disfavor on any monolithic type of educational structure; we shrink from any idea of regimentation, of uniformity as to the details of the many phases of secondary education. Unity we can achieve if our public schools remain the primary vehicle for the education of our youth, and if, as far as possible, all the youth of a community attend the same school irrespective of family fortune or cultural background. Diversity in experimentation we maintain by continued emphasis on the concept of local responsibility for our schools. Both these ideas are to a considerable degree novel in the development of civilization; a combination of them is to be found nowhere in the world outside of the United States.

By organizing our free schools on as comprehensive a basis as possible, we can continue to give our children an understanding of democracy. Religious tolerance, mutual respect between vocational groups, belief in the rights of the individual are among the virtues that the best of our high schools now foster. Any understanding of the political machinery of our federal union, of the significance of the Anglo-Saxon tradition of the common law, of the distinction between decisions arrived at by "due process" and those obtained by social pressures and by duress, all this is now being achieved to some degree in the free tax-supported schools of this country.

What the great "Public Schools" of England accomplished for the future governing class of that nation in the nineteenth century the American high school is now attempting to accomplish for those who govern the United States, namely, all the people. Free Schools where the future doctor, lawyer, professor, politician, banker, industrial executive, labor leader, and manual worker have studied and played together from the ages of 15 to 17 are a characteristic of large sections of the United States; they are an American invention. That such schools should be maintained and made even more democratic and comprehensive seems to me to be essential for the future of this republic.

Those who would grant all this but still question our free schools on religious grounds I would refer to a recent publication on "Moral and Spiritual Values in the Public Schools." There is set forth in strong terms the belief of many of us that in spite of their nondenominational character, our tax-supported schools have had as a great and continuing purpose the development of moral and spiritual values.

Diversity in American secondary education will be assured if we continue to insist on the doctrine of local control. We have few restrictions on the variety of approaches to secondary education presented by our thousands of local boards. Indeed, to an outsider I should think our diversity would look like educational chaos. But this is a characteristic of our flexible decentralized concept of democracy. The time may conceivably come when a state or the Federal Government may jeopardize this concept, but as far as secondary education is concerned, I do not detect any danger signals in that direction. The National Youth Administration threat, which was real in the 1930's, has almost been forgotten. In short, the answer to the question, "Can we achieve national unity through our public schools and still retain diversity?" is that we can if we so desire. My own personal answer would be that we must.

And now one final look ahead. In spite of the inadequacies of many of our high school programs and the undeveloped nature of our two-year community colleges, we have made great progress in the last twenty-five years in our attempt to provide adequate schools for *all* American youth. For the future we must endeavor to combine the British concern for training the "natural aristocracy of talents" with the American insistence on general education for *all* future citizens. If we can do that, then our industrialized society will prosper and at the same time the necessary degree of instruction will be provided for all the people so that in their hands "our liberties will remain secure."

The Organization of American Schools

THE American school system is organized on a single track, ladder basis with the major institutions being the elementary schools, the secondary schools, and the colleges and universities. In most states children enter the first grade of the elementary school at age six. They cannot enter before their sixth birthday but are compelled by law to do so at the beginning of the first school term following the sixth birthday. Some schools admit pupils at mid-year, but the great majority admit them only in September. If the school has a kindergarten the child may enter at five or five and one-half, but attendance is not compulsory. The kindergarten is generally in session for half a day. The pupil may attend the public school in his district without charge. He may attend a public school in another district if that school will accept him and if he is willing to pay tuition. A few school systems have nursery schools for children from two and one-half to five years. As in the kindergarten attendance at the nursery school is voluntary.

The elementary school is almost always at least a six-year institution and in some systems consists of eight grades, although in recent years some school systems have been establishing three-year primary neighborhood schools. This is being done most in the large cities and seems to be a very encouraging trend. These schools are smaller and more numerous and naturally closer to the pupil's home. Equally important with the small size is the homelike, neighborly atmosphere of a community school in which personal relationships which are so important, especially in the early years, can be established. If it is a six-year school, the pupil will graduate (with or without a formal ceremony) into a junior high school which is sometimes a two-year but more often a three-year school. After graduation from the junior high school the student will generally enter a comprehensive high school which is either a three or a four-year school depending on the nature of the junior high school. In many large cities students may enter vocational or technical high schools but only a small percentage of the total number of students do so. In some instances high schools that were originally designed and actually operated as vocational or technical schools have been converted into comprehensive high schools which offer not only the technical programs but college preparatory and general programs as well.

After graduation from the senior high school most of the students do not continue their formal education. Those who do then enter either a four-year college or a two-year junior college. If he attends a junior college, the student may terminate his study at the end of the two years or he may transfer to a four-year college for his last two years of work and receive his bachelor's degree. Some of the professional schools, such as medicine, require the bachelor's degree prior to entrance. Others, such as law, may admit a student with two or sometimes three years of college work and then provide three years of specialized training. Some professional schools, such as engineering, take students directly from high school and provide a four-year program leading to the bachelor's degree in the profession. To be admitted to the graduate schools which grant the master's and the doctor's degrees a student must have a bachelor's degree and a fairly good undergraduate record. Generally the master's degree requires one year of full-time study beyond the bachelor's. The student may or may not take the master's degree on his way to the doctorate. In most instances the most rigid selective process in the entire American school system occurs when the student applies for admission to the doctoral program.

There is no special school system in American education for adults. In many systems, especially in the cities and larger towns, the public schools conduct special classes open to all adults. Sometimes these classes are free and sometimes a small tuition charge is made. In some programs courses are offered to enable adults to complete their high school work, but most of them offer courses of special professional or cultural interest. These courses given by the public school system may or may not be taken for high school credit. Education beyond the secondary schools for which college credit is granted as well as the work leading to college degrees is generally handled by the evening division of the local college or university.

The American public school system is administered and operated on three levels: the local, the state, and the national. As we shall see, the administrative emphasis in the system is upon decentralization and particularly upon local control. However, from the beginning in the 1830's the tendency has been toward more and more centralized administrative control *within* states. This tendency has not grown out of a desire on the part of the state to dictate to the local districts, but rather from a desire to improve education by requiring that certain minimum standards be maintained. From the historical analysis in Chapter 6 the manner in which this administrative organization developed in American education can be understood. Now let us turn to the specific ways in which the school system is administered on the three levels.

The primary responsibility for education in America rests with the states, not with the federal government. The source of this authority is the Tenth Amendment to the Constitution which states that "the powers not delegated to the United States by the Constitution nor prohibited by it to the States, are reserved to the States respectively, or to the people." Education falls into this category, and it is therefore a state function.

It is important to remember that neither the U.S. Office of Education nor the U.S. Commissioner of Education has any direct control over the public schools of America. Unlike the European systems, which are generally highly centralized, the American pattern has emphasized decentralization. This is partly a historical accident and partly a result of the real fear of a strong central government that has been a potent influence in American history. Nevertheless, an able U.S. commissioner can exert a real influence upon American education. Moreover, as the world grows smaller through technical progress in transportation and communication, and our contact with other nations increases, it seems probable that the international aspects of American education will be receiving added emphasis. If so, the U.S. Office of Education would seem to be the logical agency to represent the fifty school systems in the United States.

The educational activity of the federal government is not limited to the Office of Education. In fact, so many different agencies have a hand in educational programs sponsored by the government that recommendations have been made to bring them together under one agency. For example, the school lunch program is handled by the Department of Agriculture, while the GI bill was under the jurisdiction of the Veterans Administration. Of course, the main branches of the government are involved in educational matters from time to time. For example, the Congress of the United States, through its legislative enactments, has contributed to education in the past and will probably continue to do so in the future. The Supreme Court of the United States as the final authority on the constitutionality of all laws also has had and will continue to have a profound effect upon the schools. Consider the impact of the decisions in the Oregon Case, the Everson Case, the McCollum Case, the Zorach Case, and the recent decision on segregation. Thus the federal government has a demonstrated interest in and an influence over the American schools, even though education is primarily a function of the state.

As has been pointed out, there is no mention of education in the Constitution; therefore, under the reserved power clause of the tenth amendment, the control of education is retained by the states. Each state, through its constitution or its laws, has made provision for a system of public schools. The provision for education in the Arizona Constitution is typical. It reads as follows:

> The legislators shall enact such laws as shall provide for the establishment and maintenance of a general and uniform public school system, which system shall include kindergarten schools, common schools, high schools, normal schools, industrial schools, and a university (which shall include an agricultural college, a school of mines, and such other technical schools as may be essential, until such time as it may be deemed advisable to establish separate state institutions of such character). The legislature shall also enact such laws as shall provide for the education and care of the deaf, dumb, and blind.

With this mandate in the state constitution, the state legislatures have enacted laws providing for the establishment of schools within the states. This was done by delegating to the local districts the authority to set up schools. The assemblies also created machinery on the state level to see that the laws were carried out. The pattern that has been followed over the nation was developed in Massachusetts under the leadership of Horace Mann. Three basic offices or agencies were established: the State Board of Education, the State Superintendency, and the State Department of Education. Not all of the states followed Massachusetts immediately, but gradually in the second half of the nineteenth century it became evident that some machinery was necessary to see to it that the districts met their responsibility to operate schools. Eventually all of the states created the office of superintendent of schools and state departments of education, while the majority have set up state boards of education.

The over-all responsibility for the management of the public schools in most states is assigned by law to the state board of education. The board usually consists of eight members who are either elected or appointed, ordinarily by the governor of the state, for rather lengthy terms. The members of the state board are required to be citizens of the state, and of high moral standing. Some states require that some members of the board be professional educators, while others stipulate that they must be laymen, and still others have no requirement either way. Some states try to keep the board bipartisan by providing that not more than half of the members can be of one political party. In most states the terms of office of the board members are staggered so that there are always veteran members in the group. The prevailing pattern is not to pay these men (or if a payment is made, the amount is small) except for expenses incurred in the performance of their duties. Usually an attempt is made to see to it that all sections of the state are represented, and some states provide that not more than one member from a single county or congressional district may serve on the board at one time.

The powers and duties of the state boards vary from state to state, but usually their job is to formulate policy and to oversee the management of the school system while the actual administration is in the hands of the state superintendent. In the states where the state board appoints the state superintendent, the board is in a very strong position. In many states there are separate state boards that control each university and college. However, the trend seems to be in the direction of having one board for all the institutions of higher learning in addition to the board that oversees the elementary and secondary schools.

The state superintendent, or state commissioner of schools as he is sometimes entitled, is the chief administrative officer on educational matters in the state. In some states he is elected by the people; in others he is appointed either by the state board or by the governor. But however he is chosen, he is always a professional educator and he always has direct responsibility for administering the state laws pertaining to education. Many of the state laws are quite specific and need only be enforced, but others, for example the certification laws, require that the state superintendent and his staff in the state department of education actually make the decisions as to what the specific requirements for certification will be. In most states the superintendent or commissioner has a real opportunity to provide leadership necessary to improve the schools. This can be done through budgetary recommendations, through establishing high minimum standards for teachers and administrators, and by working with local districts in improving their programs and salary schedules. In some states the state superintendent regards the state office as being primarily a service agency whose main function is to keep the status quo instead of providing vigorous leadership. This philosophy might be acceptable if the schools were perfect, but unfortunately they are not.

There has been much discussion in recent years over whether the superintendent should be elected or appointed. Most experienced educators have contended that by having the superintendent appointed, especially by the state board, the chances of getting a well-qualified individual are better. They have also pointed out that with this system the superintendent doesn't have to spend a great deal of time campaigning and can devote his attention to education. The advantage of the elective system is that the superintendent is secure in his job for four years and is in a position to exert strong leadership. One disadvantage of the appointive system is that in some states the superintendent is hired for an indefinite period and can be fired at any time by the board. In this situation the temptation to straddle the fence on issues in order to keep his position might be great. However, even if the superintendent were appointed for a four-year term and it developed that some of the board members violently objected to his policies, a man with a sense of professional ethics would probably resign. The problem is to establish the best system possible for selecting a competent person and allowing him freedom to carry out his policies.

The state departments of education have the responsibility for carrying out the programs formulated by the state boards of education and the state superintendent. For the most part the state departments are divided into specialized areas such as instruction, certification, finance, school buildings, research, guidance, agriculture, etc., with a professionally qualified person in charge of each division. These men are appointed by the state superintendents and are regarded as his staff. The state departments have grown tremendously in the last century as the state has assumed more and more responsibility for the schools. In many states the staff of the state department consists of well over a hundred persons. The diagram of the organization of the Department of Education in California is typical of the pattern of organization found in other state departments.

One of the chief functions of the state department is to provide professional service to the local district. Thus, if a local district needs help on school building problems, it can get such assistance from specialists in that field in the state department. The departments also publish materials which are helpful to the teachers and administrators throughout the state. For example, most states publish courses of study for elementary and secondary schools which may be used by the local districts.

In summary it can be said that the function of the state in the American school system is one of providing some compulsion and some stimulation to the local district. It attempts to establish minimum standards, to equalize opportunity, and, in general, to improve the quality of education in the schools. Service and leadership are provided but the major responsibility for formulating educational policy and operating the schools is left to the local districts. It can be said that the state attempts to provide a framework within which the local district can function. There is, of course, the danger that the states will become too strong and impose a deadening uniformity upon the schools, but so far the states have acted with restraint and the local districts have plenty of freedom to develop their educational programs.

The basic unit of organization so far as the public schools are concerned is the local district. It is the local district that actually operates

STATE OF CALIFORNIA, DEPARTMENT OF EDUCATION
CHART INDICATING LINES OF AUTHORITY

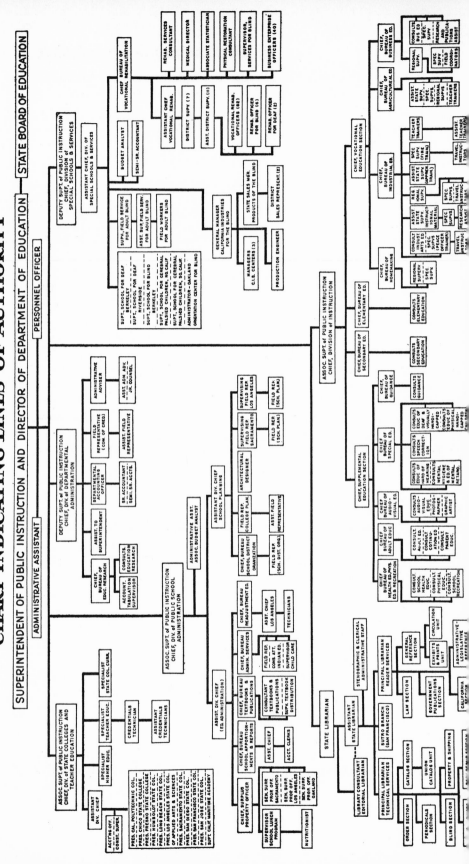

and controls the 160,000 public elementary and secondary schools of America. The state, through the various state boards or through the state commissioner, operates only the colleges and universities and a few special schools, such as schools for the blind. The federal government operates only the military colleges and, through the U.S. Office of Education, the schools in the territories and on the Indian reservations. To be sure, the authority to establish, operate, and control education is delegated to the districts by the states, but the actual operation from building schools to hiring teachers and creating a school program is in the hands of the local communities.

The school district is a quasi-corporation created by the state to establish and maintain schools. These local districts, of which there are some 45,000 in the nation, vary in size from a district, such as New York City, with several million people, hundreds of schools, and thousands of teachers to a small rural district with one school, one teacher, and a handful of pupils.

Despite this difference in size and wealth, the basic structure and the pattern of operation is similar in all school districts. Each district is represented by a board of education of from three to twelve members who are usually elected by the people in the district. Once elected, the board of education is in charge of the schools. In most large cities, for example, the mayor and the city aldermen have no authority over the schools. Even in the few districts where the board of education is a part of the municipal government, the board is responsible to the state, not the city council.

The pattern of having a locally elected board responsible for the schools originated in New England and has spread over the nation. It has served the purpose of keeping the schools out of politics, at least officially, and its organization and operation are certainly in the democratic tradition. In the middle of the nineteenth century, when the public school system was in its infancy, the boards actually assumed the responsibility of running the schools. But as the schools grew in number and in complexity, it became obvious that a professional educator who would devote full time to the job was essential. Today the most important task of the school board is selecting a competent superintendent who, together with his teachers, will actually run the schools. Once the superintendent is selected, the board accepts his recommendations as to school matters, such as school buildings, hiring teachers, budget, etc., although not always without question. If the board loses confidence in its superintendent, his contract is not renewed and a new person is hired. In general, the function of the board is to represent the people, establish the broad lines of educational policy, and exercise over-all supervision and control of the schools, while the actual administration and operation is left to the superintendent and the staff.

The nature and social composition of boards of education were studied by George Counts in an extensive nation-wide survey in 1927. The purpose of the study was to find out:

Who are the men and women composing the boards that control public education in the United States? From what social classes do they come? What training do they bring to the task of determining the educational policies to be adopted by the schools? What particular prejudices or special points of view may they be expected to exhibit? In a word, what is their intellectual and moral equipment for bearing the heavy responsibilities which society has placed upon them? How much time do they devote to those duties which devolve upon them as members of boards of education? What is the probability that they will support a type of education which seeks to make the coming generation genuinely intelligent about the present complex civilization and its numerous problems. Are the means which society has evolved for the control of education commensurate with the burden to be borne? These and many other questions of a similar character ought to receive the earnest consideration of students of education.[2]

After assembling and analyzing the data Dr. Counts wrote a short description of "typical" county, city, and state boards. As he points out, such a board does not exist but it does give a representative picture of the average board. His description of the typical city board is as follows:

The typical city board of education in the United States is composed of six members. These members are elected at large for a term of three years. One of the six members is a woman, who follows the occupation of housewife. Of the five men, one is a merchant; one, a lawyer; one, a physician; one, a banker, manufacturer, or business executive; and one, a salesman, clerk, or laborer. Three of the members have children attending the public schools of the city. From the standpoint of formal education, they constitute, in comparison with the city population as a whole, a highly selected group. But one of the members is a product of the elementary school only; two have attended the secondary school; and three have enjoyed college or university privileges. In age, they exhibit a range of twenty-six years, or a range from thirty-seven to sixty-three years. The remaining four members are distributed between these two extremes at the ages of forty-two, forty-six, fifty, and fifty-four years. In length of service on the board, they likewise show considerable diversity. At the one extreme is a novice who is serving his first year, while at the other is a

[2] George S. Counts, The Social Composition of Boards of Education (Chicago: University of Chicago Press, 1927), p. 1. Copyright 1927 by the University of Chicago.

veteran who has already given fifteen years of service to the board. The others show tenures of office of two, three, five, and eight years, respectively. On the average, these members devote approximately fifty-one hours a year to board duties. For this service they receive no financial compensation.[3]

Despite the fact that this study was conducted thirty years ago, its findings, with some slight changes still apply today. Today organized labor is generally represented more adequately, there are more women on the boards, and the educational background of the members has improved, but the social composition remains much the same. Even in the smaller towns the majority of board members are merchants or professional people.

The organizational and administrative arrangements within the district so far as the operation of the schools is concerned depend primarily on the size and population of the district. In large cities the organization resembles the state departments of education in complexity. Invariably there will be a superintendent who is in over-all control and several assistant superintendents, each responsible for a segment of the school system, e.g. elementary, secondary, vocational instruction, finance, guidance, personnel, buildings and grounds, etc. Most large systems today have specialists and consultants in curriculum, guidance, reading, supervision, audio-visual, and many other areas plus a large office and janitorial staff, hundreds of principals, and thousands of teachers. In a smaller district with three elementary schools and a high school the superintendent will probably have a principal, in charge of each school, who may or may not teach part time, and perhaps a business manager. In the very small districts with a one-room school the teacher will be principal, teacher, and probably janitor. In those districts without administrators, the county superintendent usually supervises the school.

One important fact that needs to be mentioned about the local district is the movement toward consolidation that has been underway in the last thirty years. There were approximately 150,000 school districts in America in 1933 while today there are approximately 60,000. The main reason for this consolidation of districts is that it makes possible a better quality of education for children. For example, if several small districts, each with a small elementary school, consolidate and pool their resources they probably would be able to provide a graded elementary school and a high school for all the children. Of course the progress in transportation, including better roads, has made consolidation possible. Most of the consolidation has gone on in the rural areas, but many suburban districts have also joined together in recent years. No one can predict where the consolidation movement will stop, but there are fac-

[3] *Ibid.*, p. 79.

tors that limit the size of districts. The first is distance. Even with modern transportation, there is a limit to the amount of time a student can be expected to sit in a school bus and still attend classes six hours a day. As it is, many students in rural consolidated districts spend an hour going to school and an hour coming home. The problem is not so acute on the elementary level because the schools can be smaller and scattered geographically throughout the district. But high schools, because they require more teachers, must be larger and therefore fewer in number. The second factor that should limit consolidation is the number of pupils to be taught. There is a point in school enrollments where schools become too large and too machinelike and impersonal. Of course, small schools can be maintained in very populous districts, but usually they are not and the idea very often seems to be the bigger they are, the better.

The basic pattern of local organization described in the preceding pages applies in general all over the nation, but with some variations. In some states, for example in New England, the "town" is the local unit instead of the "district." The town unit includes urban and rural areas and is administered by a single school board so the "town," educationally speaking, is analogous to the school "district." Some states, notably in the north-central section of the country, have similar rural-urban local educational units that are known as townships. Indiana, for example, has over 1,000 townships each of which has a single trustee who is elected by the people and serves the same function as the board of education in other states. This trustee system does not apply in the large cities of Indiana; Indianapolis, for example, has a conventional school board which runs the schools. In some states a combination of township and district exists. In Illinois, several small districts may form a township unit and build a township high school. Under this arrangement each of the districts has its own school board and in addition has membership on the board of education which operates the high school.

Another kind of local organization in American education is the county type, which is used extensively in the southern states. In these states each county has an elected school board which appoints a county superintendent, and the entire organization and operation is similar to the district, the only difference being that the counties are generally much larger. In the states where the county is the local unit, the larger cities and towns have their own board and are not under the authority of the county board or the county superintendent. In some states the county organization exists alongside the local districts. In Missouri, for example, the state is divided into 114 counties, each of which has an elected county superintendent. Within each county are numerous school districts each with its own board of education. If the district does not employ a superintendent who devotes at least half of his time to administration and supervision the county superintendent assumes responsibility for the general supervision of the schools within the district. He has no authority whatsoever over those districts within his county which have a full-time or even a half-time superintendent.

The International Aspects of American Education

AMERICAN education has been projected onto the international scene chiefly through American membership in the United Nations Educational, Scientific, and Cultural Organization. It is true that Americans, on both an individual and an organizational basis, have been participating in international educational activity since the nineteenth century. But America's membership in UNESCO involved the official approval of the government of the United States. This was given in 1946 in the form of a joint resolution approved by both houses of Congress. This was as much a landmark in American educational history as our membership in the United Nations constituted a landmark in American political history.

The entrance of the United States into UNESCO was the culmination of a series of steps in the direction of international co-operation in education. After World War I an unsuccessful attempt was made to make education a part of the League of Nations Covenant. But in 1921 the Council of the League created the International Commission on Intellectual Co-operation and this commission became the nucleus of the Institute of Intellectual Co-operation which was supported largely by the French and had its headquarters in Paris. The Institute was active in the period between the wars in promoting the exchange of students and scholars, the study of international relations, and the improvement of textbooks. In 1929 the International Bureau of Education was established, originally under the University of Geneva, but later on an international basis. The Bureau collected statistics and published a yearbook on education. Despite the fact that the United States was not a member of the League, American educators participated in all of these organizations. In America some progress was being made in international education. Shortly after World War I the Institute of International Education was established in New York to promote the exchange of teachers and students, and this organization is still operating an extensive program. In the late twenties the International Institute of Education was established at Teachers College under the leadership of such outstanding American educators as Isaac Kandel and George Counts, for the purpose of promoting the study of educational systems all over the world.

In the mid-thirties the Department of Cultural Affairs was created in the United States State Department and much of its activity was educational in nature. These efforts to use education as a means of improving international understanding of course failed to prevent World War II; in fact, since many German and Japanese students used skills learned through exchange programs against America during World War II many American educators questioned the value of the programs. However, the general consensus was that the programs had been too limited to be effective, and the result was a determination not to abandon the idea but to do a better job.

The horror and destructiveness of World War II stirred some educators into a realization that men would either learn to live together in peace or they eventually would destroy themselves. They were well aware that education, far from helping to create a peaceful world, had actually been the means through which war had been nurtured. Men could be taught to hate and to kill as effectively as they could be taught to love and live in peace. The challenge was clear cut. Either men would be educated to live in peace or they probably would not be alive to educate at all. As a result UNESCO was created as a specialized agency of the United Nations to carry out the purposes of the United Nations in the field of education. The basic philosophy of the organization is stated clearly in the Preamble to its Constitution. It reads as follows:

The Governments of the States parties to this Constitution on behalf of their peoples declare,

that since wars begin in the minds of men, it is in the minds of men that the defenses of peace must be constructed;

that ignorance of each other's ways and lives has been a common cause, throughout the history of mankind, of that suspicion and mistrust between the peoples of the world through which their differences have all too often broken into war;

that the great and terrible war which has now ended was a war made possible by the denial of the democratic principles of the dignity, equality, and mutual respect of men, and by the propagation, in their place, through ignorance and prejudice, of the doctrine of the inequality of men and races; that the wide diffusion of culture and the education of humanity for justice and liberty and peace are indispensable to the dignity of man and constitute a sacred duty which all the nations must fulfill in a spirit of mutual assistance and concern;

that a peace based exclusively upon the political and economic arrangements of the governments would not be a peace which could secure the unanimous, lasting, and sincere support of the peoples of the world, and that the peace must therefore be founded, if it is not to fail, upon the intellectual and moral solidarity of mankind.

For these reasons, the States parties to this Constitution, believing in full and equal opportunities for education for all, in the unrestricted pursuit of objective truth, and in the free exchange of ideas and knowledge, are agreed and determined to develop and to increase the means of communication between their peoples and to employ these means for the purposes of mutual understanding and a truer and more perfect knowledge of each other's lives.

In consequence whereof they do hereby create the United Nations Educational, Scientific, and Cultural Organization for the purpose of advancing, through the educational and scientific and cultural relations of the peoples of the world, the objectives of international peace and of the common welfare of mankind for which the United Nations was established and which its Charter proclaims.

The Constitution of the new organization was adopted in London in November of 1945 by representatives from more than thirty nations. The organization has three major organs. The first is the General Conference, a legislative body in which each nation has representation. The Conference meets every two years and approves the budget and program of the organization. The second major organ is the Executive Board, composed of twenty members elected by the General Conference. The Board, which meets frequently, acts for the General Conference during the period between its meetings and supervises the program of UNESCO. The third major organ is the Secretariat, which administers the business and professional affairs of the organization. The Secretariat, with its headquarters in Paris, has a staff of 800 international civil servants and is headed by the Director General who is elected by the General Conference. The Director General and his staff have the task of initiating and carrying out the program of UNESCO.

The present membership of UNESCO stands at about eighty countries. During the first eight years of the organization's existence (1946–54) the Soviet Union refused to join, and at times actually opposed it. However, in 1954 the Russians joined, and when they did Czechoslovakia, Hungary, and Poland renewed their active membership. UNESCO raises its own funds through contributions by the member states. The budget for the two-year period 1959–60 was approximately $13,000,000 per year. The United States contributes thirty-one per cent of the total budget, which meant that in each of those years UNESCO cost each American three cents.

Within many of the member states the work of UNESCO is carried on by the various national commissions. In America the United States National Commission, established by Congress, consists of one hundred members appointed by the Secretary of State. Sixty of the members are nominated by national associations in the fields of education, science, and culture, such as the National Education Association, the American Association for the Advancement of Science, and the American Academy of Arts and Sciences. Twenty are chosen from agencies of the federal, state, and local governments, and the remaining fifteen are chosen at large. These members, who include many of America's top educators, scientists, and artists, serve without pay. The National Commission has a biennial national conference to which all interested organizations are invited and at which the activities of UNESCO are discussed. The delegates to the General Conference of UNESCO are selected largely from the National Commission. In addition to the National Commission many states have organized UNESCO agencies. For example, the Missouri Coordinating Council for UNESCO helps to carry out the program of UNESCO in that state. To illustrate the kind of work that the state and national commissions do, the program for the 1953 Missouri State Conference has been included below. The theme was *What Is Your Part in Peace through World Understanding?* and the topics discussed were as follows:

Is Our Foreign Policy Promoting World Understanding?
What's Going On in the UN Today?
What Can I Do to Promote World Understanding in My Community?
How Can My Church Further World Understanding?
How Shall We Teach World Understanding in the Elementary School?
How Shall We Teach World Understanding in the High School?

When the new international educational organization was created in 1946 its leaders had high hopes and great expectations. So much needed to be done and man had so much to offer his fellow men. Great plans were laid and they were discussed eagerly. Then came the problem of financing the new organization. In the end UNESCO had to settle for a budget of $5,000,000. The readjustment was difficult and the frustration was great. What emerged from the floundering was a determination to make the best of the limited budget, and under the leadership of Torres Bodet of Mexico, UNESCO concentrated upon programs that would bring the greatest results with the least expenditure. This has been the philosophy guiding UNESCO ever since and it is reflected in the program that is described briefly below.

Perhaps the most important part of UNESCO's activity has been its program in fundamental education. From the beginning the leaders of the organization were aware of the problem of illiteracy, with its consequent ignorance, poverty, and suffering and its shackling of human growth and development. Unfortunately, limited funds did not permit a wide-scale attack on the problem. Instead, fundamental education centers were planned to prepare teachers who would then return to their native land and teach others. Two of these centers have been established, one at Patzcauro, Mexico, and the other at Sirs-el-Layyan near Cairo in Egypt. The center at Patzcauro in the first four years of its existence produced 227 graduates from 18 Latin American countries. At these centers the emphasis is upon a functional program related to the needs of the people. The fundamentals of reading and writing are taught, but the content of the materials used stresses basic facts about health and sanitation, diet and nutrition, and the elements of sound agriculture. For UNESCO learned quickly that trying to teach men who were hungry and disease-ridden to learn to read was impossible. One of the most difficult problems in this program is that of language. Many of the illiterate people have no written language. Therefore materials must be produced. Moreover there is little future in teaching men to read dialects in which no literature exists. On the other hand, many educators have been reluctant to impose upon these people foreign languages, such as English or Spanish, which have extensive literature. In many instances the beginning is made in the native dialect, and then a second language is introduced. The fact that teaching men to read and write does not guarantee that they will develop free humanitarian patterns of life also bothers some educators who believe deeply in fundamental education. Unfortunately men who know how to read but who read uncritically may be more effectively controlled by dictators, who of course have supported the "right kind" of education for this very reason. It is a risk but a risk that must be taken. As a result, in work that is being done by UNESCO in this area freedom and the dignity of man are being stressed along with the technical knowledge so necessary for a decent life.

UNESCO's program includes work in the international exchange of teachers and students, and, although its effort in this field is necessarily limited (for financial reasons), it is regarded as highly important. It is in line with the UNESCO thesis that "ignorance of each other's ways and lives has been a common cause, throughout the history of mankind, of that suspicion and mistrust between the peoples of the world through which their differences have all too often broken into war." It is realized that mere exchange may be ineffective and even harmful to international understanding. For example, many colored exchange students have left America with a bitterness in their hearts because of the way they have been treated while they were here. For this reason it is essential to select the right kind of individuals in the program and then to provide an opportunity for them to study all aspects of the culture into which they have been placed. In America, for example, they should see us as we really are, not all good, but not all bad.

UNESCO has sponsored many conferences and seminars on various subjects such as public education, teacher education, music, art, science, and the meeting of East and West. The idea is to get men together to discuss their common problems in the hope that a better understanding will emerge and that all may profit from the achievement of others.

UNESCO devotes a part of its budget to promoting research that seems to have some potential for improving international understanding. A research project has been supported that has investigated the tensions that cause wars, and some of this research has been published. Educational experts have been hired to study textbooks in the hope that these books could be improved so as to contribute to understanding or at least not to contribute to misunderstanding. A group of historians has been engaged by UNESCO to write a history of mankind from an international rather than a national point of view. Another project has been launched to study the effects of industrialization upon the lives of people, particularly in the underdeveloped areas of the world. On these problems and on many others UNESCO has engaged some of the finest scholars in the world in the belief that knowledge can help men to live together in peace.

Another major aspect of UNESCO's program is its publication and dissemination of materials. Again limited by lack of funds, it does its best to make available all kinds of materials pertaining to education, science, culture, and international understanding. It publishes material on the United Nations (including films), on subjects such as the Declaration of Human Rights, and on the teaching of reading. It attempts to act as a clearing house for all nations and especially to provide materials to the underdeveloped countries.

As a part of its program UNESCO has sponsored numerous educational missions in which experts are sent to assist the underdeveloped countries of the world. This aspect of UNESCO's program overlaps some others but it constitutes one of its most important and most effective activities. The educational mission is initiated by a country's request to UNESCO for assistance. The request is evaluated and if found to be promising, a team of experts is sent into the country to work on the matter. The cost is borne jointly by the country seeking assistance and by UNESCO. Frequently experts from other specialized agencies such as the World Health Organization and the Food and Agricultural Organization work with UNESCO in providing a team of experts, if this is necessary for the success of the mission. The following account of such a mission to Liberia in 1952 written by Professor David Scanlon of Newark State Teachers' College illustrates the way in which this aspect of UNESCO's program functions.

DAVID SCANLON

FROM

"Fundamental Education in Liberia, West Africa" [4]

In February, 1952, the Joint UNESCO Liberian Education agreement was signed by representatives of UNESCO and the Liberian government in Monrovia, Liberia. UNESCO had been invited by the Liberian government to inaugurate a Fundamental Education project which would assist this underdeveloped country to improve its standard of living. Under the direction of Dr. Joseph Jablow, an anthropologist from Brooklyn College, and Mr. W. S. deGuide Rankin, a former British Colonial Education Officer, a survey had been conducted to determine a suitable site for a Fundamental Education Pilot Project and the staff that would be needed in order to carry out the program successfully.

As conceived by Dr. Jablow and Mr. Rankin, during the first stage of the Pilot Project all work would be carried on at the village level. Eventually, a Fundamental Education Center would be built and from this Center young men and women trained as agriculturalists, teachers, health workers, and women's education workers would be assigned to villages that requested assistance. Villages used as demonstration centers during the first stage would be used as training areas when the permanent Center was constructed.

PERSONNEL FOR PROJECT

To carry out the work envisaged for the Pilot Project, four specialists were requested by the Government of Liberia. The Food and Agriculture Organization of the United Nations sent a member to be responsible for agricultural development and experimentation. From UNESCO came a woman who was responsible for women's education, which includes prenatal and baby care as well as domestic science and handicraft. UNESCO also sent a man to direct the organization of schools and the training of teachers. Mr. Rankin remained as co-ordinator of the Project. A request for a doctor from the World Health Organization has not as yet been filled, but the Liberian government assigned a nurse to maintain the clinic in the center of the area. In addition, a doctor from

[4] David Scanlon, "Fundamental Education in Liberia, West Africa," *Teachers College Record*, November 1953, pp. 70–6.

the Government Hospital in Monrovia visits the clinic once a week to treat those cases beyond the capabilities of the nurse. Since it soon became apparent that the services of a male handicraft expert were also needed, a request was made to the International Labor Organization for a specialist in this field.

In all cases a Liberian, whose salary was paid by the Liberian government, was assigned to each "foreign" specialist as a co-worker. He or she was selected by the Government of Liberia on the basis of past training, experience, and probably of prime importance, interest in bush life. Eventually, as the Liberian co-workers become adequately trained in their positions, they will replace the foreign specialists. A Fundamental Education Project is considered successfully completed when trained local personnel are able to maintain the program without foreign assistance. In several instances a Liberian co-worker has maintained his section of the program during intervals in which the international specialist was on leave or when the post has been vacated before the arrival of a replacement. The success with which the Liberians have been able to carry out this responsibility is a tribute to their zeal and enthusiasm. They are typical of the young Africans today who are anxious to build a better nation.

Plans and policies for Fundamental Education were made in weekly meetings of the complete team—foreign and Liberian. While it was recognized that each member of the team was a specialist in his field, the opportunity to exchange opinions and discuss aspects of each other's work helped to create a spirit of co-operative effort. In this way any undertaking by a member of the team represented the combined thinking of the whole team. The Liberian co-workers were particularly valuable at these meetings, inasmuch as they were the experts in the culture of the people. Joint meetings were held under the chairmanship of the Secretary of Public Instruction, to discuss over-all policy and administration of Fundamental Education.

AREA AND PEOPLE

The area chosen for the Fundamental Education program has a population of approximately twenty-five thousand people. The center of the area, about forty miles from the capital, Monrovia, is accessible during the dry season by a motor road. To reach the majority of the larger villages, however, involves a trek of two to ten hours over bush trails.

There are three major chiefdoms in the Fundamental Education area —the Dei, Gola, and Vai. The last constitutes one of the largest tribes in West Africa and is one of the few that has a written language. Each tribe has its own language. A Dei, for example, needs an interpreter to talk to a Vai, and a Vai, in turn, needs an interpreter to talk to a Gola.

Although a district is administered by a Commissioner appointed by the government, the various tribal chiefs are extremely powerful and are often considered rulers over their particular chiefdoms. Because of their influence among the people, their support was essential for success of the Project.

The co-operation of the Poro, the men's secret society, was vital for any form of organized educational effort in the area. The power of the Poro has decreased as the power of the federal government has increased, but the elders of the Poro can still remove any chief, including the Paramount Chief, who is the representative of the government, upon protest to the government. Boys are taken into the Poro for a circumcision rite when they are five or six. This is called the Little Bush, and they remain for a few days. When they are seven or eight they enter the Big Bush, where they may remain for years. During this period they are in a restricted area of the forest and attend a Bush School, where they are taught the fundamental laws of the tribe, agriculture, and hutbuilding and are given sex instruction.

Members of the team approached the elders of the Poro and explained to them the plans for raising the standard of living in the area. The elders questioned various aspects of the program and in many instances made valuable suggestions. At the end of the conference the elders agreed to co-operate in the program.

A comparable organization for girls is called the Sande. The period of training is much shorter than that for the boys. The Bush School attended by the girls emphasizes those things a future bride should know, such as cooking, agriculture, and her responsibilities to her husband, and offers sex instruction. While participation in the Sande is not mandatory today, a girl is not considered really ready for marriage until she has graduated from the Bush School. In addition, the village head of the Sande, the Ma Zo, is usually the midwife of the area. If a girl is not a member of the Sande she cannot expect to receive the full benefit of the Ma Zo's magic in child delivery. Thus, in an area where many children and women die in childbirth, the healing and "magical" powers of the Ma Zo are regarded as essential.

Agriculture is the main occupation of the men and women. The low productivity of the soil requires the farmer to let his field lie fallow for seven years. Because of the rapid growth of bush in West Africa, the farmer is forced to clear a forest area every year for his farm. His tools are few and his methods primitive. The men clear bush and plant; the women harvest the crop.

Cassava, rice, and palm oil constitute the main diet of the people. Cassava, a bulbous root plant which is practically pure starch, is prepared many ways. Rice, however, is the staple food. There is a popular saying among the Dei people that a man who does not eat rice for a year will die. No matter what food he eats, rice is considered the source of energy and good health. One healthful factor in the diet is palm oil, rich in vitamins. The palm oil is poured over the cooked rice. Except for a few goats, chickens, and fish, meat is scarce. Cattle in the area have long since died of sleeping sickness. A few hunters are found in the larger villages but the small game, deer, and bush cow (wild boar) are not plentiful.

The absence of cattle and the scarcity of goats eliminates milk from the diet of children. Once the child is weaned, and very often before, he is fed rice and water. The resulting malnutrition, characterized by a swollen stomach and swollen feet, causes a high infant mortality rate.

If the non-literate people of the area could be taught to boil water, wear a protective covering for their feet, and use pit latrines, a high percentage of the diseases could be eliminated. The spread of amoebic dysentery, schistosomiasis, guinea worm, and yaws could certainly be considerably reduced by following the methods mentioned above. Other diseases prevalent in the area are malaria, venereal diseases, and tuberculosis. Leprosy is also found, despite government efforts to confine lepers to restricted areas.

ORGANIZATION OF VILLAGE SCHOOLS

The members of the team decided that during the Pilot Project Fundamental Education would be primarily concerned with the development of village schools. These schools would be concerned not only with literacy but also with other aspects of Fundamental Education such as health and agriculture. In the beginning the schools would be modeled after the village kitchen, simple structures approximately 20 feet wide and 36 feet long open on all sides except for a low wall of rammed earth. The village craftsman who produced the woven squares of palm thatch used for the roof estimated the cost at $6.25—the only expense for building the school, since the village provided other materials and labor. The floor was covered with sand brought from a near-by river. Until the arrival of paper and other supplies ordered from abroad, sand was used for paper and bamboo sticks for pencils. Blackboards and furniture were of course nonexistent in the beginning. Each child brought a mat made of bamboo, upon which he sat. These simple, practical structures and materials of instruction can be obtained immediately in every Liberian village; more elaborate buildings might have discouraged the development of a school system in the interior.

The schools were to be organized on a four-year plan. For the majority this would represent terminal education in the formal sense. Those who showed promise and ability would be sent to an advanced elementary school, high school, and eventually the University of Liberia. The curriculum of the four-year school would include agriculture, health, reading, writing, oral English, and art. All instruction except oral English would be given in the local language. The Laubach System was to be used in reading and writing. It was expected that at the end of the third year all instruction could be carried on in English, as English is the official language of the country.

There was no difficulty in arousing parent interest in the school. Every day the open sides would be rimmed with parents watching the proceedings and occasionally shouting instructions to the children or the teacher. Although the West African seldom beats his child, on opening day of each school parents would provide the teacher with a heavy stick, for they had heard that children do not "learn" unless they are beaten.

AGRICULTURE, HEALTH, HANDICRAFTS

Attached to each school was a garden. The area, cleared by the men of the village, provided a garden for each child in addition to a communal school garden. During the gardening period, children learned general gardening principles and were taught how to sterilize soil, grow individual plants in bamboo cups, and estimate the amount of shade needed to protect newly planted seeds. New plants were introduced in an effort to provide a more healthful diet. Peanuts and soybeans were particularly stressed, in the hope that they would help compensate for the lack of protein in the diet of the majority of the people. The children proved to be extremely interested in gardening and it is difficult to imagine more neatly kept gardens anywhere. The men of the village, who visited the school garden daily, had been told they could have plants from the school seedbed; but first, as conservative farmers, they watched the school garden. When the gardens proved successful they asked for help from the FAO agriculturalist or one of the six Liberian assistants he was training as a type of county agent.

In teaching health the team stressed practical example rather than formal study. For instance, a high percentage of students had craw-craw, a skin disease common among children in West Africa. By mixing sulphur and palm oil and applying it generously to the infected areas the disease can be cured. But this would simply be the cure; the disease could be prevented if the children and adults washed daily with soap. The typical African family bathes every evening with just water. Unfortunately, soapmaking has practically died out in the area, and unless the family can afford to buy soap from the traders, no soap is used. By experimenting, the team discovered that a satisfactory soap could be made from papaya ashes and palm oil. It was decided to start soapmaking in the school. To obtain the necessary palm oil, a meeting was called of the parents. It was explained to them that use of soap could eliminate craw-craw and that if they would provide the palm oil, soap could be made for the children. Lengthy discussions took place in which, for the first time in a Mohammedan area, women took an active part. At the end of the discussion the parents agreed to provide the palm oil. From the school, soapmaking spread to the villages, where many women for the first time began making soap. With the increased use of soap, craw-craw was practically eliminated.

Every school had a pit latrine, and materials adapted from the Indian *Village Life Series* showed the spread of yaws, hookworm, and general infection from contaminated ground. Drinking water was boiled in the classroom, and individual drinking cups were made from bamboo poles.

The Liberian nurse made regular visits to the schools, and children needing a doctor's care were brought to the weekly clinic. These visits by the nurse were also used in training teachers to recognize the early stages of tropical ulcers, yaws, and other common diseases. For less serious complaints, teachers were provided with first-aid kits.

The Women's Education Specialist planned to work in the villages where schools were established, but first it was necessary to gain the support of the Ma Zos, leaders of the Sande. The Ma Zos had been invited to work with the nurse and to assist the doctor on clinic days that were devoted to women and children. By asking and using the help of the Ma Zos, a very cordial relationship had been built between the team and the secret society. However, while the support of the Sande was genuine, it was quite another matter to fit classes in child care and handicraft into the already crowded day of the village women. After trying unsuccessfully to conduct classes in the village, the Women's Education Specialist began conducting the classes in the rice fields, where most of the women worked during the day.

TRAINING OF TEACHERS

To recruit prospective teachers for training in the Fundamental Education schools, word was sent to the leading chiefs that teachers would be needed for the project and that young men and women who were elementary school graduates and interested in teaching would be interviewed. Since it was soon apparent that it would be impossible to find enough elementary school graduates to train, the formal education requirement was reduced to six years. After interviewing a number of candidates, five men were selected to be trained. While the search for teacher candidates was being conducted, the first Fundamental Education school was opened. This school was to serve as a demonstration school for the training of teachers and was taught by a Liberian who had been selected by the government as a co-worker in teacher training. This teacher, in co-operation with the UNESCO Teacher-Training Specialist, had been oriented to the Fundamental Education philosophy and had been given a brief course in teaching methods. With the arrival of the new trainees, the training program was begun. The trainees were given a six-week intensified course in teaching methods, health, and agriculture. Mornings were spent observing and participating in the demonstration school. In the afternoon, classes were held using what the student-teachers had seen in the morning as the basis for future discussion. During the evening the trainees learned how to make teaching aids from available native materials.

At the end of the six-week period three trainees were considered capable of being responsible for their own schools. Two remained for additional training. Classes were held two afternoons a week for those teachers who now taught in the Fundamental Education schools. In addition, the Teacher Training Specialist visited the schools twice each week and discussions were held regarding their teaching techniques and problems.

This program was considered an emergency training course that would be used until the completion of the Training Center. Once the Center is established, the "emergency" teachers will gradually be replaced by Center graduates and will then have the opportunity of taking the two-year training program at the Center.

At the end of eight months, twelve schools had been opened in widely scattered villages, with a total enrollment of 420 children. Every day a number of children would be found waiting at the school, hoping that one of the students would be absent and he or she would have the opportunity to "sit in" for the day; it had been necessary, though difficult, to restrict the number of children to 35 per class. Truancy is no problem here.

COMMUNITY CO-OPERATION

Films were found to be invaluable in teaching health and village development. In addition to those used in the teacher-training program, films were also shown in the villages. An experience with the village of Besao proved to be typical. With the permission of the chief it was announced in the village that films would be shown in the evening. Over three hundred people of all ages gathered, many having walked for hours to reach the village. For the vast majority it was the first time they had seen films. Plugged into the speaker was a microphone by means of which a teacher translated the English dialogue into the native language. The films, provided by the United States Information Service, were Walt Disney's *Careless Charlie*, a health film illustrating the need for pit latrines, and *Daybreak in Udi*, a British film showing co-operation in community development in native villages of Nigeria. The team, not expecting any results from the showing of the films, reasoned that the people would be impressed by the color and sound but probably would miss the message of the film, as this was their first experience.

The day following the showing of the film, the chief and elders announced that they could do as well as the people in the film. A pit latrine was dug, and those people not making use of the latrine were laughingly called "Charlie" by the rest of the village. The chief said that his people, not satisfied with building only a simple thing like a latrine, wanted to build something "big," as had the people in *Daybreak in Udi*. They had decided to build a school that would be an improvement over the usual village kitchen. The team, with the chief and elders, planned a two-room school that would also serve as a community center. An earthen block-building machine arrived from South Africa in time to be used in the construction of the new school. The chief and elders distributed the work among the men of the village. One group was responsible for clearing bush for the site; a second group made the blocks; a third laid the blocks; a fourth group of selected men were trained in elementary carpentry. The building of this school not only provided an adequate school and community center for the villagers but also served as an example of what other villages could do if they were willing to work together. Other chiefs who had heard of the undertaking visited Besao, and soon the team received many requests for assistance from villages who wanted to build a more adequate school.

Thus, in accordance with the basic philosophy of the UNESCO Technical Assistance program, the non-literate peoples of Liberia are learning to help themselves. The full co-operation of the people of the area has been won. The program described represents the first stage of Fundamental Education in Liberia. During the coming years a more rapid development can be expected. This success can be attributed largely to the support of the Liberian government and to the young Liberians who are now in training for leadership in the program after the departure of the international team.

Suggested Readings

Allen, Hollis P.: *The Federal Government and Education*. New York: McGraw-Hill Book Company, 1950.

Caswell, Hollis L., ed.: *The American High School*. New York: Harper & Brothers, 1946.

Conant, James B.: *Education and Liberty*. Cambridge, Mass.: Harvard University Press, 1953.

Counts, George S.: *The Social Composition of Boards of Education*. Chicago: University of Chicago Press, 1927.

DeYoung, Chris A.: *Introduction to American Education*. New York: McGraw-Hill Book Company, 1951.

Educational Policies Commission: *Education for All American Children*. Washington, D.C.: National Education Association, 1944.

————: *Education for All American Youth*. Washington, D.C.: National Education Association, 1944.

————: *The Structure and Administration of Education in American Democracy*. Washington, D.C.: National Education Association, 1938.

Shane, Harold C., ed.: *The American Elementary School*. New York: Harper & Brothers, 1953.

Warner, W. Lloyd; Havighurst, Robert J.; and Loeb, Martin B.: *Who Shall Be Educated?* New York: Harper & Brothers, 1944.

CHAPTER 10

THE LEGAL FOUNDATIONS OF
AMERICAN EDUCATION

THE LEGAL BASIS FOR THE AMERICAN SCHOOL SYSTEM HAS BEEN EStablished through provisions in our state constitutions, state and federal statutes, court decisions, and rulings of the attorney generals. The ultimate source of all law, educational or otherwise, in the United States is, of course, the people. It is the people of America, through their elected representatives, who have created the basic law of the land—the Constitution and the thousands of state and federal statutes that have been passed. It is the people therefore who, through their Constitution, have created the courts and the office of attorney general. There are no laws or legal institutions, including the Constitution of the United States and the Supreme Court, which cannot be changed if enough Americans want to change them.

Since no legal provision for education is made in the federal Constitution, the organization and administration of education in the United States is legally a function of the states. Each state has provided for a public school system in its constitution, and these provisions have been implemented and made specific through laws passed by the state legislatures. These laws have in turn been interpreted by the courts and through the rulings of the attorney generals.

The Public School and the State

THE public school in America is a state institution created by the state for its own preservation. This is made quite clear in the various state constitutions, and it has been reiterated again and again in numerous court decisions. Although it is common to think of the school as an institution primarily designed to promote the well-being of individuals, in legal theory the school exists because the continuation of the democratic state depends upon it. So far as the state is concerned education is not as much a right to which the pupil is entitled as it is a duty imposed upon him.

As we have seen, the establishment of the public school system in the mid-nineteenth century was based upon the needs of a democratic society. If men were to govern themselves and to participate intelligently in the affairs of state, they had to be educated and so the state legislatures compelled the local districts to establish schools. In the early years schools had to be established but attendance was voluntary. When it became obvious that many pupils were not being sent to school and that others were attending irregularly, the states, led by Massachusetts and Horace Mann in 1852, began to pass compulsory education laws. Today all states have such laws. The power to establish schools and to compel attendance is regarded by the court as a part of the power of the state to govern and is justified on the same grounds that the state's power to levy taxes or to raise armies is justified—that is, because the welfare of the state depends upon it.

The Individual and the State

THE question may be asked as to whether this power of the state in compelling children to attend school does not violate the rights of the individual and is not therefore undemocratic. Related to this is the question of whether the parents or the state or perhaps the church should control the education of the child. Until the Reformation the church was in complete control of education. Since then the tendency has been toward state control in most countries although some of the religious groups, notably the Roman Catholic, still maintain that education should be controlled by the church. Because public education is controlled by the state in the United States the basic issue concerns the parents and the state. (It should be remembered that since America is a democracy the state is the people. It is not the all-powerful agency beyond the reach of the individual that it is in many countries.) The legal view is that forcing a child to attend school is no more a violation of his rights than forcing an adult to pay taxes or forcing him to serve in the armed forces. Both are essential to the preservation of the state.

For the most part this question is a theoretical one since the overwhelming majority of the American people have accepted the idea of compulsory attendance at school as natural and beneficial. In fact American parents have accepted school attendance in such a responsible way, and are so sold on the benefits that can be derived from schooling that, despite the masses of children attending school, truancy is not much of a problem. However, the issue has been raised by a few parents and for them and their children it is important. It is equally important to students of education because the basic principles that are involved add to an understanding of the school system.

So far as the individual (or the parent and child) and the state are concerned, the issue is generally whether the parents have the right to educate their own child or whether they must send him to a school. The issue has usually had to be settled in the courts even though some states in their compulsory education laws specifically require attendance at school. The courts have held that parents may educate their own children or may have them educated at home, but the instruction must be equivalent to that given in the public school. In these cases the parent must prove to a court of competent jurisdiction that such instruction is being given. If the court is not satisfied that the instruction is equivalent, the child may be forced to attend school. There is, of course, no doubt of the legality of educating the child at home where the law is quite specific in this respect. For example, the compulsory attendance law in Ohio reads in part as follows:

Every parent, guardian, or other person having charge of any child of compulsory school age who is not employed under an age and schooling certificate and who has not been determined to be incapable of profiting substantially by further instruction, must send such child to a public, private or parochial school for the full time the school attended is in session, which shall not be for less than thirty-two weeks per school year . . .

Excuses from future attendance at or past absence from school may be granted for the causes, by the authorities, and under the following conditions:

(A) The superintendent of schools of the district in which the child resides may excuse him from attendance for any part of the remainder of the current school year upon satisfactory showing of either of the following facts:

(1) That his bodily or mental condition does not permit his attendance at school during such period;

(2) That he is being instructed at home by a person qualified to teach the branches in which instruction is required, and such additional branches, as the advancement and needs of the child may, in the opinion of such superintendent, require. In each such case the issuing superintendent shall file in his office, with a copy of the excuse, papers showing how the inability of the child to attend school or the qualifications of the person instructing the child at home were determined. All such excuses shall become void and subject to recall upon the removal of the disability of the child or the cessation of proper home instruction; and thereupon the child

or his parents, guardians, or other persons having him in charge may be proceeded against after due notice whether such excuse be re-called or not.[1]

On the other hand, in other states such as Illinois and Indiana where the law specifically requires attendance at school the issue has had to be settled in the court. The Illinois law reads in part as follows:

Whoever has custody or control of any child between the ages of seven and sixteen years shall cause such child to attend some public school in the district wherein the child resides the entire time it is in session: provided, that the following children shall not be re-quired to attend the public schools:

1. Any child attending a private or parochial school where chil-dren are taught the branches of education taught to children of corresponding age and grade in the public schools, and where the instruction of the child in the branches of education is in the English language;

2. Any child who is physically or mentally unable to attend school, such disability being certified to the county or district truant officer by a competent physician; or who is excused for temporary absence for cause by the principal or teacher of the school which the child attends.[2]

In the cases in which these laws had to be interpreted the decision hinged upon what constituted a "school." The following excerpt from an opinion of an Indiana court shows that a parent educating his child at home was in fact obeying the law.

A school, in the ordinary acceptation of its meaning, is a place where instruction is imparted to the young. If a parent employs and brings into his residence a teacher for the purpose of instructing his child or children, and such instruction is given as the law contemplates, the meaning and spirit of the law have been fully complied with. This would be the school of the child or children so educated, and would be as much a private school as if advertised and conducted as such. We do not think that the number of persons, whether one or many, makes a place where instruction is imparted any less or more a school.[3]

The compulsory attendance laws are of course not absolute, as indicated by the exceptions made for handicapped children. The courts have de-

---

[1] Ohio Statutes, Published in *Baldwin's Ohio Revised Code Annotated*, Chap-ter 3321 "School Attendance" Section 3321.04 (4849–3).

[2] Illinois Statutes, Published in *Smith-Hurd Illinois Annotated Statutes*, Chap-ter 122, "Schools" (26–1).

[3] State v. Peterman, 32 Ind. App. 665, 70 N.E. 550, 551 (1904).

cided that the compulsory attendance laws must be tempered by reason. For example, if a child is ill he is not required to attend school. Or, if he lives too far from the school to walk and no transportation is provided, the attendance laws cannot be enforced. In one case the court ruled that a child who had to cross railroad tracks which were not adequately protected and which endangered his life could not be forced to attend school.

On the other hand the parent does not have the right to refuse his child education. If he refuses, the state could and would take custody of the child. The same principle applies to local school boards. They must establish and maintain schools. Moreover the state can not only require that the parent educate the child, but it can also prescribe what the child shall be taught just as it can prohibit the teaching of doctrines that threaten the well-being of the state. Thus a parent would not be allowed to teach his child to be a thief or a murderer, nor would a school be permitted to teach and advocate the overthrow of the government.

The Rights of Private Schools

WHILE the states can compel a child to attend school, they cannot compel him to attend a public school. This issue was settled in the Oregon case. In 1922 the legislature of Oregon passed a law requiring all children to attend the public schools. The Supreme Court of the United States ruled that the law was unconstitutional on the grounds that it unreasonably interfered with the right of the parents to educate their children and that it deprived the owners of the private schools of their property rights. And so the private and parochial schools have the right to operate in America and parents have the right to send their children to these schools if they so desire. The Supreme Court did not, however, free the private schools of state control as the following excerpt from the opinion of the Court indicates:

> No question is raised concerning the power of the state reasonably to regulate all schools, to inspect, supervise and examine them, their teachers and pupils; to require that all children of proper age attend some school, that teachers shall be of good moral character and patriotic disposition, that certain studies plainly essential to good citizenship must be taught, and that nothing be taught which is manifestly inimical to the public welfare.[4]

Thus the legislature cannot prohibit the establishment of a private school unless it can be shown that the school is in some way endangering the public welfare. Neither can the state alter or revoke a charter granted

[4] Pierce v. Society of Sisters, 268 U.S. 510, 534 (1924).

to a private school unless provision for such action was contained in the charter. These charters are regarded by the courts as contracts, and the Constitution of the United States prohibits the state from violating them. This issue was decided in the famous Dartmouth College case in 1821.

The Power of the State Legislatures

THE state legislatures hold the real power in American education. Their members are the representatives of the people and are empowered to pass any laws which they deem necessary, subject only to the provisions and restrictions placed upon them by the state and federal constitutions. The state constitutions provide that the legislature must establish free public schools, and they generally prohibit the use of public funds for sectarian schools. Therefore, the legislatures have no choice but to establish free, public, nonsectarian schools. Many state constitutions had provisions prohibiting Negro and white pupils from attending the same public schools, and until the Supreme Court ruled that these provisions violated the Constitution of the United States the legislatures in these states could not provide for racially integrated schools. Some state constitutions require the legislatures to spend a certain percentage of the state revenue for schools, and the legislature must comply. But within this framework the legislatures have free rein. By their very nature, they are empowered to legislate, and this includes enacting laws pertaining to education and the schools. It is possible, of course, to change the state constitution, and this has been done in some of the southern states in an effort to get around the Supreme Court ruling on segregation. In these states either the governor or the legislature took the initiative in submitting proposals for the passage of permissive legislation giving the legislature the power to amend the Constitution and to do away with the public school system. If this is done, the question has been raised as to whether the federal government under the general welfare clause would have the right to establish public schools in these states. Some educators have also questioned the right of the states to abolish the public schools since they were accepted into the Union with provisions for the public schools in their constitutions and presumably these provisions were part of the basis for their being accepted; at least one state was refused admission into the Union until its constitution was changed to provide for public schools. But these questions will have to be decided by the courts in the years ahead.

In carrying out the mandate to establish a system of public schools the state legislatures have passed thousands of laws. Through these laws the legislature can and does determine such matters as the kinds and types of schools to be established, the number of days and the number of hours per day they are to be in session, the content of the curricula, the certification requirements for teachers, and the nature of the organization and administration of the school system. As was pointed out in the preceding chapter, the states have generally provided a broad framework for the school system within the state and then delegated the authority for actually operating and maintaining the schools to the local units.

The Power of the Courts

THROUGHOUT the history of American education the courts, both state and federal, have been called upon again and again to decide whether certain laws were or were not constitutional and to make decisions that involved an interpretation of existing laws. In both ways the courts have shown the power and influence they exert over the American schools. In any matter of educational law, the Supreme Court of the United States is the final judge. The Supreme Court derives its authority to pass on state legislation from the Fourteenth Amendment which provides that:

> No state shall make or enforce any law which shall abridge the privileges or immunities of citizens of the United States; nor shall any state deprive any person of life, liberty, or property without due process of law; nor deny to any person within its jurisdiction the equal protection of the laws.

In any dispute the Supreme Court is the final judge of whether the Constitution or any of its amendments has been violated. The McCollum case in which the Supreme Court ruled that the practice of granting released time to allow religious classes to be held in the school violated the First Amendment and was unconstitutional offers a good illustration of the power of the courts. The majority opinion also shows how the judges reasoned and how the public schools must operate within the framework of the Constitution. The opinion of the Court reads in part as follows:

> This case related to the power of a state to utilize its tax-supported public school system in aid of religious instruction insofar as that power may be restricted by the First and Fourteenth Amendments to the Federal Constitution.
>
> The appellant, Vashti McCollum, began this action for mandamus against the Champaign Board of Education in the Circuit Court of Champaign County, Illinois. Her asserted interest was that of a resident and taxpayer of Champaign and of a parent whose child was then enrolled in the Champaign public schools. Illinois has a compulsory education law which, with exceptions, requires

parents to send their children, aged seven to sixteen, to its tax-supported public schools where the children are to remain in attendance during the hours when the schools are regularly in session. Parents who violate this law commit a misdemeanor punishable by fine unless the children attend private or parochial schools which meet educational standards fixed by the State. District boards of education are given general supervisory powers of the use of the public school buildings within the school districts.

Appellant's petition for mandamus alleged that religious teachers, employed by private religious groups, were permitted to come weekly into the school buildings during the regular hours set apart for secular teaching, and then and there for a period of thirty minutes substitute their religious teaching for the secular education provided under the compulsory education law. The petitioner charged that this joint public-school religious group program violated the First and Fourteenth Amendments to the United States Constitution. The prayer of her petition was that the Board of Education be ordered to "adopt and enforce rules and regulations prohibiting all instruction in and teaching of religious education in all public schools in Champaign School District Number 71, . . . and in all public school houses and buildings in said district when occupied by public schools. . . .

The foregoing facts, without reference to others that appear in the record, show the use of tax-supported property for religious instruction and the close co-operation between the school authorities and the religious council in promoting religious education. The operation of the State's compulsory education system thus assists and is integrated with the program of religious instruction carried on by separate religious sects. Pupils compelled by law to go to school for secular education are released in part from their legal duty upon the condition that they attend the religious classes. This is beyond all question a utilization of the tax-established and tax-supported public school system to aid religious groups to spread their faith. And it falls squarely under the ban of the First Amendment (made applicable to the States by the Fourteenth, as we interpreted it in *Everson v. Board of Education*, 330 U.S. 1. There we said: "Neither a state nor the Federal Government can set up a church. Neither can pass laws which aid one religion, aid all religions, or prefer one religion over another. Neither can force or influence a person to go to or to remain away from church against his will or force him to profess a belief or disbelief in any religion. No person can be punished for entertaining or professing religious beliefs or disbeliefs, for church attendance or nonattendance. No tax in any amount, large or small, can be levied to support any religious activities or institutions, whatever they may be called, or whatever form they may adopt to teach or practice religion. Neither a state nor the Federal Government can, openly or secretly, participate in the affairs of any religious organizations or groups and vice versa. In the words of Jefferson, the clause against establishment of religion by law was intended to erect 'a wall of separation between church and State.'" Id. at 15–16. The majority in the Everson case, and the minority as shown by quotations from the dissenting views in our notes 6 and 7, agreed that the First Amendment's language, properly interpreted, had erected a wall of separation between Church and State. They disagreed as to the facts shown by the record and as to the proper application of the First Amendment's language to those facts.

Recognizing that the Illinois program is barred by the First and Fourteenth Amendments if we adhere to the views expressed in the Everson case, counsel for the respondents challenge those views as dicta and urge that we reconsider and repudiate them. They argue that historically the First Amendment was intended to forbid only government preference of one religion over another, not an impartial governmental assistance of all religions. In addition they ask that we distinguish or overrule our holding in the Everson case that the Fourteenth Amendment made the "establishment of religion" clause of the First Amendment applicable as a prohibition against the States. After giving full consideration to the arguments presented we are unable to accept either of these contentions.

To hold that a state cannot consistently with the First and Fourteenth Amendments utilize its public school system to aid any or all religious faiths or sects in the dissemination of their doctrines and ideals does not, as counsel urge, manifest a governmental hostility to religion or religious teachings. A manifestation of such hostility would be at war with our national tradition as embodied in the First Amendment's guaranty of the free exercise of religion. For the First Amendment rests upon the premise that both religion and government can best work to achieve their lofty aims if each is left free from the other within its respective sphere. Or, as we said in the Everson case, the First Amendment has erected a wall between Church and State which must be kept high and impregnable.

Here not only are the State's tax-supported school buildings used for the dissemination of religious doctrines. The State also affords sectarian groups an invaluable aid in that it helps to provide pupils for their religious classes through use of the State's compulsory public school machinery. This is not separation of Church and State.[5]

[5] McCollum v. Board of Education, 333 U.S. 203, 205–12 (1947).

The segregation case in which the Supreme Court ruled in a unanimous decision that the provisions in the state constitutions separating Negro and white students in the public schools were unconstitutional is another example of the way in which the courts influence the schools. The reasoning of the Court in this case was as follows:

We conclude that in the field of public education the doctrine of "separate but equal" has no place. Separate educational facilities are inherently unequal. Therefore, we hold that the plaintiffs and others similarly situated for whom the actions have been brought are, by reason of the segregation complained of, deprived of the equal protection of the laws guaranteed by the Fourteenth Amendment. This disposition makes unnecessary any discussion whether such segregation also violates the due process clause of the Fourteenth Amendment.[6]

The Supreme Court has been involved in the most spectacular cases, at least in recent years, because the really controversial cases are eventually heard there. But the state and lower federal courts have also exerted a powerful influence over the schools. In many other instances school problems involving an interpretation of school law never reach the courts but are decided by rulings of the state attorney general. If his ruling is contested then the case comes before the courts.

The Authority of the Local School Boards

THE local school district and the school board are creatures of the state and have no authority that is not expressly or impliedly granted by the state. Thus for example, a local board may issue bonds but only to the amount authorized by the state. However, since school districts are quasi-corporations created by the state to establish and maintain schools, the courts have held that they have the legal right to create whatever rules and regulations are necessary in order to carry on their assigned task as long as these rules are reasonable. For example, although the state law requires that the pupil attend school, the courts have decided that it is reasonable for a school board to refuse to admit pupils who reach the admission age late in the school year until the following September. In general, the courts have upheld the actions of the local boards on matters over which the board has jurisdiction so long as the rules were not arbitrary, unreasonable, or malicious. The attitude of the court in this matter can be illustrated by an excerpt from a case in Kentucky in which a student was expelled for writing an insulting composition. The court held that:

[6] Brown v. Board of Education, 347 U.S. 483, 495 (1953).

It necessarily follows that those in charge of said school must be allowed to judge of and determine as to the propriety of expelling scholars therefrom, and it is manifest that those in charge of the school are better qualified to judge of and determine as to what offenses justify expulsion than the courts can ordinarily be . . . Our conclusion is that those in charge of such schools have a right to formulate such necessary rules as, in their judgment, will best promote the public good; and, if such rules are violated by any pupil, the right to expel such pupil exists, and may be exercised by the proper school authorities; and the question as to the guilt or innocence of the accused cannot be reviewed by the courts unless it appears that such pupil was expelled arbitrarily or maliciously. We do not feel called upon to determine in this case whether the plaintiff was guilty of the offense for which it seems she was expelled from school. It may be that she did not mean to insult her teacher. That question was determined by the superintendent, and his action ratified by the board of education, and we do not think we have the authority to weigh and determine the evidence in respect thereto. We are not of the opinion that the evidence in this case tends to show that the teacher, superintendent or board of education acted maliciously or unfairly in the matter under consideration. . . . [7]

For similar reasons the courts have ruled that school districts may require a physical examination of pupils. The states may require local districts to have children vaccinated whether an epidemic of smallpox exists or not. If no specific state requirement or authority exists, the authority of the local district to require vaccination usually depends upon whether there is danger of an epidemic. So far as the curriculum or courses of study are concerned the local board, through its administrative and teaching staff, have a free hand within the limitations set by the state and federal law.

Control of Pupil Conduct by the School

BY SENDING a child to school a parent delegates a certain amount of authority over the child to the teacher or the school authorities. According to one of the authoritative treatises on American law, the legal control of the pupil by the teacher is as follows:

As a general rule a school teacher, to a limited extent at least, stands in loco parentis to pupils under his charge and may exercise such powers of control, restraint, and correction over them as may be reasonably necessary to enable him properly to perform his duties

[7] Board of Education v. Booth, 110 Ky. 807, 812 (1901).

as teacher and accomplish the purposes of education subject to such
limitations and prohibitions as may be defined by legislative enact-
ment.[8]

If the teachers did not have such control over pupils the schools would
be in a chaotic condition. However, the teacher does not have the same
authority over the child as the parent, especially when it comes to
punishing children. The legal facts are that teachers or school authorities
have the right to inflict reasonable corporal punishment upon the child
for offenses committed by the child while he is under the jurisdiction of
the school authorities. But if the teacher inflicts permanent injury upon
the child or acts with malice toward the child the punishment is illegal
and the teacher is held liable. Fortunately the issue is becoming less
important since corporal punishment is rapidly disappearing from American schools and American homes. As we learn more about children and
why they behave as they do we are in a better position to help and guide
their development without beating them.

The school authorities may control the conduct of pupils in many
other ways. Schools may require children to salute the flag, although the
Supreme Court has ruled that where this action violates the religious
convictions of a pupil he may be excused. Public school authorities may,
with or without the support of a state statute, prohibit fraternities,
sororities, or secret societies in their schools if in their judgment such
organizations are hampering the program of the school. The school
board has the authority to suspend or expel any pupil who breaks the
rules of the school if such rules are reasonable and within the jurisdiction
of the board to make. Moreover a school board may expel a pupil even
if no rule has been broken if that pupil is interfering with the proper
functioning of the school. It is clear then that the public school authorities have broad powers in regulating the conduct of the pupils under their
jurisdiction. But they must always act within the law (e.g., they could
not force a child to study a particular religion) and they must act reasonably and with discretion.

Suggested Readings

Duke University School of Law: "School Pupils and the Law." *Law and
Contemporary Problems.* Vol. 20 (Winter 1955) No. 1.

Edwards, Newton: *The Courts and the Public Schools.* Chicago: University of Chicago Press, 1933.

Hamilton, Robert R., and Mort, Paul R.: *The Law and Public Education.* Chicago: The Foundation Press, 1941.

[8] Control of Pupils and Discipline, 56 Corpus Juris, 1088 (1932).

CHAPTER 11

FINANCIAL SUPPORT OF AMERICAN EDUCATION

ONE OF THE MOST IMPORTANT ASPECTS OF ANY EDUCATIONAL SYStem is the way in which it is supported financially, for no matter how intelligently a school system is organized it cannot function without adequate funds. It is true that generous financial support does not, in and of itself, guarantee an excellent school system, but an excellent school system cannot exist without adequate support. Before getting into the problems of the support of American education, however, let us turn to the present arrangements whereby the American schools are supported. Once this is done, an attempt will be made to judge the adequacy of these arrangements and to consider some of the problems connected with them.

Our concern will be primarily with the public schools, especially on the elementary and secondary levels, since better than ninety per cent of American children attend these schools. The private nondenominational schools are supported by tuition charges to students and endowments, while the religious schools are supported by the churches and to some extent through tuition charges to students. The public schools are supported by taxes paid by all adults whether they have children or not. According to the U.S. Office of Education, a total of $20,000,000,000 was spent on the American school system in 1957–58. This figure includes both operational costs and capital outlay (for buildings and interest on bonds) for all public and private schools.

The public schools are financed by taxes collected from the local districts, the states, and the federal government. For the nation as a whole, approximately fifty-five per cent of the school's funds are derived from local districts, about forty-one per cent from the states, and less than four per cent from the federal government. There is great variation among the states in respect to the percentage of funds derived from local sources and from state sources. In Nebraska and New Hampshire, for example, approximately ninety-five per cent of school funds come from *local* sources. At the other extreme, Delaware derives eighty-three per cent of its funds from *state* sources, while Alabama derives seventy-nine per cent. The trend for the nation as a whole to have a larger share of the support borne by the states is evidenced by the fact that the states supplied only seventeen per cent of the total revenue in 1930, whereas they supplied about forty-one per cent in 1957–58. Between two thirds and three fourths of the school revenue is used for instructional purposes— that is, for teachers' salaries—with the remainder being spent on supplies, operation and maintenance of buildings, etc.

Local Support of Public Schools

THE pattern of support for the American public schools parallels the legal and organizational arrangements. The state creates the local district and delegates to it the responsibility for the maintenance and operation of the schools. In the same pattern, the states require the local districts to levy taxes to raise funds to support the schools but usually set limits on the taxes which may be levied. These funds are obtained through a tax on real estate levied on all property owners in the district. The amount of money a local district has for operating its schools depends upon (1) the assessed valuation of the real property in the district, and (2) the amount of the tax levy. Obviously a district which is poor —that is, one with a low property value—may have less revenue than a wealthy district even if its tax levy is higher.

In general, the local district is permitted by the state to levy a minimum tax on each $100 of the assessed value of all real estate in the district without a vote of the people. If the school board in the district wishes to raise the tax levy beyond the minimum, a vote of the people is required. In Missouri, for example, school boards in the local districts may levy, without a vote, a tax of $0.65 per $100 assessed valuation in rural districts. This levy is raised to $1.00 in districts with an incorporated town and to $0.89 in the city of St. Louis. By a simple majority vote this levy may be increased by $1.30 per $100 in rural districts, $2.00 in districts with incorporated towns, and $1.78 in St. Louis, but these increases may be voted only for the period between school elections, which is normally one year. By a *two-thirds* majority vote, the tax levies may be raised beyond these limits and the increases may be voted for a four-year period, but the money may be used only for current school purposes, which means for all phases of the school program except capital outlay. There are variations of this pattern in all the states. Thus many of the states place an upper limit on the tax that can be levied in the local districts regardless of the vote.

The funds raised from these taxes are generally used for operating the schools and, as we have seen, the bulk of it for teachers' salaries. If new school buildings are needed, the usual procedure is to raise the money by borrowing and issuing bonds which are then paid off with interest over an extended period of time with the money obtained through the tax levy. As in the case of the tax levy the state prescribes the limit of bonded indebtedness which a district may incur, usually a small percentage (five to ten per cent) of the total assessed valuation of the property in the district. These bond issues must be approved by the voters in the district, generally by a simple majority but sometimes by a two-thirds majority. It is permissible for school districts to set aside a part of the regular school revenue for school building purposes, but few are able to do so.

The local revenue is used primarily for elementary and secondary schools, with the state colleges and universities being financed with state funds. If a local district (usually a city district) maintains a college as a part of the local school system, it is supported by local funds. If the local district receives state funds for the partial support of the college, it is generally required to admit students from all over the state, although it remains under city control.

The procedure for determining how much revenue is needed for the schools in a district is similar to the procedure for the determination of other school policy. The superintendent, with the assistance of his staff, makes an estimate of the financial need and submits his recommendations to the school board. If the board approves the budget and the revenue of the district is adequate, nothing else need be done. If additional funds are needed, the superintendent makes an estimate of the tax increase that will be necessary and submits it to the board. If the school board approves the request the proposal is then submitted to the voters at the next school election. If the district is already taxing itself up to the limit set by the state, it must get along on what it has. If a bond issue is necessary, it is the superintendent's job to bring a recommendation before the board, which in turn submits it to the people.

This system of local taxation on real property which has provided the bulk of the funds for the public schools since their establishment has been a subject of controversy among educators for years. This system of taxation is the basic cause of the gross inequality between districts within states. With this system of support the wealthier districts obviously have more money to spend on schools and the poorer districts have less. This means, of course, that the wealthy districts have better schools, better teachers, smaller classes, and better materials. The net result is that our children do not have equality of educational opportunity. It is also contended that the real-estate tax as such is outmoded and inadequate. It was developed at a time when America was an agrarian country and land was the basis of wealth. Today, however, America is an industrial nation, and, while the assessed valuation of land is generally related to its wealth and value, it is believed that other forms of taxation are more effective and more equitable.

State Support of Public Education

THE second major source of revenue for public schools in America is the state. As was pointed out above, for the nation as a whole forty-one per cent of the funds spent on public schools are derived from this source. All states spend a substantial portion of their total revenue for public schools. Most states are required by law to spend a certain percentage, say one-fourth, of their total revenue for schools, and many regularly go beyond this minimum and spend as much as one-third of their revenue for this purpose. There is great variety among the states in the kinds of taxes which provide the revenue, but sales taxes, motor vehicle and gasoline taxes, income taxes, and property taxes are most common.

The decisions regarding how much money is needed and how it is to be spent are made by the state superintendent of schools. He draws up the budget with the help of his staff and submits it to the state board of education. If they approve it, the budget then must be approved by the legislature. If revenue beyond the existing limit is needed, the legislature must approve the increase and then enact the legislation necessary to secure it.

For the most part state funds are granted directly to the local districts. Exceptions occur in the case of the state colleges and universities and for special schools such as schools for the blind. One of the vexing problems in the American public school system is how to apportion these state funds to the local districts. The principles upon which the states act in this matter are quite simple and uniform. All states in their programs of supporting the local districts attempt to (1) establish minimum standards in all the districts of the state and (2) equalize opportunity. In pursuing these objectives no attempts are made to bring all districts down to a common level. On the contrary, all districts are encouraged to raise their levels of support as high as possible. The goal is to see to it that *all* districts achieve at least a minimum level of support. Ideally, under the theory of equalization, the poorer districts receive more money from the state and the wealthier districts receive less.

But the ideal is difficult to realize because of the difficulty of determining the local district's ability to support its schools and of gauging the effort it is making. The problem is complicated by the lack of standardization in assessing property valuations. The result is that there is great variation in these assessments from district to district. Therefore it is impossible to determine from the tax levy alone how much effort the local district is making to support its schools. It has been estimated by the Committee on Tax Education and School Finance of the National Education Association that property in some districts is assessed at only ten per cent of its actual value, whereas in others the figure is as high as ninety per cent.

The problem of the apportionment of state funds to the local districts in order to equalize educational opportunity is aggravated by practical politics within the states. Obviously the districts that have not been pulling their share of the load but which have been receiving state funds on the basis of pupil attendance are not willing to give up their state aid and pay more for the support of their local schools without a struggle. However, despite the difficulties, the states have been making real progress in their efforts to apportion state funds so that all children within the state, even those in the poorest districts, will receive a good education. Some states have developed a system of having a state agency estimate the full valuation of property within the local districts; the state aid is then apportioned on this basis. Since 1935 educational finance experts in seeking an answer to this problem have been working on "ability indexes" which compute ability to support schools on a combination of factors other than property valuation indicating the wealth of a community. This type of ability index is already being used in six states and is being considered in others. It seems reasonable to assume that further progress in this direction is likely as a result of research that is being conducted. It is also possible that some of the techniques being developed by economists might be adapted and used to help solve this problem of educational finance.

One of the facts of life so far as the financial support (from state and local sources) of the public school system is concerned is the great variation between the states in their ability and their willingness to support their schools. The truth is that some of our states, despite the fact that they tax themselves heavily, simply do not have much wealth and therefore do not have adequate funds for their schools. In 1957, for example, Mississippi had available for educational purposes an income per pupil of $3,806, as compared with $17,305 in Delaware and $16,149 in New York. Yet the state of Mississippi spent a larger percentage of its income in that year for education than either of the other, wealthier states (3.37 per cent in Mississippi, 2.21 per cent in Delaware and 2.78 per cent in New York). It should be remembered that these figures are *averages* for the entire state and that within some of the poorer states there are wealthy districts with well-financed schools, just as there are poor districts with poorly supported schools in the richer states. Nevertheless there is gross inequality among the states and this means that some of our children are being cheated. This real inequality is the most powerful argument for federal aid to education for if a reasonable degree of equality of educational opportunity is our goal, then federal aid is a must. Just as the state is the only agency that can counteract inequality in districts *within* the state, so the federal government is the only agency that can achieve a measure of equality of educational opportunity *among* the states. This basic inequality of the states in the ability to support schools is also the strongest argument against the matching principle in the apportionment of federal funds, for under this system the wealthy states, which already have more money, are given more by the federal government.

Federal Support of Public Education

THE federal government, as has already been noted, contributes only a small percentage of the total amount spent on public education, for education is a state function which has been largely delegated to the local districts. Nevertheless, the federal government has made, and probably will make in the future, significant financial contributions to the public school system. In the land ordinance of 1785, for example, the federal government granted to each state entering the Union sections of land to be used for public education. By the time all the states had received these grants of land, the federal government had given the states a total of 90,000,000 acres, or an area almost as large as the state of Texas. During and after the Civil War the federal government passed a series of laws aiding mechanical, agricultural, and vocational education. Since then other acts have been passed in which federal funds have been made available to the states. And while it is true that these funds generally represent only a small fraction of the total spent on education, in some years the percentage has been much greater. For example, in 1950 the federal government spent $3,500,000,000 for educational purposes, of which $3,000,000,000 went to veterans under the provisions of the G.I. bill. This figure becomes significant when it is realized that the total amount spent on public schools in the states in that year was about $5,000,000,000.

The following is a list of the more important acts and programs through which the federal government has aided the American schools.

The Ordinance of 1785. Provided that lot number 16 of every township be reserved for the maintenance of public schools in each state being admitted to the Union. Later this was extended to two sections and then to four sections in each township for some of the western states.

The Morrill Act of 1862. Provided that each state receive 30,000 acres of land for each senator and representative then in Congress. The money derived from the sale of this land was to be invested and used for the establishment and support of colleges devoted to the agricultural and mechanical arts. In 1890 the second Morrill act provided for annual appropriations of $15,000 per year to the land-grant colleges and for annual increments of $1,000 for ten years so that by 1900 the annual grant was $25,000.

The Hatch Act of 1887. Provided $15,000 per year to each state having an agricultural college. The money was to be used to promote research in agricultural science.

The Smith-Lever Act of 1914. Provided funds on a matching basis for agricultural extension work so that the benefits of scientific work in agriculture and home economics would be brought into the American home. Although the matching principle had been proposed earlier it was incorporated into a federal program for the first time in this bill. The federal government spent $48,000,000 in 1952–53 for education in the field of agriculture and mechanical arts.

The Smith-Hughes Act of 1917. Provided funds, again on a matching basis, to promote vocational education in public schools below the college level. The funds were to be used to pay the salaries of teachers of agriculture, home economics, and trade and industrial subjects; and to promote research in vocational education. For the first time in an education act, the federal government applied controls and limitations. A federal Board of Vocational Education was set up to supervise the program, and the state established state boards to administer the federal funds. The conditions under which federal vocational funds may be used are as follows:

1. Federal funds may be used only for education which is of less than college grade. A program of vocational education is considered to be of less than college grade when all of the following conditions are met:

   a) The objective is to provide training which will be advantageous in entering upon, or continuing in, employment in specific occupations or fields of work.

   b) Admission is based upon the ability of pupils to profit by the instruction offered rather than upon the possession of secondary school credits required for college entrance.

   c) The instruction offered is based upon the needs of workers in the occupations for which training is given.

   d) The instruction is terminal in nature and not a part of a course which is to be continued in a college or other higher institution.

   e) The instruction does not lead to a baccalaureate degree and is not organized to conform to the requirements of a course which does lead to such a degree.

2. Federal funds may be used when such vocational education shall

be given in schools or classes under public supervision or control. A school or class is considered to be under public supervision or control, within the requirements of the federal vocational acts when it meets all of the following criteria:

a) It is organized and operated under the direction of a state or local board responsible for the expenditure of public school funds for vocational education in the state or community.

b) The teachers are paid from public funds in the same way as other public school teachers employed by the state or local board responsible for vocational education are paid.

c) Officials on the staff of a state or local board responsible for vocational education have full charge of:

(1) Selection, salaries, and length of term of the teachers.

(2) Qualifications and admission of pupils.

(3) Content and organization of all courses and curricula.

3. Federal funds may be used when each dollar of federal money is matched by a dollar of state or local funds, or both. In order that state and local expenditures may be used to match federal funds, it is necessary that such expenditures be made only for work which meets all of the conditions essential for federal reimbursement that are set up in the state plan.

The Smith-Hughes Act has been supplemented by other acts, such as the George-Reed Act in 1929, the George-Ellzey Act in 1934, the George-Deen Act in 1936, and the George-Barden Act in 1946.

The Vocational Rehabilitation Act of 1920. This act provided funds to the states for the purpose of rehabilitating handicapped persons. The program was expanded under the Social Security Act of 1936 and has been extended under the G.I. Bill.

The Servicemen's Readjustment Act of 1944. Better known as the G.I. Bill, this act provided aid to veterans of World War II to enable them to further their education. Tuitions were paid directly to the schools and colleges while the veterans received a monthly stipend for living expenses. The amount of education to which the veteran was entitled depended on his length of service but could not exceed four calendar years. A total of more than $14,000,000,000 was spent on this program, and more than 8,000,000 veterans received benefits. A similar bill for veterans of the Korean War was passed in 1952.

The School Lunch Acts of 1946. Funds on a matching basis are provided to the states by this act for the establishment and support of nonprofit school lunch programs. Under this program, which is supervised by the Department of Agriculture, the federal government contributes one dollar for every three dollars put into the program by the state. In this program the federal government has again set up specific requirements that the states must meet. Among other things, the state must demonstrate that there is need, that there is no discrimination in the use of funds, and that minimum nutrition and sanitation standards are being maintained.

Public Laws 874 and 815. The first of these acts provides federal funds for current expenditures of school districts in areas affected by federal activities related to defense effort. The second provides funds on a matching basis for conducting state-wide surveys of school building facilities and provides more funds for school construction in federally affected areas.

The National Defense Education Act of 1958. In this bill Congress authorized almost a billion dollars, most of which was to be used for loans to college students and for grants to the states (on a matching basis) to improve the teaching of science, mathematics, and foreign languages. Money was also provided in smaller amounts for assisting the states in improving guidance, counseling, and testing programs, for establishing institutes to improve the competence of foreign language teachers, and for creating fellowships to increase the number of college teachers.

In addition to these major programs, the federal government has provided funds during the thirties for the support of such educational agencies as the Civilian Conservation Corps, the National Youth Administration, and the Public Works Administration. Since World War II a great deal of money has been spent to support scientific research in the universities and the exchange of teachers and students under the Fulbright and Smith-Mundt Acts.

This completes the picture of the present system of financing the American schools. The next question to be asked is whether the funds available for American schools, especially public schools, are adequate.

The Adequacy of Current Revenues

WHILE it is probably true that more Americans receive more formal education than any other people, there is little doubt that our present efforts are inadequate in terms of the quality of education needed in the modern world. Moreover, we are supporting our schools at a level far below that at which we are financially able. One of the best statements of the inadequacy of our support of education was made by Walter Lippmann in a speech before the National Citizens Commission for the Public Schools at its meeting in San Francisco early in 1954, and excerpts from that speech are reprinted here. Mr. Lippmann is one of America's most distinguished writers and political analysts and speaks from broad knowledge and experience in both domestic and world affairs.

WALTER LIPPMANN

FROM

"Educating for Leadership" [1]

. . . We have been raised to the first place in the leadership of the Western society at a time when the general civilization of the West has suffered a spectacular decline and is gravely threatened. We, who have become so suddenly the protecting and the leading power of that civilization, are not clear and united among ourselves about where we are going and how we should deal with our unforeseen responsibilities, our unwanted mission, our unexpected duties.

It is an awe-inspiring burden that we find ourselves compelled to bear. We have suddenly acquired responsibilities for which we were not prepared—for which we are not now prepared—for which, I am very much afraid, we are not now preparing ourselves.

We have had, and probably we must expect for a long time to have, dangerous and implacable enemies. But if we are to revive and recover, and are to go forward again, we must not look for the root of the trouble in our adversaries. We must look for it in ourselves. We must rid ourselves of the poison of self-pity. We must have done with the falsehood that all would be well were it not that we are the victims of wicked and designing men.

In 1914, when the decline of the West began, no one had heard of Lenin, Trotsky, Mussolini, Hitler, Stalin, and Mao Tse-Tung. We have not fallen from our pre-eminence because we have been attacked. It would be much truer to say, and it is nobler to say it, that we have been attacked because our capacity to cope with our tasks had begun to decline.

We shall never have the spirit to revive and to recover so long as we try to console ourselves by shutting our eyes, and by wringing our hands and beating our breasts and filling the air with complaints that we have been weakened because we were attacked, and that we have been making mistakes because we were betrayed.

We must take the manly view, which is that the failure of the western democracies during this catastrophic half of the 20th Century is due to the failings of the democratic peoples. They have been attacked and brought down from their pre-eminence because they have lacked the clarity of purpose and the resolution of mind and of heart to cope with the accumulating disasters and disorders. They have lacked the clarity of purpose and the resolution of mind and of heart to prevent the wars

[1] Walter Lippmann, "Educating for Leadership," *School Life*, XXXVI (April 1954), p. 97.

that have ruined the West, to prepare for these wars they could not prevent, and, having won them at last after exorbitant sacrifice and at a
ruinous cost, to settle those wars and to restore law and order upon the
face of the globe.

EDUCATIONAL EFFORTS

I have said all this because it is only in the context of our era that we
can truly conceive the problem of educating the American democracy.
When we do that, we must, I believe, come to see that the effort we are
making to educate ourselves as a people is not nearly equal to our needs
and to our responsibilities.

If we compare our total effort—in public and private schools, and
from kindergarten through college—with what it was 50 years ago, the
quantitative increase is impressive. We are offering much more schooling
of a more expensive kind to very many more pupils. By every statistical
measure, the United States has made striking quantitative progress during the past century towards the democratic goal of universal education.
The typical young American is spending more years in school than his
father or grandfather; a much higher proportion of young people are going to high school and beyond; and more dollars—even discounting the
depreciation of the dollar—are being spent for each person's education.

Now, if it were no more difficult to live in the United States today
than it was fifty years ago, that is to say if life were as simple as it was
then—if the problems of private and community life were as easily understood—if the task of governing the United States at home, and of
conducting its foreign relations abroad, were as uncomplicated and no
more dangerous than it was fifty years ago—then we could celebrate, we
could be happy, we could be congratulating ourselves that we are making great progress in the task of educating ourselves as a democracy.

But we cannot make the comforting comparison without deceiving
ourselves seriously. We cannot measure the demands upon our people in
the second half of the 20th Century—the demands in terms of trained
intelligence, moral discipline, knowledge, and, not least, the wisdom of
great affairs—by what was demanded of them at the beginning of the
first half of this century. The burden of living in America today and of
governing America today is very much heavier than it was 50 years ago,
and the crucial question is whether the increase of our effort in education is keeping up with the increase in the burden.

When we use this standard of comparison, we must find, I submit,
that the increase in our effort to educate ourselves is of a quite different
—and of a very much smaller—order of magnitude than is the increase
in what is demanded of us in this divided and dangerous world. Our
educational effort and our educational needs are not now anywhere

nearly in balance. The supply is not nearly keeping up with the demand. The burden of the task is very much heavier than is the strength of the effort. There is a very serious and dangerous deficit between the output of education and our private and public need to be educated.

How can we measure this discrepancy? I am sorry to say that I shall have to use a few figures, trusting that none of you will think that when I use them, I am implying that all things can be measured in dollars and cents. I am using the figures because there is no other way to illustrate concretely the difference in the two orders of magnitude—the difference between what we do to educate ourselves, on the one hand, and on the other hand, what the kind of world we live in demands of us.

EDUCATIONAL DEFICIT

What shall we use as a measure of our educational effort? For the purpose of the comparison, I think we may take the total expenditure per capita, first in 1900, and then about half a century later, in 1953, on public and private schools from kindergarten through college.

And as a measure of the burden of our task—of the responsibilities and of the commitments to which education has now to be addressed— we might take federal expenditures per capita, first in 1900, and then in our time, half a century later.

We differ among ourselves, of course, as to whether we are spending too much, too little, or the right amount, on defense, and on the public services. But these differences do not seriously affect the argument. For all of us—or nearly all of us—are agreed on the general size and the scope of the necessary tasks of the modern federal government, both in military defense and for civilian purposes. Between the highest and the lowest proposals of responsible and informed men, I doubt that the difference is as much as 20 percent. That is not a great enough difference to affect the point I am making. That point is that the size of the public expenditure reflects—roughly, of course, but nevertheless, fundamentally —the scale and scope of what we are impelled and compelled to do. It registers our judgment on the problems which we must cope with.

Now in 1900, the educational effort—measured in expenditures per capita—was $3.40. The task—as measured by federal expenditure per capita—was $6.85. What we must be interested in is, I submit, the ratio between these two figures. We find, then, that in 1900 the Nation put out $1 of educational effort against $2 of public task.

How is it now, half a century or so later? In 1953, the educational effort was at the rate of about $76 per capita. Federal expenditures—including defense—had risen to $467 per capita. The ratio of educational effort to public task, which in 1900 was as one is to two, had fallen, a half century later, to a ratio of one to six.

Perhaps I should pause at this point for a parenthesis, to say for those who may be thinking how much the value of the dollar has depreciated since 1900, that I am aware of that, but for the purposes of this comparison, it makes no difference. For while the dollar was worth probably three times as much in 1900 as in 1953, we are interested only in the relative effort in 1900 and in 1953. The ratio would be the same if we divided the 1953 expenditures by three, or if we multiplied the 1900 expenditures by three.

You have now heard all the statistics that I shall use. The two ratios, the one at the beginning of our rise to the position of the leading great power of the world and, the other ratio a half century later, when we carry the enormous burden abroad and at home—these two ratios show, I submit, that the effort we are now making to educate ourselves has fallen in relation to our needs.

I must now remind you that this disparity between the educational effort and the public task is in fact greater than the figures suggest. For in this half century there has been a momentous change in the structure of American society and it has added greatly to the burden upon the schools.

The responsibility of the schools for educating the new generation has become very much more comprehensive than it used to be. Ever so much more is now demanded of the schools. For they are expected to perform many of the educational functions which used to be performed by the family, the settled community, the church, the family business, the family farm, the family trade.

This is a very big subject in itself—much too big for me tonight—except to mention it as a reminder that the comparison between our real educational effort and our real public need is less favorable than the figures of one as to two in 1900, as against one as to six today. For the school today has a much larger role to play in the whole process of education than it needed to play in the older American society.

Can it be denied that the educational effort is inadequate? I think it cannot be denied. I do not mean that we are doing a little too little. I mean that we are doing much too little. We are entering upon an era which will test to the utmost the capacity of our democracy to cope with the gravest problems of modern times—and on a scale never yet attempted in all the history of the world. We are entering upon this difficult and dangerous period with what I believe we must call a growing deficit in the quantity and the quality of American education.

There is, I believe, compelling proof that we are operating at an educational deficit. It is to be found in many of the controversies within the educational system. I am not myself, of course, a professional educator. But I do some reading about education, and I have been especially interested in the problem of providing education for the men and women who must perform the highest functions in our society—the elucidation and the articulation of its ideals, the advancement of knowledge, the making of high policy in the government, and the leadership of the people.

How are we discussing this problem? Are we, as we ought to be doing, studying what are the subjects and what are the disciplines which are needed for the education of the gifted children for the leadership of the Nation? That is not the main thing we are discussing. We are discussing whether we can afford to educate our leaders when we have so far to go before we have done what we should do to provide equal opportunities for all people.

Most of the argument—indeed the whole issue—of whether to address the effort in education to the average of ability or to the higher capacities—derives from the assumption that we have to make that choice. But why do we have to choose? Why are we not planning to educate everybody as much as everybody can be educated, some much more and some less than others?

This alleged choice is forced upon us only because our whole educational effort is too small. If we were not operating at a deficit level, our working ideal would be the fullest opportunity for all—each child according to its capacity. It is the deficit in our educational effort which compels us to deny to the children fitted for the leadership of the Nation the opportunity to become educated for that task.

NEW PLATEAU IN EDUCATION

So we have come to the point, I would contend, where we must lift ourselves as promptly as we can to a new and much higher level of interest, of attention, of hard work, of care, of concern, of expenditure, and of dedication to the education of the American people.

We have to do in the educational system something very like what we have done in the military establishment during the past 15 years. We have to make a breakthrough to a radically higher and broader conception of what is needed and of what can be done. Our educational effort today, what we think we can afford, what we think we can do, how we feel entitled to treat our schools and our teachers—all of that—is still in approximately the same position as was the military effort of this country before Pearl Harbor.

In 1940 our armed forces were still at a level designed for a policy of isolation in this hemisphere and of neutrality in any war across the two oceans. Today, the military establishment has been raised to a different and higher plateau, and the effort that goes into it is enormously greater than it was in 1940.

Our educational effort, on the other hand, has not yet been raised to the plateau of the age we live in. I am not saying, of course, that we should spend 40 billions on education because we spend about that much on defense. I am saying that we must make the same order of radical change in our attitude towards education as we have made in our attitude towards defense.

We must measure our educational effort as we do our military effort. That is to say, we must measure it not by what it would be easy and convenient to do, but by what it is necessary to do in order that the nation may survive and flourish. We have learned that we are quite rich enough to defend ourselves, whatever the cost. We must now learn that we are quite rich enough to educate ourselves as we need to be educated.

There is an enormous margin of luxury in this country against which we can draw for our vital needs. We take that for granted when we think of the national defense. From the tragedies and the bitter experience of being involved in wars for which we were inadequately prepared, we have acquired the will to defend ourselves. And, having done that, having acquired the will, we have found the way. We know how to find the dollars that are needed to defend ourselves, even if we are to do without something else that is less vitally important.

In education we have not yet acquired that kind of will. But we need to acquire it, and we have no time to lose. We must acquire it in this decade. For if, in the crucial years which are coming, our people remain as unprepared as they are for their responsibilities and their mission, they may not be equal to the challenge, and if they do not succeed, they may never have a second chance in order to try again.

These views of course represent the opinions of Mr. Lippmann, a keen observer whose judgment is respected. In addition, there is other evidence of our inadequate financial support for our schools. The thousands of overcrowded classrooms, many with fifty-five and sixty students, are incontrovertible evidence. Also the fact that many teachers leave the profession each year for financial reasons, despite the fact that there is a serious shortage of teachers, is supporting evidence. This is one issue about which there is little controversy. But, despite this agreement that our schools are inadequately supported, we seem unable to grasp the fact that, as Lippmann says, it is not that we are doing a little too little, but that we are doing much too little and what is needed is a revolution in our thinking regarding the support necessary for our schools.

The Consequences of Inadequate Support

THE consequence of the inadequate support that our schools are receiving is that our children get a mediocre education at a time when an excellent education is essential for all of them. Furthermore, there is evidence that our lack of support is resulting in a loss of faith in our public school system. To the extent that this is so, our democracy itself is being undermined, because democracy and public education are interdependent. There is abundant evidence of this loss of faith. It is becoming difficult to find a newspaper or periodical that does not have at least one article complaining about the state of the nation's public schools. The children, it is claimed, are not learning the three "R's" in the elementary school, and they are leaving our high schools still practically illiterate. These same complaints are expressed with great feeling by many college instructors. The perceptive visitor to the American college will find that many professors are frustrated. They are frustrated when they give examinations and are reminded that many of their students are unable to organize and express their ideas in an intelligent way, and that their spelling and grammar are very poor. They are also reminded that many students have a very limited knowledge and a superficial understanding of some of the basic facts about subjects, such as American history or government, which they have studied *repeatedly* in the elementary and secondary schools.

Few educators would contend that these fundamentals should not have been learned in high school. There is danger that college instructors will expect college freshmen to approach their own level of understanding and competence, but plenty of evidence indicates that our students enter college far below the necessary and desirable level of achievement, and far below their level of capability. There is also evidence that students finish college unable to write effectively and with a very limited understanding of some of the subjects they have studied.

College instructors will hold that teaching students the fundamentals —writing, for instance—is not their job. Certainly it is not their job to teach the student to write, but it is a part of their job to teach the student to write more effectively. In most colleges this basic skill is taught in a special course, usually English Composition. In other courses written work is generally required in the form of examinations or term papers. These papers are marked, and in almost every case comments are made regarding spelling and grammatical errors. Sometimes the spelling and grammar are factors in the instructor's evaluation of the paper (especially in a negative way) and sometimes they are not. Often instructors do an exhaustive and detailed job of analyzing the written work of students on examinations and term papers. Usually if the written work is very poor the student receives a lower grade than he would have on the basis of factual content alone. In many instances errors are marked and comments such as "poorly written" are inserted in the margin. But only rarely does the instructor go over the examination carefully with the student in order to teach him how it could have been written more effectively. Unfortunately, this is as true of term papers as it is of examinations, and the real teaching opportunity is lost.

The fact is that in the colleges as in the high schools there is more talking at (lecturing) students than there is *teaching*. Most of what students learn, particularly of the fundamentals of writing, speaking, reading and studying, they learn on their own. Training in the fundamentals of research—gathering data, evaluating sources of information, and in general working independently—which is so badly needed in our high schools and colleges, is neglected. Too often the work is graded, handed back, and that is the end of it. Very often students are so disinterested that they don't even bother to pick up the papers, and if they do, they may glance at the grade and no more. They are not encouraged or required to correct their work and learn from their mistakes.

The basic reason for this lack of teaching and learning as opposed to lecturing and listening is the sheer, overwhelming weight of the teaching load that most high school and college instructors have to carry. In the high schools most teachers teach five classes with a minimum of 15 to 20 and a maximum of 40 to 50 students in each class. The average high school class in most large communities has about 35 students. This means that a teacher would have a minimum of 75–100 students a day, a maximum of 200–250, with the average teacher having perhaps between 125 and 175 students. In addition to this crushing teaching load, most teachers have at least one "activity" to handle after school, and, because of low salaries, a large percentage of the men also hold outside jobs. It is difficult to see how the teacher can possibly teach the individual student in such circumstances. For effective teaching, constant and continued interaction between teacher and student is essential. *The Christian Science Monitor* reported on a man who has done a tremendous job of teaching creative writing. How does he do it? The article says:

The secret of his success—if it can be called a secret—is patient, persevering work.

Students write, rewrite, rewrite—and rewrite. They may hand in the same theme five, ten or eighteen times.

Not until Mr. Newsom is satisfied that the poem is the best of which they are capable—not until then does he mark it satisfactory.[2]

[2] *The Christian Science Monitor* (Boston), December 18, 1953, p. 2.

This is successful teaching and it is *teaching*, not talking at students. But picture this kind of painstaking, individual effort with a load of one hundred and fifty students. Unfortunately, the worst is yet to come, for the increased enrollments that began in the elementary schools in 1947 are just starting to affect the high schools. Under these circumstances, it is not hard to understand why students are poorly prepared.

In the universities the average numerical load per instructor is probably not as high, although many instructors have huge lecture classes, especially in the lower divisions. Each instructor normally teaches four classes which meet three times a week, as compared with five classes meeting every day for each high school teacher. Also, while most college instructors need to supplement their incomes by teaching an extra course in the evening or in the extension division, they are generally better paid for this extra work than the high school teacher is for his part-time job. However, the real equalizer is the research function of the university instructor, for the university, unlike the high school, has the dual function of teaching and research. Most college instructors have a vital interest in this aspect of their job, for it offers a chance to do creative work and to contribute to the store of human knowledge. But even if they are not interested in research, their academic status and therefore their promotion depends upon it. Finally, many instructors teach in the graduate as well as the undergraduate school and have a heavy load of graduate students engaged in research, and this requires countless hours in conference. The result is that the college professor is consumed by his job. He has to cut down somewhere and he usually does so on his teaching, since this aspect of his work is the most difficult to evaluate and has the least to do with his promotion.

Finally, the whole problem in the secondary schools and the colleges is aggravated by the cumulating inadequacies that result from sheer numerical overloads in the elementary schools. Many elementary teachers have classes with forty, fifty, and even fifty-five children in a class. With these huge classes, students fail in grade after grade to reach the level of achievement that they should. At each level teachers realize that the pupils are behind and try to catch up but cannot. Thus students start high school poorly prepared, and the overloaded teachers there have little chance of helping them improve. As a result, many really good teachers are frustrated because the task of *teaching individuals is physically impossible*. If America were a poor country, teachers would feel better and would make the best of a bad situation.

There are some poor teachers in both high schools and colleges. There are some teachers who, while they are well qualified in their own subject matter, are contemptuous of teaching methods and ignorant of even the barest essentials of the learning process. And certainly improvement can be made within the existing framework. Steps could be taken to lessen the extreme departmentalization of the high schools and colleges in which subjects are studied in isolation from each other. Since relationships between subjects are not stressed, the quality of education is poorer than it needs to be even with the heavy overload. There are some so-called progressive teachers who in their reaction against the theory of formal discipline are unwilling to lead students into vigorous intellectual experiences. However, these factors are not the basic problems. And even these lesser problems could be solved if we had the funds to prepare more and better teachers.

Possible Solutions to the Problem of Inadequate Support

ONCE the seriousness of the situation is realized in terms of the consequences of inadequate support, the next question is: what is being done and what might be done to provide adequate support for our schools? Most educators believe that much could be done to improve the present system of support. We could improve our methods of assessing property values within the states and produce much more revenue for schools. We could change over to more equitable kinds of taxes, i.e., an income tax rather than a sales tax. At least one businessman concerned about the financial plight of the public schools has suggested that the states and local districts introduce a pay-as-you-go plan or a payroll deduction plan similar to the one used for federal income taxes. He argues that this plan is much easier on taxpayers than paying a lump sum and that people will pay higher taxes with less objection than with the present system. Much could be done through the state legislatures to help local districts, especially in freeing them of restrictions. For example, the city of St. Louis is permitted to levy a school tax of $0.89 on each $100 of assessed valuation of real property in St. Louis without a vote. The present tax rate is $1.15 and must be reapproved each two years by the voters, so there is always a chance that it will be voted down. The same procedure would apply if a higher levy were passed, except that under Missouri law it would have to be approved by a two thirds majority every four years. The result is that teachers and administrators and friends of the schools are always in doubt about future revenues and every two or four years they must carry on an intensive campaign to maintain their funds. It would seem reasonable to provide a system whereby once a tax levy was voted it would remain in force unless two thirds of the voters wanted to change it. However, even if these steps were taken there would still be gross inequality among the states because of the inability of some states to provide adequate minimum revenues regardless of the effort they make.

The Problem of Federal Aid

MOST educators and many political leaders are convinced that while some improvements can be made within the states the most logical way to solve the problem is through federal aid. This has not always been true, and even as recently as a decade ago there was strong objection to federal aid, mainly on the ground that it would bring federal control, but also because it was felt that the nation could not afford it. The Democratic Party has had a plank in its platform since 1944 favoring federal aid. The Republicans have taken the position that education is a state and local responsibility and have not supported federal aid as a party. Yet Senator Taft was one of the strongest supporters of federal aid, and in February of 1955 President Eisenhower recommended a program of federal aid to the Congress. There is little doubt that so far as the overwhelming majority of Congressmen are concerned the issue is not whether we should or should not have federal aid but rather how much and what kind.

The question is then if such strong agreement exists regarding the desirability of federal aid for general use by the public schools, why has such a program not been put into operation? The answer is that for the last decade at least the program has been bogged down over the question of whether this aid should go to public and parochial schools or only to public schools. The religious group seeking aid for its schools is the Roman Catholic Church. The other two major religious groups, the Protestants and the Jews, have officially opposed any public aid to parochial schools. The leaders of thirty Protestant churches at a meeting in Denver a few years ago took the position that:

> . . . the subsidization of education carried on under religious auspices would both violate the principle of the separation between church and state and be a devastating blow to the public school system, which must at all costs be maintained.[3]

The issue came to a head in 1949 and 1950 over the Barden bill, which provided that federal aid of approximately $300,000,000 be granted only to public schools. The Catholic position was that the Catholic schools, by educating Catholic children, were saving the American taxpayer a great deal of money. The Church pointed out that Catholic parents had to pay twice for the education of their children. Their position was that the First Amendment, which provides that "Congress shall pass no law respecting the establishment of religion," means that government cannot establish a religion or favor one religion over another but does not pre-

[3] *The St. Louis Post-Dispatch*, December 12, 1952, p. 7c.

vent action favoring all religions. Although not all Catholics accepted this view, it is essentially the official view of the Church.

Those who opposed public aid to parochial schools maintained that the government could not aid one church school without aiding all of them. Since there are some 250 denominations in the United States, each of which could qualify for funds to establish its own schools, this would mean the end of the public school system. They contended that if this happened education would revert to private hands and the great unifying force exerted by the public schools would be lost. They pointed out that such a step would violate principles of the separation of church and state and freedom of conscience, since one man would be paying taxes to support another man's church. This interpretation was bolstered by the United States Supreme Court in the New Jersey Bus case. The Court voted 5 to 4 that public aid for transporting children to parochial schools was not unconstitutional since it aided the child and not the church. But in handing down the decision the Court gave its interpretation of the First Amendment which reads in part as follows:

> The "establishment of religion" clause of the First Amendment means at least this: Neither a state nor the Federal Government can set up a church. Neither can pass laws which aid one religion, aid all religions, or prefer one religion over another. Neither can force nor influence a person to go to or remain away from church against his will or force him to profess a belief or disbelief in any religion. No person can be punished for entertaining or professing religious beliefs or disbeliefs, for church attendance or nonattendance. No tax in any amount, large or small, can be levied to support any religious activities or institutions, whatever they may be called, or whatever form they may adopt to teach or practice religion. Neither a state nor the Federal Government can, openly or secretly, participate in the affairs of any religious organizations or groups and vice versa. In the words of Jefferson, the clause against establishment of religion by law was intended to erect "a wall of separation between Church and state." [4]

As a result of this interpretation of the First Amendment, there are real doubts as to whether a bill providing aid to parochial schools would be constitutional. That this arrangement imposes a hardship on parents who wish to send their children to a parochial school few would deny. Justice Rutledge who wrote the minority opinion in the New Jersey Bus case summed up the whole problem in these words:

> No one conscious of religious values can be unsympathetic toward the burden which our constitutional separation puts on par-

4 Everson v. Board of Education, 330 U.S. 1, 15–16 (1946).

ents who desire religious instruction mixed with secular for their children. They pay taxes for others' children's education, at the same time the added cost of instruction for their own. Nor can one happily see benefits denied to children which others receive, because in conscience they or their parents for them desire a different kind of training others do not demand.

But if those feelings should prevail, there would be an end to our historic constitutional policy and command. No more unjust or discriminatory in fact is it to deny attendants at religious schools the cost of their transportation than it is to deny them tuition, sustenance for their teachers, or any other educational expense which others receive at public cost. Hardship in fact there is which none can blink. But, for assuring to those who undergo it the greater, the most comprehensive freedom, it is one written by design and firm intent into our basic law.

Of course discrimination in the legal sense does not exist. The child attending the religious school has the same right as any other to attend the public school. But he foregoes exercising it because the same guaranty which assures this freedom forbids the public school or any agency of the state to give or aid him in securing the religious instruction he seeks.

Were he to accept the common school, he would be the first to protest the teaching there of any creed or faith not his own. And it is precisely for the reason that their atmosphere is wholly secular that children are not sent to public schools under the Pierce doctrine. But that is a constitutional necessity, because we have staked the very existence of our country on the faith that complete separation between the state and religion is best for the state and best for religion.

That policy necessarily entails hardship upon persons who forego the right to educational advantages the state can supply in order to secure others it is precluded from giving. Indeed this may hamper the parent and the child forced by conscience to that choice. But it does not make the state unneutral to withhold what the Constitution forbids it to give. On the contrary it is only by observing the prohibition rigidly that the state can maintain its neutrality and avoid partisanship in the dissensions inevitable when sect opposes sect over demands for public moneys to further religious education, teaching or training in any form or degree, directly or indirectly. Like St. Paul's freedom, religious liberty with a great price must be bought. And for those who exercise it most fully, by insisting upon religious education for their children mixed with secular, by the terms of our Constitution the price is greater than for others.[5]

[5] *Ibid.*, pp. 58–9.

As if the religious issue were not enough, the problem has recently been complicated by the segregation question. In 1957, for example, a proposal by Congressman Powell of New York to attach a provision to the federal aid bill to withhold federal funds from segregated schools was approved. Southern Democrats, of course, voted against the rider, but many Republicans who had opposed federal aid joined with northern Democrats to vote its attachment to the bill. When the bill itself came up for a vote, the southerners, as expected, voted against the bill, but many of the Republicans who voted *for* the rider *voted against the bill*.

There is no doubt that federal aid to education is essential—not only to equalize educational opportunity but to raise the level of education generally. While there are many communities and some states which can support pubic education at the level suggested by Mr. Lippmann, many cannot. In addition, the federal government has greater tax resources and a more efficient taxing machinery than the states. It is certain also that federal funds can be provided while federal controls are prohibited; such an arrangement was incorporated into the Murray-Metcalf Bill (1959). But the problem is broader than any specific means of support. It is even broader than the support of education itself and involves, as economist John Galbraith has pointed out, a severe lack of balance in our spending for private goods as opposed to public services. America has become an "affluent society"—a nation of tremendous wealth. But we are pouring our wealth into consumer goods (bigger and better automobiles, television sets, etc.) and into all kinds of amusements while our schools and hospitals are overcrowded and our public services generally are neglected. Consider this picture of American life drawn by Professor Galbraith:

> The family which takes its mauve and cerise, air-conditioned, power-steered, and power-braked automobile out for a tour passes through cities that are badly paved, made hideous by litter, blighted buildings, billboards, and posts for wires that should long since have been put underground. They pass on into a countryside that has been rendered largely invisible by commercial art. (The goods which the latter advertise have an absolute priority in our value system. Such aesthetic considerations as a view of the countryside accordingly come second. On such matters we are consistent.) They picnic on exquisitely packaged food from a portable icebox by a polluted stream and go on to spend the night at a park which is a menace to public health and morals. Just before dozing off on an air mattress, beneath a nylon tent, amid the stench of decaying refuse, they may reflect vaguely on the curious unevenness of their blessings. Is this, indeed, the American genius? [6]

[6] John Kenneth Galbraith, *The Affluent Society* (Boston: Houghton Mifflin Company, 1958), p. 253.

The basic problem is one of value not of economic ability. There is no question that we can afford fine schools, as anyone who will take the trouble to examine our national income and our expenditures for consumer goods can ascertain. The question is whether we wish to do so. The choice will not be an easy one, for, as Galbraith points out "the engines of mass communication, in their highest state of development, assail the eyes and ears of the community on behalf of more beer but not of more schools." Moreover, the satisfactions to be derived from spending money on education are necessarily long-range and intangible, whereas those derived from the purchase of a new automobile or a swimming pool are immediate and tangible. Yet regardless of the difficulty, it is clear that as these choices are being made all over the nation in the years ahead the very nature of American civilization is being fashioned. We may decide to continue our policy of private opulence and public squalor, but let us not continue to maintain that we cannot afford to educate our children adequately.

Suggested Readings

Allen, Hollis P.: *The Federal Government and Education*. New York: McGraw-Hill Book Company, 1950.

Burke, Arvid J.: *Financing Public Schools in the United States*. New York: Harper & Brothers, 1951.

Fine, Benjamin: *Our Children Are Cheated*. New York: Henry Holt and Company, 1947.

Galbraith, John Kenneth: *The Affluent Society*. Boston: Houghton Mifflin Company, 1958.

Harris, Seymour E.: *How Shall We Pay for Education?* New York: Harper & Brothers, 1948.

Johns, R. L., and Morphet, E. L., eds.: *Problems and Issues in Public School Finance*. New York: Bureau of Publications, Teachers College, Columbia University, 1952.

Mort, Paul R., and Reusser, Walter C.: *Public School Finance*. New York: McGraw-Hill Book Company, 1951.

Norton, John K., and Cocking, Walter: *Still Unfinished Business*. Washington, D.C.: National Education Association, 1948.

CHAPTER 12

AIMS AND PURPOSES IN AMERICAN
EDUCATION

WE HAVE DEALT WITH THE ORGANIZATION AND ADMINISTRATION, the legal foundations, and the financial support of American education so far in this section. In this chapter we will be concerned with the aims and purposes of American education in general and of the schools in particular. Many questions might be asked. Are the present aims satisfactory? Are some educational aims to be preferred over others? If so, on what basis? Is there substantial agreement as to what these aims should be? Who decides on the aims of education in our society? Is it parents, teachers, superintendents, board members, pressure groups, university professors, or government officials? Or to go into the more fundamental aspect of the matter: what is an aim? What is its function in education? Are the aims of education similar in the United States, Great Britain, and the Soviet Union? If not, how does one account for the differences? What is the relationship between the aims of American education and American society, as a whole? Some of the answers to these questions will be obvious as a result of the material presented in previous chapters, but some will not. The problem of purpose as it has developed in American education will be discussed first.

The Problem of Purpose

A FEW years ago Professor Karl Bigelow of Teachers College, Columbia University, reported an interesting fact in discussing the findings of a group, of which he was a member, that had spent months visiting classrooms over the entire country. He said that the group had learned many things about American schools, some of them good, some of them bad. But as they evaluated the data they had gathered, one conclusion kept reappearing: Whenever they found good teaching and learning, on any level, they always found a teacher with a purpose who knew where he was going and how to get there. In other words, whatever other elements might be absent, a sense of direction could not be lacking in a good teaching-learning situation. Moreover, he said that when the class was aware of the purpose and had had some voice in forming it, another essential ingredient for a high quality education was present. John Dewey felt so strongly about this point that he wrote:

> There is, I think no point in the philosophy of progressive education which is sounder than its emphasis upon the importance of the participation of the learner in the formation of the purposes which direct his activities in the learning process, just as there is no defect in traditional education greater than its failure to secure the active cooperation of the pupil in construction of the purposes involved in his studying.[1]

While there is not a complete lack of purpose in American schoolrooms, unfortunately there is evidence that for many teachers the only functional purpose has been the teaching of the textbook or the course of study. This was one of the conclusions drawn by Professor Bigelow on the basis of his extended study. It was also one of the criticisms made of secondary education by the Commission in the Eight-Year Study. The Commission found a serious lack of direction among teachers generally, and even many principals so busy "running the machine" that they seldom asked: "Where are we going?"[2] That the problem is far from solved is evident to anyone familiar with the schools.

Undoubtedly one of the reasons for the existence of the problem is that teachers are thrust into an ongoing situation. If they actually had a part in establishing the school, they would be forced to think about the problem of purpose. As it is, our teachers are placed into schools that have been established for years with complete programs of study. The new teacher fits into this ready-made program and begins teaching the course of study. This is, of course, a natural and desirable procedure. Unfortunately, too many teachers and administrators never go beyond this step. When some thoughtful student asks why he has to study Chaucer, the teacher is likely to answer "because it is in the course of study." The result is that often the student comes out of a course originally set up to provide an opportunity for him to learn and enjoy great literature with an active dislike for this area of human experience that could have been a source of inspiration and enjoyment.

[1] John Dewey, *Experience and Education* (New York: The Macmillan Company, 1938), pp. 77–8.
[2] W. Aiken, *The Story of the Eight-Year Study* (New York: Harper & Brothers, 1942), p. 10.

Another reason for the lack of purpose in education is that a searching analysis of one's activities requires thinking, and thinking is work. It is much easier to get into a habit pattern and stay there. It is true, of course, that many teachers are so consumed by teaching duties that they scarcely have time to stop and question the worthwhileness of their activities. For this reason it would be highly desirable to free teachers for a time to think about the ends and means of education. It would be a fine thing for American education if more school districts would pay their teachers for an extra month in the summer to think through and discuss with their fellow teachers and administrators the purpose and direction of the schools and how they themselves can be most effective.

The need for a sense of direction or purpose in education on a national as well as an individual basis was brought to the fore during the critical years of the depression. Because education in America is a function of the states and not of the federal government, we had in effect forty-eight systems of education. This resulted in a decentralized system, which most American educators thought was desirable, but it also resulted in a lack of national direction in education in a period in which intelligent direction was desperately needed. The result was that the Educational Policies Commission was established as a part of the National Education Association to do just what its name implies—formulate policy. Since then, this group, made up of outstanding individuals from all areas of education, has provided invaluable leadership. Its statements of policy on communism and communists in the schools and on moral and spiritual values, as well as its publication, *The Purposes of Education in American Democracy*, have been accepted widely by American educators. This Commission has given American education more of a sense of direction than ever before.

However, one of the dangers inherent in having a high-powered group (or any group for that matter) work out objectives is that these objectives may have very little meaning to the teachers who are supposed to put them into action. It has happened frequently that groups of this kind have worked for months setting up a list of objectives. They discuss the matter among themselves, think it through, and finally come out with a very clear and concise statement which is then handed to teachers. These clear and concise statements do not have, and could not have, the same meaning to the teachers, since they did not participate in the long process of discussion and formulation. For example, in 1918 the Commission on the Reorganization of Secondary Education, under the chairmanship of Clarence D. Kingsley, published its report on the *Cardinal Principles of Secondary Education*. The Commission, which had been appointed by the National Educational Association in 1913, consisted of numerous committees (who eventually issued reports on various aspects of secondary education including the subject matter areas) and a reviewing committee whose task was to co-ordinate and review the work of the other committees. It was this reviewing committee, also chaired by Kingsley, who wrote the *Cardinal Principles* document. Kingsley, in his preface to the report, stated that the reviewing committee had spent *three years* in formulating and revising its ideas on the principles which should guide the reorganization and development of American secondary education. The results of three years of effort were then published in a concise, thirty-two-page document. The report included a list of seven objectives (and five pages were devoted to an explanation of them) which gained wide acceptance in American secondary education. The objectives were:

1. Health
2. Command of the Fundamental Processes
3. Worthy home membership
4. Vocational efficiency
5. Civic participation
6. Worthy use of leisure time
7. Ethical character

The same pattern was followed twenty years later when the Educational Policies Commission of the NEA published another statement of objectives for American education. This time the major aims were reduced to the following:

1. Self-realization
2. Human relationship
3. Economic efficiency
4. Civic responsibility

Impressive? Certainly. But what is meant by self-realization or human relationships? It is true that the groups who have published such lists have attempted to describe in great detail what they meant by each statement. But all too often lists exactly like the ones shown above are handed out in college classrooms or in courses of study. The fact is that objectives, to be effective, must be meaningful to individual teachers and students. If these objectives are to have meaning, there must be an active search on the part of teachers and students for understanding. Then and only then can these objectives be implemented. This is not to say that intelligent leaders in American education should not attempt to provide direction for our schools. It is to say that these aims must be carefully thought through and understood by teachers and students. This involves time, effort, thought, and probably much discussion, but it is essential if the work of our schools is not to degenerate into "busy work" or to teaching subjects "because they have always been taught."

Another problem related to that of developing a sense of direction in our schools is the fact that sometimes there is very little relationship between the stated objectives and the activities of the class. This is partly because the objectives are not understood, so that naturally there can be little relationship between ends and means. If there is, it is purely accidental. All too often, however, teachers have lists of objectives neatly tucked away in their desks (usually as a part of a course of study) which can be pulled out for the supervisor or for the annual open house. The most impressive list of purposes is worse than useless unless some provision is made for their achievement in the school program. Such a list may even be a substitute for action and serve as a balm for the conscience of teacher, principal, and supervisor. The same danger exists when teachers pick up and use phrases such as "meeting the needs" or "teaching the whole child." Very often teachers use these responses because they feel expected to do so. When they are asked to say precisely what these needs are or how they are meeting them, they are at a loss. Here again "meeting the needs" is a slogan, a cliché, and is used as a substitute for thought.

One attempt to get around the ever present danger of having objectives become mere verbalizations has been through the practice, developed in recent years, of stating objectives in terms of behavior. This approach tries to make abstractions like self-realization more meaningful, as does the pattern of breaking down objectives into categories such as knowledge, skills, attitudes, and understandings. The merit of these patterns is that they generally force the teacher to become specific. The objectives, therefore, have a better chance of being put into operation in the classroom. An example of objectives stated in behavioral terms and the practice of having students involved in their formulation is given by Quillen and Hanna:

> Suppose that the teachers of social education in a school decided that cooperation is a characteristic of an effective democratic citizen which they wish to develop and suppose, then, that a class of students, together with the teacher, defines a student who is cooperative as one who:
> a) Works well with a group or committee
> b) Respects constituted authority
> c) Recognizes and carries out his share of responsibilities
> d) Supports group and school activities
> e) Volunteers to bring additional data or help in group projects
> f) Meets his obligations promptly and to the best of his ability
> g) Adjusts his interests to the best interests of the group
> h) Treats others and their ideas with respect and courtesy.[3]

[3] From *Education for Social Competence* by I. J. Quillen and L. A. Hanna. Copyright, 1948, by Scott, Foresman and Company, and used with their permission.

Of course having purposes stated in this way in no way guarantees that they will not degenerate into mere verbalizations, but since the desired outcomes are more tangible the danger is not so great. Even so, this practice does not eliminate the need for serious thought, study, and work on the part of the teacher.

The Nature of Aims

BEFORE going into the question of the aims of American education and how they are evolved it is necessary to consider the nature and function of aims. For this purpose a statement by John Dewey has been included here. In reading Dewey's material, attention should of course be given to the main points of the analysis, that is, to the nature, the function, and the formulation, as well as the criteria of good aims. Attention should also be given to the way in which his ideas bear upon educational theory and practice. It might also be worthwhile to consider whether Dewey's analysis throws any light on the problems of purpose discussed in the preceding pages. Does his analysis provide any clues as to the sources of educational aims or to the related questions of *who* should decide the aims and *what* the aims should be. This statement is taken from Chapter 8 of *Democracy and Education*.

JOHN DEWEY

FROM

Democracy and Education [4]

Our first question is to define the nature of an aim so far as it falls within an activity, instead of being furnished from without. We approach the definition by a contrast of mere *results* with *ends*. Any exhibition of energy has results. The wind blows about the sand of the desert; the position of the grains is changed. Here is a result, an effect, but not an *end*. For there is nothing in the outcome which completes or fulfills what went before it. There is mere spatial redistribution. One state of affairs is just as good as any other. Consequently there is no basis upon which to select an earlier state of affairs as a beginning, a later as an end, and to consider what intervenes as a process of transformation and realization.

Consider for example the activities of bees in contrast with the changes in the sands when the wind blows them about. The results of the bees' actions may be called ends not because they are designed or con-

[4] John Dewey, *Democracy and Education*. Copyright 1916 by The Macmillan Company and used with their permission. Pp. 117–28.

sciously intended, but because they are true terminations or completions of what has preceded. When the bees gather pollen and make wax and build cells, each step prepares the way for the next. When cells are built, the queen lays eggs in them; when eggs are laid, they are sealed and bees brood them and keep them at a temperature required to hatch them. When they are hatched, bees feed the young till they can take care of themselves. Now we are so familiar with such facts that we are apt to dismiss them on the ground that life and instinct are a kind of miraculous thing anyway. Thus we fail to note what the essential characteristic of the event is; namely, the significance of the temporal place and order of each element; the way each prior event leads into its successor while the successor takes up what is furnished and utilizes it for some other stage, until we arrive at the end, which, as it were, summarizes and finishes off the process.

Since aims relate always to results, the first thing to look to when it is a question of aims, is whether the work assigned possesses intrinsic continuity. Or is it a mere serial aggregate of acts, first doing one thing and then another? To talk about an educational aim when approximately each act of a pupil is dictated by the teacher, when the only order in the sequence of his acts is that which comes from the assignment of lessons and the giving of directions by another, is to talk nonsense. It is equally fatal to an aim to permit capricious or discontinuous action in the name of spontaneous self-expression. An aim implies an orderly and ordered activity, one in which the order consists in the progressive completing of a process. Given an activity having a time span and cumulative growth within the time succession, an aim means foresight in advance of the end of possible termination. If bees anticipated the consequences of their activity, if they perceived their end in imaginative foresight, they would have the primary element in an aim. Hence it is nonsense to talk about the aim of education—or any other undertaking—where conditions do not permit of foresight of results, and do not stimulate a person to look ahead to see what the outcome of a given activity is to be.

In the next place the aim as a foreseen end gives direction to the activity; it is not an idle view of a mere spectator, but influences the steps taken to reach the end. The foresight functions in three ways. In the first place, it involves careful observation of the given conditions to see what are the means available for reaching the end, and to discover the hindrances in the way. In the second place, it suggests the proper order or sequence in the use of means. It facilitates an economical selection and arrangement. In the third place, it makes choice of alternatives possible. If we can predict the outcome of acting this way or that, we can then compare the value of the two courses of action; we can pass judgment upon their relative desirability. If we know that stagnant water breeds mosquitoes and that they are likely to carry disease, we can, disliking that anticipated result, take steps to avert it. Since we do not anticipate results as mere intellectual onlookers, but as persons concerned in the outcome, we are partakers in the process which produces the result. We intervene to bring about this result or that.

Of course these three points are closely connected with one another. We can definitely foresee results only as we make careful scrutiny of present conditions, and the importance of the outcomes supplies the motive for observations. The more adequate our observations, the more varied is the scene of conditions and obstructions that presents itself, and the more numerous are the alternatives between which choice may be made. In turn, the more numerous the recognized possibilities of the situation, or alternatives of action, the more meaning does the chosen activity possess, and the more flexibly controllable is it. Where only a single outcome has been thought of, the mind has nothing else to think of; the meaning attaching to the act is limited. One only steams ahead toward the mark. Sometimes such a narrow course may be effective. But if unexpected difficulties offer themselves, one has not as many resources at command as if he had chosen the same line of action after a broader survey of the possibilities of the field. He cannot make needed readjustments readily.

The net conclusion is that acting with an aim is all one with acting intelligently. To foresee a terminus of an act is to have a basis upon which to observe, to select, and to order objects and our own capacities. To do these things means to have a mind—for mind is precisely intentional purposeful activity controlled by perception of facts and their relationships to one another. To have a mind to do a thing is to foresee a future possibility; it is to have a plan for its accomplishment; it is to note the means which make the plan capable of execution and the obstructions in the way,—or, if it is really a *mind* to do the thing and not a vague aspiration—it is to have a plan which takes account of resources and difficulties. Mind is capacity to refer present conditions to future results, and future consequences to present conditions. And these traits are just what is meant by having an aim or a purpose. A man is stupid or blind or unintelligent—lacking in mind—just in the degree in which in any activity he does not know what he is about, namely, the probable consequences of his acts. A man is imperfectly intelligent when he contents himself with looser guesses about the outcome than is needful, just taking a chance with his luck, or when he forms plans apart from study of the actual conditions, including his own capacities. Such relative absence of mind means to make our feelings the measure of what is to happen. To be intelligent we must "stop, look, listen" in making the plan of an activity.

To identify acting with an aim and intelligent activity is enough to show its value—its function in experience. We are only too given to making an entity out of the abstract noun "consciousness." We forget that it comes from the adjective "conscious." To be conscious is to be aware of what we are about; conscious signifies the deliberate, observant, planning traits of activity. Consciousness is nothing which we have which gazes idly on the scene around one or which has impressions made upon it by physical things; it is a name for the purposeful quality of an activity, for the fact that it is directed by an aim. Put the other way about, to have an aim is to act with meaning, not like an automatic machine; it is to *mean* to do something and to perceive the meaning of things in the light of that intent.

THE CRITERIA OF GOOD AIMS

We may apply the results of our discussion to a consideration of the criteria involved in a correct establishing of aims. (1) The aim set up must be an outgrowth of existing conditions. It must be based upon a consideration of what is already going on; upon the resources and difficulties of the situation. Theories about the proper end of our activities —educational and moral theories—often violate this principle. They assume ends lying *outside* our activities; ends foreign to the concrete make-up of the situation; ends which issue from some outside source. Then the problem is to bring our activities to bear upon the realization of these externally supplied ends. They are something for which we *ought* to act. In any case such "aims" limit intelligence; they are not the expression of mind in foresight, observation, and choice of the better among alternative possibilities. They limit intelligence because, given ready-made, they must be imposed by some authority external to intelligence, leaving to the latter nothing but a mechanical choice of means.

(2) We have spoken as if aims could be completely formed prior to the attempt to realize them. This impression must now be qualified. The aim as it first emerges is a mere tentative sketch. The act of striving to realize it tests its worth. If it suffices to direct activity successfully, nothing more is required, since its whole function is to set a mark in advance; and at times a mere hint may suffice. But usually—at least in complicated situations—acting upon it brings to light conditions which had been overlooked. This calls for revision of the original aim; it has to be added to and subtracted from. An aim must, then, be *flexible*; it must be capable of alteration to meet circumstances. An end established externally to the process of action is always rigid. Being inserted or imposed from without, it is not supposed to have a working relationship to the concrete conditions of the situation. What happens in the course of action neither confirms, refutes, nor alters it. Such an end can only be insisted upon. The failure that results from its lack of adaptation is

attributed simply to the perverseness of conditions, not to the fact that the end is not reasonable under the circumstances. The value of a legitimate aim, on the contrary, lies in the fact that we can use it to change conditions. It is a method for dealing with conditions so as to effect desirable alterations in them. A farmer who should passively accept things just as he finds them would make as great a mistake as he who framed his plans in complete disregard of what soil, climate, etc., permit. One of the evils of an abstract or remote external aim in education is that its very inapplicability in practice is likely to react into a haphazard snatching at immediate conditions. A good aim surveys the present state of experience of pupils, and forming a tentative plan of treatment, keeps the plan constantly in view and yet modifies it as conditions develop. The aim, in short, is experimental, and hence constantly growing as it is tested in action.

(3) The aim must always represent a freeing of activities. The term *end in view* is suggestive, for it puts before the mind the termination or conclusion of some process. The only way in which we can define an activity is by putting before ourselves the objects in which it terminates—as one's aim in shooting is the target. But we must remember that the *object* is only a mark or sign by which the mind specifies the *activity* one desires to carry out. Strictly speaking, not the target but *hitting* the target is the end in view; one *takes* aim by means of the target, but also by the sight on the gun. The different objects which are thought of are means of *directing* the activity. Thus one aims at, say, a rabbit; what he wants is to shoot straight: a certain kind of activity. Or, if it is the rabbit he wants, it is not rabbit apart from his activity, but as a factor in activity; he wants to eat the rabbit, or to show it as evidence of his marksmanship—he wants to do something with it. The doing with the thing, not the thing in isolation, is his end. The object is but a phase of the active end,—continuing the activity successfully. This is what is meant by the phrase, used above, "freeing activity."

In contrast with fulfilling some process in order that activity may go on, stands the static character of an end which is imposed from without the activity. It is always conceived of as fixed; it is *something* to be attained and possessed. When one has such a notion, activity is a mere unavoidable means to something else; it is not significant or important on its own account. As compared with the end it is but a necessary evil; something which must be gone through before one can reach the object which is alone worth while. In other words, the external idea of the aim leads to a separation of means from end, while an end which grows up within an activity as plan for its direction is always both ends and means, the distinction being only one of convenience. Every means is a temporary end until we have attained it. Every end becomes a means of carrying activity further as soon as it is achieved. We call it end when it marks off the future direction of the activity in which we are engaged; means when it marks off the present direction. Every divorce of end from means diminishes by that much the significance of the activity and tends to reduce it to a drudgery from which one would escape if he could. A farmer has to use plants and animals to carry on his farming activities. It certainly makes a great difference to his life whether he is fond of them, or whether he regards them merely as means which he has to employ to get something else in which alone he is interested. In the former case, his entire course of activity is significant; each phase of it has its own value. He has the experience of realizing his end at every stage; the postponed aim, or end in view, being merely a sight ahead by which to keep his activity going fully and freely. For if he does not look ahead, he is more likely to find himself blocked. The aim is as definitely a *means* of action as is any other portion of an activity.

APPLICATIONS IN EDUCATION

There is nothing peculiar about educational aims. They are just like aims in any directed occupation. The educator, like the farmer, has certain things to do, certain resources with which to do, and certain obstacles with which to contend. The conditions with which the farmer deals, whether as obstacles or resources, have their own structure and operation independently of any purpose of his. Seeds sprout, rain falls, the sun shines, insects devour, blight comes, the seasons change. His aim is simply to utilize these various conditions; to make his activities and their energies work together, instead of against one another. It would be absurd if the farmer set up a purpose of farming, without any reference to these conditions of soil, climate, characteristic of plant growth, etc. His purpose is simply a foresight of the consequences of his energies connected with those of the things about him, a foresight used to direct his movements from day to day. Foresight of possible consequences leads to more careful and extensive observation of the nature and performances of the things he had to do with, and to laying out a plan—that is, of a certain order in the acts to be performed.

It is the same with the educator, whether parent or teacher. It is as absurd for the latter to set up their "own" aims as the proper objects of the growth of the children as it would be for the farmer to set up an ideal of farming irrespective of conditions. Aims mean acceptance of responsibility for the observations, anticipations, and arrangements required in carrying on a function—whether farming or educating. Any aim is of value so far as it assists observation, choice, and planning in carrying on activity from moment to moment and hour to hour; if it gets in the way of the individual's own common sense (as it will surely do if imposed from without or accepted on authority) it does harm.

And it is well to remind ourselves that education as such has no aims. Only persons, parents, and teachers, etc., have aims, not an abstract idea like education. And consequently their purposes are indefinitely varied, differing with different children, changing as children grow and with the growth of experience on the part of the one who teaches. Even the most valid aims which can be put in words will, as words, do more harm than good unless one recognizes that they are not aims, but rather suggestions to educators as to how to observe, how to look ahead, and how to choose in liberating and directing the energies of the concrete situations in which they find themselves. As a recent writer has said: "To lead this boy to read Scott's novels instead of old Sleuth's stories; to teach this girl to sew; to root out the habit of bullying from John's make up; to prepare this class to study medicine,—these are samples of the millions of aims we have actually before us in the concrete work of education."

Bearing these qualifications in mind, we shall proceed to state some of the characteristics found in all good educational aims. (1) An educational aim must be founded upon the intrinsic activities and needs (including original instincts and acquired habits) of the given individual to be educated. The tendency of such an aim as preparation is, as we have seen, to omit existing powers, and find the aim in some remote accomplishment or responsibility. In general, there is a disposition to take considerations which are dear to the hearts of adults and set them up as ends irrespective of the capacities of those educated. There is also an inclination to propound aims which are so uniform as to neglect the specific powers and requirements of an individual, forgetting that all learning is something which happens to an individual at a given time and place. The larger range of perception of the adult is of great value in observing the abilities and weaknesses of the young, in deciding what they may amount to. Thus the artistic capacities of the adult exhibit what certain tendencies of the child are capable of; if we did not have the adult achievements we should be without assurance as to the significance of the drawing, reproducing, modeling, coloring activities of childhood. So if it were not for adult language, we should not be able to see the import of the babbling impulses of infancy. But it is one thing to use adult accomplishments as a context in which to place and survey the doings of childhood and youth; it is quite another to set them up as a fixed aim without regard to the concrete activities of those educated.

(2) An aim must be capable of translation into a method of co-operating with the activities of those undergoing instruction. It must suggest the kind of environment needed to liberate and to organize *their* capacities. Unless it lends itself to the construction of specific procedures, and unless these procedures test, correct, and amplify the aims, the latter is worthless. Instead of helping the specific task of teaching, it

prevents the use of ordinary judgment in observing and sizing up the situation. It operates to exclude recognition of everything except what squares up with the fixed end in view. Every rigid aim just because it is rigidly given seems to render it unnecessary to give careful attention to concrete conditions. Since it *must* apply anyhow, what is the use of noting details which do not count?

The vice of externally imposed ends has deep roots. Teachers receive them from superior authorities; these authorities accept them from what is current in the community. The teachers impose them upon children. As a first consequence, the intelligence of the teacher is not free; it is confined to receiving the aims laid down from above. Too rarely is the individual teacher so free from the dictation of authoritative supervisor, textbook on methods, prescribed course of study, etc., that he can let his mind come to close quarters with the pupil's mind and the subject matter. This distrust of the teacher's experience is then reflected in lack of confidence in the responses of pupils. The latter receive their aims through a double or treble external imposition, and are constantly confused by the conflict between the aims which are natural to their own experience at the time and those in which they are taught to acquiesce. Until the democratic criterion of the intrinsic significance of every growing experience is recognized, we shall be intellectually confused by the demand for adaptation to external aims.

(3) Educators have to be on their guard against ends that are alleged to be general and ultimate. Every activity, however specific, is, of course, general in its ramified connections, for it leads out indefinitely into other things. So far as a general idea makes us more alive to these connections, it cannot be too general. But "general" also means "abstract," or detached from all specific context. And such abstractness means remoteness, and throws us back, once more, upon teaching and learning as mere means of getting ready for an end disconnected from the means. That education is literally and all the time its own reward means that no alleged study or discipline is educative unless it is worth while in its own immediate having. A truly general aim broadens the outlook; it stimulates one to take more consequences (connections) into account. This means a wider and more flexible observation of means. The more interacting forces, for example, the farmer takes into account, the more varied will be his immediate resources. He will see a greater number of possible starting places, and a greater number of ways of getting at what he wants to do. The fuller one's conception of possible future achievements, the less his present activity is tied down to a small number of alternatives. If one knew enough, one could start almost anywhere and sustain his activities continuously and fruitfully.

The Aims of American Education

THE question of the aims of American education is difficult to answer. Unlike many other countries, the United States does not have a centralized system of education. If we did, it would be possible for the Minister of Education to decide by decree what the objectives of education would be in the schools throughout the country, as is done in countries like France, Mexico, and the Soviet Union. But with out decentralized system in which educational policies and programs are worked out in the some 45,000 school districts, it is impossible to say categorically what the aims of education are. However, the diversity is more apparent than real, and the fact is that, while educational aims differ from district to district, the degree of similarity is very high.

The answer to this apparent paradox is that the United States as a nation is so well unified, so far as language, institutions, customs, and values are concerned, that this basic unity is reflected in the schools. There are differences, of course, but the basic characteristics of American society discussed in Chapter 7 apply to a great extent to the entire nation. As a result, statements on educational aims from school districts in Florida, California, New York, and Iowa show an amazing degree of similarity. Also of importance is the fact that many of America's leading educators have received their advanced education either directly or indirectly from a relatively small number of great universities. Institutions such as Columbia, Harvard, Chicago, Stanford, and the great state universities like Minnesota, Illinois, Michigan, Iowa, and California have prepared thousands of teachers and school administrators and sent thousands of their graduates into teacher-education institutions. Thus, despite the lack of official centralization, a high degree of unity exists in the American school system. For this reason, it is probable that most educators would agree with the following list of objectives drawn up by Sidney Hook. This list, as well as the others included, again points up the relationship between American society and American education.

1. Education should aim to develop the powers of critical, independent thought.
2. It should attempt to induce sensitiveness of perception, receptiveness to new ideas, imaginative sympathy with the experiences of others.
3. It should produce an awareness of the main streams of our cultural, literary and scientific traditions.
4. It should make available important bodies of knowledge concerning nature, society, ourselves, our country and its history.

5. It should strive to cultivate an intelligent loyalty to the ideals of the democratic community.

6. At some level, it should equip young men and women with the general skills and techniques and the specialized knowledge which, together with the virtues and aptitudes already mentioned, will make it possible for them to do some productive work related to their capacities and interests.

7. It should strengthen those inner resources and traits of character which enable the individual, when necessary, to stand alone.[5]

Nor would there be much disagreement with the following statement of the aims of a liberal education drawn up by a committee of the faculty of Washington University in St. Louis in 1952.

I. Concerning *knowledge*:
   1. Of man's physical and biological nature and environment.
   2. Of man's social environment and history.
   3. Of man's cultural history and situation.
   4. Of the processes which make for personal and group fulfillment.
II. Concerning *abilities*:
   1. To use one's own language.
   2. To think critically.
   3. To make value judgments.
   4. To participate effectively in social situations.
   5. To handle a foreign language.
III. Concerning *appreciations*:
   1. Of beauty.
   2. Of people.
   3. Of differences.
   4. Of wonder, awe and mystery.
   5. Of man's potentialities.
IV. Concerning *motivations*:
   1. To develop an adequate hierarchy of values.
   2. To adopt an affirmative, constructive orientation toward life.
   3. To achieve independence.
   4. To assume social responsibility as a participant in the world community.
   5. To include the interests of others within one's own.
   6. To seek self-realization on the highest possible level.

Evidence that Americans generally would agree with these statements of objectives for their schools was provided at the White House Conference on Education held in Washington D.C. in 1955. The Conference,

[5] Sidney Hook, *Education for Modern Man* (New York: The Dial Press, 1946), p. 2.

called by President Eisenhower, was made up of professional educators and laymen from all parts of the country. In its report on the topic "What Should Our Schools Accomplish?" the delegates agreed that the schools should develop in the student:

1. The fundamental skills of communication—reading, writing, spelling as well as other elements of effective oral and written expression; the arithmetical and mathematical skills, including problem solving. While schools are doing the best job in their history in teaching these skills, continuous improvement is desirable and necessary.
2. Appreciation for our democratic heritage.
3. Civic rights and responsibilities and knowledge of American institutions.
4. Respect and appreciation for human values and for the beliefs of others.
5. Ability to think and evaluate constructively and creatively.
6. Effective work habits and self-discipline.
7. Social competency as a contributing member of his family and community.
8. Ethical behavior based on a sense of moral and spiritual values.
9. Intellectual curiosity and eagerness for life-long learning.
10. Esthetic appreciation and self-expression in the arts.
11. Physical and mental health.
12. Wise use of time, including constructive leisure pursuits.
13. Understanding of the physical world and man's relation to it as represented through basic knowledge of the sciences.
14. An awareness of our relationships with the world community.

Despite similarities in statements of objectives, there are sharp differences of opinion as to where the emphasis should be placed. These differences have centered around the relative value of "liberal" as against "vocational" education, "cultural" versus "practical" studies. Both groups would probably agree with Hook's list of objectives but would emphasize different points. Those who advocate the "liberal" aspects of education would concentrate upon points three and four. Those for the "vocational" would place more value on his sixth point.

Because of the controversy between advocates of "liberal" and "vocational" education, and because America is an industrial society and will continue to become more highly industrialized in the years ahead this problem is an important one. Therefore it is essential to understand what "liberal" education and "vocational" education are, in order to reach an intelligent conclusion as to what the relationship is or should be between them. For this reason a statement by Sidney Hook on the subject has been included.

Sidney Hook

FROM

Education for Modern Man [6]

Nothing is more familiar than the contrast drawn by modern educators between liberal education and vocational education. But as soon as we try to track down the specific differences between them we discover that no hard and fast lines can be drawn. Usually a liberal education is so defined that if it has any other end beyond itself, if it involves more than the joys of consummatory experience, it is illiberal. It thus automatically excludes any activity connected with "earning one's living.". . .

A liberal education should do something more than prepare the student to earn his own living. But it should at least prepare him for it. The crucial question is how he should be prepared. No conception of liberal education is worth a second glance which professes to be unconcerned with the quality of the life a student will lead after he is through with his formal schooling—a life in which the fruits of his schooling first become apparent. All the great educators of the modern world, despite their differences as to what constitutes the best education, agree that it should be complete in the sense that it should fit men to grapple with their duties as citizens of the community. But a citizen of the community is not only a "political" entity. He is a producer, a consumer, a potential warrior, a critic, a teacher in some respects, a learner in others. He is sometimes more of one or another. But in the life of the citizen they are all related. This thought was expressed long ago by John Milton whose conception of a "complete" education is a measure by which we may still judge what belongs to a desirable education, and how it belongs. "A complete and generous education," he said, "is one that fits a man to perform skillfully, justly and magnanimously, all the acts, both public and private, of peace and war." Vocational education is part of a complete and generous education. . . .

The fundamental problem of vocational education today is whether it should be considered as a form of vocational *training*, serving industry and government, or whether it should be considered as an aspect of liberal education in which preparation for careers in industry and government is justified *both* by the needs of a developing personality and the interests of the community. Here, as elsewhere, we can observe a meeting of extremes which in effect makes allies of the lily-pure academician

[6] Reprinted from *Education for Modern Man* by Sidney Hook. Copyright 1946 by Sidney Hook. Used by permission of the Dial Press, Inc. Pp. 152–9, 162–4, 168–9.

and the tough-minded practical man. The first finds utterly distasteful the idea that vocational interests should obtrude on the course of study. In his heart he believes that students who study for any other reason save the sheer love of it degrade learning. They therewith prove themselves in his eyes to be no true students at all. The second regards liberal arts studies as irritating conventional preliminaries to useful subjects whose mastery has a cash value. Wherever possible, he seeks to give vocational courses a content that is directly relevant to the tasks that must be performed on the job. For all their opposition, both agree on sharply separating liberal from vocational study, although they differ in the grounds offered for the separation. Both are united in strong opposition to any plan to make vocational education integral to liberal education. . . .

Vocational education conceived as job-training represents the greatest threat to democratic education in our time. It is a threat to democracy because it tends to make the job-trained individual conscious only of his technological responsibilities, but not of his social and moral responsibilities. He becomes a specialist in "means" but indifferent to "ends" which are considered the province of another specialist. The main concern is with "getting a job" and after that with "doing a job" no matter what the political direction and moral implications of the job are. Social programs are judged simply by whether they promise to provide the jobs for which the technician is trained. If a democratic community can supply the opportunity for work, well and good; if it can't, and a totalitarian party or government offers the opportunity, why not? Observers have noted that the technically trained students in institutions of higher education in Germany and Italy have in the mass been much more susceptible to totalitarian propaganda than students whose education has primarily been in the pure sciences. An education that is narrowly vocational, without cultural perspective or social orientation, unillumined by knowledge of large scientific principles considered in a large way, undisciplined by a critical method that sets the range of relevance for methods of technical thinking, is even worse for democratic purposes than a narrow and pure scientific training which, as a special kind of professionalism, is bad in its own way. For the problems on the job are *applications* of scientific knowledge in contexts of social values and human relationships. And it is these which conventional vocational education persistently ignores.

The high incidence of interest in vocational training among youth today reflects the expectation that our economy will have a place for them. The underlying assumption is that the seller's market for the vocationally trained will indefinitely continue in peace as well as war. This is far from being a sure thing. The history of American capitalism does not provide grounds for great confidence. Vocationally trained talents rusted for almost a decade after the depression. Educators made desperate efforts to revamp curriculums so as to keep youth out of the labor market. We may witness the same thing again. Dearth of vocations may be the most powerful argument against vocational education of the present type. But it would be the weakest argument, and the wisdom it would enforce, besides being costly, would be limited. For, even if prosperity were to continue unabated in years of peace, there is no reason why a truncated vocational education should be substituted for an integrated liberal one. We could well forego the difference in national wealth that would result from keeping young people out of the labor market for a few years, if it added to the immeasurable but more genuine wealth of a well informed, critically minded youth.

Such a critically minded youth would think not only about jobs but about the economy as a whole which provided the jobs and sometimes took them away. Such a youth would not be educated to "adjust" themselves to an economic and social order as if it were as perennial as the course of the stars. They would be encouraged to view it in its historical development. They would be taught to recognize its present-day problems as *occasions for choices* which they, among others, have to make. They would adjust not to the present but to the future as if it were present. To adjust to the future as if it were present is never an automatic reaction. For it is the essence of reflection.

There is a paradox connected with vocational training. The more vocational it is, the narrower it is; the narrower it is, the less likely it is to serve usefully in earning a living. Techniques, know-hows, operative skills change so rapidly in industry that the student who has been trained to perform certain specific tasks runs the risk of suffering from what Veblen called "trained incapacity." This is particularly true for manual crafts. Those who are muscle-bound, either physically or intellectually, must unlearn and relearn, for all their previous vocational training, if they are to continue to earn their living. Proper vocational education stresses doing, of course. Its skills are largely practical, not abstract. But at the same time it must nourish and strengthen powers of flexibility which will enable students intelligently to breast the waves of vocational change. To a certain extent, this is achieved in the kind of vocational education we call "professional" about which I shall have more to say later.

The indictment against vocational education summarized above would be signed with both hands by those who desire to keep liberal education uncontaminated by concern for earning a livelihood. They offer two distinct solutions to the problem. The first is a sharp separation between liberal arts education and vocational education. Liberal arts education above the elementary level is to be open to anyone who can qualify for it. After it is completed, it may be followed by vocational education. The second solution is much more radical. It has the great merit of making the problem disappear from view. It proposes that vocational education be left to apprentice experience on the job, and that the schools abandon all vocational instruction. . . .

But it is this very *separation* between the two kinds of education which is pedagogically defective. Vocational education is simply overlaid on liberal education. The bearings of the general ideas and philosophy acquired through liberal education is not integrated with the vocational subject matter at the points where they are most important. Why a man works, the effects of his work, its relation to the tasks of the community are questions quite germane to his vocational activity. They are best studied in specific contexts. The worker remains a citizen while he is at his job. His knowledge of the fact will ofttimes make a difference even to what he does and how he does it. What is called a liberal education should be a continuous process, and there is no reason—except unfamiliarity with the idea—why vocational education should not be liberalized to include the study of social, economic, historical and ethical questions wherever relevant instead of assuming, as in the existing practice, that education in these matters is something already gone through and forever done with. . . .

The greatest obstacle to this attempt to integrate vocational and liberal education flows from the suspicions of the specialists against introducing anything outside the narrow confines of his specialty. He regards cultural studies in professional schools as a kind of academic boondoggling. It wastes time which in his eyes is already insufficient for the technical matters students should know. The specialist has a natural tendency to view the whole curriculum from the standpoint of his own professional concern. Yet he recognizes how narrowing and educationally disastrous such a perspective is when it is drawn by *other* specialists. This recognition should serve as one of the checks upon his natural appetite. Even in liberal arts colleges, as we have already observed, many subjects, particularly the sciences, are taught from the specialist's point of view to the detriment of broader understanding and abiding interest on the part of students, most of whom, if they become specialists, will be specialists in something else.

Recent tendencies in our best vocational schools, viz., our professional schools, show a growing realization that vocational and liberal education cannot be sharply separated. A dawning perception is now manifest that the best specialist is not necessarily the man who has received the most vocational training. The work of the physician, the work of the lawyer, the work of the engineer in different ways demands a *continuing* familiarity with subjects that would seem to the specialist to be utterly irrelevant to his proper vocational tasks. . . .

This is not confusing liberal and vocational education. It is relating them in such a way that no matter how a man earns his living he will not lose sight of the communal traditions to which he owes his knowledge and skills, the communal responsibilities he shares with his fellows, and the communal tasks to which he can make his distinctive contribution. Vocational education which fails to do this is illiberal and had best be abandoned.

The difficulties of giving organizational form to this integrated curriculum are tremendous. But they must be faced. There are certain healthy developments in existing practice which should be encouraged. In many courses in the liberal arts colleges today an attempt is made to provide either some work experience or firsthand contact with practical activities in which general principles are given application. Instead of being done in a haphazard and episodic way, this should be systematized. During the third and fourth years of the typical liberal arts college, studies are concentrated around a vocational interest but in isolation from the vocation. Guidance by self or others is hardly likely to be sound unless the student is given an opportunity to savor for himself the quality of his prospective vocational career.

Thus we see that "vocational" education properly understood would be liberal in the sense that it would be liberating. On the other hand, "liberal" education at its best is truly vocational in the sense that it gives direction and broad perspective to the individual in his lifework.

Agents Responsible for the Aims of Education

In general, in the United States educational aims are developed by the teachers and administrators in the local districts. Of course, these individuals are influenced by the institutions in which they receive their training. They are also influenced by groups like the Educational Policies Commission and by individual educational leaders who have written on the subject. They are also influenced to some extent by the state courses of study, which are generally the result of the co-operative efforts of teachers from all over the state and are published by the state departments of education in the various states. These courses of study need not be, and are not, always used. Frequently they are used only as source material. Finally, it must be said that textbook authors and publishers often determine the educational aims. This happens when the teacher, without thinking the problem through, simply follows the text.

The most acceptable procedure for developing the purposes of education is to have them worked out co-operatively by educators and laymen.

It is clear that educators cannot ignore the wishes of the American people in deciding on what will be taught in the public schools. On the other hand, it would be a waste of talent and professional training to have the community decide on the objectives and relegate teachers to the role of technicians whose task would be to follow orders. Educators must, of course, work with the community, but, as professional persons, they have a responsibility for providing leadership in the determination of the aims of education. And in this process the classroom teacher plays a key role. He is the one who should know the most about conditions in the classroom and what is possible and desirable for each child. He is the one who is in the best position to meet Dewey's requirements for establishing intelligent aims. He is the only person who can develop the aims of education with children and, of course, it is he who will have to maintain the connection between ends and means as he develops his program from day to day in the classroom. This responsibility requires that every teacher be something of an expert on child growth and development as well as on the society in which he lives, since these are the major factors that determine the objectives of education. If he is, the chances are that Dewey's criteria for good aims will be applied.

A final word needs to be said regarding the aims of American education. Our treatment has been largely in terms of the stated, avowed aims of educators. It would have been possible to have treated the *actual* aims of teachers (and perhaps even of students, parents, and others) insofar as these differ from the avowed aims. For example, some research has been done which indicates that some high school teachers are primarily concerned with having their students like them. This, of course, is approaching the problem from a very personal and perhaps a psychological standpoint but it sheds some light on a very interesting aspect of American education. What personal aims do teachers have in education? Obviously the answer to this question would differ for each teacher, and the same thing would apply for each individual student. Doubtless many teachers have as their central aim developing intelligent, sensitive, mature human beings and their personal satisfaction is derived from achieving this end. Others, as Riesman has pointed out,[7] satisfy their basic personality needs by being popular with students, often at the expense of sacrificing the level of academic demand. In the same way, studies of the aims of parents in regard to the education of their children indicate that, while they may agree to the aims set up by educators, they are usually most concerned with having their children learn a trade or a profession. Likewise, many pressure groups, while giving lip service to the aims discussed earlier, may be primarily concerned with having the school develop a certain economic or political philosophy in students.

[7] David Riesman, "Teachers amid Changing Expectations," *Harvard Educational Review*, XXIV (Spring, 1954), p. 112–5.

Or a school administrator may have an impressive list of professional objectives but actually be primarily concerned with keeping his job or with climbing up the social ladder. Of course the same individual school administrator may have the two sets of aims at the same time but very often the stated educational aims remain at the verbal level while the personal aims are dominant and have the greater influence upon his actions and decisions.

As our knowledge of human personality and of the motivating forces of human behavior increases, it becomes clear that there are often conflicts between real aims and avowed aims of individuals. Real and avowed aims can be and frequently are identical, but we should be aware that discrepancies sometimes exist.

Suggested Readings

Childs, John L.: *Education and Morals*. New York: Appleton-Century-Crofts, 1950.

Counts, George S.: *Education and American Civilization*. New York: Bureau of Publications, Teachers College, Columbia University, 1952.

Dewey, John: *Democracy and Education*. New York: The Macmillan Company, 1916.

Educational Policies Commission: *Education for All American Children*. Washington, D.C.: National Education Association, 1944.

————: *Education for All American Youth*. Washington, D.C.: National Education Association, 1944.

————: *Moral and Spiritual Values in the Public Schools*. Washington, D.C.: National Education Association, 1951.

————: *The Purposes of Education in American Democracy*. Washington, D.C.: National Education Association, 1938.

Hook, Sidney: *Education for Modern Man*. New York: The Dial Press, 1946.

Kearney, Nolan C.: *Elementary School Objectives*. New York: Russell Sage Foundation, 1953.

Smith, Huston: *The Purposes of Higher Education*. New York: Harper & Brothers, 1955.

CHAPTER 13

NATURE, CONTENT, AND ORGANIZATION
OF CURRICULUM

O NCE THE AIMS OF EDUCATION ARE ESTABLISHED, THE EDUCATOR HAS
to face the problem of achieving them within the school. The
all-inclusive term *curriculum* developed in education to embrace
the many facets of this problem. Derived from the Latin word *currere*
meaning to run, the word *curriculum* means a runway or a race course
over which one must travel to reach a goal. Traditionally in American
education *curriculum* was used to refer to a particular or specific course
of study that was taken in order to get a degree and was applied at first
to higher education and then to the secondary schools.

Recent Changes in Curriculum

FOR a number of reasons the curriculum of the American school has undergone a radical change in the last fifty years. One aspect of the change
has been in the direction of greater breadth and scope of content. One
reason for this change was that American society was changing, becoming more technical, more complex, and requiring an ever higher level of
formal schooling for its citizens. The vast extension of knowledge which
provided the basis for the new technological society resulted in the addition of new subjects to the traditional offerings. This was especially
true in the secondary schools and colleges, and was one of the important
reasons for the introduction of the elective system, and subsequently the
credit system, into American education. Among the new subjects introduced into colleges were the modern languages, principally French,
Spanish, and German, and the new sciences, such as biology, physics,
chemistry, and geology, while the larger colleges and universities added
entire technical schools to their institutions. These subjects were

also added in the high schools as well as new courses in drafting, mechanical drawing, and many others.

Another reason for the extension of the curriculum was that the nature of the student population in the secondary schools, and inevitably the nature of the secondary schools themselves were changing. High schools were becoming institutions devoted less exclusively to college preparation. They became concerned with providing terminal education, and the American people were demanding that this education be practical and useful. As a result, courses such as bookkeeping and typing and numerous vocational courses were added.

A third reason for the expansion of the curriculum is related to the two already given and yet is important enough to be mentioned separately. Because of the changes in American society, the school gradually took on more and more of the functions formerly handled by the home. Part of this increase in function was a direct result of the development of a modern technical industrial society. Whereas a century ago a young man would in most instances have learned his vocational skills from his father, today he will usually learn these skills in a school. But many other newly assumed responsibilities, while they were not so directly related, were still a result of the changes in society. For example, the schools, because of the alarming increase in the death and accident rate on the nation's highways began to offer courses in driver training. As a result of the awareness by educators of a lack of knowledge about sex and hygiene on the part of adolescent boys and girls, courses in these topics were brought into the high school curriculum. Likewise a growing awareness of the need for training in home economics, especially in urban centers, led to the introduction of a whole series of courses in this field. The net result has been that the curriculum in the modern schools has become not only more technical and practical but also very comprehensive.

It should be realized that there are real dangers inherent in this increase in the breadth and scope of the curriculum. It is possible that in attempting to be so comprehensive the schools may spread themselves so thin they may do nothing well. As was pointed out in the previous chapter, in the last two decades one of the over-all stated aims of education has been to meet the needs of youth. This all-embracing concept has been used as the basis for introducing the many new courses that have broadened the curriculum. Probably few would deny that the schools should attempt to meet the needs of youth. But youth has thousands of needs and it is necessary to decide which ones the schools can and should attempt to meet. For example, the boy who is a high school senior needs to know how to ask a girl for a date and he needs to understand the nature and functioning of Russian communism. Obviously in this instance the parents should deal with the dating problem and the school with the Russian communism. This is an oversimplification of course but it points up the problem of deciding what the schools can and should teach and what they cannot or should not teach. Obviously no rule, especially for the specific courses or programs to be included in the curriculum, can be made for *all* American schools. What would conceivably be a desirable and legitimate function of the school in one community might not be so in another school in the same or a different community. For example, in certain sections of our large cities, a good case can be made for a course or even a program in home economics, whereas in other communities such a course might be less important or have a different emphasis. What is the most immediately useful may not always be the most valuable or the most necessary,—the example of the choice between offering work in grooming and dating and study about Russian communism is a case in point. The problem of deciding what to include in the curriculum, always vitally important, will become increasingly difficult in the years ahead.

The change in the curriculum in the American schools has been not only in breadth and scope but also in the conception of the curriculum itself which educators have held. In modern education, *curriculum* is usually defined as "all of the learning activities, planned, organized, and carried out under the control of the school." Thus curriculum is broader than subject matter narrowly defined, and includes such activities as the student government as well as clubs and sports which were formerly considered extracurricular.

The reasons for this changed conception of the nature of curriculum are not hard to find. With the tremendous growth of the schools and the school population, two interrelated developments occurred. First, the teaching profession not only grew in size but also began seriously to improve its standards. Second, more and more attention was devoted to the study of the problems of education, and since no aspect of education was more important than the curriculum, it became one of the major areas of study. As the study of curriculum got underway in earnest after the World War I, other factors operated influencing its development. Perhaps most important was the knowledge gathered concerning the nature of the child and his development, and then its application to the aims of education and logically to the problems of curriculum. As a result of research in psychology and psychiatry, indicating the unity or wholeness of personality, it became clear that the child's intellect could not be isolated and trained irrespective of the emotional, social, or physical aspects of his personality. With these changes came changes in the aims of education. No longer was the gathering of basic skills and information regarded as sufficient. Increasingly it was felt that the kind of individual the schools turned out was important and this involved not only the problem of emphasizing understanding to make the skills and learned information more functional, but also the problem of developing proper attitudes and changing behavior patterns. Also the gradual awakening of the teaching profession to the problems of mental health led to a concerted effort to organize the curriculum for meeting the emotional needs of children. Finally the increasing knowledge of the nature of the learning process had a tremendous influence upon the curriculum. The old conception of learning either as a process of stuffing the mind with information or of training the mind like a muscle through appropriate intellectual gymnastics gave way to a conception of learning as an active process involving the reorganization of the experience of the individual, and a process inevitably connected with the past experience and the interests of the individual. As a result of these factors the conception of the school's function and the role of the teacher began to change. Also the curriculum, since it constituted the means through which the aims of education were achieved, was changed. Today at its best, the modern curriculum is planned to provide an opportunity for the child to learn the skills, the knowledge, and the understandings, and to develop the attitudes and behavior patterns to function effectively in a complex, industrial, democratic society.

For the most part this changed conception of the curriculum is most applicable in the elementary school and least applicable in the colleges, with the high schools somewhere in between. In the colleges the word *curriculum* is generally used to describe the system or pattern of courses, some elective and some required, that must be taken to receive a degree. Activities such as sports, dramatics, and social functions are regarded by most faculty members as an important part of a college education although not a part of the curriculum and the student can take them or leave them. Despite this fact there is certainly a growing realization in the colleges of the importance of "total learning environment" in which the college student lives for four years. This realization has led many colleges and universities to make some interesting changes. For example, one large private midwestern university, in planning its new library, has in mind a place where students will live and work. It will be a place where they will not only be surrounded by open shelves of books and a place conducive to serious thought and study, but a place where seminar rooms are available so that the ideal of a university as a community of scholars can more nearly be realized. There is no attempt to underestimate the importance of the social and physical aspects of campus life. But many of the faculty members at this institution felt that the intellectual activity of the students had been limited largely to the classroom for the reason that proper provisions to encourage the intellectual aspects of university life were lacking.

The Curriculum as Means and End

MENTION was made earlier of the connection between the aims of education and the curriculum, and later of the fact that curriculum is essentially a means to an end. This relationship now needs to be explored more thoroughly. In a very real sense the curriculum is a means to an end, and it is helpful to think of it in this way both from the standpoint of understanding the nature of curriculum and from the standpoint of understanding the entire educational process as carried out in the schools. If one of the aims of education is to teach children to read, provision must be made in the curriculum planning as to where and when this will be done. If another aim is to teach the student to understand and use the scientific method, provision must be made within the curriculum for the opportunity to acquire this knowledge and skill. If an aim of education is to develop democratic citizens, provision must be made within the curriculum for the student to understand the nature of democracy on an intellectual basis, as well as experiencing the democratic processes and living the values of democracy within the school. In these instances, as well as all others, the curriculum is essentially a means through which the aims of education are achieved.

But the curriculum is more than a means to an end. In a very real sense the curriculum is both means and end. It is an end in itself because its substance, its content, and its experiences should be of value to the child from day to day. This seeming paradox can be resolved by realizing that in any actual life situation means and ends can never be separated. As inevitably as the end influences the means used to achieve it, the experiences in achieving the end change and modify the end. The aim of producing democratic citizens can never be achieved through a curriculum operated in such an authoritarian manner that the student has no opportunity to think for himself, assume responsibility, or discuss and solve problems co-operatively with his peers. In the same way, the communists who say they hope to achieve a democratic, classless society by using force and coercion and denying any semblance of freedom have become so modified through these experiences that they are incapable of behaving democratically.

The value in thinking of curriculum as a means is that it places a very important part of the educational process in its proper relation to the aims of education and makes the entire process more intelligible. When the organic connection between the aims of education and the curriculum is lost, the work of the school is carried on without intelligent direction. On the other hand, to think of curriculum merely as a means leads to the possibility of considering it as an obstacle course, something to be crossed as quickly and painlessly as possible in order to reach a goal. Unfortunately this situation is all too prevalent in American high schools and colleges as students endure the course work for four years to get their gold stars. It cannot be overemphasized that the curriculum is itself important in the quality of the experience of the student from day to day, but it must also be constantly thought of in its relation to the aims of education, that is, as means.

The Nature of Subject Matter

ONE other problem needs to be considered before ending our treatment of the nature of curriculum. This problem concerns the nature of subject matter and its relationship to the curriculum. Much of the controversy over the curriculum of the schools has centered about the subject matter of instruction. It has been charged that the modern schools neglect the teaching of subject matter and are too much concerned with methods and activities. On the other side, some modern teachers apparently associate teaching subject matter with a return to the traditional school. In discussions among teachers one is likely to hear heated arguments as to whether teachers should be teaching *subject matter* or *children*, as though the two were mutually exclusive. At one teachers' meeting attended by the author, the speaker was stressing the need for higher standards of scholarship among teachers whereupon one teacher inquired whether this meant a return to teaching subject matter. Because of the controversy and the apparent confusion regarding the term and because there is such a strong connection between subject matter and curriculum, it is essential to understand clearly what subject matter is.

Subject matter is often used synonymously with curriculum but it is better to think of subject matter as an important part of the curriculum that consists of the facts, concepts, skills, and ideas to be taught. This distinction separates subject matter from activities that are a planned part of the curriculum, though in practice the two are often closely related in the actual classroom situation. For example, in a fifth-grade class taught by the author the group was studying a unit on the discovery and exploration of America. In the course of the work the students planned and put on a play depicting some of the events in the discovery and exploration. There were many anticipated outcomes including an appreciation of the heterogeneous character of the explorers and the early settlements, a knowledge of how to gather and evaluate information, an increasing ability to work in groups, and many others. The students learned many skills including some in art, as they worked on scenery. However, the subject matter of the unit consisted of the facts and understandings connected with the historical events together with their implications for modern America. The activities of the unit aided in teaching and learning the subject matter. Obviously some aspects of the curriculum cannot be classified as subject matter. For example, if a school has a recess period devoted to free play in the school yard, the objective is to provide an opportunity for physical exercise, and no subject matter is involved. If, however, the period is devoted to instruction in the skills of batting, throwing, catching, etc., these skills would be considered a part of the subject matter of instruction.

One of the difficulties in dealing with subject matter is that the term has been associated in the minds of many teachers with the teaching of subjects and with the traditional school. Thus the fear noted above was displayed on the part of teachers that any consideration of subject matter would mean teaching arithmetic, spelling, geography, grammar, history, etc., as separate subjects, instead of the integrated approach commonly used in the elementary school. Also, in the last thirty years, as teachers have developed a better understanding of the learning process, they have come to think more in terms of the experiences of the child and the resultant changes in attitudes and behavior. Because the traditional subjects were ill suited to the elementary school and often meaningless to the children as well as being difficult to teach, many teachers have regarded subject matter as a nasty word. But as we shall see, no school can function, no curriculum could exist without subject matter. Therefore every effort should be made to understand its nature and place in the curriculum. To help with our understanding of the problem, a short statement by John Dewey on the nature of subject matter, from his book *Democracy and Education*, is included. In this statement Dewey also discusses the problem created by the difference in the conception of subject matter from the standpoint of the teacher and the students. This problem was aggravated in the traditional school because quite often it was not recognized, but it is always present in any educational endeavor, including the modern school.

John Dewey

FROM

Democracy and Education [1]

. . . The educator's part in the enterprise of education is to furnish the environment which stimulates responses and directs the learner's course. In last analysis, *all* that the educator can do is modify stimuli so that response will as surely as is possible result in the formation of

[1] John Dewey, *Democracy and Education.* Copyright 1916 by The Macmillan Company, and used with their permission. Pp. 212–16.

desirable intellectual and emotional dispositions. Obviously, studies or the subject matter of the curriculum have intimately to do with this business of supplying an environment. The other point is the necessity of a social environment to give meaning to habits formed. In what we have termed informal education, subject matter is carried directly in the matrix of social intercourse. It is what the persons with whom an individual associates do and say. This fact gives a clew to the understanding of the subject matter of formal or deliberate instruction. A connecting link is found in the stories, traditions, songs, and liturgies which accompany the doings and rites of a primitive social group. They represent the stock of meanings which have been precipitated out of previous experience, which are so prized by the group as to be identified with their conception of their own collective life. Not being obviously a part of the skill exhibited in the daily occupations of eating, hunting, making war and peace, constructing rugs, pottery, and baskets, etc., they are consciously impressed upon the young; often, as in the initiation ceremonies, with intense emotional fervor. Even more pains are consciously taken to perpetuate the myths, legends, and sacred verbal formulae of the group than to transmit the directly useful customs of the group just because they cannot be picked up, as the latter can be in the ordinary processes of association.

As the social group grows more complex, involving a greater number of acquired skills which are dependent, either in fact or in the belief of the group, upon standard ideas deposited from past experience, the content of social life gets more definitely formulated for purposes of instruction. As we have previously noted, probably the chief motive for consciously dwelling upon the group life, extracting the meanings which are regarded as most important and systematizing them in a coherent arrangement, is just the need of instructing the young so as to perpetuate group life. Once started on this road of selection, formulation, and organization, no definite limit exists. The invention of writing and of printing gives the operation an immense impetus. Finally, the bonds which connect the subject matter of school study with the habits and ideals of the social group are disguised and covered up. The ties are so loosened that it often appears as if there were none; as if subject matter existed simply as knowledge on its own independent behoof, and as if study were the mere act of mastering it for its own sake, irrespective of any social values. Since it is highly important for practical reasons to counteract this tendency the chief purposes of our theoretical discussion are to make clear the connection which is so readily lost from sight, and to show in some detail the social content and function of the chief constituents of the course of study.

The points need to be considered from the standpoint of instructor and of student. To the former, the significance of knowledge of subject matter, going far beyond the present knowledge of pupils, is to supply definite standards and to reveal to him the possibilities of the crude activities of the immature. (i) The material of school studies translates into concrete and detailed terms the meanings of current social life which it is desirable to transmit. It puts clearly before the instructor the essential ingredients of the culture to be perpetuated, in such an organized form as to protect him from the haphazard efforts he would be likely to indulge in if the meanings had not been standardized. (ii) A knowledge of the ideas which have been achieved in the past as the outcome of activity places the educator in a position to perceive the meaning of the seeming impulsive and aimless reactions of the young, and to provide the stimuli needed to direct them so that they will amount to something. The more the educator knows of music the more he can perceive the possibilities of the inchoate musical impulses of a child. Organized subject matter represents the ripe fruitage of experiences like theirs, experiences involving the same world, and powers and needs similar to theirs. It does not represent perfection or infallible wisdom; but it is the best at command to further new experiences which may, in some respects at least, surpass the achievement embodied in existing knowledge and works of art.

From the standpoint of the educator, in other words, the various studies represent working resources, available capital. Their remoteness from the experience of the young is not, however, seeming; it is real. The subject matter of the learner is not, therefore, it cannot be, identical with the formulated, the crystallized, and systematized subject matter of the adult; the material as found in books and in works of art, etc. The latter represents the *possibilities* of the former; not its existing state. It enters directly into the activities of the expert and the educator, not into that of the beginner, the learner. Failure to bear in mind the difference in subject matter from the respective standpoints of teacher and student is responsible for most of the mistakes made in the use of texts and other expressions of preexistent knowledge.

The need for a knowledge of the constitution and functions, in the concrete, of human nature is great just because the teacher's attitude to subject matter is so different from that of the pupil. The teacher presents in actuality what the pupil represents only in *posse*. That is, the teacher already knows the things which the student is only learning. Hence the problem of the two is radically unlike. When engaged in the direct act of teaching, the instructor needs to have subject matter at his fingers' ends; his attention should be upon the attitude and response of the pupil. To understand the latter in its interplay with subject matter is his task, while the pupil's mind, naturally, should be not on itself but on the topic in hand. Or to state the same point in a somewhat different manner: the teacher should be occupied not with subject matter in itself but in its interaction with the pupil's present needs and capacities. Hence simple scholarship is not enough. In fact, there are certain features of scholarship or mastered subject matter—taken by itself—which get in the way of effective teaching unless the instructor's habitual attitude is one of concern with its interplay in the pupil's own experience. In the first place, his knowledge extends indefinitely beyond the range of the pupil's acquaintance. It involves principles which are beyond the immature pupil's understanding and interest. In and of itself, it may no more represent the living world of the pupil's experience than the astronomer's knowledge of Mars represents a baby's acquaintance with the room in which he stays. In the second place, the method of organization of the material of achieved scholarship differs from that of the beginner. It is not true that the experience of the young is unorganized —that it consists of isolated scraps. But it is organized in connection with direct practical centers of interest. The child's home is, for example, the organizing center of his geographical knowledge. His own movements about the locality, his journeys abroad, the tales of his friends, give the ties which hold his items of information together. But the geography of the geographer, of the one who has already developed the implications of these smaller experiences, is organized on the basis of a relationship which they bear to his house, bodily movements, and friends. To the one who is learned, subject matter is extensive, accurately defined, and logically interrelated. To the one who is learning, it is fluid, partial, and connected through his personal occupations.[2] The problem of teaching is to keep the experience of the student moving in the direction of what the expert already knows. Hence the need that the teacher know both subject matter and the characteristic needs and capacities of the student. . . .

From what has been said, it should be clear that no school program or educational activity in which teaching is involved can be carried out without teaching subject matter. However, subject matter is not necessarily limited to the information contained in textbooks or in courses of study. It is this notion that has been most harmful in education, for when teachers regard the subject matter of instruction as consisting of the facts in the textbook it is easy, as Dewey pointed out, to lose sight of its social significance for them and eventually their students. Then the subject matter of instruction becomes something to be learned in school and remote from the social reality of life outside the

[2] Since the learned man should also still be a learner, it will be understood that these contrasts are relative, not absolute. But in the earlier states of learning at least they are practically all-important.

classroom. An even more dangerous concomitant of this conception of subject matter is the idea that subject matter, and therefore knowledge, is something static, which prevents the teacher and the student from understanding how knowledge is gained. Without this understanding the work of the school is limited to learning what is known. All of the excitement, all of the pedagogical value of students actively thinking and seeking is lost, as is the potential creativeness of young minds.

So far as the question of whether or not to teach subject matter is concerned, the answer is it must be taught in every school. And in discussions of the differences between traditional and progressive schools the proper question should not be whether subject matter will or will not be taught, but rather *what* subject matter will be taught, how it will be *organized* in the curriculum, and *how* it will be taught. Likewise the old argument of whether we should teach *children* or *subject matter* is really a play on words. Subject matter is *what* is taught and children *those to whom* it is taught. Obviously no teaching or learning, formal or informal, can occur unless both are present.

Problems of Selecting Subject Matter of Instruction

It is clear that the selection of the subject matter of instruction is no simple matter and the dangers involved are real. The potential subject matter of education is the total experience of the group. In our group this means, for the most part, the knowledge accumulated in the various branches of science. But the data that has been accumulated in an area of science such as biology cannot be brought intact into the elementary schools or even into the secondary schools. There is the difficult task of selecting from this total field of knowledge the basic facts and concepts and arranging them into an intelligent sequence. Even this is not the end, for there still remains the job of relating this knowledge to the experience and interests of the child. It is at that point that the close relationship between the curriculum and instruction methods can be seen. A teacher with a thorough knowledge of biology and a carefully planned curriculum to provide sequence and continuity are largely wasted if the material cannot be presented in such a way that it is understood by the child. It is equally true that the best methods of teaching are wasted if the teacher is not well informed, and obviously both are wasted if the curriculum is not planned intelligently.

There are other aspects to the problem of selection of the curriculum. Since all that is basic from the various fields of knowledge cannot be included in the curriculum, decisions must be made as to what will be taught, and in making these decisions some criterion must be used. The question is: what criterion will be used? One group of educators believes there are certain common essentials in our cultural heritage which should form the basis of the curriculum. But the question of *which essentials* still remains. Dewey believed that the essentials should be taught first and defined the essentials as those things which were most widely shared by the community. He also took the position that the material selected in a democracy must meet the criterion of being "broadly human." Sidney Hook, taking the same position as Dewey but in a more specific manner, uses the criterion of *relevance* and defends his position as follows:

Sidney Hook

FROM

Education for Modern Man [3]

To demand that the content of instruction be relevant to the present emphatically does not preclude a study of the past. It only prevents us from getting lost in the past. It enables us to make some intelligent selection out of the limitless materials inherited from the past. . . .

To what in the present should the content of study be relevant? In the broadest sense of the term, to the fundamental problems of the age —to the social, political, intellectual and, if we like, the spiritual questions posed by our time and culture. Here the issue acquires a biting edge. It is these problems, problems which will not be denied even if we refuse to study them, that should serve as the chief subject matters around which to build educational instruction. By "chief" subject matter I mean not merely that at a certain point in schooling they become the focal problem of study, but that they become the points of departure for *planning* the content of curriculum at other levels, too. Far from unduly narrowing the course of study, we shall see that such orientation expands and enriches it without converting it into an archaic or contemporary miscellany.

The reason this approach enriches the course of study is twofold. First, the past world and the present are so continuous that there are few problems which can be intelligently understood without transcending the immediate context in which they are discovered. Second, the nature of present-day problems is such that they require the mastery of certain subject matters and techniques which are themselves not problematic, and which have no *direct* relation to these problems. The first

[3] Reprinted from *Education for Modern Man* by Sidney Hook. Copyright 1946 by Sidney Hook. Used by permission of the Dial Press, Inc. Pp. 72–6.

reason explains why the study of the past must be included in the education of modern man. For it provides the key to what to include and exclude from the past. The second reason explains why the mastery of certain skills and areas of knowledge must precede others in the organization of a curriculum: why, for example, an ability to read critically is more important than an ability to typewrite; why knowledge of the essential elements of statistics should be more generally required than knowledge of the history of astronomy. Together, these reasons explain, as we shall see, what elements in education should be constant and what not; how curriculums may be intelligently changed in content and emphasis; how they may be different and yet equally good at different times. . . .

The fundamental problems of an age are not born overnight, nor are they ever solved in a fortnight. They are not disasters before which we are helpless, nor are they business opportunities which we must snatch before they disappear. Education relevant to an understanding of the place of war in modern society is not an education relevant specifically to Pearl Harbor or to the next occasion of war. An education relevant to an understanding of economic depressions, their causes and controls, is not relevant to selling long or short on the stock market. The problem of reconciling social security and political democracy was not created by the New Deal, nor was the problem of racial conflict created by Hitler. To speak intelligently of *fundamental* problems is at the same time to distinguish between them and *ephemeral* problems. The *specific* form a fundamental problem may take will vary from situation to situation. But recognizing that it is a specific form of a *fundamental* problem is a genuine educational discovery. It is a discovery that immediately lifts the problem out of ephemeral detail, and without losing sight of its dramatic significance for the present, uncovers the connections with the past and the possible bearings on the future which are of its very nature.

It is quite possible for the criterion of relevance to be applied in such a way as to be narrowly utilitarian. There is already strong pressure from within and without the school to eliminate any aspect of the curriculum not having immediate value. The reasons for this were discussed in Chapter 8. Dewey has frequently criticized this attitude and it needs to be criticized; for if this attitude is allowed to prevail, it would mean that those aspects of our heritage such as literature, philosophy, history, and art, which cannot be converted into immediate cash value, would be eliminated from the curriculum. Obviously this criterion does not and cannot provide *specific* answers as to what the subject matter of instruction should be. This task of selecting the subject matter of instruction must be done by teachers, with help from experts, in every school in the nation. It can be done intelligently in this way only. But the criterion of relevance proposed by Professor Hook does provide a *basis* for intelligent selection.

Planning the Curriculum

Another curriculum problem that has arisen in the last three decades is whether the curriculum can be or should be planned in advance. The problem stems from our knowledge that the curriculum must vary with the background and experience of the children being taught. One of the criticisms of the traditional curriculum was that it imposed a uniform program on all children, regardless of their interests or background. It was also criticized on the ground that it did not provide an opportunity for the student to participate in planning the curriculum. This is a practice regarded as essential in modern educational theory. In reaction against the completely pre-planned, imposed curriculum with no provision for pupil participation, many schools instituted a curriculum that was virtually improvised from day to day. The result was a lack of orderly planning of learning experiences, a lack of sequence, and a lack of continuity. In addition, the training, experience, and maturity of the teacher was wasted as the *pupils* decided what would be studied. This hands-off policy on the part of the teacher has been sharply criticized by leaders in education, including John Dewey. The spectacle of having pupils plan the curriculum while the teacher stands by is comparable to a situation in which a student entering medical school would decide what he needed to study about medicine. At present there is a general consensus among teachers that the curriculum must be carefully planned in advance so that sequence and continuity can be attained. But the planning has to be flexible so that it can be adapted to the spontaneous events that offer excellent opportunities for learning and so that it can be adapted to individual and group interests, needs, and backgrounds. What has emerged is a concept of curriculum planning providing a broad framework with room for the talent and initiative of individual teachers and pupils. Such a conception requires a far more difficult type of planning than a curriculum completely preplanned and inflexible.

The actual planning of the curriculum is generally done by teachers, supervisors, and administrators. In some school systems very little curriculum planning is done and the curriculum or course of study is built around a series of textbooks. In some elementary schools teachers have texts in arithmetic, reading, language and grammar, spelling, science, and social studies, and the program of the school consists in the main in covering these texts from cover to cover. In these schools the teacher is largely a robot and the curriculum may be poorly adapted to the interests and background of the student in the class. For example some of the popular series of reading texts used in the elementary schools are oriented almost exclusively toward the middle-class socio-economic group. They depict children surrounded by typically middle-class possessions, entering into typically middle-class activities. These texts have very little meaning for children from the lower socio-economic groups. It is possible for a lively teacher to do a fine job of teaching even within what might be called a textbook curriculum. By bringing in additional material and adapting the text to the class and the local community a fairly satisfactory program can be developed.

In the better schools it is the practice of the teachers, working together and with supervisors and administrators, to plan the curriculum. This may be done in a one- or two-week period just prior to the opening of school, it may be done during the summer, or it may be done throughout the school year. Usually in the small elementary schools all of the teachers work as a committee of the whole to plan the curriculum. In the larger schools teachers may be divided into primary and intermediate groups. The general practice is for these groups to work out details for their own grades. These plans or outlines are then made available to all of the teachers so that sequence and continuity can be assured.

Unfortunately, there are many schools in which the curriculum is handed to the teachers by the administrator who in some instances expects the teachers to follow it without deviation. In others, individual teachers plan the curriculum for their grade without reference to what is being done in the other grades. In these schools sequence and continuity are either achieved through the textbooks or are not achieved at all. In other schools the state course of study provides the basis for the curriculum. As with the textbook curriculum, if this state course of study is handled intelligently and adapted to the local community, a good job can be done. Where it is followed rigidly it can be deadly.

In the secondary schools the same general patterns of curriculum planning prevail except that teachers in the same subject areas such as science, English, or social studies work together. These committees decide what will be taught in freshman English, sophomore English etc. Often there are attempts to integrate the various subject matter areas but too often there are not. With no integration the curriculum may be fragmentary, the student simply taking a series of courses having very little relationship to one another. This same pattern exists in most colleges with committees in the humanities, the natural sciences and the social sciences planning the curriculum for the first two years. In the last two years the student is expected to specialize, and his program is planned or laid out by the department in which he decides to major. Most colleges have a curriculum committee consisting of representatives of several departments which decides on over-all curriculum policy.

In theory, the best procedure for planning the curriculum should be similar to that described for the formulation of aims; that is, it should be planned co-operatively by those individuals who have knowledge or experience to contribute to this most important aspect of education. It is obvious that no one individual, even a curriculum expert, knows enough to plan a curriculum for schools in a complex society such as ours. This means that teachers need to consult with psychologists and sociologists to supplement their knowledge and understanding of the child and the community, and with specialists from the various subject matter fields, such as biology, mathematics, history, English, etc., to aid them in making decisions on the content of the curriculum. As in deciding on objectives, the teachers have primary responsibility but they obviously must have help. In recent years progress has been made in co-operative planning, especially with psychologists and curriculum experts, but little has been done to bring university experts into the work. This is partly because these specialists have little interest in the schools and partly because they have not been asked to participate. But the logic in employing such experts, in such fields as the natural and social sciences, is so sound that it is hoped in the years ahead that the co-operation being developed between the schools and the community can be extended to the universities.

Content of the Curriculum

So FAR our treatment of the curriculum has been largely in terms of content, its problems and the basis for its selection. The question as to what should be taught in the schools still remains. Specifically, what knowledge, what skills, what attitudes or appreciations should be taught?

Obviously the answers to this question will depend upon the aims of education. As was pointed out in this respect, the curriculum can be conceived as a means through which the ends of education are to be achieved. Just as the aims of education are derived from and related to the society in which schools function, so is the content of the curriculum. Thus from the study of the characteristics of American society presented in Chapter 10, valid generalizations could be made concerning subject matter being taught in the American schools. The problem deserves a more systematic treatment, and we turn again to Professor Sidney Hook for his thoughts on the content of education. This statement, taken from his *Education for Modern Man*, was written for the college, but it is applicable to the upper elementary grades and the secondary schools as well.

SIDNEY HOOK

FROM

Education for Modern Man [4]

What, concretely, should the modern man know in order to live intelligently in the world today? What should we require that he learn of subject matters and skills in his educational career in order that he may acquire maturity in feeling, in judgment, in action? Can we indicate the minimum indispensables of a liberal education in the modern world? This approach recognizes that no subject per se is inherently liberal at all times and places. But it also recognizes that within a given age in a given culture, the enlightenment and maturity, the freedom and power, which liberal education aims to impart, is more likely to be achieved by mastery of some subject matters and skills than by others. In short, principles must bear fruit in specific programs in specific times. In what follows I shall speak of studies rather than of conventional courses.

(1) The liberally educated person should be intellectually at home in the world of physical nature. He should know something about the earth he inhabits and its place in the solar system, about the solar system and its relation to the cosmos. He should know something about mechanics, heat, light, electricity and magnetism as the universal forces that condition anything he is or may become. He should be just as intimately acquainted with the nature of man as a biological species, his evolution, and the discoveries of experimental genetics. He should know something about the structure of his own body and mind, and the cycle of birth, growth, learning and decline. To have even a glimmer of understanding of these things, he must go beyond the level of primary description and acquire some grasp of the principles that explain what he observes. Where an intelligent grasp of principles requires a knowledge of mathematics, its fundamental ideas should be presented in such a way that students carry away not only the sense of mathematics as a tool for the solution of problems but as a study of types of order, system and language.

Such knowledge is important to the individual not merely because of its intrinsic fascination. Every subject from numismatics to Sanskrit possesses an intrinsic interest to those who are curious about it. It is important because it helps make everyday experience more intelligible; because it furnishes a continuous exemplification of scientific method in action; because our world is literally being remade by the consequences and applications of science; because the fate of nations and the voca-

[4] Reprinted from *Education for Modern Man* by Sidney Hook. Copyright 1946 by Sidney Hook. Used by permission of the Dial Press, Inc. Pp. 86–90, 92–9, 102–7.

tions of men depend upon the use of this knowledge; and because it provides the instruments to reduce our vast helplessness and dependence in an uncertain world.

Such knowledge is no less important because it bears upon the formation of *rational belief* about the place of man in the human universe. Whatever views a man professes today about God, human freedom, Cosmic Purpose and personal survival, he cannot reasonably hold them in ignorance of the scientific account of the world and man. . . .

(2) Every student should be required to become intelligently aware of how the society in which he lives functions, of the great forces molding contemporary civilization, and of the crucial problems of our age which await decision. The studies most appropriate to this awareness have been conventionally separated into history, economics, government, sociology, social psychology and anthropology. This separation is an intellectual scandal. For it is impossible to have an adequate grasp of the problems of government without a knowledge of economics, and vice versa. Except for some special domains of professional interest, the same is true for the other subjects as well.

The place of the social studies, properly integrated around problems and issues, is fundamental in the curriculum of modern education. It is one of the dividing points between the major conflicting schools of educational thought. The question of its justification must be sharply distinguished from discussion of the relative merits of this or that mode of approach to the social studies.

The knowledge and insight that the social studies can give is necessary for every student because no matter what his specialized pursuits may later be, the extent to which he can follow them, and the "contextual" developments within these fields, depend upon the total social situation of which they are in some sense a part. An engineer today whose knowledge is restricted only to technical matters of engineering, or a physician whose competence extends only to the subject matter of traditional medical training, is ill-prepared to plan intelligently for a life-career or to understand the basic problems that face his profession. He is often unable to cope adequately with those specific problems in his own domain that involve, as so many problems of social and personal health do, economic and psychological difficulties. No matter what an individual's vocation, the conditions of his effective functioning depend upon pervasive social tendencies, which set the occasions for the application of knowledge, provide the opportunities of employment, and not seldom determine even the direction of research.

More important, the whole presupposition of the theory of democracy is that the electorate will be able to make intelligent decisions on the issues before it. These issues are basically political, social and economic. Their specific character changes from year to year. But their generic form, and the character of the basic problems, do not. Nor, most essential of all, do the proper intellectual habits of meeting them change. It is undeniably true that the world we live in is one marked by greater changes, because of the impact of technology, than ever before. This does not necessitate changing the curriculum daily to catch up with today's newspapers, nor does it justify a concentration on presumably eternal problems as if these problems had significance independent of cultural place-time. The fact that we are living in a world where the rate of cultural change is greater than at any time in the past, together with its ramifications, may itself become a central consideration for analysis.

The construction of a social studies curriculum is a task of the greatest difficulty even after the artificiality of departmental lines of division has been recognized. For the integration of the material demands a historical approach, set not by bare chronology, but by the problems themselves. It must incorporate large amounts of philosophy and the scientific disciplines of evaluating judgments of fact and value. It must abandon misconceived interpretations of the "institutional approach" which describe social practices without confronting the challenge of theories and problems. It must not shrink from considering "solutions," and at the same time must guard against indoctrination of conclusions. It must learn how to use our life in cities, factories and fields as a kind of "laboratory," not as occasions for sightseeing excursions of dubious educational significance.

Properly organized studies of this kind are not something which already exist. They are something to be achieved. Their content must be definite and yet not fixed in detail. They do not exclude treatment of historical background but relate it to something of momentous issue in the present. They do not exclude great books of the past and present, nor bad books, nor material not found in books. . . .

(3) Everyone recognizes a distinction between knowledge and wisdom. This distinction is not clarified by making a mystery of wisdom and speaking of it as if it were begotten by divine inspiration while knowledge had a more lowly source. Wisdom is a kind of knowledge. It is knowledge of the nature, career and consequences of *human values*. Since these cannot be separated from the human organism and the social scene, the moral ways of man cannot be understood without knowledge of the ways of things and institutions.

To study social affairs without an analysis of policies is to lose oneself in factual minutiae that lack interest and relevance. But knowledge of values is a prerequisite of the intelligent determination of policy. Philosophy, most broadly viewed, is the critical survey of existence from the standpoint of value. This points to the twofold role of philosophy in the curriculum of the college.

The world of physical nature may be studied without reference to human values. But history, art, literature, and particularly the social studies involve problems of value at every turn. A social philosophy whose implications are worked out is a series of proposals that something be *done* in the world. It includes a set of *plans* to conserve or change aspects of social life. Today the community is arrayed under different banners without a clear understanding of the basic issues involved. In the press of controversy, the ideals and values at the heart of every social philosophy are widely affirmed as articles of blind faith. They are partisan commitments justified only by the emotional security they give to believers. They spread by contagion, unchecked by critical safeguards; yet the future of civilization largely depends upon them and how they are held. It is therefore requisite that their study be made an integral part of the liberal arts curriculum. Systematic and critical instruction should be given in the great maps of life—the ways to heaven, hell and earth—which are being unrolled in the world today.

Ideals and philosophies of life are not parts of the world of nature; but it is a pernicious illusion to imagine that they cannot be studied scientifically. Their historical origins, their concatenation of doctrine, their controlling assumptions, their means, methods and consequences in practice, can and should be investigated in a scientific spirit. There are certain social philosophies that would forbid such an investigation for fear of not being able to survive it; but it is one of the great merits of the democratic way of life and one of its strongest claims for acceptance that it can withstand analysis of this sort. . . .

(4) Instruction in the natural, social and technological forces shaping the world, and in the dominant conflicting ideals in behalf of which these forces are to be controlled, goes a long way. But not far enough. Far more important than knowledge is the method by which it is reached, and the ability to recognize when it constitutes *evidence* and when not; and more important than any particular ideal is the way in which it is held, and the capacity to evaluate it in relation to other ideals. From first to last, in season and out, our educational institutions, especially on the college level, must emphasize *methods* of analysis. They must build up in students a critical sense of evidence, relevance and validity against which the multitudinous seas of propaganda will wash in vain. They must strengthen the powers of independent reflection, which will enable students to confront the claims of ideals and values by their alternatives and the relative costs of achieving them. . . .

The field of language, of inference and argument, is a broad field but a definite one in which specific training can be given to all students. How to read intelligently, how to recognize good from bad reasoning, how to evaluate evidence, how to distinguish between a definition and a hypothesis, and between a hypothesis and a resolution, can be taught in such a way as to build up permanent habits of logic in action. The result of thorough training in "semantic" analysis—using that term in its broadest sense without invidious distinctions between different schools —is an intellectual sophistication without which a man may be learned but not intelligent.

Judging by past and present curricular achievements in developing students with intellectual sophistication and maturity, our colleges must be pronounced as, in the main, dismal failures. The main reason for the failure is the absence of serious effort, except in a few institutions, to realize this goal. The necessity of the task is not even recognized. This failure is not only intellectually reprehensible; it is socially dangerous. For the natural susceptibility of youth to enthusiasms, its tendency to glorify action, and its limited experience, makes it easy recruiting material for all sorts of demagogic movements which flatter its strength and impatience. Recent history furnishes many illustrations of how, in the absence of strong critical sense, youthful strength can lead to cruelty, and youthful impatience to folly. It is true that people who are incapable of thinking cannot be taught how to think, and that the incapacity for thought is not restricted to those who learn. But the first cannot be judged without being exposed to the processes of critical instruction, and the second should be eliminated from the ranks of the teachers. There is considerable evidence to show that students who are capable of completing high school can be so taught that they are aware of *whether* they are thinking or not. There is hope that, with better pedagogic skill and inspiration, they may become capable of grasping the main thought of what they are reading or hearing in nontechnical fields —of developing a sense of *what validly follows from what,* an accompanying sensitiveness to the dominant types of fallacies, and a habit of weighing evidence for conclusions advanced. . . .

(5) There is less controversy about the desirability of the study of composition and literature than about any other subject in the traditional or modern curriculum. It is appreciated that among the essentials of clear thought are good language habits and that, except in the higher strata of philosophic discourse, tortuous obscurities of expression are more likely to be an indication of plain confusion than of stuttering profundity. It is also widely recognized that nothing can take the place of literature in developing the imagination, and in imparting a sense of the inexhaustible richness of human personality. The questions that arise at this point are not of justification, but of method, technique and scope of comprehensiveness.

If good language habits are to be acquired *only* in order to acquire facility in thinking, little can be said for the conventional courses in English composition. Students cannot acquire facility in clear expression in the space of a year, by developing sundry themes from varied sources, under the tutelage of instructors whose training and interest may not qualify them for sustained critical thought. Clear thinking is best controlled by those who are at home in the field in which thinking is done. If language instruction is to be motivated only by the desire to strengthen the power of organizing ideas in written discourse, it should be left to properly trained instructors in other disciplines.

But there are other justifications for teaching students English composition. The first is that there are certain rules of intelligent reading that are essential to—if they do not constitute—understanding. These rules are very elementary. By themselves they do not tell us how to understand a poem, a mathematical demonstration, a scientific text or a religious prayer—all of which require special skills. But they make it easier for the student to uncover the nature of the "argument"—what is being said, what is being assumed, what is being presented as evidence —in any piece of prose that is not a narrative or simply informational in content. In a sense these rules are integral to the study of logic in action, but in such an introductory way that they are usually not considered part of logical study which begins its work after basic meanings have been established, or in independence of the meaning of logical symbols.

Another reason for teaching English composition independently, is its uses in learning how to write. "Effective writing" is not necessarily the same thing as logical writing. The purpose for which we write determines whether our writing is effective. And there are many situations in which we write not to convince or to prove but to explain, arouse, confess, challenge or assuage. To write *interestingly* may sometimes be just as important as to write soundly because getting a hearing and keeping attention may depend upon it. How much of the skills of writing can be taught is difficult to say. That it is worth making the effort to teach these skills is indisputable.

The place of language in the curriculum involves not merely our native language but *foreign* languages. Vocational considerations aside, should knowledge of a foreign language be required, and why? . . .

The main reason why students should be requested to learn another language is that it is the most effective medium by which, when properly taught, they can acquire a sensitivity to language, to the subtle tones, undertones and overtones of words, and to the licet ambiguities of imaginative discourse. No one who has not translated prose or poetry from one language to another can appreciate both the unique richness and the unique limitations of his own language. This is particularly true where the life of the emotions is concerned; and it is particularly important that it should be realized. For the appreciation of emotions, perhaps even their recognition in certain cases, depends upon their linguistic identification. The spectrum of human emotions is much more dense than the words by which we render them. Knowledge of different languages, and the attempts made to communicate back and forth between them in our own minds, broaden and diversify our own feelings. They multiply points of view, and liberate us from the prejudice that words—our words—are the natural signs of things and events. The genius of a culture is exemplified in a pre-eminent way in the characteristic idioms of its language. In learning another language we put ourselves in a position where we can appreciate both the cultural similarities and differences of the Western world. . . .

The place of literature in the curriculum is justified by so many considerations that it is secure against all criticism. Here, too, what is at issue is not whether literature—Greek, Latin, English, European, American—should be read and studied in the schools but what should be read, when, and by what methods. These are details, important details—but outside the scope of our inquiry.

Something should be said about the unique opportunity which the teaching of literature provides, not only in giving delight by heightening perception of the formal values of literary craftsmanship, but in giving insight into people. The opposite of a liberal education, William James somewhere suggests, is a literal education. A literal education is one which equips a person to read formulas and equations, straightforward prose, doggerel verse and advertising signs. It does not equip one to read the language of metaphor, of paradox, of indirect analogy, of serious fancy in which the emotions and passions and half-believed ideas of human beings express themselves. To read great literature is to read men —their fears and motives, their needs and hopes. Every great novelist is a *Menschenkenner* who opens the hearts of others to us and helps us to read our own hearts as well. The intelligent study of literature should never directly aim to strengthen morals and improve manners. For its natural consequences are a delicacy of perception and an emotional tact that are defeated by preaching and didactic teaching.

A liberal education will impart an awareness of the amazing and precious complexity of human relationships. Since those relationships are violated more often out of insensitiveness than out of deliberate intent, whatever increases sensitiveness of perception and understanding humanizes life. Literature in all its forms is the great humanizing medium of life. It must therefore be representative of life; not only of past life but of our own; not only of our own culture but of different cultures.

(6) An unfailing mark of philistinism in education is reference to the study of art and music as "the frill and fads" of schooling. Insofar as those who speak this way are not tone-deaf or color-blind, they are themselves products of a narrow education, unaware of the profound experiences which are uniquely bound up with the trained perception of color and form. There is no reason to believe that the capacity for the appreciation of art and music shows a markedly different curve of distribution from what is observable in the measurement of capacity of drawing in-

ferences or recalling relevant information. A sufficient justification for making some study of art and music required in modern education is that it provides an unfailing source of delight in personal experience, a certain grace in living, and a variety of dimensions of meaning by which to interpret the world around us. This is a sufficient justification: there are others, quite subsidiary, related to the themes, the occasions, the history and backgrounds of the works studied. Perhaps one should add—although this expresses only a reasonable hope—that a community whose citizens have developed tastes would not tolerate the stridency, the ugliness and squalor which assault us in our factories, our cities and our countryside.

One of the reasons why the study of art and music has not received as much attention as it should by educators, particularly on the college level, is that instruction in these subjects often suffers from two opposite defects. Sometimes courses in art and music are given as if all students enrolled in them were planning a career as practicing artists or as professional teachers of the art. Sometimes they are given as hours for passive enjoyment or relaxation in which the teacher does the performing or talking and in which there is no call upon the students to make an intelligent response.

The key-stress in courses in art and music should be *discrimination* and *interpretation*, rather than appreciation and cultivation. The latter can take care of themselves, when the student has learned to discriminate and interpret intelligently.

Briefly summarized: The answer to the question What should we teach? is selected materials from the fields of mathematics and the natural sciences, social studies, including history, language and literature, philosophy and logic, art and music. The knowledge imparted by such study should be acquired in such a way as to strengthen the skills of reading and writing, of thinking and imaginative interpretation, or criticism and evaluation.

The content of education as here described finds its most direct application on the college level. It indicates the knowledge, the values, the habits of thought and feeling which educators must have before them as objectives in constructing and revising curriculums, and in guiding and teaching students.

The same principles apply, *mutatis mutandis,* to education on the lower levels. Those who are not professional educators may feel that this is shockingly "high-brow" and unrealistic. But once due allowance is made for the differences in powers of children at various ages in the preparation of teaching materials, themes for emphasis and specific techniques of instruction, the air of paradox and unrealism disappears. It is not necessary to discuss with children in the fourth or fifth grade "the evils of capitalism"—a typical illustration employed by those who caricature the philosophy of progressive education; at that level, social studies can begin with problems that are always found whenever children work or study or play in groups. It cannot be expected that the only conclusions presented to children will be ones for which they can see the logical or empirical reasons. Otherwise, they will never learn that twice two is four, or that honesty is desirable even when it isn't the best immediate policy. But the school cannot begin at too early an age to strengthen the child's powers of intelligence and to develop habits of reasonableness even if on some crucial matters it must supplement them with other methods of suasion until he reaches maturity and can rationally test these matters for himself. The teacher may have to step in to stop a child from undertaking an experiment from which the child, or those on whom he practices it, may not recover. The direction, however, that teaching should take is such as to progressively reduce the frequency of authoritative intrusion into the learning process. . . .

Organization of the Curriculum

THE final question to be asked about curriculum concerns organization. How can the curriculum be organized so that maximum results can be achieved from the teaching-learning situation? Many a superbly trained teacher has been frustrated and unable to teach effectively because of a curriculum organization lacking in the opportunity for real teaching and learning. The best example of this exists in many of our large high schools. The school day is divided into fifty-minute periods. The average student takes five subjects and has one study period each day that, in recent years, has been used for activities. The average teacher has five classes to teach and a study hall to supervise each day. Regardless of what is going on in the class when the bell rings, everything must stop to be resumed the next day. Because of the shortness of the period and the size of the class, most teachers in such schools are virtually forced into a lecture system. The possibility of taking the class out of the school, e.g., for a field trip, is negligible for this would disrupt other classes for the entire school day. Because of the organization of the curriculum the libraries, which in many schools are excellent, are seldom used. The students simply do not have the time for library work, and the system is not flexible enough to permit working in the library for any length of time.

This pattern of curriculum organization is quite efficient and enables the school to handle masses of students in clocklike fashion. But it violates practically every principle of a good teaching-learning situation. It is impersonal, with teachers being fortunate if they become acquainted with the student, to say nothing of what he has learned. It is inflexible, because with the short period the learning situation is limited to the classroom. Because the teacher handles so many different students, certain teaching techniques are used more frequently than is warranted, such as the use of objective tests which are scored easily. When classes are small, this pattern of organization is not too bad. But where classes are large, the educational program becomes mechanical, impersonal, inflexible, formalized, and routine. Nothing could be better calculated to produce superficial learning or, what is worse, conditioning students to believe that learning and boredom are synonymous.

Thus it can be seen that the problem of curriculum organization is of vital importance and needs to be studied carefully. In the paragraphs below a general description of the four basic patterns of curriculum organization in use in the public schools at the present time are given. Students who are just entering their professional work in education will have an opportunity to go into the problem more thoroughly later in their programs. Those readers who wish to pursue the matter further, will find the references at the end of this chapter useful.

The oldest and still the most widely used pattern of curriculum organization is the subject curriculum. In this pattern the school day is divided into subjects such as mathematics, history, language, science, etc., all taught independently of one another. Formerly used from the elementary school through the university, the subject curriculum is giving way to other patterns in the elementary school but is still the basic pattern in the vast majority of secondary schools and is used almost exclusively in the colleges.

The subject curriculum is based on the division of human knowledge handed down through the years or developed by scholars in the universities. From the standpoint of research this division is probably responsible for the great progress made in the various spheres of knowledge. For a man devoting his life to the study of a narrow field has a chance to add to the store of knowledge. The subject curriculum has the great advantage of having the content of instruction organized in a systematic, coherent way, and therefore the task of maintaining sequence and continuity is simplified. A disadvantage is that the logical organization of the subject may not be logical from the standpoint of the child, and it may be meaningless to him. Other disadvantages are that the curriculum may be fragmentary and not integrated into a unified whole, and it may neglect important social problems, therefore missing the psychological advantage of being problem-centered.

The reaction against the compartmentalized nature of the subject curriculum led to the attempt to pull together material from various subjects in order that the student see the relationship between them wherever possible. Thus, instead of teaching history, geography, sociology, government, and economics as separate subjects they would be integrated into a broad field called social studies. The amount of material integrated or the number of subjects combined varies with the grade level, the base being much broader in the elementary school and much narrower in the senior high school. For example, a fifth-grade social studies program would in all probability combine material from all the social sciences, whereas in a senior high school, subjects such as government and economics or American history and American literature might be combined. There are obvious advantages to this plan. First, the teacher has a double period with each class and therefore a better opportunity to know his students and to teach them. Second, the two subjects complement each other which enables a good teacher to make both more interesting and meaningful. But this plan also requires a teacher who is competent in both subjects. If he is not, the material is bound to be watered-down and the result superficial learning. This need not be so, however, and if the teacher will take his job seriously and prepare himself, the combined program can be most effective. It is possible to draw relationships between subjects without combining them. It should be realized that not all subjects can be or should be combined and this is especially true on the higher levels. Subjects such as physics or biology for example probably should be studied separately on the senior high school level and not as a part of advanced general science. The various combinations of subject matter areas have been assigned descriptive titles such as "correlation," and "fusion," but in practice they are used almost synonymously. The combination of any two subjects, e.g., American history and American literature, in which reciprocal relationships are drawn out is generally known as *correlation*. When several subjects are brought together into a single course it is usually referred to as a *fused* pattern.

The pattern of curriculum organization known as the *core* has been one of the most important and one of the most controversial developments in education in the last three decades. Like the broad-field pattern and its many variations, the core has been used in so many different ways that it sometimes appears to have no special characteristics of its own. But there are some essential common elements. First, the "core" is, as its name implies, a center, a heart, or a vital part of anything. Applied to curriculum the core means the knowledge and skills essential to all students. Second, it involves a bloc of time, generally from one-third to one-half of the school day. Third, the core always brings together material from many subject-matter fields and integrates it, usually around socially significant problems. Often the core consists largely of material from the language arts and the social studies but material from any other area, such as science, mathematics, or art is used if it seems desirable.

The core has many obvious advantages. It gives teachers a chance to get to know students and so a personal relationship can be established between teacher and student. Since a rather large bloc of time is involved teachers have more flexibility. There is time for field trips or other community studies. There is time for extended research and for rather long discussions, and there is also time for work in the library. In the hands of a good teacher the core program can lead to an integration of knowledge from various fields. It can provide unlimited possibilities for students to draw relationships and perhaps to see the essential unity of all knowledge. Finally, if it is problem-centered, it has the possibility of evoking student interest and enthusiasm.

The one important problem with the core is the teacher. Unless the teacher is broadly educated there may be a narrowness in the program. If he does not have a real knowledge of the areas, e.g., language, social studies, etc., that form the basis of the core the program will lack substance. If the teacher does not have a real grasp of research techniques, he will be unable to teach his students these techniques and the chances are that the problems dealt with will be treated superficially. Without these qualities in the teacher the core program may be lively, active, and interesting but lack depth.

The fourth pattern of organization is usually known as the experience, the child centered, or the activity, curriculum. This pattern, whatever it is called, emphasizes basing the curriculum upon the interests and needs of pupils and not on the logic of any subject-matter field. In the experience curriculum subjects and subject matter fields as such are eliminated. There is no preplanned, uniform experience curriculum for all schools since by its very nature it must be planned with a particular class. This pattern has grown out of the knowledge that children learn through experience and that if the work of the school is not related to this experience it is bound to be meaningless.

The advantage of the experience curriculum is that it makes real learning more likely, as opposed to memorization and verbalization without understanding. Its chief disadvantage is that it may lack continuity and balance because of the lack of long-range planning.

In practice very few schools have what might be called a "pure" experience curriculum. In most of the better elementary schools the curriculum is planned with the idea of providing an environment in which students can have the desired learning experience. Subjects such as arithmetic, spelling, reading, science, and social studies are taught but usually centered around large topics or areas called units of work which are carefully planned in advance by the teacher. Pupil-teacher planning is used extensively and the teacher thinks in terms of pupil experiences but the logical arrangement of the subject is maintained for the most part. For example, in a unit on nutrition in the third grade the teacher carefully plans the broad outlines of the facts and concepts that are to be taught. She also plans for learning experiences, such as experiments, which the children have a voice in planning and carrying out. In a school in the St. Louis area in a unit on nutrition an experiment was arranged in which two mice were fed different diets. One was fed a balanced diet, the other was fed candy and soda. This was a real learning experience, as the children saw the results with their own eyes. In this instance a combination of the various curriculum patterns was used, and used effectively. There are a few elementary schools that still maintain a strict subject curriculum with the day being divided up into time allotments for the various subjects. For the most part, however, a pattern is used which provides for sequence and continuity and still allows room for flexibility so that the program can be adapted to the interests, needs, and experiences of the children.

In the junior high schools the combined subject curriculum is generally used with the work centered around areas such as social studies, science and mathematics, and language arts. Some junior high schools have strict subject curriculum patterns, while most senior high schools and colleges do. Many senior high schools use the combined subject pattern, and a few use the core.

It should be borne in mind that, in actual practice, there are no hard and fast lines dividing these four basic patterns of curriculum organization. Frequently, in a given school there may be features of two or more of these patterns, depending upon the school's philosophy of education and its concept of its purposes. And it should be remembered that good teaching is possible within each of these different types of organization. The important point in the organization of the curriculum is that whatever is done should be done to facilitate teaching and learning. In too many instances we have adopted organizational patterns for reasons of efficiency and economy or for administrative convenience. This was true in the platoon school arrangement which was widely adopted in elementary schools between 1915 and 1929. We have also adhered to organizational plans, such as the five-class-per-week schedule in the high schools, which were introduced at a time (1900–10) when quantitative standardization was desirable to bring order out of the chaos that existed in American secondary education. But this plan keeps students in class so much that they do not have enough time for study or independent work, and it prevents teachers from having enough time or energy for preparation or for working with students individually or in small groups.

Suggested Readings

The Harvard Committee, Report of: *General Education in a Free Society*. Cambridge, Mass.: Harvard University Press, 1945.

Lee, Murray J., and Lee, Dorris May: *The Child and His Curriculum*. New York: Appleton-Century-Crofts, 1950.

Leonard, J. Paul: *Developing the Secondary School Curriculum*. New York: Rinehart & Company, 1946.

Ragan, William B.: *Modern Elementary Curriculum*. New York: The Dryden Press, 1953.

Rugg, Harold, ed.: *Democracy and the Curriculum*. New York: Appleton-Century-Crofts, 1939.

Smith, O. B.; Stanley, W. O.; and Shores, Harlan J.: *Fundamentals of Curriculum Development*. New York: World Book Company, 1950.

Spears, Harold: *The Teacher and Curriculum Planning*. Englewood Cliffs, N.J.: Prentice-Hall, 1951.

Stratemeyer, Florence B.; Forkner, Hamden L.; and McKim, Margaret G.: *Developing a Curriculum for Modern Living*. New York: Bureau of Publications, Teachers College, Columbia University, 1947.

PART V

The Philosophy of Education

Greeting his pupils, the master asked:
  What would you learn of me?
And the reply came:
  How shall we care for our bodies?
  How shall we rear our children?
  How shall we work together?
  How shall we live with our fellowmen?
  How shall we play?
  For what ends shall we live? . . .
And the teacher pondered these words, and sorrow
was in his heart, for his own learning touched not
these things.

J. CROSBY CHAPMAN and GEORGE S. COUNTS, 1924

CHAPTER 14

PHILOSOPHY, EDUCATION, AND THE INTELLECTUAL VIRTUES

THE PURPOSE OF THIS SECTION IS TO INTRODUCE THE READER TO SOME of the philosophical aspects of American education. It is true that philosophical questions have been connected with much of the material already presented, especially in the chapter on aims, but it has not been dealt with in a systematic way as a philosophy of education. The approach taken in this section has been to analyze briefly the nature, function, and importance of philosophy and then to present three readings representing different positions in educational philosophy. The selection presented in this chapter is by Robert Hutchins, that in Chapter 15 is by William Bagley, and that in Chapter 16 is by John Dewey. These particular selections were chosen, first, because they are among the most important in American education and, second, because they represent sharply different points of view. No pretense is made that the readings selected present a complete picture of the philosophy of the three men, much less a total picture of American educational thought. The reader is urged to read the books, in their entirety, from which the selections presented were taken and to follow this by reading other books by the same authors. Also it is hoped that the reader, especially the prospective teacher, may be stimulated to read some of the other works in philosophy that are suggested.

This brief encounter with three of the major statements of educational philosophy cannot equip the prospective teacher with the answers to all of the educational problems he will face. This would not be possible with even a much more thorough treatment of the subject, for the problems considered cannot be as meaningful until the student has faced them in an educational situation. Yet a beginning must be made. Therefore the purpose of this section is not only to introduce the reader to three of the major philosophical positions in American education, but also to start the prospective teacher on the path toward developing and formulating a philosophy of his own. For while it is certainly desirable for the layman to reflect upon his philosophy of life with a view to being more intelligent, it is essential for a teacher, who has the responsibility for guiding thousands of young people, to do so.

The Nature of Philosophy

THE literal meaning of philosophy is love of wisdom, and certainly this is a part of any attempt to philosophize and of every philosophical system. Down through history, philosophy has been associated with outstanding individuals, such as Plato, Hegel, Dewey, who have developed elaborate and comprehensive systems of philosophy. As a result of this development, philosophy has come to be divided into the kinds of problems with which these men have dealt, such as logic, ethics, metaphysics, aesthetics, and epistemology. Thus, very often in the past when a college student took a course in philosophy, he was introduced to the systems of philosophy developed by these great thinkers treated in the terms and categories used by them. The result was that very often philosophy was divorced from real problems that occurred in the everyday life of the student. From a pedagogical standpoint the task was extremely difficult and the results were often very poor. For men like Plato and Hegel and the other great thinkers develop not only systems but also a language of philosophy—a language that is meaningful and even essential to them. This enables them to work on a very high level of abstraction, but the language is sometimes not very meaningful to students.

Because of these developments philosophy itself is often regarded as something mysterious and abstract, carried on by queer, speculative fellows in ivory towers who are far removed from the real world of men. Unfortunately this conception of philosophy has had too much basis in fact. As Dewey has said, "the student of philosophy 'in itself' is always in danger of taking it as so much nimble or severe intellectual exercise —as something said by philosophers and concerning them alone!" [1] The danger will always be great, for philosophy is essentially an intellectual activity, that is, it involves conscious reflection of human experience. Moreover any attempt to look at the whole of human experience or any phase of it, such as education, necessarily requires some degree of perspective and aloofness from the world of action. But when this perspective leads to a break with human conduct, it becomes so much verbiage and, although it may be of value to the individual philosopher, it is of limited value to society. Once we realize that philosophy has to do with

[1] John Dewey, *Democracy and Education* (New York: The Macmillan Company, 1916), p. 383.

the everyday problems of men, and that it is not the exclusive domain of a few individuals called "philosophers," we are in a position to consider what philosophy is and the kinds of problems with which it deals.

Taken from this point of view, our conception is that philosophy is an effort to make human life in all of its aspects, including education, as understandable and therefore as intelligible as possible. As Dewey has pointed out, "whenever philosophy has been taken seriously, it has always been assumed that it signified achieving a wisdom which would influence the conduct of life." [2] Apply this criterion to men like Socrates and Emerson and you will see that they certainly pass the test.

The Function of Philosophy

PHILOSOPHY has at least two functions. One is the critical analysis and appraisal of existing values and beliefs. The other is the attempt to create a consistent ordering of beliefs about the nature, origin, and purpose of human life and of the universe. To question beliefs and actions presupposes an awareness of their existence and their nature. It also presupposes some criteria, some standard for judging, testing, and appraising. Here the close relationship between philosophy and education is important. Since education is an affair of action, it provides a testing ground for theory and, as Dewey said, "if a theory makes no difference in educational endeavor, it must be artificial." [3]

Too often in human affairs, the critical function of philosophy is neglected. In the common everyday usage of the term we are apt to state our philosophy of life, or our economic philosophy, or our philosophy of government. This generally means that we declare our convictions upon one of these subjects. Only infrequently does it mean that we are holding our cherished convictions up for scrutiny and analysis. This pattern of "philosophizing" is often used in the same way by teachers with the result that conviction hardens into dogma. Therefore it is extremely important for prospective teachers to understand this aspect of philosophy. Properly used it can lead to a continuous intellectual evolution and maturity of outlook. It does not mean that convictions cannot be held or that nothing is true. On the contrary, it means that our convictions, if they can stand the test of new evidence and critical analysis, are even more valuable than if they had been held on emotional or irrational grounds. The case of philosophy can be summed up pretty well by the statement of Socrates that "the unexamined life is unfit to live." For teachers, the "unexamined life" is even worse, for it amounts to the blind leading the blind.

[2] *Ibid.*, p. 378.
[3] *Ibid.*, p. 383.

The Problems of Educational Philosophy

THE problems of educational philosophy center around the nature and function of education and the school. They merge into questions of what we should teach and why. What is education, and what is the nature of the educational process? What is the relationship between education and human experience and between education and knowledge? What is knowledge and how is it acquired? What is the relationship between knowledge and truth? What methods are used for deciding upon truth? Is there agreement upon what is true? How does the element of human bias enter into the determination of truth? Or, to ask another series of questions: What is the purpose or purposes of education? Which of these purposes can the school meet? What is the role of the school in relation to the family, the church, and the community? Is the school influenced by the society in which it functions or is education always and everywhere the same? To be more specific about our own society, is there anything special about the school system in a democracy? What about the underlying principles of American education? Will they stand the test of critical analysis? For example, do we believe in universal education, in equality of opportunity? If the answer is yes, on what grounds can they be justified?

These are some of the important questions that teachers must attempt to answer—though not, to be sure, the only ones. But more important than any questions is the *basis* upon which they are answered. For the answers to many, if not most of the fundamental questions in education it is essential to rely upon all available evidence which is relevant. Thus questions concerning the nature and conditions of learning cannot be answered adequately without considering evidence gathered in research studies on these topics by psychologists. Even questions which demand value judgments, such as whether equality of opportunity is desirable, cannot be answered intelligently without a knowledge of the nature and development of American civilization—information that has been gathered by historians and sociologists. In some instances, of course, there is not enough evidence to provide a conclusive answer, but it is essential to use all available knowledge in arriving at a solution. This point should be kept in mind in evaluating the following statements by Hutchins, Bagley, and Dewey.

Education and the Intellectual Virtues

THE first position presented in our comparative study of philosophies of education is that of Robert Maynard Hutchins, former Chancellor of the University of Chicago and now President of the Fund for the Republic.

He has been one of the most controversial figures in American education in the last three decades. His career at Chicago was a stormy one, and he rocked the academic world with his innovations. Still active, he has a large following, especially in university circles where his attention and his writings have been directed. He has been a bitter critic of business methods in education as well as the overemphasis or professionalization of sports in the colleges and universities. He has been and continues to be one of the stanchest defenders of academic freedom, and all teachers owe him a debt of gratitude for his efforts in this area.

So far as his educational ideas are concerned our intent is to let Mr. Hutchins speak for himself. It should be pointed out, however, that his views are similar to Mortimer Adler's, who in turn is very close to the thinking of the Frenchman Jacques Maritain, the leading Catholic philosopher-educator. Despite the similarities in outlook between Hutchins and Adler, and Adler and Maritain, there are important differences and these differences are accentuated when Hutchins' views are compared with those of Catholic educators such as W. J. McGuchen, S.J., of St. Louis University. The reader is urged again to read the complete works of Mr. Hutchins as well as Mr. Adler and M. Maritain, some of which are included in the bibliography at the end of this chapter. The statement from Mr. Hutchins is from his book *The Higher Learning in America,* published in 1936.

ROBERT M. HUTCHINS

FROM

The Higher Learning in America [4]

In this chapter I should like to talk about content, not about method. I concede the great difficulty of communicating the kind of education I favor to those who are unable or unwilling to get their education from books. I insist, however, that the education I shall outline is the kind that everybody should have, that the answer to it is not that some people should not have it, but that we should find out how to give it to those whom we do not know how to teach at present. You cannot say my content is wrong because you do not know the method of transmitting it. Let us agree upon content if we can and have faith that the technological genius of America will solve the problem of communication.

Economic conditions require us to provide some kind of education for the young, and for all the young, up to about their twentieth year. Probably one-third of them cannot learn from books. This is no reason why

[4] Robert M. Hutchins, *The Higher Learning in America* (New Haven: Yale University Press, 1936), pp. 59–87.

we should not try to work out a better course of study for the other two-thirds. At the same time we should continue our efforts and experiments to find out how to give a general education to the hand-minded and the functionally illiterate. Even these attempts may be somewhat simplified if we know what a general education is.

Please do not tell me that the general education I propose should not be adopted because the great majority of those who pass through it will not go on to the university. The scheme that I advance is based on the notion that general education is education for everybody, whether he goes on to the university or not. It will be useful to him in the university; it will be equally useful if he never goes there. I will admit that it will not be useful to him outside the university in the popular sense of utility. It may not assist him to make money or to get ahead. It may not in any obvious fashion adjust him to his environment or fit him for the contemporary scene. It will, however, have a deeper, wider utility: it will cultivate the intellectual virtues.

The trouble with the popular notion of utility is that it confuses immediate and final ends. Material prosperity and adjustment to the environment are good more or less, but they are not good in themselves and there are other goods beyond them. The intellectual virtues, however, are good in themselves and good as means to happiness. By the intellectual virtues I mean good intellectual habits. The ancients distinguish five intellectual virtues: the three speculative virtues of intuitive knowledge, which is the habit of induction; of scientific knowledge, which is the habit of demonstration; and of philosophical wisdom, which is scientific knowledge, combined with intuitive reason, of things highest by nature, first principles and first causes. To these they add the two virtues of the practical intellect: art, the capacity to make according to a true course of reasoning, and prudence, which is right reason with respect to action.[5]

In short, the intellectual virtues are habits resulting from the training of the intellectual powers. An intellect properly disciplined, an intellect properly habituated, is an intellect able to operate well in all fields. An education that consists of the cultivation of the intellectual virtues, therefore, is the most useful education, whether the student is destined for a life of contemplation or a life of action. I would remind you of the words of Newman:

> "If then the intellect is so excellent a portion of us, and its cultivation so excellent, it is not only beautiful, perfect, admirable, and noble in itself, but in a true and high sense it must be useful to the possessor and to all around him; not useful in any low, mechanical, mercantile sense, but as diffusing good, or as a blessing, or a gift, or

[5] Cf. *Summa Theologica*, Part II, Q. 57, Art. 2–4.

power, or a treasure, first to the owner, then through him to the world." [6]

I shall not be attentive when you tell me that the plan of general education I am about to present is remote from real life, that real life is in constant flux and change, and that education must be in constant flux and change as well. I do not deny that all things are in change. They have a beginning, and a middle, and an end. Nor will I deny that the history of the race reveals tremendous technological advances and great increases in our scientific knowledge. But we are so impressed with scientific and technological progress that we assume similar progress in every field. We renounce our intellectual heritage, read only the most recent books, discuss only current events, try to keep the schools abreast or even ahead of the times, and write elaborate addresses on Education and Social Change.

Paul Shorey said:

> "If literature and history are a Heraclitean flux of facts, if one unit is as significant as another, one book, one idea, the equivalent of another . . . , we may for a time bravely tread the mill of scholastic routine, but in the end the soul will succumb to an immense lassitude and bafflement. But if . . . the flux is not all, if the good, the true, and the beautiful are something real and ascertainable, if these eternal ideals re-embody themselves from age to age essentially the same in the imaginative visions of supreme genius and in the persistent rationality and sanity of the world's best books, then our reading and study are redeemed, both from the obsessions of the hour, and the tyranny of quantitative measures and mechanical methods."

Our erroneous notion of progress has thrown the classics and the liberal arts out of the curriculum, overemphasized the empirical sciences, and made education the servant of any contemporary movements in society, no matter how superficial. In recent years this attitude has been accentuated by the world-wide depression and the highly advertised political, social, and economic changes resulting from it. We have been very much upset by all these things. We have felt that it was our duty to educate the young so that they would be prepared for further political, social, and economic changes. Some of us have thought we should try to figure out what the impending changes would be and frame a curriculum that embodied them. Others have even thought that we should decide what changes are desirable and then educate our students not merely to anticipate them, but also to take part in bringing them about.

---

[6] Cf. Aristotle, *Politics*, VIII, e: "To be always seeking after the useful does not become free and exalted souls."

One purpose of education is to draw out the elements of our common human nature. These elements are the same in any time or place. The notion of educating a man to live in any particular time or place, to adjust him to any particular environment, is therefore foreign to a true conception of education.

Education implies teaching. Teaching implies knowledge. Knowledge is truth. The truth is everywhere the same.[7] Hence education should be everywhere the same. I do not overlook the possibilities of differences in organization, in administration, in local habits and customs. These are details. I suggest that the heart of any course of study designed for the whole people will be, if education is rightly understood, the same at any time, in any place, under any political, social, or economic conditions. Even the administrative details are likely to be similar because all societies have generic similarity.

If education is rightly understood, it will be understood as the cultivation of the intellect. The cultivation of the intellect is the same good for all men in all societies. It is, moreover, the good for which all other goods are only means. Material prosperity, peace and civil order, justice and the moral virtues are means to the cultivation of the intellect. So Aristotle says in the *Politics*: "Now, in men reason and mind are the end towards which nature strives, so that the generation and moral discipline of the citizens ought to be ordered with a view to them." An education which served the means rather than their end would be misguided.

I agree, of course, that any plan of general education must be such as to educate the student for intelligent action. It must, therefore, start him on the road toward practical wisdom. But the question is what is the best way for education to start him and how far can it carry him. Prudence or practical wisdom selects the means toward the ends that we desire. It is acquired partly from intellectual operations and partly from experience. But the chief requirement for it is correctness in thinking. Since education cannot duplicate the experiences which the student will have when he graduates, it should devote itself to the developing correctness in thinking as a means to practical wisdom, that is, to intelligent action.

As Aristotle put it in the *Ethics*, ". . . while young men become geometricians and mathematicians and wise in matters like these, it is thought that a young man of practical wisdom cannot be found. The cause is that such wisdom is concerned not only with universals, but with particulars, but a young man has no experience, for it is length of time that gives experience." Since practical wisdom is "a true and rea-

[7] "It is therefore evident that, as regards the general principles whether of speculative or practical reason, truth or rectitude is the same for all, and is equally known by all." *Summa Theologica*, Part II, Q. 94, Art. 4.

soned capacity to act with regard to the things that are good or bad for man," it would seem that education can make its best contribution to the development of practical wisdom by concentrating on the reasoning essential to it.

A modern heresy is that all education is formal education and that formal education must assume the total responsibility for the full development of the individual. The Greek notion that the city educates the man has been forgotten. Everything that educated the man in the city has to be imported into our schools, colleges, and universities. We are beginning to behave as though the home, the church, the state, the newspaper, the radio, the movies, the neighborhood club, and the boy next door did not exist. All the experience that is daily and hourly acquired from these sources is overlooked, and we set out to supply imitations of it in educational institutions. The experience once provided by some of these agencies may be attenuated now; but it would be a bold man who would assert that the young person today lived a life less full of experience than the youth of yesterday. Today as yesterday we may leave experience to other institutions and influences and emphasize in education the contribution that it is supremely fitted to make, the intellectual training of the young. The life they lead when they are out of our hands will give them experience enough. We cannot try to give it to them and at the same time perform the task that is ours and ours alone.

Young people do not spend all their time in school. Their elders commonly spend none of it there. Yet their elders are, we hope, constantly growing in practical wisdom. They are, at least, having experience. If we can teach them while they are being educated how to reason, they may be able to comprehend and assimilate their experience. It is a good principle of educational administration that a college or university should do nothing that another agency can do as well. This is a good principle because a college or university has a vast and complicated job if it does what only it can do. In general education, therefore, we may wisely leave experience to life and set about our job of intellectual training.

If there are permanent studies which every person who wishes to call himself educated should master; if those studies constitute our intellectual inheritance, then those studies should be the center of a general education. They cannot be ignored because they are difficult, or unpleasant, or because they are almost totally missing from our curriculum today. The child-centered school may be attractive to the child, and no doubt is useful as a place in which the little ones may release their inhibitions and hence behave better at home. But educators cannot permit the students to dictate the course of study unless they are prepared to confess that they are nothing but chaperons, supervising an aimless, trial-and-error process which is chiefly valuable because it keeps young people from doing something worse. The free elective system as Mr. Eliot introduced it at Harvard and as Progressive Education adapted it to lower age levels amounted to a denial that there was content to education. Since there was no content to education, we might as well let students follow their own bent. They would at least be interested and pleased and would be as well educated as if they had pursued a prescribed course of study. This overlooks the fact that the aim of education is to connect man with man, to connect the present with the past, and to advance the thinking of the race. If this is the aim of education, it cannot be left to the sporadic, spontaneous interests of children or even of undergraduates.[8]

Mr. Gladstone once remarked that it is difficult to discern the true dimensions of objects in that mirage which covers the studies of one's youth. Even at stages beyond general education, when the student because he has had a general education and because he is more mature might be given wider latitude in selecting the subjects interesting to him, this can be permitted only to a limited degree. If there are an intellectual tradition and an intellectual inheritance in the law, for example, law schools must see to it that they are transmitted to law students even if law students are more interested in the latest devices for evading the Sherman Antitrust Act.

It cannot be assumed that students at any age will always select the subjects that constitute education. If we permit them to avoid them, we cannot confer upon them insignia which certify to the public that they are in our opinion educated. In any field the permanent studies on which the whole development of the subject rests must be mastered if the student is to be educated.

The variations that should be encouraged fall not in the realm of content but in that of method. Allowances for individual differences should be provided for by abolishing all requirements except the examinations and permitting the student to take them whenever in his opinion he is ready to do so. The cultivation of independent thought and study, now almost wholly missing from our program, may thus be somewhat advanced. And this may be done without sacrificing the content of education to the obsessions of the hour or the caprices of the young.

If we are educators we must have a subject matter, and a rational, defensible one. If that subject matter is education, we cannot alter it to

[8] Plato, *Republic*, Book IX: " 'And it is plain,' I said 'that this is the purpose of the law, which is the ally of all classes in the state, and this is the aim of our control of children, our not leaving them free before we have established, so to speak, a constitutional government within them and, by fostering the best element in them with the aid of the like in ourselves, have set up in its place a similar guardian and ruler in the child, and then, and then only we leave it free.' "

suit the whims of parents, students, or the public. Whewell, Master of Trinity College, Cambridge, one hundred years ago, said:

"Young persons may be so employed and so treated, that their caprice, their self-will, their individual tastes and propensities, are educed and developed, but this is not Education. It is not the Education of a Man; for what is educed is not what belongs to man as man, and connects man with man. It is not the Education of a man's Humanity, but the Indulgence of his Individuality."

In general education we are interested in drawing out the elements of our common human nature; we are interested in the attributes of the race, not the accidents of individuals.

If our course of study reflects today an interest in the accidents of individuals; if the permanent studies are conspicuous by their absence from it, I can only say that these are the reasons why our course of study is bad. We know that our course of study leads to the most unfortunate results in the organization of education, in the qualities and activities of professors and students, and in the cultivation of our people. It is surely not a criticism of the permanent studies that they have had no share in producing these results.

By insisting on the permanent studies as the heart of a general education I do not mean to insist that they are the whole of it. We do not know enough to know whether certain technological work, for example, may not have certain subsidiary value in general education for some students. Nor do I overlook the fact that since by hypothesis general education may be terminal for most students, it must connect them with the present and future as well as with the past. It is as important for them to know that thinking is still going on as it is for them to know what has been thought before.

The question whether certain technical work shall be allowed to be a part of general education is rather a question of method than of content, a question how to teach rather than what. Technology as such has no place in general education. If it can be justified at all, it can only be because we discover that certain principles can best be communicated through technical work. The question of present thought is largely answered by saying that it is impossible to think of a teacher who contented himself with elucidating the thought of the past without intimating that these ideas have a history running to the present day.

The proponents of current events as the subject matter of education gain little by insisting on the importance of present thought; for they are not much interested in thought of any kind. They would be only less horrified if contemporary thought were made the heart of general education than they would be if St. Augustine or Spinoza were central in it. They would get little consolation from the remarks of Whewell about what he called the progressive studies, which were to make their first appearance at a much later stage of education than the one we are here considering. He said:

"It is not enough that we take for this purpose any expression of the present activities of men's minds. Progressive studies, too, must be a part of the development of humanity in its general form. They must express an activity which belongs to man as man. They must be, though not permanent in their form, universal in their principles. They must be the results, not of individual caprice, or fancy, but of human Reason. They must aim, not at mere change or novelty, but at Truth. And since the progress of the human mind is from Truth to Truth, the new Truths must be founded upon the old ones. The progressive studies which education embraces must rest upon the permanent studies which it necessarily includes. The former must be its superstructure, the latter, its foundation."

Again he says:

"A man who really participates in the progress of the sciences, must do so by following their course when the time of education is past. . . . Modern Science and Philosophy ought to be introduced into education so far as to show their nature and principles; but they do not necessarily make any considerable or definite part of it. The intellectual culture, though it will be incomplete if these are excluded, may still be a culture which connects him with the past, and prepares him for the present; but an education from which classical literature or mathematical reasoning is omitted, however familiar it may make a man with the terms of modern literature and philosophy, must leave him unprepared to understand the real purport of literature and philosophy, because he has not the intellectual culture which the greatest authors in literature and philosophy have always had." [9]

Let us avoid all questions of administration and method. Let us assume that we have an intelligible organization of education under which there is a four-year unit, beginning at about the beginning of the junior year in high school and ending at about the end of the sophomore year in college. Let us assume that we are going to try to teach in that unit everybody who can learn from books. Let us assume further that the conclusion of their work in this unit will mark the end of formal instruction for most students. They will not go on to the university. Nevertheless we must have a curriculum which will, in the main, do as well

[9] Consider the importance to English law of Aristotle's distinctions of misadventure, mistake, an act of injustice, and the unjust act of an unjust man. *Ethics*, 1135B. Consider also the influence on Anglo-Saxon jurisprudence of Locke's *Second Essay on Civil Government.*

for those who are going on as those who are not. What shall this curriculum be?

We have excluded body building and character building. We have excluded the social graces and the tricks of trades. We have suggested that the curriculum should be composed principally of the permanent studies. We propose the permanent studies because these studies draw out the elements of our common human nature, because they connect man with man, because they connect us with the best that man has thought, because they are basic to any further study and to any understanding of the world. What are the permanent studies?

They are in the first place those books which have through the centuries attained to the dimensions of classics. Many such books, I am afraid, are in the ancient and medieval period. But even these are contemporary. A classic is a book that is contemporary in every age. That is why it is a classic. The conversations of Socrates raise questions that are as urgent today as they were when Plato wrote. In fact they are more so, because the society in which Plato lived did not need to have them raised as much as we do. We have forgotten how important they are.

Such books are then a part, and a large part, of the permanent studies. They are so in the first place because they are the best books we know. How can we call a man educated who has never read any of the great books in the western world? Yet today it is entirely possible for a student to graduate from the finest American colleges without having read any of them, except possibly Shakespeare. Of course, the student may have heard of these books, or at least of their authors. But this knowledge is gained in general through textbooks, and textbooks have probably done as much to degrade the American intelligence as any single force. If the student should know about Cicero, Milton, Galileo, or Adam Smith, why should he not read what they wrote? Ordinarily what he knows about them he learns from texts which must be at best second-hand versions of their thought.

In the second place these books are an essential part of general education because it is impossible to understand any subject or to comprehend the contemporary world without them. If we read Newton's *Principia*, we see a great genius in action; we make the acquaintance of a work of unexampled simplicity and elegance. We understand, too, the basis of modern science. The false starts, the backing and filling, the wildness, the hysteria, the confusion of modern thought and the modern world result from the loss of what has been thought and done by earlier ages. The Industrial Revolution begins our study of history and the social sciences. Philosophy begins with Descartes and Locke and psychology with Wundt and William James. Natural science originates with the great experimenters of the nineteenth century. If anything prior is mentioned, it is only as a reminder that our recent great achievements in these fields must, of course, have had some primitive beginnings in the dark earlier centuries. The classics, if presented at all, are offered in excerpts out of context, and for the most part for the sake of showing the student how far we have progressed beyond our primitive beginnings.

Yet we may with profit remember the words of Nicholas Murray Butler:

"Only the scholar can realize how little that is being said and thought in the modern world is in any sense new. It was the colossal triumph of the Greeks and Romans and of the great thinkers of the Middle Ages to sound the depths of almost every problem which human nature has to offer, and to interpret human thought and human aspiration with astounding profundity and insight. Unhappily, these deep-lying facts which should be controlling in the life of a civilized people with a historical background, are known only to a few, while the many grasp, now at an ancient and well-demonstrated falsehood and now at an old and well-proved truth, as if each had all the attractions of novelty."

You will note that Mr. Butler says that only a scholar can realize these things. Why should this insight be confined to scholars? Every educated person should know the colossal triumph of the Greeks and Romans and the great thinkers of the Middle Ages. If every man were educated—and why should he not be?—our people would not fall so easily a prey to the latest nostrums in economics, in politics, and I may add, in education.

You will observe that the great books of the western world cover every department of knowledge. The *Republic* of Plato is basic to an understanding of the law; it is equally important as education for what is known as citizenship. The *Physics* of Aristotle, which deals with change and motion in nature, is fundamental to the natural sciences and medicine, and is equally important to all those who confront change and motion in nature, that is, to everybody. Four years spent partly in reading, discussing and digesting books of such importance would, therefore, contribute equally to preparation for specialized study and to general education of a terminal variety. Certainly four years is none too long for this experience. It is an experience which will, as I have said, serve as preparation for advanced study and as general education designed to help the student understand the world. It will also develop habits of reading and standards of taste and criticism that will enable the adult, after his formal education is over, to think and act intelligently about the thought and movements of contemporary life. It will help him to share in the intellectual activity of his time.

In order to read books one must know how to do it. The degeneracy of instruction in English grammer should not blind us to the fact that only through grammatical study can written works be understood. Grammar is the scientific analysis of language through which we understand the meaning and force of what is written. Grammar disciplines the mind and develops the logical faculty. It is good in itself and as an aid to reading the classics. It has a place in general education in connection with the classics and independently of them. For those who are going to learn from books learning the art of reading would seem to be indispensable.

I do not suggest that learning the languages or the grammar in which the ancient classics were written is necessary to general education. Excellent translations of almost all of them now exist. Unless it can be shown that the study of Greek and Latin grammar is essential to the study of English grammar or that the mastery of the Greek and Latin languages is essential to mastery of our own, I see no reason for insisting on these languages as part of general education. The modern languages, of course, are no necessary part of it. Time should be allowed for students to acquire them; but the examinations reflecting general education should not contain them. They are an extracurriculum accomplishment or a tool for advanced work rather than a fundamental portion of general education.

I add to grammar, or the rules of reading, rhetoric and logic, or the rules of writing, speaking, and reasoning. The classics provide models of excellence; grammar, rhetoric, and logic are means of determining how excellence is achieved. We have forgotten that there are rules for speaking. And English composition, as it is commonly taught, is a feeble and debased imitation of the classical rules of writing, placing emphasis either on the most trivial details or on what is called self-expression. Self-expression as here understood is, of course, the exact reverse of the discipline which rhetoric in all ages up to the present was used to give. Logic is a statement in technical form of the conditions under which reasoning is rigorously demonstrative. If the object of general education is to train the mind for intelligent action, logic cannot be missing from it.

Logic is a critical branch of the study of reasoning. It remains only to add a study which exemplifies reasoning in its clearest and most precise form. That study is, of course, mathematics, and of the mathematical studies chiefly those that use the type of exposition that Euclid employed. In such studies the pure operation of reason is made manifest. The subject matter depends on the universal and necessary processes of human thought. It is not affected by differences in taste, disposition, or prejudice. It refutes the common answer of students who, conformable to the temper of the time, wish to accept the principles and deny the conclusions. Correctness in thinking may be more directly and impressively taught through mathematics than in any other way.[10] It is depressing that in high schools and junior colleges mathematics is not often taught in such a way as to achieve these ends. Arithmetic and geometry are there usually presented to the student as having great practical value, as of course they have.[11] But I have had students in the freshman year in college who had never heard that they had any other value, and who were quite unwilling to consider mathematical questions until their practical possibilities had been explained. To this pass has our notion of utility brought us.

We have then for general education a course of study consisting of the greatest books of the western world and the arts of reading, writing, thinking, and speaking, together with mathematics, the best exemplar of the processes of human reason. If our hope has been to frame a curriculum which educes the elements of our common human nature, this program should realize our hope. If we wish to prepare the young for intelligent action, this course of study should assist us; for they will have learned what has been done in the past, and what the greatest men have thought. They will have learned how to think themselves. If we wish to lay a basis for advanced study, that basis is provided. If we wish to secure true universities, we may look forward to them, because students and professors may acquire through this course of study a common stock of ideas and common methods of dealing with them. All the needs of general education in America seem to be satisfied by this curriculum.

What, then, are the objections to it? They cannot be educational objections; for this course of study appears to accomplish the aims of general education. One objection may be that the students will not like it, which is, as we have seen, irrelevant. But even if it were relevant, it is not true. Since the proposed curriculum is coherent and comprehensible, and since it is free from the triviality that now afflicts our program, students will respond to it if the teachers will give them a chance to do it.

It may be said that the course of study is too difficult. It is not too difficult for students who can read or who can be taught to do so. For ease of reading, as well as other qualities, *The Federalist*, an American classic, is superior to some recent treatises on government and public administration; Herodotus is more sprightly than most modern historians of the ancient world; and Plato and Aristotle are as intelligible as contemporary philosophers.

No, the students can do the work if the faculties will let them. Will the faculties let them? I doubt it. The professors of today have been

---

[10] " 'You see, then, my friend,' said I, 'that this branch of study really seems to be indispensable for us, since it plainly compels the souls to employ pure thought with a view to truth itself.' " Plato, *Republic*, Book VII.

[11] Plato on geometers: "Their language is most ludicrous, though they cannot help it, for they speak as if they were doing something and as if all their words were directed toward action. For all their talk is of squaring and applying and adding and the like, whereas the real object of the entire study is pure thought." *Ibid.*, Book VII. See also Aristotle, *Ethics*, 1098a.

brought up differently. Not all of them have read all the books they would have to teach. Not all of them are ready to change the habits of their lives. Meanwhile they are bringing up their successors in the way they were brought up, so that the next crop will have the habits they have had themselves. And the love of money, a misconception of democracy, a false notion of progress, a distorted idea of utility, and the anti-intellectualism to which all these lead conspire to confirm their conviction that no disturbing change is needed. The times call for the establishment of a new college or for an evangelistic movement in some old ones which shall have for its object the conversion of individuals and finally of the teaching profession to a true conception of general education. Unless some such demonstration or some such evangelistic movement can take place, we shall remain in our confusion; we shall have neither general education nor universities; and we shall continue to disappoint the hopes of our people.

Suggested Readings

Brubacher, John S.: *Modern Philosophies of Education.* New York: McGraw-Hill Book Company, 1950.

Hutchins, Robert M.: *Education for Freedom.* Baton Rouge, La.: Louisiana State University Press, 1943.

———: *The Higher Learning in America.* New Haven, Conn.: Yale University Press, 1936.

———: *No Friendly Voice.* Chicago: University of Chicago Press, 1936.

———: *University of Utopia.* Chicago: University of Chicago Press, 1953.

Maritain, Jacques: *Education at the Crossroads.* New Haven, Conn.: Yale University Press, 1943.

National Society for the Study of Education: *Forty-first Yearbook, Part I. Philosophies of Education.* Bloomington, Ill.: Public School Publishing Company, 1942. (Contains concise statements of the major philosophies of education, including a chapter by Mortimer Adler and the Catholic position by W. J. McGuchen, S.J.)

———: *Fifty-fourth Yearbook, Part I. Modern Philosophies and Education.* Chicago: University of Chicago Press, 1955.

Park, Joe, ed.: *Selected Readings in the Philosophy of Education.* New York: The Macmillan Company, 1958.

Redden, J. D., and Ryan, F. A.: *A Catholic Philosophy of Education.* Milwaukee: The Bruce Publishing Company, 1942.

Schneider, Herbert W.: *A History of American Philosophy.* New York: Columbia University Press, 1946.

Van Doren, Mark: *Liberal Education.* New York: Henry Holt and Company, 1943.

CHAPTER 15

THE ESSENTIALIST PHILOSOPHY OF
EDUCATION

THE SECOND MAJOR POINT OF VIEW PRESENTED IS WHAT IS KNOWN
in educational circles as the essentialist philosophy. The selection
chosen is by one of it's leading advocates, William C. Bagley. In
1917 he joined the faculty of Teachers College, Columbia University and
was a part of that institution through the years in which such outstanding men as Counts, Childs, Kilpatrick, Rugg, Hopkins, Raup, Kandel,
Newlon, Norton, and Mort were making the institution world famous
in the field of education. In the great debate over educational theory and
practice that raged in the twenties and thirties he, along with Kandel
and others, was a part of the conservative group that criticized aspects
of the progressive movement. His primary concern was with the improvement of teaching in the classroom and the classroom teacher. This
concern was illustrated in his well-known book *The Educative Process*,
published in 1905. He was not trained as a philosopher and did not consider himself one, but his interest in theory brought him into the field
and his ability carried him to prominence.

The selection below was prepared as a paper and presented by Bagley
to a small group of educators in Atlantic City in February of 1938. The
group adopted the name The Essentialist Committee for the Advancement of American Education, and Bagley's paper became a virtual platform for the group.

WILLIAM C. BAGLEY

FROM

"An Essentialist's Platform for the Advancement of American Education" [1]

I. THE SITUATION

In spite of its vast extent and its heavy cost to society, public education in the United States is in many ways appallingly weak and ineffective. For the sake of brevity only a few outstanding evidences of this weakness will be set forth here:

1. Age for age, the average pupil of our elementary schools does not meet the standards of achievement in the fundamentals of education that are attained in the elementary schools of many other countries. In so far as English-speaking countries are concerned, this statement can be and has been substantiated by the scores made in the elementary schools of these countries on American achievement tests, the norms of which represent the average scores of large, unselected groups of American pupils. In the most extended investigation [2] of this type, the differences revealed are so wide as to justify no other inference than that American elementary-school achievement is far below what it could be and what it should be.

2. Similar comparisons relative to secondary education cannot be made because the secondary schools of practically all other countries are not intended for "all the children of the people" as are our high schools. It is generally agreed among competent students of the problem that our average 18-year-old high-school graduate is scholastically far behind the average 18-year-old graduates of the secondary schools of many other

[1] William C. Bagley, "An Essentialist's Platform for the Advancement of American Education," *Educational Administration and Supervision*, XXIV (April, 1938), pp. 241–56.

[2] The study here referred to was published by the University of London Press in 1934 for the Scottish Council for Research in Education. (MacGregor, G.: *Achievement Tests in the Primary Schools: A Comparative Study with American Tests in Fife.*) A battery of American achievement tests was given to every eleven-year-old child in the County of Fife—about seven thousand in all. Even mentally defective children were included. While the findings are somewhat difficult to evaluate because Scottish children enter school at five rather than six, the conclusion stated in the text is clearly justified. The use of achievement tests in Canadian schools tells a similar story, for example in the province-wide survey of the schools of British Columbia conducted by Professor Peter Sandiford. One of the writer's colleagues who has constructed many tests reports that when he has included significant numbers of Canadian pupils in "standardizing" the tests, the norms have been raised to a point where the tests could not be used equitably with American pupils.

countries. This difference has been recognized in the practice of admitting the latter to junior-year standing in many American colleges. But even granting that secondary education elsewhere is in general selective, there is abundant evidence that in our laudable efforts to send everyone to and through high school standards have been unnecessarily lowered. Both the bright and the slow pupils are handicapped by weaknesses in the fundamentals that all except those hopelessly subnormal are able to master. Within the past decade the effectiveness of high-school instruction has been weakened by increasing disabilities in so basic an accomplishment as reading. It is scarcely too much to say, indeed, that increasing proportions of pupils in the junior and senior high schools are essentially illiterate. Failures in such high-school studies as mathematics and natural science are in many cases traceable to the fact that pupils cannot read effectively. Classes in "remedial" reading are now necessary on the secondary level to bring pupils to a standard of literacy that primary- and intermediate-grade instruction could and should have insured. Equally lamentable weaknesses in basic arithmetic are reported. And it is now taken for granted by high-school teachers of Latin and modern languages that one of their chief duties is to teach their pupils the rudiments of English grammar.

3. In other and not at all exclusively scholastic accomplishments, American education is relatively ineffective. A recent study suggests that juvenile delinquency may be correlated in many cases with these reading disabilities which we contend are almost always unnecessary and easily avoidable by appropriate elementary education. And while no causal relationship is claimed, it is well to know that during the one hundred years in which universal elementary education has been increasingly the policy of all civilized countries, ours is apparently the only country in which the expansion of the universal school has not been paralleled by a significant and in some cases a remarkable decrease in the ratios of serious crime.

II. THE CAUSES: A. GENERAL ECONOMIC AND SOCIAL FACTORS

4. American education has been confronted with uniquely difficult and complicated problems which have arisen from a rapid growth in population; from a constantly advancing frontier; from the increase in national wealth; from the arrival year after year and decade after decade of millions of immigrants of widely diverse national origins; from the complex social and political situations involved in racial differences; from the profound changes brought about by the transition from a predominantly agricultural to a predominantly industrial civilization; from the growth of cities; from an ever-increasing mobility of the population; and from a multitude of other factors which have operated here

with a force unprecedented in history and unparalleled in any other part of the world.

The American public school has met some of these problems with a notable measure of success. Of outstanding significance is the fact that among the states which by any test would be rated as the most advanced in civilization are those which have had the heaviest burden of immigration from backward countries to assimilate. And it should be said that, in general, the states that have had the most substantial (but not necessarily the most "Progressive") school systems have by far the lowest ratios of serious crime. In a notable degree, too, these same states, many of which do not rank high in *per capita* wealth, are those that have been least dependent upon the federal government for "relief" during the depression years. Beyond all this, the schools can claim a very high degree of definitely measurable success for their programs of physical development and health education.

5. The upward expansion of mass-education first to the secondary and now to the college level, which is probably the chief cause of our educational ineffectiveness, has been an outcome, not alone of a pervasive faith in education, to the realization of which the material wealth of the country was fairly adequate, but also and perhaps more fundamentally of economic factors. Power-driven machinery, while in many cases reducing occupational opportunities on the purely routine levels, quite as markedly opened new occupational opportunities in types of work that could not be done by machinery; work that involved deliberation and judgment; work for which a broad foundation in general education as well as specialized technical and vocational training was advantageous and often essential. That increasing numbers of young persons should seek the advantages of an extended education has been inevitable. Fortunately the wealth of the country has enabled the people of many sections to meet this demand. In opening the high schools and colleges to ever-increasing numbers, however, it was just as inevitable that scholastic standards should be relaxed, and when such a need arises it is only natural that those responsibile for the administration of education should welcome any theory or philosophy which justifies or rationalizes such a policy—any theory of education which can make a virtue of necessity. Under such a condition, it is easy to understand why the relaxation of standards has been carried far beyond the actual needs of the case.

III. THE CAUSES: B. EDUCATIONAL THEORIES THAT ARE ESSENTIALLY ENFEEBLING

6. Throughout the long history of education—and organized education is practically as old as civilization—two opposing theories have been

in evidence. Although over-simplification is always dangerous, one with this caution may contrast these two theories of education by certain conflicting concepts summed up in pairing such opposites as "individual vs. society," "freedom vs. discipline," "interest vs. effort," "play vs. work,"—or to use more recently current expressions, "immediate needs vs. remote goals," "personal experience vs. race experience," "psychological organization vs. logical organization," "pupil-initiative vs. teacher-initiative." The fundamental dualism suggested by these terms has persisted over the centuries. It came out sharply in Greek education during the Age of the Sophists. It was reflected in the educational changes brought about by the Italian Renaissance. It appeared in the 17th Century in a definite school of educational theory the adherents of which even at that time styled themselves the "Progressives." It was explicit in the successive educational reforms proposed by Rousseau, Pestalozzi, Froebel, and Herbart. In American education it was reflected in the theories advocated and practiced by Bronson Alcott, in the work of Horace Mann, and later in the work of E. A. Sheldon and Francis W. Parker; while the present outstanding leader, John Dewey, first came into prominence during the last decade of the 19th Century in an effort to resolve the dualism through an integration expressed in the title of his classic essay, now called "Interest and Effort in Education."

7. Under the necessity which confronted American education of rationalizing the loosening of standards and the relaxation of rigor if mass-education were to be expanded upward, the theories which emphasized interest, freedom, immediate needs, personal experience, psychological organization, and pupil-initiative, and which in so doing tended to discredit and even condemn their opposites—effort, discipline, remote goals, race-experience, logical sequence, and teacher-initiative—naturally made a powerful appeal. Over more than a generation these theories have increasingly influenced the lower schools.[3] They find

---

[3] Dr. H. C. Morrison (*School and Commonwealth*, Chicago, 1937, p. 11) states that an educational philosophy embodying such theories has been gradually taking form in American education during the past fifty or sixty years. The present writer has publicly called attention for more than thirty years to manifestations of this influence, and to its weakening tendencies. His charges, with evidence supporting them, are matters of published record, duly documented. They have been frequently denounced, but never answered. In addition to published articles, the following books by the present writer make references to the problem: *The Educative Process*, 1905; *Classroom Management*, 1907; *School Discipline*, 1914; *Determinism in Education*, 1925; *Education, Crime, and Social Progress*, 1932; *Education and Emergent Man*, 1934. The theories were influencing the schools long before the terms "activity program," "integrated curriculum," "child-centered school," and the like came into vogue or had even been coined. It should be noted, too, that these theories have had no comparable recognition in the school systems of other countries except the Soviet Union, where after twelve years of consistent application they were abandoned in 1933 as hopelessly weak and ineffective.

specific expression today in a variety of definite movements so numerous that even the more outstanding can here be listed.

(a) *The complete abandonment in many school systems of rigorous standards of scholastic achievement as a condition of promotion from grade to grade, and the passing of all pupils "on schedule."* This policy which found a strong initial support thirty years ago in the studies of "retardation and elimination" has of late been given even a wider appeal by the teachings of mental hygiene regarding the possible effects of failure in disintegrating personality. The problem is extremely complicated as a later reference to it will show, but the movement has already resulted in at least one very important change. Instead of having "overage" pupils piling up in the intermediate grades, we now have "overgraded" pupils handicapped in the work of the junior and senior high schools by their lack of thorough training in the fundamentals already referred to.

(b) *The disparagement of system and sequence in learning and a dogmatic denial of any value in, even of any possibility of learning through, the logical, chronological and causal relationships of learning materials.* This has led to an enthronement of the doctrine of incidental learning. Only as one becomes acquainted with facts and principles through applying them to vital problems that appeal to one as worth solving at the moment (so the theory holds) can one truly learn such facts and principles. And on the side of skills—such as the fundamental arts of language, measurement, and computation—mastery as far as possible should await an occasion when one of them is needed. As someone has said in effect, "These things are only tools, and when a workman needs a tool he goes to the shop and gets it." And yet this theory that "mind will not learn what is alien to its fundamental vital purposes," Thorndike has pronounced on the basis of extended experimentation, "to be attractive and plausible but definitely false." [4] The disparagement of systematic and sequential learning has also been criticized in no uncertain terms by John Dewey.[5]

(c) *The wide vogue of the so-called "activity movement."* This is an outgrowth of the so-called "project-method" which in its turn was an effort to find, or to encourage the learner to find, problems or vital purposes in the solution of which desirable learnings could be effected. The activity movement and the resulting "activity programs" and "activity curricula," like the project-method, have an important place— a central function in the primary school, and a very useful supplementary function on all educational levels. The tendency to make them a substitute for systematic and sequential learning and to go even further and regard activity as a sufficient end in itself irrespective of whether or

---

[4] Thorndike, E. L.: *Adult Interests.* New York, 1935, p. 52.
[5] Especially in an article in *The New Era* referred to below.

not anything is learned through the activity is another matter. It is, however, an intriguing proposal. As one enthusiastic activist said, "Let us not use activities as pegs on which to hang subject-matter." If the schools only provide an abundance of "rich experiences" for the learner, it seems, other things will miraculously take care of themselves. This is not at all absurd if one accepts the premises; it is a thoroughly consistent result of the theory of incidental learning carried to its logical conclusion.

(d) *The discrediting of the exact and exacting studies.* The most significant barrier to opening the high schools to the masses was at the outset the practically universal requirement of Latin, algebra, and geometry in the secondary program. Perhaps inherently and certainly as commonly taught, the difficulties in mastering these subjects were quite beyond a large proportion of pupils. At the same time the practical value of the subjects was difficult to defend. Their central place in the curriculum, however, was believed to be justified in a high degree by the mental discipline that their mastery involved. Anything that would tend to discredit this justification was seized upon by those responsible for the upward expansion of mass-education. Most fortunately for their purposes there appeared just at the turn of the century the report of the first careful psychological experiments testing the validity of the theory of mental discipline. These really classic experiments of Thorndike and Woodworth were followed by a long series of similar investigations that aimed to determine how far learnings acquired in one subject were, or could be, applied in other situations. The results in general indicated that such a "transfer" was far from inevitable and in some cases either quite negative or so slight as to bring the whole theory into question.

The proponents of the universal high school and of other educational movements that were impeded by the requirement of subjects inherently difficult to the average mind were not slow to capitalize these experimental findings. As is natural under conditions of this sort, the evidence was generalized to a far greater extent than the experiments warranted, and with far-reaching results in school practice. Although the absolute number enrolled in Latin classes has increased, only a small proportion of pupils graduating from the high schools during the past ten years have even been exposed to Latin. Increasing proportions, too, are quite innocent of any training in elementary mathematics beyond the increasingly ineffective modicum of arithmetic acquired in the elementary schools. But the important fact is that there has been a growing practice of discouraging even competent learners from undertaking the studies that are exact though exacting; hence the upward expansion of mass-education, while sincerely a democratic movement, is not guarding itself against the potentially most fatal pitfall of democracy. It has deliberately adopted the easy policy of leveling-down rather than facing resolutely the difficult task of leveling-up—and upon the possibility of leveling-up the future of democracy indisputably depends. As John Dewey has contended, the older curriculum of classics and mathematics does have a unique value to those competent to its mastery—a value for which the so-called reform movements have not as yet, in his judgment, provided a substitute.[6]

(e) *An increasingly heavy emphasis upon the "social studies."* While the exact and exacting studies were in effect being discredited, the primrose path of least resistance was opened ever wider in the field known as the social studies. The argument here is plausible and appealing. "Education for citizenship" is a ringing slogan with limitless potentialities, especially in an age when high-sounding shibboleths, easily formulated, can masquerade as fundamental premises and postulates wrought through the agony of hard thinking.

Obviously no fundamental premise in educational thinking could fail to recognize the importance of a firm foundation in the history of human institutions, or of an acquaintance with present and pressing social problems especially in the light of their genesis, or of an acquaintance with such principles of economics, sociology, and political science as have been well established.

But just as obviously the social sciences, so called, are not in the same class with the natural sciences. Their generalizations permit trustworthy predictions only in a few cases and then only in a slight degree. When the human element enters, uncertainty enters—else the world could have anticipated and adjusted itself to Hitler and Mussolini and Stalin and the military oligarchy of Japan and would not be standing dazed and impotent as it stands today. And while to expect an educational pabulum of social studies in the lower schools essentially to overcome this inherent limitation of the social sciences is an alluring prospect, it is to expect nothing less than a miracle. It is, indeed, just as sensible as would be a brave and desperate effort to incite immature minds to square the circle.

(f) *Using the lower schools to establish a new social order.* The proposal definitely and deliberately to indoctrinate immature learners in the interest of a specific social order and one that involves wide de-

[6] "Development . . . is a continuous process, and continuity signifies consecutiveness of action. Here was the strong point of traditional education at its best . . . The subject-matter of the classics and mathematics involved of necessity, for those who mastered it, a consecutive and orderly development along definite lines. Here lies, perhaps, the greatest problem of the newer efforts in education." Dewey, J.: "The Need of a Philosophy of Education." *The New Era*, London, November, 1934, pp. 214 f.

partures from that which prevails in our country is to be questioned, if for no other reasons, upon the grounds set forth in the preceding paragraphs. With the growing ineffectiveness of the lower schools in failing to lay adequate foundations in fundamental and established learnings of unquestioned permanence and value, such efforts would necessarily be superficial in the last degree. It would be an extreme case of building what may be characterized for the sake of argument as a perfectly splendid edifice on shifting sands—in this case, quicksands would be the more appropriate metaphor. And here we might well study certain peoples that have actually achieved a social order which is pointed to by our idealists as exemplifying in many ways the realization of their dreams. Reference is made, of course, to such countries as Sweden, Denmark, Norway, and New Zealand. An outstanding fact of fundamental significance is that these countries have *not* achieved these laudable results by emasculating their educational systems. Their peoples indeed would stand aghast at the very suggestion.

(g) *The "curriculum-revision" movement and its vagaries.* The various reform proposals just discussed have culminated in the general movement known as curriculum-revision which has dominated the lower schools for nearly twenty years. A primary emphasis has been the alleged need of building the programs of instruction around the local community. As long ago as 1933 more than 30,000 different curricula were on file in the curriculum-laboratory of Teachers College, Columbia University. Most of these had been prepared during the preceding decade by committees of teachers in local school systems throughout the country. Sometimes the committees were personally directed by a "curriculum-expert"; in practically all cases a rapidly developing theory evolved by these specialists guided the work. In so far as we can learn, this theory has never explicitly recognized that the state or the nation has a stake in the content of school instruction. The need of common elements in the basic culture of all people, especially in a democracy, has in effect been denied. Furthermore, with the American people the most mobile in the world, with stability of residence over the period of school attendance the exception and not the rule in many sections of the country, and with a significantly higher average of school failure among pupils whose parents move from place to place than among those who remain in the same community, the curriculum theorists have been totally insensitive to the need of a certain measure of uniformity in school requirements and in the grade-placement of crucial topics. In addition to all this, the clear tendency of the curriculum-revision movement has been to minimize basic learnings, to magnify the superficial, to belittle sequence and system, and otherwise to aggravate the weakness and ineffectiveness of the lower schools.

IV. THE PROBLEM AND THE PLATFORM

8. It is particularly unfortunate that American education should be unnecessarily weak at a time when the situation both at home and abroad is critical in the last degree.

The American people are facing an economic problem which both in nature and in magnitude is without an even remotely similar precedent in all history. In the richest country in the world, two-thirds of the world's unemployment is now concentrated. In the midst of potential abundance, the cogs in the wheels of production, distribution, exchange, and consumption have lamentably failed to mesh.

It is the indicated and imminent task of the present dominant generation to solve this problem under whatever expert guidance at the hands of the economist and the social engineer it may find and accept. The student of education must co-operate with all other citizens in this task. It is his own specific duty, however, to consider the problems in his field that are bound to arise in the changes that seem now to be inevitable, regardless of the form which the solution of the present desperate economic situation may take—this with one exception, for if in desperation the American people discard democracy and yield to a dictator the sincere student of education will have no function and consequently no duty. The yes-man and the rubber-stamp will take his place. He will be a luxury without a purpose; and the dictators have standardized a simple but effective technique for liquidating luxuries of this sort.

9. We shall assume, however, that "it can't happen here" and that, whatever may be the new economic and social order, the political order based upon representative government and the Bill of Rights will persist. Hence a primary function of American education will be to safeguard and strengthen these ideals of American democracy with especial emphasis upon freedom of speech, freedom of the press, freedom of assembly, and freedom of religion. It is clear enough now that whenever any one of these is permitted to collapse, the whole democratic structure will topple like a house of cards. These, then, are among the first essentials in the platform of the Essentialist.

10. Democracy is now distinctly on trial. It is under criticism and suspicion. Every weakness will be watched for and welcomed by its enemies. Inevitably the future will bring competition if not clashes and conflicts with the now militantly anti-democratic peoples. Democratic societies cannot survive either competition or conflict with totalitarian states unless there is a democratic discipline that will give strength and solidarity to the democratic purpose and ideal. If the theory of democ-

racy finds no place for discipline, then, the theory will have before long only historical significance. French education, much closer to the danger, has recognized this imperative need. Still unswerving in fidelity to the ideals of democracy, and still giving its first emphasis to clarity of thought and independence in individual thinking as the time-honored objectives of French education, it recognizes no less the fundamental importance of social solidarity in the defense of democracy.[7]

American educational theory long since dropped the term "discipline" from its vocabulary. Today its most vocal and influential spokesmen enthrone the right even of the immature learner to choose what he shall learn. They condemn as "authoritarian" all learning tasks that are imposed by the teacher. They deny any value in the systematic and sequential mastery of the lessons that the race has learned at so great a cost. They condone and rationalize the refusal of the learner to attack a task that does not interest him. In effect they open wide the lines of least resistance and least effort. Obedience they stigmatize as a sign of weakness. All this they advocate in the magic names of "democracy" and "freedom."

Now, obviously, the freedom of the immature to choose what they shall learn is of negligible consequence compared with their later freedom from the want, fear, fraud, superstition, and error which may fetter the ignorant as cruelly as the chains of the slave-driver—and the price of this freedom is systematic and sustained effort often devoted to the mastery of materials the significance of which must at the time be taken on faith.

11. This problem is far more than merely personal or individual in its reference. A democratic society has a vital, collective stake in the informed intelligence of every individual citizen. That a literate electorate is absolutely indispensable not only to its welfare but to its very survival is clearly demonstrated by the sorry fate that so speedily overtook every unschooled and illiterate democracy founded as a result of the War that was to "Make the world safe for democracy."

And literacy in this sense means, of course, far more than the mere ability to translate printed letters into spoken words; it means the development and expansion of ideas; it means the basis for intelligent understanding and for the collective thought and judgment which are the essence of democratic institutions. These needs are so fundamental to an effective democracy that it would be folly to leave them to the whim or caprice of either learner or teacher.

Among the essentials of the Essentialist, then, is a recognition of the right of the immature learner to guidance and direction when these are needed either for his individual welfare or for the welfare and progress

[7] See the concluding paragraphs of Bouglé, C.: "The French Conception of 'Culture Générale,'" a series of lectures at Teachers College, Columbia University, April, 1938. Published by the Teachers College Bureau of Publications.

of the democratic group. The responsibility of the mature for the instruction and control of the immature is the biological meaning of the extended period of human immaturity and necessary dependence. It took the human race untold ages to recognize this responsibility. It is literally true that until this recognition dawned man remained a savage. Primitive societies, as numerous students have observed (and their testimony seems to be unanimous), pamper and indulge their young. Freedom of children from control, guidance, and discipline is with them a rule so nearly universal that its only brief but significant exception during the nearly universal savage ceremonies marking the adolescent onset of maturity is regarded as the first faint beginning of consciously directed human education.

It would be futile to deny that control and discipline may be stupid and brutal and used for unworthy ends. It would be futile to deny the need for the development of self-discipline and for the relaxation of external discipline with the growth of volitional maturity. But all this does not alter the fundamental truth that freedom must go hand in hand with responsibility, and that responsible freedom is always a conquest, never a gift.

12. An effective democracy demands a community of culture. Educationally this means that each generation be placed in possession of a common core of ideas, meanings, understandings, and ideals representing the most precious elements of the human heritage.

There can be little question as to the essentials. It is by no means a mere accident that the arts of recording, computing, and measuring have been among the first concerns of organized education. They are basic social arts. Every civilized society has been founded upon these arts, and when these arts have been lost, civilization has invariably and inevitably collapsed. Egypt, Asia Minor, and Mesopotamia are strewn with the ruins of civilizations that forgot how to read and write. Contemporary civilization, for the first time in history has attempted to insure its continuance by making these arts in so far as possible the prerogative of all.

Nor is it at all accidental that a knowledge of the world that lies beyond one's immediate experience has been among the recognized essentials of universal education, and that at least a speaking acquaintance with man's past and especially with the story of one's own country was early provided for in the program of the universal school. Widening the space horizon and extending the time perspective are essential if the citizen is to be protected from the fallacies of the local and the immediate.

Investigation, invention, and creative art have added to the heritage and the list of recognized essentials has been extended and will be further extended. Health instruction and the inculcation of health practices are now basic phases of the work of the lower schools. The elements of natural science have their place. Neither the fine arts nor the industrial arts are neglected.

We repeat that there can be little question as to the essentials of universal education. As Charles A. Beard has so well said: "While education constantly touches the practical affairs of the hour and day, and responds to political and economic exigencies, it has its own treasures heavy with the thought and sacrifice of the centuries. It possesses a heritage of knowledge and heroic examples—accepted values stamped with the seal of permanence." [8]

13. A specific program of studies including these essentials should be the heart of a democratic system of education. In a country like ours with its highly mobile population there should be an agreement as to the order and grade-placement of subjects and especially of crucial topics.[9] There is no valid reason for the extreme localism that has come to characterize American education. There is no valid reason for the failure of the American elementary school to lay as firm a foundation in the fundamentals of education as do the elementary schools of other democracies. It is especially regrettable that contemporary educational theory should in effect condone and rationalize scamped work by ridiculing such traits as thoroughness, accuracy, persistence, and the ideal of good workmanship for its own sake. One may be very sure that democracy schooled to the easy way will have short shrift in competition or conflict with any social order dominated by objectives which, however reprehensible, are clear-cut and appealing, and are consequently embraced even by disenfranchised masses.

14. Generally speaking, the recognized essentials should be taught as such through a systematic program of studies and activities for the carrying out of which the teachers should be responsible. Informal learning through experiences initiated by the learners is important, and abundant opportunities should be provided for such experiences throughout the range of organized education. Beyond the primary grades, however, where as we have said it may well predominate, informal learning should be regarded as supplementary rather than central.

15. Failure in school is unpleasant and the repetition of a grade is costly and often not very effective. On the other hand, the lack of a stimulus that will keep the learner to his task is a serious injustice both to him and to the democratic group which, we repeat, has a fundamental stake in his effective education. Too severe a stigma has undoubtedly been placed upon school failure by implying that it is symp-

[8] *The Unique Function of Education in American Democracy.* Washington, D.C.: The Educational Policies Commission of the National Education Association, 1937, p. 71.

[9] Fortunately the National Society for the Study of Education is sponsoring a *Yearbook* dealing with this problem. This will be published in 1939.

tomatic of permanent weakness. By no means is this always the case. No less a genius than Pasteur did so poorly in his first year at the Higher Normal School of Paris that he had to go home for further preparation. One of the outstanding scientists of the present century had a hard time in meeting the requirements of the secondary school, failing, it is said, in the most elementary work of the field in which he later became world-famous. The list could be extended almost indefinitely.

Obviously not all learners can progress at the same rate. Some will go very, very slowly. Others will have trouble in getting started but will progress rapidly when they overcome the initial handicaps. Let us not stigmatize failure as we have done in the past. On the other hand, if education abandons rigorous standards and consequently provides no effective stimulus to the effort that learning requires, many persons will pass through twelve years of schooling only to find themselves in a world in which ignorance and lack of fundamental training are increasingly heavy handicaps. This in an all too literal sense is to throw the baby out with the bath.

16. The transition from a predominantly rural to a predominantly urban life has laid increasing burdens upon American education. For four decades or more we have been told that the school must provide opportunities for types of education that the normal bringing-up of children once provided on the farm and in the home. Manual training and the household arts were among the first responses to this demand. The parallel development of physical training with its later ramifications into various forms of health education are traceable in part to the same causes. Playgrounds, gymnasiums, and swimming pools are material expressions of the effort to meet these recognized needs. School and college athletics are lusty by-products representing in a very real sense the importance of finding a substitute for the vigorous physical work that once devolved of necessity upon the great majority of young people.

With the profound changes in the conditions of life already in progress, and with their clearly predictable extension and intensification in the immediate future, analogous substitutes must be sought for other educative experiences which the simpler conditions of life naturally and normally provided. Bread-winning employment is now postponed for vast numbers of young people. Willy-nilly they must remain dependent upon society, whether in attendance at school or college, or in such highly important educational enterprises as the Civilian Conservation Corps, or in "made work" of one variety or another.

The analogy of our civilization with the older civilizations based upon slavery is in no sense far-fetched. It has, indeed, a profound significance. Our slaves, it is true, are mechanical and not human. They are power-driven and increasingly they are being automatically controlled. They can do much more economically than human slaves the heavy work and the routine work. In some tasks they can perceive distinctions far too fine to be detected by the human senses, and they can respond far more quickly and far more accurately and dependably than can human nerves and muscles. Fortunately they can neither feel nor suffer, and so the grossest evils of the old slave civilizations are avoided. The fact remains, however, that the perils to those who are the supposed beneficiaries of a slave civilization are in no significant degree changed, whether the slaves be men or robots. Every slave civilization has within it the seeds of degeneration, decay, and ultimate extinction. Struggle and competition, selection and rejection, have often been cruel, but in both biological and social evolution they have been primary factors of progress. In societies that have lifted themselves above the plane of the brute and the savage, a most powerful steadying and civilizing force has been the ideal of personal economic responsibility for one's own survival and for one's old age and the care of one's dependents.

Generally speaking, then, "social security," like responsible freedom, has been a conquest, not a gift. Making it a gift involves some definite dangers. In our own country, few families have long survived the social security that comes through inherited wealth. "Three generations from shirt-sleeves to shirt-sleeves" has usually told the story. But this rule has had its exceptions. Here, as in some other countries, social security has, with occasional families, remained secure over a much longer time—but under the condition that each generation has been rigorously disciplined to its responsibilities and made clearly aware of the pitfalls that await the spendthrift and the idler. These exceptions, and especially those among them that have exemplified the development in each generation of a vigorous and highly sensitized social conscience, warrant the hope that an economy of abundance with social security for all may be so organized that our machine-slave civilization can escape the fate of the slave civilizations that have gone before. Herein lies an educational problem of the first magnitude which our educational theorists seem not even dimly to have sensed—so busy have they been in condemning out of hand the economic system which has made possible an economy of abundance based upon a machine-slave civilization.

A clear and primary duty of organized education at the present time is to recognize the fundamental character of the changes that are already taking place, and to search diligently for means of counteracting their dangers. Let us repeat that an educational theory to meet these needs must be strong, virile, and positive not feeble, effeminate, and vague. The theories that have increasingly dominated American education during the past generation are at basis distinctly of the latter type. The Essentialists have recognized and still recognize the contributions of real value that these theories have made to educational practice. They believe, however, that these positive elements can be preserved in an educational theory which finds its basis in the necessary dependence of the immature upon the mature for guidance, instruction, and discipline. This dependence is inherent in human nature. "What has been ordained among the prehistoric protozoa," said Huxley, "cannot be altered by act of Parliament"—nor, we may add, by the wishful thinking of educational theorists, however sincere their motives. "Authoritarianism" is an ugly word. But when those who detest it carry their laudable rebellion against certain of its implications so far as to reject the authority of plain facts, their arguments, while well adapted perhaps to the generation of heat, become lamentably lacking in light.

Suggested Readings

Brameld, Theodore: *Patterns of Educational Philosophy*. New York: World Book Company, 1950.

Brubacher, John S.: *Modern Philosophies of Education*. New York: McGraw-Hill Book Company, 1950.

Demiashkevich, Michael: *Introduction to the Philosophy of Education*. New York: American Book Company, 1935.

The Harvard Committee, Report of: *General Education in a Free Society*. Cambridge, Mass.: Harvard University Press, 1945.

Horne, Herman H.: *A Democratic Philosophy of Education*. New York: The Macmillan Company, 1932.

National Society for the Study of Education: *Forty-first Yearbook, Part I. Philosophies of Education*. Bloomington, Ill.: Public School Publishing Company, 1942.

———: *Fifty-fourth Yearbook, Part I. Modern Philosophies and Education*. Chicago: University of Chicago Press, 1955.

Park, Joe, ed.: *Selected Readings in the Philosophy of Education*. New York: The Macmillan Company, 1958.

Ulich, Robert: *Fundamentals of Democratic Education*. New York: American Book Company, 1940.

CHAPTER 16

THE BASIS FOR CONTEMPORARY
EDUCATIONAL THEORY

THE THIRD AND FINAL POINT OF VIEW PRESENTED IS THAT OF THE "father" of progressive education, regarded by many as not only the greatest American philosopher but one of the great thinkers of all time, John Dewey. While the title of this chapter may seem presumptuous, it is demonstrably true that Dewey's ideas are accepted not only in public schools but in religious schools as well. As one writer has said, "Numerous classroom practices stemming directly from Dewey's philosophy are being successfully carried out in church-controlled schools. Pupil planning, creative work, group activities—all of these can be and are used in both public and private schools. But when it comes to ethical and religious training, many progressive followers of Dewey's educational theory close their copy of *Democracy and Education* on Saturday night and do not open it again until Monday morning." [1] It is true of course that most American teachers have gotten Dewey's philosophy second hand and too few even know about, much less have read, his greatest work on education, *Democracy and Education*. As a result Dewey's ideas have been distorted and misapplied. His efforts to rectify this situation are evident in his book, *Experience and Education*, sections of which are quoted below. The first half of the selection chosen is from an article entitled "The Need for a Philosophy of Education," published in 1934 and the second half from his book *Experience and Education*, published in 1938. The reader is urged to follow this material with a careful reading of his *Democracy and Education*, published in 1916, which is his most comprehensive work on education and one of the classics in the field.

[1] Clifton L. Hall, *Great Human Issues of Our Time* (Nashville: George Peabody College for Teachers, 1953), p. 58.

John Dewey

FROM

"The Need for a Philosophy of Education" [2]

The phrase "progressive education" is one, if not of protest, at least of contrast, of contrast with an education which was predominantly static in subject-matter, authoritarian in methods, and mainly passive and receptive from the side of the young. But the philosophy of education must go beyond any idea of education that is formed by way of contrast, reaction and protest. For it is an attempt to discover what education *is* and how it takes place. Only when we identify education with schooling does it seem to be a simple thing to tell what education actually is, and yet a clear idea of what it *is* gives us our only criterion for judging and directing what goes on in schools.

It is sometimes supposed that it is the business of the philosophy of education to tell what education *should* be. But the only way of deciding what education should be, at least, the only way which does not lead us into the clouds, is discovery of what actually takes place when education really occurs. And before we can formulate a philosophy of education we must know how human nature is constituted in the concrete; we must know about the working of actual social forces; we must know about the operations through which basic raw materials are modified into something of greater value. The need for a philosophy of education is thus fundamentally the need for finding out what education really *is*. We have to take those cases in which we find there is a real development of desirable powers, and then find out how this development took place. Then we can project what has taken place in these instances as a guide for directing our other efforts. The need for this discovery and this projection is the need for a philosophy of education.

What then is education when we find actual satisfactory specimens of it in existence? In the first place, it is a process of development, of growth. And it is the *process* and not merely the result that is important. A truly healthy person is not something fixed and completed. He is a person whose processes and activities go on in such a way that he will continue to be healthy. Similarly, an educated person is the person who has the power to go on and get more education. Just what do we mean by growth, by development? Some of the early educational philosophers, like Rousseau and his followers, made much use of the analogy of the development of a seed into the full-grown plant. They used this analogy

[2] John Dewey, "The Need for a Philosophy of Education," *The New Era* (November 1934). Reprinted in *Education Today* by John Dewey (New York: G. P. Putnam's Sons, 1940), pp. 288–98.

to draw the conclusion that in human beings there are latent capacities which, if they are only left to themselves, will ultimately flower and bear fruit. So they framed the notion of *natural* development as opposed to a directed growth which they regarded as artificial.

But in the first place the growth of a seed is limited as compared with that of a human being; its future is largely prescribed by its antecedent nature. It has not got the capacities for growth in different directions toward different outcomes that are characteristic of the more flexible and richly endowed human young. The latter is also, if you please, a seed, a collection of germinal powers, but he may become a sturdy oak, a willow that bends with every wind, a thorny cactus or a poisionous weed.

This fact suggests a second fallacy. Even the seed of a plant does not grow simply of itself. It must have light, air and moisture in order to grow. Its development is after all controlled by conditions and forces that are outside of it. Native inherent forces must interact with those of its surroundings if there is to be life and development. In fact, development, even with a plant, is a matter of the *kind of interaction* that goes on between itself and the conditions and forces that form its environment. A stunted oak, a stalk of maize that bears few ears with only a few scattered grains, exhibit so-called natural development as truly as does the noble tree with expanding branches or the ear of maize that wins the prize at an exhibition. The difference in result may in part be due to native stock, but it is also due in part to what the environment has provided. And even the finest native stock would come to an untimely end or result in a miserable product if its own energies could not interact with favorable conditions of light, moisture, air, etc.

Since there are two factors involved in the existence of any interaction, the idea and ideal of education must take account of both. Traditional school methods and subject-matter failed to take into account the *diversity* of capacities and needs that exist in different human beings. It virtually assumed that, for purposes of education at least, all human beings are as much alike as peas in a pod, and it therefore provided a uniform curriculum for all.

In the second place, it failed to recognize that the *initiative* in growth comes from the needs and powers of the pupil. The *first* step in the interaction that results in growth comes from the reaching out of the tentacles of the individual, from an effort, at first blind, to procure the materials that his potentialities demand in order that they may come into action and find satisfaction. As with the body, hunger and power of taking and assimilating nourishment are the first necessities. Without them, the food that is theoretically most nutritious is offered in vain. Nothing would be more extraordinary if we had a proper system of education than the assumption, now so commonly made, that the mind of the individual is naturally averse to learning, and has to be either browbeaten or coaxed into action. Every mind, even of the youngest, is naturally or inherently seeking for those modes of active operation that are within the limits of its capacities—precisely as the body of the baby is constantly active as long as the infant is awake. The problem, a difficult and delicate one, is to discover what tendencies are especially seeking expression at a particular time and just what materials and methods will serve to evoke and direct a truly educative development.

The practical counterpart of the failure of traditional education to see that the initiative in learning and growth is with the individual learner lay in the method of imposition from the side of the teacher and reception, absorption, from the side of the pupil. Unwillingness to learn naturally follows when there is failure to take into account tendencies that are urgent in the existing make-up of an individual. All sorts of external devices then have to be resorted to in order to achieve absorption and retention of imposed subject-matter and skills. This method of teaching may be compared to inscribing records upon a passive phonographic disc to result in giving back what has been inscribed when the proper button is pressed in recitation or examination.

It is impossible, of course, for any teacher not to observe that there *are* real differences among pupils. But because these differences are not carried back to concrete differences in individuality, to differences in needs, in desires, in direction of native interest, they are too often generalized by being summed up under two main heads. Some pupils are just naturally bright while others are dull and stupid! Some are docile and obedient and others are unruly and troublesome! Conformity then becomes the criterion by which the pupil is judged in spite of the fact that initiative, orginality and independence are precious qualities in life.

While the raw material and the starting-point of growth are found in native capacities, the environing conditions which it is the duty of the educator to furnish are the indispensable means by which intrinsic possibilities are developed. Native capacities are the beginning, the starting-point. They are not the end and they do not of themselves decide the end. A gardener, a worker of metals, will not get far in his work if he does not observe and pay attention to the properties of the material he deals with. But if he permits these properties to dictate what he does, he will not get *anywhere*. Development will be arrested, not promoted. He must bring to his consideration of what he finds an ideal of possibilities not realized. This idea and ideal must be in line with the constitution of the raw material; it must not do violence to them; it must express their possibilities. But, nevertheless, it cannot be extracted from any study of them as they now exist. It must come from seeing them imaginatively, reflectively; and hence it must come from a source other than what is already at hand.

In the case of the educator the demand for imaginative insight into possibilities is greater. The gardener and worker in metals may take as their measure of the end to be accomplished the things that have already been done with plants and ores, although if they are original or inventive they will introduce some variation. But human individuals vary in their structure and possibilities as plants and metals do not. While the educator must use results that have already been accomplished he cannot, if he is truly an educator, make them his final and complete standard. Like the artist he has the problem of creating something that is not the exact duplicate of anything that has been wrought and achieved previously.

In any case, development, growth, involve change, modification, and modification in definite directions. It is quite possible for a teacher, under the supposed sanction of the idea of cultivating individuality, to fixate a pupil more or less at his existing level. Respect for individuality is primarily *intellectual*. It signifies studying the individual to see what is there to work with. Having this sympathetic understanding, the practical work then begins, for the practical work is one of modification, of changing, of reconstruction continued without end. The change must at least be towards more effective techniques, towards greater self-reliance, towards a more thoughtful and inquiring disposition, one more capable of persistent effort in meeting obstacles.

The weakness of some schools and teachers that would like to claim the name of progressive is that in reaction from the traditional method of external and authoritative imposition, they stop short with the recognition of the importance of giving free scope to native capacities and interests. They do not, in the first place, examine closely enough and long enough to find out what these actually may be. In the second place, they are inclined to take the individual traits that are showing themselves as finalities, instead of possibilities which by suitable direction can be transformed into something of greater significance, value and effectiveness. There is still current in many quarters the idea that evolution and development are simply matters of unfolding from within and that the unfolding will take place almost automatically if hands are kept off.

This point of view is natural as a reaction from the manifest evils of external imposition. But there is an alternative; and this alternative is not just a middle course or compromise between the two procedures. It is something radically different from either. Existing likes and powers are to be treated as possibilities, as starting-points, that are absolutely necessary for any healthy development. But development involves a point *towards* which as well as one *from* which; it involves constant movement in a given direction. Then when the point that is for the time being the goal and end is reached, it is in its turn but the starting-point of further reconstruction. The great problems of the adult who has to deal with the young is to see, and to feel deeply as well as merely to see intellectually, the forces that are moving in the young; but it is to see them as possibilities, as signs and promises; to interpret them, in short, in the light of what they may come to be. Nor does the task end there. It is bound up with the further problem of judging and devising the conditions, the materials, both physical, such as tools of work, and moral and social, which will, once more, so *interact* with existing powers and preferences as to bring about transformation in the desired direction.

The essential weakness of the old and traditional education was not just that it emphasized the necessity for provision of definite subject-matter and activities. These things *are* necessities for anything that can rightly be called education. The weakness and evil was that the imagination of educators did not go beyond provision of a fixed and rigid environment of subject-matter, one drawn moreover from sources altogether too remote from the experiences of the pupil. What is needed in the new education is more attention, not less, to subject-matter and to progress in technique. But when I say more, I do not mean more in quantity of the same old kind. I mean an imaginative vision which sees that no pre-scribed and ready-made scheme can possibly determine the exact subject-matter that will best promote the educative growth of every individual young person; that every new individual sets a new problem; that he calls for at least a somewhat different emphasis in subject-matter presented. There is nothing more blindly obtuse than the convention which supposes that the matter actually contained in textbooks of arithmetic, history, geography, etc., is just what will further the educational development of all children.

But withdrawal from the hard and fast and narrow contents of the old curriculum is only the negative side of the matter. If we do not go on and go far in the positive direction of providing a body of subject-matter much richer, more varied and flexible, and also in truth more definite, judged in terms of the experience of those being educated, than traditional education supplied, we shall tend to leave an educational vacuum in which anything may happen. Complete isolation is impossible in nature. The young live in some environment whether we intend it or not, and this environment is constantly interacting with what children and youth bring to it, and the result is the shaping of their interests, minds and character—either educatively or mis-educatively. If the professed educator abdicates his responsibility for judging and selecting the kind of environment that his best understanding leads him to think will be conducive to growth, then the young are left at the mercy of all the unorganized and casual forces of the modern social environment that inevitably play upon them as long as they live. In the educative environment the knowledge, judgment and experience of the teacher is a greater, not a smaller factor, than it is in the traditional school. The difference is that the teacher operates not as a magistrate set on high and marked by arbitrary authority but as a friendly co-partner and guide in a common enterprise.

Development, however, is a *continuous* process, and continuity signifies consecutiveness of action. Here was the strong point of the traditional education at its best. The subject-matter of the classics and mathematics involved of necessity, for those who mastered it, a consecutive and orderly development along definite lines. Here lies perhaps the greatest problem of the newer efforts in education. It is comparatively easy to improvise, to try a little of this today and this week and then something else tomorrow and next week. Things are done on the basis of some immediate interest and stimulation but without sufficient regard to what it leads to, as to whether or not something more difficult, setting new demands for information, need for acquisition of greater adequacy in technique and for new modes of skill, is led up to and grows naturally out of what is started. The need for taking account of spontaneous and uncoerced interest and activity is a genuine need; but without care and thought it results, all too readily, in a detached multiplicity of isolated short-time activities or projects, and the continuity necessary for growth is lost. Indeed, the new education processes require much more planning ahead on the part of teachers than did the old—for there the planning was all done in advance by the fixed curriculum.

I have spoken of the importance of environment, but a sound philosophy of education requires that the general term environment be specified. It must be seen to be dominantly human and its values as social. Through the influence of the social environment each person becomes saturated with the customs, the beliefs, the purposes, skills, hopes and fears of the cultural group to which he belongs. The features of even his physical surroundings come to him through the eyes and ears of the community. Hills and plains, plants and animals, climate and change of seasons, are clothed with the memories and traditions, and characteristic occupations and interests, of the society of which he is part. In the earlier years of education, it is particularly important that subject-matter be presented in its human context and setting. Here is one of the commonest failures of the school. We are told that instruction must proceed from the concrete to the abstract, but it is forgotten that in the experience of the child only that which has a human value and function is concrete. In his nature study and geography, physical things are presented to him as if they were independent and complete in themselves. But in the actual experience of a child, these things have a meaning for him only as they enter into human life. Even those distinctively human products, reading, and writing, which have developed for the purposes of furthering human association, of making human contacts closer and richer, are treated as if they were subjects in themselves. They are not used as friendly speech is used in ordinary life, and so for the child they become abstract, a kind of mystery that belongs to the school but not to life outside the school.

As the material of genuine development is that of human contacts and associations, so the end, the value that is the criterion and directing guide of educational work, is social. The acquisition of skills is not an end in itself. They are things to be put to use, and that use is their contribution to a common and shared life. They are intended, indeed, to make an individual more capable of self-support and of self-respecting independence. But unless this end is placed in the context of services rendered to others, skills gained will be put to an egoistic and selfish use, and may be employed as means of a trained shrewdness in which one person gets the better of others. Too often, indeed, the schools, through reliance upon the spur of competition and the bestowing of special honors and prizes, only build up and strengthen the disposition that makes an individual when he leaves school employ his special talents and superior skill to outwit his fellows without respect for the welfare of others.

What is true of the skills acquired in school, is true also of the knowledge gained there. The educational end and the ultimate test of the value of what is learned is its use and application in carrying on and improving the common life of all. It should never be forgotten that the background of the traditional educational system is a class society and that opportunity for instruction in certain subjects, especially literary ones and in mathematics beyond the rudiments of simple arithmetical subjects, was reserved for the wellborn and the well-to-do. Because of this fact, knowledge of these subjects became a badge of cultural superiority and social status. For many persons the possession of knowledge was a means of display, almost of showing off. Useful knowledge, on the other hand, was necessary only for those who were compelled by their class status to work for a living. A class stigma attached to it, and the uselessness of knowledge for all purposes save purely personal culture was proof of its higher quality.

Even after education in many countries was made universal, these standards of value persisted. There is no greater egoism than that of learning when it is treated simply as a mark of personal distinction to be held and cherished for its own sake. Yet the only way of eliminating this quality of exclusiveness is that all conditions of the school environment should tend in actual practice to develop in individuals the realization that knowledge is a possession held in trust for the furthering of the well-being of all.

Perhaps the greatest need of and for a philosophy of education at the present time is the urgent need that exists for making clear in idea and effective in practice that its end is social, and that the criterion to be applied in estimating the value of the practices that exist in schools is also social. It is true that the aim of education is development of individuals to the utmost of their potentialities. But this statement in isolation leaves unanswered the question as to what is the measure of the development. A society of free individuals in which all, through their own work, contribute to the liberation and enrichment of the lives of others, is the only environment in which any individual can really grow normally to his full stature. An environment in which some are practically enslaved, degraded, limited, will always react to create conditions that prevent the full development even of those who fancy they enjoy complete freedom for unhindered growth. . . .

John Dewey

FROM

Experience and Education [3]

If one attempts to formulate the philosophy of education implicit in the practices of the newer education, we may, I think, discover certain common principles amid the variety of progressive schools now existing. To imposition from above is opposed expression and cultivation of individuality; to external discipline is opposed free activity; to learning from texts and teachers, learning through experience; to acquisition of isolated skills and techniques by drill, is opposed acquisition of them as means of attaining ends which make direct vital appeal; to preparation for a more or less remote future is opposed making the most of the opportunities of present life; to static aims and materials is opposed acquaintance with a changing world. . . .

I take it that the fundamental unity of the newer philosophy is found in the idea that there is an intimate and necessary relation between the processes of actual experience and education. If this be true, then a positive and constructive development of its own basic idea depends upon having a correct idea of experience. Take, for example, the question of organized subject-matter—which will be discussed in some detail later. The problem for progressive education is: What is the place and meaning of subject-matter and of organization *within* experience? How does subject-matter function? Is there anything inherent in experience which tends towards progressive organization of its contents? What results

[3] John Dewey, *Experience and Education* (New York: The Macmillan Co., 1938), pp. 5–10, 12–14, 16–17, 86–90, 95–6, 103–4, 108–10. Printed with permission of Kappa Delta Pi.

follow when the materials of experience are not progressively organized? A philosophy which proceeds on the basis of rejection, of sheer opposition, will neglect these questions. It will tend to suppose that because the old education was based on ready-made organization, therefore it suffices to reject the principle of organization *in toto*, instead of striving to discover what it means and how it is to be attained on the basis of experience. We might go through all the points of difference between the new and the old education and reach similar conclusions. When external control is rejected, the problem becomes that of finding the factors of control that are inherent within experience. When external authority is rejected, it does not follow that all authority should be rejected, but rather that there is need to search for a more effective source of authority. Because the older education imposed the knowledge, methods, and the rules of conduct of the mature person upon the young, it does not follow, except upon the basis of the extreme *Either-Or* philosophy, that the knowledge and skill of the mature person has no directive value for the experience of the immature. On the contrary, basing education upon personal experience may mean more multiplied and more intimate contacts between the mature and the immature than ever existed in the traditional school, and consequently more, rather than less, guidance by others. The problem, then, is: how these contacts can be established without violating the principle of learning through personal experience. The solution of this problem requires a well thought-out philosophy of the social factors that operate in the constitution of individual experience.

What is indicated in the foregoing remarks is that the general principles of the new education do not of themselves solve any of the problems of the actual or practical conduct and management of progressive schools. Rather, they set new problems which have to be worked out on the basis of a new philosophy of experience. The problems are not even recognized, to say nothing of being solved, when it is assumed that it suffices to reject the ideas and practices of the old education and then go to the opposite extreme. Yet I am sure that you will appreciate what is meant when I say that many of the newer schools tend to make little or nothing of organized subject-matter of study; to proceed as if any form of direction and guidance by adults were an invasion of individual freedom, and as if the idea that education should be concerned with the present and future meant that acquaintance with the past has little or no role to play in education. . . . I assume that amid all uncertainties there is one permanent frame of reference: namely the organic connection between education and personal experience; or, that the new philosophy of education is committed to some kind of empirical and experimental philosophy. But experience and experiment are not self-explanatory ideas. Rather, their meaning is part of the problem to be explored. To know the meaning of empiricism we need to understand what experience is.

The belief that all genuine education comes about through experience does not mean that all experiences are genuinely or equally educative. Experience and education cannot be directly equated to each other. For some experiences are mis-educative. Any experience is mis-educative that has the effect of arresting or distorting the growth of further experience. An experience may be such as to engender callousness; it may produce lack of sensitivity and of responsiveness. Then the possibilities of having richer experience in the future are restricted. Again, a given experience may increase a person's automatic skill in a particular direction and yet tend to land him in a groove or rut; the effect again is to narrow the field of further experience. An experience may be immediately enjoyable and yet promote the formation of a slack and careless attitude; this attitude then operates to modify the quality of subsequent experiences so as to prevent a person from getting out of them what they have to give. Again, experiences may be so disconnected from one another that, while each is agreeable or even exciting in itself, they are not linked cumulatively to one another. Energy is then dissipated and a person becomes scatterbrained. Each experience may be lively, vivid, and "interesting," and yet their disconnectedness may artificially generate dispersive, disintegrated, centrifugal habits. The consequence of formation of such habits is inability to control future experiences. They are then taken, either by way of enjoyment or of discontent and revolt, just as they come. Under such circumstances, it is idle to talk of self-control. . . .

It is not enough to insist upon the necessity of experience, nor even of activity in experience. Everything depends upon the *quality* of the experience which is had. The quality of any experience has two aspects. There is an immediate aspect of agreeableness or disagreeableness, and there is its influence upon later experiences. The first is obvious and easy to judge. The *effect* of an experience is not borne on its face. It sets a problem to the educator. It is his business to arrange for the kind of experiences which, while they do not repel the student, but rather engage his activities are, nevertheless, more than immediately enjoyable since they promote having desirable future experiences. Just as no man lives or dies to himself, so no experience lives or dies to itself. Wholly independent of desire or intent, every experience lives on in further experiences. Hence the central problem of an education based upon experience is to select the kind of present experiences that live fruitfully and creatively in subsequent experiences. . . .

One consideration stands out clearly when education is conceived in terms of experience. Anything which can be called a study, whether arithmetic, history, geography, or one of the natural sciences, must be derived from materials which at the outset fall within the scope of ordinary life-experience. In this respect the newer education contrasts sharply with procedures which start with facts and truths that are outside the range of the experience of those taught, and which, therefore, have the problem of discovering ways and means of bringing them within experience. Undoubtedly one chief cause for the great success of newer methods in early elementary education has been its observance of the contrary principle.

But finding the material for learning within experience is only the first step. The next step is the progressive development of what is already experienced into a fuller and richer and also more organized form, a form that gradually approximates that in which subject-matter is presented to the skilled, mature person. That this change is possible without departing from the organic connection of education with experience is shown by the fact that this change takes place outside of the school and apart from formal education. The infant, for example, begins with an environment of objects that is very restricted in space and time. That environment steadily expands by the momentum inherent in experience itself without aid from scholastic instruction. As the infant learns to reach, creep, walk, and talk, the intrinsic subject-matter of its experience widens and deepens. It comes into connection with new objects and events which call out new powers, while the exercise of these powers refines and enlarges the content of its experience. Life-space and life-durations are expanded. The environment, the world of experiences, constantly grows larger and, so to speak, thicker. The educator who receives the child at the end of this period has to find ways for doing consciously and deliberately what "nature" accomplishes in the earlier years.

It is hardly necessary to insist upon the first of the two conditions which have been specified. It is a cardinal precept of the newer school of education that the beginning of instruction shall be made with the experience learners already have; that this experience and the capacities that have been developed during its course provide the starting point for all further learning. I am not so sure that the other condition, that of orderly development toward expansion and organization of subject-matter through growth of experience, receives as much attention. Yet the principle of continuity of educative experience requires that equal thought and attention be given to solution of this aspect of the educational problem. Undoubtedly this phase of the problem is more difficult than the other. Those who deal with the pre-school child, with the kindergarten child, and with the boy and girl of the early primary years do not have much difficulty in determining the range of past experience or in finding activities that connect in vital ways with it. With older children both factors of the problem offer increased difficulties to the educator. It is harder to find out the background of the experience of individuals and harder to find out just how the subject-matters already contained in that experience shall be directed so as to lead out to larger and better organized fields.

It is a mistake to suppose that the principle of the leading on of experience to something different is adequately satisfied simply by giving pupils some new experiences any more than it is seeing to it that they have greater skill and ease in dealing with things with which they are already familiar. It is also essential that the new objects and events be related intellectually to those of earlier experiences, and this means that there be some advance made in conscious articulation of facts and ideas. It thus becomes the office of the educator to select those things within the range of existing experience that have the promise and potentiality of presenting new problems which by stimulating new ways of observation and judgment will expand the area of further experience. He must constantly regard what is already won not as a fixed possession but as an agency and instrumentality for opening new fields which make new demands upon existing powers of observation and of intelligent use of memory. Connectedness in growth must be his constant watchword. . . .

That up to the present time the weakest point in progressive schools is in the matter of selection and organization of intellectual subject-matter, is I think, inevitable under the circumstances. It is as inevitable as it is right and proper that they should break loose from the cut and dried material which formed the staple of the old education. In addition, the field of experience is very wide and it varies in its contents from place to place and from time to time. A single course of studies for all progressive schools is out of the question; it would mean abandoning the fundamental principle of connection with life-experiences. Moreover, progressive schools are new. They have had hardly more than a generation in which to develop. A certain amount of uncertainty and of laxity in choice and organization of subject-matter is, therefore, what was to be expected. It is no ground for fundamental criticism or complaint.

It is a ground for legitimate criticism, however, when the ongoing movement of progressive education fails to recognize that the problem of selection and organization of subject-matter for study and learning is fundamental. Improvisation that takes advantage of special occasions prevents teaching and learning from being stereotyped and dead. But the basic material of study cannot be picked up in a cursory manner. Occasions which are not and cannot be foreseen are bound to arise wherever there is intellectual freedom. They should be utilized. But there is a decided difference between using them in the development of a continuing line of activity and trusting to them to provide the chief material of learning.

Unless a given experience leads out into a field previously unfamiliar no problems arise, while problems are the stimulus to thinking. That the conditions found in present experience should be used as sources of problems is a characteristic which differentiates education based upon experience from traditional education. For in the latter, problems were set from outside. Nonetheless, growth depends upon the presence of difficulty to be overcome by the exercise of intelligence. . . .

We are told almost daily and from many sources that it is impossible for human beings to direct their common life intelligently. We are told, on one hand, that the complexity of human relations, domestic and international, and on the other hand, the fact that human beings are so largely creatures of emotion and habit, make impossible large-scale social planning and direction by intelligence. This view would be more credible if any systematic effort, beginning with early education and carried on through the continuous study and learning of the young, had ever been undertaken with a view to making the method of intelligence, exemplified in science, supreme in education. There is nothing in the inherent nature of habit that prevents intelligent method from becoming itself habitual; and there is nothing in the nature of emotion to prevent the development of intense emotional allegiance to the method. . . .

When education is based in theory and practice upon experience, it goes without saying that the organized subject-matter of the adult and the specialist cannot provide the starting point. Nevertheless, it represents the goal toward which education should continuously move. It is hardly necessary to say that one of the most fundamental principles of the scientific organization of knowledge is the principle of cause-and-effect. The way in which this principle is grasped and formulated by the scientific specialist is certainly very different from the way in which it can be approached in the experience of the young. But neither the relation nor grasp of its meaning is foreign to the experience of even the young child. When a child two or three years of age learns not to approach a flame too closely and yet to draw near enough a stove to get its warmth he is grasping and using the causal relation. There is no intelligent activity that does not conform to the requirements of the relation, and it is intelligent in the degree in which it is not only conformed to but consciously borne in mind. . . .

I see at bottom but two alternatives between which education must choose if it is not to drift aimlessly. One of them is expressed by the attempt to induce educators to return to the intellectual methods and ideals that arose centuries before scientific method was developed. The appeal may be temporarily successful in a period when general insecurity, emotional and intellectual as well as economic, is rife. For under these conditions the desire to lean on fixed authority is active. Nevertheless, it is so out of touch with all the conditions of modern life that I believe it is folly to seek salvation in this direction. The other alternative is systematic utilization of scientific method as the pattern and ideal of intelligent exploration and exploitation of the potentialities inherent in experience.

The problem involved comes home with peculiar force to progressive schools. Failure to give constant attention to development of the intellectual content of experiences and to obtain ever-increasing organization of facts and ideas may in the end merely strengthen the tendency toward a reactionary return to intellectual and moral authoritarianism. The present is not the time nor place for a disquisition upon scientific method. But certain features of it are so closely connected with any educational scheme based upon experience that they should be noted.

In the first place, the experimental method of science attaches more importance, not less, to ideas as ideas than do other methods. There is no such thing as experiment in the scientific sense unless action is directed by some leading idea. The fact that the ideas employed are hypotheses, not final truths, is the reason why ideas are more jealously guarded and tested in science than anywhere else. The moment they are taken to be first truths in themselves there ceases to be any reason for scrupulous examination of them. As fixed truths they must be accepted and that is the end of the matter. But as hypotheses, they must be continuously tested and revised, a requirement that demands they be accurately formulated.

In the second place, ideas or hypotheses are tested by the consequences which they produce when they are acted upon. This fact means that the consequences of action must be carefully and discriminatingly observed. Activity that is not checked by observation of what follows from it may be temporarily enjoyed. But intellectually it leads nowhere. It does not provide knowledge about the situations in which action occurs nor does it lead to clarification and expansion of ideas.

In the third place, the method of intelligence manifested in the experimental method demands keeping track of ideas, activities, and observed consequences. Keeping track is a matter of reflective review and summarizing, in which there is both discrimination and record of the significant features of a developing experience. To reflect is to look back over what has been done so as to extract the net meanings which are the capital stock for intelligent dealing with further experiences. It is the heart of intellectual organization and of the disciplined mind. . . .

Suggested Readings

Bode, Boyd A.: *How We Learn*. Boston: D. C. Heath and Company, 1940.

Brameld, Theodore: *Patterns of Educational Philosophy*. New York: World Book Company, 1950.

Brubacher, John S.: *Modern Philosophies of Education*. New York: McGraw-Hill Book Company, 1950.

Childs, John L.: *Education and Morals*. New York: Appleton-Century-Crofts, 1950.

————: *Education and the Philosophy of Experimentalism*. New York: Appleton-Century-Crofts, 1938.

Dewey, John: *A Common Faith*. New Haven, Conn.: Yale University Press, 1934.

————: *Democracy and Education*. New York: The Macmillan Company, 1916.

————: *Education Today*. New York: G. P. Putnam's Sons, 1940.

————: *Experience and Education*. New York: The Macmillan Company, 1938.

————: *Experience and Nature*. Chicago: The Open Court Publishing Company, 1925.

————: *Human Nature and Conduct*. New York: Henry Holt and Company, 1922.

————: *Logic, the Theory of Inquiry*. New York: Henry Holt and Company, 1938.

————: *Reconstruction in Philosophy*. New York: Henry Holt and Company, 1920.

————: *School and Society*. Chicago: University of Chicago Press, 1900.

James, William: *Pragmatism*. New York: Longmans, Green & Co., 1907.

Kilpatrick, William H.: *Philosophy of Education*. New York: The Macmillan Company, 1951.

National Society for the Study of Education: *Fifty-fourth Yearbook, Part I. Modern Philosophies and Education*. Chicago: University of Chicago Press, 1955.

Park, Joe, ed.: *Selected Readings in the Philosophy of Education*. New York: The Macmillan Company, 1958.

Schneider, Herbert W.: *A History of American Philosophy*. New York: Columbia University Press, 1946.

The
American Teacher

*There is no office higher than that of a teacher of
youth; for there is nothing on earth so precious as
the mind, soul, character of the child. No office
should be regarded with greater respect. The first
minds in the community should be encouraged to
assume it. Parents should do all but impoverish
themselves, to induce such to become the guardians
and guides of their children. To this good, all their
show and luxury should be sacrificed. Here they
should be lavish, whilst they straiten themselves in
every thing else. They should wear the cheapest
clothes, live on the plainest food, if they can in no
other way secure to their families the best instruction. They should have no anxiety to accumulate
property for their children, provided they can place
them under influences which will awaken their faculties, inspire them with pure and high principles, and
fit them to bear a manly, useful, and honorable part
in the world. No language can express the cruelty or
folly of that economy, which, to leave a fortune to a
child, starves his intellect, impoverishes his heart.*

WILLIAM ELLERY CHANNING, 1833

CHAPTER 17

HISTORY OF THE TEACHING PROFESSION IN AMERICA

THE HISTORY OF THE TEACHING PROFESSION IN AMERICA HAS OF necessity paralleled the development of the American school system and of American society. In the colonial period there were no teacher training institutions as such and no professional organizations. In the seventeenth century formal education was limited, for most persons, to the primary grades and, for a small percentage, to the Latin grammar schools and Harvard College. Through the eighteenth century the situation improved as more schools on all levels were established. Even so, only a small percentage of persons went beyond the primary grades and many individuals received no formal schooling at all. The schools that did exist, especially in the rural areas, were very poor with few books and other materials of instruction, and with students ranging in age from five to fifteen or older. Under these conditions the relatively low standards characteristic of the teaching profession in colonial America are understandable.

The Colonial Teacher

THE evidence from the colonial period suggests that teachers varied greatly in educational background. Some were college graduates, some were graduates of Latin grammar schools, and some had evidently received very little formal schooling and were barely able to read and write. Those who were educated in the colleges, whether in America or in England, had received the standard training in Latin, Greek, and religion. These men would be hired to teach in the Latin grammar schools and later the academies, and in the colleges. Generally the less formal education a teacher had, the lower the grade level he taught, and his salary and social status varied accordingly. Until Franklin's Academy was established in 1750, there were no teacher training institutions in the colonies and even in this institution little attention was given to teaching as such.

During the colonial period there were three basic qualifications for teaching. First, the individual had to have an adequate academic background. If he were applying for a position in a Latin grammar school, he obviously had to know Latin and Greek and this generally meant, especially in the better schools, that he had attended college. In the elementary schools a knowledge of reading, writing, arithmetic, and religion was necessary. The second qualification was religious orthodoxy and good moral character. This qualification was applied in all of the colonies since the schools were controlled either directly or indirectly by the various religious groups. This requirement is understandable when it is recalled, for example, that in Massachusetts the chief function of the schools was to teach the principles of religion and the reason for teaching reading was to enable the individual to read the Bible. The third qualification was loyalty to the government. This requirement has been applied to almost every teacher since the beginning of the history of education and is still being applied today in the United States and elsewhere. Thus, although the issue of whether loyalty oaths should be required of teachers has been one of the most controversial issues before American education since World War II, there is no question of the necessity for having "loyal" teachers. The issue is whether teachers, in order to prove their loyalty, should be required to take an oath and, to some extent, what the nature of the oath should be.

An example of the nature of the qualifications for teaching in the Colonial period is contained in a document issued by the Society for the Propagation of the Gospel in Foreign Parts in 1711. This English society was very active in establishing schools and supporting education in the eighteenth century and apparently made a real effort to get good teachers for its schools. The qualifications for teachers in the Society were as follows:

That no person be admitted as Schoolmaster till he bring Certificates of the following particulars
1. his age
2. his condition of life whether single or mary'd
3. his temper
4. his prudence
5. his learning
6. his sober and pious conversation
7. his Zeal and the Xtian Religion and diligence in his calling
8. his affection to the present government

9. his conformity to the doctrine and discipline of the Church of England [1]

Teachers were appointed in colonial America in several different ways. In New England and in Pennsylvania among the Quakers teachers were generally hired by committees appointed for that purpose, although often the final decision on hiring would involve both election in the town meeting and approval by the local minister. Teachers in the English schools in New York and Virginia were often appointed and paid by the Society for the Propagation of the Gospel in Foreign Parts. The procedure for hiring was set forth in the document quoted above. It stated that:

> . . . no person Shall be employ'd as a Schoolmaster by the Society till he has been tryed and approved by three members appointed by the Society or Committee who Shall testify by word or writing his ability to teach reading, writing and the Catechism of the Church of England and Such exposition thereof as the Society Shall order.[2]

Where tutors were employed, for example on the large plantations in the south, the appointment was a matter of personal selection by the owner.

The problem of certification was dealt with, when it was dealt with, in a more direct and personal way than it is today. In most instances the teacher was approved by some members of the community without the formality of a license. There are indications that from time to time attempts were made to force teachers to obtain a license either from the Bishop of London (Virginia), from the Royal Governors, from local magistrates, or from the Colonial Assemblies. It is impossible to determine how successful these more or less official efforts at certification were, but there is evidence that some difficulty was encountered in enforcing the license requirements. There is also evidence that the purpose of these early attempts at "certification" was not only (as today) to insure academic standards but also to insure religious and political orthodoxy in the teacher.

With very few exceptions the teachers in colonial America were men. When women did teach, it was in the elementary schools and most often in the dame school. The reasons for this are not hard to find. Since a woman's place was in the home, and the professions, e.g., the ministry, law, medicine, etc., were not open to her, there was no need for her to be educated. It was not until the Revolutionary War that girls were admitted to anything equivalent to a secondary school or college. Also, the teacher's job often included extra duties which

[1] Quoted in E. W. Knight and C. L. Hall, *Readings in American Educational History* (New York: Appleton-Century-Crofts, 1951), p. 28.
[2] *Ibid.*

could not be handled easily by women. For example, Johannes von Eckkellen, teacher in Flatbush, Long Island, in 1682, was expected to perform the following tasks in addition to his teaching:

> He shall be chorister of the church, keep the church clean, ring the bell three times before the people assemble, and read a chapter of the Bible in the church between the second and third ringing, he shall read the Ten Commandments and the twelve articles of our faith, and then set the psalm. In the afternoon, after the third ringing of the bell, he shall read a short chapter or one of the psalms of David, as the congregation are assembling; afterwards he shall again sing a psalm or hymn.
>
> When the minister shall preach at Brooklyn or Utrecht, he shall be bound to read twice before the congregation, from the book used for the purpose. He shall hear the children recite the questions and answers out of the catechism on Sunday, and instruct them therein.
>
> He shall provide a basin of water for the administration of holy baptism and furnish the minister with the name of the child to be baptized. He shall furnish bread and wine for the communion, at the charge of the church. He shall also serve as messenger for the consistory.
>
> He shall give the funeral invitations, dig the graves, and toll the bell. . . .[3]

When it is realized that many schools were in session from 7 a.m. to 5 p.m. in the summer and 8 a.m. to 4 p.m. in the winter and that children were released from school only for the major holidays, it is not difficult to see why teaching school was a man's job. Nevertheless, there were women teachers, especially in Pennsylvania among the Quakers where the discrimination against them was not as strong, but also in other areas including the south. Where women were employed as "schooldames" they received less pay, which probably was an incentive for hiring them when they were available.

The salaries of the colonial teachers varied, as they do today, with the qualifications of the teacher, the level of his teaching, and the locale. In the larger towns such as Boston, New York, Philadelphia, and Charleston, grammar school teachers received as much as one hundred pounds per year while others in smaller towns received as little as ten pounds annually. Teachers in colleges and grammar schools were paid the highest salaries, while elementary teachers were paid the lowest. Frequently the salaries, especially in the rural areas, were paid in kind, i.e., corn, wheat, or beaver skins, and payments were usually on a semi-

[3] Quoted in W. S. Elsbree, *The American Teacher* (New York: American Book Company, 1939), pp. 63-4.

annual or a quarterly basis. In some instances, in addition to the salary, dwellings with a few acres of ground were provided. In others, provisions for room and board were a part of the contract. It was a standard practice for teachers to supplement their income by receiving tuition payments from students. In comparing the salaries of teachers to other workers in the colonies, Elsbree states that:

> . . . it appears that colonial teachers were probably paid higher wages than common laborers in most sections of the country; that the total yearly wages of teachers, including perquisites, were not greatly different from those of skilled carpenters, bricklayers, and other craftsmen; that clergymen usually received two or three times as much salary as teachers; and that physicians and lawyers also fared better than pedagogues.[4]

Apparently the majority of teachers in the colonial period regarded teaching as a temporary position rather than a life career although many teachers were permanent members of the profession. For example, Ezekiel Cheever, who was one of the most well-known and respected teachers, taught for some fifty years, thirty-seven of which were in the Boston Latin Grammar School. For the most part, however, teaching was a temporary expedient until other arrangements could be worked out. Often teachers in the grammar schools used teaching as a steppingstone to the ministry. Often it was a means of livelihood while the individual studied law or saved enough money to buy a farm or go into business. The result was that finding teachers and keeping them was a real problem. One solution was to use indentured servants and the following advertisement, which appeared in a Baltimore newspaper in 1786, indicates that a supply of such schoolmasters was available. The advertisement reads as follows:

Men and Women Servants
Just Arrived
In the Ship Paca, Robert Caulfield, Master, in five Weeks from Belfast and Cork, a number of healthy men and Women SERVANTS.
Among them are several valuable tradesmen, viz.
Carpenters, Shoemakers, Coopers, Blacksmiths, Staymakers, Bookbinders, Clothiers, Diers, Butchers, Schoolmasters, Millwrights, and Labourers.
Their indentures are to be disposed of by the Subscribers. Baltimore, May 29, 1786

BROWN, and MARIS,
WILLIAM WILSON.[5]

[4] *Ibid.*, p. 97.
[5] Quoted in Knight and Hall, *op. cit.*, p. 15.

There is also evidence that these men frequently jumped bail as the following advertisement which appeared in the *Pennsylvania Gazette,* February 4, 1735, indicates:

> Run away on the 28th of last month, from his bail, Samuel Jaques, and James Marshall, of Elizabeth town, Essex county, in East New-Jersey, one Edward Kite, an English man, about 30 years of age, of middle stature, brown complexion, has a fresh colour, black eyes, and has a bold look: Had on when he went away an old green jacket, an old bob wig, and a speckled shirt. He had some time ago broke one of his Legs, which by observing, will be found to be a little crooked, and is somewhat thicker than the other. He is a cooper by trade, but has lately taught school, and writes a good round hand. Whoever takes up and secures said Edward Kite, so as his bail may have him again, shall have Four Pounds reward, and reasonable Charges, paid by
>
> SAMUEL JAQUES, and JAMES MARSHALL
>
> N.B. All masters of vessels, and others, are forbid to harbour or carry him off, at their peril.[6]

From all that has been said it is not difficult to understand the instability of the teaching profession in early America. To receive a decent salary and to achieve social status as a teacher in a community a man had to be well educated. If he were well educated the ministry or law was more lucrative and carried more prestige. If he were poorly educated, he could probably do better on his own in rich, expansive America. At best he had a difficult, arduous job. At worst he was poorly paid and his conditions of work, especially outside of the towns, were anything but pleasant.

The Beginning of Teacher Education

IN 1750 Franklin's Academy was established primarily to provide a more functional type of secondary school than the Latin grammar school, but also to provide a school to prepare teachers for the common schools. The population of the country increased gradually during the eighteenth century and the colonies were becoming more prosperous and more complex. The result was that more schools were being established on all levels and the need for teachers was increasing. From 1750 on, many academies were established and, although many were closed during the war, their numbers increased rapidly once the treaty of peace was signed. For the better part of the first half of the nineteenth century

---

[6] Quoted in E. P. Cubberley, *Readings in Public Education in the United States* (Boston: Houghton Mifflin Company, 1934), p. 70.

the academy was the institution in which most teachers received their formal education. These schools were privately controlled but often received public funds which were sometimes given expressly to subsidize the preparation of teachers.

There was evidently a great deal of dissatisfaction with the academy as a teacher training institution. It was charged that not enough attention was being given to teaching and that prospective teachers were receiving the same education as other students. It was further criticized on the ground that little was done to teach students how to teach and no model or practice schools were available for apprentice teaching. For a time while the monitorial schools were in vogue, several demonstration schools in which methods were taught were established, and some individuals thought these institutions were an answer to the problem. But teachers schooled in the monitorial methods were only valuable if the monitorial schools themselves were accepted and established, and the record shows that they were not.

In the early 1820's the need for some kind of teacher training institution began to be felt, and the story of the effort that was made, the foresight that was shown, and the success that was achieved in the forty years preceding the Civil War rivals the story of the establishment of the common school itself as an example of humanitarian democracy at its best. Fortunately the leaders in the movement had the advantage of the work of Pestalozzi, and of the Prussians who established normal schools between 1810 and 1820. In the period between 1825 and 1845 many Americans, including such educational leaders as Henry Barnard and Calvin Stowe, studied the European schools at first hand. Barnard traveled in Europe in the late thirties and upon his return wrote lengthy accounts of the teacher training institutions of most of the countries of Europe.

The Normal School

According to Henry Barnard the movement for the establishment of special schools for the purpose of preparing teachers began with the separate but almost simultaneous publication of a series of articles on education in the newspapers of Hartford and Boston in 1825. The Hartford articles were written by Reverend Thomas H. Gallaudet and included one entitled "Plan of a Seminary for the Education of Instructors of Youth." The Boston articles were written by James G. Carter and included one entitled "Outline of an Institution for the Education of Teachers." These two essays were reprinted and circulated widely in New England and started a chain reaction that resulted in having the problem of teacher education discussed widely in newspapers and periodicals and had the effect of bringing the issue before the literate public. Because it was so widely read and quoted, and because it reflects the thinking of the educational leaders of the time, parts of James Carter's essay are included here. As will be seen, the basic elements of his outline will coincide with the characteristics of the teacher education institutions that were established all over the country throughout the nineteenth century. The article is taken from a volume prepared by Henry Barnard entitled *Normal Schools and Other Institutions, Agencies, and Means Designed for the Professional Education of Teachers* published in 1851.

JAMES G. CARTER

FROM

"Outline of an Institution for the Education of Teachers" [7]

It will do but little good for the Legislature of the State to make large appropriations directly for the support of the schools, till a judicious expenditure of them can be insured. And in order to do this, we must have skillful teachers at hand. It will do but little good to class the children till we have instructors properly prepared to take charge of the classes. It will do absolutely no good to constitute an independent tribunal to decide on the qualification of teachers while they have not had the opportunities necessary for coming up to the proper standard. And it will do no good to overlook and report upon their success, when we know beforehand that they have not the means of success. It would be beginning wrong, too, to build houses and to tell your young and inexperienced instructors to teach this or to teach that subject, however desirable a knowledge of such subjects might be, while it is obvious that they cannot know how, properly, to teach any subject. The *science of teaching*—for it must be made a science—is first in the order of nature, to be inculcated. And it is to this point that the public attention must first be turned, to effect any essential improvement.

And here let me remark upon a distinction in the qualifications of teachers, which has never been practically made; though it seems astonishing that it has so long escaped notice. I allude to the distinction between the possession of knowledge, and the ability to communicate it to other minds. When we are looking for a teacher, we inquire how much he knows, not how much he can communicate; as if the latter qualification were of no consequence to us. Now it seems to me that

[7] James G. Carter, *Outline of an Institution for the Education of Teachers.* As quoted in Henry Barnard, *Normal Schools and Other Institutions, Agencies, and Means Designed for the Professional Education of Teachers* (Hartford: Case, Tiffany & Co., 1851), I, pp. 91–9.

parents and children, to say the least, are as much interested in the latter qualification of their instructor as in the former.

Though a teacher cannot communicate more knowledge than he possesses, yet he may possess much, and still be able to impart but little. And the knowledge of Sir Isaac Newton could be of but trifling use to a school, while it was locked up safely in the head of a country schoolmaster. So far as the object of a school or of instruction, therefore, is the acquisition of knowledge, novel as the opinion may seem, it does appear to me that both parents and pupils are even more interested in the part of their teacher's knowledge which they will be likely to get, than in the part which they certainly cannot get.

One great object in the education of teachers which it is so desirable on every account to attain, is to establish an intelligible language of communication between the instructor and his pupil, and enable the former to open his head and his heart, and infuse into the other some of the thoughts and feelings which lie hid there. *Instructors and pupils do not understand each other.* They do not speak the same language. They may use the same words; but this can hardly be called the same language, while they attach to them such very different meanings. We must either, by some magic or supernatural power, bring children at once to comprehend all our abstract and difficult terms, or our teachers must unlearn themselves, and come down to the comprehension of children. One of these alternatives is only difficult, while the other is impossible.

The direct, careful preparation of instructors for the profession of teaching, must surmount this difficulty; and I doubt if there be any other way in which it can be surmounted. When instructors understand their profession, that is, in a word, when they understand the philosophy of the infant mind, what powers are earliest developed, and what studies are best adapted to their development, then it will be time to lay out and subdivide their work into an energetic system of public instruction. Till this step toward a reform, which is preliminary in its very nature, be taken, every other measure must be adopted in the dark; and therefore, be liable to fail utterly of its intended result. Houses, and funds, and books are all, indeed, important; but they are only the means of enabling the minds of the teachers to act upon the minds of the pupils. And they must, inevitably, fail of their happiest effects, till the minds of the teachers have been prepared to act upon those of their pupils to the greatest advantage.

If, then, the first step toward a reform in our system of popular education be the scientific preparation of teachers for the free schools, our next inquiry becomes, How can we soonest and most perfectly achieve an object on every account so desirable? The ready and obvious answer is, establish an institution for the very purpose. To my mind, this seems to be the only measure which will insure to the public the attainment of the object. It will be called a new project. Be it so. The concession does not prove that the project is a bad one, or a visionary, or an impracticable one. Our ancestors ventured to do what the world had never done before, in so perfect a manner, when they established the free schools. Let us also do what they have never so well done yet, and establish an institution for the exclusive purpose of preparing instructors for them. This is only a second part, a development or consummation of the plan of our fathers. They foresaw the effect of universal intelligence upon national virtue and happiness; and they projected the means of securing to themselves and to us universal education. They wisely did a new thing under the sun. It has proved to be a good thing. We now enjoy the results of their labors, and we are sensible of the enjoyment. Their posterity have praised them, loudly praised them, for the wisdom of their efforts. Let us, then, with hints from them, project and accomplish another new thing, and confer as great a blessing on those who may come after us. Let us finish the work of our fathers, in regard to popular education, and give to it its full effect. Let us double, for we easily may, the happy influences of an institution which has already attracted so much notice from every part of our country, and drawn after it so many imitations, and send it, thus improved, down to posterity for their admiration.

If a seminary for the purpose of educating teachers scientifically be essential in order to give the greatest efficacy to our system of popular education, then, in the progress of the discussion, the three following questions arise in the order in which they are stated. By whom should the proposed institution be established? What would be its leading features? And what would be some of the peculiar advantages to the public which would result from it? To answer these several questions at length would require a book; while I have, at present, only leisure to prepare one or two newspaper essays. A few hints, therefore, upon the above three topics are all that I dare profess to give, and more than I fear I can give, either to my own satisfaction or that of those readers who may have become interested in the subject.

The institution, from its peculiar purpose, must necessarily be both literary and scientific in its character. And although, with its design constantly in view, we could not reasonably expect it to add, directly, much to the stock of what is now called literature, or to enlarge much the boundaries of what is now called science, yet, from the very nature of the subject to which it would be devoted, and upon which it would be employed, it must in its progress create a kind of literature of its own, and open a new science somewhat peculiar to itself—the science of the development of the infant mind, and the science of communicating knowledge from one mind to another while in a different stage of maturity. The tendency of the inquiries which must be carried on, and the discoveries which would be constantly made, in a seminary for this new purpose, would be to give efficacy to the pursuits of other literary and scientific institutions. Its influence, therefore, though indirect, would be not the less powerful upon the cause of literature and the sciences generally. These remarks may seem to anticipate another part of my subject; but they are introduced here to show that a seminary for the education of teachers would stand, at least, on as favorable a footing in relation to the public, as other literary and scientific institutions. It seems now to be believed that the Legislature of the State are the rightful proprietors of all public institutions for the diffusion of knowledge. And if they are of any, they certainly ought to be of one for such a purpose. Because there are none in which the public would be more deeply interested. There are none which would tend so much to diffuse knowledge among the whole mass of the people. And this, as has been before remarked, is a solemn duty enjoined upon our government by the constitution under which they are organized, and from which they derive their authority. Besides, it is the first impulse of every government, operating as quickly and steadily as instinct, to provide for its own preservation. And it seems to be conceded on all hands, by the friends as well as the enemies of freedom, that a government like our own can only exist among a people generally enlightened; the only question as to the permanency of free institutions being, whether it be possible to make and to keep the whole population of a nation so well educated as the existence of such institutions supposes and requires. . . .

An institution for the education of teachers, as has been before intimated, would form a part, and a very important part, of the free-school system. It would be, moreover, precisely that portion of the system which should be under the direction of the State, whether the others are or not. Because we should thus secure at once, a uniform, intelligent, and independent tribunal for decision on the qualifications of teachers. Because we should thus relieve the clergy of an invidious task, and insure to the public competent teachers, if such could be found or prepared. An institution for this purpose would become, by its influence on society and particularly on the young, an engine to sway the public sentiment, the public morals, and the public religion, more powerful than any other in the possession of government. It should, therefore, be responsible immediately to them. And they should carefully overlook it, and prevent its being perverted to other purposes, directly or indirectly, than those for which it is designed. It should be emphatically the State's institution. And its results would soon make it the State's favorite and pride, among other literary and scientific institutions. The Legislature of the State, should, therefore, establish and build it up, without waiting for individuals, at great private sacrifices, to accomplish the work. Such would be the influence of an institution for the education of teachers; and such is the growing conviction of the strength of early associations and habits, that it cannot be long before the work will be begun in some form. If it be not undertaken by the public and for public purposes, it will be undertaken by individuals for private purposes. . . .

The next question, mentioned above, as arising in the progress of this discussion, was, what would be the leading features of an institution for the education of teachers. If the institution were to be founded by the State, upon a large scale, the following parts would seem to be obviously essential.

1. An appropriate library, with a philosophical apparatus. 2. A principal and assistant professor in the different departments. 3. A school for children of different ages, embracing both those desiring a general education, and those designed particularly for teachers. 4. A Board of Commissioners, or an enlightened body of men representing the interests and the wishes of the public. . . .

2. The institution should have its principal and its assistant professors. The government and instruction of a seminary for the education of teachers would be among the most responsible situations which could be assigned to men in literary or scientific pursuits. As many of the objects of the institution would be new, so the duties of its instructors would also be new. No commanding minds have gone before precisely in the proposed course, and struck out a path which others may easily follow. There are no *rules* laid down for the direction of those who will not think upon, or who cannot understand the subject. Men must, therefore, be brought to the task who have the ability to observe accurately and to discriminate nicely. They must also collect the results of what experience they can from books and from others, in order to enable themselves to form some general principles for the direction of their pupils, who will go abroad to carry their improvements to others. It is not supposed for a moment that all who may receive instruction at the proposed institution with the intention of becoming teachers, will necessarily be made thereby adepts in the science, any more than it is believed that all who happen to reside four years within the walls of a college are necessarily made expert in the mysteries of syllogism and the calculus. But having seen correct general principles of education successfully reduced to practice, they may, at least, become *artists* in the profession, and be able to teach pretty well upon a system, the philosophy of which they cannot thoroughly comprehend.

3. A school of children and youth of different ages and pursuing different branches of study would form an essential part of the institution. . . .

After the young candidate for an instructor, therefore, has acquired sufficient knowledge for directing those exercises and teaching those branches which he wishes to profess, he must then begin his labors under the scrutinizing eyes of one who will note his mistakes of government and faults of instruction, and correct them. . . .

4. The fourth branch, which I mentioned above as constituting an important part of an institution for the education of teachers, was a Board of Commissioners. Although they would, probably, have little to do with the immediate government and instruction of the institution, they would be valuable to it by representing the wishes of the community, and by bringing it more perfectly in contact with the public interests. . . .

One-third of our whole population are now at that period of life when their principles and characters are rapidly forming. Habits, both moral and intellectual, are taking their direction, and acquiring the strength of age. In all this, the schools must have a deep influence. Both the degree and the kind of influence are, to a certain extent, within our control, and consequently depend upon our efforts. In twenty years, and surely twenty years are not beyond the ken of a tolerably clear-sighted politician, this part of our population will succeed to most of the responsible places and relations of their fathers. They must receive all that we have to leave for them. They must take our names, and attach to them honor or infamy. They must possess our fortunes, to preserve or disperse them. And they must inherit our free institutions, to improve, pervert, or destroy them. Here, then, are the strongest political motives, as well as paternal affection, urging upon us attention to all the means of forming correctly the characters of those who are to receive from us our choicest blessings. And what means within our control can be devised more efficient for this purpose, than those primary seminaries for instruction, where the mass of the people must receive several years of their education? Find, if they are to be found, or create, if they are not now to be found, a class of teachers *well skilled* in their profession, and put them into all our free schools. What an effect would soon be produced in their condition! And what a renovating influence these same schools would soon have upon the character of the whole people who have access to them!

The challenge thrown down by James Carter was picked up by Horace Mann, Henry Barnard, Calvin Stowe, William Ellery Channing, Governor Clinton, and many others. Carter himself presented a memorial to the Massachusetts legislature in 1827 asking for the establishment of a seminary for the education of teachers with a model school attached, but the bill making an appropriation was defeated by one vote. In 1830 the American Institute of Instruction was organized in

Boston by a group of educators and Carter was able to get the organization to support the normal school idea. In the thirties Channing wrote articles in favor of the plan while Mann in Massachusetts and Barnard in Connecticut wrote plea after plea to the legislatures of their respective states. In the west Calvin Stowe kept the issue before the public in a speech in Cincinnati in 1837. His proposals resembled Carter's of a decade earlier but on some points he was more specific than Carter had been. His plan was included by Barnard in his volume mentioned above.

CALVIN STOWE

FROM

A Speech in Cincinnati, 1837 [8]

Having devoted some attention to this subject, and having spent considerable time in examining institutions of the kind already established in Europe, I propose in this paper to exhibit the result of my investigations. In exhibiting this result, I have thought proper to draw out, somewhat in detail, what I suppose would be the best plan, on the whole, without expecting that all parts of the plan, in the present state of education in our country, will be carried into immediate execution. I propose what I think ought to be aimed at, and what, I doubt not, will ultimately be attained, if the spirit which is now awake on the subject be not suffered again to sleep.

The sum of what I propose is contained in the six following propositions, namely:

I. The interests of popular education in each State demand the establishment, at the seat of government, and under the patronage of the legislature, of a NORMAL SCHOOL, that is, a *Teachers' Seminary and Model-school,* for the instruction and practice of teachers in the science of education and the art of teaching.

II. Pupils should not be received into the Teachers' Seminary under sixteen years of age, nor until they are well versed in all the branches usually taught in common schools.

III. The model-school should comprise the various classes of children usually admitted to the common schools, and should be subject to the same general discipline and course of study.

IV. The course of instruction in the Teachers' Seminary should include three years, and the pupils be divided into three classes, accordingly.

V. The senior classes in the Teachers' Seminary should be employed,

[8] Quoted in Henry Barnard, *Normal Schools and Other Institutions, Agencies, and Means Designed for the Professional Education of Teachers* (Hartford: Case, Tiffany & Co., 1851), I, 123–5.

under the immediate instruction of their professors, as instructors in the model-school.

VI. The course of instruction in the Teachers' Seminary should comprise lectures and recitations on the following topics, together with such others as further observation and experience may show to be necessary.

1. A thorough, scientific, and demonstrative study of all the branches to be taught in the common schools, with directions at every step as to the best method of inculcating each lesson upon children of different dispositions and capacities, and various intellectual habits.

2. The philosophy of mind, particularly in reference to its susceptibility of receiving impressions from mind.

3. The peculiarities of intellectual and moral development in children, as modified by sex, parental character, wealth or poverty, city or country, family government, indulgent or severe, fickle or steady, &c., &c.

4. The science of education in general, and full illustrations of the difference between education and mere instruction.

5. The art of teaching.

6. The art of governing children, with special reference to imparting and keeping alive a feeling of love for children.

7. History of education, including an accurate outline of the educational systems of different ages and nations, the circumstances which gave rise to them, the principles on which they were founded, the ends which they aimed to accomplish, their successes and failures, their permanency and changes, how far they influenced individual and national character, how far any of them might have originated in premeditated plan on the part of their founders, whether they secured the intelligence, virtue, and happiness of the people, or otherwise, with the causes, &c.

8. The rules of health, and the laws of physical development.

9. Dignity and importance of the teacher's office.

10. Special religious obligations of teachers in respect to benevolent devotedness to the intellectual and moral welfare of society, habits of entire self-control, purity of mind, elevation of character, &c.

11. The influence which the school should exert on civilization and the progress of society.

12. The elements of Latin, together with the German, French, and Spanish languages.

Despite the impressive efforts of these men progress of the normal schools was slow. The private academies, which were training and continued to train most of the teachers until the Civil War, opposed the movement for obvious reasons, and their opposition was instrumental in delaying the establishment of special teacher-training institutions in many states. Just as important, perhaps, was the attitude inherited from the colonial period that teaching in the common schools could be entrusted to anyone of good character who had a knowledge of the fundamentals. Another factor was the spread at this time of the Jacksonian idea that any citizen, because he was a citizen, had the qualifications for any public office. This fact, plus the emphasis upon economy, was largely responsible for the increasing use of young, unskilled women in the schools.[9]

A few private preparatory schools had been established in the 1820's. The first was the seminary with a model-school attached established by Samuel R. Hall at Concord, Vermont, in 1823. A few years later Hall was asked to direct a teacher education program at Phillips Academy at Andover. In 1827 James Carter, with the aid of a grant of land and the use of an academy building from the city of Lancaster, Massachusetts, established a *public* teachers' seminary but the plan was shortlived because, according to Barnard, the people of Lancaster:

> did not comprehend the full and ultimate public benefits of the new institution, began to manifest opposition, and threw such obstacles in his way, that he was obliged to abandon his project as a public enterprize after having embarrassed himself by his pecuniary outlays for buildings and teachers.[10]

These schools, which compared in grade level and curriculum to the academies, offered work in teaching methods and classroom management. These ventures were apparently not too successful. Hall remarked in a speech in 1833 that "there is not in our whole country one seminary where the educator of children can be thoroughly qualified for his important work." [11] But these early efforts were of great importance since they got the normal school movement started and they had some effect on the academies where, despite the establishment of the normal schools between 1839 and 1860, many common-school teachers were trained.

It was in 1839, fourteen years after Carter's proposal was made, that the first public normal school was established in America. As in so many other ways it was Massachusetts, with Horace Mann leading the fight, that took the honors. Mann had induced a friend to contribute $10,000 for the support of a new institution but the money was offered on condition that the state would appropriate an equal amount. After a bitter struggle the effort was successful and the new school was established at Lexington. A few months later a second normal school was opened at Barre, followed by a third a year later at Bridgewater, Massachusetts. From this point the normal school idea spread until by 1900

[9] R. F. Butts and L. A. Cremin, A *History of Education in American Culture* (New York: Henry Holt and Company, 1953), pp. 283–4.
[10] Barnard, *op. cit.*, p. 101.
[11] Quoted in Elsbree, *op. cit.*, p. 145.

all of the forty-five states in the Union had established normal schools.

In no state was the battle won without a struggle. In Connecticut, Henry Barnard, although he recommended the establishment of normal schools every year in his position as State Superintendent of Schools, did not succeed in having one established until 1849 in the town of New Britain. In Missouri the chief educational official in the state (at times the Secretary of State and at times the Superintendent of Schools) urged the legislature to establish normal schools in official reports every year from 1840 to 1870 (excluding the Civil War years) before they were finally successful. During this interval other individuals and groups, including several of the governors of the state, joined in support of the measure. Indeed, in 1866 the Missouri State Teachers Association under the leadership of William Torrey Harris sent a memorial to the legislature urging the creation of normal schools and stating the reasons for their action. This memorial is included below because it provides valuable insight into the teacher situation immediately following the Civil War and because the situation in Missouri was typical of that in the other states. It also shows that professional teacher organizations were beginning to make themselves heard in the struggle for better schools.

Memorial of the Missouri State Teachers' Association to the General Assembly, for the Establishment of a Normal School [12]

The teachers of the State of Missouri, through the undersigned committee, appointed for the purpose at the convention held in St. Louis, in June, 1866, beg leave to present their memorial, praying your honorable body to consider the expediency of establishing, at some convenient locality, a normal school, for the sole purpose of training teachers of both sexes in what pertains to their profession. And, in presenting this memorial, they beg leave to state the reasons which impel them to offer this request. They feel confident that nothing need be said upon the paramount importance of a system of public schools in a commonwealth like our own; and that anything which can be shown to be of essential aid in furthering the efficiency of such a system will meet with your hearty approval. And they feel the more assured of this when they remember the thorough going legislation of last year, which conceived and adopted the present school law of the state. They would respectfully call attention to the following considerations:

I

That there is a manifest lack of efficient teachers to supply the present and increasing demand in this state; this is evident from the fact that the supply comes in large measure, from other states.

[12] Quoted in E. M. Violette, *History of the First District State Normal School, Kirksville, Missouri* (Kirksville, Mo.: Journal Printing Company, 1905), pp. 19–22.

II

That there is a lack of institutions which give the special training requisite to fit the abundant native talent of the state for the responsible calling of teachers. Notwithstanding the excellence of this native element, which has been shown by the marked success it has achieved after proper training, yet the professional school is wanting, and the want is more keenly felt, because the dearth of higher institutions in the state extends even to seminaries and colleges, although these can give only one side of the education necessary to a teacher—namely the general culture.

III

That the economy is very obvious. If teachers were educated and trained in this state, better schools with less cost would result. For if the best talent is drawn here from other states, it must be because higher salaries are paid here than at home. That Missouri must be content with a poorer grade of teachers, at the same cost that other states pay for better ones, or else increase a disproportionate expense for the right quality. By a small comparative outlay, a normal school may be established that will save this extra cost.

IV

The most enlightened governments of Europe, consider the normal school as an essential appendage to the state. Prussia, since 1735, has increased her normal schools to fifty. France has established ninety since 1810; England has forty, and Switzerland, thirteen, while the system has been adopted in Saxony, Hanover, Bavaria, Sardinia, Greece, and Belgium.

The movement extended to this country during the first quarter of the present century, and has resulted in establishing such schools in Massachusetts, New York, Connecticut, Rhode Island, Michigan, South Carolina, New Jersey, Pennsylvania, Illinois, Minnesota, Maine, and Wisconsin, as State Institutions; while the larger cities, Boston, New York, Brooklyn, Philadelphia, St. Louis and others, have their own normal schools as a matter of economy.

Experience has demonstrated that it is better to have a school exclusively devoted to the training and culture of teachers, than to make it the department of another institution. The department system is not much in vogue since its failure in Germany, and the experiments with it in New York and Kentucky.

V

In order to get in a clear light the benefits to be derived from normal schools, your memorialists further beg leave to recapitulate briefly the arguments used by its advocates, which have been confirmed by the test of one hundred years.

1. There is an obvious distinction between the ability to acquire knowledge and the ability to communicate it. Again there is a difference in modes of communication.

A man may be very learned, and able to express his knowledge in rigid scientific forms, while he is utterly unable to explain anything so a child can understand it; the teacher, however, must above all, be able to translate his knowledge into the form adapted to the youthful mind.

The normal school is the only school that professes to attempt this art.

2. The history of education is made a special object of investigation in the normal school. All past experience is thoroughly discussed, and the causes of success or failure set forth. It is seen that eminent teachers of all times have followed essentially the same method. It is further seen that this method involves the waking up of all the faculties to activity; how to stimulate the mind to self activity in the proper manner; how to govern the school in accordance with the spirit of our national idea, by training the pupil to self government; how to avoid these evil customs that have rendered the name pedagogue odious from time immemorial: to teach things constitutes the business of a normal school.

3. Thorough indoctrination in the true principles of instruction saves long and unfortunate experience; unfortunate for the scholars who are practiced upon for the teacher's benefit; unfortunate for the teacher who is forced to waste his time in groping about in the dark for that knowledge of method which he might have acquired at the normal school.

4. The same sentiment that refuses to place confidence in the uneducated lawyer or physician should refuse to entrust the children of the community to the care of the empiric, to serve as waste material upon which he experiments while learning the art of teaching.

Moved by these considerations your memorialists respectfully pray you to consider the expediency of establishing at some convenient locality one normal school for the purposes above mentioned.

In behalf of the Missouri State Teachers' Association,

WM. T. HARRIS
IRA DIVOLL
E. B. NEELEY
G. P. BEARD
T. A. PARKER
Committee

The nature of the normal schools that were established varied from state to state and from town to town, but they were remarkably similar considering the decentralized nature of the American school system. Therefore, while it is impossible to say positively what, for example, the admission requirements or course of study was at a particular school, it is possible to get an idea of them by looking at one school, especially if there is reason to believe that the school being studied served as a model. For this reason the State Normal School at Lexington was selected. The purpose of the school was set forth by its first principal, Mr. Cyrus Peirce, as follows:

> It was my aim, and it would be my aim again, in a Normal School, to raise up for our common schools especially, a better class of teachers,—teachers who would not only teach more and better than those already in the field, but who would govern better; teachers, who would teach in harmony with the laws of juvenile development, who would secure diligent study and good lessons and sure progress, without a resort to emulation and premiums, and good order from higher motives than the fear of the rod or bodily pain; teachers, who could not only instruct well in the common branches, as reading, writing, arithmetic, &c., but give valuable information on a variety of topics, such as accounts, history, civil institutions, political economy, and physiology; bring into action the various powers of children, and prepare them for the duties of practical life; teachers, whose whole influence on their pupils, direct and indirect, should be good, tending to make them, not only good readers, geographers, grammarians, arithmeticians, &c., but good scholars, good children, obedient, kind, respectful, mannerly, truthful; and in due time, virtuous, useful citizens, kind neighbors, highminded, noble pious men and women. And this I attempted to do by inculcating the truth in the art of teaching and governing, —the truth in all things; and by giving them a living example of it in my own practice.[13]

Mr. Peirce was in a good position to carry out these aims since he taught most of the courses, supervised the model school, prepared the professional materials, and served as janitor of the building. But his efforts were not in vain since his work was "watched carefully by admiring educators everywhere and gave impetus to the establishment of other normal schools, both inside and outside of the state.[14] The fact that the Lexington school was the first, plus Peirce's ability and the widespread acclaim he received as a leader in the field, lend support to

[13] Quoted in Barnard, op. cit., p. 77.
[14] Elsbree, op. cit., p. 148.

the use of this school as typical of the early normal schools. The following is an official statement of the organization and operation of the school. It is taken from Barnard's volume on Normal Schools.

Organization and Operation of the Lexington State Normal School[15]

THE State Normal Schools, of which there are three in Massachusetts, are designed for those *only* who purpose to teach, and especially for those who purpose to teach in the common schools. The school at West Newton is for females.

It was opened at Lexington, July 3rd, 1839, with the examination of three pupils, who were all that presented themselves as candidates. At the close of the first term it numbered twelve pupils.

The school continued at Lexington five years. In May, 1844, having by far outgrown its accommodations, it was removed to West Newton, where the liberality of the Hon. Josiah Quincy, Jr., of Boston, had provided for it by the purchase of a building, formerly used as a private academy, which he generously gave to the Institution.

The whole number of graduates is 423, nearly all of whom have engaged in teaching, the most of them in the public schools of this state.

CONDITIONS OF ENTRANCE.—1. The applicant must be at least sixteen years old.

2. She must make an *explicit declaration of her intention to become a Teacher.*

3. She must produce a certificate of good PHYSICAL, INTELLECTUAL, and MORAL CHARACTER, from some responsible person. It is exceedingly desirable that this condition be strictly complied with on the part of those who present candidates.

4. She must pass a satisfactory examination in the common branches, viz:—Reading, spelling and defining, arithmetic, grammar, writing and geography.

5. She must give a pledge to remain in the school at least *four consecutive terms,* and to observe faithfully all the regulations of the Institution, as long as she is a member of it.

6. All candidates for admission must be at the school-room on the morning of the day which precedes that on which the term commences, at half-past eight o'clock. None will be admitted after the *day of examination.*

7. Each pupil, at entrance, must be supplied with slate and pencil, blank book, Bible, Worcester's Comprehensive Dictionary, and Morse's

---

[15] Quoted in Barnard, *op. cit.,* pp. 71–3.

Geography. Many of the other books used will be furnished from the library of the school.

STUDIES.—The course of study in each of the State Normal Schools begins with a review of the studies pursued in the Common Schools, viz:—Reading, writing, orthography, English grammar, mental and written arithmetic, geography and physiology.

The attention of pupils is directed, 1st, to a thorough review of elementary studies; 2d, to those branches of knowledge which may be considered as an expansion of the above-named elementary studies, or collateral to them; to the art of teaching and its modes.

The advanced studies are equally proportioned, according to the following distribution, into three departments, viz:—1. The mathematical, including algebra through quadratic equations; geometry, to an amount equal to three books in Euclid; book-keeping and surveying. 2. The philosophical, including natural philosophy, astronomy, moral and intellectual philosophy, natural history, particularly that of our own country, and so much of chemistry as relates to the atmosphere, the waters, and the growth of plants and animals. 3. The literary, including the critical study of the English language, both in its structure and history, with an outline of the history of English literature; the history of the United States, with such a survey of general history as may be a suitable preparative for it; and historical geography, ancient and mediaeval, so far as is necessary to understand general history, from the earliest time to the period of the French Revolution.

"The art of teaching and its modes," includes instruction as to philosophy of teaching and discipline, as drawn from the nature and condition of the juvenile mind; the history of the progress of the art, and the application of it to our system of education; and as much exercise in teaching under constant supervision, toward the close of the course, as the circumstances and interests of the Model schools may allow.

Members of the higher classes give teaching exercises before the whole school, several each week. Members of the senior class spend three weeks, each, in the public grammar school of District No. 7, which is connected with the institution as its Model department.

Pupils who have had considerable experience in teaching, and are otherwise qualified for it, will be allowed to enter existing classes.

Pupils who may desire to study the Latin and French languages, and to prepare themselves to instruct in those branches usually taught in High Schools, can have an opportunity to do so, by giving a pledge to remain in the school for a term of three years, provided the number is sufficient to warrant the forming of a class.

EXAMINATIONS.—The school is visited and examined by the Visiting Committee of the Board of Education, at the close of each term; and a public examination is held whenever a class graduates. The school is open to visitors at all times.

LIBRARY AND APPARATUS.—A well-selected library, consisting mostly of works on education, belongs to the school, and also a well-assorted Apparatus, for the illustration of principles in natural philosophy, chemistry, mathematics, &c. &c.

TUITION.—For those who purpose to teach in the public schools of the state, tuition is free; for such as intend to teach elsewhere, it is $10 per term, payable at entrance, and such can not be admitted to the exclusion of those first mentioned. At the beginning of each term, each pupil pays to the Principal $1.50, to meet incidental expenses.

BOARD.—Board may be had in good families at from $2 to $2.50 per week, including washing and fuel. Some of the pupils take rooms and board themselves at a lower rate. The whole annual expense is about $100.

TERMS AND VACATIONS.—There are three terms in the year. The winter term commences on the second Wednesday in December, and continues fifteen weeks. The summer term commences on the second Wednesday in April, and continues fifteen weeks. The autumn term commences on the first Wednesday in September, and continues twelve weeks. Between the summer and autumn terms, there is a vacation of six weeks; between the other terms a vacation of two weeks. No session is held on the week of the anniversaries in Boston.

Pupils who reside in the vicinity, and whose friends request it, have leave to go home on Saturday morning and stay until Monday morning, provided this can be done without interference with school duties.

Pupils are not permitted to board at such a distance from the institution, as to render it impracticable for them to be present during all regular exercises.

STUDY HOURS &C.—It is expected, as a matter of course, that the young ladies will conform to the general order and usage of the families in which they reside. Where it can be done conveniently, it is desirable that they should breakfast about one hour after rising, dine at a quarter past two o'clock, and sup from six to six and a half o'clock.

The hours for rising, studying, &c., will vary somewhat with the season of the year. For the winter and autumn terms, the pupils will rise at six o'clock, and study one hour, either *before or after* breakfast, as may suit the custom of the family. In the summer term, they will rise at five o'clock and study two hours. In the afternoon, they will study from four till five and a half o'clock. Evening study hours for the winter and autumn terms commence at seven o'clock, and continue two hours, with a short recess; for the summer term, evening study hours commence at eight o'clock, and continue one hour.

All study hours are to be spent in *perfect quietness*. At all seasons of the year pupils are to retire at *ten* o'clock. Every light must be extinguished at half-past ten, *at the utmost*.

It is expected that the pupils will attend public worship on the Sabbath, health, weather, and walking permitting; preserve order and quiet in their rooms, and throughout the house; and refrain from everything like a desecration of the day.

ORDER, PUNCTUALITY AND NEATNESS, *in their persons and in their rooms*, and a kind and respectful demeanor, are expected of all.

It is expected that the young ladies will avoid all ground of complaint, and endeavor to make themselves agreeable in their family intercourse, thus securing honor to themselves and the institution.

The Principal requests that any marked and continued disregard of these regulations may be reported to him.

The school sessions commence at eight and a half o'clock. A.M., and close at two o'clock. P.M. On Saturday no session is held.

Pupils who desire to leave town for home, or for other places, are expected to confer with the Principal.

It can be seen that in these early days the normal schools corresponded roughly to the academies and high schools of the time. Gradually through the nineteenth century, standards were raised until by 1900 Massachusetts required a high school education or the equivalent for admission. It is true that Massachusetts had the highest standards and many states lagged far behind, yet the trend toward raising standards is evident all over the country. The trend was manifested in the raising of admission requirements, an up-grading of the work, and a lengthening of the program. In most instances the requirements for teaching in the secondary schools were greater than for teaching in the elementary schools. In all schools an attempt was made to provide a general academic program and a series of professional courses.

Despite the progress of the normal schools, most of the teachers in the public schools had not attended these schools and of those that did only a small percentage completed a four-year course. In most schools various types of diplomas or certificates were granted after the successful completion of each year. In 1898 in Massachusetts (one of the leaders in teacher education) only 38.5 per cent of the public school teachers had attended normal schools and only 33.5 per cent had completed a normal-school course. Doubtless many of the teachers in the Massachusetts schools had received their training at academies, but it is also probable that many of them had no professional training and very meager academic preparation.

From Normal Schools to Teachers Colleges

THE rapid growth of the normal schools continued in the twentieth century, both in terms of the number of institutions established and in the extension upward of their programs. As the requirements for entrance were raised to graduation from high school and the program of study was extended to four years, a movement began to convert the normal schools into teachers *colleges*. The Michigan State Normal School at Ypsilanti was the first school to make the change, being converted into a teachers college by an act of the legislature in 1897. In 1903 the new school was authorized to grant the B.A. degree and the movement was underway. By 1920 forty-six other teachers colleges were in existence.

The evolution of the normal schools into teachers colleges in America in this period can be illustrated by developments in Missouri after 1870. Between 1870 and 1906 five state normal schools were established, the first at Kirksville in 1870; the second at Warrensburg in 1872; the third at Cape Girardeau in 1873; the fourth at Maryville in 1905; and the fifth at Springfield in 1906. These schools were in addition to the University of Missouri, which also provided work in teacher education, and the municipal normal school in St. Louis. In 1915 the school at Warrensburg was converted into a four-year college. In 1919 this step was recognized by the state legislature which officially authorized it and the other four normal schools to become state teachers colleges with the power to grant the bachelor's degree. Between 1945 and 1949 all of the schools, except the one at Kirksville, acting under permissive legislation from the state dropped the word *teachers* from their name and became *state colleges*. Today these schools offer general and preprofessional programs in addition to their work in teacher education, and some offer graduate work on the master's level.

Teacher Education in Colleges and Universities

MANY of the men who taught in the colleges, the academies, and the Latin schools during the seventeenth, eighteenth, and nineteenth centuries in America were educated in colleges. But there was no provision made in the program of study for preparing the student for teaching. It should be remembered that until the middle of the nineteenth century the traditional, classical, fully prescribed curriculum was standard for American colleges. Then, under the impact of the great social and economic changes taking place, the colleges were forced into adapting their programs to the needs of American society and this meant offering professional, scientific, and technical courses, including some in pedagogy.

Some courses were offered in the "art and science of teaching" prior to the Civil War, e.g., at Brown in 1850, but the movement did not really spread until after 1865. The pattern followed in most schools was to establish first a chair in education or pedagogy, then to expand it into a department as additional staff members were added, and finally into a school or college of education which was a separate administrative unit controlling its own program and granting its own degrees. Not all universities that educate teachers have schools or colleges of education. Some have kept the departmental arrangement which means that education is one of many departments within the college of liberal arts.

The steps in the development of teacher education programs at the larger state universities can be illustrated by a look at the University of Michigan in this period. The State Normal School of Ypsilanti, started in 1852, was providing instruction for elementary teachers but many educators, including Michigan University's President Tappan, believed that the higher institutions of learning had to provide programs for teachers on the higher levels. His statement to the Board of Regents in 1856 indicates his position.

> The highest institutions are necessary to supply the proper standard of education, to raise up instructors of the proper qualifications, to define the principles and methods of education, to furnish cultivated men to the professions, to civil life, and to the private walks of society, and thus diffuse everywhere the educational spirit. The common schools can be perfected only through competent teachers. These can be provided only by institutions like the normal school, which belong to the intermediate or second grade of education. But the teachers of the normal schools, again, require other and higher institutions to prepare them, such at least as the academy, gymnasium, or college; and these, the highest forms of the intermediate grade, can only look to the university for a supply of instructors. He who has passed through a common school is not fitted to teach a common school. He who has passed through a normal is not prepared to teach a normal school. He who has passed through a union school or an academy is not prepared to teach it. The graduate of a college is not prepared to become a college professor. But the direct object of a university is to prepare men to teach in the university itself, or in any other institution." [16]

In addition to pressure from within the university, there was pressure from outside, particularly by the superintendents of public instruction who year after year urged the school to offer work in the art of teaching.

[16] Quoted in A. S. Whitney, *History of the Professional Training of Teachers at the University of Michigan* (Ann Arbor, Mich.: George Wahr Publishing Co., 1931), p. 17.

As a result President Angell in 1874 recommended the offering of instruction of "pedagogies" but no action was taken. In 1878 he repeated the recommendation as follows:

> I venture to repeat a suggestion I have made in a previous report, that it would be of essential service to the cause of education in the State, if a course of lectures on Pedagogics could be given here by some competent man. A large proportion of our students engage in teaching after graduation. Some adequate exposition of the Science and the Art of Teaching, some methodical discussion of the organization and superintendence of schools, would be most helpful. Our new system would easily yield a place for such instruction. Perhaps for a time at least a non-resident lecturer occupying a part of a year might meet the wants of our students and might afford us an opportunity to test the value of such a course as is here suggested.[17]

This time the recommendation was accepted and in 1879 a chair of the "Science and Art of Teaching" was established on a permanent basis. Gradually the chair grew into a department and then into a school of education in 1921.

Similar developments occurred throughout the colleges of the country. By 1900 over one-fourth of them were offering courses in education and at the present time most of them do. The offerings and program vary from the wide range at the large universities with hundreds of faculty members in education to the small colleges in which one individual teaches all of the courses required for certification. In this development, state certification laws have been decisive. Since no public school could legally employ a teacher who had not been certified and since certification required courses in education, colleges and universities were forced (often against their will) to offer work in education if they wanted to attract students.

The Teachers' Institute

ANOTHER important agency that was used in the nineteenth century for the instruction of teachers was the teachers' institute. Introduced by Henry Barnard in Hartford, Connecticut, in 1839, the institute was a stop-gap measure designed to provide some instruction for the teachers in the common schools. Barnard's first institute was attended by twenty-six young men and women who were given six weeks of instruction in pedagogy and a review of the subjects taught in the elementary school. During the next two decades the teachers' institute was used extensively in many states. Elsbree states that between 1843 and 1845 institutes were

[17] *Ibid.*, p. 27.

held in thirty-nine counties in New York State with a total attendance of over a thousand teachers.[18]

The men who established these institutes had no illusion that these short periods of instruction were an adequate substitute for the normal schools, but they provided at least some instruction for thousands of teachers who otherwise would have had none at all. Originally teachers were required to pay their own way to these institutes, but after 1845 the states began contributing funds for their support.

The institutes varied in length from two to eight weeks and in the early years, at least, there is evidence that most of this time was devoted to teaching reading, writing, and arithmetic. As time went by and teachers came to the institutes with a better background, more attention was given to methods of teaching and even to problems of the profession. For example, at the teachers' institute held at Jamestown, Pennsylvania, in 1858 the following questions were discussed:

Is it better for teachers to board around?
Should the teachers encourage pupils to chew tobacco?
Should teachers open their schools in the morning by reading a portion of the scripture?
Should the door be closed against pupils, who are not present at 9 o'clock in the morning?
Should the rod be used in school?
Should the wages of females be equal to those of male teachers? [19]

Compared with our modern conception of the nature and extent of education needed by teachers in the elementary schools, the institutes were inadequate indeed. Yet some instruction was better than none. Since the institute served to some extent as a forerunner of the summer school and the workshop and since it helped to pull the teachers together in a professional way, it served a useful purpose in the evolution of the profession.

The Certification of Teachers

THROUGHOUT the history of education men have attempted in many ways to insure the quality of their teachers. In the colonial period this was done either on a personal basis by those persons charged with the responsibility for hiring the teachers, or by a bishop or governor who had the power to license teachers. If the teacher was a graduate of a college or of a well-known Latin school or academy, this would be evidence enough of his academic qualification. The information concerning his character, loyalty, and religious views would be obtained through interview and from recommendations. If the teacher were not a graduate of a recog-

[18] Elsbree, *op. cit.*, p. 155.
[19] Quoted in Elsbree, *op. cit.*, p. 159.

nized institution, evidence of his academic qualification would be obtained through some kind of examination. Although attempts were made to establish some certification standards, the chronic shortage of teachers made any effective certification extremely difficult before 1900. Even when certificates were granted after the Civil War, they were often granted by local or county authorities on the basis of examinations which varied greatly from place to place, with the result that no effective standards were maintained.

Gradually in the late nineteenth and early twentieth centuries the situation began to improve. One reason was that as the years passed the task of certification tended more and more to be vested in one agency— the state. Another reason was the acceptance of the idea that graduation from a recognized teacher-education institution should replace the examination system. By 1911 a majority of states had passed certification laws and in fifteen of those states all of the certificates were issued by the state. In 1921 the number had risen to twenty-six, by 1926 to thirty-six, and by 1933 to thirty-nine. In general, these law' specified the minimum prerequisites for teaching in terms of years of schooling and they also specified a certain amount of work in professional education. Thus Indiana in 1907 required high school graduation as a prerequisite to certification for teaching in the elementary schools, and other states gradually increased their minimum up to this level. The work in professional education varied from state to state but tended to include requirements in educational psychology, history of education, methods of teaching, and practice teaching.

At the present time all states require a bachelor's degree from an accredited college along with certain academic and professional requirements for a permanent certificate. And, although no two states are exactly alike, in general they are quite similar. The following requirements from the state of New York are representative.

Certification Requirements for the State of New York
(Exclusive of Buffalo and New York City)

ELEMENTARY SCHOOL

Permanent Certificate
  I. Bachelor's degree (approved four-year curriculum for elementary school teachers) or equivalent.
 II. Professional requirements—in semester hours 36
    A. Observation and Supervised Student Teaching in elementary schools including conferences on teaching problems 12–15
    B. Elementary School Methods and Materials 8–12

C. Psychology for Teachers and Child Development or Child Psychology 6–10
D. History, Philosophy, Problems and/or Principles of Education 2–6

JUNIOR HIGH SCHOOL

Requirements the same as for High School.

HIGH SCHOOL (Provisional Certificate)

I. Bachelor's degree (an approved four-year curriculum).
II. Academic requirements (*minimum*) in specific fields in semester hours:
    A. English including English and American Literature, advanced composition; and speech to a maximum of 6 hours 24
    B. A foreign language (may include a maximum of 6 hours of entrance credit 18
    C. Mathematics, including an introduction to differential and integral calculus (may include a maximum of 9 hours of entrance credit) 18
    D. Citizenship education, including 12 hours in history of which 6 must be in American history plus one course in each of two of the following fields: political science, economics and geography 24
    E. General science (grades 7, 8, 9) including biology, chemistry, physics, and earth science 18
    F. Biology 12
    G. Chemistry 12
    H. Physics 12
    I. Earth science 12
III. Professional requirements—semester hours in professional courses approved for secondary school teaching 18
    A. Human growth and development, including learning and behavior problems of the adolescent 3
    B. Methods and materials relating to the major field of teaching, including educational measurements and evaluation 3
    C. Supervised practice teaching in secondary school including conferences on teaching problems of which 4 semester hours shall be in actual classroom teaching 6
    D. History, principles and/or philosophy of education and secondary education including special problems of the junior high school 3
    E. Additional hours in above fields 3

JUNIOR COLLEGE

No State regulations governing the preparation required of Junior College organizations.

ADMINISTRATION AND SUPERVISION

Elementary School Principal (Provisional Certificate)
 I. Bachelor's degree (or approved equivalent preparation) plus six semester hours in approved graduate courses.
 II. Teacher's certificate valid in elementary schools.
 III. Candidate's total program of graduate and undergraduate preparation must include in semester hours:
  A. Professional preparation approved for elementary school teaching 24
  B. Approved courses in the field of elementary school administration 4
 IV. Experience—3 years of approved and appropriate teaching and/or supervision.

Junior High School Principal
 I. Bachelor's degree plus a year of appropriate graduate preparation.
 II. Academic requirements—valid certificate for teaching an academic subject on the junior high school level.
 III. Professional requirements—minimum in professional preparation to include: Secondary school administration and supervision—semester hours:
  A. For the provisional certificate 6
  B. For the permanent certificate 10
 IV. Experience—secondary teaching:
  A. For the provisional certificate .... 2 years
  B. For the permanent certificate .... 5 years

Secondary School Principal (Provisional Certificate)
 I. Bachelor's degree plus six semester hours in approved graduate courses.
 II. Teacher's certificate valid in secondary schools.
 III. Professional requirements—candidate's total program of undergraduate and graduate preparation must include, in semester hours:
  A. Professional courses approved for secondary school teaching 12
  B. Approved courses in the field of secondary school administration 6
 IV. Experience—2 years of teaching and/or supervision.
  Note: In lieu of each year of experience, 6 additional semester hours in approved graduate courses may be offered.

Superintendent
 I. Bachelor's degree and 30 semester hours in approved graduate courses.
 II. Professional requirements—20 semester hours in approved education courses, 8 of them in school administration or organization and in school supervision to include one course in public school administration and *one course in supervision.* Other courses which may be offered toward the eight-semester-hour requirement are: curriculum organization and administration, elementary school administration, elementary school supervision, experimentation in education, high school administration, high school supervision, organization and administration of the extra-curricular program, organization and administration of the guidance

program, problems of the school superintendent, research in education, school business administration, school finance, school plant planning, school survey, social aspects in school administration, vocational school administration, vocational school supervision.

III. Experience—5 years of teaching and/or supervision in public schools.

GUIDANCE COUNSELOR (Provisional Certificate)

    I. Bachelor's degree plus 30 semester hours in approved graduate courses.

   II. Certificate or a statement of eligibility for teaching in the public schools of New York state.

 III. Professional requirements—undergraduate and graduate preparation—semester hours as follows: 16
- A. Understanding the individual .... 2 to 4
- B. Principles and practices of guidance .... 2 to 4
- C. Techniques of counseling .... 2 to 4
- D. Measurement and appraisal for the use of counselors   2 to 6
- E. Survey, organization and use of educational and occupational information .... 2 to 4

 IV. Experience—approved and appropriate experience ....   3 years
- A. Teaching experience in an approved school ......   2 years
- B. Experience other than teaching ....   1 year
- Note: May be an additional year of teaching combined with an approved field work course in which there is observation, study and discussion of occupational and training opportunities and community resources.

Whatever the specific requirements in each state, a teaching certificate is a legal requirement. It is a license which the teacher must have before he can teach in the *public* schools. Generally the state board of education is the agency that officially issues the certificate, but the whole program, including the establishment or change of requirements as well as the actual handling of the certification, is done by the state department of education. In most states graduates of state colleges and universities receive their teaching certificate upon receiving their bachelor's degree; private schools generally must certify by sending in college transcripts indicating that each of its students has met the requirements set up by the state, whereupon the individual receives his teaching certificate.

There has been much criticism of state certification laws (especially those that require courses in professional education), by individuals in the colleges and universities. They claim that these laws are a result of the action of a vested-interest group, namely, professional educators. It is undoubtedly true that some special course requirements have been the pet project of some officials in state departments of education. Perhaps of more importance is the fact that the state requirements are often inflexible and do not allow for the knowledge and experience gained by the individual outside of formal courses. For example, the author has had students who had studied and taught music for years, but since they had no credits in music on a college transcript, they were forced to take some credits in music in order to get their state teaching certificate. Of course, it is possible that despite the preparation and experience of the individual he would need additional work and study before he began teaching; if so, he should be required to have it. But in many states no evaluation of individual teachers is made. All are required to have credits in music regardless of their knowledge, ability, and experience. The main reason for this educational boondoggling is a system so big that it cannot be administered intelligently on an individual basis. Most states have an office in the state department of education to handle the problems of certification. Like any bureaucracy, it has the task of interpreting the laws and then making decisions. In making these decisions it is always easier and safer to stick to the letter of the law. Doubtless in many instances certification officers would apply the certification laws more liberally if they had the time and staff to investigate and judge the merit of each case. Unfortunately, because there are thousands of teachers in every state and the certification staff and funds are limited, they cannot.

The problems of certification are of vital importance to the teaching profession and ultimately to our free society. And while the inflexibility of the requirements and the administrative difficulties described in the previous paragraphs are irritating, especially to the individuals involved, they are not the basic problems. *There is no question that certification in education is as essential as it is in medicine. It is just as important to ensure that only qualified teachers will teach our children as it is to ensure that they will be treated for their physical ailments by competent physicians.* The crucial questions are: What is to be the nature and extent of the requirements for certification? Who shall decide on these requirements? How and by whom shall they be administered? [20]

It would be difficult if not impossible to get a consensus of opinion from educators on the first of these questions, although there would be substantial agreement that standards need to be raised both for teachers in the schools and for those entering the profession. There would also be substantial agreement that before they begin teaching, all teachers must have a good liberal education and a thorough professional preparation. The latter would include as a minimum extensive work in the teaching fields, an understanding of the nature and development of the public schools, a knowledge of human growth and development, including the nature and conditions of learning, and a student-teaching experience. But agreement on specific requirements is less important than an awareness by teachers (in the schools and in the universities) that *they* have

[20] For an excellent and challenging analysis of the certification problem see Myron Lieberman's *Education as a Profession* (Englewood Cliffs, N.J.: Prentice-Hall, Inc., 1956).

a professional responsibility to control certification. Who else is qualified to decide what the qualifications for teaching should be? Unfortunately, the lingering heritage of the simple nature of teaching (especially in the elementary schools), together with the rapid growth of our school system, has caused us to employ many individuals who were inadequately prepared for teaching. This fact is in turn partly responsible for the lag in the development of a sense of professional responsibility on the part of teachers. The result has been that teachers as a group have allowed laymen on state boards or small groups of educators in state departments of education or state colleges that prepare teachers to establish certification requirements.

It is clear that if and when the teaching profession—and I include in this category college as well as elementary and secondary teachers—takes the certification process more firmly in its own hands, there will be difficult problems to solve. For example, what mechanism or procedure should be established for deciding on specific requirements? Certainly the profession will have to give a great deal of time and thought to this as well as to other questions. There are, of course, some features of any certification program which would seem to be desirable. One of these is that at the very least the certification requirements be enforced (as they are now) at the state level, and it is possible that a national minimum standard would be desirable. Another is that various certification requirements be established by those members of the profession who are best qualified. Since there are common elements in the preparation of all teachers, it would seem that for this part of the requirements a certification board made up of representatives of the various institutions —elementary, secondary, liberal arts, and professional—would function most effectively. But requirements in the specialized aspects of the teacher's preparation should be determined by those who are most competent in that field. Thus decisions concerning the subject-matter requirements for teaching biology in the secondary schools should be made jointly by biology teachers in the high schools and professors of biology in the universities. The same procedure could be applied in all the subject matter areas: history, mathematics, English, physics, art, music, etc.[21] This procedure will be difficult to establish because of the gap which has developed between the elementary and secondary schools and the universities, but it is the only intelligent solution. And it can be predicted that it will be difficult to achieve a balance in the expectations of the various groups (advocating general education, specialized subject-matter study, and professional training) whose competence is needed for establishing sound certification requirements. Finally, it will be difficult but desirable

[21] The Teacher Education and Professional Standards Commission of the N.E.A., in considering questions of certification has for the past several years, been attempting to bring these various groups into a more active role.

to state the requirements in terms of broad areas of knowledge and competence and not in terms of specific courses. This latter practice, so prevalent in certification procedures at the present time, turns teacher education into a collection of discrete courses instead of a unified program of study.

Suggested Readings

Butts, R. Freeman, and Cremin, Lawrence A.: *A History of Education in American Culture*. New York: Henry Holt and Company, 1953.

Cremin, Lawrence A.; Shannon, David A.; and Townsend, Mary E.: *A History of Teachers College, Columbia University*. New York: Columbia University Press, 1954.

Curti, Merle: *The Social Ideas of American Educators*. New York: Charles Scribner's Sons, 1935.

Elsbree, Willard S.: *The American Teacher*. New York: American Book Company, 1939.

Russell, James Earl: *Founding Teachers College*. New York: Bureau of Publications, Teachers College, Columbia University, 1937.

Violette, E. M.: *History of the First District State Normal School, Kirksville, Missouri*. Kirksville, Mo.: Journal Printing Company, 1905.

Whitney, Allen S.: *History of the Professional Training of Teachers at the University of Michigan*. Ann Arbor, Mich.: George Wahr Publishing Co., 1931.

CHAPTER 18

THE TEACHING PROFESSION IN PRESENT-DAY AMERICA

THE TEACHING PROFESSION, WITH ITS 1,200,000 MEMBERS, IS BY FAR the largest profession in the country, although not as well organized or as strong as medicine or law. The development of the teaching profession has almost paralleled the development of the public school system in America. As the schools have grown in number and quality, the profession itself has followed along to its present size, which, incidentally, is still only about half the size it needs to be. If the future growth is anything like the past, we can expect to have this quantitative and qualitative growth of the teaching profession continue.

Before going into an account of the organization of the profession or into an analysis of some of its basic problems, it is necessary to ask whether teaching is in fact a profession. Throughout this volume, and especially in the preceding chapter, the assumption has been made that teaching is a profession. But, as Lieberman has pointed out we have "seldom questioned or seriously criticized" this assumption.[1] Perhaps education is not a profession after all but merely a large occupational group. To answer this question it will be necessary to define a profession and then to determine whether teaching can be so classified.[2]

The Nature of a Profession

THE task of defining a profession is easier said than done. *Webster's International Dictionary* defines it as "the occupation, if not commercial, mechanical, agricultural, or the like, to which one devotes oneself; a call-

[1] Myron Lieberman, *Education as a Profession* (Englewood Cliffs, N.J.: Prentice-Hall, Inc., 1956), p. vii.

[2] In the brief analysis of the profession which follows I am indebted to Lieberman's analysis in his volume cited above. Students who are interested in examining the problem more thoroughly will find this study invaluable.

ing; as, the *profession* of arms, of teaching; . . ." This definition settles
the question about teaching, but it opens other questions that are connected with the common usage of the term. We speak of a "professional
athlete" or a "professional model." What we mean by these descriptive
phrases is that the person is engaged full-time and earns his living in one
of these occupations; we mean that he is not an amateur. Certainly we
would not mean that the professional athlete was a member of a profession in the same sense that a physician was a member of the medical
profession or in the same way that a lawyer was a member of the legal
profession. Perhaps the distinction which is most applicable is one that
has been used for centuries—that is to set certain occupational groups
off as *learned*. Thus from the middle ages on the learned professions
have been theology, medicine, and law. These groups, of course, had
different functions, but all had certain common characteristics, the most
basic of which was a lengthy period of training before individual members could begin practice.

In the modern period, with the expansion of knowledge and the growing complexity of societies, new groups of experts, such as engineers,
have appeared and have claimed professional status. Partly as a result of
the confusion of claims (in 1915 Louis Brandeis discussed "business as a
profession") scholars have attempted to establish criteria for determining whether a particular occupational group was in fact a profession. The
method they have used has been to study the groups which are clearly
recognized as professions, such as medicine and law, and on the basis of
their characteristics to establish a set of criteria for determining professional status. Of course, there is nothing absolute or sacred about these
criteria but they are useful. Without some acceptable definitive criteria
the term *profession* would have little meaning, and it would be impossible to determine the legitimacy of the claims of groups who have called
themselves professional.

One of the first efforts in the recent period to establish definitive criteria for a profession was made by Abraham Flexner—a man whose studies of the medical profession had resulted in a great improvement in the
preparation of physicians. According to Flexner,[3] there are six criteria of
a profession. The first is that a profession is essentially intellectual.
Tools and manual labor may be employed, but they are incidental and
the problems that are encountered are solved through the use of intelligence. Because of this, the professional person must assume great personal responsibility. His task is not routine but involves judgment and
a certain amount of risk. The second criterion is that a profession is based
upon a vast amount of scientific knowledge and requires a great deal of
learning on the part of its members. Obviously, if the knowledge of a

[3] Abraham Flexner, "Is Social Work a Profession?" *School and Society*, June 26,
1915, p. 904.

professional person, say, a physician, were generally known by all persons in the society, there would be no need for a profession. The third criterion is that a profession must be essentially practical as opposed to being merely theoretical. It must have some purpose and serve some concrete function in society. The fourth criterion is a body of knowledge and a number of well-established techniques that can be communicated. For the most part the members of a profession are in substantial agreement concerning the knowledge and skills that must go into the preparation of a person seeking to enter the profession. Also every profession in establishing these standards seeks to control the quality of the new members. The fifth criterion is a high degree of organization. Because of common interest and preparation among the members of a profession, something analogous to a class consciousness develops. While the several professions have a degree of selectivity which is inherent, they are not aristocratic, but rather democratic because the selection is not based upon birth or wealth, but upon the nature of the abilities required and upon a willingness to assume responsibilities. The final criterion is that professions are concerned with the welfare of society. Although individual interest and even selfish interests can never be eliminated, Flexner believed that professions were becoming more altruistic and responsive to public interest.

A more recent analysis of the nature of a profession was made by Myron Lieberman, formerly a professor at the University of Oklahoma. Lieberman regards as a profession an occupation which exhibits the following characteristics:

1. A unique, definite, and essential social service.
2. An emphasis upon intellectual techniques in performing its service.
3. A long period of specialized training.
4. A broad range of autonomy for both the individual practitioners and for the occupational group as a whole.
5. An acceptance by the practitioners of broad personal responsibility for judgments made and acts performed within the scope of professional autonomy.
6. An emphasis upon the service to be rendered, rather than the economic gain to the practitioner, as the basis for the organization and performance of the social service delegated to the occupational group. [Lieberman adds that this does not mean that members of the profession are not motivated along economic lines. It does mean that professional people have obligations that go beyond economic considerations.]
7. A comprehensive self-governing organization of practitioners (this includes control over standards for entrance into, or exclusion from, the profession, etc.).

8. A code of ethics which has been clarified and interpreted at ambiguous and doubtful points by concrete cases.[4]

Education as a Profession

AN application of these criteria to the teaching profession indicates that it is very far from being a true profession. It is true, despite the controversy about what the schools should be doing, that teachers have a unique, fairly definite, and certainly an essential social service to perform in our society. It is also true that the teacher's work is essentially intellectual in character. Teaching qualifies, too, on the criterion of requiring a long period of formal training (although in some places it is still possible to enter the field with little more than two years of college). Finally, teaching has, perhaps more than other professions, emphasized service over economic gain to the practitioner. It is in the area of professional autonomy and of controlling its own affairs—establishing and enforcing entrance and training standards and controlling the professional behavior of its members—that the education group falls short as a profession. The need to have the teaching profession control the certification of new teachers was discussed in the previous chapter. Regarding professional autonomy in general, educators have in too many instances abdicated their professional responsibilities by turning *educational* matters over to lay groups. Because of the American pattern of local control through elected officials and because the public schools must serve society, there will always be differing opinions over which matters are strictly professional and should be handled by educators and which are the proper province of laymen on school boards. Actually, the school boards have the *legal* right to decide on such strictly professional matters as how reading should be taught. Whether legal limitations need to be or could be imposed on school boards to keep them from interfering in strictly professional matters poses some interesting questions, not the least of which would be the determination of what constitutes a "professional matter." But, with or without legal changes, to the extent that laymen make professional decisions teachers have correspondingly less of a claim to professional status. Lieberman, discussing this question, has listed a number of matters he believes are among those which should definitely be decided by educators who claim professional standing. They are the following:

The subjects to be taught and the materials (such as textbooks) to be used in teaching them; the criteria to be used in deciding who should be admitted, retained, and graduated at all levels; the forms

[4] Lieberman, *op. cit.*, pp. 2–6.

to be used in reporting pupil progress; school boundary lines and the criteria for permitting students to attend schools outside the boundary lines; the qualifications for entrance into teacher training; the length and content of the teacher training program; the standards for entry into and expulsion from education; the standards of professional conduct and the power to judge if and when practitioners have violated these standards; and who should lead the profession and speak for it on matters of broad professional concern.[5]

There are a number of reasons why teachers as a group have not had more professional autonomy. The American pattern of control is important, but there are other reasons. One is the inadequate preparation of so many teachers, even of some who have met formal certification requirements. Even with our pattern of local control (which, it should be remembered, has its advantages) there would be less lay interference if teachers could defend their professional actions, but too often they cannot. For example, when critics of the schools charged that reading was not being taught properly too many teachers were unable to defend their procedures by reference to research studies on the teaching of reading. This inability can be traced to the teacher-training institutions who have taught teachers how to teach reading without showing them the evidence available as to why it should be taught in a certain way. Teachers and administrators in the schools are sometimes suspicious of and antagonistic toward professors engaged in research in the universities. But their professional competence and therefore their professional status is dependent upon the evidence being accumulated in the universities. If the teaching profession is to be improved, much more attention and support, both moral and financial, will have to be given to research. And a mere verbal commitment to the sacred cow "research" will not suffice. What is needed is intensive investigation of fundamental problems, such as those of attitude change or of increasing motivation for learning. Inquiry into these and countless other problems, which can be carried out only by highly trained personnel, is required if the education profession is to build up a body of reliable, specialized knowledge which will enable us to move in the direction of better prediction and control of our classroom procedures. As this body of knowledge is accumulated and made available to students in education, and subsequently brought to bear on classroom practice, education will be moving in the direction of a true profession.[6]

There are other important reasons for the relatively low status of the teaching profession, such as the large number of women who go into

[5] *Ibid.*, p. 91.

[6] See the material on the art and science of teaching in Chapter 19 for additional material on this point.

teaching as an interim occupation until they are married. It is understandable, though unfortunate, that such women would not be vitally concerned about long-range professional problems. Another is the fact that to educate forty-five million Americans under our present arrangement means that we have a chronic teacher shortage. Education must of course compete with other occupational groups for manpower, and in such a situation the tendency is to keep requirements low. Lieberman has suggested—as have many other educators—that "subprofessionals" be utilized in education, just as technicians are used in medicine, and he discusses the advantage of such a plan as follows:

> It might be that a more effective utilization of subprofessional assistants would pave the way for a profession of teachers at all grade levels fully comparable to the leading professions; an elementary school with twenty-five teachers with master's degrees might be better and more economically served by five teachers with Ph.D. degrees and twenty professional assistants with bachelor degrees. In this situation, the elementary *teachers* might no longer be an inferior caste within the teaching profession. Their time on the job could be devoted to professional tasks with the professional assistants carrying out tasks analogous to those performed by the auxiliary professions in medicine. The problem of teacher turnover might be substantially reduced if not solved, because the turnover would come mostly at the level of the auxiliary personnel. The need for fewer *professional* personnel would permit larger salaries to be paid to the professionals. Such an approach might attract more men into elementary teaching, without making any special concession to them because of their sex. Relieved of the obligation to support a mass profession whose work is excessively subprofessional, communities could well afford to pay salaries to the professionals comparable to those prevailing in the leading professions.
>
> The utilization of subprofessional personnel openly controlled by a professional group could have many advantages in public education. This conclusion rests upon an awareness of the undesirable consequences of the current situation with respect to educational personnel. Teachers who are professional workers are forced to do a great deal of subprofessional work. This leads to the requirement of a higher number of professional level personnel than would be needed if professional personnel did only professional work. Obviously, if doctors were required to do the work of nurses, X-ray technicians, and laboratory assistants, it would be necessary to have a tremendous increase in the number of doctors. This would create strong and probably irresistible pressures to lower the standards for entry to the medical profession. The status and compensation of

doctors would decline. Ultimately, the quantity and quality of medical services would suffer.[7]

After they have considered the problems carefully, educators themselves will have to decide whether these ideas should be experimented with. Similarly they will have to decide whether as a group they wish to deal with the problem of professional ethics, and then whether they want to define more carefully and attempt to enforce the code of ethics of the National Education Association or to draw up and enforce a new code. But more important than any of these steps and prerequisite to them is the need for an awareness on the part of teachers of what is involved in achieving professional status. As Lieberman has said:

> The experience of the established professions clearly indicates that occupational groups do not achieve professional status until the members of the groups concerned participate en masse in the movement to achieve professional status. This they cannot do unless they understand the significance of professional status and the problems of professionalization confronting their occupational group.[8]

When it is realized that as recently as 1920 the majority of American teachers had the equivalent of a high school education, and when this fact is coupled with the tremendous quantitative growth of our school system, it must be granted that tremendous progress toward genuine professional status has been made by teachers. But if we are to improve the teaching profession qualitatively to the extent that conditions in the modern world require, vigorous concerted actions will have to be taken by teachers. One final word needs to be said in connection with professionalization. It is not an end in itself, and it is to be sought not for the improved social status and increased remuneration it will bring its members. These are important and desirable outcomes, but they are not the primary purpose. The basic reason for seeking true professional status, with all that this entails, is that it is a means through which the quality of education our children will receive in the classrooms of America can be improved.

The Education Associations

IF the teaching profession has not developed the professional strength characteristic of the American Medical Association or the American Bar Association, it is not because teachers have been unwilling to join together in various kinds of organizations. Teachers in the United States

[7] *Ibid.*, pp. 502–3.
[8] *Ibid.*, p. vii.

belong to a complex variety of local, state, national, and international educational organizations and, in addition, may belong to numerous associations or departments within the larger organizations. For example, a teacher in a suburb of St. Louis may belong to a community teachers' association, a county association, a state association, a national association, and a world association. At the same time, she may be a member of a classroom teachers' association which is a part of the national organization and may belong to a similar subgroup of her state organization. In addition, there are numerous fraternities and honor societies in education to which teachers may belong, as well as organizations such as mental health associations which are not, technically speaking, in the field of education but are certainly closely related to it. This amazing development, most of which has occurred in the last thirty-five years, has caused many teachers to be more selective in joining organizations because of the impossibility of keeping up with all of them.

It is difficult to say precisely how many local teacher associations exist in the United States, but the National Education Association is currently affiliated with 5,100 such groups, so there are at least that many. There are no standardized organizational or procedural patterns for these associations, but they have at least two things in common. One is that they are concerned with the improvement of the public schools and the teachers in them. The other is that they operate more or less democratically through elected officers, committees, etc. Most of these groups have a small dues payment, and many of them publish newsletters. They may include among their members all of the teachers who teach in a district or they may be limited to a special group such as high school teachers or English teachers. In most instances these local groups affiliate with related groups within the state and with national organizations.

All of the states, including Alaska and Hawaii, have state teachers' associations, and all these are affiliated with the National Education Association. Many of the southern states have separate associations for Negro teachers. The first state association was organized in Alabama in 1840, and groups were formed in New York and Rhode Island a few years later. By 1860 twenty states had state organizations. By 1870 the number had jumped to thirty, and all but two states had organizations by 1900. The membership has grown from slightly more than ten per cent of the teachers in 1900 to about ninety per cent in 1954. At the present time most of the state associations have a full-time staff. All but a few of the associations publish professional journals, and all engage in numerous activities in behalf of public education, including lobbying. The general pattern is to have a state convention once a year, and teachers are generally given time off to attend the meetings. Usually a small annual membership fee is charged to support the organization. Since their beginning a century ago, these associations have worked to improve

CHARTERED BY ACT OF CONGRESS—1906

NATIONAL EDUCATION ASSOCIATION
OF THE UNITED STATES

627,836 individual members   1,085,000 affiliated members

OUR UNITED PROFESSION

65 STATE AND 5815 LOCAL AFFILIATED ASSOCIATIONS

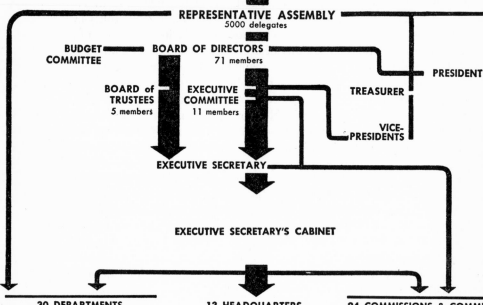

REPRESENTATIVE ASSEMBLY
5000 delegates

BUDGET COMMITTEE — **BOARD OF DIRECTORS**
71 members

PRESIDENT

BOARD of TRUSTEES
5 members

EXECUTIVE COMMITTEE
11 members

TREASURER

VICE-PRESIDENTS

EXECUTIVE SECRETARY

EXECUTIVE SECRETARY'S CABINET

30 DEPARTMENTS

- Administrative Women
- Art Education
- Audio-Visual Instruction
- Business Education
- Classroom Teachers
- Deans of Women
- Educational Research
- Elementary School Principals
- Exceptional Children
- Health, Physical Education, Recreation
- Higher Education
- Home Economics
- Industrial Arts
- Journalism Directors
- Kindergarten-Primary Education
- Mathematics Teachers

- Music Educators
- Public School Adult Educators
- Retired Teachers
- Rural Education
- School Administrators
- School Public Relations
- School Secretaries
- Science Teachers
- Secondary-School Principals
- Social Studies
- Speech
- Supervision and Curriculum Development
- Teacher Education
- Vocational Education

13 HEADQUARTERS DIVISIONS

- Accounts
- Adult Education Service
- Audio-Visual Service
- Business
- Legislation—Federal Relations
- Membership
- NEA Journal
- Press and Radio
- Publications
- Records
- Research
- Rural Service
- Travel Service

24 COMMISSIONS & COMMIT

- Auditing
- Budget
- Bylaws and Rules
- Citizenship
- Credentials
- Credit Unions
- Defense Commission
- Educational Policies Commission, NEA, AASA
- Elections
- International Relations
- Legislative Commission
- NEA and American Legion
- NEA and American Library Association
- NEA and American Medical Association

- NEA and Ame Teachers Association
- NEA and Mag Publishers Association
- NEA and Nati Congress of P and Teachers
- Professional Et
- Resolutions
- Safety Commis
- Tax Education
- Teacher Educa and Profession Standards
- Teacher Retire
- Tenure and Academic Free

education and have been responsible for much of the progress that has been achieved. Many of the state associations have helped to protect the rights of teachers and all of them have helped in the struggle for improved salaries, retirement, tenure, and other benefits.

The largest professional organization in the world, with 562,000 individual and over a million affiliated members, is the National Education Association (NEA). Organized originally in 1857 as the National Teachers' Association, it combined in 1870 with the National Association of School Superintendents and the American Normal School Association and assumed its present name. The purpose of the group as stated at that time was "to elevate the character and advance the interests of the teaching profession and to promote the cause of education throughout the country." The organization struggled along until 1884 with a small membership and a program limited to an annual meeting. In that year the new president of the group toured the country publicizing the organization and urging teachers to attend the convention. The result was a huge turnout at the convention held at Madison, Wisconsin, which established the association in the minds of teachers and put it in better shape financially. With a surplus in the treasury, the young organization entered the field of investigation by appointing the famous Committee of Ten in 1892, and from that time on the NEA was firmly established.

In 1906 a charter was granted by Congress and in 1920 a permanent headquarters was established in Washington, D.C. In 1920 the membership became so large that a representative assembly, composed of delegates from local and state associations, was created. In 1921 the Association began to publish the *Journal*. In 1922 a research division was added. Gradually the Association grew in size and complexity (indicated by the chart on page 424).

Although the NEA has been criticized for not being forceful enough and for allegedly being dominated by the school administrators, there is no doubt that it has been an important force in improving American education. Since the mid-thirties it has assumed a role of leadership, chiefly through one of its most important agencies, the Educational Policies Commission. The organization has taken a strong positive stand on such issues as federal aid, and academic freedom, and has opposed communists teaching in the schools and loyalty oaths. Through its many publications, its departments and commissions, and its affiliated local and state associations, it has consistently helped to raise the standards of education over all the nation. It has developed a code of ethics and has had a Committee on Professional Ethics since 1924. It has a National Commission on Teacher Education and Professional Standards whose purpose is to help to establish and raise professional standards in education. The NEA has had a research division since 1922, which publishes *Research Bulletins* on various educational matters four times a year and issues a periodical—*The Review of Educational Research*— which in the opinion of many educators is the organization's most professional publication.

Much smaller than the NEA but nonetheless of importance in the teaching profession is the American Federation of Teachers (AF of T) which is affiliated with the American Federation of Labor. The AF of T was formed in 1916 when eight local teacher unions decided to form a national organization as a part of the American Federation of Labor. The membership in the organization has fluctuated sharply and has tended to increase during periods of economic trouble. For example, the membership had declined from 12,000 in 1920 to 3,000 in 1926, but by 1939 it was up to 35,000 and it currently stands at about 50,000. The organization consists of twenty state federations with 375 locals. Most of its membership is concentrated in the large industrial centers.

The AF of T has had difficulty gaining acceptance by teachers because it is a "union" and not a "professional" organization, and many teachers feel that joining would lower their status. Also, most teachers are from middle-class families in which unions are often regarded at best as necessary evils and at worst as "socialistic." In many districts school administrators are actively opposed to having their teachers join a union. It is also true that many teachers and administrators who have no objection to joining unions believe that it is unwise for teachers to be affiliated with either labor or management. The result of all these factors has been that the AF of T has remained relatively small. Nevertheless, it has been a vigorous champion of the public schools and their teachers. Through its journal, *The American Teacher*, and through its many local and national committees, the AF of T has consistently defended academic freedom and has been a strong advocate of higher salaries, smaller teaching loads, effective tenure provisions, adequate pensions, and federal aid.

As a result of World War II, the NEA in August of 1946 invited representatives from teacher associations all over the world to attend a conference at Endicott, New York, to discuss common problems. The conference, which was attended by delegates from thirty-eight national educational associations, drafted a constitution for a World Organization of the Teaching Profession (WOTP). The purposes of the new organization as stated in Article II of the Constitution are as follows:

The purposes of this Organization shall be to secure world wide cooperation among recognized organizations of teachers, in order:
Sec. 1. To make the highest standards of full and free education available to all without discrimination.
Sec. 2. To improve the professional status of the teachers of the

world and to promote their intellectual, material, social, and civic interests and rights.

Sec. 3. To promote world wide peace through the building of good will founded upon cooperation between nations in educational enterprises, based upon pertinent and accurate information.

Sec. 4. To advise the appropriate organs of the United Nations and of other international bodies on educational and professional matters.

The first meeting of the Delegate Assembly of the new organization took place the following year in Glasgow, Scotland. Offices were established, officers were elected, a budget was approved, and a program of study for the following year was laid out. It included the study of the following topics:

1. International exchange of pupils and teachers
2. The extension of literacy
3. The problem of an international language
4. The teaching of social studies and current affairs
5. Health education.

In subsequent meetings the World Organization has discussed and studied a wide range of problems important to teachers such as salaries and tenure, and has maintained an active connection with the United Nations and UNESCO.

In August of 1952 the WOTP joined with the International Federation of Secondary Teachers to form the World Confederation of Organizations of the Teaching Profession (WCOTP). The new organization has member associations in more than forty countries. In the United States three associations are members: the AF of T, the NEA, and the American Teachers' Association (an organization of Negro teachers). Neither the Soviet Union nor any of the nations behind the Iron Curtain, including Red China, is a member. The aims of the WCOTP, which are similar to those of the WOTP are as follows:

> The Confederation aims at gathering into one powerful organization professional teachers from all stages of education, with a view to enabling them to exert an influence corresponding to the importance of their social function. The Confederation proposes, in cooperation with the constituent International Federations:
>
> To foster a conception of education directed toward the promotion of international understanding and goodwill, with a view to safeguarding peace and freedom and respect for human dignity;
>
> To improve teaching methods, educational organization and the

academic and professional training of teachers so as to equip them better to serve the interests of youth;

To defend the rights and the material and moral interests of the teaching profession;

To promote closer relationships between teachers in the different countries.

While the world organization of teachers has not turned the world upside down in its short life, it is certainly a step toward strengthening the profession all over the world and could be a powerful force in helping to improve international relations.

The professional organizations already mentioned draw the great bulk of their membership from teachers in the elementary and secondary schools. The professional organization for college and university teachers is the American Association of University Professors (AAUP) established in 1915. The nature and purposes of the AAUP as formulated at that time were as follows:

> To bring about more effective cooperation among the members of the profession in the discharge of their special responsibilities as custodians of the interests of higher education and research in America; to promote a more general and methodical discussion of problems relating to education in institutions of higher learning; to create means for the authoritative expression of the public opinion of the body of college and university teachers; to make collective action possible, and in general to maintain and advance the ideals and standards of the profession.

The membership has grown steadily from the original charter membership of 1,362 up to better than 42,000, or roughly one fourth of all eligible college and university teachers at the present time. The Association has approximately 450 organized chapters and its membership is distributed throughout 928 accredited colleges. The AAUP publishes a quarterly bulletin and from time to time has conducted special studies and published reports on various aspects of college teaching. Perhaps the greatest contribution the AAUP has made is its defense of academic freedom and its promotion of tenure.

Problems of the Profession

THROUGHOUT this volume many of the problems facing the education profession have been considered in connection with the descriptive account of the nature and development of the American school system; thus some of the issues concerning aims and purposes, support and control, and curriculum have been discussed. But there are some problems which have not been dealt with which are of vital importance to the teaching profession in our democratic society. These include the problems connected with academic freedom and tenure, loyalty oaths, and the education of teachers.

Academic freedom. One of the foremost problems facing the teaching profession today and one of the perennials of education is the problem of freedom of teaching and learning and of inquiry, generally known as academic freedom. Stripped down to its essentials, academic freedom is the freedom of teachers and students to seek after knowledge for the purpose of establishing truth. Teachers and students should be free to inquire into any area of human experience, and to question, analyze, and criticize any belief or institution. It is the freedom to question, challenge, and inquire into some of our most cherished beliefs, such as our belief in democracy, or our belief in freedom of inquiry itself. Teachers should be free to teach the truth as they see it wherever it may lead.

However, with these freedoms go responsibilities. Freedom to teach the truth requires an obligation on the part of the teacher to consider all of the available evidence and to sift and weigh its reliability before drawing conclusions. It involves a responsibility on the part of the teacher to entertain inquiries by others (even by his students), into his own knowledge and beliefs and to change his position if the evidence proves that he has been mistaken. It involves a responsibility on the part of the teacher to be aware of his own bias or point of view and, especially in a controversial issue, to carefully present all of the relevant facts fairly.

The question arises as to the justification for academic freedom. One answer that could be given is that such freedom is implicitly guaranteed to Americans in the First Amendment. Or we might agree with Jefferson that freedom of the mind is a natural, inalienable right which is in harmony with God's plan for a rational universe. But perhaps these justifications will not suffice. Saying that freedom of teaching and learning is implied in the Constitution does not explain *why* it is desirable. Maybe the Constitution should be changed? Neither are we as certain as Jefferson that these rights are in the nature of things; at least they are not a part of the natural order in the totalitarian states. Another reason for believing that freedom of teaching and learning has some "fundamental and enduring significance in the life of man" has been given by one of America's outstanding historians, Carl Becker. Looking at the record of history, Becker points out that man has continually sought after knowledge and that this "impulse to know seems to be an inherent and ineradicable human trait." [9] Whether Becker is right in saying that

<hr />

[9] C. L. Becker, *Freedom and Responsibility in the American Way of Life* (New York: Alfred A. Knopf, Inc., 1945), p. 50.

the desire to know is an ineradicable human trait or whether it can be stifled by a conditioning process started at an early age would evoke considerable difference of opinion among scholars, particularly among psychologists and anthropologists. Certainly it is true that this impulse, whatever its nature and source, has contributed to the advancement of civilization by enabling man to "emancipate himself from bondage to ignorance and superstition, to subdue the physical world to his needs, and to shape his life in closer accord with the essential nature of men and things." [10]

It is clear that freedom to learn has contributed to human progress; if progress is desirable, it follows that freedom to learn is desirable and can be justified. But there is still another important reason for desiring academic freedom: it is necessary for the existence of a democratic society. For democracy is a form of society which depends upon an intelligent, informed citizenry and this kind of citizenry can be developed only in a free society with free schools, a free press, and in general, free access to information. Of course, this presupposes that a democratic society is what we want. We might then ask whether basing our justification upon the fact that it is essential to democracy does not beg the question. Why then do we prefer democracy? Because it is our way of life and we have grown used to it? But these are causes not reasons. Why *should* we prefer democracy? One answer, and an excellent one, was given by John Dewey, and it is worth repeating here:

> Can we find any reason that does not ultimately come down to the belief that democratic social arrangements promote a better quality of human experience, one which is more widely accessible and enjoyed, than do non-democratic and anti-democratic forms of social life? Does not the principle of regard for individual freedom and for decency and kindliness of human relations come back in the end to the conviction that these things are tributary to a higher quality of experience on the part of a greater number than are methods of repression and coercion or force? Is it not the reason for our preference that we believe that mutual consultation and convictions reached through persuasion, make possible a better quality of experience than can otherwise be provided on any wide scale. [11]

Thus if it is a better quality of human life for all people that we seek, then we should prefer the democratic pattern, and if we do, then academic freedom is essential. On the other hand, if we believe in fascism or communism or in any form of society in which there is government

[10] *Ibid.*, p. 49.
[11] John Dewey, *Experience and Education* (New York: The Macmillan Company, 1938), pp. 25–26.

by the few, freedom of learning is not essential but is really dangerous, as Plato recognized in the *Republic*.

The reasons for preferring academic freedom seem self-evident. Therefore, the question may be raised as to the reason for listing it one of the foremost problems facing the teaching profession. The fact is that many Americans do not believe in academic freedom or if they do, they believe in only the "principle." Generally this means that they believe in it for themselves but not for others; they believe in it insofar as those views being taught and learned coincide with their own. Frequently these attitudes are held by powerful groups who attempt, often successfully, to impose their will upon the schools and even upon governmental agencies. As mentioned earlier, in some of our cities in recent years materials on UNESCO have been banned from the schools. In New York City a few years ago one of the best periodicals in the country, *The Nation*, was barred from the schools because it had published articles which were critical of a religious group. In other instances textbooks by certain authors with the "wrong" point of view have been banned. A few years ago a group in Indiana tried to get the time-honored stories of Robin Hood removed from schools and libraries on the ground that the idea of robbing the rich to feed the poor was subversive. In government the recent efforts to intimidate scientists such as Edward Condon in the Bureau of Standards were examples of this pressure, as was the removal of certain books from our overseas libraries because Senator MacCarthy thought that they were dangerous. It is clear in all of these instances that what these individuals desire in a school or in a library is not freedom but propaganda and indoctrination.

It is not only special interest groups who have restricted freedom of teaching and learning in our schools and libraries. Very often these actions are taken by educators themselves. In 1954 the students at several teachers colleges in Nebraska and at the military academies at West Point and Annapolis were forbidden to debate whether Red China should be recognized by the United States. In a fifth-grade class in one of our large cities, books on Russia that had been obtained for the children from the public library were removed by the principal. In many other classrooms these actions do not occur simply because teachers avoid controversial issues and concentrate upon what is safe. In these situations it is probably not so much a matter of the lack of belief of the teacher or principal in academic freedom as the fear of offending powerful individuals and ultimately losing their jobs. It is doubtful that teachers, or any other group, could do more harm to the fiber of democracy than through these acts of commission or omission. As Harold Benjamin has so aptly put it: "Free men cannot be taught properly by slaves. Courageous citizens cannot be well educated by scared hired men."

We need to ask whether teachers who do not or are not able to inquire freely can possibly develop these abilities in students. It is true of course that many teachers and administrators do not have a clear conception of academic freedom and are therefore unaware of the consequences of their actions. But to the extent that freedom of inquiry is being throttled or not encouraged, to that extent is the heart and soul of democracy being destroyed.

It must be granted that there are risks involved in freeing the mind, for once human beings begin to think there is no telling where their thinking will end. As Dewey has said:

> Let us admit the case of the conservative: if we once start think-ing, no one can guarantee where we shall come out, except that many objects, ends and institutions are doomed. Every thinker puts some portion of an apparently stable world in peril and no one can wholly predict what will emerge in its place.

It is for this reason that attempts to restrict freedom of the mind are more numerous in times of tension. For example, during and immedi-ately following World War I many German teachers were fired, and in some schools German music and literature was banned. At the present time the fear of communism has led to many restrictions on the study of the ideas of Marx and Lenin and even Russian history. In many schools where such matters are studied, care is taken to see that it is done in such a way as to prove their evil nature and to show how superior American democracy is in comparison.

But if freeing the mind is dangerous it must also be granted that there are even greater risks involved in suppressing freedom. Even from the standpoint of expediency, it is doubtful that, for example, preventing our students from studying about communism is an intelligent approach to the problem. This approach is based on the premise that ignorance of communism is the best way to combat it, or that a head-in-the-sand atti-tude of ignoring problems is the best solution. But more serious prob-lems are involved. If censorship is to be carried out, who is to do the censoring? And who is to censor the censors? And once we start censor-ing, where do we stop? These are patterns of totalitarianism not of de-mocracy. The men and women who would restrict freedom of teaching and learning are afraid and have probably lost faith in democracy. And a sturdy faith is required in democratic education—faith that the mind set free is the best hope for the future of mankind. This does not mean that teachers must be neutral regarding values. We are certainly concerned that our students turn out to be democrats, not fascists or communists, but a part of democracy is freedom of choice and students must be al-lowed, after studying the facts, to make their own decisions.

It must be realized also that there is a difference between teaching mature college students or high school students and teaching children in the elementary school. Surely teachers in the elementary schools must make a selection of the materials for children to study. Surely they will do their best to see that these young minds are nourished on what we consider to be good literature, as opposed to some of the flashy, sadistic crime comics. Moreover, second- or third-graders do not have the background or maturity to handle complex problems involving subtle differences in value. But even on this level, teachers have a responsibility to see that the material presented is true and not false, and that in matters involving controversy an objective approach is used. Even in the elementary schools children can be taught to inquire freely, to ask questions and seek answers, and to develop habits of critical thinking. There is no room for dogmatism even in an elementary school.

On the higher levels the student must be given more and more opportunity for assuming the responsibility for intellectual honesty and proving his statements. For the high school senior or the college student (and of course for all citizens) all areas of human experience must be open—nothing must be censored. Unless students are taught to inquire freely and to think critically, it is difficult to see how they can function effectively in a democratic society. As has been pointed out, it is impossible for teachers who are themselves unwilling or unable to think critically to develop this ability in students. The most essential characteristic of a good teacher—more essential than all the best techniques—is intellectual curiosity. The teacher who ceases to be a student will be a poor teacher.

There is one final point that needs to be remembered in any discussion of academic freedom. The point is that this freedom has always to be worked for—has always to be achieved. As historian Carl Becker has pointed out:

> In the long history of civilization there have been relatively few systems of government that accepted in theory and applied in practice the dangerous notion that learning and teaching should be perfectly free. Modern liberal democracy is one of the few.[12]

The stories of Socrates and Galileo are well known, as are the limitations placed upon academic freedom in our own times. Probably until we reach Utopia there will always be those who fear freedom and try to curb it. We in America today have as much freedom as any nation in history has ever had, but there are still too many schools in which freedom is an empty word. Achieving freedom of teaching and learning will always take effort and courage. It is never acquired automatically. Whether this precious freedom is maintained and extended in our society will depend in large part upon the teachers of America.

[12] Becker, *op. cit.*, p. 45.

Tenure. Closely related to academic freedom is the problem of tenure. Tenure is defined as the "act or right of holding" and as applied to education is the right of the teacher to hold his job without fear of arbitrary dismissal. This does not mean that teachers on tenure cannot be fired. It does mean that the reasons for which a teacher may be dismissed must be known, and that if the teacher is dismissed, he is entitled to receive a fair hearing under a carefully laid out procedure which provides adequate safeguards. In Illinois, for example, a teacher may be dismissed for incompetence, cruelty, negligence, immorality, for not being qualified to teach, or because the interest of the school requires it. It is also possible for teachers in Illinois to be dismissed for failure to comply with *reasonable* regulations of the school board, such as the requirements to give evidence of physical fitness.

The relationship between freedom of teaching and learning and tenure is so close that it amounts to virtual interdependence. For if the teacher fears the loss of his job, the chances are that he will avoid teaching that which is offensive to individuals or groups who may be in a position to cause him to be dismissed. In the history of education in the United States much evidence has been gathered which indicates that superintendents, principals, supervisors, board members, politicians, and various types of pressure groups have been successful in coercing teachers. When this pressure is exerted the teacher without tenure has two choices: he can resist the pressure and run the risk of being fired or he can submit and avoid trouble. The case of the teacher who was forced by her principal to remove from her classroom the books she had gathered on Russia is an illustration of this process. Even with tenure, it takes courage for a teacher to resist these infringements on his academic freedom, but if he has permanent tenure he is in a strong position. If we want to have teachers in our schools who are free to teach the truth, it is essential that they have tenure.

Since 1900 there has been a growing awareness on the part of American teachers that education in a democratic society requires free teachers under obligation to no man or group. If this was to be achieved, some institutional arrangement was necessary. The arrangement developed was to grant teachers tenure. The problem of placing teachers in a strong, independent position is analogous to the problem of placing judges in a strong position. One of the great bulwarks of our legal system has been the independent position of our federal judges. They are appointed for life and probably have the maximum safeguard that an institution can provide to enable them to dispense justice.

The achievement of tenure legislation has been a slow process. By 1918 only seven states had such laws, and some of these were apparently so loosely worded as to be virtually useless. A recent study has shown that fifteen states have tenure laws, while a few others have them only in cities of a certain size. Many other cities, towns, and districts have tenure arrangements set up by the local school boards within the district. Obviously the tenure provisions provided by state law are the strongest, because any board ruling can be changed by a majority vote of the board. State legislation can be repealed, but this is a more difficult task.

The procedures established can be illustrated by reference to the tenure system in effect in Illinois. The tenure law was passed in 1940 and provides that the teacher serve a probationary period of not less than two and not more than three years. At the end of that time, if the teacher is rehired, he has tenure and can be removed only for just cause. If a teacher is dismissed, it must be done by a majority vote of the board, and the reasons must be stated in writing and submitted to the teacher. He can, if he wishes, ask for a hearing before the board of education and at that hearing may be represented by counsel and has the right to call in witnesses in his behalf. If the teacher feels that he has been unfairly treated, he may appeal and take his case to the courts. The result is that very few teachers who are on tenure are ever removed, for something like incompetence, negligence, or immorality is difficult to prove. Of course, if the teacher is convicted of robbing a bank, the issue is clear cut, but in most instances such gross evidence is not available. For this reason the tenure laws have been opposed by some educators. Like freedom of teaching and learning, tenure has its disadvantages. It is possible for a poor teacher who has tenure to remain in the schools for years, but the same logic could be applied to a Supreme Court justice. The decision should be made during the probationary period. Once it is made, teachers should be secure and independent. For their part, teachers have the responsibility not to take advantage of the protection that tenure affords by becoming complacent or indifferent.

This is not to say that wherever teachers do not have tenure there is no academic freedom. In many schools teachers have complete freedom without such arrangements, but they have no protection and must rely on the beneficence of their superiors. In many states and districts where tenure laws do not exist the professional teacher organizations are often of great help to teachers. If teachers have been dismissed without cause the state teachers' association will often investigate the cases and publish its findings. These recommendations have no legal force, but they have often brought unsavory practices into the open and in many cases resulted in teachers being rehired. In states where tenure laws do exist, the local or state teachers' association may be called upon by either the teacher or the school board or both to help settle a dispute. Again their recommendations carry great weight even without legal backing.

Loyalty Oaths. Another of the persistent problems that has faced teachers, and one that becomes more acute in a time of trouble, concerns loyalty and the signing of loyalty oaths. As was shown in the preceding chapter, since colonial times attempts have been made to insure the loyalty of teachers. These attempts are quite natural at any time, but with the uncertainty of the modern world plus our awareness of the nature of the communist conspiracy, they have been intensified in the last decade. The problem of rooting out subversives and of determining loyalty in government officials has of course received most of the attention. The struggle over loyalty in the schools, although it has received less publicity, is of vital importance to our free schools. The loyalty oath has been the defense mechanism most often used to fight subversion in the schools, and at the present time thirty states require such oaths of their teachers. These oaths range from a simple statement requiring the teacher to support the Constitution to complicated oaths requiring the teacher to swear that he has not been a member of the Communist Party or any other organization listed as subversive. Some of these oaths, such as those in California and Oklahoma, have been declared unconstitutional by the courts on the ground that they infringed upon freedom of speech, thought, and association. Teachers generally have opposed these oaths and the most important teacher organizations, including the NEA and the AF of T, have gone on record as opposing them. The opposition to the oaths is based upon the belief that, first, they are unnecessary, since the overwhelming majority of American teachers are loyal and there is no reason to question their loyalty, and second, that the oath is an ineffective way of solving the problem, since no real communist would hesitate to sign it. The result is that even after the oath is taken, the task of finding the communist still exists. However, the fact remains that some individuals and groups believe these oaths to be necessary, and they have been able to get laws requiring them through the legislatures. The situation is comparable to the passage of laws requiring the study of the state and national constitutions in the schools on the ground that these requirements will somehow produce loyal American citizens.

Probably the two most important and certainly the bitterest struggles over the loyalty issue have taken place in California and New York. In 1949 the Board of Regents of the University of California introduced a special oath for all faculty members, and all who refused to sign were to be discharged. The action stirred a storm over the entire country. Many faculty members resigned and sought jobs elsewhere, while others took the case to the courts. A year or so later the Board of Regents dropped the oath, and subsequently the courts held that it was unconstitutional. In New York the state legislature passed the Feinberg Law which provided that any teacher who held membership in an organization listed as subversive by the state Board of Regents would not be permitted to teach in the public schools. The Board of Regents delegated to the local boards of education the authority to investigate all teachers and to determine whether the law was being violated and whether charges should be preferred. The law was ruled to be unconstitutional by a district court, but this decision was reversed by a higher court. This reversal was upheld by the U.S. Supreme Court in a six-to-three vote. The majority opinion was that the state had the right to determine the fitness and loyalty of its teachers and that a teacher's associates as well as the organizations to which he belonged were important factors in determining fitness and loyalty. The court also held that excluding a person from teaching did not deny him his right of freedom of speech or assembly. In the dissent the minority contended that the law upheld the concept of guilt by association and that its effect would be to turn the school system into a spying project, to frighten and intimidate teachers, and to stifle free and critical inquiry.

Probably few teachers will rise in armed rebellion against an oath requiring them to swear that they are loyal to America or that they are not affiliated with a subversive organization. But they ask why it is necessary. There are over 1,200,000 teachers in the United States, and only an insignificant number have been accused, much less found guilty, of being disloyal. And what is the nature of the loyalty that is sought? How does a teacher who is disloyal behave? Is teaching the violent overthrow of the government being disloyal? If so, the Smith Act has been violated, and there is no need of a loyalty oath. Or is criticizing or questioning the current foreign policy of the United States being disloyal? Or is criticizing the Constitution itself being disloyal? And who is to decide who is loyal and who is not?

In every state these loyalty oaths have been promoted by small groups of superpatriots who insist that for a man to be patriotic he must be willing to proclaim it loudly before the world. These groups have been helped by a large group of legislators who are unwilling to vote against the oath for fear *they* might be branded as disloyal and not re-elected. Their answer to the question of what is loyalty is simple. It is conformity —conformity and acceptance of the *status quo*: No dissent, no criticism, no rebellion. To be loyal to America one must believe as they do politically, economically, socially, and morally. The ironic part of the whole situation is that there is no surer way to subvert, to undermine, and eventually to destroy freedom than by discouraging dissent and criticism. For America was born in rebellion and nurtured on dissent. If conformity, sheep-like acceptance of the *status quo*, and the avoidance of controversial issues is being loyal to America, then Washington, Jefferson, Lincoln, Emerson, Thoreau, Whitman, and John Dewey were disloyal. Actually a good case could be made to show that the conformity and docile behavior aimed at and achieved by the sponsors of the loyalty oaths is in reality the grossest betrayal of democracy.

On the basis of our experience with loyalty oaths since World War I the judgment on them can be clearly drawn. They do not achieve their purpose because taking an oath will not make a person loyal and because a person who is really disloyal would have no qualms about taking the oath. Therefore even after the oath is given, there still remains the task of finding out who is actually disloyal. This can of course be done— Gestapo style—by having teachers investigated constantly. But then we would have to investigate the investigators ad infinitum, and this pattern is characteristic of a police state, not of a free society. About all that can be said for the oath is that if a teacher who signed one is eventually proved to be subversive, he could be charged with and punished for perjury. But if he is found guilty of such acts, there are other, stronger laws that he has violated, and he could be punished more effectively. And the gain seems slight when the harmful moral and psychological effects of the oath are considered. The oath is harmful morally because individuals who have given us little reason for doubting their loyalty and plenty of reason for trusting it are now forced by their countrymen into the humiliating experience of having to swear that they are loyal. It is harmful psychologically because it makes teachers fearful conformists, unwilling to participate in any activities either in or out of the classroom that are not "safe."

America has no need of loyalty oaths for teachers. Requiring American teachers to take them is both unnecessary and harmful. It is a sign of weakness—an act of fear—and America is not weak and has no reason to be afraid. If we insist on giving loyalty oaths to teachers we should, for the sake of logical consistency, require all *parents* to take an oath, since the parents have much more influence over the child than the teacher has. When this step is taken and all Americans have loudly proclaimed their loyalty, we shall be right back where we started.

Teacher Education. Much has been said and written in recent years about the poor quality of many of the teachers in the American schools. There is little doubt that teachers are not as well prepared as they could be or should be, but when the problem is seen in historical perspective it becomes more understandable. The record presented in the preceding chapter on the development of teacher education shows that it is only in recent years that the majority of American teachers have received college degrees. Unquestionably much progress has been made in the last fifty years in improving teacher education. But there is evidence that we are moving too slowly in times too critical for slowness. More important perhaps is our failure to understand how the improvement is to be brought about. It is not only a matter of requiring more years of schooling or more college credits. Some educators believe that what is needed is a change in our whole approach to the education of teachers. For a discussion of the changes needed a statement by one of the leaders in American education, George S. Counts, has been selected. This statement was published in 1952 as part of the chapter on "The American Teacher" in his book *Education and American Civilization.*

GEORGE S. COUNTS

FROM

Education and American Civilization [13]

THE TEACHER IS INADEQUATELY EQUIPPED TO DISCHARGE THE DUTIES OF HIS PROFESSION IN THE PRESENT AGE

Although great advances have been made during the past two generations, the teacher is the victim of a severe cultural lag. While the demands made upon the school by the changed conditions of life have greatly increased, the popular conception of the calling remains rooted largely in the pre-industrial epoch.

The difficulty may be traced in part to the origins of our system of common schools. That system was not imposed from above by a strong central government or an influential intellectual class. Rather were its foundations laid by relatively untutored farmers who established one-room district schools in rural neighborhoods as they moved across the continent. In their eyes the school was a minor social and educational institution. Its work was encompassed by "book larnin," and "book larnin" was a simple matter of reading, writing, and arithmetic. They could therefore see little reason for an elaborate program of teacher training. To them it seemed entirely appropriate to ask a bright boy or girl graduate of the eighth grade to return to school and teach the things he or she had just learned. Thus there developed in the United States the tradition of the professionally untrained teacher. In a later generation many of our people viewed with scorn and ridicule the proposal that farm boys and girls should study agriculture and housekeeping.

Under these conditions teaching was not taken too seriously. It ranked low among the occupations as a life career. It was poorly paid, marked by insecurity of tenure, and hedged about by all sorts of petty restrictions and annoyances. It was regarded as a task suited to the undeveloped powers of youth approaching manhood and womanhood, as a stepping-stone to marriage or some adult calling or profession. As late as the middle of the nineteenth century many teachers in the most progressive states were under twenty-one years of age and the great majority departed the school after one, two, three, four, or five years of teaching.

[13] George S. Counts, *Education and American Civilization* (New York: Bureau of Publications, Teachers College, Columbia University, 1952), pp. 453–5, 457, 459–68.

Those who remained longer were often looked upon as a "little queer," as human culls who could not "make the grade" in the rough and tumble of life, as women who failed to find husbands or as men who feared to compete with their peers in the economic struggle.[14] This conception of the teacher was given satirical expression by Washington Irving in the character of Ichabod Crane. Many an American citizen doubtless has greeted with a chuckle of approval the observation of Henry L. Mencken: "The average schoolmaster . . . is and always must be essentially an ass, for how can one imagine an intelligent man engaging in so puerile an avocation?" [15] And how often have we heard a banker, a physician, or even a teacher evoke condescending laughter with George Bernard Shaw's famous gibe, "He who can, does: he who cannot, teaches?" But how many know that the great dramatist also said, "He who can do, does: he who can think, teaches"? [16] . . .

From earliest historical times the word teacher has generally carried a lofty connotation. The great prophets of mankind have been called teachers. According to an old Chinese saying, which reflects the high regard for learning of this enduring civilization, "a great teacher is like a spring breeze and seasonal rain." Cicero inquired: "What greater or better gift can we offer the republic than to teach and instruct our youth?" Franklin, Washington, Jefferson, and others among our founding fathers regarded teaching as a noble profession. And throughout our history men and women of highest idealism and talents have given themselves unsparingly to the cause of education. Moreover, the improvement of the preparation and the raising of the status of the teacher have advanced notably during the last several generations. Today, in terms of social idealism and devotion to the general welfare, teachers as a group are unsurpassed by any other comparable body of citizens. Yet, as we shall see later, much remains to be done. The old heritage lingers on. In 1947–48 many teachers in the American common schools had received no college training whatsoever, and less than fifteen per cent held the master's or a higher degree.[17] Moreover, in five states more than forty per cent of the teachers received less than fifteen hundred dollars a year.[18] Clearly the task of building a profession capable of discharging the heavy responsibilities of public education in the present epoch is only well begun. Our American conception of the teacher still lags far behind our expressed convictions regarding the worth and power of education. . . .

[14] See Willard S. Elsbree, The American Teacher (New York, 1939), Chaps. XXI–XXII, pp. 271–305.
[15] Henry L. Mencken, Prejudices (New York, 1922), Third Series, p. 244.
[16] The W. E. A. Education Year Book (London, 1918), pp. 20–1.
[17] The Council of State Governments, The Forty-eight State School Systems (Chicago, 1949), p. 70.
[18] Ibid., p. 209.

THE TRAINING OF THE TEACHER MUST BE GREATLY
BROADENED AND DEEPENED

THE central theme of this volume is that education always expresses some conception of civilization and that, regardless of the efficiency of its procedures, it can rise no higher than the conception of civilization which determines its substance and purpose. Since the teacher must ever be the living embodiment of this conception, it follows that the education of a society can rise no higher than the qualifications, physical, intellectual, aesthetic, and moral, of its teachers. The conception of civilization developed in these pages obviously requires profound changes in the program of professional preparation.

First of all we must abandon or enrich much that is in our heritage. We must abandon completely the idea that teaching at any level is a simple process whose elements can be mastered in a few months or even several years by bright boys and girls in the period of late adolescence. We must abandon completely the tradition derived from our simple agrarian past that teaching is a matter of keeping order and transmitting verbal skills to embellish the genuine education acquired in the home and on the farm. We must abandon also the tradition derived from the class societies of the Old World that teaching in the common school involves merely giving to the offspring of the "hewers of wood and drawers of water" the narrow training required by that humble station in the social order to which they are called by the laws of God and man. We must abandon too the idea derived from the early period of industrialization that teaching has as its main object the preparation of ambitious youth to "get ahead" of their fellows in the race for preferred positions in the economic and social order. We must abandon likewise the assumption that teaching is essentially a process of passing on to the young various bodies of knowledge and that the level of teaching bears a direct relation to the abstruseness of the knowledge involved. We must abandon finally the idea derived from business management that the teacher is merely a semi-skilled worker in the assembly line who is expected to follow without question the orders of his immediate superior in a mass-production enterprise.

We must see teaching as the tremendous and difficult task that it is. We must see that it involves nothing less than the guiding of the individual to full maturity and freedom, of inducting him into the most complex and dynamic society of history, of preparing him to assume the heavy duties of managing that society and of transmitting its heritage of liberty unimpaired and even enhanced to his children. The assumption of the post of teaching at any level of the school system is indeed a sobering and challenging responsibility, and hardly to be assigned to the ill-prepared or the ill-disposed. Who can say that the task is easier in the kindergarten than in the university, in the guiding of the total personality of the child than in the teaching of higher mathematics? About this we need not quarrel. We know that either requires not only professional skill and knowledge of the first order, but also charity, understanding, and wisdom.

Since the days of Samuel R. Hall and James G. Carter, who toward the close of the first quarter of the nineteenth century founded the first institutions to prepare young people for "school keeping," the need for the professional training of the teacher has been increasingly recognized in America. With the unparalleled expansion of the common school during subsequent generations, and particularly since the opening of the present century, the program for the training of teachers has been greatly extended. Today the need for such a program is generally accepted. Yet the actual practice lags far behind the evolution of American civilization and the conception of education. The professional training of the teacher continues to bear the stamp of its humble origins in the agrarian age. It is severely limited in both scope and content. In terms of depth and breadth of preparation teaching remains today a skilled or at best a semi-professional occupation. The emphasis is still on the mechanics of education, on methods of teaching, on "school keeping," on mastery of narrow subject matter, on financial and material operations. All of these things are of course necessary, but they are scarcely sufficient to equip even the most gifted to discharge the obligations of rearing the young in the atomic age. The time has come for us to consign to the wastebasket of history the idea that teaching requires less severe selection and training than the practice of medicine, law, engineering, or theology. Indeed, from the standpoint of the values and responsibilities involved teaching is probably the most difficult and important of all the professions.

In addition to the mastery of techniques and specialized subject matter, every teacher should be expected to acquire a basic understanding of the nature of the child and of man. This would of course mean knowledge of the biological constitution of the species, of the role of hereditary forces, of the laws of growth, learning, and maturation, of the development of character and personality, of the whole process of the induction of the young into the life of the group. It would mean also the acquisition of those insights and perspectives which can come only from some acquaintance with man in the natural order, in history, and in diverse cultures. The value of knowledge of psychology has of course long been recognized, and with the revolutionary advances in the science during the past two generations it has thoroughly established itself in the program. However, even today the emphasis is placed too largely on the relation of the individual to the learning of "subject matter." The educational psychology of the future must be increasingly social in character. It must devote far more attention than heretofore to the relation of the individual to the group and the entire field of human relations. The complexity and dynamism of industrial society, as well as the moral commitments of democracy, make this shift in emphasis clearly necessary.

At this point we come to the central and crucial deficiency in our program of teacher training—a deficiency which is derived from the limitations of our traditional conception of education. According to that conception education should and can be conducted in conformity with the universal laws of the organism and its own nature. Adequate understanding of the process can therefore be gained through the study of the child and the school. The thesis of the present volume, on the other hand, is that the whole enterprise of education is a function of a particular society at a particular time and place and must express some conception of life and civilization supported by the social group involved. This view vastly complicates the task of the teacher in a free society and, if consistently applied, would call for nothing less than a revolution in the program of professional training.

If the education of the young involves in some measure not only the fortunes of individuals, but also the future of our society and civilization, of our democratic institutions and free way of life, as it clearly does, then the selection and preparation of teachers should be recognized by all as a major concern of the Republic, certainly as important as the production of material things or even the maintenance of the national defense. Indeed, if conceived in appropriate terms and with adequate vision, it is the most basic and decisive factor in survival and progress. Johann Valentin Andreae, seventeenth century humanist, long ago gave voice to an ideal which free society should always cherish. "Their instructors," he said of teachers in his mythical community of Christianopolis, "are not men from the dregs of human society nor such as are useless for other occupations, but the choice of all the citizens, persons whose standing in the republic is known and who very often have access to the highest positions in the state." [19] In these words Andreae was merely saying that our children, all of our children, constitute our most precious resource.

For a teacher to be ignorant of the history of his people, of their triumphs and failures, of their basic ways and institutions, of their points of weakness and strength, of their moral commitments and ideals, of the great patterns of their civilization, of the dangers which threaten them, and of the opportunities which confront them is to invite catastrophe in the present age. Yet it must be conceded that our program

[19] Johann Valentin Andreae, *Christianopolis*, edited by Julius Goebel (New York, 1916), p. 207.

of teacher training today must plead guilty in considerable measure to this indictment. The fact is that few American teachers are able to outline except in most superficial terms the basic features of our civilization or our way of life. Fewer still have reasoned and informed convictions regarding the foundations of free society and the forces at home and abroad which place in jeopardy our entire heritage of human liberty. And yet fewer have more than a most superficial knowledge of the great ethical, aesthetic, philosophical, and religious traditions of Western man on which our entire civilization rests. The explanation of this situation undoubtedly must be attributed largely to deficiencies in their training. They are simply not expected to be interested in or to probe deeply into such questions.

Whatever may be said about other forms of professional preparation a teacher-training institution should make central the study of our American civilization in both its historical and its world setting, from its origins in antiquity to its relations with all nations and peoples. Whether the individual is to practice his calling in the kindergarten or the university, in the teaching of literature or science, he should know both the society and the culture which the school is supposed to serve. To aspire to less than this in the contemporary world is certain to provide an education of inferior quality and possibly to court catastrophe. Clearly, if teachers are to assist effectively in the rearing of a generation of free men, they must themselves have the knowledge and the loyalties necessary to set and keep men free. This of course does not mean that they should be required to transmit to the young an official body of doctrine or a set of fixed allegiances beyond the reach of informed criticism. The adoption of such a policy would be disastrous and would mark the end of liberty in America. The spirit of freedom cannot be evoked on command, even by the highest authority. On the contrary, it is a tender plant that can be nurtured in the young only by those who practice, understand, and love it. . . .

THE LIFE OF THE TEACHER MUST BE GREATLY ENRICHED

First of all the teacher must be relieved from excessive demands on his time and energies. He must be assured those working conditions which are essential to the successful discharge of his heavy responsibilities. This means the reduction of class size and teaching load to the point that makes it possible for him to know his pupils individually, to become acquainted with their parents and home surroundings, and to participate effectively in the formulation of school policy and the development of the curriculum. It means also the complete abandonment of the tradition that the teacher is merely a more or less high-grade servant who may be called upon at will by members of the board of education or private persons of power and influence in the community to perform manifold duties ranging from the teaching of Sunday school to the administration of an essay contest on the virtues of advertising. Only when an individual feels that he is doing his job well can he experience that sense of personal dignity and satisfaction in his calling which is the highest reward of socially useful and creative labor. It is only then, too, that the community is likely to appreciate fully the work of the teacher.

In the second place, the teacher must be free to participate as a mature person in the life of the community—local, state, and national. Indeed, such participation should be encouraged and rewarded. This calls for the abandonment of the tradition that the teacher should be something less than a whole human being, that he should lead a cloistered existence, that he should always remain as immature as the boys and girls who wielded the "hickory stick" and taught "readin', 'ritin', and 'rithmetic" in the one-room district school of hallowed memory. Teachers today, whether men or women, should be expected to engage in courtship, to marry and to have children of their own. They should be expected to join and aspire to leadership in organizations devoted to the promotion of the general welfare, the advancement of the arts and sciences of life, or the simple enjoyment of good fellowship. They should be expected to pursue avocational interests of the greatest variety, from hiking to music and from stamp collecting to horticulture. Through appropriate conditions of work and adequate remuneration they should be assured leisure and funds necessary for travel, purchase of books, attendance at the theatre, and general cultivation of personal interests. Perhaps even more than other citizens they should set an example to the young by taking an active part in civic affairs and exercising responsibly all the rights of citizenship. They should join political parties, make political speeches, and run for public office. There is of course no suggestion here that every teacher should do all of these things. Like others of his generation he should be allowed freedom of choice. The point to be emphasized is merely that by living a full and rich life he will be a better teacher. No one can truly understand our American community by reading books and following the role of a spectator.

In the third place, teachers should be as free to form their own organizations as any other group of citizens. This right is implied in the foregoing paragraph. But the issue is so important that it merits special consideration. It is of course well known that teachers today have many organizations. They are organized at all levels and in all specialties, and they have several organizations which aspire to embrace and represent the profession as a whole. Yet the fact remains that as yet they are not effectively organized to present their case as a whole to the American community.

The object of an adequate organization, aside from the improvement of processes and purposes of education, should be threefold. It should strive to remove the many disabilities and frustrations under which the teacher labors and to which attention has already been directed. In a world marked by organized pressures, no group is likely to be heard or even respected if it lacks the resources which come from association. Also the organization should battle for the common school, for the welfare of the younger generation, and for a conception of education appropriate to the present age. Being closer to these interests than any other group of citizens, teachers naturally have a special obligation here to the whole community. Finally, through their organization they should endeavor to express with power their special point of view with respect to all the great issues confronting the American people. In their varied struggles teachers will inevitably work with other groups which share their values and purposes. Whether they should affiliate organically with any one element in the population, such as organized labor, is a highly complicated question whose merits will not be discussed in these pages. The point to be emphasized here is that teachers need a powerful organization and that they will find themselves closely associated with those groups which are devoted to the cause of public education and democracy.

Acceptance of the philosophy of education underlying Professor Counts' statements will have definite and concrete implications for institutions that prepare teachers. It will mean that the professional aspects of the program must be linked very closely with the college of liberal arts, and it will mean that the education of teachers will become more of a university-wide concern although centered in the schools or departments of education. It will mean not only that the length of the preparatory programs will be extended, but that all teachers will be required to have done extensive work in American studies, especially history and literature, political science, economics, and sociology. Finally, it will mean that prospective teachers, in addition to their major subject-matter work, will be required to take far more work than they have been in psychology, sociology, and social psychology.

Suggested Readings

Barzun, Jacques: *Teacher in America.* Boston: Little, Brown & Company, 1944.
Beale, Howard K.: *Are American Teachers Free?* New York: Charles Scribner's Sons, 1936.

Beale, Howard K.: *A History of Freedom of Teaching in American Schools*. New York: Charles Scribner's Sons, 1941.

Becker, Carl: *Freedom and Responsibility in the American Way of Life*. New York: Alfred A. Knopf, 1945.

Butts, R. Freeman, and Cremin, Lawrence A.: *A History of Education in American Culture*. New York: Henry Holt and Company, 1953.

Counts, George S.: *Education and American Civilization*. New York: Bureau of Publications, Teachers College, Columbia University, 1952.

Elsbree, Willard S.: *The American Teacher*. New York: American Book Company, 1939.

Hook, Sidney: *Education for Modern Man*. New York: The Dial Press, 1946.

Lieberman, Myron: *Education as a Profession*. Englewood Cliffs, N.J.: Prentice-Hall, Inc., 1956.

CHAPTER 19

TEACHING AS A CAREER

THE READER HAS PROBABLY GATHERED BY THIS TIME THAT ONE OF the basic premises of this volume concerns the key role that the teacher has to play in American society. The belief is that the education of the young is an important task in any society but in a free society it is a more important task. The parents, particularly the mother, have the greatest influence upon the development or education of the child, and we know that the early years are the important ones. Without the parents' love and attention the child, regardless of his native ability, is retarded mentally, emotionally, and physically. But in our society next to the parents and the family come the teachers in terms of relative educative influence upon the child. Of course, there are exceptions to this statement. If a child is in very large classes throughout his school years, the influence of the teacher is bound to be lessened, and in this situation the influence of the family, the neighborhood, and the peer group becomes proportionately greater. But with a decent class size and a nondepartmentalized program such as prevails in our elementary schools, the influence of the teacher can be tremendous, since the child is under his direct supervision six hours a day for nine months out of the year.

Factors in Choosing a Teaching Career

FROM all of the material that has been presented about American education in previous chapters the reader should have formed some opinion as to whether he would be interested in teaching as a career. If this volume has been read in connection with an introductory course in education, the chances are that some opportunity for visiting and observing schools was presented. If so, a more adequate basis for making a decision exists. However, whether or not a fairly definite decision has already been made, there are some factors that need to be considered before the decision is final.

In selecting a vocation or a career or a profession, there are two major factors that need to be taken into consideration. One is the nature of the vocation itself—that is, the type of work involved, the probable remuneration (both immediate and long range), and the job opportunities. The other factor is the interest and ability of the individual. In the pages that follow an attempt will be made to indicate the nature of the teacher's job, and more specifically the extent to which teaching is an art and the extent to which it is a science. Then attention will be given to the opportunities available, the areas of specialization possible, and the probable salary schedules to be expected. Finally, to help the student determine whether he has the kind of ability necessary for teaching, a statement is included by a leading American educator on the qualities deemed essential.

Teaching—An Art Based on Science

THE job of teaching always entails working with people and generally with children. On every level the teacher's job is to guide the learning and to stimulate the intellectual development of students. On all levels, but especially in the elementary school, teachers attempt to help the student to develop physically, socially, emotionally, and morally. The task at all levels is to help the student to understand himself and the world in which he lives, and this requires a tremendous amount of knowledge. In the primary grades strong emphasis is placed upon the basic skills of reading and writing, but these skills must continue to be developed even in the colleges. With each class, with each student, the teacher's job is one of opening doors into new areas of knowledge, of awakening latent interests and of developing special talents. On every grade-level the teacher's job is to make learning an adventure, to nurture the native curiosity of the child and channel it into a skilled search for knowledge. Above all, the teacher's task is to nourish those moral qualities, such as gentleness, humility, and concern for others, without which a civilization degenerates into barbarism regardless of its technical and material progress. All the American teacher is asked to do is to help develop the knowledge, skills, attitudes, and understandings that will enable our children to assume the responsibility for guiding the destiny of the most complex civilization in history, and for not only preserving but also improving our great heritage of freedom and democracy and then passing it on to future generations.

There would probably be substantial agreement among educators with the preceding account of the nature of the teacher's job. But especially since 1910 or so, with the effort to study education scientifically, controversy has arisen as to whether education is an art or a science. The dispute which continues down to the present time was polarized by the unwillingness of some educators to entertain even the possibility that human behavior could be studied scientifically and by the extravagant claims of other educators who believed that teaching could be reduced to a precise science. This latter group underestimated the difficulty of analyzing the complexities of human learning in the classroom; when they did not produce miracles, those educators who were skeptical of educational science said, "I told you so!" This has resulted in numerous charges and countercharges and a delay in genuine understanding.

There is no question that teaching in its actual practice is an art. It is also clear that education is not a separate science but, like engineering and medicine, it is based upon science—especially the behavioral sciences, psychology, social psychology, and sociology-anthropology—as well as upon other disciplines, such as history and philosophy. The engineer in building a bridge must have a knowledge of mathematics and of physical, mechanical principles as well as a knowledge of the nature and strength of the materials with which he works. Bridges were built before the modern scientific era, but no one would suggest that engineers ignore and fail to utilize whatever knowledge from the physical sciences and mathematics would enable them to build better bridges. The same applies in education. Children were being taught before psychologists began to study learning and before sociologists and anthropologists began to study human societies. But can we seriously doubt that such knowledge would enable teachers to do a more effective job in the classroom?

For a number of reasons the teaching profession has lagged behind engineering and medicine in basing its practice upon scientific evidence. First, in the early years of this century many educators who were anxious to put education on a scientific basis failed to understand that, as Dewey pointed out, "Material drawn from *other* sciences furnishes the content of educational science when it is focused on the problems that arise in education." [1] This led them to attempt to study educational problems without mastering what these sciences had to offer, and much superficial work was done while many of the real problems were neglected. Second, the sciences upon which educational practice must be based—the behavioral sciences—are relatively new sciences and the problems with which they deal—human behavior—are very complex. Third, in many instances when these sciences, especially psychology, *were* drawn upon they were rushed into classroom practice prematurely. These actions are understandable, for educators were under pressure to

[1] John Dewey, *The Sources of a Science of Education* (New York: Liveright Publishing Corp., 1929), p. 36.

show immediate results. However, when the expected results were not forthcoming, many teachers as well as laymen became skeptical that educational practice could ever be "scientific." This same situation exists in the professional programs in teacher education when students expect educational psychologists to tell them exactly how to teach in much the same way they would get a recipe for baking a cake. When the psychologist cannot provide such a recipe they become skeptical. Finally, the scientific study of education has lagged because of a combination of a lack of adequate time and money for research and the failure of men trained in the social sciences and professional educators (including teachers) to collaborate in studying educational problems.

Even though the progress in establishing a scientific basis for educational practice has not been as rapid as might have been desired, the important point for prospective teachers to remember is that such a basis is not only possible but is already partly established. And one has only to consider the impact that the work of such outstanding social scientists as Thorndike, Terman, Lewin, Pavlov, and Warner has had upon educational theory and practice to understand potential influence of the social sciences upon classroom procedures. For those individuals who are considering teaching as a career this means that they will be required to study seriously in the behavioral sciences, but it also means that as a result of this study they will be more effective teachers. It is also possible that as classroom teachers are more adequately prepared in the social sciences they will be able to collaborate with specialists from the universities in attacking and solving teaching problems in the schools. Certainly this would add an element of intellectual stimulation to the work of the teacher.

Opportunities for Teaching Positions

THE opportunities for teaching positions in the United States in the foreseeable future are virtually unlimited. The teacher shortage which is severe today is bound to get worse as the population continues to increase. There are approximately 44,000,000 students in American schools at the present time, and that figure is expected to rise to 53,000,000 in 1964. The American Schools in 1959–60 needed approximately 195,000 additional teachers, and this figure will undoubtedly continue to rise. The fact is that in the foreseeable future well-qualified teachers will be in such great demand that they will be virtually able to pick the jobs they want. It is true today, and it is quite likely to continue to be true in the future, that the greatest opportunity will be in the elementary schools although any qualified person wanting to teach in the secondary schools will have no difficulty finding a position. The reasons for the greater opportunity in the elementary schools are, first, that the enrollment in the elementary schools is four times as great as in the secondary schools and, second, that the great majority of teachers in the elementary schools are women who get married, have children, and therefore drop out of teaching for several years. However, since positions in the secondary schools will be plentiful, students should make decisions as to their areas of specialization on the basis of interests. In other words, anyone who really prefers to teach in the secondary school should not go into elementary work just because of the greater opportunity there. However, there are great opportunities, especially for men, in elementary education.

Areas of Specialization

As THE teaching profession gradually raises its standards, the tendency is toward more and more specialization. Thus at the present time in the better teacher-education institutions, a student planning to teach in the primary grades of the elementary schools is given courses specifically related to the problems of teaching on that level. It is true of course that much of the professional knowledge needed by teachers is common to all levels, just as all physicians receive a great deal of similar work whether they plan to specialize in pediatrics or surgery. The list of areas of specialization in teaching given below is certainly not complete, but it will indicate the major types of teaching positions which are open to prospective teachers.

> *Nursery School*—The demand for teachers in the nursery school has been growing steadily in the last two decades. Today many public schools maintain nursery schools, but more frequently they are maintained by social agencies or are privately owned and operated.
>
> *Kindergarten*—The kindergarten is rapidly becoming a standard part of the American public school system and so the demand for kindergarten teachers is great.
>
> *The Primary Grades*—This area includes grades one, two, and three. The emphasis here is upon the basic skills of reading, writing, spelling, and arithmetic as well as on continuing the socialization and creative elements of the nursery school and kindergarten. It is also true that more and more science and social studies are being taught in the primary grades. Generally teachers who specialize in this area are qualified to teach any of the three grades as well as the kindergarten, although more attention is being given to specialized training for the work in early childhood. In some schools primary teachers remain with a class for two and sometimes three years.
>
> *The Intermediate Grades*—This area includes grades four, five, and six. While the work in the basic skills, e.g., reading, is continued,

generally in the intermediate grades the job is one of widening horizons through work in the social studies and in science and through providing opportunities for the further development of the basic skills. Teachers in these grades need to be broadly trained in the social sciences, the natural sciences, and the humanities. A teacher who enjoys working with ideas and yet wishes to avoid the departmentalized system of the high school will find that the children in these grades can provide a real challenge.

Specialized Positions in the Elementary School—In addition to the types of positions described, there are many special teaching jobs, especially in the larger systems. Some schools have special teachers for art, music, physical education, and foreign languages. Many schools have special reading teachers who work with retarded readers, while others have special teachers for classes of slow learners.

The Junior High School—In most places *this* area is considered a part of the secondary school system and is departmentalized. Teachers in the junior high school teach either social studies, general science, mathematics, or English (grammar, composition, and literature) and sometimes a combination of two such as social studies and English.

The Secondary Schools—Teaching in the secondary schools requires specialization in one or more of the following areas:

English—Includes grammar, composition, and literature.

Social Studies—Includes American and world history, government, economics, sociology, psychology, and geography. Often courses in American problems or citizenship are a part of the teaching in this area.

Foreign Language—Most schools offer Spanish, French, German, and Latin.

Science—Includes general science, biology, chemistry, and physics.

Mathematics—Most high schools offer work in algebra, geometry, and trigonometry.

Speech—This position generally entails corrective speech work as well as debating, dramatics, radio, etc.

Physical Education—Includes coaching, classes in physical education and health and hygiene.

Home Economics—Generally involves teaching cooking, sewing, home management, etc.

Industrial Arts—Includes teaching mechanical drawing, machine shop, wood turning.

Music—Most schools require work in chorus and offer opportunities for individual instrumental instruction.

Art—Most schools offer courses in drawing and painting and some offer work in sculpturing and ceramics.

Commerce—Includes courses in typing, shorthand, bookkeeping, business law, etc.

Agriculture—Positions in this field are of course primarily offered in the rural areas.

In addition to these types of positions, there are others in the secondary schools in specialized fields such as guidance and counseling, curriculum, and administration. For the most part, these types of jobs are available only in the larger school systems and require a background of teaching experience plus advanced graduate preparation.

Teaching in Colleges and Universities—The teaching positions on this level are more highly specialized than those in the high schools. With few exceptions these positions require a Ph.D. in the subject field in which one desires to teach: English, history, political science, science, sociology, psychology, chemistry, physics, biology, philosophy, education, music.

Special Education—In the last thirty years more and more opportunities have become available in the teaching of handicapped children. These include teaching the blind, the deaf, and the physically and mentally handicapped.

Guidance and Counseling—American schools have assumed responsibility for the development and guidance of the individual as well as for providing instruction for students as members of classes. Increasing diversity of student interest, multiplying school programs from which to choose, and intensifying pressures upon students have created need for guidance counselors. Persons experienced in teaching, with advanced training in psychology and vocational and educational counseling, and with sympathetic insight into the problems of young people, may prepare for positions as guidance teachers, as directors of guidance programs, or as school psychologists.

Supervision—Well-qualified teachers have a distinct opportunity with their own students to improve the quality and excitement of education. Especially capable teachers may wish to extend the range of their influence by seeking positions as supervisors, or more properly, consultants to other teachers. School systems increasingly employ such specialists to aid the less experienced teacher and to help keep the entire staff informed of broad developments in subject matter, psychology, and methods of teaching.

School Principalship—The word *principal* is an abbreviation of an older term, *principal teacher,* and implies responsibility in improving instruction and in supervising teachers. The principal enjoys a particularly advantageous position, for the quality of his leadership in large part determines whether a given school will be a static or a dynamic institution.

School Superintendency—The superintendent is the chief administrative officer of the school system. He devotes the major portion of his time to the administration and supervision of the entire system under his control. He is the official most counted upon to provide effective educational leadership to the Board of Education, to all members of the staff, and to the community. He recommends and executes personnel policies, budgets, building programs, plans for curricular development, the improvement of instruction, and public relations programs.

Salaries

REGARDLESS of how interesting or promising a particular career may appear, before choosing it as a career the inevitable question of how well does it pay must be answered. It is impossible to say precisely, of course, what salary schedules are or will be in the thousands of school districts across the country, but some general statements can be made. At the present time a teacher with a bachelor's degree and no teaching experience can expect to receive between $3,000 and $5,000 per school year. In all but the poorest districts the usual pattern is to provide yearly increments of $200 up to a maximum of between $6,000 and $7,000, and some go as high as $10,000. Some districts without adequate finances offer comparatively high starting salaries, but have little or no increment from year to year and very low maximum salaries. Where this condition prevails, there is usually a large turnover of personnel, since the teachers naturally seek positions that offer better long-range salaries.

The most recent recommendation of the NEA (whose past recommendations have been gradually accepted) is for a salary schedule with a minimum of $3,800 and a maximum of $8,400. Benjamin Fine, the education editor of the *New York Times*, has suggested that we set our teaching minimum at $5,000 and our maximum at $10,000. He believes this kind of schedule is imperative if we are to attract and keep able people in the profession. For these salaries, Mr. Fine points out, he would expect highly trained, well-qualified teachers, who have a minimum of five years of college work. This is not to say that all is rosy regarding teachers' salaries. Too many teachers receive far too little compensation and many have actually been forced out of the profession for this reason. But salaries can be and are being raised. It must be conceded that some of the responsibility for poor salaries rests with teachers themselves. We can be certain that as long as there are poorly qualified teachers there will be low salaries. We can be equally sure that as long as there are teachers who timidly accept any salary, however low, little can be done. However, the problem of adequate salaries for teachers (along the scale set by Mr. Fine) is part of the larger problem which was discussed in Chapter 11 of securing adequate support for education in all of its aspects.

In general, it can be said that the principle of the single-salary schedule has been adopted in the United States. This principle is that teachers should receive equal pay, regardless of their sex and regardless of whether they are teaching in the first grade or the twelfth, if they have comparable training and experience. This principle is also being applied to Negro teachers, although many states maintain higher scales for white teachers. Most salary schedules also provide higher salaries for advanced degrees. Having a master's degree, for example, generally means an increase of $250 to $350 per year for a teacher. Many districts also make their annual salary increment dependent upon evidence of professional growth, such as additional university work.

As might be expected, the salaries of teachers vary between states and within states, and between rural and urban areas. Teachers in states such as New York and California have high salary schedules, while the average salary of teachers in some of the poorer states is much lower. But in some of the states where average salaries are low there are districts in which they are as high as any in the country. As a general rule, salaries tend to be higher in large cities and suburban areas and lower in the rural areas. However, the fact that the cost of living in rural areas is generally lower tends to offset this difference somewhat.

The Qualities of a Good Teacher

WITH this brief account of the nature of the job and of the remuneration and opportunities that can be expected, it is time to turn to the second major consideration involved in choosing a career—namely, the interests and abilities of the individual. In attempting to decide this important question, alternatives have to be weighed and values examined carefully. In the last analysis, the decision will depend upon what the individual thinks is important in life. Obviously if the most important thing in an individual's life is accumulating money, teaching should not be chosen. But if the important thing is to engage in work that offers an opportunity to make a contribution to individual and social well-being, teaching might be chosen. This is not to say that going into the business world does not contribute to the welfare of society. Nor is it to say that teaching is the only career that offers an opportunity for real service. In this respect careers in medicine, law, engineering, nursing, and many others offer ample opportunity. It is to say that teaching presents a unique opportunity to the individual to contribute to the progress of the human race. All of us can remember from our own experience the influence that some fine teacher had upon our lives. And every veteran teacher can recall the satisfaction derived from igniting a spark and awakening latent talent in a student. The fact is that a good teacher is a most important person. His work makes a real difference to a whole generation of students. If an individual likes working with people and ideas in a position that is pregnant with social significance, teaching might well be chosen.

But interest in teaching is not enough. Equally important is the individual's ability. Many individuals would like nothing better than to be great athletes, surgeons, scientists, yet they simply do not have the ability. This is equally true of teachers, as anyone who has suffered under a poor teacher can attest. What are the qualities that a good teacher should have? No two people, not even two teachers, would agree completely, but there are certain essential qualities that must be present. One of the best statements on this topic that the author has ever read is a statement by Professor Sidney Hook in his book *Education for Modern Man*, written in 1946. The major portion of that statement is printed below. The prospective teacher should read it carefully and apply the criteria to himself.

SIDNEY HOOK

FROM

Education for Modern Man [2]

The major role of the teacher in the educational process has led some writers to the conclusion that, once students have been assembled for purposes of instruction the good teacher is all sufficient. Given a good teacher, they assume, further concern with educational content and method is unnecessary. He has an unfailing natural sense of what is right to teach and how to teach it. He does not even need a well appointed classroom. One end of a log will do. Invariably someone will recall an individual of whom he will say: "He did not know anything about pedagogy but he was a great teacher."

Such a position is understandable as a reaction to the view that anybody can be educated to be an educator. It manifests a healthy skep-

[2] Reprinted from *Education for Modern Man* by Sidney Hook. Copyright 1946 by Sidney Hook. Used by permission of the Dial Press, Inc. Pp. 173–4, 180–9, 192–3.

ticism towards the over-developed curriculums of professional schools of education in which courses are needlessly proliferated. But there is little to be said for it as a serious response to the problems of instruction. If what a student learns depends altogether on who his teacher is, the result is sure to be a disorderly cross-patch pattern. The traditions and knowledge and skills which our age requires as a common soil in which to cultivate individual variety could hardly be developed. The diversity in temperament of these uniquely endowed persons, and in the direction of their interests as well as ideas, is much greater than among those who cannot spin an entire educational curriculum out of their innards. Such diversity within limits is desirable, provided students are exposed to the varied stimuli of several outstanding personalities. But this is not likely to be the case. For the number of these extraordinary teachers is not enough to go around. And what the educational system of America needs is at least a million good teachers.

Teaching is an art and like all arts it can be learned with varying degrees of proficiency. Some are so gifted by nature that they can perform as good teachers without learning the arts of teaching, just as some singers can have brilliant musical careers without studying voice culture. On the other hand, there are some individuals who are naturally so handicapped for a teaching career that instruction in the teaching arts can do as little for them as musical study for the tone deaf. Most teachers fall between these two extremes. It is a crime against students to permit individuals of the second kind to enter the ordinary classroom as teachers, no matter how great their gifts may be in other respects or in other fields. Whatever teaching is, it should at least not be an obstruction to learning. But it is certainly no crime, it is not even a hardship, to require of naturally gifted teachers—those who are to the teaching manner born—that they learn the formal rudiments of the art of teaching. They can always improve their skills. An enormous amount of time can be saved by familiarizing oneself with teaching devices and techniques even if one already possesses the educators's insight and an adequate educational philosophy. No one who has not actually attempted to teach the details of a curriculum can properly appreciate the great difference that mastery of specific ways and means can make in motivating interest, facilitating communication and starting a train of thought in students which runs its course to the click of understanding. There are some things that are best learned *not* on the job. And although we can rely on any teacher to learn by trial and error experience, why should the students pay the price for that experience? . . .

A good teacher is not good for all purposes and in all circumstances. In the army, in the church, in the political party, in the penitentiary, as they are presently constituted, a good teacher as we shall define him cannot be used. What makes a good teacher, like what makes a good education, must be considered in relation to certain values. What we are seeking are the criteria of a good teacher in a democratic society whose educational system has embraced the fundamental aims we have previously outlined.

(a) The first criterion is intellectual competence. By this I mean not only the truism that the teacher should have a mastery of the subject matter he is teaching and that he should keep abreast of important developments in his field, but that he should have some capacity for analysis. Without this capacity, he cannot develop it in his students. There are different levels and types of analysis but what they have in common is an understanding of how to approach problems, of how to take ideas apart, of how to relate our language habits to our intellectual practices. Capacity of analysis is something different from mere possession of the dry-bones and heaps of knowledge. Insofar as the distinction can be made, it is bound up more with method than content. Whatever information a teacher imparts, he must know (and wherever relevant be able to explain) how it is reached, what its validity depends on, and the role of empirical and conventional elements in the answer.

Another element in intellectual competence is a sense of relevant connection. The good teacher should be well oriented in some other fields besides the one in which he may claim to be a specialist. He should be able to follow the thread of an argument or the ramifications of a problem without concerns for what a subject is called or for departmental non-trespass signs. I have heard a professor of political science bitterly complain that the economics department was teaching government, too! If the teaching was good, he should have applauded it. On the other hand, not everything in the world is interrelated and, if it were, not all of it would be equally relevant to a specific problem. The most obvious evidence of bad teaching is classroom "thinking by association," in which by a series of grasshopper jumps topics are dwelt on that have no logical connection with each other. The usual result is that the original problem, where there is one, is lost sight of.

Related to intellectual competence is the willingness to countenance, if not to encourage, rational opposition and spirited critical dissent by students. The inquiring mind even among youth sometimes probes deeply. Only a teacher unsure of himself will resent embarrassing questions to which the only honest reply must be a confession of ignorance. Intellectual independence is such a rare virtue that the good teacher positively welcomes it despite the occasional excess of youthful dogmatism and exuberance. For many years I refused to believe that any liberal arts teacher would actually penalize a student for intellectual disagreement. But the evidence is overwhelming that in many colleges this is far from exceptional, and that students are often fearful of venturing a defence of ideas and attitudes incompatible with those held by their teachers. In one institution, a teacher of philosophy did not conceal from his students his conviction that to embrace the metaphysics of materialism was to reveal a moral deficiency in character. Anyone who expected a recommendation from him was warned to look to his philosophy. In another institution, a bright member of the Young Communist League bitterly complained to his English teacher who had given him the lowest possible passing grade. In answer, he was told that anyone who believed in dialectical materialism deserved nothing better. A few years later, a young woman who had a perfect record in all her subjects took the same course with the same teacher and received the only C in her college career. On inquiring the reason she was told that no student who *disbelieved* in dialectical materialism deserved anything better. The teacher had become converted and had changed his mind about dialectical materialism—a speculative doctrine really irrelevant to the subject matter of his course. But he had not changed his intellectual ways. He was sincerely convinced that he had the truth on both occasions, but lacked the wit to realize that the students' *reasons* for embracing truth or error were far more important, in their educational experience, than the question of the validity of dialectical materialism. In the last decade, more than one class of students has been punished for the tortuous intellectual pilgrimages of their teachers—particularly at the hands of a certain school of militantly doctrinaire teachers, who, despite the fact that their opinions veer as if by order from year to year, regard themselves as qualified to settle the most delicate problems of economics, politics, history, philosophy and religion with a zeal and confidence that specialists, handicapped by genuine knowledge, shrink from assuming.

(b) Intellectual competence is necessary but not sufficient for good teaching. It must be accompanied by a quality of patience towards beginners which accepts as natural the first groping steps toward understanding by the uninitiated. The "simple" and the "obvious" are relative to antecedent skills and knowledge. Failure to see and act on this is responsible for intellectual browbeating by otherwise competent teachers and for the air, deliberately only half-concealed, of suffering the hopeless stupidity of those who are stumbling their way forward. The intellectually quick, and all teachers should be quick, have a tendency towards intellectual impatience. The impatience but not the quickness must be curbed. Patience is something that can be learned, except by certain temperaments who should never be entrusted with a class. Good teaching is not found where a star teacher holds forth for the benefit only of his star pupils, but where some participating response is evoked from every normal member of the class. Nothing is easier than to yield to the pleasures of colloquy with the exceptional students of a class—and nothing more unfair to the rest, in whom this builds up intense resentments, oddly enough not against the teacher, but against their exceptional classmates. Special provision should be made for the instruction of superior students but a good teacher does not let their special needs dominate the class.

(c) The third characteristic of good teaching is ability to plan a lesson, without mechanically imposing it on the class, in those subjects where basic materials have to be acquired, and to guide the development of discussion to a cumulative result in subjects in which the seminar method is used. The bane of much college teaching is improvisation. Improvisation is not only legitimate but unavoidable in motivating interest and finding points of departure or illustration for principles. But it cannot replace the planful survey of subject matter and problems, nor provide direction to discussion. It is delightful to follow the argument wherever it leads. But it must be an argument.

Where improvisation is chronic and draws its materials from autobiography, teaching sinks to its lowest level. In my own experience I recall teachers who rarely knew what they were going to talk about before they came to class. Usually they would talk about themselves or their families. Over the years, when members of their successive classes came together, they were able to construct a fairly accurate composite family portrait. The personalities of such teachers rarely possessed a richness or power that might justify taking themselves as subject matter. The contempt in which intelligent students held them was checked only by the teachers' power to distribute grades—a power which they wielded with a whimsical irresponsibility.

Naturally, the responsibility of the teacher for the progressive organization of subject matter varies with elementary and advanced classes, and he will proceed differently in presenting a lecture and in conducting a tutorial. Nothing I have said suggests the necessity of a detailed lesson plan which is as often a drawback as an aid even in the secondary schools. What the teacher must aim at is to make each class hour an integrated experience with an aesthetic, if possible a dramatic, unity of its own. Without a spontaneity that can point up the give and take of discussion, and a skill in weaving together what the students themselves contribute, preparation will not save the hour from dullness. The pall of dullness which hangs over the memories of school days in the minds of many unfortunately envelops the whole question of education.

(d) Another important quality the good teacher possesses is knowledge of human beings. He is in a sense a practical psychologist. He knows something more about people than the laws of their learning curves, and what he knows he has not found in textbooks on psychology. The more one studies students, the more difference they reveal. These differences need not be relevant to what they are trying to learn; but sometimes they are. A teacher devoid of this knowledge cannot solve the problem of motivation or evoke full participation from his class. Nor can he tell when to temper the wind, when to let it blow, when to build up self-assurance in the pathologically shy, when to deflate the bumptious. Unable to diversify his challenges, he cannot teach with proper justice and discipline in a class of miscellaneous talents. He may have a standard for the group; he should have a standard for each individual in terms of his special needs—whether they be disabilities or advantages.

Except on the frontiers of knowledge, subject matter cannot be continuously fresh. The great bulk of what is taught to students in every institution except the graduate schools of universities is "old stuff" to their teachers. To stay intellectually alive as one traverses familiar ground year in and year out is not easy. It can be done, of course, by rotating assignments, by taking sabbaticals and, most important of all, by strong theoretical interests in one's own field and related fields. But to stay intellectually alive in the classroom is something else again. Yet for the sake of students one must be alive there if nowhere else. The new developments in one's field seldom bear upon the fundamentals of college instruction and the minutiae of scholarship have meaning only to those who are already well instructed.

The secret of intellectual vitality in the classroom, when a theorem is being derived for the twentieth time or when an elementary point in the grammar of a foreign language is being explained, or when the nerve of an old philosophic argument is being laid bare, lies in experiencing the situation as a fresh problem in communication rather than one in personal discovery. Or, putting it a little differently, it consists in getting the students to reach the familiar conclusion with a sense of having made their own discovery. The task is to make as many as possible see as much as possible of what they have not seen before. It is this perennial challenge, which cannot be adequately met without a knowledge of people, that keeps the good teacher alive. If he does not recognize it, he is a pedagogical automaton, and almost always a bore.

Where knowledge has not yet been won and the authority of method does not point to inescapable and well-tested conclusions, the love of truth can be relied on to generate its own enthusiasm. But where knowledge is already warranted by methods that are themselves warranted, and where originality is likely to be little more than a craving for attention or an expression of conceit, the love of truth by itself cannot be relied upon to make a lesson exciting. . . .

There is a crackle of interest always present in the classroom of a good teacher no matter how trite or time-worn the theme. It is supplied not merely by the teacher's love of truth but by the students' desire to discover the truth, and by the teacher's interest in that desire and in the art of gratifying it. In the end, the good teacher makes himself superfluous and the good student learns the art of self-education. But it is literally in the end.

(e) He knows man best who loves him best. A teacher can not love all his students, nor is it wise to love any of them. The knowledge appropriate for good teaching requires an emotion not so strong as love but also not so irrational. This emotion is sympathy. The good teacher must like people and be interested in them as people, and yet he need not like or be interested in everyone. I am speaking of a general personality trait. It need not find universal expression in every action. But without it an intellectually competent teacher may do more harm than good. There is such a thing as sadism in educational life. Teachers have enormous powers to make students miserable; and, where they are chosen haphazardly, there will always be some who will visit their frustrations and disappointments upon those before them, usually under the guise of being strict disciplinarians. The incidence of insanity is higher among teachers than among any other profession, and the academic community is no freer from phobias like antisemitism than the rest of the community. It requires only one teacher to ruin a student's career.

Sympathy is a positive attitude of imaginative concern with the personal needs of others. Benevolent neutrality and mechanical application of rules, no matter how scrupulous, are no substitutes for it. If justice is based on understanding, then without sympathy there cannot be true justice. For understanding is never complete without the sympathy that awakens our organs of perception. Those who teach large numbers and never get to know their students have a tendency to regard all but a brilliant few as a dull, cloddish mass. Reduce the number of each class, foreshorten the perspective, and no one worthy of being a teacher will fail to see the interesting variety of potentiality in every group. Even outside the classroom it takes two people to make one bore. And, next to ideas, persons are the most interesting things in the world. In each person there is some unique quality of charm, intelligence or character, some promise and mystery that invites attention and nurture. The teacher who seeks it will find it.

Students respond to sympathy for their special intellectual needs like plants to sunshine and rain. They undertake more and achieve more. A certain danger exists that they may at the beginning undertake tasks in order to please their teacher or not to disappoint him but, if proper guidance is furnished, their own sense of growing mastery of a task and its increasing significance, provides intellectual momentum. The function of the teacher at this point is unobtrusively to raise the stick of achievement higher and to offer criticism without killing self-confidence. Students rarely disappoint teachers who assure them in advance that they are doomed to failure. They do not, of course, always live up to the more optimistic expectations of their teachers but they invariably do the better for it.

It is easy to caricature what I am saying by pretending that this is a demand that the teacher be a nurse or a psychiatrist to his students or that he serve literally in *loco parentis*. It would be helpful, naturally, if a teacher were to know the chief relevant facts about those students who need psychiatrists or nurses, if only to put them in proper professional hands and thus prevent them from serving as a drag on other students. But the teacher should not essay the role of amateur psychiatrist or nurse. His sympathy must be primarily directed to his students as growing intellectual organisms in a growing intellectual community, in the faith that they will become integrated persons capable of responsible choice. He cannot cope with all their emotional needs or assume the responsibilities of family and society, priest or judge. He must be friendly without becoming a friend, although he may pave the way for later friendship, for friendship is a mark of preference and expresses itself in indulgence, favors and distinctions that unconsciously find an invidious form. There is a certain distance between teacher and student, compatible with sympathy, which should not be broken down—for the sake of the student. A teacher who becomes "just one of the boys," who courts popularity, who builds up personal loyalties in exchange for indulgent treatment, has missed his vocation. He should leave the classroom for professional politics. . . .

(f) The good teacher, to close our inventory of his traits, possesses vision. It is the source both of his intellectual enthusiasm and his detachment in the face of inevitable failures and disappointments. Without vision he may become a kindly technician, useful in a limited way. But he cannot inspire a passion for excellence. The vision may take many forms. It may be a doctrine—but he must not preach it. It may be a dream—but he must not keep talking about it. It may be a hope, an ambition, a work in progress, so long as it is not merely personal and has a scope or sweep of some imaginative appeal. But it must not obtrude itself into the details of instruction. Its presence should be inferrable from the spirit with which the instruction is carried on. It should operate in such a way as to lift up the students' heart and minds beyond matters of immediate concern and enable them to see the importance of a point of view. Wherever an intellectually stimulating teacher is found, there will also be found some large perspective of interest that lights up the corners of his subject matter. If students catch fire from it, it should not be in order to believe some dogma but to strengthen them in the search for truth and to become sensitive to visions that express other centers of experience.

The best teacher possesses all of the qualities we have mentioned to a pre-eminent degree. But the best teacher is to be found only in a Platonic heaven. Good teachers, however, who exhibit some or all of these qualities are to be found on earth. They can become, can be helped to become, and can help others to become better teachers. If a resolute beginning is made by those who educate and select teachers, in time the community will discover that a new spirit and morale is abroad in the teaching profession. It will discover that a good teacher is a dedicated person, strong in his faith in what he is doing, worthy not only of honor in a democracy but of a place in its councils.

The Need for Specialization

It is clear that not everyone has the natural ability to become a teacher and of those who have, almost all can improve their skill in the art of teaching. But one more aspect of teaching as a career needs to be considered. Formal education in America has become an enormous, complex endeavor, and as a result there is and will be a continually growing need for many kinds of individuals with many different kinds of ability and talents. Not everyone interested in education needs to have all of the qualities described by Professor Hook, nor does he have to be a master-teacher. Although every educator should have experience in the classroom, since it is there that the process of education actually occurs, increasingly in the years ahead there will be need for specialists. For example, there is a need for individuals who are interested in concentrating upon research—that is, gathering knowledge—on the many problems of education. These individuals, in order to be effective, may need to be highly trained in one of the fields of knowledge, such as psychology, sociology, history, economics, philosophy, literature, physics, biology, chemistry, music, art, etc. With a strong background plus knowledge, experience, and an interest in education, such individuals will be in a position to make real contributions to American education. For the fact is that in many aspects of education precious little is *known*, and in many instances a great deal of educational literature is based on very limited and unsubstantial knowledge. In the years ahead, we will need a great deal of knowledge about all the aspects of education, and this knowledge can be gathered only by intelligent, well-trained individuals interested in research, in experimentation, in asking questions, and in seeking answers that will broaden and deepen our understanding and enable us to do a better job for all of our children.

In addition to the pure research jobs, there are opportunities for individuals who are interested in combining the theoretical and the practical aspects of education on a high level by preparing themselves to teach teachers. There will be a growing need for such individuals in the major areas of elementary education—for example, early childhood and the intermediate grades—as well as in special fields such as the teaching of reading and the other basic skills. There is also a need for specialists in elementary curriculum and in administration. These positions which are open for individuals with the necessary ability and interest are especially available to men. In these highly specialized jobs (and there are similar ones open in secondary education) the individual needs to have a strong background in the social sciences and a lively interest in theoretical work on the frontiers of education.

Certainly it is true that we need and will continue to need thousands of excellent teachers of all kinds, but we also need to encourage young men and women with exceptional ability to prepare themselves to handle these special jobs. Just as the biochemist working in his laboratory provides the knowledge of the functioning of the human body upon which medicine is based, so too can the psychologist-educator, the sociologist-educator, and the philosopher-educator provide a solid base of scientifically warranted knowledge for education. This is not to say that classroom teachers cannot be or should not be concerned with research and experimentation, for they should. The classroom is a natural laboratory, and the opportunity for research is there. Also, this approach to teaching keeps the teacher seeking and questioning, which provides an excellent atmosphere in the classroom. And, equally important, it provides an interesting intellectual outlet for the teacher above and beyond her regular teaching.

In conclusion, the prospective educator should realize that the education profession is still in an embryonic stage. In the years ahead there is a great deal of important and exciting work to be done, both in teaching and in educational research. These jobs will pay at least as well as jobs in engineering or junior executive positions, they will be exciting and satisfying personally, and they will be terribly important to our nation and the world. It is no exaggeration to say that in education in American society the horizons are virtually unlimited.

Suggested Readings

Barzun, Jacques: *Teacher in America*. Boston: Little, Brown & Company, 1944.

Counts, George S.: *Education and American Civilization*. New York: Bureau of Publications, Teachers College, Columbia University, 1952.

Dewey, John: *The Sources of a Science of Education*. New York: Liveright Publishing Corp., 1929.

Hook, Sidney: *Education for Modern Man*. New York: The Dial Press, 1946.

Palmer, George H.: *The Ideal Teacher*. Boston: Houghton Mifflin Company, 1910.

Peterson, Houston, ed.: *Great Teachers, Portrayed by Those Who Studied under Them*. New Brunswick, N.J.: Rutgers University Press, 1946.

Rasey, Marie I.: *It Takes Time*. New York: Harper & Brothers, 1953.

Tenenbaum, Samuel: *William Heard Kilpatrick, Trail Blazer in Education*. New York: Harper & Brothers, 1951.

INDEX

A NOTE ON THE TYPE

THIS BOOK was set on the Linotype in ELECTRA, designed by W. A. Dwiggins. The Electra face is a simple and readable type suitable for printing books by present-day processes. It is not based on any historical model, and hence does not echo any particular time or fashion. It is without eccentricities to catch the eye and interfere with reading—in general, its aim is to perform the function of a good book printing-type: to be read, and not seen.

The book was composed, printed, and bound by Kingsport Press, Inc., Kingsport, Tennessee. Paper manufactured by P. H. Glatfelter Co., Spring Grove, Pa.

A